Notable Figures in African American History

James Forten
(1766–1842)

Jarena Lee
(1783–unknown)

Prince Hall
(1735–1807)

Thomas Peters
(1738–1792)

Crispus Attucks
(c. 1723–1770)

Absalom Jones
(1746–1818)

Paul Cuffe
(1759–1817)

David Walker
(1785–1830)

1720	1740	1760	1780

Benjamin Banneker
(1731–1806)

Phillis Wheatley
(1753–1784)

Denmark Vesey
(1767–1822)

Sojourner Truth
(1798–1833)

Venture Smith
(c. 1729–1805)

Olaudah Equiano
(c. 1745–1797)

Richard Allen
(1760–1831)

Martin Delany
(1812–1885)

Joseph Cinque
(c. 1811–1879)

Mary Ann Shadd Cary
(1823–1893)

Harriet Tubman
(1820–1913)

George Washington Carver
(1864–1943)

Madam C. J. Walker
(1867–1919)

Mary Church Terrell
(1863–1954)

Nat Turner
(1800–1831)

Henry Bibb
(1815–1854)

Frances Ellen Watkins Harper
(1825–1911)

Ida B. Wells-Barnett
(1862–1931)

W. E. B. Du Bois
(1868–1963)

Emanuel Fortune
(1832–1903)

| 1800 | 1820 | 1840 | 1860 |

Maria Stewart
(1803–1874)

Hiram Revels
(1822–1901)

Scott Joplin
(1868–1917)

Henry Highland Garnet
(1815–1882)

Booker T. Washington
(1856–1915)

Paul Laurence Dunbar
(1872–1906)

Frederick Douglass
(c. 1817–1885)

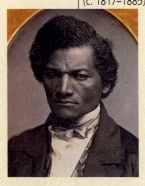

Claude McKay
(1890–1948)

A. Philip Randolph
(1889–1979)

Rosa Parks
(c. 1913–   )

Marcus Garvey
(1887–1940)

Charles Houston
(1895–1950)

Pauli Murray
(1910–1985)

Dorie Miller
(1919–1943)

Richard Wright
(1908–1960)

Billie Holiday
(1915–1959)

Jack Johnson
(1878–1946)

Ralph Bunche
(1903–1971)

1870	1880		1900	1910

Zora Neale Hurston
(1891–1960)

Louis Armstrong
(1901–1971)

Bayard Rustin
(1912–1987)

Paul Robeson
(1898–1976)

Fannie Lou Hamer
(1917–1977)

Mary McLeod Bethune
(1875–1955)

Jackie Robinson
(1919–1972)

Thurgood Marshall
(1908–1993)

Muhammed Ali
(1942–   )

Malcolm X
(1925–1965)

Louis Farrakhan
(1933–   )

Stokely Carmichael
(1941–1998)

Eldridge Cleaver
(1935–1998)

Alice Walker
(1944–   )

Condoleeza Rice
(1954–   )

Shirley Chisolm
(1924–   )

1920	1930	1940	1950	1960

Harold Washington
(1922–1987)

Oprah Winfrey
(1954–   )

Hank Aaron
(1934–   )

Angela Davis
(1944–   )

Tupac Shakur
(1971–1996)

Colin Powell
(1937–   )

Huey Newton
(1942–1989)

Spike Lee
(1957–   )

Martin Luther King, Jr.
(1929–1968)

Diane Nash
(1938–   )

Jesse Jackson
(1941–   )

Andrew Young
(1932–   )

Toni Morrison
(1931–   )

African American Lives

The Struggle for Freedom

Volume I

Clayborne Carson
Stanford University

Emma J. Lapsansky-Werner
Haverford College

Gary B. Nash
University of California, Los Angeles

PEARSON

Longman

New York San Francisco Boston
London Toronto Sydney Tokyo Singapore Madrid
Mexico City Munich Paris Cape Town Hong Kong Montreal

Publisher: Priscilla McGeehon
Senior Development Editor: Dawn Groundwater
Executive Marketing Manager: Sue Westmoreland
Media and Supplements Editor: Kristi Olson
Production Manager: Charles Annis
Project Coordination, Text Design, and Electronic Page Makeup: Electronic Publishing Services Inc., NYC
Cover Design Manager: Wendy Ann Fredericks
Cover Designer: Kay Petronio
Cover Photos: *top left:* Daniel Freeman, albumen print, 1900, woman seated wearing mourning, man holding hat, Dr. James Hill
    Collection, Washington, DC; *bottom left:* cooks, chambermaids, and one hostler, St. Augustine, Florida, The New York Public
    Library/Art Resource, NY; *right:* Taylor, the drummer boy with the 78th Regt. U.S. Colored Infantry, poses with his drum during the
    U.S. Civil War, © Corbis
Photo Researcher: Photosearch, Inc.
Manufacturing Buyer: Roy Pickering
Printer and Binder: Quebecor World Taunton
Cover Printer: Phoenix Color Corp.

For permission to use copyrighted material, grateful acknowledgment is made to the copyright holders throughout this book, which is
hereby made part of this copyright page.

Library of Congress Cataloging-in-Publication Data
Carson, Clayborne, 1944–
    African American lives : the struggle for freedom / Clayborne Carson, Emma Lapsanksy-Werner, Gary Nash.
        p.   cm.
    Includes bibliographical references and index.
    ISBN 0-321-02586-5 (hardcover)—ISBN 0-201-79487-X (pbk. : v. 1)—ISBN 0-201-79489-6 (pbk. : v. 2)
1. African Americans—History.   I. Lapsanksy-Werner, Emma.   II. Nash, Gary B.   III. Title.
E185.C356 2005
973'.0496073—dc22

                                                                                                                    200411882

Please visit our website at http://www.ablongman.com.

ISBN 0-321-02586-5 (Single Volume Edition)

ISBN 0-201-79487-X (Volume I)

ISBN 0-201-79489-6 (Volume II)

1 2 3 4 5 6 7 8 9 10—QWT—07 06 05 04

Brief Contents

Detailed Contents

CHAPTER 11

Post–Civil War Reconstruction: A New National Era 268

First Person Documents

Preface

Those who profess to favor freedom and yet depreciate agitation, are people who want crops without ploughing the ground; they want rain without thunder and lightning; they want the ocean without the roar of its many waters. The struggle may be a moral one, or it may be a physical one, or it may be both. But it must be a struggle. Power concedes nothing without a demand; it never has and it never will.

—*Frederick Douglass*

African American Lives: The Struggle for Freedom is designed to help students in the survey course gain an understanding of that struggle. It introduces the concepts, milestones, and significant figures of African American history. Inasmuch as that history is grounded in struggle—in the consistent and insistent call to the United States to make good on constitutional promises made to all its citizens—this book is also an American history text. Hence, the milestones of mainstream American history, economy, politics, arts and letters are interwoven in its pages.

But *African American Lives: The Struggle for Freedom* seeks to do something more. It engages the reader in viewing history through the lens of many biographies and through the perspectives of people who lived those struggles to ensure, in the words of Langston Hughes' famous poem, that "America Will Be." This unique biographical approach to African American history positions African American lives at the center of the narrative and as the basis of analysis.

BIOGRAPHICAL APPROACH

African American Lives: The Struggle for Freedom tells the stories of the lives of both the illustrious (abolitionist Martin Delany) and the ordinary (planter Isaiah Montgomery), the public and the private perspectives of those who shaped the African American story. Some individuals are famous for their specific contributions; other individuals are representative of a larger idea, a concept of a people who have inhabited the American continent for more than half a millennium.

Throughout the book we examine the struggles of African Americans to define their own identities, the development of nationalist ideas and rhetoric, Americans' struggle with the concept of race, and the growth of the politics of race from the Republican Party to the Rainbow Coalition. Wherever possible, we enliven and give authenticity to the story through the words of contemporary participants. With all that, we keep the story concise, fast-paced, and compelling.

Within these pages, we try to capture the essence of the African American experience. The book presents African American voices; it sees history through African American eyes. The events and the themes around which these lives were organized are defined so as to impose order on the often disorderly past and to interpret that past as modern historical research has revealed it. The biographical approach both guides the story and animates the history. In each chapter, individual African Americans are the pivot points that provide a window on the historical changes of their generation. Life stories capture the rush of events that envelop individuals and illuminate the momentous decisions that, collectively, frame the American past and present.

While humanizing history, the biographical approach has another important advantage: It is an antidote to the poisonous notion of historical inevitability. Too often, expressions such as *the sweep of history, the transit of civilization, manifest destiny,* and *the march of progress* plant the idea that history is inexorable, unalterable, and foreordained—beyond the capacity of men and women to change. That idea has been used to justify a winner's history—an approach that diminishes the full humanness of those who were captured and traded as slaves. Books with a winner's history approach also work to absolve those who traded in slaves and profited from their labor. To promote the understanding that no individual is forever trapped within iron circumstances beyond his or her ability to alter, we ground every chapter in the experience of *people* rather than *forces*.

The interwoven human stories in this textbook demonstrate that in every age, in every part of the country, at every level of society, African Americans refused to allow history to crush them. Instead, they were shakers and shapers of their own world insofar as this was possible. Whether in the small space of plantation quarters or Harlem walkups, or criss-crossing a nation, or calling for the unity of Africans dispossessed and dispersed around the globe, African Americans have shaped their world even as they contested and transformed their subordinate roles in American society. That often they did not succeed in their plans or could not fully realize their hopes does not diminish their strivings. It does not alter the fact that for many, nothing was passively accepted; everything was contested or negotiated. The struggle for dignity and respect is part of the human condition. It has been no different for a dispossessed African American minority determined to transcend the contempt of their fellow Americans.

Just as African American lives are inarguably part of the long process by which Americans have strived to achieve the promise of the national motto *E pluribus unum*—from the many, one—so too *African American Lives: The Struggle for Freedom* is not a story set in stone. It is the product of our constantly changing understandings of the past, new insights about historical possibilities, and new historical research. In that ongoing effort, African American history has achieved breadth and depth in recent decades, indeed has become one of the most vibrant components of American history, reshaping the way we understand everything from the American economy to innovations in science, politics, and the arts. Drawing on the last half-century of recast historical narrative, *African American Lives: The Struggle for Freedom* crafts a new synthesis that not only enriches our understanding of the black experience in America but alters our conception of American history in the whole.

COVERAGE AND ORGANIZATION

In *African American Lives: The Struggle for Freedom,* the distinctive people and events of American history are all here: the Europeans' first encounter with new people and a new environment, the American Revolution and its shaping of humanitarian ideals, the War of 1812, the Missouri Compromise, sectional conflicts, wars from the Civil War through this century's war against terrorism, cultural trends from the resistance poetry of revolutionary-era Phillis Wheatley through modern-day hip hop.

African American Lives: The Struggle for Freedom comprises twenty-one chapters. Chapters 1–7 explore the period up to 1830, when most Africans in North America were enslaved. The book begins, as all human history begins, in Africa with ancient history and the rise of empires in West and Central Africa during the period American and western historians think of as the Middle Ages. European contact and the growth of the slave trade are followed by an analysis of the new conditions of slavery in the Americas. To understand how Africans were not all enslaved in the same ways and in the same conditions, the chapters treat the formation of notions about race and how they figured in the descent into slavery in different zones of European settlement—French, Dutch, and Spanish as well as English—in the Americas. The galvanizing effect of the American Revolution and the decades thereafter during which free black people in the North and in the South built families, founded churches, forged friendships and communities, and struggled for autonomy and dignity are central themes.

Chapters 8–14 examine pivotal junctures in African American history that parallel the American focus on reform and nationality. The 1830s marked the first years when the majority of black Americans were not forced immigrants but rather born on American soil. Echoing the religious reawakening that undergirded both abolitionism and a vigorous defense of slavery, slave and free African Americans alike claimed their voice in an international antebellum debate about the future of American democracy. Then, through a long and merciless Civil War, the end of slavery, and the South's attempt to recreate the essence of slavery, black Americans persisted in holding forth, before white Americans and the world, the guarantees of equality and citizenship built into the new constitutional amendments. The post–Civil War dispersal of newly freed African Americans to every corner of North America shows how, in the face of a still-hostile white America that abandoned Reconstruction, black people built families, communities, and viable economic lives; established churches, mutual aid and literary societies, and businesses; and launched schools and publishing ventures as they sought to transform themselves from slaves to soldiers and citizens and to wrest equality and justice from white America.

Chapters 15–21 address African American life in modern America. We devote attention to the increasing diversity of African Americans and how—during world wars, the Great Depression, and other momentous national and international transformations—they struggled for full participation in a society still marred by racist attitudes and practices. Throughout twentieth-century scientific, technological, and economic changes, one theme permeates African American strategies for securing justice and equal opportunity: the ongoing struggle for a positive sense of identity amidst racism and destructive racial stereotypes. Whether in fighting the nation's wars; helping build the modern economy; adding to the explosion of cultural creativity through innovations in music, art, film, dance, and literature; or emerging on the political stage at the local, state, and national level, African Americans in the last century are portrayed as the principal innovators of the nation's most important liberation movement.

SPECIAL FEATURES AND PEDAGOGY

Complementing the multitude of stories connecting African American lives and American history, this book has several features we consider essential elements of a braided analytic narrative.

- *First Persons:* Each chapter contains several primary documents called "First Person" that bring authentic firsthand accounts from the past to the page. These written and spoken words help us comprehend, as no modern paraphraser can do, how African Americans such as Olaudah Equiano, Mary Ann Shadd Cary, and Pauli Murray understood their world and sought to transform it. A headnote puts each primary document in context. Many documents end with a reference to the book's companion website (www.ablongman.com/ carson/documents), encouraging students to view a longer version of the document online.

- *Timelines:* Timelines help students fix the most significant developments in African American history as they are framed in the larger, more familiar American story. These are positioned at the beginning of each chapter directly following an opening vignette.

- *Chapter-opening Vignettes:* Focusing on personal stories such as the rebelliousness of Venture Smith or the wartime experience of First Lieutenant Thomas Edward Jones, these vignettes draw students into the chapter period and herald the chapter's events and themes.

- *Conclusions:* A summary of the main ideas and events of each chapter, and a look ahead to the next, can be found in the Conclusion.

- *Further Reading:* At the end of each chapter are suggestions for further reading. Here we provide a sampling, rather than an exhaustive list, of fresh histories as well as classics, engaging autobiographies and historical novels students can explore for primary sources, visual material, historical essays, and personal interpretations.

- *Visual History:* Each chapter includes a complement of graphic materials and illustrations—maps, charts, photographs, lithographs, and paintings—that provide a visual window on the past. These visual materials are intended to unfold an additional dimension of the narrative, reinforcing the student's sense of seeing history as participants saw it. To sharpen complex or subtle concepts, tables efficiently convey a sequence of events or milestones—for example, judicial decisions, legislative acts, and protest movement flashpoints.

SUPPLEMENTS

For Qualified College Adopters
Instructor's Manual
ISBN 0-321-10852-3
Written by Jane Dabel, California State University–Long Beach, and Ann Grogg. This resource contains learning objectives, significant themes, chapter outlines, enrichment ideas, and further resources for each chapter.

Test Bank
ISBN 0-321-10854-X
Written by Beverly Bunch-Lyons of Virginia Polytechnic Institute and State University. The test bank contains multiple-choice, true/false, and essay questions for each chapter. Multiple-choice and true/false questions are referenced by topic and text page number.

TestGen-EQ Computerized Testing System
ISBN 0-321-10733-0
This flexible, easy-to-master computerized test bank on a dual-platform CD includes all the test items in the printed test bank. The software allows instructors to select specific questions, edit existing questions, and add their own items to create exams. Tests can be printed in several fonts and formats and can include figures, such as graphs and tables.

Supplements Central
http://ablongman.com/suppscentral
A helpful website where instructors can download supplements for this text including the *Instructor's Manual, Test Bank,* and the *TestGen-EQ.* Instructors will need to request a password from their sales representative to gain access.

For Students
Sources of the African-American Past, Second Edition
ISBN 0-673-99202-0
Edited by Roy Finkenbine of the University of Detroit at Mercy, this collection of primary sources covers themes in

the African American experience from the West African background to the present. Balanced between political and social history, the documents offer a vivid snapshot of the lives of African Americans in different historical periods. The collection includes documents representing women and different regions of the United States. Just $2.00 when bundled with *African American Lives: The Struggle for Freedom*.

Companion Website

www.ablongman.com/carson

Students will find summaries, practice test questions, and flashcards for every chapter at this site. Longer versions of the First Person documents are also available for reference and further study.

Student Resources CD-ROM

Available free to qualified college adopters if requested when bundled with the book, this CD-ROM contains dozens of documents, images, maps, and video clips from African American history.

Research Navigator Guide

ISBN 0-205-40838-9

This guidebook includes exercises and tips on how to use the Internet. It also includes an access code for Research Navigator™—the easiest way for students to start a research assignment or research paper. Research Navigator™ is composed of three exclusive databases of credible and reliable source material, including EBSCO's ContentSelect™ Academic Journal Database, New York Times Search by Subject Archive, and "Best of the Web" Link Library. This comprehensive site also includes a detailed help section.

Penguin Books

The partnership between Penguin-Putnam USA and Longman Publishers offers your students a discount on many titles when bundled with any Longman survey text. Available titles include *Narrative of the Life of Frederick Douglass* by Frederick Douglass; *Why We Can't Wait* by Martin Luther King Jr.; *Beloved* by Toni Morrison; and *Uncle Tom's Cabin* by Harriet Beecher Stowe.

ACKNOWLEDGMENTS

We gratefully acknowledge the many colleagues who took the time to review our manuscript. Their useful comments and keen insights have made this a stronger book. Thank you:

Leslie Alexander, *Ohio State University*

Kwame Alford, *Texas Tech University*

Julius A. Amin, *University of Dayton*

Melissa Anyiwo, *University of Tennessee at Chattanooga*

Joseph Appiah, *J. S. Reynolds Community College*

Felix L. Armfield, *State University of New York, Buffalo*

Charles Pete Banner-Haley, *Colgate University*

Abel A. Bartley, *University of Akron*

Donald Scott Barton, *East Central University*

James M. Beeby, *West Virginia Wesleyan College*

Diane L. Beers, *Holyoke Community College*

Nemata Blyden, *George Washington University*

Robert Bonner, *Amherst College*

Ronald E. Brown, *Westchester Community College*

Kimn Carlton-Smith, *Ferris State University, Long Beach*

Stephanie Cole, *University of Texas, Arlington*

Jane E. Dabel, *California State University, Long Beach*

Bruce J. Dierenfield, *Canisius College*

A. G. Dunston, *Eastern Kentucky University*

Patience Essah, *Auburn University*

Melvin Lee Felton Jr., *James Sprunt Community College*

Paul S. George, *Miami-Dade College*

Brian Gordon, *St. Louis Community College*

Lenworth Gunther, *Essex County College*

Laura Graves, *South Plains College*

Olivia B. Green, *Miles College*

Kevin Joseph Hales, *Parkland College*

Carmen V. Harris, *University of South Carolina at Spartanburg*

James Harrison, *Portland Community College, Cascade*

Sharon A. Roger Hepburn, *Radford University*

Ranford B. Hopkins, *Moorpark College*

Carol Sue Humphrey, *Oklahoma Baptist University*

Creed Hyatt, *Lehigh Carbon Community College*

Eric R. Jackson, *Northern Kentucky University*

W. Sherman Jackson, *Miami-Ohio University*

Randal M. Jelks, *Calvin College*

Cherisse R. Jones, *Arkansas State University*

Theodore Kallman, *San Joaquin Delta College*

Maghan Keita, *Villanova University*

Ben Keppel, *University of Oklahoma*

Daniel Kilbride, *John Carroll University*

Lisa King, *Morgan State University*

William M. King, *University of Colorado*

Alec Kirby, *University of Wisconsin at Stout*

Anne Klejment, *University of St. Thomas*

Alan Lamm, *Mount Olive College*

Linda Rochell Lane, *Benedict College*

Howard Lindsey, *DePaul University*

Arletha D. Livingston, *Georgia State University*

Elizabeth MacGonagle, *University of Kansas*

Kenneth Mason, *Santa Monica College*

David McBride, *Pennsylvania State University*

Larry McGruder, *Abraham Baldwin College*

Karen K. Miller, *Boston College*

Jacqueline M. Moore, *Austin College*

Sheila H. Moore, *Hinds Community College*

Earl F. Mulderink, *Southern Utah University*

Cassandra Newby-Alexander, *Norfolk State University*

Julius F. Nimmons Jr., *University of the District of Columbia*

Phillip Oguagha, *Medgar Evers College, City University of New York*

Anthony Parent, *Wake Forest University*

John B. Reid, *Truckee Meadows Community College*

Tara Ross, *Onondaga Community College*

Jerrold W. Roy, *Hampton University*

Paul Siff, *Sacred Heart University*

Bradley Skelcher, *Delaware State University*

Dorothy A. Smith-Akubue, *Lynchburg College*

Melissa Soto-Schwartz, *Cuyahoga Community College*

Darlene Spitzer-Antezana, *Bowie State University*

Donald Spivey, *University of Miami*

Marian Strobel, *Furman University*

Michael David Tegeder, *Santa Fe Community College*

Linda D. Tomlinson, *Clark Atlanta University*

William L. Van Deburg, *University of Wisconsin*

Cheryl R. Vinson, *Miles College*

Melissa Walker, *Converse College*

Irma Watkins-Owen, *Fordham University*

Vernon J. Williams Jr., *Purdue University*

Leslie Wilson, *Montclair State University*

Keith A. Winsell, *Talladega College*

Marilyn Leonard Yancy, *Virginia Union University*

The authors would like to thank the staff of Special Collections at Haverford College and the Crisis Publishing Co., Inc., the publisher of the magazine of the National Association for the Advancement of Colored People, for the use of material published in the November 1935 and June 1938 issues of *Crisis*. The project also owes a monumental debt of gratitude to Ann Grogg. Ann was by turns editor, counselor, circuit rider, diplomat, and loyal friend. Her broad and subtle knowledge of history and of those who teach and learn it were crucial to our progress. So too was her deft editing without altering the authors' voices or meaning. We are grateful to our Longman editor, Dawn Groundwater, for sticking with us and never losing sight of the book's vision and goals.

Clay Carson offers particular thanks to Damani Rivers and Caitrin McKiernan of the King Papers Project at Stanford University for their exceptional research assistance. Susan A. Carson also helped with editing the manuscript. Tenisha Armstrong, Miya Woolfalk, and other King Project staff members and student researchers offered useful comments on the manuscript at various stages of its development. Emma Lapsansky-Werner extends a special thank you to student research assistant James Chappel and her ever-patient husband, Dickson Werner. Gary Nash thanks research assistants Grace Lu and Marian Olivas for good cheer in carrying out many tasks.

All three authors wish to thank three history editors at Longman who supported this book and facilitated its completion: Bruce Borland, Jay O'Callaghan, and Ashley Dodge.

Meet the Authors

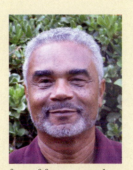

Clayborne Carson was born in Buffalo, New York. He received his BA, MA, and PhD from the University of California, Los Angeles, and has taught at Stanford University since 1974. Active during his undergraduate years in the civil rights and anti-war movements, Carson's publications have focused on African American protest movements of the post–World War II period. His first book, *In Struggle: SNCC and the Black Awakening of the 1960s* (1981), won the Frederick Jackson Turner Award from the Organization of American Historians. He has also edited *Malcolm X: The FBI File* (1991) and served as an advisor for the award-winning PBS series on the civil rights movement entitled *Eyes on the Prize*. Since 1985, Carson has been editor and director of the Martin Luther King Jr. Papers Project, which has produced five of fourteen volumes of a comprehensive edition of King's speeches, sermons, and unpublished writing. The biographical approach of *African American Lives: The Struggle for Freedom* grew out of Carson's vision. He has used it with remarkable results in his course at Stanford.

Emma J. Lapsansky-Werner received her BA, MA, and PhD from the University of Pennsylvania. From 1973 to 1990 she taught at Temple University, University of Pennsylvania, and Princeton University. Since 1990 she has been a professor of history and curator of special collections at Haverford College. From her experience with voter registration in Mississippi in the 1960s, she became an historian to try to set the records straight. Her professional and research interests include family and community life, antebellum cities, Quaker history, and religion and popular culture in nineteenth-century America. Lapsansky-Werner has written or edited several volumes, including *Neighborhoods in Transition: William Penn's Dream and Urban Reality* (1994) and *Quaker Aesthetics: Reflections on a Quaker Ethic in American Design and Consumption, 1720–1920* (2003), and a forthcoming volume on Quaker abolitionist Benjamin Coates. She has also contributed to several anthologies on the history of Pennsylvania. She hopes that *African American Lives: The Struggle for Freedom* will broaden the place of African American history in academia, helping to transform studies so that black people are seen as more than just objects of public policy, and better understood as leaders in the international struggle for human justice. Through stories, black Americans are presented as multidimensional, alive with their own ambitions, visions, and human failings.

Gary B. Nash was born in Philadelphia and received his BA and PhD in history from Princeton University. He taught at Princeton briefly and since 1966 has been a faculty member at the University of California, Los Angeles, teaching colonial American, revolutionary American, and African American history. In 1990 he won the school's Distinguished Teaching Award. Nash's many books on early American history include *Quakers and Politics: Pennsylvania, 1681–1726* (1968); *Red, White, and Black: The Peoples of Early North America* (1974; Second ed., 1982; Third ed., 1992; Fourth ed., 2000); *The Urban Crucible: Social Change, Political Consciousness, and the Origins of the American Revolution* (1979); *Race, Class, and Politics: Essays in American Colonial and Revolutionary Society* (1986); *Forging Freedom: The Formation of Philadelphia's Black Community, 1720–1840* (1988); *Race and Revolution* (1990); *Forbidden Love: The Secret History of Mixed-Race America* (1999); *First City: Philadelphia and the Forging of History Memory* (2001); *Landmarks of the American Revolution* (2003); and *The American People* (Sixth ed., 2004). Nash wanted to coauthor this book with two good friends and esteemed colleagues because of their common desire to bring the story of the African American people before a wide audience of students and history lovers. African American history has always had a central place in his teaching, and it has been pivotal to his efforts to bring an inclusive, multicultural American history into the K-12 classrooms in this nation and abroad.

African American Lives

The Struggle for Freedom

CHAPTER 1

■ Ornamental mask of a Benin oba (king) from the sixteenth century.

Ancient Africa

African Storytelling and African American History

The storytellers of the Yoruba people of West Africa, the *griots,* have a saying passed down for generations: "However far the stream flows, it never forgets its source." This wisdom is as fresh today as it was a thousand years ago.

From their first arrival in the Americas, Africans knew that without history they would be water without a source, trees without roots. Those roots derive from oral cultures in Africa, where young people heard adults tell stories about the origins of their own village-based people. Other stories taught children what it means to live properly. Still others "handed on the torch," as many Africans say, by capturing the sweep of a people's long history.

Once they were wrenched from their homelands, enslaved Africans continued to keep ancient traditions alive—passing down to their children the stories, morals, and values of their ancestors. Under slavery, the desire to preserve memory of long-ago traditions as well as more recent experiences intensified. As soon as they could, Africans began recounting the horrors of capture and transport to the Americas (the middle passage), the desperate struggle for survival under slavery, and the bravery and resolve of those who struck out for freedom. History could not ward off a brutal master's blows or break slavery's chains. Nevertheless, it sustained Africans' souls and nourished their hopes for a better life.

For many generations, Africans in America nurtured the collective memory of their history through oral storytelling. They had few opportunities to publish written accounts because most of them were in bondage to masters who forbade them to learn how to read and write. That began to change in the era of the American Revolution. Enslaved Africans such as Phillis Wheatley and free black people such as Venture Smith were the first black writers to find white patrons who helped publish their recorded thoughts and experiences. In the decades before the Civil War, a handful of black historians, such as Boston's William C. Nell and Philadelphia's William Douglass, published the first histories

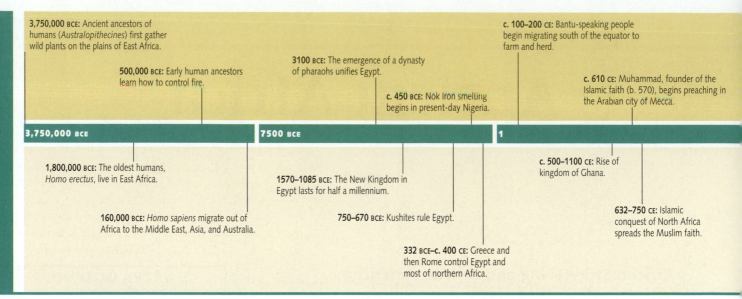

3,750,000 BCE: Ancient ancestors of humans (*Australopithecines*) first gather wild plants on the plains of East Africa.

500,000 BCE: Early human ancestors learn how to control fire.

3100 BCE: The emergence of a dynasty of pharaohs unifies Egypt.

c. 450 BCE: Nok iron smelting begins in present-day Nigeria.

c. 100–200 CE: Bantu-speaking people begin migrating south of the equator to farm and herd.

c. 610 CE: Muhammad, founder of the Islamic faith (b. 570), begins preaching in the Arabian city of Mecca.

3,750,000 BCE   **7500 BCE**   **1**

1,800,000 BCE: The oldest humans, *Homo erectus*, live in East Africa.

160,000 BCE: *Homo sapiens* migrate out of Africa to the Middle East, Asia, and Australia.

1570–1085 BCE: The New Kingdom in Egypt lasts for half a millennium.

750–670 BCE: Kushites rule Egypt.

332 BCE–c. 400 CE: Greece and then Rome control Egypt and most of northern Africa.

c. 500–1100 CE: Rise of kingdom of Ghana.

632–750 CE: Islamic conquest of North Africa spreads the Muslim faith.

(BCE means "Before Common Era"; CE means "Common Era", with years coinciding with Christian dates)

of black people in North America. Meanwhile, former bonds-man Frederick Douglass wrote an autobiographical account of his travails in slavery and his long walk to freedom. His story carried such power and poignancy that it made him an international figure. A people whose memory had been officially suppressed began to regain their voice.

Most nineteenth-century African American histories did not enjoy a wide readership. White Americans, in particular, ignored them. In recent years, however, these accounts have been republished and attracted a growing audience. They have also inspired contemporary black historians to build on their work. Twentieth-century historians such as W. E. B. Du Bois, Rayford Logan, Carter Woodson, and John Hope Franklin insisted that African American history be included in the American story. A half-century ago, a young preacher named Martin Luther King, Jr. prophesied on the night of the Montgomery bus boycott in 1955, "When the history books are written in future generations, the historians will say, 'There lived a great people—a black people— who injected new meaning and dignity into the veins of civilization.'" King's prophecy has come to be.

The story of humankind began several million years ago in East Africa, where, according to archaeologists, humans first made their appearance on Earth. Egypt gave birth to the first great African civilization. That civilization in turn shaped

■ Storytelling continues in West African villages today. When American author Alex Haley wrote *Roots* (1965), he returned to West Africa to find clues to his family's past in the oral history still recounted there.

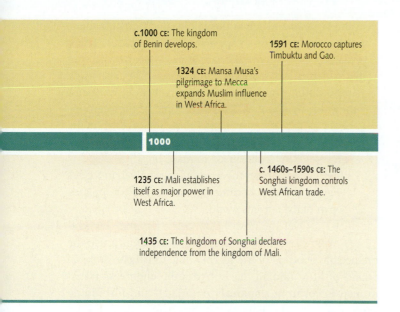

c.1000 CE: The kingdom of Benin develops.

1324 CE: Mansa Musa's pilgrimage to Mecca expands Muslim influence in West Africa.

1591 CE: Morocco captures Timbuktu and Gao.

1000

1235 CE: Mali establishes itself as major power in West Africa.

c. 1460s–1590s CE: The Songhai kingdom controls West African trade.

1435 CE: The kingdom of Songhai declares independence from the kingdom of Mali.

ancient Greece and Rome. The spread of Islam and the emergence of West and Central African kingdoms set the stage for an era in which millions of African people were torn from their homelands and forced across the Atlantic to serve as slaves in the Americas.

This chapter looks at the cultures of these African peoples—and some of the individuals who embodied those life ways. By understanding the societies these men and women came from, the gods they worshiped, the family traditions they cherished, and the social systems and artistic works they created, we will see them as more than faceless units of labor carried across the ocean. By seeing them as peoples with long, rich histories, we can better understand their—and our own—experiences in the Americas.

FROM HUMAN BEGINNINGS TO THE RISE OF EGYPT

For generations, Yoruba storytellers told young people how Olodumare, the god of the sky, sent two sons down to Earth with a bag, a hen, and a chameleon. The bag contained soft white sand and rich black soil. One son sprinkled the white sand on the water's surface. From the sand sprouted a palm tree. The chameleon gingerly stepped across the sand, discov-

ering that the grains supported its weight. Seeing this, the other son spread the soil over the sand. Then the hen scratched in the dark earth, scattering it in all directions. Pleased with his sons' work, Olodumare sent Aje—prosperity—from Heaven to dwell there for the rest of her life. The sky god sent his sons additional gifts: maize to plant for food; cowrie shells for trading; and iron bars for forging hoes, knives, and other tools. In this way, Olodumare created Yorubaland.

Like the Yoruba, every human society has developed creation myths to make sense of its beginnings and to understand the mighty forces of nature. Since the emergence of humankind, a rich array of creation stories has arisen. Around the world, these stories yield many interpretations of the first stirrings of humankind. The Yoruba creation story leads us to consider the long history of ancient Africa—from human beginnings through the flourishing of Egyptian civilization to the Roman and Greek conquest of North Africa.

Human Beginnings in East Africa

Scientists offer several explanations of how the Earth was formed and how human beings came to inhabit it. Though much remains to be discovered, the common scientific understanding is that all humans descended from hominids. These humanlike primates had enlarged brains and could walk upright on two legs. Archaeologists have found the oldest fossilized remains of these hominids in eastern Africa. As early as 1871, Charles Darwin proposed in his *Descent of Man* that Africa was probably the birthplace of humankind. But this notion offended Europeans, who saw their own race as superior to that of the African. Some Europeans thus maintained that human life began not in Africa but in Europe—specifically in Germany's Neander Valley, where fossil remains of an early human species dubbed *Neanderthal man* were discovered in 1856.

Not until 1925, when an archaeologist found a child's skull in a limestone cave at Taung, in South Africa, did the European origins thesis come under scientific scrutiny. Apelike in appearance, the skull also had human characteristics in its forehead and nose structure. Examination revealed it as the most ancient example of *Australopithecine*—a creature who walked upright around three million years ago. Once again, the notion that humans emerged in Africa gained credence.

Then, in the 1950s, the British anthropologists Louis and Mary Leakey found additional fossils of the *Australopithecine* species in East Africa's Olduvai Gorge. Scholars soon felt convinced that human life indeed began in Africa. In 1961, the Leakeys found confirming evidence of the evolution from primate to human being—fossil bones resting alongside simple stone tools. Dating technology revealed that this first group of human ancestors were toolmakers who lived between 1.5 and 3.75 million years ago in East Africa.

More evidence came to light in 1974 in Hadar, Ethiopia. There, paleoanthropologists (who study human origins) discovered "Lucy," the first example of *Homo erectus*, or upright human. This exceptionally complete skeleton, about 3 1/2 feet tall, dates back about 1.8 million years. Thanks to this finding, scientists now widely accept the idea that the ancient ancestors of all humans originated in Africa about 120,000 to 160,000 years ago. These ancestors are called *Homo sapiens*—meaning "wise human."

Though a small group of dissenters argue that hominids originated in several regions of the world and evolved separately in Africa, the Middle East, Europe, and Asia, new discoveries have consolidated the "out of Africa" scenario. In 2002, for example, three fossilized *Homo sapien* skulls excavated in Herto, Ethiopia, were dated through argon-isotope analysis to about 160,000 years ago, solidly supported the "out of Africa" theory. Though many African Americans speak of "Mother Africa" to signify the homeland of their forebears, most modern scientists agree that Africa is the mother of *all* humans.

Rise of Egyptian Civilization

By at least 60,000 years ago, humans began to migrate out of East Africa to what we today call the Middle East, Asia, and Australia. About 20,000 years later, they appeared in Europe. There they made spear and harpoon points for hunting large fish and big animals such as the wild ox and hippopotamus, and they crafted thin scrapers for cleaning hides. These nomadic groups discovered ways to increase their food supply by domesticating and herding animals. They also made simple clothing out of hides to protect themselves against the cold. By about 10,000 BCE, some of these groups began settling along the banks of the Jordan River in the Middle East. By 6000 BCE, they were harvesting millet and sorghum (grains used to make bread) as they settled along the Nile, the world's longest river, in today's Egypt. This area became the most densely populated part of the ancient world.

Over the next 4,000 years, Egyptian civilization flourished and spread. Learning to use the predictable flooding of the mighty Nile to irrigate crops in a land of little rainfall, early hydraulic engineers transformed Egypt from a sparsely populated and forbidding desert into a thriving civilization. By about 3100 BCE, local kingdoms began to emerge throughout Egypt, led by rulers called *pharaohs*. Over many centuries, rival kingdoms set aside their differences and united along the Nile's 4,000-mile-long banks.

Strong, centralized governments evolved out of these kingdoms, headed by pharaohs who claimed godlike power. These rulers commanded the labor of a vast peasantry. They amassed enough wealth from the production of crop surpluses to erect royal tombs, temples, and pyramids that showcased their power. Pharaohs drew their strength from civil servants who collected taxes and supervised irrigation projects. These same servants also compiled and maintained tax and administrative records. To record infor-

■ Funerary figurines, called *shabtis*, played a crucial role in the pharaohs' burial rituals. This one comes from the reign of Amenhotep III (c. 1391–1353 BCE). Such figurines were inscribed with orders to perform agricultural tasks that would ease the deceased royal person's way through the underworld. This practice later became common in West and Central Africa.

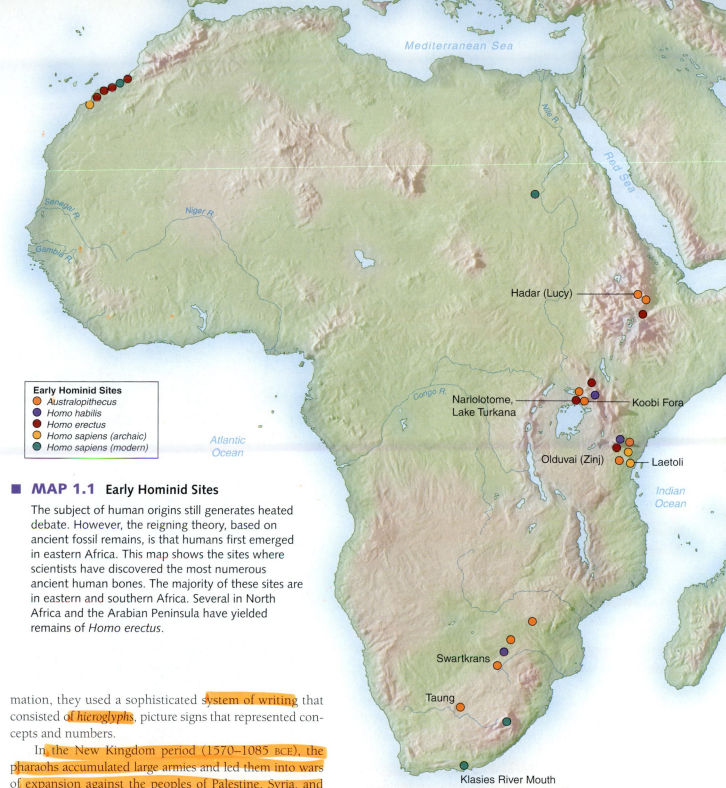

Early Hominid Sites
- 🟠 *Australopithecus*
- 🟣 *Homo habilis*
- 🔴 *Homo erectus*
- 🟡 *Homo sapiens* (archaic)
- 🟢 *Homo sapiens* (modern)

Hadar (Lucy)

Nariolotome,
Lake Turkana — Koobi Fora

Olduvai (Zinj) — Laetoli

Swartkrans

Taung

Klasies River Mouth

Mediterranean Sea

Nile R.

Red Sea

Senegal R.

Niger R.

Gambia R.

Congo R.

Atlantic
Ocean

Indian
Ocean

■ **MAP 1.1** Early Hominid Sites

The subject of human origins still generates heated debate. However, the reigning theory, based on ancient fossil remains, is that humans first emerged in eastern Africa. This map shows the sites where scientists have discovered the most numerous ancient human bones. The majority of these sites are in eastern and southern Africa. Several in North Africa and the Arabian Peninsula have yielded remains of *Homo erectus*.

mation, they used a sophisticated system of writing that consisted of hieroglyphs, picture signs that represented concepts and numbers.

In the New Kingdom period (1570–1085 BCE), the pharaohs accumulated large armies and led them into wars of expansion against the peoples of Palestine, Syria, and Nubia. The massive statues and temples built by Rameses II, which visitors to Egypt can view today, testify to the power of the empire forged out of conquered lands. As the realm extended its reach, cultural change accelerated as well. Ancient Egypt became a crossroads for merchants and other enterprising men and women seeking to trade with other societies. Within this vast realm, a composite culture arose that comprised Mediterranean peoples from the west, Semitic nomads from the east, and dark-skinned traders and farmers from Kushite and Ethiopian societies to the south.

The Egyptian civilization dominated the lands bordering the Mediterranean Sea for 3,000 years—from about 3100 to roughly 332 BCE, when the Greeks invaded the kingdom. Indeed, ancient Egypt stands as the longest-lasting civilization in human history. Scholars trace about thirty dynasties during this epoch. Perhaps no dynasty has captured the imaginations of students of history more than that of the female pharaoh Hatshepsut, who reigned during the New Kingdom period. This shrewd and skillful ruler built a great temple on the banks of the Nile and restored numerous old temples that foreign invaders had destroyed. Hatshepsut's successor, Thutmose III, became one of Egypt's mightiest pharaohs. Through military expeditions into the eastern Mediterranean region, he extended his empire into Palestine and Syria. Later rulers continued to enlarge the realm while building impressive monuments at home. For example, the three pyramids at Giza still testify to Egyptian achievements in hydraulic engineering, architecture, and sculpture.

Owing to its location, Egypt played virtually no role in the forced migration of Africans to the Americas that unfolded centuries later. Rather, it became a trans-shipment point for West Africans slated for Muslim slave markets to the east.

Debates over Black Egypt

Since the eighteenth century, African Americans have cited Egypt's greatness as a way to counter charges that "the dark continent" was home to "savages" useful only as labor for other, more civilized peoples. Europeans had long recognized ancient Egypt as a cradle of civilization and the source of many ideas that powerfully shaped ancient Greece and Rome. In denigrating African peoples, however, these same Europeans mentally plucked Egypt out of Africa and Africans out of Egypt. Yet as any glance at a world map shows, Egypt is solidly part of the African continent.

For generations, African Americans fought the notion that Egypt was not part of Africa. They referred to Egypt as an African society, and many called the Egyptians "Ethiopians." This name was a reference to nearby Ethiopia, with which Egypt had traded extensively over many centuries. By the 1870s, the first historians who tried to write a comprehensive African American history—such as George Washington Williams and Edward Blyden—pointedly began their narratives with accounts of Egypt (see chapter 11.)

Today, scholars still argue passionately over whether Cleopatra and other ancient Egyptians were "black," "white," or racially mixed. They continue to debate the question of how much Egypt influenced ancient Greece and Rome—the regions many historians regard as the cradles of Western civilization. In 1987, Martin Bernal, a professor of government at Cornell University, set off a furious controversy with his book *Black Athena: The Afroasiatic Roots of Classical Civilization*. In the book, Bernal argued that since the eighteenth century, white scholars have suppressed the fundamental role Egyptian and Semitic peoples played in

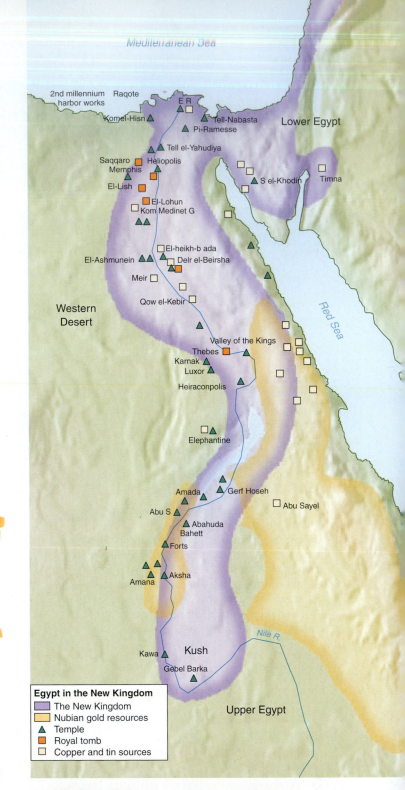

■ MAP 1.2 Egypt in the New Kingdom

Visitors to Egypt today flock to see the Luxor Temple and other monumental buildings at Karnak and other Egyptian sites that recall the New Kingdom. This map shows the major temple sites in Egypt as well as temples and fortifications in Kush, which was part of the New Kingdom.

■ Detail of statue of Cleopatra VII, c. 51–30 BCE.

the making of Greek civilization. In particular, he maintained, these ancient dark-skinned peoples invented the mathematics, philosophy, and religion on which classical Greece was built. Bernal's focus on the Egyptian roots of Greek civilization gave a tremendous boost to black Americans' efforts to reconnect with their African origins, reclaim "a stolen legacy," and bury forever the notion of an Africa culturally empty before European contact. If Egypt was the source of much that we admire about the arts, science, and political theory of classical Greece, then modern Western civilization owes a great debt to ancient Africa.

Black Athena sent a "mythic message," as one historian has said, "that asserts future great cultural achievements [of African Americans] to be a continuation of the past rather than a radical break with it." A loose reading of *Black Athena* fosters the idea that everyone today who defines himself or herself as "black" has an ancestral claim to the loftiest ideas and institutions of Western civilization.

Though many scholars dispute Bernal's findings, few deny that he has inspired much new research on the circulation of ideas throughout the Mediterranean basin. Traditional scholarship on ancient Greece now looks much more carefully at Egyptian influences. However, numerous schol-

ars have found the uses of *Black Athena* disturbing. Some scholars exploited the book to argue their side of several burning questions—such as whether "race" is biologically determined, whether identity is primarily determined by race, and whether race should be the basis of political empowerment and entitlement programs.

But what do these questions about identity and race mean, exactly? Many scholars argue that the ancient Egyptians had no concept of "race" or even "blackness." Rather, this school of thought holds, white people invented these notions to exclude and exploit people of color. One Howard University historian contends that Bernal should have titled his book *Egyptian Africa* to emphasize Egypt's influence on Africa. The title *Black Athena*, this historian maintains, feeds into the discredited notion of humankind as divided into biologically determined "races" defined by skin color. Bernal now agrees that he might have more appropriately titled his book *African Athena*. But for all the contradictory uses to which *Black Athena* has been put, the book has enriched our understanding of the connections among the ancient peoples living around the Mediterranean Sea.

Egypt and Nubia

Nubia, the state the Egyptians called Kush, has also caught the attention of modern-day African Americans seeking to reclaim a noble past. In ancient times, Nubia lay to the south of Egypt, along the lower Nile from the first great cataract (waterfall) to below the fifth cataract. For centuries, Egypt's rulers sent ships south along the Nile to trade with the dark-skinned Nubians living in Kush. Both societies benefited from this trade. Still, the pharaohs considered Kush part of their empire, so from time to time they sent armies into the region to maintain their control of its valuable assets.

Although Kush adopted many elements of Egyptian culture, it retained its individual character and political structures. Yet power shifted back and forth between Egypt and Kush. By about 1070 BCE, Egypt fell into decline. Emboldened, the Kushite rulers broke away from Egyptian control. By 750 BCE, the Kushite kings had conquered Upper Egypt and its capital city, Thebes, and seized Memphis, the main Egyptian capital. Later, Shabaka became the first Kushite monarch to control all of Egypt. Yet governing a vast empire is complex, difficult work. The Kushites' rule lasted for less than one hundred years. Slowly, Egypt regained its former stature. During the centuries that followed, the two civilizations—each with its own distinct legacy—remained closely connected. Intermarriage, trade, and the exchange of artistic traditions renewed the fusion of peoples living in the vast Nile River region.

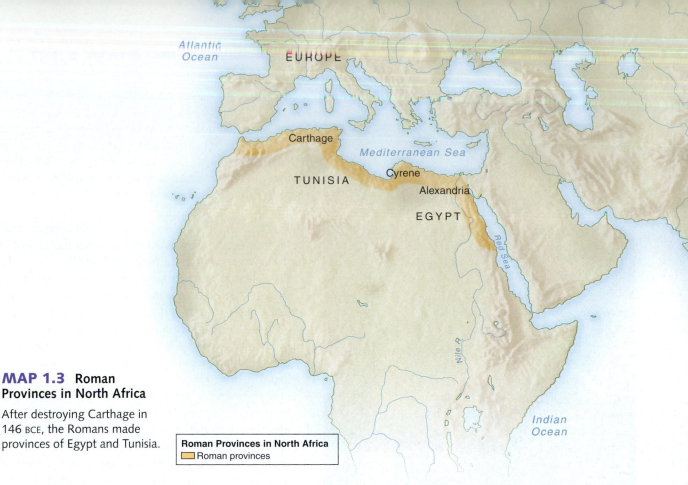

■ **MAP 1.3** Roman Provinces in North Africa

After destroying Carthage in 146 BCE, the Romans made provinces of Egypt and Tunisia.

Roman Provinces in North Africa
☐ Roman provinces

Egypt after the Greek Conquest

In 332 BCE, the twenty-four-year-old Macedonian warrior Alexander the Great swept into Egypt with his armies and added the region to his rapidly expanding collection of conquests. Though the last Egyptian dynasty came to an end, Egypt continued to serve as a cultural crossroads in the ancient Middle East as its Greek rulers spread their influence. For the next three centuries, Alexander's general, Ptolemy, and his successors governed Egypt. As one of their most striking achievements, they founded the city of Alexandria, named after the conquering Macedonian king. A port city on the Mediterranean Sea, Alexandria became a vibrant trading and cultural hub. As a crossroads, the city enabled those who lived around the Mediteranean to exchange goods and ideas with people living in the mineral-rich African interior and in Alexander's conquered lands east into India.

Egypt maintained this central cultural position when, around 500 BCE, the Romans began conquering lands as far west as Spain and dominating the Mediterranean. By about 146 BCE, the Romans had supplanted Greek control in northern Africa. The Roman government made Tunisia and Egypt dependent provinces, extracting from them grain, papyrus for papermaking, and even wild animals that were pitted against one another in the vaunted Roman circus games.

In Roman Africa, trade and periodic warfare accelerated the intermingling of peoples. A new faith, Christianity, spread through the Roman Empire as a result of this intermingling. Christianity sank its roots deep into Egypt in the first century CE. Alexandria, Egypt's commercial center, became one of the most vital hubs of early Christendom. Gradually, Christianity spread west across North Africa among Berber-speaking peoples. It also moved south from Egypt into Nubia where today, in Ethiopia, it still flourishes.

THE SPREAD OF ISLAM

"The seat of Mansa Sulayman [the sultan] was a sprawling, unwalled town set in a 'verdant and hilly' country," wrote seasoned traveler Abu Abdallah Ibn Battuta in 1351 CE after visiting the capital of Mali, a kingdom in northwest Africa. "The sultan had several enclosed palaces there . . . and covered [them] with colored patterns so that it turned out to be the most elegant of buildings. Surrounding the palaces and mosques were the residences of the citizenry, mud-walled houses roofed with domes of timber and reed. . . . Amongst their good qualities is the small amount of injustice amongst them, for of all people they are the furthest from it. Their sultan does not forgive anyone in any matter to do with injustice. . . . There is also the prevalence of peace in their country, the traveler is not afraid in it nor is

> **"T**here is also the prevalence of peace in their country."
> —Abu Abdallah Ibn Battuta

he who lives there in fear of the thief or of the robber by violence. They do not interfere with the property of the white man who dies in their country even though it may consist of great wealth, but rather they entrust it to the hand of someone dependable among the white men until it is taken by the rightful claimant."

This vivid excerpt from one of the greatest travelers of premodern times opens a window onto the theme of this section: the spread of Islam in Africa beginning in the seventh century. Enslaved Africans later carried this faith to North America. The excerpt's author, Ibn Battuta, embodied the rise of Islam. Born in 1304 CE into a family of Muslim legal scholars in Tangier, Morocco (on the southern shore of the Mediterranean Sea), he came of age as Islam was connecting Europe, Asia, and Africa by dint of religious, cultural, and military force. At age twenty-one, Ibn Battuta made a pilgrimage along well-beaten trading routes to the sacred Muslim city of Mecca in Arabia. For more than twenty years he traveled through much of the eastern hemisphere. He visited territories equivalent to forty-four present-day countries and covered about 73,000 miles—three times the distance covered by the legendary Marco Polo. He recorded the words in the excerpt above as he journeyed in 1351 from Fez across the Atlas Mountains to Sijilmasa, a bustling trade center in southern Morocco. Ibn Battuta's careful record-keeping provides a rare glimpse into a vibrant era in African history.

The Origins of Islam

Islam, meaning "submission to Allah," was born in 610 CE. That year, a young warrior named Muhammad began preaching in his Arabian village after he saw a vision of the angel Gabriel. The angel, Muhammad claimed, had commanded him to spread messages from God to peoples throughout the land. A gifted orator, Muhammad attracted numerous followers and became the founder of the new faith. Like Christianity, Islam is monotheistic; it recognizes only one god. Muhammad preached that he was God's final prophet. The Qur'an, he avowed, was God's word revealed to him. According to Muhammad, the messages he received from God completed the earlier revelations of the Hebrew prophets and Jesus.

Muhammad won many converts because his message had great appeal. The theological foundation of the faith he advocated was easily understood; it did not require an exclusive, elite class of priests. All believers, Muhammad preached, were equal in the eyes of Allah. Through private prayer, kindness and generosity, and fasting before the holy feast of Ramadan, anyone could embrace the will of the One True God. Islam also provided a code for right living. For example, the rich must demonstrate compassion, share their wealth with the poor, and contribute to public charities such as hospitals. Every Muslim (follower of Islam) must forswear drinking alcohol and gambling. Adherents to the faith must struggle to resist temptation and overcome evil. Muslims also held scholarship in high regard and established strict rules governing commercial activities such as bookkeeping, credit arrangements, and dispute resolution.

Islam's Great Reach

Like Christians, Muslims believed they had a mandate from God to convert all people to their faith. Within a century of Muhammad's death in 632, his followers had reached out aggressively, often militarily, and established control over regions larger than those making up the Roman Empire.

Spreading rapidly in Arabia, the new faith soon extended into Syria and Mesopotamia. It then moved east all the way to China, west across Mediterranean North Africa to Spain, and south along the Red Sea coast of East Africa. Invaded by Arab Muslims in 639 CE, Egypt became Islamized, just as it had earlier been Christianized under Roman influence. By the tenth century CE, Egypt had a predominantly Muslim population. Islam then spread south from Mediterranean North Africa across the Sahara Desert into the savannah region of western Africa, then called the Sudan. (The word *Sudan* is Arabic for "black people." Today's Sudan is an East African nation bordering the Red Sea.)

Islam initially made little headway among villagers in the Sudanese countryside because these men and women lived far from the trading routes that accelerated the spread of ideas. But Islam began to build momentum, first along trading routes and in urban commercial centers and then deeper into the countryside. Five centuries later, when Portuguese traders initiated the slave traffic in West Africa, they found that many of the Africans they packed into Atlantic slave ships were devout Muslims.

Along with Muslim conquering armies, relying heavily on camels, came the exchange of Muslim goods, ideas, technologies, and religious belief. With its emphasis on

 **First Person**   Leo Africanus Describes Timbuktu

When his History and Description of Africa *was published in Italian in 1550, Leo Africanus greatly extended European knowledge of the continent. Africanus was born in 1489 in Granada, the Muslim stronghold in Spain, with the name Al-Hasan Ibn Muhammad al-Wazzan al-Fasi. Trained in Arabic as a Muslim scholar, he made lengthy trips through northern and western Africa. In 1518, he was captured by Sicilian pirates and offered as a slave to Pope Leo X. In Rome, he converted to Christianity and took the name Leo Africanus. His book was translated into English and published in 1600. In the excerpt below, Africanus describes the cultural riches of Timbuktu.*

[In Timbuktu] there is a most stately temple to be seen, the walls whereof are made of stone and lime; and a princely palace also built by a most excellent workman of Granada. Here are many shops of artificers [artisans] and merchants. . . . And hither do the Barbary merchants bring cloth of Europe. . . . Here are many wells, containing most sweet water; and so often as the river Niger overfloweth, they convey the water thereof by certain sluices into the town. Corn, cattle, milk, and butter this region yieldeth in great abundance; but salt is very scarce here. . . . Here are great stores of doctors, judges, priests, and other learned men that are bountifully

maintained at the king's cost and charges. And hither are brought diverse manuscripts or written books out of Barbary, which are sold for more money than any other merchandise. . . . The inhabitants are people of a gentle and cheerful disposition, and spend a great part of the night in singing and dancing through all the streets of the city; they keep great store of men and women-slaves.

—*from* The History and Description of Africa *by Leo Africanus.*

To view a longer version of this document, please go to *www.ablongman.com/Carson/documents.*

scholarship, the religion fostered the spread of literacy and book-learning throughout West Africa. African rulers began embracing the Muslim faith.

Islam spread much faster in East Africa, the region south of Egypt and bordering the Red Sea and Indian Ocean. From its origins in Arabia, it spread through India, Ceylon, the East Indies, and China. As trading flourished in this region during the tenth century, Arab traders settled in the ports along Africa's east coast and intermarried with native people. A blended culture emerged. Muslim city-states arose across the continent, with Kilwa and Sofala, the southernmost ports on the Indian Ocean trade route, controlling the export of gold and ivory to the east. Visiting the immense palace, vast irrigated gardens, and imposing Muslim mosque in Kilwa in 1331, that avid traveler Ibn Battuta described the city as "one of the most beautiful and well-constructed towns in the world. . . . The whole of it is elegantly built."

THE EMERGENCE OF WEST AFRICAN KINGDOMS

In 951, a Muslim traveler and geographer named Ibn Hawkal journeyed from Baghdad (in modern-day Iraq) to Sijilmasa, the Moroccan trade center that lay north of the Sahara. There he heard reports that convinced him that the king of Ghana was the wealthiest of all monarchs on Earth. Traveling south across the Sahara, Ibn Hawkal entered Awdaghost, an ancient city now buried in the sands of today's Mauretanian town of Tagdaust. In his *Opus Geographicum,* he described the brisk trade he saw taking place in what was the Ghanaian gateway to the Sahara. Ibn Hawkal claimed to have seen the accounts of one trans-Saharan merchant who had a credit for 42,000 gold dinars'

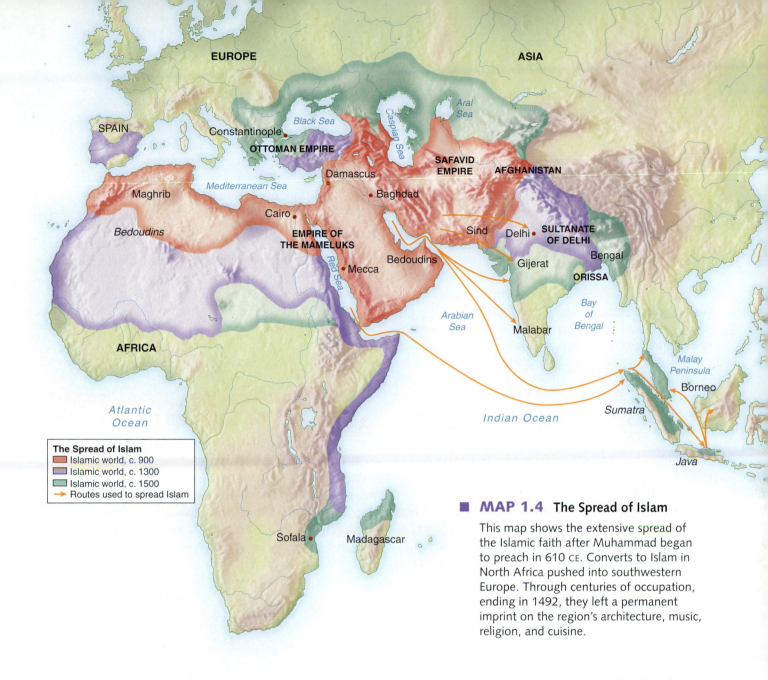

EUROPE

ASIA

SPAIN

Black Sea

Aral Sea

Constantinople

OTTOMAN EMPIRE

SAFAVID EMPIRE

AFGHANISTAN

Maghrib

Mediterranean Sea

Damascus

Baghdad

Sind

Delhi

SULTANATE OF DELHI

Bengal

Bedoudins

Cairo

EMPIRE OF THE MAMELUKS

Bedoudins

Gijerat

ORISSA

Mecca

Arabian Sea

Malabar

Bay of Bengal

AFRICA

Atlantic Ocean

Indian Ocean

Malay Peninsula

Borneo

Sumatra

Java

The Spread of Islam
- Islamic world, c. 900
- Islamic world, c. 1300
- Islamic world, c. 1500
- → Routes used to spread Islam

Sofala

Madagascar

■ **MAP 1.4** The Spread of Islam

This map shows the extensive spread of the Islamic faith after Muhammad began to preach in 610 CE. Converts to Islam in North Africa pushed into southwestern Europe. Through centuries of occupation, ending in 1492, they left a permanent imprint on the region's architecture, music, religion, and cuisine.

worth of trade. He also found that the Ghana king's title was *Kaya-Maghan*—Lord of the Gold.

Ibn Hawkal's account, written more than a millennium ago, sheds light on why West African kingdoms proliferated with such energy during the tenth century. The gold trade—and the control of the cross-Sahara traffic it required—united peoples of many cultures living in the grasslands of western Africa. Societies built on the wealth made possible by the gold trade developed along the trading routes. Over time, ambitious local rulers strengthened their control over their own and nearby groups, creating centralized kingdoms.

By the tenth century, Islam had spread across the Sahara Desert to West Africa. This vast region comprised an array of ecological zones—desert, grasslands, forests, and woodlands. Like Europeans, most West Africans tilled the soil, developing sophisticated agricultural and livestock

management practices. The West Africans' ironmaking skills enabled them to hone their agricultural talents further.

Iron production began among the Nok in present-day Nigeria about 450 BCE—long before peoples living on the European continent mastered this technology. By crushing iron ore and smelting it in a forced-air blast furnace, these early Iron Age Africans produced molten metal that they forged into finely crafted tools for cultivating and harvesting crops. Their agricultural productivity soared, igniting a population boom. With larger populations came greater specialization of tasks. Now different groups of individuals became experts in specific kinds of work such as toolmaking and leatherworking. Specialization in turn catalyzed greater efficiency and additional technical improvements. This pattern resembled that of the so-called agricultural revolution that independently transformed the Americas, Europe, the Middle East, and elsewhere.

West African societies evolved on the southern flank of the Sahara at different rates. Villages and towns in regions blessed by fertile soil, adequate rainfall, and abundant minerals, as in coastal West Africa, grew rapidly, especially with the advent of interregional trade. Meanwhile, groups living in inhospitable deserts or impenetrable forests remained small and changed slowly.

People tend to migrate when their natural environments changes for the worse. For example, the vast Sahara, once a land of flowing rivers and lush pastures and forests, became uninhabitable to humans owing to climate changes that raised temperatures and lowered rainfall. As the region dried up between about 4000 and 2500 BCE, Saharan peoples moved south in search of more fertile land. First they migrated to oases situated along a strip of grassland, or savannah, on the desert's southern border. Then they headed farther south to the fertile rainforests of the Niger River basin. In these forests, they built some of Africa's greatest kingdoms. All of them were inland civilizations whose trading routes ran overland rather than by sea.

The Kingdom of Ghana

The first of these inland civilizations was the kingdom of Ghana. Developing between the fifth and eleventh centuries CE (after the Roman Empire collapsed and medieval Europe fell into decline), Ghana occupied a huge territory that stretched between the Sahara Desert and the Gulf of Guinea, from the Niger River to the Atlantic Ocean. Ghana evolved from a collection of small villages into a major kingdom noted for its extensive urban settlements, skillfully designed buildings, elaborate sculpture, and effective political and military structure.

The gold trade fueled Ghana's growth and success. The precious metal made Kumbi-Saleh, Ghana's capital, the busiest and wealthiest marketplace in West Africa. The Soninke people of Ghana took advantage of their geographic position just south of the Sahara and north of the goldfields of the Senegal River region. They flourished by cultivating trading contacts with Muslim Arabs, who had crossed the Sahara Desert in camel caravans by the eleventh century. In this cross-desert trade, the Soninke swapped gold for imported items such as ceramics, glass, oil lamps, and salt from Saharan mines—essential for preserving and flavoring food. From the south, they traded for kola nuts, palm oil, copper, and gold. Their customers carried gold back to Europe, the Middle East, and North Africa, where people used the precious metal to make coins and jewelry.

Gold proved so plentiful that Ghanaian kings felt compelled to devise ways to keep its value high. For example, they maintained a royal monopoly over gold bars, allowing

traders to deal only in gold dust. The exhaustion of gold mines in Europe and the Middle East helped boost the value of Ghanaian gold. Even so, salt was so equally coveted that it carried the same value, pound for pound, as gold.

By the time of the western Middle Ages, two-thirds of the gold circulating in the Christian Mediterranean region had originated in Ghana. Moreover, the Soninke—now numbering in the hundreds of thousands—had gained control of more than 100,000 square miles of land. Minted in Morocco, Ghanaian gold had become the most favored currency throughout the vast Muslim trading network centered in Cairo.

By the eleventh century, a thriving caravan trade with Arab peoples across the Sahara to Morocco and Algeria spread Muslim influence deep into West Africa. By this time, the Soninke king of Ghana boasted an army of 200,000 and maintained trading contacts as far east as Cairo and Baghdad. As trade in Ghana accelerated, enterprising Arab merchants came to settle in the empire, especially in Kumbi-Saleh.

With the trading of goods came the exchange of ideas. Arabs brought the first system of writing and numbers to West Africa. The Ghanaian kings adopted Arab script and appointed Arabs to government positions in charge of trade and taxation. As these Arabs gained influence in Ghana, they spread the Islamic faith. Many Ghanaian rulers kept their traditional religion, however, which emphasized worship of the natural world. These monarchs were politically threatened by the Muslim principle of patriarchy, whereby royal succession followed the ruling father's lineage. (In many West African societies, royal succession followed the lineage of the king's sister.) But numerous Ghanaians, especially those living in the cities, converted to Islam. By 1050, Kumbi-Saleh boasted twelve Muslim mosques.

The Kingdom of Mali

Beginning in the late eleventh century, Muslim Berber warriors swept into Ghana from the north, weakening the realm and sowing religious and political strife. The resulting instability emboldened a ruler of Mali, a state within Ghana, to make war against his overlords. The troops of the Mali king Sundiata crushed Ghanaian warriors in 1235 at the Battle of Kirina, dealing the deathblow to the crippled realm. The Islamic kingdom of Mali, populated primarily by Mandingo people, rose in Ghana's place. The Mandingo quickly mastered agricultural production and seized control of the gold trade. They also cultivated rice and harvested inland deltas for fish, augmenting trade in salt, gold, and copper. Like Ghana before it, Mali grew wealthy from long-distance trade.

Under Sundiata's grandson Mansa Musa, a devout Muslim who assumed the throne in 1307, Mali came to control

Legend of King Sundiata's Triumph over the Ghanaian King

To this day, Mandingo griots—storytellers, counselors to kings, and tutors to young princes— pass along the legend of the rise of Mali and the illustrious start of King Sundiata's reign. King Sundiata met Ghana's King Soumaoro on the battlefield at Kirina in 1235. According to the legend, both rulers possessed magical power, and the superior magic would decide the battle's victor. The excerpt below describes the climax of the battle as recounted by storytellers for eight centuries.

Sundiata struck out right and left and the Sossos [Ghanaians] scrambled out of his way. The king of Sosso, who did not want Sundiata to get near him, retreated far behind his men, but Sundiata followed him with his eyes. He stopped and bent his bow. The arrow flew and grazed Soumaoro on the shoulder. The cock's spur [on the arrow] no more than scratched him, but the effect was immediate and Soumaoro felt his powers leave him. His eyes met Sundiata's. Now trembling like a man in the grip of a fever, the vanquished Soumaoro looked up towards the sun. A great black bird flew over above the ray and he understood. It was a bird of misfortune. "The bird of Kirina," he muttered. The king of Sosso let out a great cry and, turning his horse's head, he took to flight. The Sossos saw the king and fled in their turn. It was a rout.

—from D. T. Niane, Sundiata: An Epic of Old Mali, *trans. G. D. Pickett, p. 65. © Présence Africaine 1960 (original French version). © Longman Group Ltd. (English version) 1965. Reprinted by permission of Pearson Education Ltd.*

To view a longer version of this document, please go to *www.ablongman.com/carson/documents*.

territory three times as great as Ghana. Mansa Musa won fame when he made a 3,500-mile pilgrimage across the Sahara and through Cairo all the way to Mecca in 1324, accompanied by an entourage of 50,000. The young ruler played to Mediterranean merchants all along his route. Dispensing lavish gifts of gold as he wended his way east, he made Mali gold legendary. His image on maps of the world for centuries thereafter testified to his importance in promoting West Africa's treasures.

Returning home after several years of pilgrimage, Mansa Musa brought Muslim scholars and artisans with him who helped establish the inland city of Timbuktu, which stood as the gateway to the Sahara in the Sudanese region of Songhai. Traveling to Timbuktu in the 1330s, the Arab geographer Ibn Battuta wrote admiringly of "the discipline of [the city's] officials and provincial governors, the excellent condition of public finance, and . . . the respect accorded to the decisions of justice and to the authority of the sovereign."

Noted for its extensive wealth, Timbuktu was also home to an Islamic university with a distinguished faculty who wrote on legal, historical, geographical, and moral topics. Two of the first histories of the western Sudan, both completed in 1665, were written by Timbuktu scholars, Mahmud Kati and Abd al-Rahman as-Sadi. North Africans and southern Europeans flocked to the university to study.

The Kingdom of Songhai

After Mansa Musa died in 1332, his successors could not maintain Mali's dominance in West Africa. The Songhai, a subject people living along the Niger River, saw an opportunity to regain their freedom from the Mandingo. A mixture of farmers, traders, fishermen, and warriors, the Songhai broke away from Mali in 1435 and began waging wars to conquer new territories. Just as Mali had grown out of a state within the empire of Ghana, the new Songhai empire grew out of a region that had once been part of Mali. At its height, Songhai equaled France in size.

By the time Portuguese traders began establishing commercial links with the Kongo (an African region far south of

Songhai) in the late 1400s, the Songhai empire reached its peak under the Muslim rulers Sonni Ali (1468–1492) and Askia Muhammad (1493–1528). Yet Songhai, too, collapsed, as some tribes, resentful of Muslim kings, began to break away. But the worst threat came from Morocco, in North Africa. There, rulers coveted Songhai's control of salt and gold—the two critical commodities of African trade. Armed with guns procured in the Middle East, Morocco's ruler captured the major Songhai towns of Timbuktu and Gao in 1591. The North Africans maintained loose control of western Sudan for more than a century as the last great trading empire of West Africa faded into history.

During an era when centralized kingdoms began emerging in Europe, West Africa devolved into smaller states. By the time Europeans reached the continent's Atlantic coast, most Africans resided in states no larger than Switzerland or Denmark. As discussed in the next chapter, conflicts among these small states enabled European slave traders to gain a foothold in the region by persuading tribal leaders to send out warrior parties to capture slaves.

The Forest Kingdoms of Ife and Benin

To the south of Songhai, Yoruba-speaking peoples lived in villages and towns of considerable size. Their territory

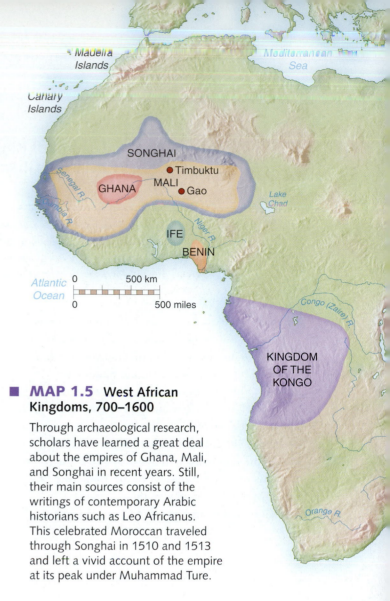

■ **MAP 1.5** **West African Kingdoms, 700–1600**

Through archaeological research, scholars have learned a great deal about the empires of Ghana, Mali, and Songhai in recent years. Still, their main sources consist of the writings of contemporary Arabic historians such as Leo Africanus. This celebrated Moroccan traveled through Songhai in 1510 and 1513 and left a vivid account of the empire at its peak under Muhammad Ture.

■ This horseman was cast in terra cotta by a Mali artist. Experts date the figure somewhere in between 1240–1460. Note the erect pose of the rider and the horse's decorative collars. The rider sports embroidered pants, a helmet and heavy necklace, and a dagger strapped to his left arm.

stretched from the inland savannah woodlands to the long Gulf of Guinea on the Atlantic coast. These peoples—hunters, farmers, and craftsmen—began to cluster in states during the eleventh and twelfth centuries. The kingdoms of Ife and Benin were among the most influential of these states. In both kingdoms, inland cities developed, and their rulers governed the surrounding peoples. Ife's settlement dates to about the eighth century. It became a religious and cultural center of the Yoruba people.

To the south of Ife stood Benin, which arose about 1000 CE west of the Niger Delta. About 50 miles from the Gulf of Guinea lay Benin City, a major West African center of metalworking and ceramic production. When the Portuguese arrived in Benin in 1485, they found a highly organized society governed by an absolute monarch. The king was attended by an elaborate court of aristocrats and served by an efficient bureaucracy and powerful military force. The first Europeans to reach Benin City found a walled urban complex boasting broad streets and hundreds of buildings. In 1602, when a Dutch artist visited the city, he compared

First Person   Praise-chant for Ogún, Deity of War and Iron

The Yoruba-speaking people have produced and used iron for centuries. They prize the metal so fervently that they invest it with mystical powers and pray for divine protection of their iron specialists. Indeed, many Ife and Benin metalsmiths traditionally recite prayers while pouring molten metal. Even today, Yoruba-speaking people revere Ogún, a deity of war and iron. From Ogún's iron come machetes, knives, and hoes for clearing forests to make way for farmland. By worshiping Ogún, Yoruba-speaking people give thanks for his gifts and honor him with iron and brass jewelry. This chant comes from the ancient town of Ketu.

Ogún, allied to the man with a quick hand
Ogún, owner of high fringes of palm fronds
Ogún, ties on his cutlass with a belt of cotton
Ogún of the sharp black cutlass

Hoe is the child of Ogún
Axe is the child of Ogún
Gun is the child of Ogún

Ogún, salute of iron on stone
The blacksmith of all heaven.

—*from* Flash of the Spirit *by Robert Farris Thompson.*
© *1983 by Robert Farris Thompson. Used by permission of Random House, Inc.*

To view a longer version of this document, please go to *www.ablongman.com/carson/documents*.

its fine houses, wide streets, and royal court favorably with those of Amsterdam, the Dutch capital.

Owing to their location on the African coast and their military might, the leaders of the Yoruba-speaking peoples became powerful slave traders. They captured thousands of slaves from the African interior and sold them in Benin City to the Portuguese. Later, they sold bondspeople to the English at the coastal city of Calabar, the site of a major slave fort. Both Ife and Benin enjoyed fertile soil and plentiful rainfall. These advantages, along with knowledge of ironworking, enabled the two kingdoms to cultivate surplus cereal and root crops as well as raise domestic animals. This bounty in turn supported trade with outside states. The wealth pouring in from trade freed enough leisure time for some people to explore artistic endeavors such as making jewelry and decorative ceramics.

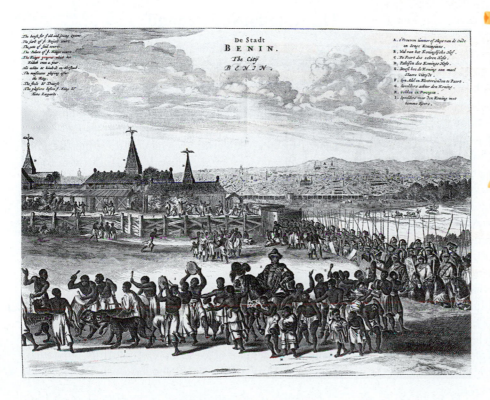

■ In this view of Benin, a Dutch artist shows the procession of the *oba* ("king") through the city.

CENTRAL AFRICAN KINGDOMS

West Africa became the biggest source of slaves shipped across the Atlantic. Nevertheless, an area farther south along the Atlantic coast and in Central Africa ultimately provided another major catch basin for slave traders. Hundreds of thousands of modern-day African Americans trace their ancestry to this region, which included the vast kingdoms of Kongo and Ndongo (Angola). The religious, musical, medical, and burial traditions that first emerged in Central Africa still find expression in the United States today.

The Kingdom of Kongo

Kongo, which Europeans first encountered in 1482, was home to the Bakongo people, some two million strong by the 1400s. Their origins trace to Bantu-speaking farmers who began a great migration out of Central Africa in the first few centuries CE. Some traveled east, all the way to the Indian Ocean, while others made their way south to the Kongo Basin. Among those migrating south, the Nok—one of many Bantu-speaking groups—carried with them the knowledge of smelting iron ore and fashioning the metal into spears, axes, fishhooks, and hoes. Thanks to these tools, farmers and fishers could accumulate more food than they needed to survive. So renowned was Nok knowledge of ironmaking that one historian has called Kongo "the land of the blacksmith kings." The technological knowledge of ironmaking spread from the Kongo Basin through much of West Africa.

The combination of ironworking skills and fertile river valleys enabled the Kongo Basin settlers to flourish in the millennium after the Nok's migration. Ironworking was widespread by the eighth century. Fertile river valleys aided the spread of population. As the centuries unfolded, hunter-gatherer groups who already had been living in the region made permanent homes in the agricultural villages that dotted the vast Kongo Basin. Gradually, strong leaders loosely united these villages into a kingdom that had its royal city at Mbanza Kongo.

Built on a fertile plateau surrounded by rainforests, Mbanza lay 100 miles east of the coast and 50 miles south of the Kongo River. In this lively trade center, artisans, craftspeople, and manufacturers conducted an energetic business. Using the fibers of the raffia palm tree, skilled weavers wove fine cloth, which they traded to merchants from the north for salt and for seashells, used as local currency. From the wheels of hundreds of potters came decorative and functional bowls for carrying water and grain. As

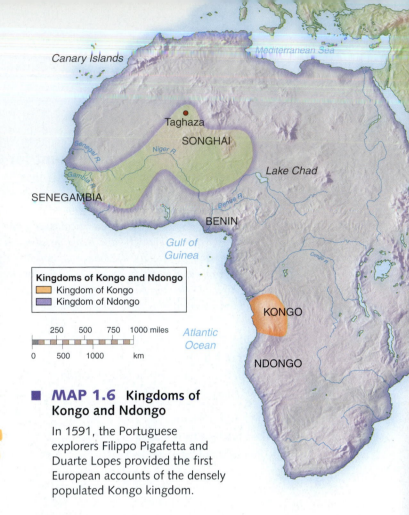

 MAP 1.6 Kingdoms of Kongo and Ndongo

In 1591, the Portuguese explorers Filippo Pigafetta and Duarte Lopes provided the first European accounts of the densely populated Kongo kingdom.

discussed in chapter 2, Mbanza also became a slave-trading center after the Portuguese arrived on the Atlantic coast of Kongo in 1482.

The Kingdom of Ndongo

South of Kongo, along the Atlantic coast, arose another kingdom: Ndongo (modern-day Angola). Like Kongo, Ndongo played a central role in the slave trade after the Portuguese reached Africa. By the 1300s, the Ndongo region consisted of three main chiefdoms: the Pende, Libolo, and Ndongo. Talented ironworkers, these peoples had established thriving, powerful societies by the time the Portuguese began wending their way down Africa's west coast. By about 1500, the Ndongo chieftains had welded the local groups together into a unified state. Chapter 2 shows how this centralization enabled the Portuguese to establish solid trade relationships with the kingdom as well as spread the Catholic belief among the Ndongo peoples.

AFRICAN CULTURE

Many of the peoples of West and Central Africa—Ndongo, Mandingo, Yoruba, Fon, Hausa, Ibo, Bakongo, Whydah, Ga, and others—eventually saw some of their members sent away in slave ships. Though their societies and languages varied greatly, most shared certain ways of life that differentiated them from Europeans. By understanding these cultures, we can better appreciate how Africans refashioned themselves in the Americas and how they built defenses against the cruelties inflicted on them during four centuries of enslavement.

Family and Community

In ancient and medieval Africa, as elsewhere, the family served as the basic unit of society. Most families lived in villages, though by the 1200s, cities of many thousands dotted the continent. In most villages, people were part of a single lineage—a large, extended family claiming a common ancestor. Thus each person felt closely linked by family ties to others in the village. Individuals defined themselves in terms of their place in a constellation of fathers, mothers, aunts, uncles, brothers, sisters, and cousins. In such close-knit village life, it is not surprising that elders commanded profound respect.

Unlike Europeans, who put fathers and husbands at the center of family life and political power, Africans organized themselves according to a rich variety of kinship systems. Though some were patrilineal, most were matrilineal: Property rights and political power descended through the mother rather than the father. Thus, when a chief died, his sister's son claimed the throne. After a wedding, the new husband joined his bride's people. This matrilineal tradition carried over into slavery, as African women continued to wield influence in their families in ways not typically seen in European families.

Regardless of the kinship system they lived by, all Africans emphasized the interdependencies among people over their roles as individuals. Indeed, African languages did not contain a word for *individualism*. When black slaves first encountered the notion of individualism in North America, they found it alien, distasteful, and nearly meaningless. As historian Nathan Huggins has explained, "Alone, a person was nobody. Alone, one was helpless before all that was unknown. The smallest thing could threaten the isolated person—the elements, inanimate objects, animals, and above all, other people."

Many Africans practiced polygamy, so most adult women were co-wives. In many of these family units, one woman ranked as the senior wife and had authority over the others. Outside their dwelling, women cultivated the land and tended the family's livestock and fowls. They also did the marketing, bartering surplus produce such as yams, peppers, rice, chickens, millet, and nuts in return for other produce or household items they wanted.

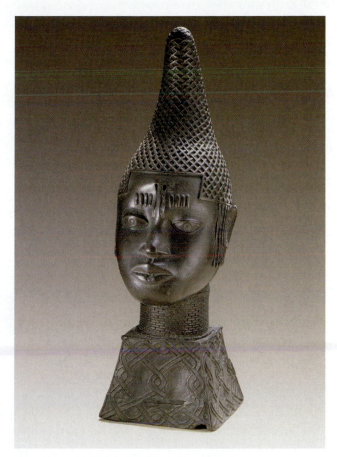

■ The tall, netted headdress on this sculpture identifies the figure as a Benin Queen Mother. In the Benin kingdom, the Queen Mother participated in state affairs with her son, the king.

Many Africans revered female deities. For example, the Yoruba worshiped the river goddess Oshun for giving them life force, fertility, family, power, and wealth. According to legend, Oshun bore twins with a fiery god of thunder, accumulated great wealth, and carried her treasures to the bottom of the Niger River, where she still reigns. Many Yoruba-speaking people today visualize Oshun as wielding a sword, always ready to slay the immoral. They thank her for protecting the people of the Niger River basin from witchcraft.

Religion

As in almost every human society, religious thought and practice in Africa made life's challenges meaningful and bearable. Across Africa, numerous people believed that a supreme being had created the universe. They also associated a pantheon of lesser gods with phenomena they saw in nature, such as rain, animals, mountains, and the fertility of the

Earth. Many people considered the Supreme Creator good and merciful. Sayings such as "Rejoice, God never does wrong to people" and epithets like the God of Pity, the Merciful One, and the Kind One reveal the belief in a kind rather than an angry and vengeful god.

> "Rejoice, God never does wrong to people."
> —*West African saying*

Because they believed lesser deities also could intervene in human affairs, Africans honored them with elaborate rituals. West Africans maintained that spirits dwelled in the trees, rocks, and rivers around them. Thus they exercised care in their treatment of these natural objects. For example, men who went fishing in a great river or tried to cross it in a canoe asked for the blessings of the river divinity through offerings or prayers. When drought struck their crops, they implored the rain gods to show mercy.

Africans also believed their ancestors retained a life force after death. Ancestors thus had the power to affect a village's welfare by mediating between the Supreme Creator and the living. Because the dead could exert a significant impact on the living, their surviving relatives held elaborate funeral rites to ensure a deceased person's proper entrance into the spiritual world. The more ancient an ancestor, the greater this person's power became. Therefore, villagers and townspeople invoked the "ancient ones" in prayers and honored them with shrines. Deep family loyalty and regard for family lineage flowed naturally from this reverence of ancestors.

West Africans also believed in spirit possession—gods speaking to men and women through priests, other religious figures, and natural forces and objects. Olaudah Equiano, who wrote an autobiographical account of his enslavement and his later purchase of his freedom, recalled, "Though we had no places of public worship, we had priests and magicians, or wise men . . . held in great reverence by the people. They calculated time, foretold events, . . . and when they died, they were succeeded by their sons." In some African societies, evil spirits caused misfortune, sickness, and even death. People beset by an evil spirit often sought the aid of a diviner or medicine man to drive off the troublesome or malicious spirit.

Beginning in the eighth century, the spread of Islam across North Africa into the sub-Saharan Sudan and down the coast of the Red Sea through large regions of East Africa brought thousands of Africans into the Muslim faith. Islam's acceptance of polygamy, which most African societies practiced, facilitated this spread. By the late fifteenth century, as Muslim Arab traders migrated into Africa and believers launched wars of conquest and conversion, Islam had begun displacing traditional African religions in many parts of West and Central Africa, where the Atlantic slave trade began to gather momentum.

This was the complex religious heritage enslaved Africans brought to the Americas. No amount of desolation or physical abuse could wipe out these deeply rooted beliefs. In fact, it was their spiritual traditions that enabled many slaves to bear the hardships inherent in the master-slave relationship.

Yet despite many cultural differences, slaves and their Western owners also shared common ground. For example, people of both cultures recognized a physical world in which the living dwelled and an "other world" inhabited by the souls of the dead. Both believed that this "other world" could not be seen. However, people could come to know it by listening to revelations interpreted by spiritually gifted persons.

These shared foundations of religious belief enabled a hybrid African Christianity to develop in both Africa and the Americas. For example, in the kingdom of Kongo and several small realms close to the Niger Delta, extensive contact between Africans and the Portuguese interwove Christian beliefs with African religious beliefs in the seventeenth century. The worship of the Christian god did not eliminate the reverence for traditional African gods. Although enslavement suppressed some African religious customs, many spiritual beliefs and practices survived and are embraced by some African Americans today.

Social Organization

When Africans first welcomed Europeans to their lands, they were surprised to discover that Europeans had political organizations as sophisticated as their own. At the top of society stood the king. Landowning nobles, military leaders, and priests (usually elderly men) collected the monarch. Beneath them were bureaucrats who collected taxes, kept records, and oversaw commerce. The next layer down comprised the craftspeople, traders, teachers, and artists of the villages and towns. The broad base of this hierarchy consisted of the great mass of people, most of whom cultivated the soil. "Agriculture is our chief employment," recalled Olaudah Equiano, "and every one, even the children and women, are engaged in

> "Everyone contributes something to the common stock."—*Olaudah Equiano*

 **First Person**   ## African Proverbs

Like people in other parts of the world, the peoples of Africa have created many proverbs and passed them down through the generations. Representing a society's wisdom, some proverbs have been told for centuries, while others are relatively new. Through repeated telling, proverbs instruct, warn, encourage good behavior, stimulate the imagination, and even dare to predict the future.

A lion does not eat its own cubs. *(Kenya)*

Do not abandon a child when it has an itching sore. *(South Africa—Azania)*

A woman is a flower in a garden; her husband is the fence around it. *(Ghana)*

He who eats alone, dies alone. *(Kenya)*

The creature is not greater than its Creator. *(Burundi)*

The way to overcome cold is to warm each other. *(South Africa—Azania)*

We do not see God, we only see His works. *(Ethiopia)*

You do not become a chief simply by sitting on a big stool. *(Ghana)*

The earth is the mother of all. *(Uganda)*

We are born from the womb of our mother; we are buried in the womb of the earth. *(Ethiopia)*

—from John S. Mbiti, Introduction to African Religion, *2d ed. (Oxford, Heinemann, 1991), pp. 208–212.*

To view a longer version of this document, please go to *www.ablongman.com/carson/documents*.

it. Thus we are habituated to labour from our earliest years." Equiano continued: "Everyone contributes something to the common stock."

African societies also included slaves—men and the women who had the least status and the least freedom. Slavery was not new to Europeans or Africans—or to any other peoples. It had flourished in ancient Greece and Rome, in Russia and eastern Europe, and in southwestern Asia. Conquering peoples everywhere sold captured enemies into slavery because they could not tolerate holding massive numbers of the enemy in their midst. Selling them to distant lands as slaves neutralized their threat, was more merciful than killing them, and generated profit.

Like peoples living almost everywhere else in the world, Africans accepted enslavement as a condition of servitude and considered slaveholding a mark of wealth. Owning slaves made a person wealthy; trading them boosted his or her wealth. The trade in other humans thus gave upper-crust men and women access to coveted European goods such as Venetian beads, fine cloth, and horses. Equiano described how his tribe traded slaves to "mahogany-coloured men from the south west" of his village: "Sometimes we sold slaves to them but they were only

prisoners of war, or such among us as had been convicted of kidnaping, or adultery, and some other crimes which we esteemed heinous."

In this way, African societies conducted a small but far-reaching slave trade that carried bondspeople across the Sahara Desert to the Christian Roman Europe and the Islamic Middle East. From the tenth to fifteenth centuries, about 5,000 enslaved West Africans each year crossed the Sahara Desert to toil as sugar workers in Egypt, as domestic servants and artisans throughout the Arabic world, and as soldiers in North Africa. These slaves rarely ended up as field hands. Islam facilitated this process by establishing secure trade routes connecting West Africa with the Mediterranean world and the regions to the east. By the time Songhai rose to prominence in West Africa, that kingdom was the major supplier of enslaved captives across the Sahara to North Africa. Songhai warriors especially valued horses, which enabled them to wage war against neighboring peoples and thus capture still more slaves. Though this slave traffic was on the rise, it remained an occasional rather than a highly organized trade.

Africans' conception of slavery contrasted sharply with the notion that developed in European colonies in the Americas during the sixteenth century. Whereas most

أغلب حيث شرف رزقاه سنظر تنطيفه اخبار وكت

فإن مولاه عليه النحق والمولى برك موته وخفت عنه اذا رزقت العبد ان قال

■ This rare image of three Africans at a
Yemen slave market shows the sale
price weighed in gold.

شوان مائة من ثمنه تخفف بأن النبك الكلام هذا ترضبح لا

الغال الرخص انتقدني كما الجار في المبلغ فإنه ماجنيت وانكرى

slaves in overseas European colonies engaged in field labor, generally for life, the majority of slaves within African societies supplied personal service to their masters for a limited period. "Those prisoners which were not sold or redeemed," remembered Equiano, "we kept as slaves; but how different was their condition from that of slaves in the West-Indies! With us, they do no more work than other members of the community, even their master. Their food, clothing, and lodging were nearly the same as theirs, except they were not permitted to eat with the free-born and there was scarce any other difference between them, than a superior degree of importance which the head of a family possesses in our state, and that authority which, as such, he exercises every part of his household. Some of the slaves even have slaves under them as their own property and for their own use."

The kind of slavery Equiano described was also well known in Europe. It emerged when Christians and Muslims enslaved one another during centuries of religious wars in the Middle Ages. In these times, some people became slaves by being "outsiders" or "infidels" (nonbelievers) captured in war. Others voluntarily sold themselves into slavery to obtain money for their family. Still others were enslaved as punishment for committing a heinous crime.

Enslavement in Africa or Europe severely restricted a person's rights and prevented that individual from improving his or her lot in life. Yet these slaves still had certain protections. For example, they could obtain an education, marry and raise families, and count on decent treatment from their owners. In fact, some slaves in Africa were so highly trusted that they served as soldiers, administrators, royal advisors, and even occasionally as royal consorts.

But African slavery differed from that in North America in two important ways. First, slavery was not a lifelong condition in Africa. Second, it did not automatically pass on to a slave woman's children. Because of these differences, black slaves in North America faced a far bleaker existence than slaves elsewhere.

Music and Dance

Aesthetics—what a society considers beautiful, moving, and life-sustaining—constituted a core value in traditional African society. People expressed their love of beauty through music, dance, and art as well as through body decoration, hair styling, and the concoction of elaborate, savory meals. For that reason, these expressions of aesthetics played a vital role in helping Africans endure enslavement in North America. Later chapters show how these forms of expression took deep root in the soil of African American life and embedded themselves in the larger American culture.

Africans engaged in dance and music-making to celebrate life and wove these activities into communal religious observances and festivals. For example, they developed a technique known as *antiphony*: the call of a religious leader and the spoken or sung responses of the worshipers. Antiphony characterized most religious gatherings in Africa and prevails today in African American church services. Drums, rattles, flutes, bells, banjoes, other stringed instruments, and the balafo (similar to a xylophone) also enhanced religious rejoicing—the ecstatic singing and shouting that characterizes many African American spiritual services. In addition, Africans engaged in singing and dancing at funeral observances. For example, at Bakongo funeral ceremonies in today's southern Nigeria, bare-chested dancers perform in a counterclockwise circle to drum rhythms around the body of their chief, which funeral workers lay out on a wooden platform in the center of the circle.

Music and dance served a playful purpose as well as religious one. Ibn Khaldun, one of the first Arab Muslim historians of Islamized Africa, observed of the Africans he encountered in the fourteenth century that "they are found eager to dance whenever they hear a melody." An early English visitor, several centuries later, maintained "there is, without doubt, no people on the earth more naturally affected to the sound of music then these people." Dancing, singing, and playing instruments enabled Africans to celebrate life together. Indeed, throughout Africa, entire villages participated in dances and songs. Musical performance by one individual at a time, a practice widespread in Europe, was foreign to African village life.

Often dancing and music-making bridged the sacred and the secular. From ancient times, African societies performed ceremonies honoring rain, sun, and other important natural phenomena. For instance, the Dinka people conducted rain ceremonies each year at the start of the rainy season. The purpose of these ceremonies was not to open the skies again; rather it was to celebrate rain as an indispensable force on which life depended. African music featured antiphony, syncopation, and a percussive style characterized by multiple rhythms unfolding simultaneously. The drum, in its many forms, played an essential part in the music. African musicians also prized improvisation—the continual changing and honing of a piece of music. With improvisation, musicians felt they shared ownership of a musical composition rather than attributing a work to a single creator, as was the case in Europe. This sense of sharing echoed the emphasis on community and interdependence apparent in other African cultural features.

> "They are found eager to dance whenever they hear a melody." —*Ibn Khaldun*

Art

Most traditional African artists worked in stone, wood, pottery, and metal. They created objects of great beauty and functionality rather than paintings of scenes or individuals. Some works served the same purpose as European court art.

■ A Benin sculptor created this brass bas-relief in the sixteenth or seventeenth century. The work shows a Benin *oba*, or king, astride a small animal. Attendants shade the royal figure with palm leaves. Such bas-reliefs provide a valuable record of court life and rituals.

For example, Benin artists carved their kings' likenesses in stone or wood to glorify and commemorate their power. But much of African art reflected themes from everyday life.

From Ife, Benin, and other parts of West and Central Africa came a diverse array of sculptures and carvings fashioned from wood, terra cotta, ivory, copper, brass, and bronze. Inheritors of the ancient knowledge of iron production and metal casting from Nok culture, the artists of Ife and Benin were prized for their abilities. Many people believed these individuals possessed spiritual powers that found expression in their work. Archaeologists have recovered numerous examples of these works dating to the twelfth through the fifteenth centuries. Today, visitors can admire these treasures in the major museums of art and natural history in African, European, Asian, and American cities.

In other parts of West Africa, craftspeople carved elephant tusks into delicate pedestals surmounted by containers meant to hold salt, a precious mineral. When Portuguese traders first encountered the Sapis in what is now Sierra Leone, they were dazzled by such carvings.

Especially intriguing to Europeans was the African ability to meticulously carve ivory to an almost lace-like appearance. In 1520, the German artist Albrecht Dürer was so struck by the beauty of African art that he purchased two ivory saltcellars created in Africa that he found in the Netherlands, where a slave ship captain had likely transported them.

African craftspeople working in brass, wood, and gold created equally impressive works. For example, in Senegambia, European traders found elaborately carved antelope headdresses worn by masked young Bambara men dancing in agricultural rites. On the Gold Coast, they found intricately carved royal stools fashioned out of wood and enhanced with inlaid gold and silver. One Frenchman, Jean Barbot, described "very fine gold casting that even a European artist would find difficult to imitate." In Benin, Europeans encountered impressive bronze funerary portraits depicting the mothers of Benin's kings.

Like European artists, Bini bronzecasters organized into guilds that established standards of quality and regulated the training of apprentices. Private collectors and museums around the world nowadays avidly bid for carvings in various materials, not only for their beauty and sophistication but also for what they reveal about the cultural interchange of Europeans and Africans. For example, Kongo craftsmen working in bronze began to include statues of the Madonna, crosses, and saints after the Portuguese began to spread the Catholic faith in that kingdom.

■ A Benin artist carved this saltcellar from an elephant tusk in the early sixteenth century. Europeans were so struck by the virtuosity of Benin carvers that they commissioned ivory pieces, sometimes providing sketches of decorative motifs. This saltcellar features a king or warrior with a spear in one hand, a sword in the other, and a cross hanging from a beaded necklace.

CONCLUSION

In ancient and medieval times, a rich variety of African societies arose in the distinct ecological zones that made up the vast and diverse continent. By the fifteenth century, intercultural contacts within Africa—as well as trade among Mediterranean Europe, North Africa, Egypt, and parts of eastern Africa—knit an elaborate web of connections among these diverse peoples. The rise of Islam accelerated this interweaving. By the early fifteenth century, peoples previously unknown to each other began to trade, exchange ideas, and intermingle throughout various parts of the continent. Though the slave trade was a minor part of this mingling and trading, it was to become the most dominant and tragic aspect of African–European–Middle East contact, as discussed in Chapter 2.

FURTHER READING

Adams, William Y. *Nubia: Corridor to Africa* (Princeton, NJ: Princeton University Press, 1984).

Bernal, Martin. *Black Athena: The Afroasiatic Roots of Classical Civilization* (New Brunswick, NJ: Rutgers University Press, 1987).

Bovill, Edward William. *The Golden Trade of the Moors,* rev. ed. (Princeton, NJ: Markus Wiener, 1995).

Brooks, George E. *Landlords and Stranger: Ecology, Society, and Trade in Western Africa, 1000–1630* (Boulder: University of Colorado Press, 1993).

Courlander, Harold. *A Treasury of African Folklore* (New York: Crown, 1975).

Curtin, Philip D. *Economic Change in Precolonial Africa: Senegambia in the Era of the Slave Trade* (Madison: University of Wisconsin Press, 1975).

Davidson, Basil. *The African Genius: An Introduction to African Social and Cultural History* (Boston: Little, Brown, 1969).

—. *A History of West Africa, 1000–1800* (London: Longman, 1977).

Drewal, Henry John, John Pemberton, and Rowland Abiodun. *Yoruba: Nine Centuries of African Art and Thought* (New York: Center for African Art, 1989).

Drewal, Henry John, and Margaret Thompson Drewal. *Art and Female Power Among the Yoruba* (Bloomington: Indiana University Press, 1983).

Ehret, Christopher. *The Civilizations of Africa: A History to 1800* (Charlottesville: University Press of Virginia, 2002).

Heywood, Linda M., ed. *Central Africans and Cultural Transformation in the American Diaspora* (Cambridge: Cambridge University Press, 2001).

Isichei, Elizabeth A. *Igbo Worlds: An Anthology of Oral Histories and Historical Descriptions* (Philadelphia: Institute for the Study of Human Issues, 1978).

Grimal, Nicholas C. *A History of Ancient Egypt* (Oxford: Blackwell, 1993).

Hilton, Ann. *The Kingdom of Kongo* (Oxford: Oxford University Press, 1985).

Levtzion, Nehemia, and Randall Pouwels, eds. *A History of Islam in Africa* (Athens: Ohio University Press, 2000).

Lovejoy, Paul E. *Transformation in Slavery: A History of Slavery in Africa* (Cambridge: Cambridge University Press, 1983).

Mbiti, John S. *An Introduction to African Religion* (London: Heinemann, 1975).

Niane, D. T., ed. *General History of Africa. Vol. 3: Africa From the Seventh to the Eleventh Century; Vol. 4: African from the Twelfth to the Sixteenth Century* (Paris and London: UNESCO and Heinemann Educational Books, 1984 and 1988).

Northrup, David. *Africa's Discovery of Europe, 1450–1850* (Oxford: Oxford University Press, 2002).

Oliver, Roland, and Anthony Atmore. *The African Middle Ages, 1400–1800* (Cambridge: Cambridge University Press, 1981).

Reader, John. *Africa: A Biography of the Continent* (New York: Alfred A. Knopf, 1998).

Ryder, A. F. C. *Benin and the Europeans, 1485–1897* (London: Longmans, 1969).

Segal, Ronald. *Islam's Black Slaves: The Other Black Diaspora* (New York: Farrar, Straus, Giroux, 2001).

Shillington, Kevin. *A History of Africa,* rev. ed. (New York: St. Martin's, 1995).

Thompson, Robert Farris. *Flash of the Spirit: African and Afro-American Art and Philosophy* (New York: Random House, 1983).

Trigger, Bruce G., B. J. Kemp, et al. *Ancient Egypt: A Social History* (New York: Cambridge University Press, 1983).

Willis, John Ralph, ed. *Slaves and Slavery in Muslim Africa* (London: Frank Cass, 1985).

CHAPTER 2

■ Bronze figurine of slaves chained together in a coffle.

Africa and the Atlantic World

King Nomimansa Meets Diego Gomes

In 1456, the Mandingo king Nomimansa welcomed Diego Gomes, a Portuguese ship captain and emissary, into his home. The king was curious about these light-skinned people who called themselves "Christians." A gracious host, he presented them with generous gifts of ivory and gold. Living near the mouth of the Gambia River, the Mandingo people in the Songhai kingdom were eager to establish mutually advantageous trade arrangements like those they had forged with other foreign travelers to their coast. But Nomimansa also knew that during the previous decade, marauding Europeans had made war against Africans on offshore islands and seized some of them. So the king decided to step carefully in cultivating relations with these newcomers.

Nomimansa listened as Gomes explained how his sovereign, Prince Henry, had sent him to negotiate trade. True, the Portuguese had prospered by using the raid-and-trade tactic, Gomes admitted. But now, the captain reassured his host, they wanted peaceful, well-regulated trade. The Mandingo king agreed to deal. Gomes sealed the commercial treaty by presenting Portugal's new trading partner with damask cloth from Flanders, huge brass pots from Germany, glass beads from Venice, and swords and knives from Spain. Nomimansa understood that his people were about to become participants in a trading network that could bring them valuable goods and luxuries in return for their gold, ivory, and salt.

But that night, King Nomimansa learned his guest's true intentions. As Gomes tells the story, "Twenty-two people were sleeping. I herded them as if they had been cattle towards the boats." Disobeying Henry's instructions, Gomes seized the people of the Gambia River and forced them onto his three ships. "We captured on that day . . . nearly 650 people, and we went back to Portugal, to Lagos in the Algarve, where the prince was, and he rejoiced with us."

1417: Portuguese seize deserted Madeira Islands and begin colonizing in 1420s.

1420s–1430s: Prince Henry's Portuguese sailors explore Saharan coast of Africa and engage in raiding for slaves.

1427: Portuguese seize unoccupied Azores and begin colonizing in 1440.

1453: Turks' capture of Constantinople blocks western European access to traditional slave markets in Russia and the Balkans, intensifying demand for African slaves.

1492: The Spanish King Ferdinand and Queen Isabella drive the last Muslims out of Spain and dispatch Christopher Columbus to search for a water route to the East Indies.

1498: Vasco da Gama, sailing for the Portuguese, reaches East African ports after being the first European to sail around Africa's southern tip.

1400

1450

1500

1402: Castile sponsors first permanent colony in the Canary Islands.

1434: Portuguese sea captain Gil Eannes navigates south of Cape Bojardor and returns home.

1444: The Portuguese import enslaved Africans to Madeiras to work on sugar plantations.

1460s: Portugal colonizes Cape Verde Islands off West Africa's coast.

1456: Diego Gomes, representing the Portuguese king, negotiates first treaties of commerce and peace with African coastal rulers, initiating an official slave trade.

1496: Kongo king converts to Roman Catholicism. His son, Nzinga Mbemba, proclaims Christianity as the royal court's religion.

1502: First enslaved Africans reach the Western Hemisphere on the Spanish ship *Hispaniola*.

Gomes's act prefigured a tragic aspect of European-African relations that would unfold for four centuries to come. From the mid-fifteenth century to the late nineteenth century, European slave traders carried off huge numbers of the most able-bodied members of African societies, especially in West and Central Africa. The Africans' fate? To toil in the new colonies European nations were founding on islands off the West African coast and in the Americas. As it turned out, ship captains who followed Gomes would not find it necessary to kidnap slaves because the Portuguese and then other Europeans found willing African trading partners to supply captives. Four years after his first meeting with King Nomimansa, Captain Gomes was trading again near the mouth of the Gambia River. But this time, he complained, "the natives used to give twelve Negroes for one horse, now they gave only six."

This chapter describes the first encounters between the Portuguese and Africans as the former worked their way down Africa's west coast. It examines the impact of the slave trade on both Europeans and Africans. The Europeans transformed an ancient, widespread practice into a harsh, lifelong bondage where skin color and African origins became the distinguishing marks of bondage. Black men, women, and children became commodities—not much different from horses or casks of tobacco. The Portuguese used slave labor first to cultivate sugar on the Atlantic islands off the coast of West Africa, creating what became known as the plantation system.

Understanding how this system worked reveals insights into the experience of enslaved Africans in the Americas. A closer look at "the middle passage," the waterborne journey to the Western Hemisphere that huge numbers of Africans endured, sheds additional light on African lives under slavery. Once across the Atlantic, the lives of slaves owned by Spanish explorers differed markedly from those of Africans who worked on Portuguese and English plantations. Many slaves became part of the Spanish conquest of an immense part of the Western Hemisphere in the late fifteenth and early sixteenth centuries.

AFRICA AND EUROPE: THE FATEFUL CONNECTION

The point of no return was Cape Bojador. Beyond it lay "the green sea of darkness." Cape Bojador, just south of the Canary Islands off West Africa's shore, struck fear into the hearts of European and Muslim sailors riding the Atlantic Ocean current along the Saharan coast from Portugal and Spain. Ship captains dared not venture south of the cape because they had no way of defying the prevailing wind and current to return to their point of origin. But all that changed in 1434, when the bold Portuguese ship captain Gil Eannes sailed south on "seas none had sailed before" and managed to make his way back home. How did Eannes

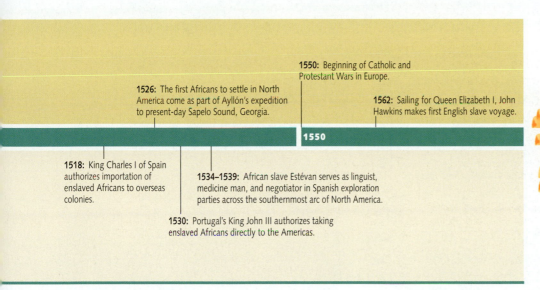

1518: King Charles I of Spain authorizes importation of enslaved Africans to overseas colonies.

1526: The first Africans to settle in North America come as part of Ayllón's expedition to present-day Sapelo Sound, Georgia.

1530: Portugal's King John III authorizes taking enslaved Africans directly to the Americas.

1534–1539: African slave Estévan serves as linguist, medicine man, and negotiator in Spanish exploration parties across the southernmost arc of North America.

1550: Beginning of Catholic and Protestant Wars in Europe.

1562: Sailing for Queen Elizabeth I, John Hawkins makes first English slave voyage.

1550

accomplish this feat? He modified Moorish-designed small wooden ships with lanteen (three-cornered) sails. Now he could sail into the wind and return to Portugal.

With Eannes's successful voyage, a new era of high-seas sailing had dawned. The Atlantic basin now lay open to any sailor who had the technology and nerve to navigate it. This revolution in trans-Atlantic navigation would have profound consequences for both Europeans and Africans. Most important, it cast a dark shadow over Africa that has not altogether lifted even today.

Portugal Colonizes the Atlantic Islands

Prince Henry, son of Portugal's king João I, earned his name as Henry the Navigator. Politically ambitious, energetic, and experienced on the battlefield, the young monarch brimmed with both business and religious zeal. Henry sponsored improvements in navigation and energetically promoted his kingdom's expansion into the Atlantic Ocean. In 1417, he ordered the seizure of the unoccupied Madeira Islands off the northern part of West Africa. In 1427, he took the Azores just northwest of the Madeira Islands. Several other European groups had earlier reached the Canary Islands, close to the African coast, but they did little more than trade with the people they found living there. In 1424, Henry seized the Canaries for Portugal.

During the first half of the fifteenth century, the Portuguese put down roots in these islands. At first they merely gathered treasures from the wild, such as honey and indigenous plants from which they made dyes to trade. Then they

began experimenting with growing wheat and grapevines in the islands' rich volcanic soils. Around the same time, they sent infrequent raiding parties to the African coast in search of a few slaves to work the fields on these island colonies. By the 1470s, the Portuguese had sailed farther south to forge trading agreements along the coast of what is today's Ghana. They also struck deals with the African kingdom of Benin, trading in exchange for the "grains of paradise"—high-quality pepper that fetched a handsome price in Europe.

The Portuguese combined their cautious, small-scale experiments on the Atlantic islands with slave raiding on the West African coast. Initially they supplied slaves to Europe, where landowners kept up a modest demand for raw labor. But as populations on the European continent boomed in the late fifteenth century, landowners had plenty of human muscle to work the fields. Demand for slaves in Europe began to dry up, leaving the Portuguese with little reason to continue slave raiding in Africa. But all this shifted when the Portuguese began cultivating sugar on the Madeiras in the 1450s.

The Plantation System: A Model for Misery on the Atlantic Islands

Produced in the temperate Mediterranean world since the eighth century, sugar had long been an exotic and expensive luxury. Only the wealthiest families could afford to sweeten their diets with the precious flavoring. Yet by the mid-1400s, the demand for sugar spread. On islands hundreds of miles from the African coast, Portuguese settlers spotted an opportunity. They experimented with growing sugarcane first on the Madeiras. To their delight, the plant flourished. Now these entrepreneurs needed laborers—not a few, but many. The plantation system they established became the first of its kind. It comprised three interwoven components: large landholding, the forced labor of gangs of enslaved peoples, and a cash crop that commanded steep prices in distant places. The plantation system meshed perfectly with the emerging European notion of *mercantilism*, whereby overseas colonists combined land and labor to produce wealth for the benefit of their home countries.

On the Madeiras, enslaved Africans initially toiled alongside slaves procured from Russia and the Balkans,

Azores (1427)

Madeiras (1418–19)

Canaries (1424)

Cape Nun

Cape Bojador (1434), *Gil Eannes*

Angra dos Runvos (1435), *Gil Eannes and Afonso Gonçalves*

Cape Blanco (1441), *Nuno Tristão and Antão Gonçalves*
Arolin (1445), *Nuno Tristão*

Cape Verde Islands

Cada Mesto (1456)

Cape Verde (1444), *Dinis Dias*

Diago Afanso (1462)

Bessados Islands

Senegal R.

Niger R.

Gambia R.

Cape Palmas (1460–61), *de Sintra*

Atlantic
Ocean

João de Santarím
and
Paro Escobar
(1471–72)

O Principe
São Tomé

Ano Bom

Fernando Po (1471), *Fernão de Po*

Congo R.

Cape Lopez (1472), *Duarte Lopes*

Cape Catarina (1475–76), *Rui de Sequeira*

Congo River (1483)

| 0 | 500 | 1000 | 1500 | 2000 Miles |

Cabo Cruz (1484), *Diago Cão*

Cape of Good Hope
(1488), *Bartolomas Dias*

■ MAP 2.1 Portuguese Colonization of Atlantic Islands

The earliest European expeditions took sailors along the eastern shores of the
Atlantic and onto the islands off West Africa's coast in the mid-fifteenth
century. Europeans would not venture across the Atlantic to the "strange new
lands" of the Americas for a few more years.

where slavery was common. The Portuguese had imported
these light-skinned individuals because they had long experience with planting and chopping cane in the sugar fields
of Cyprus and Sicily. They also knew how to extract sugar
from the cane. But the Portuguese found it far cheaper to
import black men and women from the nearby West African
coast than from distant Mediterranean locations. Thus the
forced migration of Africans started unofficially in the 1440s,
when Portuguese ship captains like Diego Gomes started
kidnapping them for lifelong labor on the Atlantic islands.

The successful experiment with sugar on the Madeiras
revealed the value of the previously uninhabited Atlantic
islands. The Portuguese began cultivating the crop on other
islands they had claimed, especially São Tomé, off Angola's

coast. By 1500, the
Portuguese were import-
ing about five thousand
African slaves annually,
most to toil on the sugar
plantations off the West
African coast. Now available in
huge quantities, sugar became more affordable. By about
1750, the saying went, even the wife of the poorest English
laborer took sugar in her tea.

Pleased with their success on the Atlantic islands, the
Portuguese took the next steps in leveraging their new-
found assets: They launched commercial ventures farther
west across the Atlantic and began using the islands as

 **First Person**

A Portugese Courtier Describes Enslaved Africans

In 1444, Gomes Eannes de Zurara, a Portuguese courtier to Prince Henry, chronicled the arrival of 235 African slaves on several ships at Lagos, Portugal. The expedition to seize Africans was led by Lançorte de Freitas, a young officer in a company created to trade on West Africa's coast.

What heart could be so hard as not to be pierced with piteous feeling to see that company? For some kept their heads low, and their faces bathed in tears, looking one upon another. Others stood groaning very dolorously. Looking up to the height of heaven, fixing their eyes upon it, crying out loudly, as if asking help from the Father of nature; others struck their faces with the palms of their hands, throwing themselves at full length upon the ground; while others made lamentations in the manner of a dirge, after the custom of their country. . . . But to increase their suffering still more there now arrived those who had charge of the division of the captives, and . . . then was it needful to part fathers from sons, husbands from wives, brothers from brothers. No respect was shown to either friends or relations, but each fell where his lot took him.

—*from Gomes Eannes de Zurara*, Chronicle of the Discovery and Conquest of Guinea, *trans. and ed. C. R. Beazley and Edgar Prestage (London: Printed for the Hakluyt Society, 1896–1899).*

To view a longer version of this document, please go to *www. ablongman.com/carson/documents.*

---

slave-trading centers. Slave raiding could backfire if it ruined profitable trading arrangements. But slave *trading* offered less risky—and more lucrative—opportunities to satisfy a growing worldwide demand for captive labor.

Demand for slaves had accelerated after Turks conquered Constantinople in 1453. With the fall of the great city, a major crossroads for east-west trade routes, Europeans lost their access to the slave markets in Russia and the Balkans. For generations, they had relied on these sources for domestic and agricultural laborers. It was precisely for these reasons that Prince Henry had sent Diego Gomes to negotiate treaties with African rulers. Though Gomes betrayed his charge—stealing rather than bartering for slaves—the Portuguese entrepreneurs who followed him chose instead to establish a purely reciprocal trade with West African leaders. Soon they struck mutually beneficial deals with several African coastal rulers.

> "**N**o respect was shown to either friends or relations, but each fell where his lot took him."—*Gomes Eannes de Zurara*

AFRICA AND THE RISING ATLANTIC WORLD

In 1486, the Spanish king put his seal on a grant to Fernão Dulmo, a military commander with a taste for exploration. The grant entitled Dulmo to all lands he could discover in the vast Atlantic Ocean—including "a great island or islands, or coastal parts of a mainland." European adventurers had no idea where they might find such islands. Moreover, they assumed that the "mainland" referred to in the grant was far-away China, or Cathay. Despite his determined forays throughout the Atlantic, Dulmo found nothing. But six years later, in 1492, Christopher Columbus reached what he believed were parts of Asia. Continued improvements in European navigation that for half a century had allowed colonization and trade along the African coast enabled the intrepid Genoese sailor to make his way across the entire Atlantic. In an instant, the momentum of European overseas colonization shifted from the Portuguese to the Spanish. This change would redirect the entire course of African history.

■ Sugar production in Brazil. The demand for sugar led to the cultivation of the crop in the Atlantic islands and in the Americas.

Initiating the Atlantic Slave Trade

After 1492, Europeans began settling in the Americas (including the Caribbean), where they cultivated valuable cash crops such as sugar, coffee, tobacco, and rice. Sensing new opportunities, European merchants and investors turned their attention from the Mediterranean Sea in Old World Europe to the Atlantic Ocean in the New World. As investment capital began flowing into the plantations dotting the Americas, a far-reaching new trade network took shape and expanded throughout the Atlantic basin. The continent of Africa provided this network with the labor and agricultural expertise plantation owners in the Americas needed to sell their bounty to the merchant houses of England, France, Spain, Portugal, and the Netherlands. Individuals fortunate enough to hold favored positions in this network—slave traders, ship-builders, land speculators, and plantation owners—amassed great wealth. Almost every European nation sent ships to trade in Africa for slaves in addition to the usual gold, ivory, and other luxuries.

As Europeans launched themselves across the Atlantic, conquering and colonizing vast territories, their nearly insa-

tiable demand for labor transformed the entire calculus of African trade. In the plantation system, colonists looked to their large tracts of land to produce crops that they could then sell for hefty profits in Europe. More than anything else, plantation owners needed human beings with strong backs. Soon they began referring to African slaves as "black gold."

For almost four centuries after Columbus's voyages to the Americas, European colonizers transported Africans out of their homelands in the largest forced migration in human history. Estimates vary widely, but the number of Africans hauled across the Atlantic who survived the trip probably reached more than 10 million. Several million more perished during the forced marches from the African interior to coastal trading forts or during the ocean voyage west to the Americas.

In Angola, the Portuguese used their considerable military might to capture and enslave Africans beginning in 1491—a change from earlier policy. Elsewhere in Africa, local rulers controlled the process of raiding for slaves, marching captives to the coast, and selling bondspeople to European merchants and ship captains. Coastal political authorities extracted taxes and tolls from the Europeans according to African law and custom. Not every

■ TABLE 2.1 Number of Enslaved Africans Arriving in the Americas, 1500–1800	
Dutch colonies	490,000
Spanish colonies	970,000
French colonies	1,550,000
English colonies	1,950,000
(West Indies)	1,523,000
(North America)	427,000
Portuguese colonies	3,647,000
Total	8,607,000

اوست ویوقار و اولدیلر اخراللامرانی دیخمی بصیدی خلایق
جانشیدیلر افزون قلد یلر بوجهلی و کد یلر ایت د یلرجون

■ Portrait of an African slave wrestling with Abu Jahl, an Arab *sayyid* (Islamic leader), 1594–1595.

side societies because they had been doing so for centuries, both in Africa itself and with Muslim societies far to the east. Black rulers and their agents did not think of themselves as Africans capturing and selling other Africans. Rather, they viewed themselves as raiding members of outside—and thus inferior—societies. In many cases, peoples from different societies saw one another as enemies. There was no unified African identity. For example, the people of Mali or Benin did not identify themselves as Africans any more than the people of France or Portugal identified themselves as Europeans.

Thus Africans felt no moral distaste for the practice of capturing and selling slaves. Indeed, as early as the 1650s, they had been selling captives to Muslim slave traders. These entrepreneurs then transported the hapless men and women in caravans across the Sahara to slave markets around the Red Sea and Indian Ocean. Estimates suggest that as many enslaved Africans went east by land between the 1650s and 1800 as went west by water from the 1490s to 1800.

The circumstances of slaves sold in Muslim lands differed markedly from those sold in the New World. Because most Muslim societies had large peasant populations, they did not need numerous additional bodies to work the land. Rather, Muslims wanted slaves who could serve as porters, soldiers, concubines (mistresses), cooks, and personal attendants. Therefore, Muslim masters valued their slaves for the personal services they provided rather than exploiting them to boost farmland production. For this reason, slave traders sent roughly two captured African women east for every man—the reverse of the gender ratio for slaves sent across the Atlantic for male dominated field labor in the plantation system.

Other differences distinguished Africans' experience as slaves to Muslims as opposed to Europeans in the Americas.

African ruler engaged in the Atlantic slave trade. For example, those governing the region between today's northern Liberia and the Ivory Coast traded with Europeans eager to obtain ivory and pepper, but they declined to enter the slave business. In all, over a period of four centuries, the leaders of some two hundred African societies participated in the trade.

Why did some African leaders engage in the slave raiding and selling process? In part, the answer lies in the long history of slave trading among a variety of peoples in West and Central Africa. Human beings' tendency to mistreat those perceived as different from themselves also offers some insight into this question. There was nothing unnatural about participating in a slave trade with people of out-

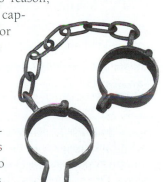

■ Don Alvare, King of Kongo, gives audience to Dutch ambassadors, c. 1580.

Whereas their masters in the Americas viewed slaves as non-human possessions, Muslim masters saw bondsmen and women as people, though to be sure, they treated them harshly. In the east, slaves had more rights than in the Americas. Some had the right to embrace the religion of their captors, while others were obligated to convert on the pain of death. Muslim masters freed more of their slaves than owners in the Americas did. Once they gained their freedom, many Africans living in Muslim society had the same rights as non-Africans and blended into the general population, as seldom was the case in the Americas. A final difference is that Islam emphasized a universal community that transcended race, so former African slaves who had embraced the faith found it easier to feel united spiritually with other Muslims. This was not the case in the Americas.

The African rulers who negotiated the first trade treaties with Europeans could not have predicted the damage that these new partnerships would ultimately do to their own kingdoms. One example from the Atlantic slave trade reveals some

> "**M**erchants are taking every day our natives, sons of the land and sons of our noblemen,"—*Kongo King Afonso I*

of the dire consequences involved. By the early 1500s, when the Portuguese began growing sugar on the island of São Tomé, they turned eagerly to their Kongo trading partners for slaves to toil in the sugarcane fields. By this time, Portuguese Catholic missionaries had already reached the court of Kongo king Mani-Kongo. The monarch proved receptive to their religious message, even allowing his son to be baptized with the Christian name Afonso I. In this spirit of cordiality, the Europeans and Africans confined their bartering to coastal fortresses. There, slaves (most of them captured in the interior by the Kongo or their subject tribes) were sold on terms agreeable to the Kongo rulers. In return for gold, ivory, and slaves, Kongo merchants received Portuguese guns, knives, horses, bars of iron, brass pots and tankards, glass, beads, rum, and textiles.

Before long, Kongo degenerated into a maelstrom of conflict. By 1526, in hopes of increasing the number of captured slaves, Portuguese merchants from São Tomé were urging village chiefs to declare war on each other and supplying them with guns. When Afonso succeeded his father as monarch, he asked the Portuguese king to ban slave trading in Kongo. "Merchants are taking every day our natives, sons of the land and sons of our noblemen," he wrote. "So great is the corruption and licentiousness that our country is becoming completely depopulated." But Afonso's request fell on deaf ears. Trapped in a web of guns, slaves, and power,

■ In 1624, Queen Njinga took the throne of Ndongo (present-day Angola), defying a custom that prohibited women from ruling. She quickly solidified her rule by contesting Portuguese incursions into her domain. When the Portuguese went on the offensive in a series of wars after 1624 to secure territory as well as access to the slave trade, Queen Njinga led the resistance. Her fierce battle cry, which reportedly could be heard from miles away, established her as a heroic figure who has become an enduring legend. Here, the kneeling Queen Njinga receives a blessing from the standing Portuguese governor with African and Portuguese attendants looking on. Three hundred years after her death in 1663, Angolans fighting for independence from Portugal went into battle inspired by the woman who had come to symbolize resistance to European imperialism in Africa.

the beleaguered ruler could not find a way out. In 1540, giving up on his attempt to withdraw from the trade, he wrote, "No other king in all these parts esteems Portuguese goods so much or treats the Portuguese as well as we do." Unable to extricate themselves from the European agreements they had made, the king and his successors continued the slave raiding that devastated Africa's heartlands. By the early seventeenth century, rebels throughout Kongo's provinces rose up, igniting a civil war that crippled the kingdom.

Sugar and Slavery

The African slave trade would never have become more than a minor commerce without the burgeoning labor shortage created by Europeans' overseas expansion and the intensifying hunger for sugar. Were it not for Europe's colonization of the Americas, the early slave trade that brought limited numbers of African slaves to southern Europe and the Atlantic islands might have ceased and been remembered simply as a short-lived phenomenon stemming from early European contacts with Africa. Sugar changed all that. When the Spanish and Portuguese stepped up their colonizing in the Caribbean and South America during the sixteenth century, they quickly learned that sugarcane grew just as easily in these lands as it did in the Atlantic islands. Once the newcomers had subdued the native peoples they encountered, they moved to transplant the plantation system they had installed on the

Atlantic islands. Now demand for slaves came from the Caribbean and South America.

At first, the Spanish and Portuguese looked to the native peoples of the Americas as an obvious source of forced gang labor. In some areas, such as Mexico and Brazil, the newcomers coerced local men and women into working on plantations and in mines. But diseases to which native Americans were not immune—such as smallpox, influenza, and scarlet fever—soon devastated the local populations. Far more familiar with their surroundings than their white captors, slaves who survived these plagues often escaped and ran back to their villages.

> African slaves are "the strength and the sinews of this western world."
>
> —Seventeenth-century Englishman

Now in need of a new source of labor, the Europeans turned their attention to the huge supply of labor available in Africa. Whereas they previously traded *with* Africans, they now began trading *in* Africans. By the mid-1500s in Portuguese Brazil, and by the early 1600s on islands throughout the Caribbean, enslaved Africans were hacking out sugar plantations from tropical forest. By the mid-eighteenth century, about nine out of every ten West Africans captured for export across the Atlantic went to labor in New World sugarcane fields. After finding gold and silver mines in Mexico and Peru, the Spanish stepped up their purchase of African laborers. After successfully introducing additional cash crops—coffee, tobacco, rice, and indigo—the Spanish and Portuguese sent thousands of ships to the West African coast and packed them with slaves. Dutch, French, and English vessels followed. Hardly anyone would have disagreed with one seventeenth-century Englishman who called African slaves "the strength and the sinews of this western world."

Once established on a large scale, the Atlantic slave trade transformed slave recruitment in Africa. At first, African leaders had sold criminals or prisoners of war. But the intensifying demand for workers in the New World presented irresistible new opportunities. Now African kings waged war against their neighbors to secure sufficient quantities of the "black gold" for which the Europeans paid so handsomely. European guns perpetuated this shift. By 1730, Europeans were providing about 180,000 arms a year to African slave traders. The availability of guns enabled unscrupulous traders to kidnap slaves and set up paramilitary organizations throughout Africa. Eager to maintain their lucrative commercial relations with European powers, some African rulers declined to stop the kidnapping and organized violence. In several cases, their decision cost them their kingdoms. Others used the situation to strengthen their own militaries.

As the demand for African slaves multiplied in the eighteenth century, the armies and agents of coastal and interior kings repeatedly invaded the hinterlands of western and central Africa. At least half of the slaves transported to English North America came from the part of western Africa that lies between the Senegal and Niger rivers and the Gulf of Biafra. Most of the others were enslaved in Angola, on the west coast of central Africa. By the end of the eighteenth century, slaving had devastated these regions' populations.

European Competition for the Slave Trade

For Europeans, the slave trade generated immense profits. Even as early as 1550, one chronicler asserted that "slaves are something that is always valuable and will triple your investment." As a result, European nations warred incessantly for trading advantages on the West African coast during the sixteenth and seventeenth centuries. The coastal forts, the focal points of the trade, became key strategic targets in the European wars of empire. For example, the major Portuguese slaving fort at Elmina on the Gold Coast, first constructed in 1481, was captured a century and a half later by the Dutch and then by the English. The primary fort on the Guinea coast, started by Swedish traders, passed through the hands of the Danish, the English, and the

■ **TABLE 2.2** **African Slaves Exported across the Atlantic, 1520–1870**

The figures in this table represent current estimates of the number of Africans delivered to European colonies on the West African coast for transport to the Americas. By a recent estimate, about 920,000 of these died during the sea voyage across the Atlantic. The number of Africans who died during capture, the march to the coast, long confinement on the coast, and the ocean crossing probably reached several million. When the Islamic slave trade is included, some estimates place the number of Africans taken from the continent, or the number who died in Africa after capture, as high as 40 million. However, we can never know the total with certainty.

1520–1600	367,000
1601–1700	1,868,000
1701–1800	6,133,000
1801–1870	3,330,000
Total	11,698,000

Source: Adapted from Table I from Paul E. Lovejoy, "The Volume of the Atlantic Slave Trade: A Synthesis," *Journal of African History*, Vol. 23, No. 4 (1982). Reprinted with the permission of Cambridge University Press.

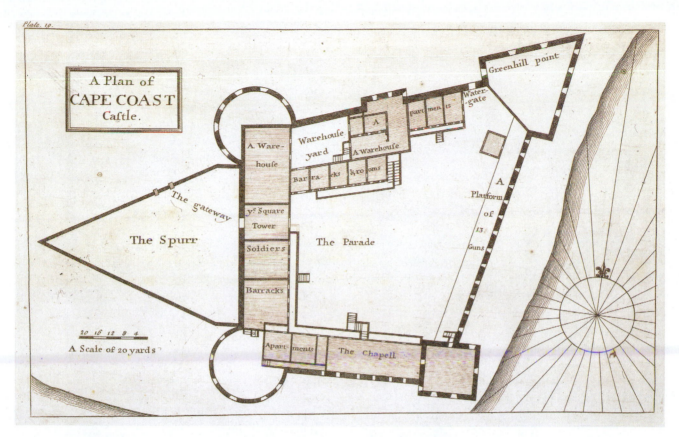

A Plan of CAPE COAST Castle.

Greenhill point

Water-gate

Warehouse yard

A Ware-house

A Warehouse

Bar-racks & rooms

The gateway

yᵉ Square Tower

Soldiers

The Spurr

The Parade

A Platform of 13 Guns

Barracks

20 16 12 8 4
A Scale of 20 yards

Apartments   The Chapell

■ This plan of England's Cape Coast Castle, where Africans marched from inland huddled until slave ships arrived to carry them across the Atlantic, shows the military force required in the Atlantic slave trade. The platform for 13 guns (at the right) is faced seaward to repel assaults by ships from other European nations.

Dutch between 1652 and 1664. As demand for slaves in the Americas exploded after 1650, European competition for trading rights on the West African coast stiffened. By the end of the century, European diplomats were negotiating to gain for their home countries the sole right to supply European plantations in the Americas with their annual quotas of slaves.

Not until the last third of the seventeenth century did the English become major players in the slave trade dominated by the Portuguese. Sponsored by Queen Elizabeth I, John Hawkins made the first English slave-trading voyage to West Africa in 1562. Horning in on what the Portuguese regarded as their exclusive right to form trading alliances with African rulers, Hawkins snared a shipful of captives, carried them across the Atlantic to Spanish colonizers, and returned home with a fat profit for his queen. Thereafter the English gave priority to supplying the Spanish colonies with slaves.

But the English would not secure their grip on the profitable trade for another century. In 1663 Charles II, recently restored to the English throne, granted a charter

to the Royal Adventurers to Africa—a joint-stock company headed by the king's brother, the Duke of York. Superseded by the Royal Africa Company in 1672, these organizations enjoyed the exclusive right to carry slaves to England's overseas colonies. For thirty-four years after 1663, each slave transported across the Atlantic bore the brand "DY" for the Duke of York. The duke himself ascended the throne in 1685. In 1698, individual merchants eager to jump into the fray pressured Parliament to break the Royal Africa Company's monopoly. Thrown open to individual entrepreneurs, the English slave trade ballooned—from about 5,000–6,000 slaves carried out of Africa a year in the 1680s to more than 20,000 a year in the early 1700s. By the 1790s, England became the foremost slave-trading nation in all of Europe.

Though European conduct of the Atlantic slave trade was rooted in advantage, racist sentiment soon began to build. Coming to regard black Africans as an inferior species enabled Europeans to rationalize their brutal traffic in human beings they had engineered. Ethnocentrism was not unknown in Africa.

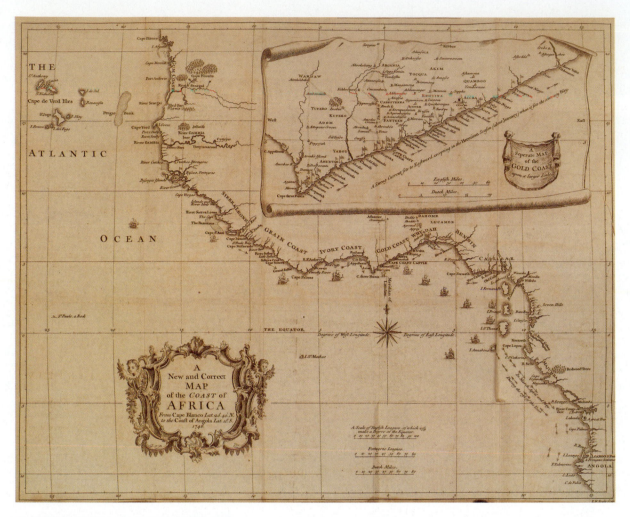

■ **MAP 2.2** **English Slave Trade**
This map appeared in a pamphlet promoting the English slave trade. The pamphlet author described the British empire in gushing terms as "a magnificent superstructure of American commerce and naval power on an African foundation." The Gold Coast, the Bight of Biafra, and the Bight of Benin—all on West Africa's coast—became major slave-trading centers for English traders.

Almost from the start Europeans thought of these captives as heathen, savage, and deserving of their fate. Notions of African "backwardness" and cultural impoverishment soon became prevalent as the slave trade became so extensive that Europeans needed to justify it. In time, Europeans began to gauge how "human" a person was not by his or her religion or cultural background but by his or her race as evidenced by skin color. These notions of Africans as ignorant heathens in turn led to the belief that they were better off toiling in the sugar, rice, and tobacco fields of the Americas than living where they were born. In the Americas, Europeans believed, the black "savages" could be "civilized" through exposure to Christianity and European culture.

THE TRAUMA OF ENSLAVEMENT

"The first object which saluted my eyes when I arrived on the coast [in about 1755]," wrote Olaudah Equiano, "was the sea, and a slave-ship, which was then riding at anchor, and waiting for its cargo." The eleven-year-old Equiano had arrived at the old slave fort at Calabar, which still stands. One of Benin's most accomplished chroniclers, he was about to endure the so-called middle passage across the Atlantic. This journey constituted the second leg of the three-part

 **First Person**   ## Olaudah Equiano Recalls His Enslavement

In his much-published Interesting Narrative, *the Ibo-born Equiano recounts his enslavement and that of his sister by an African raiding party. He obtained his freedom after ten years in slavery, probably by self purchase. He then married an Englishwoman with whom he raised a family. Equiano published an autobiographical memoir to support himself and help expose a long, dark epoch of human brutality. He wanted to "excite in your august assemblies a sense of compassion for the miseries which the Slave Trade has entailed on my unfortunate countrymen."*

One day, when all our people were gone out to their works as usual, and only I and my dear sister were left to mind the house, two men and a woman got over our walls, and in a moment seized us both; and, without giving us time to cry out, or make resistance, they stopped our mouths, tied our hands, and ran off with us into the nearest wood. . . . They offered us some victuals; but we refused them; and the only comfort we had was in being in one another's arms that night, and bathing each other with our tears. . . . I cried and grieved continually, and for several days I did not eat any thing but what they forced into my mouth.

—*from Olaudah Equiano as* The Interesting Narrative of the Life of Olaudah Equiano, or Gustavus Vassa, The African in London, *1794.*

To view a longer version of this document, please go to *www. ablongman.com/carson/documents.*

transit that for captives began in the African interior and concluded with the march to a final destination after they were purchased as slaves in the Americas.

Born in a village in a "charming fruitful vale," Equiano regarded his homeland as "the most considerable" of a variety of kingdoms in the "part of Africa known by the name of Guinea." His story echoes the experiences of millions of Africans who were born in West and Central Africa—the ancestral homelands of most of today's African Americans.

What happened to Equiano after he reached the African coast became almost a blur to the youngster. Some thirty-five years later, when he published his autobiography, he confessed that he was "yet at a loss to describe" the horror that unfolded before him. "When I was carried on board, I was immediately handled, and tossed up, to see if I were sound, by some of the crew; and I was now persuaded that I had gotten into a world of bad spirits, and that they were going to kill me." Frightened by their long hair, their strange language, and their bleached skin, the Ibo youth concluded that "if ten thousand worlds had been my own, I would have freely parted with them all to have exchanged my condition with that of the meanest slave in my own country."

■ Nobody has discovered who painted this handsome picture of Olaudah Equiano, completed probably when he was in his forties. Equiano saw nine editions of his *Interesting Narrative of the Life of Olaudah Equiano* published in London, Dublin, Edinburgh, and Norwich before he died in March 1797. After his death, enterprising printers republished his *Narrative* in many cities. Today, Equiano's *Narrative* is republished every several years, is read by thousands of people, and has won widespread recognition as the most compelling first-person story of enslavement and liberation from the pen of an African American or Afro-Briton. Equiano was enslaved a few decades after the map shown on page 38 was drawn, but this map accurately depicts the region where he first saw the slave ship that took him to Barbados and then Virginia.

 **First Person** | Slave Ship Captain Explains Bargaining for Slaves

Employed by the English Royal African Company, Welshman John Phillips commanded the slave ship Hannibal, *one of the largest ships in the trade. In 1693, he reached the coast of West Africa, where he traded guns, gunpowder, and cloth for slaves and gold. After delivering the slaves to Barbados and St. Thomas (two English sugar islands in the Caribbean), Phillips loaded his ship with sugar for the return trip to London. Here he describes his purchase of seven hundred slaves.*

Our factory [trading post] stands low near the marshes . . . , 'tis compassed round with a mud-wall about six foot high . . . within which is a large yard. . . . The king's slaves, if he had any, were first offered to sale. . . . Our surgeon examin'd them . . . to see they were sound of wind and limb, making them jump, stretch out their arms swiftly, looking in their mouths to judge of their age . . . but our greatest care of all is to buy none that are pox'd [diseased], lest they should infect the rest aboard. . . . Our surgeon is forced to examine the privities of both men and women [for signs of venereal disease]. When we had selected from the rest such as we liked, we agreed what goods to pay for them . . . how much of each sort of merchandise we were to give for a man, woman, child. . . . Then we mark'd the slaves . . . in the breast, or shoulder, with a hot iron having the letter of the ship's name on it, the place before being anointed with a little palm oil, which caused but little pain, the mark being usually well in four or five days, appearing very plain and white after.

—from the journal of Welsh sea captain John Phillips in spring 1693.

To view a longer version of this document, please go to *www. ablongman.com/carson/documents.*

On board the slave ship, matters took an even worse turn. "The stench of the hold [below decks] while we were on the [African] coast was so intolerably loathsome, that it was dangerous to remain there for any time, and some of us had been permitted to stay on the deck for fresh air; but now that the whole ship's cargo were confined together, it became absolutely pestilential. . . . The closeness of the place, and the heat of the climate," Equiano continued, "added to the number in the ship which was so crowded that each had scarcely room to turn himself, almost suffocated us. This . . . produced copious perspirations, so that the air soon became unfit for respiration, from a variety of loathsome smells, and brought on a sickness amongst the slaves of which many died, thus falling victims to the improvident avarice, as I may call it, of their purchasers."

> "The stench of the hold while we were on the coast was so intolerably loathsome, that it was dangerous to remain there for any time." —Olaudah Equiano

The Middle Passage: A Floating Hell

Equiano's account of his capture and the stupefying trip across the Atlantic is the most vivid of the few to survive Africans' centuries-long diaspora. Many enslaved Africans would have told stories different from Equiano's, for each experience was unique. But most who reached the shores of the Americas did not live long enough to record their experiences. On average, they died just seven years after arriving. So Equiano's story, covering fifty-three years, has assumed a place in historical literature far greater than he could have hoped for. Yet even his account cannot fully convey the agony and demoralization of the forced march to the west coast of Africa, the subsequent loading of captives onto wooden-hulled ships, and the miserable journey across the ocean.

European slave traders preferred young men over women because they knew that buyers on the other side of the Atlantic valued physical strength over everything else. Most captives were in their teens, twenties, and thirties. Only about 10 percent were under ten years of age or elderly.

Once captured, slaves were marched to the sea in "coffles," or trains, or brought by large canoes down the rivers

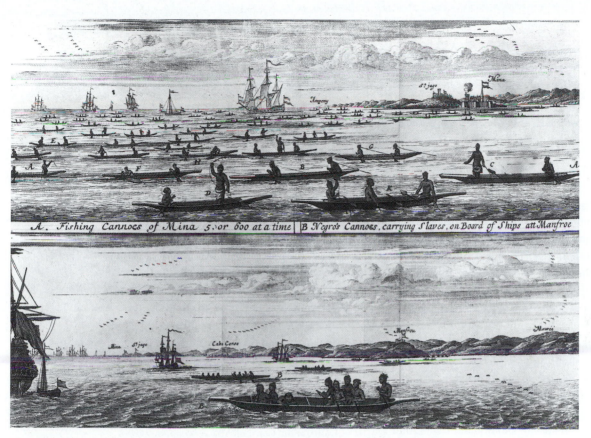

A. Fishing Cannoes of Mina 5 or 600 at a time | B Negro's Cannoes, carrying Slaves, on Board of Ships att Manfroe

■ Along much of West Africa's "Slave Coast," the lack of natural harbors, coupled with rough coastal surf, made it impossible for deep-drafted slave ships to anchor closer than half a mile or so from land. Slave traders thus needed local African canoemen, experienced in negotiating the dangerous surf, to row captives out to the ships.

that emptied into the Atlantic Ocean. A Scotsman, Mungo Park, described the coffle he marched with for 550 miles through Gambia in the 1790s. According to Park, seventy-three men, women, and children were tied together by the neck with leather thongs. Several captives attempted to commit suicide by eating clay. Another was abandoned after being badly stung by bees. Still others died of exhaustion and starvation. After two months, depleted by thirst, hunger, and exposure, the prisoners reached the coast. There their captors herded them into fortified enclosures called barracoons.

The anger, bewilderment, and desolation Africans experienced during the forced march, the first leg of the 5,000-mile journey, only worsened when they arrived at the slave ships. "As the slaves come down to Fida from the inland country," wrote one slave trader, "they are put into a booth or prison built for that purpose, near the beach . . . and when the Europeans are to receive them, they are brought out into a large plain, where the [ships'] surgeons examine every part of every one of them, to the smallest member, men and women, being all stark naked."

Once the surgeons had completed their examinations, the bargaining process began. Negotiating the purchase price of slaves proved a complicated, capricious affair. African sellers were wily barterers. "The natives have a splendid mental capacity with much judgment and sharp and ready apprehension," wrote one slave ship captain. "They have so good a memory that it is beyond comprehension, and although they cannot read or write, they are admirably well-organized in their trading and never get mixed up." African sellers drove hard bargains for the trade goods they wanted; for example, they demanded thirteen bars of iron for a male slave and nine bars and two brass rings for a female. Often the bargaining dragged on for days as sellers held out for the best price. In addition to slaves, they sold the provisions (such as yams and other foods) that the slaves and ship crews would consume during the fifty to eighty days it took to cross the ocean.

Death and Survival Aboard Ship

Once the bargaining had ended, the slaves were ferried in large canoes, manned by local Africans, to the ships waiting

 **First Person**   ## A Slave Ship Surgeon Describes the Middle Passage

Most of what historians know about the middle passage comes from slave ship captains and ship surgeons who later regretted their participation in the dirty business and published accounts that would further the cause of abolishing slavery. The excerpts below come from ship surgeon Alexander Falconbridge's An Account of the Slave Trade on the Coast of Africa, *published in London in 1788.*

The men Negroes, on being brought aboard the ship, are immediately fastened together, two and two, by hand-cuffs on their wrists, and by irons riveted on their legs. They are then sent down between the decks, and placed in an apartment partitioned off for that purpose. The women likewise are placed in a separate apartment between decks, but without being ironed. . . . The place allotted for the sick Negroes is under the half deck, where they lie on the bare planks. By this means, those who are emaciated, frequently have their skin, and even their flesh, entirely rubbed off, by the motion of the ship, from the prominent parts of the shoulders, elbows, and hips, so as to render the bones in those parts quite bare. And some of them, by constantly lying in the blood and mucus, that had flowed from those afflicted with the flux (diarrhea), and which . . . is generally so violent as to prevent their being kept clean, have their flesh much sooner rubbed off, than those who have only to contend with the mere friction of the ship. The excruciating pain which the poor sufferers feel from being obliged to continue in such a dreadful situation, frequently for several weeks, in case they happen to live so long, is not to be conceived or described. Few, indeed, are ever able to withstand the fatal effects of it. The utmost skill of the surgeon is here ineffectual.

—*from Alexander Falconbridge,* An Account of the Slave Trade on the Coast of Africa *(London, 1788).*

To view a longer version of this document, please go to *www. ablongman.com/carson/documents*.

at anchor offshore. Some tried to swallow handfuls of sand in a desperate effort to maintain a link to their homeland. Now they met with an ordeal beyond their imagination. Often branded with a hot iron and shackled in pairs, they huddled on deck, watching other prisoners being hauled aboard. Sometimes weeks passed before the captain had packed the ship with as many slaves as possible. During those weeks, some of the captives succumbed to disease or killed themselves.

Ready to depart, the ship captain ordered his crew to thrust the Africans below into half-decks with little more than four feet of headroom. If the ship that carried Equiano away from his homeland was typical, he would have been jammed below decks among roughly three hundred other slaves. Like him, about forty-five of them would have been under fourteen years of age.

Confined below decks, the Africans lost all hope of seeing their families and homelands again. As European slave traders knew, this was the moment when the chance of suicide or an uprising was greatest. "From the moment that the slaves are embarked," one slaver counseled, "one must put the sails up. . . . These slaves have so great a love for their country, that they despair when they see that they are leaving it forever; that makes them die of grief, and I have heard merchants . . . say that they die more often before leaving the port than during the voyage." One English captain described the desperation of slaves who were about to lose touch with their ancestral land: "The Negroes are so wilful and loathe to leave their own country, that they have often leap'd out of the canoes, boat and ship into the sea, and kept under water till they were drowned, to avoid being taken up and saved by our boats, which pursued them; they having a more dreadful apprehension of Barbados than we can have

> "These slaves have so great a love for their country, that they despair when they see that they are leaving it forever." —*Slave trader*

■ European ships had transported enslaved Africans across the Atlantic for nearly four centuries before any European sketched or painted a below-decks scene from such a vessel. In about 1840, an officer of HMS *Albatross*—a British Royal Navy ship intercepting Portuguese slave ships carrying Africans to Brazil—painted this haunting scene, which he witnessed on the *Albanez*.

of hell." In part, this fear stemmed from the widespread belief among Africans that they would encounter white "savages" on the other side of the ocean who would eat them. "I was persuaded that I had gotten into a world of bad spirits," wrote Equiano, "and that they were going to kill me. Their complexions, too, differing so much from ours, their long hair, and the language they spoke . . . united to confirm me in this belief."

The fear that inspired suicide while still on African soil lessened on the "middle passage," but the chance of death by disease or privation increased. Even on the better ships, the shackled Africans found that their cramped quarters made it impossible to walk unless their captors dragged them on deck for exercise. On the worst ships, they could barely turn over in the holds. "They had not so much room as a man in his coffin," testified one ship's surgeon. "This wretched situation," Equiano wrote in his narrative, "was again aggravated by the galling of the chains, now become insupportable; and the filth of the necessary tubs, into which the children often fell, and were almost suffocated. The shrieks of the women, and the groans of the dying, rendered the whole scene of horror almost inconceivable."

Even though it was to the advantage of the ship captains to deliver sellable slaves on the other side of the Atlantic, few stocked their ships properly. They assumed that many of the captives would die anyway during the ocean crossing. Pitiful rations led to undernourishment, confinement below decks in leg irons spread disease, and the impossibility of basic hygiene eroded the Africans' self-respect. Equiano described how he was "put down under the decks, and there I received such a salutation in my nostrils as I had never experienced in my life: so that with the loathsomeness of the stench and crying together, I became so sick and low that I was not able to eat." But "refusing to eat, one [sailor] held me fast . . . while the others flogged me severely." Many slaves like Equiano tried to starve themselves to death. To keep them alive, the ship's crew used tortures such as applying hot coals to force the Africans' lips open. When this did not work, the crew employed an instrument, the *speculum oris* (mouth opener), to wrench apart the jaws of a stubborn slave.

Dehydration imperiled the captives as well. On one ship, the captain provided just one coconut shell filled with water with each meal—which amounted to less than two pints of liquid a day. On many ships, the slaves had even less water. As their sodium and potassium levels dropped due to dehydration, they lost weight, grew listless, and fell into a dazed state. The slavers called this condition "melancholy"

 **Ottobah Cugoano Describes a Mid-Atlantic Slave Mutiny**

Born about 1757 in a Fante village, in what is today's Ghana, Ottobah Cugoano was captured at about age thirteen. His captors marched him to the Cape Coast Castle to await sale to the captain of a British slave ship. En route to the Caribbean sugar island of Grenada, Cugoano joined a shipboard slave rebellion. Recent scholarship has uncovered evidence of more than three hundred such rebellions during the middle passage.

When we found ourselves at last taken away, death was more preferable than life, and a plan was concerted amongst us that we might burn and blow up the ship, and to perish all together in the flames. But we were betrayed by one of our own countrywomen who slept with some of the head men of the ship, for it was common for the dirty, filthy sailors to take the African women and lie upon their bodies; but the men were chained and pent up in holes. It was the women and boys which were to burn the ship, with the approbation and groans of the rest; though that was prevented, the discovery was likewise a cruel and bloody scene.

—*from Ottobah Cugoano,* Thoughts and Sentiments on the Evil and Wicked Traffic of the Slavery and Commerce of the Human Species, Humbly Submitted to the Inhabitants of Great Britain. *London, 1787.*

To view a longer version of this document, please go to *www. ablongman.com/carson/documents*.

and believed it set in as slaves willed themselves to die. But some perceptive observers, such as the port physician in Charleston, South Carolina, knew otherwise. After inspecting the inhabitants of incoming slave ships, he opined that "it is a wonder any escape [the malnutrition and dehydration] with life."

For enslaved African women, the middle passage had one additional terror and humiliation. Slavers of all European nations separated African men and women during the ocean crossing, in part because they feared the women would incite the men to mutiny. But the arrangement also gave sailors access to their female captives, whom they regarded as fair sexual prey. They brought women above decks often only to rape them. Equiano had "even known them [sailors] to gratify their brutal passion with females not ten years old." A British surgeon on one slave ship described the captain's repeated rape of the African women. Said another observer, "It frequently happens that the Negroes on being purchased by Europeans become raving mad and many of them die in that state, particularly women."

Desperate for deliverance from this living hell, some enslaved Africans plotted mutiny. Experienced English ship captains tried to prevent conspiracy by obtaining their human cargo from different regions along the African coast. They knew that captives from the same area, speaking the same language, were the most likely to mutiny. To stifle insurrection, ship captains also used stark brutality to squelch any attempts at rebellion. If they identified leaders of a planned uprising, they flogged them to death or dismembered them in full view of the others to send a warning. John Atkins, aboard an English slave vessel in 1721, described how the captain "whipped and scarified" several plotters and sentenced others "to cruel deaths, making them first eat the Heart and Liver of one of them killed." The captain hoisted one female resistor up by the thumbs, then "whipp'd and slashed her with knives, before the other slaves, till she died."

Sale in the Americas

Probably not more than two of every three captured Africans lived to see the Americas. Those who survived were psychologically numb and physically depleted. But stumbling ashore, they had to endure yet another horror: being sold as chattel to a European master and then transported to a new place of residence. For Equiano, this final stage proved as devastating as the physical agony of the crossing. In Barbados, a slave-based English sugar colony in the West Indies, he trembled as merchants and planters clambered

> "It is a wonder any escape with life."—*South Carolina physician*

aboard ship. He believed that "we should be eaten by these ugly men, as they appeared to us." But the merchants informed the slaves that they "were not to be eaten, but to work, and were soon to go on land, where we should see many of our country people." Taken ashore, Equiano shrank in terror as "the buyers rush at once into the yard where the slaves are confined, and make choice of that parcel they like best. The noise and clamour with which this is attended, . . . serve not a little to increase the apprehensions of the terrified Africans. . . . In this manner, without scruple, are relations and friends separated, most of them never to see each other again."

No one bought Equiano; he was too young and weak. So he was shipped off to North America, where many "refuse" (damaged) slaves eked out their days in perpetual labor. Far up a river emptying into the Chesapeake Bay, the owner of a small plantation in Virginia purchased the boy. There, torn from all that was familiar to him, he had "now totally lost the small remains of comfort I had enjoyed in conversing with my countrymen; the women too, who used to wash and take care of me, were all gone different ways, and I never saw one of them afterwards." Isolated in Virginia, Equiano remembered being "exceedingly miserable, and thought myself worse off than any of the rest of my companions; for they could talk to each other, but I had no person to speak to that I could understand. In this state I was constantly grieving and pining, and wishing for death rather than anything else."

From capture in Africa to arrival at the plantation, farm, or city home of a European master may have averaged six months. During this time the African was completely cut off from everything that was familiar—family, home, community life. The body was tortured, the spirit shocked and seared. Now the African had to learn a new language, adjust to a new diet, adapt to a new climate and physical environment, and master new work routines. Most important, he or she had to find a way to live in a state of bondage intended to drag on forever. But for many, "forever" proved short. Every fourth African arriving on American soil died within just four years.

EARLY AFRICANS IN NORTH AMERICA

"We commended ourselves to God Our Lord and made our escape. . . . As we traveled that day, in considerable fear that

the Indians would follow us, we saw some smoke and, toward the end of the day, reached it, where we espied an Indian who, when he saw us coming toward him, fled without waiting for our arrival. We sent the black after him, and when the Indian saw that he was alone, he waited for him." With these words, Alvar Núñez Cabeza de Vaca, a Spanish *conquistador* (conqueror), told the story of his epic escape from enslavement by Florida Indians in the 1530s and the start of a five-year journey through the southern reaches of North America. The "black" he referred to was Estévan, also called Estéban, Estévanico, and sometimes "the black Arabian." "The black," continued de Vaca, "told [the Indian] that we were looking for the people who were making that smoke. He replied that . . . he would guide us to them: and so we followed him and he ran to tell the people that we were coming; at sunset, . . . we reached them . . . and they indicated that they were happy to have our company; and so they took us to their houses and lodged Dorantes [de Vaca's compatriot] and the black in the house of one medicine man."

This encounter among Spanish explorers, a black Arabian, and Native Americans in the forests of Florida occurred in 1534. Fifty years later, the English would make their first attempt to plant a colony in North America. Nearly a century later, the young Equiano would labor in

the fields and houses of Virginia. The incident de Vaca describes shows how cultures converged and the definitions of race blurred in this early era in North American history.

Africans and the Spanish Conquest in the Americas

Estévan was the product of three cultures coming together along the western edge of the Atlantic. He embodied the beginning of a long process by which the notion of race first emerged in Europe, Africa, and the Americas. The Spanish referred to him as "a black," "a Moor," or "an Arabian." But these words merely described his skin color (dark), his religion (Islam), and his homeland (Morocco). De Vaca never called him a slave— though he was owned by Andrés Dorantes. Nor did de Vaca ever suggest that Estévan was inferior, primitive, or savage. Rather, de Vaca's account described how four men—three Spanish and one African—became the first non-natives to penetrate the vast interior of North America. What mattered in this strange and often hostile land was not Estévan's blackness or even his slave status. It was his linguistic abilities, his fortitude, and his cleverness as a go-between. Estévan was an Atlantic Creole—a person from the east side of the Atlantic who acquired new cultural and linguistic attributes

■ Born in Africa, Juan Garrido accompanied Juan Ponce de León on his expeditions to Puerto Rico and Florida. This image shows Garrido with de León astride a Spanish horse as the two approach several Indian chiefs in about 1519. The picture appeared in Diego Duran's *Historia de las Indias de Nueve España e Islas de la Tierra Firme*, published in Spain in 1581.

on the other side of the Atlantic. His owner and companions counted on him to help them navigate the challenges of their daunting journey.

Seventy-five years before the English first tried to establish colonies in North America, Africans had been in the Americas. By 1580, 45,000 of them had arrived in the Spanish colonies in Florida and present-day New Mexico. Africans had also come to South America. About 13,000 had been shipped to Brazil, where Portuguese entrepreneurs had set up huge sugar and coffee plantations.

Many Spanish explorers and settlers came to the Americas with enslaved Africans who had valued, essential skills, such as the ability to soldier and to learn native languages that made them valuable negotiators with native peoples. For example, two Africans with Hispanicized names—Juan Garrido and Juan González—were on Juan Ponce de León's expedition to explore and seize Puerto Rico in 1508. Garrido and González obtained their freedom and stayed on in Puerto Rico to mine gold. Some Africans also aided the Spanish in slaving raids against the Caribs on the islands of Guadalupe, Dominica, and Santa Cruz. In 1513, when Vasco Nuñez de

Balboa became the first European to cross the Isthmus of Panama and see the Pacific Ocean, he had thirty Africans with him. Africans also accompanied Hernán Cortés during his siege of the Aztec capital of Tenochtitlán (in modern-day Mexico) in 1521. Cortés's entourage included Garrido, who later became a gold miner, landowner, and caretaker of one of the conquered city's aqueducts. He also served as gatekeeper of the Mexico City *cabildo* (city hall). Likewise, Africans participated in Francisco Pizarro's conquest of the Incas in Peru in 1532. Later, when local Indians murdered Pizarro, Africans carried his body to the Catholic cathedral that the Spanish had built in Lima. Some historians have claimed that one of Columbus's mariners, Pedro Alonso Niño, was an African, though this is disputed.

Africans in Early Spanish North America

As early as 1513, when the Spanish first set foot ashore on what would become the United States, they had African slaves with them. As he had in Puerto Rico, Ponce de León included Juan Garrido and Juan González, as well as African scouts and ship handlers, in his expedition to Florida. In 1521, they returned with de León to Florida to help stake Spain's claim to the entire eastern coast of North America. To make good on this claim, six hundred Spanish settlers—led by Lucas Vásquez de Ayllón and accompanied by many black slaves—tried to plant a permanent colony in La Florida (as the Spanish called it) in 1526. The group settled near present-day Sapelo Sound in Georgia. When starvation, disease, and a leadership crisis beset the expedition and Guale Indians attacked, some Africans fled and joined the Guale tribe. They married Guales, started families, and began the mixing of Africans and Native Americans that would continue in North America for centuries.

In 1528, Estévan arrived in Florida with his Spanish master as part of Pánfilo de Narváez's expedition. There, the five hundred Spanish and Africans settled near the swamplands of Tampa Bay. The colony fared as poorly as the one at Sapelo Sound had; only four members survived. These included de Vaca (whose account of the group's five-year, 2,500-mile odyssey across the continent would make him famous) as well as Estévan. A nearby tribe of Native Americans enslaved the four survivors. During his captivity among the Indians, Estévan became a linguist, healer, guide, and negotiator.

One day, the four survivors of the Spanish settlement managed to escape. They fled Florida and headed west. As they journeyed, Estévan negotiated with the hostile Indians they encountered. In the course of the men's arduous travels, his status as the slave of a Spanish adventurer all but dissolved. Paddling crude boats across the Gulf of Mexico, the tiny group shipwrecked on the Texas coast and took refuge among merciful natives. They recuperated for some time, then plunged into the Texas interior in 1534, heading west from present-day Galveston. Following Indian guides for the next two years, the travelers came to be regarded as holy men who possessed the power to heal. Indians in Spanish New Mexico described them as "four great doctors, one of them black, the other three white, who gave blessings [and] healed the sick." On one occasion, Indians gave Estévan a sacred gourd rattle—a rare honor. Making their way southwest across the continent, the foursome eventually met with Spanish settlers in Mexico. Evidence suggests that they may have reached the Pacific Ocean in 1536.

In 1539, Estévan joined a new Spanish expedition. Departing from Mexico City and heading north into Spanish New Mexico, the group blazed a trail for Francisco Vásquez de Coronado's expedition of 1540. In what would later be Arizona, the Spanish selected Estévan to forge ahead into Zuni country with Indian guides in search of the fabled seven gold-filled cities of Cíbola. His gift for acquiring native languages and his long experience with the peoples living in the vast territory north of New Spain made him the logical choice. Estévan became the first outsider to penetrate the vast Colorado Plateau. Unfortunately for him and his group, the Zuni saw him as an intruder and killed him.

In the same year that Estévan set out in advance of Coronado, Hernando de Soto, another Spaniard, made a further attempt to settle La Florida. Like every other Spanish expedition, this one included free and enslaved Africans. One slave helped a headwoman from an Indian tribe on the South Carolina coast to escape her Spanish captors. The two married and then headed back to her village near present-day Camden, South Carolina. De Soto, for his part, launched an ill-fated attempt to plunder the country of the Creeks, a native people living in Florida. Hoping to repeat his success in silver-rich Peru—where he had helped defeat the Incas eight years before—de Soto instead perished at the hands of the Indians. Half of his soldiers and the accompanying Africans died as well. Those who survived limped back to Mexico "dressed only in animal skins."

Late in the sixteenth century, the Spanish—again accompanied by free and enslaved Africans—finally established a secure presence in La Florida. When French Huguenots (Protestants) planted a small rival colony near present-day Jacksonville in 1562, the Spanish sent Pedro Menéndez de Avilés, captain general of the Spanish fleets in the West Indies, to crush them. Avilés quickly identified a talented free mulatto (part European and part African) named Luis living with the Calusa tribe south of St. Augustine. He came to depend on Luis to negotiate with the native people to gain their support. Avilés found other Africans living with Indian tribes as well. Many of them had fled their French masters to find freedom and shelter in local Indian communities. Avilés destroyed the French outpost and established a Spanish colony in Florida that lasted for two centuries.

Life in La Florida was harsh for Spaniards and Africans alike. But the scarcity of capable workers and skilled linguists gave enslaved Africans a higher status and a greater degree of freedom than they would have after the English set up colonies in North America. By the time the English had mounted their Jamestown expedition in 1606, about one hundred African slaves and a small number of free black people, many of them married to Indians or Spaniards, lived in La Florida.

The role of Africans on these grueling expeditions through mapless territory gave slavery a distinct character in the early Spanish settlements. The slaves did much of the back-breaking work as laborers in fields, on supply trains, and in fort and church construction. But they also served as soldiers, guides, and linguists. Along the west coast, Africans were a significant fraction of settlers in Mexico's northern frontier, including what would become the American Southwest, and there they also served in a variety of roles. On both the east and west coasts, Africans forged sexual unions and raised children with Native Americans and with Spanish people. This genetic blending blurred the definition of slavery. Officially, the Spanish regarded purity of lineage as the entitlement to elite status and ranked people on a social scale according to their ancestry. But pure lineage meant little on the frontiers of New Spain. There, Spanish, Native Americans, and Africans intermingled so much that traditional social categories broke down. A person's value to the community mattered far more than his or her "race." By the early 1700s, one observer of New Spain's northern frontier remarked that "practically all those who wish to be considered Spaniards are people of mixed blood."

CONCLUSION

When Diego Gomes first reached the coast of West Africa in 1456 to arrange treaties of commerce with African rulers, he unwittingly formed links between Europeans and Africans that would lock the two in a shameful embrace. Struggling to establish plantations on the islands off Africa's coast, the Portuguese began depending on enslaved Africans to produce highly profitable sugar. By the end of the 1400s, the Portuguese had extended the plantation system to the other side of the ocean. Europe, Africa, and the Americas were now bound together in a vast, Atlantic-wide system of trade and cultural exchange. The system would exert a disastrous impact on the peoples of Africa—not only those left behind but also those who survived the brutal journey to the Americas.

From the mid-fifteenth to the late nineteenth centuries, Europeans tore millions of Africans from their ancestral homelands and shipped them to the Atlantic islands and the Americas to labor in their colonies. No account of the enslavement of Africans can quite convey the demoralization and agony that accompanied the forced march to the coast of Africa and the subsequent loading aboard of the unfortunate captives. One historian has called it "the most traumatizing mass human migration in modern history."

Africans who ended up in North America met with profoundly different experiences, depending on who owned them, when they arrived on the coast, and where they ended up living. In the 1500s, only a few thousand Africans arrived in the Americas in chains. Many of them assumed roles based on their valuable skills, not on their "race." Moreover, they raised families with Native American and with Spanish partners, contributing to a blending of cultures that would powerfully shape the New World. But during the 1600s, the trickle of Africans across the Atlantic burgeoned into a steady stream. By the time Equiano arrived in the mid-eighteenth-century, it was a torrent. With increasing numbers, the English entry into the Atlantic slave trade, and English challenges to the footholds established by Spain, France, and the Netherlands in North America came changing attitudes toward Africans and changes in the practice of slavery itself.

FURTHER READING

Birmingham, David. *Trade and Conflict in Angola: The Mbundu and Their Neighbours Under the Influence of the Portuguese, 1483–1790* (Oxford: Oxford University Press, 1966).

Curtin, Philip. *Economic Change in Precolonial Africa: Senegambia in the Era of the Slave Trade* (2 vols.; Madison: University of Wisconsin Press, 1975).

Diedrich, Maria, Henry Louis Gates Jr., and Carl Pedersen, eds. *Black Imagination and the Middle Passage* (New York: Oxford University Press, 1999).

Eltis, David, David Richardson, Stephen D. Behrendt, and Herbert S. Klein, eds. *The Atlantic Slave Trade, 1527–1867: A Database on CD-ROM* (Cambridge: Cambridge University Press, 1999).

Galenson, David. *Traders, Planters, and Slaves: Market Behaviour in Early English America* (Cambridge: Cambridge University Press, 1986).

Klein, Herbert S. *The Middle Passage: Comparative Studies in the Atlantic Slave Trade* (Princeton: Princeton University Press, 1978).

Klein, Martin, ed. *Breaking the Chains: Slavery, Bondage, and Emancipation in Modern Africa and Asia* (Madison: University of Wisconsin Press, 1993).

Landers, Jane. *Black Society in Spanish Florida* (Urbana: University of Illinois Press, 1999).

Lovejoy, Paul. *Transformations in Slavery: A History of Slavery in Africa* (Cambridge: Cambridge University Press, 1983).

Manning, Patrick. *Slavery and African Life: Occidental, Oriental, and African Slave Trades* (Cambridge: Cambridge University Press, 1990).

Mariner's Museum. *Captive Passage: The Transatlantic Slave Trade and the Making of the Americas* (Washington: Smithsonian Institution Press, 2002).

Miller, Joseph. *The Way of Death: Merchant Capitalism and the Angolan Slave Trade, 1730–1830* (Madison: University of Wisconsin Press, 1988).

Patterson, Orlando. *Freedom in the Making of Western Culture* (New York: Basic Books, 1991).

Rawley, James A. *The Transatlantic Slave Trade: A History* (New York: W. W. Norton, 1981).

Segal, Ronald. *The Black Diaspora* (New York: Farrar, Straus, and Giroux, 1995).

Thomas, Hugh. *The Slave Trade: The Story of the Atlantic Slave Trade, 1440–1870* (New York: Simon and Schuster, 1997).

Thornton, John K. *Africa and the Africans in the Making of the Atlantic World, 1400–1600*, 2nd ed. (Cambridge: Cambridge University Press, 1991, 1998).

———. *The Kingdom of Kongo: Civil War and Transition, 1641–1718* (Madison: University of Wisconsin Press, 1983).

———. *Warfare in Atlantic Africa, 1500–1800* (London: Cambridge University Press, 1999).

Weber, David J. *The Spanish Frontier in North America* (New Haven: Yale University Press, 1992).

CHAPTER 3

■ Fleet Street: The Virginia Planter Trade Sign, c. eighteenth century. In this sign hanging outside a London tobacconist's shop, a happy planter observes tobacco production—a romanticized image created for English consumers.

Africans in Early North America, 1619–1726

Anthony Johnson and His Family in the Early Chesapeake

Antonio had been in Virginia only a year before a furious assault by Powhatan Indians nearly destroyed Warresquioke, his master's tobacco plantation. The day was March 22, 1622—Good Friday. Antonio survived, along with just four others of the fifty-seven people (mostly field laborers) living on the plantation. Opechancanough, the Indian leader intent on driving the English back into the ocean after fifteen years of clashes, led the well-planned attack. Antonio was no stranger to violence, having been wrenched from his home in Africa. Now he witnessed firsthand the bitter conflicts between indigenous people and Europeans seeking to establish settlements in North America.

Antonio was almost certainly brought to the Americas on a Portuguese slave ship from the Kongo-Angolan region of Africa. Then he was likely captured by a Dutch ship and sold in Jamestown, the center of the Virginia colony the English had founded in 1607. The young African labored on the plantation for nearly twenty years after his owner recovered his losses and replenished his supply of slaves.

After the Powhatan attacks, Antonio found a wife—quite a feat in a colony that now had only a handful of women. He married Mary, an African woman who had just recently arrived in Virginia, and they started a family. The couple lived together for more than forty years. One of their grandchildren honored the family's heritage by naming his 44-acre Maryland farm Angola.

Sometime in the 1640s, Antonio and Mary gained their freedom. They chose the names Anthony and Mary Johnson to signify their new status and made a place for themselves in Northampton County, on Virginia's eastern shore. By 1651, they had acquired 250 acres of tobacco land, built up a small herd of

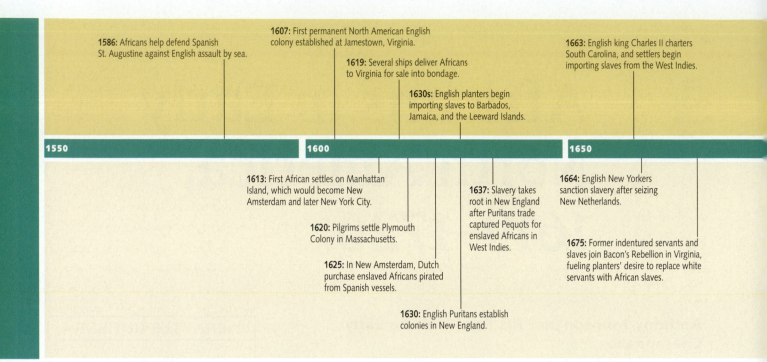

1586: Africans help defend Spanish St. Augustine against English assault by sea.

1607: First permanent North American English colony established at Jamestown, Virginia.

1619: Several ships deliver Africans to Virginia for sale into bondage.

1630s: English planters begin importing slaves to Barbados, Jamaica, and the Leeward Islands.

1663: English king Charles II charters South Carolina, and settlers begin importing slaves from the West Indies.

1550   **1600**   **1650**

1613: First African settles on Manhattan Island, which would become New Amsterdam and later New York City.

1620: Pilgrims settle Plymouth Colony in Massachusetts.

1625: In New Amsterdam, Dutch purchase enslaved Africans pirated from Spanish vessels.

1637: Slavery takes root in New England after Puritans trade captured Pequots for enslaved Africans in West Indies.

1664: English New Yorkers sanction slavery after seizing New Netherlands.

1675: Former indentured servants and slaves join Bacon's Rebellion in Virginia, fueling planters' desire to replace white servants with African slaves.

1630: English Puritans establish colonies in New England.

cattle and hogs, and had two black servants. In this corner of North America, where slave status and racial boundaries had not yet hardened in legal terms, the Johnsons were among many small planters scrambling to improve their lot in life. They apparently enjoyed respect from the authorities; in 1653, the county court forgave their taxes after a fire destroyed their dwelling. As Anthony Johnson told the court, "[Our] hard labors and known services for obtaining [our] livelihood were well known."

Both of Anthony and Mary's sons acquired homesteads—one of 550 acres; the other, 100 acres. One of the young men married a white woman. This wasn't unusual at a time when an African man could offer a woman just as decent a life as a white man could.

However, by the 1640s slave status and racial boundaries began to harden. Virginia's planter-lawmakers moved to regulate human bondage and interracial relations. Yet because slavery did not exist in England, they had no laws to copy. They began to create laws of their own, just as English settlers had done in the West Indies. Bit by bit, court judges and legislators established precedents that assigned Africans to lifelong slavery. The newly defined institution contrasted sharply with indentured servitude, an ancient English labor contract into which master and servant entered freely. Most indentured

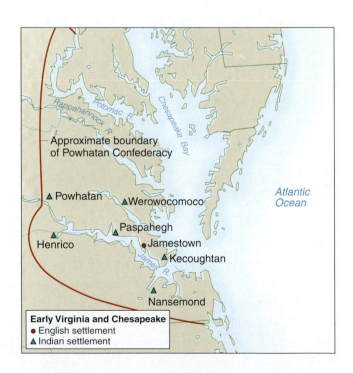

■ MAP 3.1 **Early Virginia and Chesapeake**

The homesteads of pioneering Virginians and Marylanders from England are often marked by roadside plaques, but no landmarks yet commemorate African pioneers such as Anthony and Mary Johnson.

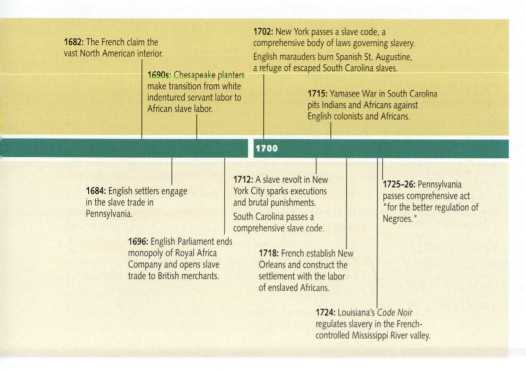

Timeline:

1682: The French claim the vast North American interior.

1690s: Chesapeake planters make transition from white indentured servant labor to African slave labor.

1702: New York passes a slave code, a comprehensive body of laws governing slavery.
English marauders burn Spanish St. Augustine, a refuge of escaped South Carolina slaves.

1715: Yamasee War in South Carolina pits Indians and Africans against English colonists and Africans.

1700

1684: English settlers engage in the slave trade in Pennsylvania.

1696: English Parliament ends monopoly of Royal Africa Company and opens slave trade to British merchants.

1712: A slave revolt in New York City sparks executions and brutal punishments.
South Carolina passes a comprehensive slave code.

1718: French establish New Orleans and construct the settlement with the labor of enslaved Africans.

1724: Louisiana's *Code Noir* regulates slavery in the French-controlled Mississippi River valley.

1725–26: Pennsylvania passes comprehensive act "for the better regulation of Negroes."

servitude agreements specified terms of five to seven years. During that time, the servant was entirely at the master's disposal but looked forward to regaining his or her freedom at the end of the term.

In 1655, Anthony Johnson himself became involved in distinguishing between servant and slave. A neighboring white planter had taken up the case of John Casor, the Johnsons' servant. The Johnsons, the neighbor argued before the county court, had held Casor beyond the agreed-upon seven years specified in most indentured servitude terms. Johnson retorted that he and Casor had not made an indenture. In fact, he added, neither Casor nor the neighbor could produce the indenture they claimed Johnson had violated. In the end, the court accepted Johnson's argument that he had purchased the lifelong labor of Casor—that, in effect, Casor was a slave. Because Casor had been enslaved in his African homeland, the court decided that anyone who bought him—even a fellow African—could count on his service for life. Losing his case, Casor served the Johnsons for another seventeen years before they gave him his freedom. Eventually, he succeeded in his own right as a tobacco planter.

By 1664, perhaps sensing diminishing opportunities for their children and their mixed-race grandchildren in Virginia, the Johnsons and one son began selling their land to white

neighbors. They then moved north to Maryland, a colony founded in 1632 as a refuge for English Catholics. Renting land there, they took up farming and cattle raising again. Six years later, when Anthony died, Virginia's tightening restrictions on Africans thwarted the execution of his will. A jury of white men declared that because Johnson "was a Negroe and by consequence an alien," the 50 Virginia acres he had deeded to his son Richard before moving to Maryland should go to a local white planter. In a colony filled with unfree laborers of many skin hues, the legal net began tightening around the small number of free Africans and their children.

By the late seventeenth century, enslaved Africans laboring in Maryland and Virginia became trapped in a legal system designed to keep them in perpetual bondage. Those who did manage to win their freedom were forced to the margins of society by whites eager to claim the fruits of former slaves' initiative and hard work. In just this way, Anthony and Mary Johnson's family suffered a slow decline from landowners to tenant farmers. In the early 1680s, one of the couple's sons, John, moved north into Delaware. There, one of his daughters married a local Indian and became part of a triracial community that survives to the present day. The other son, Richard, stayed behind in Virginia. Stripped of the land left him by his parents, he worked as a carpenter and had little to leave his own sons when he died in 1689. Anthony and Mary Johnson's grandchildren in Virginia worked as tenant farmers and servants, laboring on plantations owned by white people.

The Johnson family's story mirrors the plight of many African newcomers in the seventeenth and early eighteenth centuries. During the first few decades of English settlement along the Atlantic coast of North America, slave status and racial boundaries were fluid. Black people born and enslaved in Africa could marry in the young Virginia colony, earn their freedom, farm "myne owne ground," testify in court, and see a son marry a white woman. But after the mid-eighteenth century, new laws eroded Africans' standing and security and eventually defined slavery solely on the basis of race. In Virginia, Maryland, and the Carolinas, a few Africans captured as slaves initially mingled with white indentured servants and eventually obtained their freedom. Now plantation owners—increasingly dependent on the labor of captives from Africa—had a vested interest in consigning black people to lifelong slavery.

As this momentous change transformed the southern colonies, slavery began to take root in the northern colonies as well, though not on the same scale. The institution also emerged along the boundaries of English settlement, in the Spanish and French colonies of Florida and Louisiana. However, the shape and character of these Afro-Spanish and Afro-French societies contrasted sharply with those of the English settlements. Those differences exerted an impact that persists today.

THE FIRST AFRICANS IN ENGLISH NORTH AMERICA

"Your country? How came it yours? Before the Pilgrims landed we were here." Thus wrote W. E. B. Du Bois, the pioneering black historian and political leader who in 1895 became the first African American to receive a PhD in history at Harvard University. Du Bois posed this question many decades ago, prompted by history textbooks' almost total silence on the subject of Africans' contributions to the building of European colonies in North America. As he rightly pointed out, Africans were present at the beginning of almost every European settlement. Probably 75 percent of all the people who crossed the Atlantic to take up life in the Americas in the three centuries after Columbus's first voyage in 1492 were Africans. In North America, the number reached more than 50 percent.

> "Your country? How came it yours? Before the Pilgrims landed we were here."—W. E. B. Du Bois

By the end of the 1600s, use of African slaves had enabled plantation owners to rake in whopping profits. The slave trade catalyzed other changes as well—namely exchanges of valuable crops, agricultural techniques, and medical knowledge that redefined ways of life not only in the Americas but also in Europe and Africa. During this period, the earliest settlements of enslaved Africans appeared along the eastern coast of North America, white indentured labor transitioned to slave labor in the English colonies, and colonial legislators created laws to sanction, justify, and administer the emerging slave system.

The Chesapeake Colonies

When Anthony Johnson reached Virginia in 1621, he probably met countrymen and women who had arrived in 1619 from the Kongo-Angola region of West Central Africa. Most of them had been caught in the slave network operating out of Luanda, the primary port of Angola, a Portuguese colony in Africa. Luanda shipped about 8,000 slaves across the Atlantic each year. The vast majority were sold in Spanish and Portuguese New World colonies where white settlers had established the plantation system. By 1640, the Spanish had imported at least 335,000 slaves to their colonies in the West Indies and Mexico. The Portuguese, for their part, had brought upwards of 215,000 Africans to labor in the coffee and sugar fields of Brazil. Thus, Anthony Johnson was among the handful of Africans forced to North America before the slave trade boomed there.

English plantation owners in Virginia and Maryland, which bordered the Chesapeake Bay, needed field hands to work their money-generating tobacco fields. Because they found plenty of white indentured servants and English prisoners eager to contract their labor for passage to the Americas, they expressed scant interest in investing in black slaves from Africa. After all, it was much cheaper to transport the poorest of English and Irish society in English ships than to purchase enslaved Africans from the Portuguese and Dutch slave traders, who monopolized the African slave trade and therefore charged hefty prices.

By 1650, Virginia's white settlers had weathered early conflicts with Native Americans and had grown to about 18,300 in number—including thousands of white indentured servants. Only about 400 Africans lived in Virginia—a stark contrast to European-African population ratios in the Caribbean and South American colonies. Maryland, England's Catholic colony, also had few Africans. Like their Virginian counterparts, many of Maryland's settlers used white indentured servants and white convicts to plant, weed, harvest, cure, and pack tobacco.

As late as 1680, when the Chesapeake colonies' populations had swelled to about 57,000 in total, little more than 4,600 were slaves (about 8 percent of the Chesapeake population). Maryland and Virginia imported just a trickle of black slaves, while owners of more firmly established plantations in other parts of the Americas bought up waves of

First Person

Francis Payne Leaves a Will

Appearing first in the Virginia land records as "Francisco a Negroe," Francis Payne was likely brought to the Americas by a Portuguese slave trader. He spent several decades on Virginia's eastern shore, cultivating tobacco as a slave. During his remaining seventeen years, he was free. About four years after obtaining his freedom, he married an English woman named Agnes, who apparently bore him no children. His will gives important clues to Africans' lives in seventeenth-century Virginia.

In the Name of god Amen, I, Francis Payne of Northampton County in Virginia being sick of body but of perfect knowledge and understanding and being willing to ease my mind of all worldly care do make this my last will and testament as follows:

I bequeath my soul to my loving Father my creator and to Jesus Christ who by his blood and passion suffered for my sins and all the world, trusting through his merit to enjoy that heavenly portion prepared for me and all true believers. And as for my body, I bequeath it unto the ground from whence it came there to receive a Christian burial. And as for my worldly estate, I do give and bequeath it unto my loving wife Agnes, making her my indubitable executrix of this my last will and testament. And do here declare that by virtue of these presents all former wills by me made and signed are rebuked and made void, and this is to be my last will and testament. And desire that my debts may in the first place be paid. In testimony whereof I have subscribed my hand put my seal this 9th day of May Anno Domini 1673. Unto each of our good children a cow calf apiece when they attain to lawful age. But as for Driggins, he is to have nothing by this will.

Francis X Paine
his marke

—*Will of Francis Payne, May 9, 1673.*

---

them. Despite the boom in tobacco production in Virginia and Maryland by the 1680s, indentured white people still made up the majority of the people working the fields.

New England

Anthony and Mary Johnson were among the first of just a few Africans to trickle into the English colonies in the early 1600s. But as the century wore on, that trickle expanded to a flood. The Puritans of Massachusetts Bay colony, founded in 1630, first imported Africans in 1637 after enslaving Pequot Indian survivors of the bloody Puritan-Pequot war. Knowing they could not hold the Pequots in slavery in an area where they knew the landscape better than their captors, the Puritans shipped them to Providence Island, off the coast of South America, where Puritan planters had already begun using African slaves. Here, the Massachusetts planters exchanged the captive Indians for Africans.

Even though Massachusetts law books didn't specify slavery terms, buyers expected that Africans brought to the Puritan colony would serve a lifetime in bondage. Within a few years, one leading Massachusetts settler pronounced that "the colony will never thrive until we get . . . a stock of slaves sufficient to do all our business."

> "The colony will never thrive until we get . . . a stock of slaves sufficient to do all our business."
> —*Massachusetts settler*

Just south of Massachusetts, Rhode Islanders purchased slaves when they could find them. However, like the Virginians, they employed mainly white indentured servants for most of the seventeenth century. The number of Africans grew slowly in New England, in part because the climate didn't support year-round farming. In addition, most white settlers prized homogeneous Christian communities and

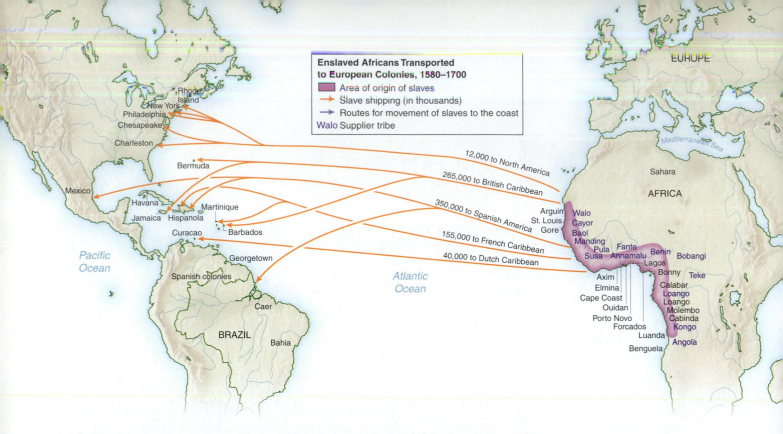

Enslaved Africans Transported
to European Colonies, 1580–1700
■ Area of origin of slaves
→ Slave shipping (in thousands)
→ Routes for movement of slaves to the coast
Walo Supplier tribe

12,000 to North America
265,000 to British Caribbean
350,000 to Spanish America
155,000 to French Caribbean
40,000 to Dutch Caribbean

■ **MAP 3.2** Enslaved Africans Transported to European Colonies, 1580–1700

This map contrasts the small number of enslaved Africans transported to the North American colonies in the seventeenth century with the number imported to the Carribean and Spanish America. For example, from 1660 to 1700, about 120,000 Africans arrived in Barbados. During that same time, only about 10,000 came to Maryland and Virginia.

had little interest in seeing Africans "do all our business." As late as 1700, slaves made up less than 3 percent of New England's population. Most of them served as domestic laborers in the port towns dotting the rocky coastline.

Nonetheless, New Englanders did have connections to the slave trade. For example, they supplied grain, flour, wood products, and salted fish to the large slave plantations in the West Indies. Moreover, they constructed and sailed ships to the English-run sugar and tobacco islands, where they dealt in slaves and rum. New Englanders also began consuming slave-produced sugar, coffee, rice, tobacco, and indigo—and prizing these luxuries. Not until the late 1690s did England allow New Englanders to enter the slave trade directly by sailing their ships to Africa's west coast. Nonetheless, New England's economy, almost as much as the Chesapeake's, came to rely on the slave system. By the eighteenth century, many upper-class officials, merchants, and ministers measured their status by the number of slaves they owned.

The Mid-Atlantic Colonies

Just south of New England, the Dutch established New Netherlands in 1624. (Later, when the English wrested control of New Netherlands from the Dutch, they renamed the colony New York.) In this mid-Atlantic settlement, slavery

eventually took root more firmly and deeply than it did in seventeenth-century Virginia and Maryland. But at first, some newly arriving Africans had opportunities to build lives based on freedom. For example, Jan Rodrigues—an African probably transported across the Atlantic by a Portuguese slaver—was left on the mid-Atlantic shore in 1613 by a Dutch ship captain. The first non-Indian resident of Manhattan Island, Rodrigues learned the Indian language, married a Rockaway woman, and fathered several children. He also initiated trade between the Indians and Europeans, which eventually formed the foundation of the New Netherlands colony the Dutch established eleven years later.

But as Dutch settlers flocked to the colony, their interest in African slaves intensified. When the agricultural families, soldiers, and officials of the Dutch West Indies Company set up farms along the banks of the Hudson River in 1624–1625, they wasted no time in satisfying their labor needs with Africans. In 1625, the Company purchased sixteen black slaves from pirates who had stolen them from Spanish vessels. Their names—including Paul D'Angola, Simon Congo, Anthony Portuguese, and Anthony Portuguis Gracia—suggest that they had either come from Angola or were captured by Portuguese slavers. The Dutch bought additional captive Africans and set them to work building forts, constructing roads, clearing land, and sawing boards out of trees.

Like Anthony and Mary Johnson, these people were slaves, but not necessarily forever. To be sure, Europeans had begun to consider a person's skin color a mark of his or her slave or free status. However, these Africans with Portuguese names still had opportunities to regain their freedom, accumulate land, and mix with white neighbors. They could also drill with the Dutch militia, sue and be sued in court, and trade independently. For example, Ascento Angola, Lewis Guinea, and Jan Guinea successfully sued in New Amsterdam, the colony's capital, for release from their servitude in 1664. Some former slaves, like Anthony Jansen van Vaes, "noted for his size and strength," took Dutch wives, joined the Dutch Reformed Church, and acquired farmland as free persons. Indeed, van Vaes was Coney Island's first farmer and later worked as a merchant in what would become Manhattan. By 1660, free Afro-Dutch farms were sprinkled along lower Manhattan in the area known today as the Bowery, and black residents had established a "negro burying ground" that symbolized an emerging free black community.

But just as the first Angolans shipped to New Netherlands were working their way free of servitude, more and more Africans slated for lifelong bondage began arriving at the colony. By 1650, New Netherlands ranked as the largest slave importation center in North America. The Dutch also moved to control the source of slaves in Africa. In 1637, they captured Castle Elmina, the Portuguese slave trading center on West Africa's Guinea coast, and in the 1640s, they seized Portuguese slaving posts along the coast of present-day Angola and Zaire. Now the Dutch monopolized the flow of slaves up and down Africa's west coast. When the English captured New Netherlands in 1664, they found a colony where one-tenth of the population, and nearly one-quarter of its capital, was African—a far greater black presence than in the Chesapeake.

Small numbers of enslaved Africans arrived in other mid-Atlantic colonies besides New Netherlands. For example, when the Swedes and Finns planted a small colony along the Delaware River in the 1630s, they imported a few Africans. The Dutch seized this colony in 1655 and brought in additional African slaves. After England captured New Netherlands in 1664, English settlers streamed into East Jersey across the Hudson River in search of good land. These settlers included planters from the West Indies island of Barbados seeking larger land holdings. Many of them brought dozens of slaves from Barbados. Lewis Morris, with more than sixty slaves, and John Berry, with thirty-two, were the largest East Jersey slaveholders. The settlers also brought particularly harsh attitudes toward slaves, viewing them as chattel no different from horses or oxen. These attitudes came to infect the thinking of European settlers in North America who had not yet seen the harsher slavery practiced in the Caribbean. European newcomers prized the opportunity to acquire land as free men and to control their own labor, but they saw no irony in working their land using slave labor.

In the 1670s, more Europeans flocked to the New World's mid-Atlantic coast. English, Irish, and German Quakers fleeing religious persecution began journeying to East and West Jersey and then to William Penn's new colony of Pennsylvania. These newcomers found only small numbers of slaves in the Delaware River valley region. But within two years of its founding, Philadelphia became a slave trading and slaveholding hub. When the English slave ship *Isabella* arrived in 1684, 150 dazed Africans staggered ashore. Pioneering Quakers, living

■ Probably more Africans passed through Elmina, on the present-day Ghanaian coast, than any other port in Africa. The Portuguese built Elmina in 1481–1482. The Dutch captured it in 1637. In the centuries afterward, Europeans battled for control of this gateway to the lucrative slave trade.

in riverbank caves and crude buildings at first, snapped up the Africans and put them to work. Black men and women set about clearing trees and brush, splitting wood and sawing boards, digging house foundations, and laying out streets. In a town comprising about 800 settlers, these 150 Africans nearly doubled the workforce while relieving white craftsmen of heavy labor.

As members of what they called the Society of Friends, the Quakers followed a "peace testimony," rejecting any form of violence in human affairs. Slave ownership put them in a morally awkward position. When bondspeople resisted captivity, many principled Quakers refused to mete out physical punishment. Yet some German Quakers lamented the very nature of slavery and refused to own slaves. One wrote, "Quakers do here handle men" as people in Europe "handle their cattle."

How would the Society of Friends handle an outright slave revolt—the kind that erupted periodically in the English West Indies? Word had already reached Philadelphia of a blood-drenched revolt that scourged Jamaica in 1685–1686. On that lush island, slaves had murdered several dozen white people. In retaliation, authorities caught every slave they could and burned them at the stake, had them torn apart by hunting dogs, or ordered them drawn and quartered. In Barbados, too, Quakers learned, slaves had mounted a massive uprising in 1675 and plotted further revolts in 1683 and 1686.

Most Quakers held just one or a few slaves and tried to treat them humanely. Deeply disturbed by antislavery protests, they wrestled with their consciences for many years. But less conscientious Quakers joined other colonists in exploiting black labor, trading beef, wheat, and wood products for slaves, sugar, and rum in the British islands. Gradually, they entrenched themselves in the Atlantic basin human trade network connecting West Africa with the Caribbean and the North American mainland.

South Carolina

While Quakers and other settlers began populating the sparsely settled mid-Atlantic region in the 1670s and 1680s, South Carolina also received an influx of colonizers. Chartered by the English king Charles II in 1663, South Carolina soon (and to Charles's surprise) became the center of a thriving southern plantation system. More than half of all the enslaved Africans brought to the mainland colonies would flow through Charleston, South Carolina's capital, in the eighteenth century.

Unlike most Quakers, South Carolina's white settlers were well acquainted with slavery. About half of them came from the overcrowded island of Barbados, and most of these showed up with slaves in tow. For the next two generations, slaveowning English Barbadians controlled South Carolina's political process, commercial activities, and social hierarchy. They found an ideal place to extend their power: a semi-tropical environment and plenty of fertile land that yielded cash crops of rice and indigo. Anthony and Mary Johnson relocated to Maryland in 1664, before the Barbadians started streaming into South Carolina. Fortunately for the Johnsons, the move took them a safe distance from a full-fledged plantation system imported directly from the English West Indies.

■ The marriage of Anthony and Mary Johnson's black son to an Englishwoman in the mid-seventeenth century occasioned little comment in the historical record. But by 1820, the approximate year this anonymous crude painting was done, interracial sex and interracial violence were seen as two sides of the same coin. Though a new Virginia law forbade interracial marriage in 1691, legal efforts could not stop such relationships.

THE FATEFUL TRANSITION

Anthony and Mary Johnson did not live to see what their children witnessed—the emergence of slave societies in which imported Africans performed the majority of field labor. The Johnsons had lived in a place and time in which slavery provided just one of many sources of labor. But their children experienced a pivotal changeover when slavery became the foundation of North America's southern economy—the primary means of producing goods and providing services. In Spanish Mexico, Cuba, and Peru; in Dutch Surinam; in Portuguese Brazil; and in the French Caribbean, European colonists had already seen the advantage of combining legions of enslaved Africans and fertile land to produce staple crops that fetched handsome prices in their home countries. Now white planters in North America, inspired by this success, set out to acquire as much land and black muscle as possible.

England Enters the Slave Trade

The English were the last Europeans to participate in the slave-based plantation system, mostly because they had a late start colonizing the Caribbean. Not until the 1640s did English settlers in Barbados, Jamaica, and the Leeward Islands begin copying their European rivals by purchasing thousands of enslaved Africans, mostly from Dutch ships. By 1680, when about 65,000 Africans were laboring in the sugar and coffee fields in the English West Indies, no more than 7,000 slaves toiled in all of England's North American colonies. On tiny Barbados, the population was half European and half African in 1660; two generations later, Africans outnumbered

Europeans three to one. Once the English gained a foothold in the West Indies, they embraced slavery enthusiastically. In North America, their fellow colonists inched toward it.

After 1680, white English settlers' increasing reliance on forced black labor transformed England's southern North American colonies. After defeating the Dutch in three wars over commercial shipping between 1650 and 1674, the English seized control of the Atlantic slave trade. Now English and New England ship captains brought their human cargoes directly from Africa to Virginia, Maryland, and the Carolinas. In the northern colonies, small numbers of slaves still worked alongside free laborers, except in a few pockets where planters cultivated large fields of tobacco. But by the early 1700s, southern planters relied almost exclusively on enslaved black men and women to tend and harvest huge tracts of cash crops.

South Carolina Descends into Slavery

In South Carolina, slave importations began rising after 1700. Planters wanted strong backs to do the difficult work of digging ditches and draining the swampy coastal country for rice cultivation. By the 1720s, most field laborers were enslaved Africans. About two-thirds of all imported Africans were male, most of them in their teens or early twenties. South Carolinian planters bought large volumes of slaves and worked them mercilessly. On average, Africans in this colony died earlier than they did in the Chesapeake. As in the West Indies and Brazil, South Carolina planters began to treat slaves as replaceable commodities with little regard for how long they lived. Owing to the high death rate and the constant need to replace slaves in South Carolina, most bondspeople in this colony originated in Africa. In the Chesapeake, by contrast, more and more slaves were born in North America.

■ **TABLE 3.1** **Regional African Population in English America, 1630–1710**

This table reveals that the rate of growth in African populations was four times as high in the southern colonies as in New England. The table also shows that throughout the seventeenth century, slaves in the English colonies lived and worked mostly in the West Indies

	New England	Mid-Atlantic	South	West Indies	Total	% of Slaves in West Indies
1630	—	20	50	10,000	10,070	99.3
1650	400	520	700	20,000	21,620	92.5
1670	500	800	3,400	40,000	44,700	89.5
1690	950	2,500	13,300	90,000	106,750	84.3
1710	2,600	6,200	29,000	148,000	185,800	79.6

As the number of slaves rose in South Carolina, the slave system grew harsher. Francis Le Jau, an Anglican missionary, cringed in 1709 to see a slave woman burned alive and an African man put into "a hellish Machine" in the form of a coffin. Slave masters "hamstring, maim, and unlimb those poor Creatures for small faults," Le Jau lamented. A few years later, South Carolina's legislature sanctioned such grisly punishments and more. A 1714 law made a black person's striking of a white man punishable by death. Other laws permitted retaliations unheard of in other colonies. For example, slaveowners could slit the nose or cut the ankle tendons of disobedient slaves.

Bacon's Rebellion and Slavery in the Chesapeake

In the Chesapeake, an uprising by angry, poor white settlers unwittingly drew the region deeper into slavery. It started in 1675, when the brash young Nathaniel Bacon, a recent immigrant from England, raised a small army of landless but well-armed poor white people. Mostly former indentured servants, Bacon's followers chafed at their limited opportunities in Virginia's Tidewater region. In particular, the rebels resented an arrangement the royal governor

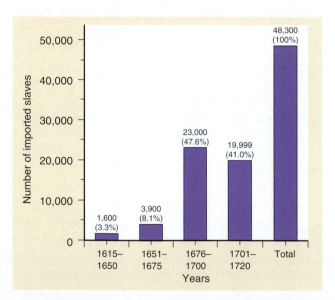

■ FIGURE 3.1 **Number of Slaves Imported from Africa to North America, 1615–1720**
This figure shows the sharp increase in the number of African slaves brought to England's North American colonies after 1675. Births to slaves added to the numbers of those brought from Africa so that by 1720, about 70,000 slaves lived in the English mainland colonies. The numbers suggest that births of slaves greatly outnumbered deaths.

had made to avert conflicts with Native Americans in the region. Specifically, the governor had promised that Virginians would not encroach on inland frontier land —precisely where poor men looked to secure their future.

What began as a frontier war against local Native Americans waged by Bacon's men soon turned into a civil war. As free black people and runaway slaves joined the poor white rebels, Bacon's forces turned their wrath against planter aristocrats who supported the governor. By the time the violence ebbed, the rebels managed to burn Jamestown; destroy the statehouse, church, and other buildings; and put the governor to flight across Chesapeake Bay.

Shaken, white planters became attracted to the notion of securing a permanent labor force that had no claims to liberty or equality. Turning away from the idea of recruiting indentured men and women from the rural villages of England and Ireland, plantation owners began looking to the villages of West Africa to satisfy their labor needs.

In addition to fear, several other forces drove Chesapeake colonists to rely more heavily on black slave labor. First, economic opportunities in England improved, so fewer white men and women were venturing across the ocean to the New World in search of employment. Moreover, indentured white servants who did cross the Atlantic flocked to the northern colonies, where terms of servitude were shorter and less harsh than in the Chesapeake. Second, Virginia and Maryland clamped down on the shipment of white convicts to the Chesapeake in 1670 and 1676, trying to stop the flow of men to the mass of discontented servants.

Third, just as the supply of indentured servants and convicts in the Chesapeake dwindled, the supply of Africans boomed. The slave trade itself began flourishing—especially after 1696, when English merchants persuaded Parliament to break the monopoly of the Royal Africa Company, which the king's brother controlled. With hundreds of private merchants now sailing their ships to West Africa, the flow of imported slaves to North America swelled. With greater supply, the price of slaves dropped—so southern planters now had an opportunity to purchase Africans more easily and cheaply than ever.

Africans Resist

As white colonists soon learned, their dependence on black labor came at great cost. White New Yorkers discovered this in the most frightening way. On a Monday morning in April 1712, white residents awoke to a horrific sight: white bodies lying in the streets, most of them bleeding from knife and ax wounds. Three of the dead were English, three were French, two were Dutch, one was a German, and another was a Wal-

Lament of a Convict Laborer in Virginia

James Revel was one of thousands of convicted criminals sent overseas from English and Irish jails to toil for extended periods in the Americas. Arriving in Virginia about 1665, Revel served time as a convict for fourteen years. He recounted his experience in verse.

> Forc'd from your friends and country for to go,
> Among the Negroes to work at the hoe;
> In distant countries void of all relief,
> Sold for a slave because you prov'd a thief
> We and the Negroes both alike did fare,
> Of work and food we had an equal share

> —*from James Revel, "The Poor Unhappy Transported Felon's Sorrowful Account of His Fourteen Years Transportation at Virginia in America." London, 1767.*

To view a longer version of this document, please go to www.ablongman.com/carson/documents.

loon (from what today is called Belgium). Seven other white people who had come under attack survived their wounds. The perpetrators were a group of more than twenty Africans who set fire to a building and then lay in wait for whites to come extinguish the flames. Some of the attackers were newly arrived African slaves; one was a free black man who claimed mystical powers and distributed a powder that, spread on the clothing, would reputedly make a person invulnerable to European weaponry. "Had it not been for the garrison [of English soldiers] there," reported one New Yorker, "that city would have been reduced to ashes, and the greatest part of the inhabitants murdered."

After quelling the revolt, white New Yorkers took about seventy slaves into custody. They tried forty-three of them and convicted twenty-five, including three women and several enslaved Indians. Determined to raise the price of rebellion, white magistrates imposed a series of grisly death penalties: thirteen slaves died on the gallows, three were burned at the stake, one was starved to death in chains, and one was broken on the wheel. Six others killed themselves to escape this kind of retribution. Though the

A Negro hung alive by the Ribs to a Gallows.

white leaders hoped to set an example with these punishments, neither they nor Africans felt entirely convinced that fear could force human beings to resign themselves to everlasting bondage.

DEFINING SLAVERY, DEFINING RACE

John Punch stood before Virginia's high court alongside his friends Victor and James Gregory in 1640. Their heads no doubt bowed, the three indentured servants waited anxiously for the judge's decision. They must have suspected that the court would punish them severely for fleeing their Welsh master, Hugh Gwyn, despite their vivid descriptions of his brutality. After escaping, the trio had managed to reach Maryland, but there they were captured. John Punch, an African; Victor, a Dutchman; and James Gregory, a Scot—all of them were fugitives from a harsh master who owned every minute of their time during the term of their servitude.

John Punch listened to the judge read out the sentence: Victor and James were to receive thirty lashes, serve Hugh Gwyn an extra year after fulfilling their term of servitude, and then labor an additional three years for the colony. Next came the astonishing words from the bewigged governor presiding over the court: "Being a negro, . . . John Punch shall serve his said master or his assigns for the time of his natural life here or elsewhere."

John Punch left no testimony revealing his response to being singled out because he was "a negro." But his unique sentence revealed a profound shift in white people's attitudes toward black people. During the sixteenth and early seventeenth centuries, the English had called Africans and Native Americans "heathens," and Christian tradition had long sanctioned the enslavement of heathen peoples. Up until the mid-seventeenth century in Virginia, being a heathen had defined slavery far more than being dark-skinned did.

Yet neither piety nor pigmentation had much to do with a person's ability to cultivate tobacco. So why did Virginia's high court cite John Punch's race to justify handing him a life sentence? Did simple economics lie behind the decision? Was the court acting on behalf of premier planters—seeking to secure Virginia's labor force by converting black servants' transgressions into a lifetime of hard labor? How could Punch have reasoned otherwise, if no other runaway servant had received such a sentence?

A well-known case ten years before Punch's sentencing had made clear that white Virginians viewed Africans as not just different but inferior. In 1630, the court had ordered that Hugh Davis, a white man, was "to be soundly whipt before an assembly of negroes & others for abusing himself to the dishonor of God and shame of Christianity by defiling his body in lying with a negro which fault he is to acknowledge next sabbath day." By shaming Davis "before negroes and others," the court hoped to stop interracial sex. Social biases were turning into harsh legal decisions in which the highest authorities meted out justice with partiality. Racial prejudice had begun paving the way for laws defining race-based slavery.

Laws Defining Social and Racial Relations

The legal decisions in the Punch and Davis cases set precedents defining how people of different races could relate. These precedents eventually influenced how white authorities defined slavery and what kinds of restrictions applied to bondspeople. As Virginia's African population grew slowly between 1640 and 1680, the legislature and courts gradually stripped away their rights and forged the fatal link between slavery and race. Step by step, the terms *English, Christian, white,* and *free* became nearly synonymous in the minds of white colonizers. Meanwhile, the words *African,*

heathen, black, and *slave* became equally interchangeable in these same minds. By 1680, Virginia's Reverend Morgan Godwyn could say with certainty that "these two words, *Negro* and *Slave*" were "by custom grown Homogeneous and Convertible; even as *Negro* and *Christian, Englishman* and *Heathen,* are . . . made Opposites."

In gradually associating slavery with race, the English drew from the experience of their countrymen in the West Indies. In the Caribbean, English settlers had already worked out definitions of slavery and pieced together a slave code—a comprehensive series of laws regulating the governance of bondspeople. As one historian puts it, "Every time a black man did something objectionable the English drew up a rule against it, until in a few years they had erected a wall of taboos around the slave." English authorities in Virginia and Maryland repeated this codification process.

In their lifetimes, Anthony and Mary Johnson witnessed the piecemeal development of a slave code. Race-based punishments and privileges first made their appearance in 1630, when authorities whipped Hugh Davis to discourage sexual relations between Europeans and Africans. Nine years later, white fear of African rebelliousness assumed legal force when the Virginia court ruled that "all persons except Negroes" were to be provided with arms and ammunition for militia duty. Precedents in court rulings and language in legal documents distinguished between white and black, servant and slave. In 1643, the Virginia assembly levied a tax on African women, making it more expensive for Africans to marry, purchase their freedom, and establish independent households. Wills written by white colonists in the 1640s bequeathed Africans and their children "forever."

The earliest Virginian slaveowners likely assumed the Africans they imported would serve them for life. But in the 1640s, such assumptions were crystallized in law. As early as 1642, county courts began recording sales of Africans and their children into lifelong bondage to their white owners. In 1660, the legislature implicitly acknowledged the lifelong servitude of Africans when it pinned extra years of indentured servitude on any white servant who ran away with an African—since "Negroes . . . are incapable of making satisfaction by addition of time."

In 1662, the legal system dealt Africans another blow. Virginia's House of Burgesses ruled that "all children borne in this country shall be held bond or free only according to the condition of the mother." The legislature passed this law because "some doubts have arisen whether children got by any Englishman upon a negro woman should be slave or free." With this latest ruling, the ambiguous legal status of

First Person

A White Virginian Defines Slavery (1705)

In the same year that Virginia's legislative body, the House of Burgesses, passed a comprehensive slave code (1705), Robert Beverley, a prominent Virginia slaveowner, penned The History and Present State of Virginia. *Published in London, the book celebrated the simplicity of Virginia life but also lauded a society that had raised itself out of misery and frontier rawness. Beverley included a section on servants and slaves—the foundation of landowners' wealth in Virginia.*

Their servants, they distinguish by the names of slaves for life, and servants for a time. Slaves are the Negroes, and their posterity, following the condition of the mother, according to the maxim, *partus sequitur ventrem* [status proceeds from the womb]. They are called slaves, in respect of the time of their servitude, because it is for life. Servants are those which serve only for a few years, according to the time of their indenture, or the custom of the country. . . . The male-servants, and slaves of both sexes, are imployed together in tiling and manuring the ground, in sowing and planting tobacco, corn, etc. Some distinction indeed is made between them in their cloaths and food; but the work of both is no other than what the overseers, the freemen, and the planters themselves do.

Sufficient distinction is also made between the female-servants and slaves; for a white woman is rarely or never put to work in the ground, if she be good for anything else. And to discourage all planters from using any women so, their law imposes the heaviest taxes upon female-servants working in the ground, while it suffers all other white women to be absolutely exempted. Whereas, on the other hand, it is a common thing to work a woman slave out of doors; nor does the law make any distinction in her taxes, whether her work be abroad or at home.

—*from Robert Beverley,* The History and Present State of Virginia *(1705).*

To view a longer version of this document, please go to *www.ablongman.com/carson/documents*.

Africans ended. Here were the two crucial distinctions that set enslavement of Africans throughout the Americas apart from slavery elsewhere in the world: Slave status was life-long, and it was inherited through enslaved mothers.

Religious and cultural prejudices no doubt had a role in this legal definition of slavery. The economic advantages of consigning black people to lifelong labor in the Chesapeake's booming tobacco economy played a part as well. While Virginia's 1662 law reflected a growing abhorrence of interracial sex, its chief importance lay in the economic benefits it gave white slaveowners. By legislating that an enslaved black woman's child took the mother's status, the opposite of the English legal doctrine where the child's status was determined by that of the father, Virginia lawmakers guaranteed that the colony's black labor force would reproduce itself.

Every child conceived by a white master, in either a coercive or consensual relationship with an African woman,

added to that labor force—at no extra cost to the master. By extending slave status to the womb, planter-politicians ensured that the *reproductive* as well as *productive* work of black women belonged to their master and that a child's paternity had no relevance in the eyes of the law. Now African women were more vulnerable than ever to white men's sexual exploitation.

In 1664, legislators in Maryland enacted a law that went even further than Virginia's and that nearly every mainland colony copied within a few decades. Existing Maryland law stated that "All Negroes" in servitude already in Maryland, along with all those imported into the colony, must serve for life, as must their children. That ruling duplicated the Virginia statute. But to stop white women from making matches with black men, the Maryland law also provided that any freeborn white wife of an African slave must serve her husband's master for as long as her husband

■ **TABLE 3.2** The Descent into Slavery in the Chesapeake Colonies

Laws defining race-based slavery in Virginia and Maryland were neither imported intact from other European colonies nor invented all at once. Rather, these mandates developed slowly. By 1705, legislators and courts had crystallized them in comprehensive slave codes.

1630: Virginia court condemns interracial sex in Hugh Davis case.

1639: Maryland law, declaring that all Christians were entitled to all the rights, liberties, and privileges "as any natural born subject of England," exempts "slaves" from these provisions.

1640: African-born servant John Punch is sentenced to serve his master for life for running away with two whites who received light sentences, thus establishing precedent for lifelong slavery in Virginia.
       Virginia law denies Negroes "the right and obligation to bear arms."

1643: In Virginia, first law in North America directly involving race establishes tax on African women but exempts white women.

1640s: Virginia county courts record sale of "Negroes" "for their life time" or "forever . . . with all their issue."

1662: Virginia law requires heavy fines for any white person having sexual relations with a black man or woman.
       Virginia legislates that children of enslaved mothers must also be slaves.

1664: Maryland law specifies that Negroes must serve *durante vita* (for life).
       Maryland bans interracial marriage and decrees that white women marrying enslaved Africans must themselves serve as slaves for life.

1667: Virginia legislates that Christian baptism no longer entitles slaves to freedom.

1668: Virginia law declares, in deliberately vague language, that a free "negro woman" "ought not in all respects" enjoy "a full fruition of the exemptions and impunities of the English"—that is, though free, a black woman still did not have all the rights of a white woman.

1669: Virginia law exempts from punishment slaveowners whose resistant slave dies "by the extremity of the [master's] correction" because it is presumed that no owner would "destroy his owne estate" without good reason.

1691: Virginia bans interracial marriages under pain of banishment from the colony; most other colonies follow suit in next thirty-five years.
       Virginia prohibits slaveowners from freeing slaves unless the owners provide for transporting freed persons out of the state within six months.

1705: Virginia passes a comprehensive slave code, including masters' right to dismember runaway slaves after their capture and white citizens' right to kill runaway slaves "without accusation or impeachment of any crime for the same."

lived. Moreover, any child born of such a mixed-race marriage would be enslaved for life as well.

Restrictions on Free Black People

These noxious laws may have figured in Mary and Anthony Johnson's decision to move out of Virginia. In 1645, "Anthony the negro" (probably Anthony Johnson) had appeared before a court of law in Virginia's Northampton County and demonstrated his confidence in his status as a free planter when he told the court, "I know myne owne ground and I will worke when I please and play when I please." But in the 1660s, the vise tightened around black servitude in the form of new restrictions on the rights of free black

> "I know myne owne ground and I will worke when I please and play when I please."
> —Anthony Johnson

colonists. These rulings struck at Africans' economic opportunities by preventing them from acquiring land and, in some cases, taking land away from them.

The statutes also intruded on family relations. Mary and Anthony Johnson's new daughter-in-law, wife of their son Richard, was an Englishwoman; indeed, half of the ten black freeholders in Northampton County were married to white women in this era. The evolving law set out to prohibit such unions. Nowhere else in English America did legislators enact rulings prohibiting interracial marriage except in tiny Antigua and Bermuda. Nowhere in the Dutch, Spanish, or Portuguese colonies did courts ban interracial marriage. Now such bans proliferated in North America—in Maryland in 1664 and Virginia in 1691. Ultimately, more than thirty states adopted such rulings—and these laws remained on the books until as late as the 1970s.

Mary and Anthony Johnson's descendants who remained in Virginia after Anthony's death in 1670 must have watched with dismay as Virginia's legislature tightened the screws on Africans. In 1668, a new law had special meaning for the

Johnsons' freeborn daughters: "Negro women, though permitted to enjoy their freedom, yet ought not in all respects to be admitted to enjoy a full fruition of the exemptions and immunities of the English." The writers of this law deliberately refused to specify which privileges given to the English might be denied to free black women. In this way, they gave *carte blanche* to future legislators who might want to restrict free black rights even further.

In 1691, when slave ships were unloading Africans in unprecedented numbers, white Virginia legislators availed themselves of this slippery language. To prevent "that abominable mixture and spurious issue [that is, offspring] . . . by Negroes, mulattoes [mixed-race people] and Indians intermarrying with English or other white women," Virginia's lawmakers ordered the banishment from the colony of any white man or woman who married an Indian or African person—whether free or enslaved. The law also provided that an indentured white woman who bore an illegitimate child by a black man must serve five additional years as a servant; her child was bound to indentured labor for thirty years. Now the kind of marriages made by one of Anthony and Mary Johnson's sons and several of their grandsons were considered criminal.

Like other free black people, the Johnsons' children and grandchildren struggled to navigate around these hardening racial distinctions. Some of them joined triracial communities in southern Delaware, where Nanticoke Indian, African, and European bloodlines criss-crossed. Others, with white wives or mothers, identified loosely with full-blooded Africans but strove as free, light-skinned Negroes to maintain ties with white neighbors, patrons, and employers.

In basing the definition of slavery on race, Virginian planters took two additional steps to make the system inescapable. In 1667, Virginia's House of Burgesses cut off conversion to Christianity as an avenue to freedom for blacks. A new law declared that "the conferring of baptism doth not alter the condition of the person as to his bondage or freedom." Christianity had enabled the English to justify their domination of "heathens." Consequently, many Africans converted to Christianity in an effort to extinguish the mark of inferiority and make themselves ineligible for enslavement. Like many other black servants who had gained their freedom before 1660, Mary and Anthony took Christian vows, baptized their children, and attended church. Enslaved Africans also converted, then made their bid for freedom. With the new ruling, this door slammed shut in Virginia.

The second step came in 1691, when Virginia lawmakers prohibited masters from freeing their slaves unless the owners provided for the transportation of freed persons out of the colony within six months. This ruling punished both kindhearted masters and grateful slaves. Moreover, it emphasized that only enslaved Africans were welcome in Virginia. For many bondspeople, the idea of leaving family, friends, and familiar surroundings—and facing uncertain prospects in a new home—dampened any joy they may have felt at the thought of escaping lifelong enslavement.

South Carolina's Slave Code

South of Virginia, the newly established Carolinas started out dependent on slavery. Building on the assumption encoded in the 1669 Fundamental Constitutions of Carolina (which became South Carolina) that "every freeman . . . shall have absolute power and authority over Negro slaves, of what opinion or religion soever," white planters legislated the most complete deprivation of freedom found in the mainland colonies. More fully developed than anywhere else, South Carolina's slave laws included a compulsory pass system that required slaves to carry a pass when traveling on their own away from their owner's plantation. This system was intended to limit slaves' mobility. Runaways received brutal punishment—whipping for men for the first offense, branding for the second, mutilation or even castration for the third. Anyone who captured an escaped slave received a reward.

> "Every freeman . . . shall have absolute power and authority over Negro slaves, of what opinion or religion soever."—*1669 Carolina Constitution*

Living among legions of enslaved Africans and Indians, as well as indentured whites, Carolina lawmakers also imposed the death penalty on white servants who ran away with enslaved Africans. This unusual measure reflected planters' fear that cross-color alliances at the bottom rungs of society, such as Bacon's Rebellion in Virginia, might topple the slave labor system entirely. In 1712, South Carolina brought its scattered laws together in a comprehensive slave code.

Though South Carolina developed the most severe racial code in English North America, the colony did so amid a remarkable tolerance for interracial sex between white men and black women specifically. Why? Few white women had any interest in building a life on a raw plantation frontier, a situation paralleled in the English West Indies. By the early eighteenth century, white men had more access to the rapidly growing number of enslaved African women than they did to white women. As on Caribbean islands such as Jamaica and Barbados, people in South Carolina accepted sexual relations between white men and enslaved black women as a given. The rising mulatto population testified to this attitude. In addition, in deference to white fathers, mulatto offspring of these liaisons were given a favored status, most importantly the chance to become free.

While tolerating sex between white men and black women, South Carolina's lawmakers tried to prevent white women from engaging in sex with black men. All male legislators viewed white women as the prized possessions of white men. Under a new law passed in 1717, any white woman who delivered a child fathered by a black man was sentenced to seven years' servitude. Her child, if a girl, had to serve eighteen years; if a boy, twenty-one years. To keep white women away from free black men, the law further provided that any free black father of a child born of a white woman must serve as a slave for seven years.

Despite the severity of these laws, South Carolinian legislators never prohibited interracial marriages, nor did they employ the emotionally loaded language used in other colonies, where legal terminology described children of mixed parentage as "abominable mixture," "spurious issue," or "disgrace of the nation." As white people in the West Indies did, white South Carolinians increasingly accepted interracial sexual relations—as long as the lines of slave-versus-free status remained crystal clear. Only sexual contact between white women and black men remained abhorrent to white settlers in this colony.

SLAVERY AND RACE NORTH OF THE CHESAPEAKE

Black Alice, as she was known, was born in slavery in Philadelphia along the banks of the Delaware River in 1686. Two years earlier, her parents had been brought from Barbados to the capital city of William Penn's Pennsylvania. Alice died in 1802—at the age of 116. Few enslaved Africans left recorded traces of their life experiences, but Black Alice's story has survived because her extraordinary longevity and remarkable character interested white Philadelphians. Black Alice became a venerated keeper of Pennsylvania's past. She recounted stories in the tradition of an African *griot*—archivist of a tribe's collective memory. Years later, she told Pennsylvanians she remembered the land on which Philadelphia stood "when it was a wilderness, and when the Indians hunted wild game in the woods, while the panther, the wolf, and the beasts of the forest were

prowling about the wigwams and cabins in which they [the first colonists] lived." She remembered lighting the pipe of William Penn, a slaveowner himself.

In time, Black Alice became a devout Christian. She joined Philadelphia's largely white Christ Church, an affiliation that would have been nearly impossible in the southern colonies by the 1730s. In her recollections, the first crude Anglican church had ceilings so low that "she could reach [them] with her hands from the floor." After she moved with her master outside the city, Black Alice served as the toll keeper for forty years at Dunk's Ferry on the Delaware River. She rode to her Philadelphia church on a horse until she reached ninety-five years of age. "The veneration she had for the bible," claimed one notice after her death, "induced her to lament that she was not able to read it; but the deficiency was in part supplied by the kindness of many of her friends, who, at her request, would read it to her, when she would listen with great attention, and often make pertinent remarks."

Black Alice's experience was far from typical, but her story reveals the flexible definitions of slavery and race that characterized the northern colonies in this era. Gaining admission to a white church, working as toll keeper, socializing with important white figures, and winning respect and admiration for her memory of Philadelphia's earliest history, Black Alice had experiences that simply weren't possible in the southern colonies—though she was a slave her entire life.

Unlike Virginia, Maryland, and North and South Carolina, the northern colonies did not make slave labor the main prop of their economy. Nonetheless, white settlers in the North participated eagerly in the African slave trade and created slave codes that remained in force until the American Revolution and beyond.

Slave Codes in New England

During the seventeenth century, New Englanders held more enslaved Indians than imported African slaves. They never specifically legislated perpetual and hereditary slavery. However, surviving legal documents such as wills show that slaveowners regarded their human property as lifelong servants as early as 1641. By at least 1660, many white people living in the New England colonies also assumed that children born of slaves would be lifelong slaves themselves.

Yet Africans teetered between extended servitude and lifelong bondage while occupying an indeterminate status between that of property and that of person. Though they associated slavery with African origins, New Englanders gave their bondspeople many privileges that masters in the southern colonies denied them—for example, the right to testify in court, to sue in court and make contracts, and to bear arms with masters' consent in colonial wars. Northern slaves could also acquire, hold, or transfer property and even petition the legislature for their freedom. Even more significant, slaves working in New England had the right to life: Their masters could not kill them without legal repercussions, as they could in Maryland and Virginia after 1705. New Englanders never passed laws preventing masters from freeing their slaves.

Slavery and the Law in the Mid-Atlantic

The vise of slavery tightened more rapidly around black life in New Netherlands than in the New England colonies farther north—but not nearly as quickly as it did in Virginia and Maryland. While the Dutch ruled New Netherlands, men who had capital to invest in imported Africans held slaves for life. They also regarded the offspring of enslaved African women as slaves at birth, even though no law mandated this condition.

But the legal fog enshrouding Africans evaporated immediately after the English conquered New Netherlands in 1664 and named it New York. Within a year, the first legislative assembly in the colony sanctioned lifelong servitude for black slaves. Another ruling that quickly followed specified that "no Negro slave who becomes a Christian after he had been bought shall be set at liberty." In 1702, after importing substantial numbers of Africans, the English devised a fully developed slave code. The new body of laws stripped away many entitlements slaves had treasured under Dutch rule, such as the right to earn money for themselves on leisure days, bear arms, and secure their freedom through self-purchase. The English slave code gave masters the right to inflict any punishment they wanted on a slave,

■ Lithographs, paintings, or sketches of Africans in early North America are rare because artists almost always worked entirely by commission. Few black Americans, whether free or slave, could afford to pay for portraits. The visual record of the early black experience is even sketchier than the literary record. This engraving of Black Alice thus provides a unique glimpse into early North American life. At age ninety-six, the redoubtable Black Alice began to lose her eyesight, but her deteriorating vision hardly slowed her down. Frequently she rowed into the middle of the Delaware River "from which she seldom returned without a handsome supply of fish for her master's table."

short of dismemberment and death. It also outlawed the assembly of more than three slaves without their masters' consent. It prohibited slaves from buying or selling property, and it removed their right to testify in court except when providing evidence against another slave for running away, destroying his or her master's property, or conspiring to revolt.

South of New York, Quakers in Pennsylvania, New Jersey, and Delaware practiced a milder form of slavery than other white colonists did. However, Quakers still feared slave resistance and revolt. Out of this fear came slave codes meant to limit enslaved black peoples' privileges and control their activities. But in Pennsylvania, Quaker and German influence at least lessened discrimination against black transgressors. For example, in the early years, African and European servants received the same penalties for running away. Also, free black people had equal access to the courts. To illustrate, Francis Johnson (Anthony and Mary Johnson's grandson who had moved to southern Delaware and become part of a triracial community) successfully sued a white man in 1687 and continued to work as a free farmer. White Pennsylvanians also did not impose special penalties on interracial sex. Francis Johnson, for instance, married a white woman.

Yet even in William Penn's Quaker haven, a slave code slowly took shape, accompanied by discriminatory treatment of free black people. By 1693, Philadelphia courts forbade slaves from traveling on Sundays without passes from their owners. In 1700, the legislature authorized special courts to try, judge, and convict black persons charged with criminal offenses. Race-based justice made African Americans liable to capital punishment for burglary and to castration for the rape of a white

 **First Person**

The First Antislavery Protest

In 1688, four years after the arrival of the first enslaved Africans in Philadelphia, a quartet of Rhineland craftsmen who had settled in nearby Germantown met to discuss what seemed to them an immoral anomaly. In Pennsylvania, they found that men of peace, belonging to the Society of Friends, used violence against fellow humans by depriving them of their liberty and consigning them and their offspring to perpetual slavery. The Germantown protest was the first committed to paper and the first publicized. It did not stop Quakers from holding and trading slaves in Pennsylvania. However, it demonstrated that some European settlers saw chattel slavery a reprehensible, blatant offense to the Quakers' vision of a world at peace.

These are the reasons why we are against the traffic of men-body. . . . Is there any that would be done or handled at this manner? . . . Now, though they are black, we cannot conceive there is more liberty to have them slaves as it is to have other white ones. There is a saying, that we shall do to all men like as we will be done ourselves, making no difference of what generation, descent or color they are. . . . Here is liberty of conscience, which is right and reasonable; here ought to be likewise liberty of the body. . . . But to bring men hither, or to rob and sell them against their will, we stand

against. In Europe there are many oppressed for conscience sake; and here there are those oppressed which are of a black color. . . . This makes an ill report in all those countries of Europe where they hear of that the Quakers do here handle men as they handle there the cattle. . . . Have these Negroes not as much right to fight for their freedom as you have to keep them slaves?

—*First printed as "Germantown Friends' Protest against Slavery, 1688."*

To view a longer version of this document, please go to *www.ablongman.com/carson/documents*.

---

woman—a form of retaliation reserved for them only. In 1725–1726, much later than in other colonies, Pennsylvania passed a comprehensive "act for the better regulation of Negroes." The code placed new restrictions on free African Americans. For example, any free black person convicted of fornication or adultery with a white person could be sold into servitude for seven years.

Facing a rising tide of imported Africans in all colonies, lawmakers gradually compiled a package of statutes governing slave behavior. These laws defined how much labor white owners could extract from black slaves and what kinds of punishments they could mete out for infractions of work rules, running away, and attacks on masters' property. In general, the higher the proportion of Africans in a particular society, the harsher the slave codes became.

But slave codes could not entirely control enslaved Africans. So long as bondsmen and women had the will to resist their plight, slavery remained unstable. White colonists had to constantly negotiate the legal details of

the institution as well as continually patrol their human holdings.

BEYOND ENGLISH BOUNDARIES

Juan Fernandez was a black soldier in the Spanish garrison town of St. Augustine, Florida. One morning in 1586, he awoke to a startling sight: A fleet of twenty heavily armed ships flying English flags was tacking along the north Florida coast. Led by England's famous explorer Francis Drake, the ships commenced a two-day bombardment of the garrison. Fernandez and the garrison's remaining soldiers fled to Indian villages in the nearby wilderness and made guerrilla strikes against the English to prevent them from coming ashore. But their efforts came to nothing. The invaders looted the town, set it aflame, and departed. When the garrison's occupants returned, they found nothing more than a smoking ruin where St. Augustine had once stood.

Determined to have the last say, the Spanish and African soldiers rebuilt St. Augustine. The nagging presence of the small Spanish outpost plagued the English for more than a century. Indeed, the English took particular offense when their slaves began defecting to St. Augustine because they heard rumors of sanctuary there.

Africans in Spanish America

By the time of Drake's attack, Africans had lived in Spanish Florida for many decades. Their presence gave the early Spanish settlements a distinct character. Some Africans were royal slaves, owned by the Spanish king, who put them to work in the garrisons. Others belonged to Spanish settlers. Some had gained their freedom in ways not revealed in the historical records. This mixture mirrored Africans' situation in Spain, where Muslim North Africans and black men of the African continent had mingled with the native Spaniards known as Castilians for centuries. In Spain, Castilian law offered many avenues out of slavery, and the Catholic church welcomed African souls into the fold.

The character of slavery in Spanish colonies such as Florida has led some historians to see a paradox: Enslaved Africans in autocratically run Spanish colonies seemed to fare better than Africans in English colonies, where white lawmakers emphasized representative government. In Spanish Florida, African slaves did the most back-breaking work—as field laborers, supply train workers, and fort and church builders. Yet they, along with free black men, also served as soldiers, guides, and linguists. Like many Spanish soldiers, black slaves mingled and started families with neighboring Indians so frequently that the Spanish didn't associate slavery with skin color or African heritage nearly as much as did the English. Historian Frank Tannenbaum noted how slaves fared better in Spanish colonies more than half a century ago in his *Slave and Citizen: The Negro in the Americas* (1946). The Spanish, Tannenbaum explained, treated slaves more humanely, gave them numerous opportunities to gain their freedom, and permitted them to become full citizens after emancipation.

Tannenbaum offered several explanations for this situation. First, Catholic priests—numerous in Spain—viewed every slave as a potential soul to be protected and added to the Christian community. Second, the Spanish colonies practiced a form of law inherited from the Romans that delineated slaves' rights and their masters' obligations to them. Third, Spain's government, built on monarchy and aristocracy, extended its power overseas—where local officials could easily enforce the Catholic church's protection of slaves.

By contrast, England's kings and aristocrats did not project their power quite so effectively overseas, nor did the Church of England do much to Christianize slaves or demand respect for their souls. Unlike Roman law, Anglo-Saxon law said nothing on the subject of slavery. Thus, English colonists were free to establish slave codes as harsh as they wished. African slaves in England's colonies, Tannenbaum argued, were at the complete mercy of their masters.

However, unique conditions within the Spanish colonies played just as large a role in shaping slavery as the institutions transported by European settlers from their homelands. Among these conditions, climate, crops, and the size of the slave population had the most decisive impact. In tropical Caribbean and Latin American regions, for example, slaves were driven to human limits in the difficult work of cultivating sugar and coffee, which grew only in tropical zones. Also, slaves vastly outnumbered white settlers, which led masters to treat bondspeople far more harshly than did owners in temperate zones where the white-black ratio was more balanced. Wherever slaves became more numerous than white people, masters' fear of a slave revolt—and their compulsion to crack down on black people—intensified.

Florida: A Slave Sanctuary

St. Augustine recovered slowly from the English assault. From the 1580s through the 1660s, the population grew only gradually. Yellow fever in 1649 and smallpox in 1654 claimed numerous African and Spanish lives. The town also suffered neglect from Spain's government. The Spanish monarchy focused its commercial efforts on the West Indies and Central and South America, where enslaved Africans and native peoples mined silver and gold and cultivated the sugar and coffee Europeans prized. The Spanish authorities viewed Florida as a mere outpost on the fringe of Spain's New World empire. Left to their own devices, settlers in Florida established numerous cattle ranches, where some Africans became North America's first black *vaqueros* (cowboys).

After the 1660s, when English sugar planters arrived from Barbados to acquire new lands in South Carolina, the slaves they brought with them learned about the freedom available to Africans in Spanish Florida. Controlled by

Catholic Spain, Spanish administrators tolerated a racially mixed population and enlisted free black men and slaves as militiamen. St. Augustine, with its massive stone fort and the promise of sanctuary, had particular appeal for slaves toiling on South Carolinian plantations. Not surprisingly, the garrison town unnerved English Protestant Carolinians.

Irritated by St. Augustine's presence, the English forged alliances with Indians and began harassing the garrison and surrounding Spanish settlements in the early 1680s. The Spanish governor retaliated in 1686 with the help of free and enslaved Africans as well as Indians. His strike force even managed to steal several of the Carolina governor's slaves—a particularly humiliating blow. Border warfare between the two colonies raged for years, fueled by an incessant leakage of Carolinian slaves into Spanish territory. Once they had escaped the clutches of their masters, many of these slaves requested baptism into the Catholic church. They knew this sacrament would give them protections and opportunities, such as the right to marry, that the English no longer extended.

Between 1687 and 1690, Africans fled from South Carolina to northern Florida. As South Carolina's governor lamented to his Florida counterpart, slaves run "daily to your town." When Spain's Charles II issued a royal proclamation in 1693 granting liberty to all enslaved men and women who reached Florida, he set the stage for the formation of a free black community in this Spanish outpost.

Matters in Florida grew even more turbulent in 1702, when the War of Spanish Succession (known in North America as Queen Anne's War, after the English queen) erupted in Europe. The English battered the Spanish sanctuary. War engulfed the region as the English and Spanish vied for control of Indian allies. That same year, South Carolina's governor led a mixed force of Yamasee Indian

allies, African slaves, and white settlers to set St. Augustine aflame for the second time. Two years later, the English destroyed most of the town of Apalachee in a follow-up strike. These raids devastated the Indian villages and took the lives of many Afro-Spanish, both enslaved and free. The Carolinians also captured some 24,000–50,000 Indians, marched them north to Charleston, and sold them into slavery. Many of the captives were shipped to the West Indies and to Boston and other New England towns.

Despite the violence, Africans in English Carolina and Spanish Florida maintained lines of communication. Slaves in South Carolina increasingly associated Florida with Catholicism and the freedom and protections it offered. In 1706, their interest in Florida intensified when a triracial Spanish force invaded Charleston. Former Carolina slaves who had escaped to Florida now attacked the men who had owned them. Though Charleston's residents repulsed the assault, the experience inspired many Africans still in South Carolina to make a bid for freedom. In 1711 and 1714, a number of Carolina slaves revolted and headed south for Florida.

In 1715, the Yamasee Indians, South Carolina's former allies, launched an attack on the English that united fragmented remains of the coastal tribes and the powerful interior nations of Creeks, Choctaws, and Cherokees. Inspired by the Yamasee War, runaway slaves from Carolina joined the effort. Such collaboration between blacks and Native Americans had gone on for some years. In one expedition against Tuscarora Indians in 1712, Carolina's most experienced military leader found an elaborately designed Indian fort featuring two tiers of port holes, large tree limbs strewn to

■ The Tuscaroras, at war with the Carolinians, captured prominent Indian trader John Lawson and his slave. They also took Baron von Graffenried, who led German and Swiss colonists to South Carolina in 1709. This contemporary drawing shows Tuscaroras torturing Lawson and von Graffenried, but not Lawson's slave. The African probably had already defected to the Tuscaroras.

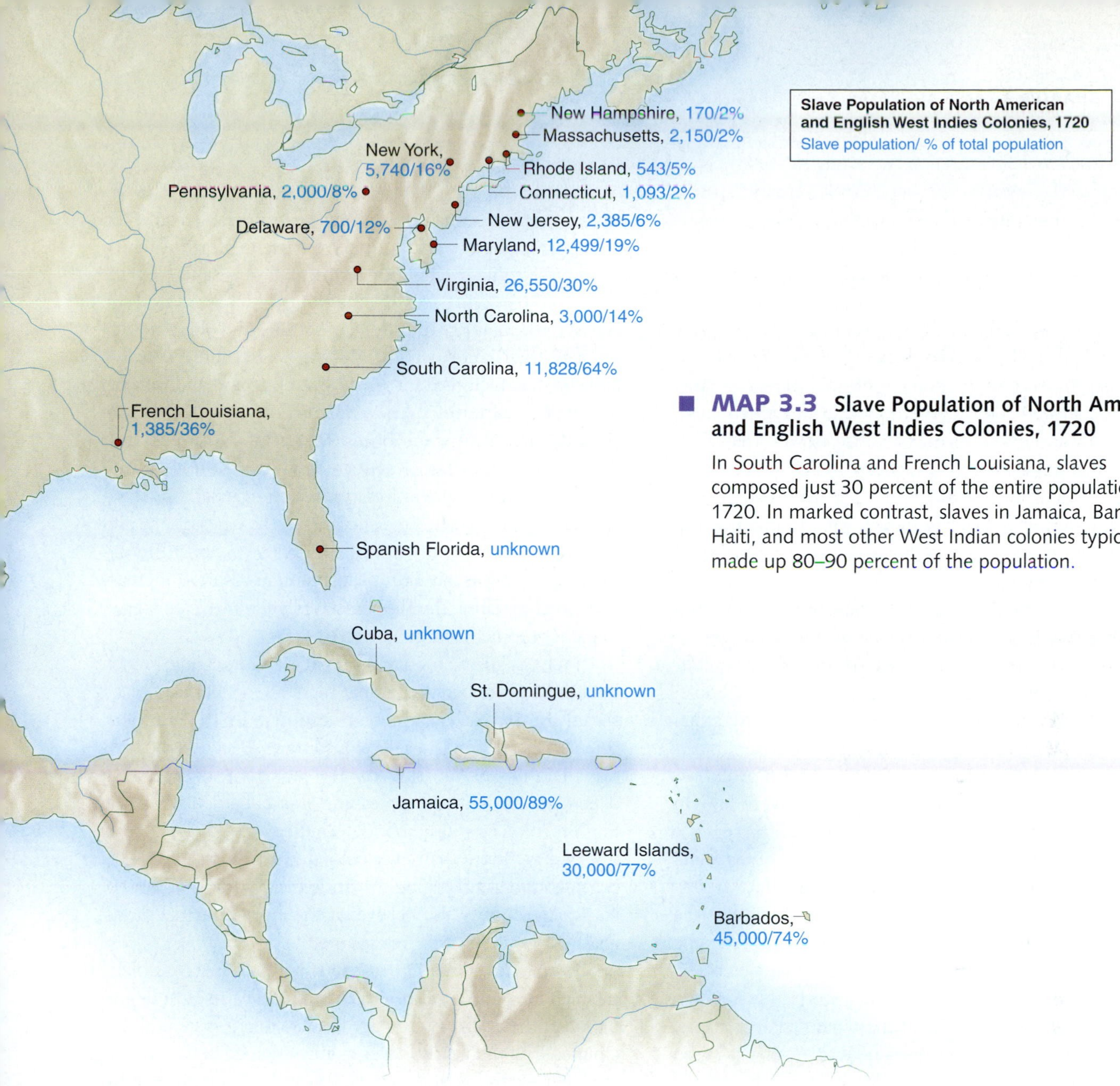

Map 3.3 Data

New Hampshire, 170/2%
Massachusetts, 2,150/2%
New York, 5,740/16%
Rhode Island, 543/5%
Pennsylvania, 2,000/8%
Connecticut, 1,093/2%
Delaware, 700/12%
New Jersey, 2,385/6%
Maryland, 12,499/19%
Virginia, 26,550/30%
North Carolina, 3,000/14%
South Carolina, 11,828/64%
French Louisiana, 1,385/36%
Spanish Florida, unknown
Cuba, unknown
St. Domingue, unknown
Jamaica, 55,000/89%
Leeward Islands, 30,000/77%
Barbados, 45,000/74%

Slave Population of North American and English West Indies Colonies, 1720
Slave population/ % of total population

■ **MAP 3.3** Slave Population of North American and English West Indies Colonies, 1720

In South Carolina and French Louisiana, slaves composed just 30 percent of the entire population in 1720. In marked contrast, slaves in Jamaica, Barbados, Haiti, and most other West Indian colonies typically made up 80–90 percent of the population.

discourage an approach to the fort, and "large reeds and canes to run into people's legs." Capturing the fort after a long siege, Colonel John Barnwell wrote that he "never saw such subtle contrivances for defence." As it turned out, a runaway slave who had fled to the Tuscarora tribe had used skills he learned in Africa and "taught [the Indians] to fortify thus."

Slavery in French Colonies

While the Spanish quickly incorporated Africans into mission and ranching life in the Southeast, the French settlers who preceded the English in Carolina hardly lasted long enough for Africans to establish a presence there. The small French settlement planted in 1562 near the mouth of St. John's River in Florida crumbled under a Spanish assault three years later. Farther north, in Canada, the French estab-

lished their main North American base. Initially, they had little use for enslaved Africans because the climate did not support intensive agriculture; their interest was more in fur-trading than raising cash crops. When French explorer Robert de LaSalle canoed through the Great Lakes and down the Mississippi River to its mouth in 1682, the French king claimed for France the vast North American interior stretching from Spanish Florida to the Mississippi River. Hoping to outflank the English colonies—or at least pin them to the Atlantic coast—the French began building trading posts and garrisons in the heart of Indian America. Now they made liberal use of Indian and African slaves to establish settlements in 1699 on the Biloxi and Mobile rivers, which emptied into the Gulf of Mexico east of the Mississippi River.

In 1718, the French stepped up their effort to occupy the immense territory they had claimed, which they dubbed

Louisiana. Establishing their capital at New Orleans, members of the French Company of the Indies began building what they envisioned would become a tobacco- and indigo-based bonanza port city. In time, they hoped, their presence in New Orleans would enable them to control the vast lower Mississippi Valley. They accomplished this feat of construction almost entirely with coerced labor: 1,900 Africans, some 1,200 *engagés* (criminals emptied from French jails), several thousand indentured servants, fewer than 200 adventurous French settlers, and a garrison of soldiers who held the unlikely mass together. This mixture of people constructed the budding port city meant to be France's strategic key to controlling the vast lower Mississippi Valley of North America.

By 1721, nearly 2,000 black slaves—more than one-fifth of the population—formed the backbone of Louisiana's economy. Skilled rice growers, indigo processors, metal-workers, river navigators, herbalists, and cattle keepers, they proved indispensable to the French. Like enslaved men living in Spanish Florida, African men in Louisiana mingled extensively with Indian women. These couples produced mixed-race children, born into slavery, who were known locally as *grifs*. Few French women ventured to the New World, so many French soldiers in search of partners formed liaisons with enslaved African women.

France's *Code Noir,* introduced in 1724 to regulate the conduct of slavery, forbade interracial marriage. But everyone in Louisiana knew that a law inscribed on the far side of the Atlantic meant little in the wilds of the lower Mississippi. To be sure, Catholic priests did not sanction interracial marriages, but a French man who took a common-law African wife raised no eyebrows in this frontier territory. Moreover, such relations often opened the door to freedom for mixed-race individuals whose white parent, usually the father, did not want his children enslaved. Many Afro-Indian, Franco-Indian, and Afro-French children born into slavery in early Louisiana won their liberty either through manumission or self-purchase. After a decade of colonization, Louisiana was still a lawless frontier zone, but it boasted a more flexible multiracial society than the English colonists had created.

tives for Africans enslaved in the West Indies. Because the Dutch controlled the Atlantic slave trade in North America during the mid-seventeenth century, slavery sank particularly deep roots into New Netherlands. But for most of the century, the majority of European settlers in North America satisfied their labor needs with white indentured servants and convicted felons transported from England and Ireland. In the last quarter of the seventeenth century, this pattern shifted, and Europeans began using far more enslaved African workers than indentured white laborers. White planters made this transition in reaction to rebellions instigated by former indentured servants in the Chesapeake and to the dwindling supply of white indentured servants coming from overseas. As European planters resorted increasingly to black labor, the slave-based plantation system began to gather momentum in North America.

From English New York to Spanish Florida and French Louisiana, white people became highly dependent on black slaves by the early eighteenth century. In the northern colonies, that dependence developed more slowly. But no matter where or how quickly slavery took root, this growing dependence redefined the meaning of race. Particularly in the English colonies, skin color determined a person's status as free or slave more than ever before. Most English colonists began considering lifelong servitude the natural condition of black people. They also believed it equally natural that slaves' children should be born into perpetual slavery.

In this new color-coded social system, enslaved black people and their families faced harsh work lives, a degradation of their African heritage, and a violent system of discipline. Most died early, never having escaped bondage. The era when Anthony and Mary Johnson had been free to till their own land, testify in court, and marry as they wished— to "know myne owne ground and . . . work . . . and play when I please"— had all but ended by the 1720s. A cruel new chapter had opened for Africans in North America. As the eighteenth century wore on, blacks had to find new ways to survive and to craft lives of dignity, pride, and hope.

CONCLUSION

Slavery took only shallow root in the North American English colonies for three-quarters of a century after a Dutch ship delivered a small number of Africans to Virginia in 1619. In 1637, Massachusetts Puritans traded Pequot cap-

FURTHER READING

Berlin, Ira. *Many Thousands Gone: The First Two Centuries of Slavery in North America* (Cambridge: Harvard University Press, 1998).

Breen, Timothy, and Stephen Innes. *"Myne Owne Ground": Race and Freedom on Virginia's Eastern Shore, 1640–1676* (New York: Oxford University Press, 1980).

Brown, Kathleen M. *Good Wives, Nasty Wenches, and Anxious Patriarchs: Gender, Race, and Power in Colonial Virginia* (Chapel Hill: University of North Carolina Press, 1996).

Charney, Judith A. *Black Rice: The African Origins of Rice Cultivation in the Americas* (Cambridge: Harvard University Press, 2001).

Deal, J. Douglas. *Race and Class in Colonial Virginia* (New York: Garland, 1993).

Diouf, Sylviane A. *Fighting the Slave Trade: West African Strategies* (Athens, OH: Ohio University Press, 2003).

Eltis, David. *The Rise of African Slavery in the Americas* (New York: Cambridge University Press, 2000).

Gallay, Alan. *The Indian Slave Trade: The Rise of the English Empire in the American South, 1670–1717* (New Haven: Yale University Press, 2002).

Hannaford, Ivan. *Race: The History of an Idea in the West* (Baltimore: Johns Hopkins University Press, 1996).

Hodges, Graham. *Root and Branch: African Americans in New York and East Jersey, 1613–1863* (Chapel Hill: University of North Carolina Press, 1999).

Holloway, Joseph E., ed. *Africanisms in American Culture* (Bloomington: Indiana University Press, 1990).

Ingersoll, Thomas I. *Mammon and Manon in Early New Orleans: The First Slave Society in the Deep South, 1718–1819* (Knoxville: University of Tennessee Press, 1999).

Jordan, Winthrop. *White over Black: Racial Attitudes Toward the Negro, 1550–1812* (Chapel Hill: University of North Carolina Press, 1968).

Kulikoff, Allan. *Tobacco and Slaves: The Development of Southern Cultures in the Chesapeake, 1680–1800* (Chapel Hill: University of North Carolina Press, 1986).

Morgan, Edmund. *American Slavery, American Freedom: The Ordeal of Colonial Virginia* (New York: W. W. Norton, 1975).

Nash, Gary B. *Red, White, and Black: The Peoples of Early North America*, 4th ed. (Englewood Cliffs, NJ: Prentice Hall, 2000).

Parent, Anthony S., Jr. *Foul Means: The Formation of a Slave Society in Virginia, 1660–1740* (Chapel Hill: University of North Carolina Press, 2003).

Solow, Barbara, ed. *Slavery and the Rise of the Atlantic System* (Cambridge: Cambridge University Press, 1991).

Thomas, Hugh. *The Slave Trade: The Story of the Atlantic Slave Trade, 1440–1870* (New York: Simon and Schuster, 1997).

Usner, Daniel H., Jr. *Indians, Settlers, and Slaves in a Frontier Exchange Economy* (Chapel Hill: University of North Carolina Press, 1992).

Wood, Betty. *The Origins of American Slavery: Freedom and Bondage in the English Colonies* (New York: Hill and Wang, 1997).

Wood, Peter. *Black Majority: Negroes in Colonial South Carolina from 1670 through the Stono Rebellion* (New York: W. W. Norton, 1974).

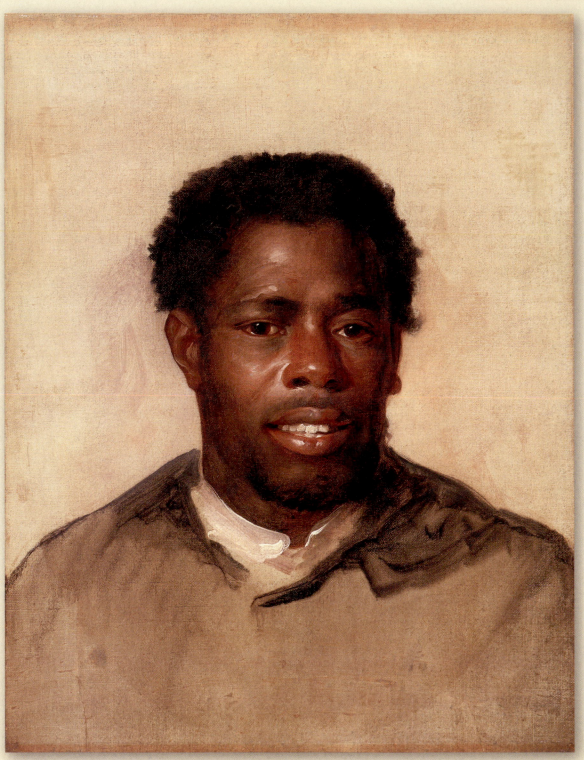

CHAPTER 4

■ *Head of a Negro* by the colonies' most noted portrait artist, John Singleton Copley.

Africans in Bondage: Early Eighteenth Century to the American Revolution

Venture Smith Defies the Colonial Slave System

Eight-year-old Broteer was the son of a king. His world collapsed in 1736 when Bambara slave raiders captured all the members of his village in Anamaboe, Guinea. The raiders killed Broteer's father and then marched the boy, along with the other villagers, to the coast. When a slaver from Rhode Island arrived to pick up the human cargo, Broteer's captors sold him to the ship's steward for "four gallons of rum and a piece of calico." The steward renamed the boy Venture. "Having purchased me with his own private venture," the steward intended to sell the youngster for a profit as soon as the ship returned to North America.

Arriving in New England by way of Barbados, Venture was purchased by a Connecticut farmer who gave him his surname—Smith. The farmer promptly set the boy to work combing sheep's wool for spinning, pounding corn for feeding the poultry, and carrying out household tasks. "My behavior had as yet been submissive and obedient," Smith related many years later. Then, at age nine, he reported, "I began to have hard tasks imposed on me . . . or be rigorously punished."

Smith grew tall and strong in his teens, and began chafing against slave life. He found his master's son James particularly galling. James "came up to me . . . big with authority" and "would order me to do *this* business and *that* business different from what my master had directed me." Tempers flared. When James

75

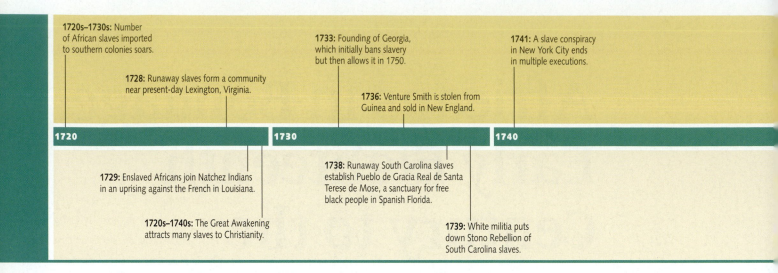

1720s–1730s: Number of African slaves imported to southern colonies soars.

1728: Runaway slaves form a community near present-day Lexington, Virginia.

1733: Founding of Georgia, which initially bans slavery but then allows it in 1750.

1736: Venture Smith is stolen from Guinea and sold in New England.

1741: A slave conspiracy in New York City ends in multiple executions.

1720   **1730**   **1740**

1729: Enslaved Africans join Natchez Indians in an uprising against the French in Louisiana.

1720s–1740s: The Great Awakening attracts many slaves to Christianity.

1738: Runaway South Carolina slaves establish Pueblo de Gracia Real de Santa Terese de Mose, a sanctuary for free black people in Spanish Florida.

1739: White militia puts down Stono Rebellion of South Carolina slaves.

flew into a rage and attacked Smith with a pitchfork, the young African defended himself and pummeled the white boy until he burst into tears. Soon other white men arrived on the scene and overpowered Smith. They suspended him from a cattle hook while another servant gathered peach-tree branches to whip the skin from the slave's back. Smith hung from the hook for an hour, anticipating the coming torment. He was spared only because James, dabbing his eyes with a handkerchief, "went home to tell his mother."

By age twenty-two, Venture Smith was a giant by eighteenth-century standards. Over six feet tall and weighing 250 pounds, he built a reputation as a prodigious worker with amazing strength. By day, he labored as a carpenter and farmhand. By night, he worked for himself, catching and selling game and fish with an eye toward purchasing his way out of slavery some day. Shortly after marrying Meg, another African slave, Smith made a break for freedom. Accompanied by three white indentured servants, he stole a boat and provisions from his master's home. The fugitives rowed across Long Island Sound for New York territory.

But Smith's freedom lasted only an instant. One of the indentured servants ran off with the group's scant provisions, leaving the others to fend for themselves. Heartsick and discouraged, Smith returned voluntarily to his master. As frequently happened with runaway slaves, his owner put him up for sale. Fortunately, his new Connecticut master, Thomas Stanton, soon purchased Smith's wife and their baby girl.

Then a battle of wills broke out between Meg and Stanton's wife. Smith recalled finding the two women shouting heatedly at one another. Meg stood her ground and ignored her husband's pleas to apologize "for the sake of peace." Then "my mistress turned the blows which she was repeating on my wife to me." Mrs. Stanton took down her horsewhip and "glutt[ed] her fury with it." Defending himself, Smith "reached out my great black hand, . . . received the blows of the whip on it," and then seized the whip and hurled it into the fireplace. Several days later, when his master returned, "he seemed to take no notice of it, and mentioned not a word of it to me. Some days after, . . . in the morning as I was putting on a log in the fireplace, not suspecting harm from anyone, I received a most violent stroke on the crown of my head with a club two feet long and as large around as a chair post." Staggering to his feet, the strapping slave threw his master to the ground and dragged him out of the house.

Smith thought himself unjustly attacked and fled to a local justice of the peace to plead his case. The justice "advised me to return to my master, and live contented with him till he abused me again, and then complain." Smith followed this suggestion, and the justice of the peace warned Stanton against abusing his slave again. But on the way home, Stanton and his brother "dismounted from their horses . . . and fell to beating me with great violence." The muscular Smith overpowered both men. "I became enraged, turned them both under me, laid one of them across the other, and stamped

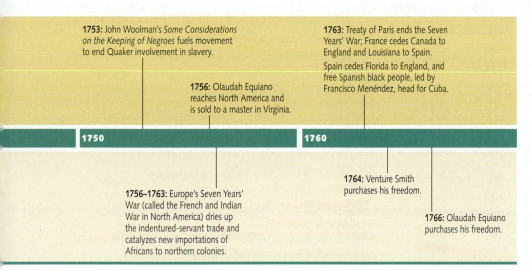

1753: John Woolman's *Some Considerations on the Keeping of Negroes* fuels movement to end Quaker involvement in slavery.

1756: Olaudah Equiano reaches North America and is sold to a master in Virginia.

1763: Treaty of Paris ends the Seven Years' War; France cedes Canada to England and Louisiana to Spain. Spain cedes Florida to England, and free Spanish black people, led by Francisco Menéndez, head for Cuba.

1750

1760

1756–1763: Europe's Seven Years' War (called the French and Indian War in North America) dries up the indentured-servant trade and catalyzes new importations of Africans to northern colonies.

1764: Venture Smith purchases his freedom.

1766: Olaudah Equiano purchases his freedom.

Another five years passed before he could purchase Meg. By the eve of the American Revolution, Smith had acquired a farm, owned his house and a second dwelling on Long Island, and had tucked away cash savings. As the war raged around him, he owned and managed a fleet of some twenty small coastal vessels that sold cordwood, fish, and garden produce along the shores of Long Island Sound. One of Smith's sons fought the British in the American Revolution.

both with my feet." Soon the town constable arrived to restrain Smith, and the local blacksmith fitted the slave with ankle and wrist shackles. When his master threatened to sell Smith to the West Indies—a fate most slaves dreaded—Smith replied, "I crossed the waters to come here, and I am willing to cross them to return."

Venture Smith's owner now knew he could never break this African's will. "I continued to wear the chain peaceably for two or three days." Smith remembered. "Not anyone said much to me, until one Hempstead Miner of Stonington asked me if I would live with him . . . and that in return he would give me a good chance to gain my freedom. I answered that I would." But Miner soon sold Smith for a quick profit to yet another owner, a Colonel Smith of Hartford. Smith toiled for this latest master for five years, working on his own time to save money coin by coin. Finally, at age thirty-six, Smith purchased his way out of twenty-eight years of slavery. But his wife, daughter, and now two sons remained trapped in bondage.

Smith worked feverishly to save enough to buy his family's freedom. "In four years, I cut several thousand cords of wood . . . I raised watermelons, and performed many other singular labors," he recalled. Described as a black Paul Bunyan "who swung his axe to break his chains," Smith "shunned all kind of luxuries" and "bought nothing that I absolutely did not want." By 1768, he had purchased his sons out of slavery and then later managed to free his daughter.

Venture Smith was one of about 255,000 slaves to arrive in North America's English colonies between 1700 and 1775, the year the American Revolution broke out. The influx of slaves in those seventy-five years dwarfed the 28,000 who arrived in the seventeenth century. Colonial slavery had reached its peak.

The struggle to survive the system of slavery, itself still in the process of formation, was a great test of human endurance. While liberty-loving European settlers paradoxically built a strict code of laws, social rules, and attitudes designed to deprive Africans and their descendants from freedom, black slaves did not simply accept this code. They made the terms of their bondage a matter of negotiation, defying the system in a continual series of abrasive and often violent encounters with their masters and mistresses.

Slavery took many forms in different English colonies and in the Spanish- and French-controlled regions of North America. Yet no matter its shape, the interactions between masters and slaves led to a gradual merging of African and European cultures. By this process, Africans in America became African Americans, while Euro-Americans adopted elements of African culture. Embedded within their story is a subplot featuring individuals such as Venture Smith, who worked their way out of bondage and inspired hope in the hearts of their enslaved fellows. Only a tiny fraction of all black Americans achieved what Smith did in this era. But they had allies: a handful of white abolitionists whose voices gathered strength by the 1770s.

COLONIAL SLAVERY AT HIGH TIDE

A year after reaching Virginia in 1756, Olaudah Equiano, the much-traveled slave autobiographer, had some good fortune: His Virginia master sold him to an English ship captain who later sold him to a merchant in Montserrat, English West Indies. Traveling as a shipboard slave among England, Caribbean ports, and North American settlements, Equiano saw how slavery functioned differently in various English colonies. In the West Indies and in southern ports, he observed colonial societies that in a single generation made slavery the key to producing goods and services and measuring wealth. In Philadelphia and other northern ports, he saw societies in which slavery was one of many forms of labor and not necessarily a mark of social status for white people. Equiano thus had a broad perspective on the workings of the entire cross-Atlantic economy.

A Rising Slave Population

After Virginia and Maryland's planters replaced white indentured servants with African slave labor in the late seventeenth century, the composition of North America's population shifted dramatically. When some 75,000 slaves, almost all coming directly from Africa, reached the Chesapeake colonies between 1700 and 1750, the agricultural and domestic labor force became mostly black. In 1736, one of Virginia's largest planters already worried that his neighbors "import so many Negroes hither that I fear this colony will be confirmed by the name of New Guinea"—referring to the African region where many of Virginia's slaves originated.

In the Lower South—Georgia and South Carolina—slave importations soared after 1710. By the 1730s, field labor became overwhelmingly black in this region. Almost half of all slaves arriving in the English colonies after 1700 first saw land at Sullivan's Island, a quarantine station in the harbor of Charleston that has been called the Ellis Island of black America. In 1737, one Swiss newcomer traveling through South Carolina thought the colony "looks more like a negro country than like a country settled by white people."

> The colony "looks more like a negro country than like a country settled by white people."
> —*A Swiss traveler*

Georgia, founded by British philanthropists in 1733, followed this pattern, though unexpectedly. Launching the colony as an experiment in settling poor English men and women on small plots of land, Georgia's founders banned slavery. But in 1750, at the insistence of the white settlers there, the colony's trustees abandoned their initial vision and permitted slavery. Now wealthy investors snapped up large tracts of land with the aim of establishing lucrative plantations. "Stark mad after Negroes," as one observer claimed, they imported shiploads of Africans. By the time the American Revolution broke out, black slaves in Georgia outnumbered the white settlers.

The flood of slaves rushing into the southern colonies originated in many parts of West and Central Africa. A small number came from Madagascar, an island off Africa's southeast coast. But southern planters were particular about the human merchandise they purchased. Moreover, they held strong—if often misinformed—opinions about which Africans were the best. Equiano claimed that West Indian planters prized "the slaves of Benin or Eboe [Ibo] to those of

■ TABLE 4.1 Growth of Slave Population in English America, 1710–1770

After 1730, the rate of slave population increase in the southern colonies (Virginia, Maryland, North and South Carolina, and Georgia) continued to outstrip that in New England (Massachusetts, New Hampshire, Connecticut, and Rhode Island) and the mid-Atlantic (New York, New Jersey, Pennsylvania, and Delaware) colonies. By 1770, the slave population in the southern colonies nearly equaled that in the British West Indies.

Years	New England	Mid-Atlantic	South	British West Indies	Total	% of African Slaves in British West Indies
1710	2,600	6,200	29,000	148,000	185,800	79.6
1730	6,100	11,700	79,200	221,000	318,000	69.5
1750	11,000	20,700	210,400	295,000	537,100	55.5
1770	15,400	34,900	406,800	434,000	891,100	48.7

Source: McCusker and Menard, The Economy of British America.

any other part of Guinea, for their hardiness, intelligence, integrity, and zeal." In Virginia, where Iboes like Equiano made up the largest ethnic group, slaveowners echoed this sentiment. Meanwhile, slave buyers in South Carolina and Georgia disdained Iboes as despondent and suicidal. In the punishing climate of the Carolina low country, planters preferred Kongolese, Angolan, and Senegambian people from West Central Africa, many of whom had cultivated rice back home. These slaveowners also valued male over female bondspeople. They imported roughly three men for every two women, keeping an eye out especially for young, strong, and healthy males.

Slave Life in the South

By the early eighteenth century, slavery had sunk deep roots into the southern English colonies. Importation of slaves into the region stretching from Maryland to Georgia began rivaling that of the West Indies. Some planters, such as Virginia's William Byrd II, worried that an "unhappy effect of [having so] many Negroes [here] is the necessity of being severe. Numbers make them insolent, and then foul means must do what fair will not." The flood of imported slaves, Byrd complained, was turning his friends into inhumane slavedrivers. But neither Byrd nor any other southern planter took steps to reverse the situation.

On South Carolina's coastal lowlands, slave importations and rice cultivation expanded together. Planters in the tidal floodplain relied on African slaves' knowledge about growing rice in such a region. Much of this "African knowledge system," as one geographer has called it, resided within women, who in Africa did most of the sowing and winnowing of rice. Though black families in Africa celebrated rice planting as a time of renewal and promise, rice cultivation in South Carolina—where the whip ruled the fields—meant just another cycle of misery and sickness.

Unlike cultivating wheat or corn in the North, growing rice demanded backbreaking year-round labor. Slaves had to clear the swampy lowlands in winter, build dykes (structures keeping seawater out of the fields), and plant rice in shallow trenches in the spring. In late summer, they harvested the crop. In the fall, they pounded the rice kernels with wooden mortars and pestles. Come wintertime, they turned the soil to prepare it for a new round of planting.

Rice "is the most unhealthy work in which the slaves were employed," wrote one English visitor to South Carolina, "and they sank under it in great numbers. The causes of this dreadful mortality are the constant moisture and heat of the atmosphere, together with the alternate floodings and dryings of the fields, on which the negroes are perpetually at work, often ankle deep in mud, with their bare heads exposed to the fierce rays of the sun." One-quarter of the Africans imported to the low country in the first half of the eighteenth century died within a year of their arrival—victims of overwork, inadequate nutrition, and respiratory disease. Still, their labor made their owners rich: By the late 1760s, white South Carolina planters were exporting more than 60 million pounds of rice annually.

As South Carolinian planters stepped up rice cultivation, they began importing ever larger numbers of Africans. Advertisements regularly announced new arrivals: "A choice cargo of about 250 fine healthy NEGROES just arrived from the Windward & Rice Coast." "An exceeding fine Cargo of 350 Healthy NEGROES, just imported in the Ship *Emporer* . . . directly from Angola." "Slaves remarkably healthy, just arrived in the ship *Sally* from Cape Mount—a rice country—on the Windward

■ This depiction of conical-roofed houses at Mulberry Plantation in South Carolina shows that Africans often built their own living quarters based on designs they knew from their West African home villages. Slaves' housing improved during the eighteenth century, as sex-segregated barracks gave way to family cabins on many plantations.

Coast, after a short passage of five weeks." Owing to these heavy importations, the proportion of slaves toiling in South Carolina who were African-born reached as high as one-third at the end of the colonial era. These slaves maintained a feeling of close connection to Africa. One visitor to the Carolina low country in 1740 noticed the "many various ages, nations, [and] languages" among the "whole body of slaves"—suggesting that numerous slaves still spoke their native languages.

The Chesapeake colonies of Virginia and Maryland experienced a similar phenomenon. After intense slave importation in the first third of the eighteenth century, plantation quarters housed diverse mixtures of Africans who spoke different languages. At the same time, slaves' working and living conditions worsened as masters strived for ever higher tobacco profits. Greedy planters lengthened the slaves' workday and reduced the number of holidays to just three (Christmas, Easter, and Whitsuntide, or Pentecost—the Christian holy day commemorating the descent of the Holy Spirit on the apostles). Whereas masters had previously let slaves rest a bit during the winter, now they ordered them to grind corn, clear stumps, and chop wood in the cold months. They also imposed stricter supervision, cracking the whip and applying the branding iron with more severity than ever.

By the time Equiano arrived in Virginia in 1756, the ratio between African-born and North American–born slaves had begun to shift. In this English colony, the number of black people born in the colonies had been rising since about 1720. Historians have several explanations for this transition from African to African American. For one thing, as large plantations began to edge out small farms, slaves began living in larger groups. In these groups, they found marriage partners more easily, created families, and built the extended kin networks that made life more bearable, even as their work routines grew more oppressive. All of this triggered a natural population increase among slaves. By the late colonial period, slaves had forged ties of kinship and friendship that criss-crossed the southern countryside. Some planters complained about the "continual concourse of Negroes on Sabbath and holy days meeting in great numbers."

■ England's booming textile industry drove demand for indigo, a plant that yielded a deep blue dye prized by textile manufacturers. Processing indigo was exhausting work. As slaves boiled the plant, a sickening stench arose from the vats. The odor attracted clouds of flies, and the boiled water polluted streams.

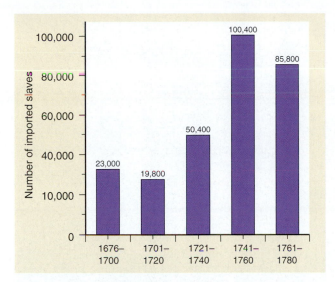

■ FIGURE 4.1 Importation of Slaves to North America, 1676–1780

Between 1701 and 1780, ship captains transported about 256,000 slaves directly from Africa to colonial ports, especially Savannah, Charleston, Philadelphia, New York, Newport, and Boston. After the Declaration of Independence in 1776, many states banned the importation of Africans, thus the lower number of incoming Africans in the 1770s. The disruption of seaborne traffic during the American Revolution further reduced these numbers. But after the war, slavers resumed the traffic, carrying as many as 100,000 slaves to South Carolina and Georgia between 1783 and 1808.

Births in Chesapeake slave families gradually evened out the gender imbalance in slave imports. At the same time, the increase in North American–born slaves gave white planters less reason to import new captives fresh from Africa. Because a more gender-balanced population provided greater opportunity for early marriages, Virginia-born slave women bore children at younger ages than their African-born mothers had. Families thus grew larger. By the 1770s, Virginia's slave population was expanding at the rate of 5,000 per year, but only about 500 to 800 of them were arriving from Africa. The rest of the increase came from American-born slaves' fertility and the rising ratio of slave births over slave deaths.

In the southern colonies overall, slave fertility exceeded that in the British West Indies. White Caribbean planters imported five times as many slaves in the colonial era as white people in the mainland southern colonies had. Yet on the eve of the American Revolution, black people in the southern colonies and in Britain's Caribbean sugar islands numbered roughly the same. In the islands, the brutal sugar

work regimen had swept away black lives with hurricane force. By 1770, more than 400,000 slaves resided in the southern colonies—a whopping increase over the 13,000 slaves who lived in the region just eighty years earlier.

Eighteenth-century plantations were small worlds in themselves. In addition to field hands and house servants, they required the labor of carpenters, blacksmiths, bricklayers, weavers, coopers (barrelmakers), butchers, and leatherworkers to keep functioning. As slaves acquired the skills necessary to provide these forms of labor, they increasingly came into contact with white workers. Slaves who possessed valued abilities were allowed to move around more freely—from home to workshop, plantation to town, warehouse to wharf—than field slaves could. Those who drove wagonloads of crops to river landings and piloted tobacco- and rice-laden rafts and boats through the inland waterways of the coastal South spent much of their time away from the plantation.

The experiences of these slaves resembled that of urban bondspeople, many of whom were also skilled artisans and shopworkers. In his visits to Charleston and Savannah, Equiano saw slave women selling goods from street carts and purchasing food for the kitchens they ran in their white masters' homes. Most urban slaves had easier lives than plantation slaves because they were spared backbreaking field labor. However, their isolation in white households made it harder for them to form families and friendships with other slaves.

Most bondsmen and women in the southern colonies labored in the fields. Nearly every black woman on a small farm or large plantation wielded a hoe and sickle as well as tended and butchered livestock, cultivated vegetable gardens, and took care of dairy cows. Slave women who worked in the houses of their masters had a more diverse work routine. They attended the births of the master's children and fed, suckled, and bathed his infants. As the children grew, slave women rocked them to sleep and supervised their play. They also washed, mended, and ironed clothes; cooked, baked, and canned; served meals and washed up afterward; and spun, wove, and stitched clothing. A few men also worked in households as waiters, coach drivers, and valets (personal attendants).

Sexual Oppression

Whether in the fields or in the master's household, slave women lived under the constant threat of sexual aggression by white men. Though written accounts by black women of their ordeal have not been found as yet, we know it was widespread. The rape of an enslaved black woman probably constituted the most destructive and disruptive weapon in

■ Enslaved Africans in South Carolina and Georgia—in the background two slaves are carrying water skimmed off indigo vats—toiled in long, exhausting work regimens much like those on tropical West Indies plantations.

the white man's arsenal. In raping black women, white men also asserted their power over black men. Indeed, to demonstrate their dominance, some white slaveowners forced black men to witness their assault on a wife, sister, or daughter. The pain stemming from these attacks disrupted black families and inflicted permanent emotional scars not only on the victims but on all who cared about them.

Interracial rape was the purview of white men. Few black men were accused of raping white women. Indeed, most sexual unions between white women and black men were consensual. Even though the laws forbade white-black marriages, the scores of white women dragged into court for bearing mulatto children testified to their willingness to choose a black mate.

Some sexual relationships between white men and black women were also consensual. For example, a slave woman might agree to have sex with a white man to gain advantages for herself or her children. In some cases, such relationships endured for many decades. But affection within such couples was rare. Moreover, these relationships, consensual or not, spawned excruciating tensions among both black and white people. They reinforced the dependency of black women on white men and were a painful reminder that black men had little power or worth in the society. The actions of these white men also put their wives in a painful position. The women could only endure silently as their husbands had adulterous relations with their slaves. When such unions produced children, these youngsters suffered as well. They lived in a kind of social no-man's land. The law said they

were slaves because their mothers were slaves. Yet some of them had the affection of their white fathers. Others received more favorable work assignments and their freedom on reaching adulthood. But despite these advantages, they rarely found acceptance in white society.

Slave Life in the North

North of the Chesapeake, Africans made up only about 5 percent of the population. Dispersed widely across the hilly terrain and living in small numbers within white households, they found themselves isolated in a sea of white people. Still, slave importations directly from Africa swelled the northern black population from 9,000 in 1710 to 32,000 in 1750. When the Seven Years' War (1756–1763) cut off the supply of white indentured servants from Ireland and Germany, it created a labor vacuum that northerners gladly filled with even more African slaves. Their numbers swelled to about 50,000 by 1770.

Like Venture Smith, most slaves in New England and the mid-Atlantic colonies had work lives characterized by variety and seasonal rhythms. Many black men and women also possessed a range of valuable skills—from farming, woodworking, and seafaring to cargo transporting, cattle tending, and cooking. Indeed, numerous slave advertisements spoke of a black man who could "turn his hand at many sorts of trades" or was "fit for town and country." A large number of black people mingled with white indentured servants and wage laborers and hired out their free time to labor for others. Many were sold from master to master, often gaining new skills. In northern cities, most wealthy households had at least one slave. By 1770, nearly one-quarter of white householders in Philadelphia and New York owned slaves—about the same proportion as in North Carolina. Even families that only recently rose to the middle class, such as Benjamin Franklin's, bought slaves to handle domestic chores.

Slaves in the North had easier work lives than those in the South, mostly because the northern climate did not permit year-round farming. But these more tolerable work lives came at the cost of family life. Like Venture Smith, most slaves ate, slept, and lived in their owner's home because no slave quarters were needed. Thus they didn't have the after-sundown privacy, away from the master's watchful eye, that southern slaves prized. Northern slaves were often the only slave in a household, so they were isolated and lacked the sense of community southern slaves treasured. An excess of black men over women prevented many of them from forming families. Only in Rhode Island's Narragansett area and in New York's Kings and Queens counties, where dozens of slaves worked large farms, did the black population prove dense enough for slaves to construct durable, extended kin groups. Elsewhere, slaves formed so-called abroad marriages, in which husbands and wives lived in different white households and only occasionally spent time together. The children of such marriages were often sold away from their mother at an early age.

African Americans in the North mingled more closely with white people than slaves in the South did. In streets, churches, and taverns, and along oceanside wharves and river-ferry landings, black and white peoples encountered one another every day as they went about their business. In many households, black slaves took their meals with white masters. One Englishwoman traveling in Connecticut marveled that masters allowed slaves "to sit at table with them (as they say to save time), and into the dish goes the black

■ Venture Smith died in 1805 at age seventy-nine. Four pallbearers struggled to hoist the coffin containing this giant man of more than 250 pounds. Stories about Smith's prodigious strength circulated around Connecticut for years after his death. One man recalled that "a noted wrestler tried his skill in wrestling with Venture but found he might as well try to remove a tree."

hoof as freely as the white hand." Yet despite these advantages, many northern slaves endured brutal treatment by masters and unequal treatment under the law.

More rapidly than in the South, black northerners became part of the wider emerging American culture. Encompassing English, Dutch, German, Scots, and Scots-Irish elements, this culture boasted a richness and variety not seen in the South. Black people and Europeans borrowed from and adapted one another's practice of medicine and other knowledge. A notable example was the West African knowledge of smallpox inoculation. The highly contagious smallpox virus was a persistent problem in the colonies, especially in densely inhabited towns. In Boston alone, seven smallpox epidemics

 **First Person** — Petitioning Boston Slaves Lament Family Life

The obstacles to forming and maintaining families in the northern colonies counted among slaves' most sorrowful burdens. In 1773, when a group of slaves in Boston petitioned the Massachusetts legislature for release from slavery, they cited the desire to create their own families as the primary reason for their plea. Below is an excerpt from their petition.

The endearing ties of husband and wife we are strangers to, for we are no longer man and wife than our masters and mistresses think proper, married or unmarried. Our children are also taken from us by force and sent many miles from us where we seldom or ever see them again, there to be made slaves of for life, which sometimes is very short by reason of being dragged from their mother's breast. Thus our lives are embittered to us on these accounts. . . .

How can a slave perform the duties of a husband to a wife or parent to his child? How can a husband leave master and work and cleave to his wife? How can the wife submit themselves to their husbands in all things? How can the child obey their parents in all things?

—*from Collections*, Massachusetts Historical Society, *5th series, III (Boston, 1877).*

To view a longer version of this document, please go to *www.ablongman.com/carson/documents*.

between 1640 and 1721 killed hundreds. In 1721, the slave of Boston's eminent minister, Cotton Mather, showed how to introduce a small amount of fluid from a smallpox blister under the skin of another person to stimulate the formation of antibodies that gave immunity. From this first experiment, called *variolation*, the practice spread to other towns. Within a single generation, smallpox no longer counted as the most dreaded epidemic of the era.

Even though northern colonists had relatively few slaves, they had strong economic links to slavery. They built and manned ships engaged in the Atlantic slave trade. Northern merchants shipped fish, meat, and grain to feed the huge West Indies slave population; brought back molasses, which they distilled into rum; and shipped the rum to Africa, where they exchanged it for slaves whom they sold in the West Indies or North America. Northern forests provided the wood for the ships and barrels that carried all these goods. Considering the wide appeal of slave-produced sugar, coffee, rice, indigo, and tobacco, and the number of colonists who participated in producing, financing, and shipping exports to the West Indies, Europe, and Africa, most northern colonists participated in or benefited from slavery directly or indirectly.

After 1720, New England merchants, especially in Rhode Island, participated in the slave trade in the most direct manner possible: transporting black people from Africa directly to North America. Though small in number compared to the

British slavers (who concentrated on the massive West Indies trade), New England captains transported a large proportion of the Africans brought to North America. England's North American colonists on the eve of revolution—both northern and southern—were immersed in race-based slavery.

NEGOTIATED BONDAGE

According to white colonists' law books, Africans brought to the colonies in chains had no power. But the day-to-day realities of living with the people they enslaved forced slave-owners to admit that absolute control over other humans was impossible. "A short time after[ward] my master carried me to Hartford," Venture Smith remembered, "and first proposed to sell me to one William Hooker of that place." Hooker would have been Smith's fourth master, and had made no mention of buying Smith's wife and children. "Hooker asked whether I would go to the German Flats [in northern New York] with him. I answered no. He said I should, if not by fair means . . . by foul. If you will go by no other measures," Hooker warned, "I will tie you down in my sleigh." Undaunted, Smith replied "that if he carried me in that manner, no person would purchase me, for it would

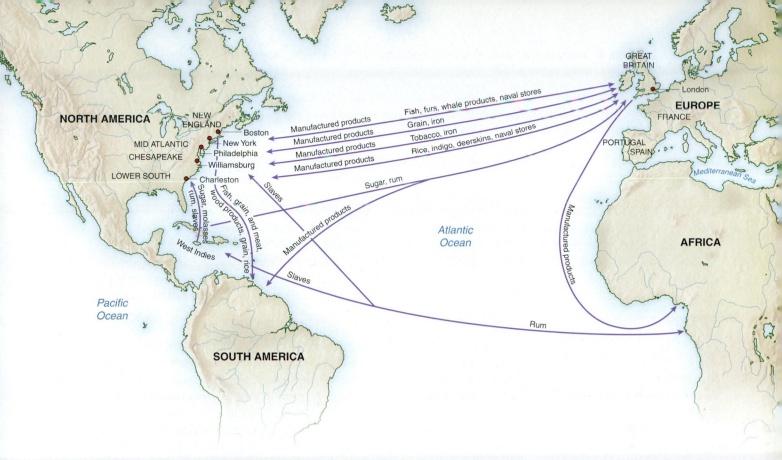

■ **MAP 4.1** **The Commercial Triangle**

Southern colonists had the most extensive daily interactions with slaves, yet northern colonists acquired the most experience in doing business with slave traders in Africa and slaveowning merchants and planters in the West Indies.

be thought that he had a murderer for sale." That ended the sale of Smith to William Hooker. "After this he tried no more, and said he would not have me as a gift."

Europeans rationalized their involvement in slavery by maintaining that Africans were subhuman heathens born for the sole purpose of serving as beasts of burden. To that end, owners sought to convert slaves into mindless drudges who obeyed every command, worked efficiently for the master's profit, and accepted their lowly status. Slaveowners used law, terror, torture, and, ultimately, the control of life and death over slaves to preserve this power imbalance. Yet masters never achieved absolute control. Not every slave had Smith's physical strength or defiance, but every master knew that slaves were volatile property. They always had to take into account what a slave might or might not do. Sometimes it was easier to compromise with a slave than to insist on total obedience. Slave advertisements give glimpses into this reality: "The cause of his being sold is that he is not inclined to farming." "They are sold for no fault, only not agreeing with the freeman of the business they are present employed in."

Slave and master were tied together in a condition of intimate interdependence. Masters could set the boundaries of the slave's existence— defining physical location, work roles, rations, and shelter. But slaveowners depended on bondsmen and women to plant, tend, and harvest cash crops, get the crops to market, construct buildings, and care for the children of the manor. Practical owners knew that if they pushed slaves too far, the work simply would not get done, or would be performed sloppily.

In addition, masters had limited power over precisely how slaves accomplished their work. Unless an owner wanted to monitor and physically control a slave's every physical action, he had to accept that the slave would make his or her own decisions about how to approach a task. Nor did masters have much say over whether and how slaves established friendships, fell in love, and formed kin groups. Finally, owners could not completely supervise the way slaves raised their children, worshiped their gods, buried their dead, and spent their scant leisure time.

Resisting Slavery

Slaveowners watched for resistance from their human property the moment African captives stepped foot on American soil. Most white people agreed that newly imported slaves, known as saltwater Africans, were far more dangerous than "country-born" slaves. "If he must be broke, either from obstinacy, or, which I am more apt to suppose, from greatness of soul, [it] will require . . . hard discipline," wrote one North Carolina planter. "You would really be surprised at their perseverance . . . they often die before they can be conquered." In South Carolina, one eighteenth-century newspaper published advertisements calling for the return of "Gambia men" or Africans from "the Fullah Country" who had fled into the countryside together immediately on arriving on North American shores. In 1773, fourteen freshly imported slaves escaped as a group from a Virginia slave merchant, plunging into unfamiliar territory before being recaptured and sold.

Resistance and the threat of violence pervaded the master-slave relationship. "When you make men slaves, you compel them to live with you in a state of war," wrote Olaudah Equiano. Every slaveowner knew this. Surely all who owned Venture Smith dared not relax. One Maryland planter claimed he had "never known a single instance of a negro being contented in slavery." A German minister acknowledged that slaves were "always on the point of rebellion." Even in the northern colonies, where owners treated slaves somewhat less harshly than they did in the South, masters held few illusions about their slaves' state of mind. Benjamin Franklin, himself a slaveowner, wrote in 1770 to a European friend: "Perhaps you may imagine the Negroes to be a mild-tempered, tractable kind of people. Some of them indeed are so. But the majority are of a plotting disposition, dark, sullen, malicious, revengeful and cruel in the highest degree." In every slaveowning region of North America, some bondsmen and women murdered their masters. Such killings kept white people on edge as long as slavery existed.

> "When you make men slaves, you compel them to live with you in a state of war."—Olaudah Equiano

Contesting Labor

Labor lay at the core of the slave's existence. Because their survival—as well as their dignity and self-respect—depended on work, slaves strove to perform their duties on their own terms. They controlled what they could, practicing African work habits in New World fields in ways that made their lives more bearable. For example, they preferred team to individual work and drew on homeland knowledge of rice cultivation to work in familiar ways. All the while, they devised strategies for defying their master's authority. By shamming sickness, breaking hoes, dropping dishes, dragging out a job, pretending ignorance, uprooting freshly planted seedlings, and harvesting carelessly, they foiled their

master's purpose. One visitor to a Maryland plantation expressed surprise at slave laborers' "Perseverance." "Let an hundred men shew him how to hoe, or drive a wheelbarrow, he'll still take the one by the bottom, and the other by the wheel," the visitor remarked. In neighboring Virginia, a planter despaired, "I find it almost impossible to make a negro do his work well. No orders can engage it, no encouragement persuade it, nor no punishment oblige it."

Masters developed many strategies for coping with this contest of wills. Some treated their slaves leniently; others applied the lash with increasing frustration. Slave owners knew that one way to maintain discipline was through terror and torture—legalized flogging, branding, burning, amputation of limbs, and murder. But they also knew that, pushed too hard, slaves would strike back. In 1732, a South Carolina "friend to the planters" wrote an article in the *South Carolina Gazette* describing increased incidents of barn burning. Such burnings, the author noted, seemed to happen particularly frequently on plantations where owners treated slaves with notable cruelty. In the most recent case, the author explained, "Mr. James Gray worked his Negroes late in his Barn at Night, and the next Morning before Day, hurried them out again, and when they came to it, found it burnt down to the Ground, and all that was in it." A decade later in Caroline County, Virginia, a slave named Phill torched his master's home, corn house, and tobacco house. Virginian legislators soon made arson a capital crime. Yet no laws could prevent all attacks on masters.

Savvy masters realized they could get the most out of their human chattel by sharing power and permitting slaves to control some aspects of their lives. For example, some owners delegated authority to black drivers. Others, especially along the rice coast of South Carolina and Georgia, used the tasking system. They assigned slaves specific tasks—such as so many baskets of rice to thresh or so many barrels of indigo to pack—and then allowed the slaves to do whatever they liked after finishing the assignments. Masters liked the tasking system because it gave slaves an incentive to get the work done. Slaves liked it because it permitted them some control over their lives.

Most slaves used their leisure time to their advantage. They cultivated garden plots and kept poultry that enriched their diets. Some also traveled to towns and neighboring plantations to market their produce. Eventually, they created their own economy within the master's economy. They saved coins to buy small things to improve their lives or, in rare cases, to purchase their freedom. To be sure, such entrepreneurial behavior created cracks in the slave system. Nevertheless, owners recognized that slaves who had the right to produce for themselves and barter what they made were less likely to run away. From the slaves' perspective, the arrangement allowed them to preserve family and friendship ties while finding satisfaction in managing a small aspect of their existence.

Sometimes slaves pilfered chickens, livestock, crops, or tools from their masters and sold the stolen goods in underground market systems spread over considerable distances. Domestic slaves took advantage of their station to pinch liquor and pocket household items. Most slaves saw no sin at all in taking crops they had planted, raised, and harvested, even if their master decried the stealing. Most masters kept the peace by looking the other way.

Creating Family Ties

In the master's view, slave family life was theoretically impossible because allegiance was supposed to run in only one direction: from slave to master. To that end, the majority of colonies prohibited marriage contracts between slaves. Yet masters also knew that slaves who forged family ties might have children, thus increasing the owner's wealth at no additional investment. (A male slave in his prime typically sold for about 50 English pounds—roughly $1,000 today.) As Thomas Jefferson put it, "A woman who brings a child every two years [is] more profitable than the best man on the farm, [for] what she produces is an addition to the capital, while his labor disappears in mere consumption." In addition to the profitability of slave families, owners also valued the power of family ties to keep slaves from fleeing. Thus many masters struck bargains with slaves regarding domestic life.

Negotiations over slave family life always involved tension. That tension reached its highest point when slaveowners contemplated auctioning off members of slave families. Often, slaves were sold after an owner's death to fulfill the terms of the deceased person's will. Aware that shattered families made for unhappy, recalcitrant slaves, a new owner might succumb to pressure from slave husbands to be allowed to visit "abroad" wives and children. Once again, slave advertisements reveal much about this aspect of slavery. In South Carolina, the flight of an enslaved man named Cuffee in 1749 was "occasion'd by his Wife and Child's being sold from him." A generation later, even an iron collar with protruding prongs could not keep a slave woman named Patt from absconding to find her husband, to whom "she [was] very much attached."

Running Away

For most slaves, running away offered the best hope of resisting their plight. Colonial newspapers recorded thousands of runaway cases, posting notices of fleeing slaves and offering rewards for their capture. Runaway-slave advertisements tell a vivid story about people who used their knowledge of a region's geography and linguistic skills to seize freedom. "Run away from Charles Town, Cecil County, Maryland, . . . two Negroe Fellows," read one notice in 1765. "One named Cuff, about 5 feet, 3 inches high, a thick well-set Lad about 17 Years of Age . . . had on, when he went away, a blue Cloth Jacket without Sleeves, . . . Shirt and Trowsers, and about 4 Weeks ago was brought home (after running away) from Philadelphia Work-house, where he was taken up and confined, and formerly belonged to Mr. Charles Moor, Hatter there."

Three years earlier, twenty-three-year-old Joe, a mixed-race Philadelphia slave, used his abundant talents to pose as a freeman. Fleeing his master in 1762, he reinvented himself as Joseph Boudron—because a free black needed a full first name and a distinctive surname. With his new identity, Boudron traded on his unusual language skills: He "speaks good English, French, Spanish, and Portuguese," read the advertisement announcing his escape. Boudron also knew his way around the landscape. Born in Guadalupe, a French sugar island in the West Indies, he had already lived in Charleston, South Carolina, and New York—where his Philadelphia master thought he was headed. "A good cook and much used to the Seas," Boudron could pose as a free black mariner or chef. Another ad in 1771 told of Violet, "about 35 years of Age . . . very Active and rather tall." Violet was "remarkably artful," having escaped twice before in the 1760s to find her three children.

Many runaway slaves changed their appearance to make good their flight from bondage. Some impersonated Native Americans. Clothing and hair offered plenty of opportunities to transform themselves. In 1751, Tom, a thirty-seven-year-old mulatto in East New Jersey, cut his coat short to make Indian stockings, lopped off his hair, and searched for a blanket "to pass for an Indian." He then headed for a Susquehannah Indian village where the German Moravian sect in Pennsylvania had established a mission. In New Jersey, a runaway slave woman named Hannah used clothes to refashion her identity, grabbing mourning attire "which she no doubt intends to Dress in, that she may not be known."

Some slaves ran away knowing they would return, often voluntarily; they just needed the comfort of a loved one, relief from a heartless overseer, or a few days in the woods on their own. But most runaways set out with the intention of winning their freedom permanently. Men fled far more often than women, who felt tied to their places of captivity by their children. Yet many women escaped, too, sometimes while pregnant or with small children clutched in their arms.

In the southern colonies, most runaways were re-captured and hauled back to their owners. A slave had to make it as far north as Philadelphia to find sanctuary in communities formed by freed slaves. A few settlements of escaped slaves survived briefly in the Carolinas and the Chesapeake. One sanctuary lay near present-day Lexington, Virginia. There, in 1728, runaway slaves built a small village of huts resembling those they had known in Africa and formed a government under a chief whose father had been a king in Africa. But owing to the determination of masters to root out these communities, they did not last long. In a region where only one or two free Africans existed for every hundred slaves, it was next to impossible to masquerade as a free person indefinitely.

Masters did everything possible to discourage slaves from running away. Some chopped off the toes of repeat offenders or hobbled them with heavy ankle chains and iron collars. Others branded and flogged recaptured runaways and vented their rage on the slaves' family members. The first African whom Equiano saw in Virginia was a woman enduring retaliation for running away: "The poor creature was cruelly loaded with various kinds of iron machines; she had one particularly on her head, which locked her mouth so fast that she could scarcely speak; and could not eat nor drink. I was much astonished and shocked at this contrivance, which I afterwards learned was called the iron muzzle." Though such treatment might cow individual slaves, it could not vanquish the collective determination of a people sharing the same fate.

Norfolk and Princess Anne. Some 300 slaves, after choosing "officers to command them," fled to the Dismal Swamp "where they commit[ted] many outrages against the [white] Christians." With the aid of local Pasquotank Indians, white Virginians suppressed the insurrection and hanged twenty-nine of the rebels.

Nine years later, an uprising known as the Stono Rebellion broke out in South Carolina. About twenty slaves along the Stono River southwest of Charleston—most of them newly arrived from Angola or Kongo—seized weapons from their masters. They killed several white people and headed for the Florida frontier. There, they hoped to find refuge among the Spanish, as handfuls of slaves had done for years. Raising banners and marching to a stirring drumbeat, they burned and plundered plantations as they moved south. The small army attracted additional slaves and swelled to about a hundred. But the colonial militia intercepted the band and, with Indian assistance, defeated them in a pitched battle. Thirty slaves lost their lives. Shaken, South Carolina's legislature halted imports of Africans for several years. Lawmakers also tightened restrictions on slaves' use of written passes from their masters to move about on Sundays and holidays. Yet even these actions could not prevent slaves from organizing resistance. Southern white authorities uncovered and squelched several other revolts in the making, such as a plot to destroy Charleston, South Carolina, in 1730 and a plan to capture Annapolis, Maryland, in 1740.

Though large-scale rebellions were rare, they occurred often enough to remind slaveowners that even the most

Rebelling

For bondspeople, organized revolt represented the highest form of resistance. The largest slave uprising in the colonies erupted in 1730 in Virginia's Tidewater counties of

■ From a century during which only a few Africans such as Venture Smith or Olaudah Equiano wrote personal accounts, runaway slave advertisements provide a rich source of information about life under slavery. This ad, for example, notes the runaway's scars and his language abilities.

Philadelphia, August 24, 1762.

RUN away from the Subscriber Yesterday, a Mulattoe Man Slave, named Joe, alias Joseph Boudron, a middle-sized Man, a brisk lively Fellow, about 23 Years of Age, was born at Guadaloupe, has lived some Time in New-York, and Charles-Town, in South-Carolina, speaks good English, French, Spanish, and Portuguese: Had on when he went away, an old whitish coloured Broadcloth Coat, faced with Plush, and Metal Buttons, a Calicoe Jacket, black knit Breeches, blue Worsted Stockings, new Shoes, with large Brass Buckles, Check Shirt, an old laced Hat, and has other Things not known; he is a good Cook, and much used to the Seas, where it is thought he intends, or for New-York. Any Person that takes up said Runaway, and brings him to me, or secures him in any Goal in this Province, shall have Two Pistoles Reward, and if in any other Province, Four Pistoles, and reasonable Charges, paid by me

THOMAS BARTHOLOMEW, junior.

N. B. All Masters of Vessels and others are desired not to carry him off, or harbour him, on any Account.

sadistic punishments could not suppress black men and women's will to regain their freedom. A wave of slave unrest that swept the northeastern seaboard in 1740–1741 affirmed this reality. The rebellion first erupted in New Jersey in 1740, in the form of an outbreak of barn burning. Authorities executed two slaves for the crime. The following year, the uprising spread to New York City, in a rash of thefts and fires. First, Fort George, the British garrison, burned to the ground. Next, fires broke out in Long Island and northern New Jersey. Because England and its colonies were at war with Spain and France (King George's War, 1739–1744), these fires triggered widespread concern among white people that slaves were about to rebel. In particular, white New Yorkers feared a group of free black Spanish sailors whom the British had captured on a Spanish sloop and sold into slavery in New York City.

Another blaze hit New York City in 1741. After authorities overheard one slave muttering "Fire, fire, scorch, scorch a little damn it," they linked the blaze to John Hughson, a white tavern keeper; his wife; and an indentured servant girl, Mary Burton, a tavern prostitute. Tortured and promised immunity, Burton confessed that her master was conspiring with several slaves and a Catholic priest to burn the town to the ground, kill all white New Yorkers, and free all slaves. This confession led to the arrests and trials of two slaves, Caesar and Prince, who died "very stubbornly" on the gallows without confessing to anything more than theft. Hughson and his wife, hanged for treason, also died revealing nothing about a slave plot. But the dragnet continued to pull in suspects, whom officials threatened with torture and execution unless they revealed the slave conspirators' identities. The authorities extracted sixty-seven confessions from terrified slaves. Trials of 150 slaves and twenty-five white people led to the hanging of seventeen slaves and four white people. Thirteen additional slaves perished in the grisliest of all executions—burning at the stake. White authorities also transported seventy-two slaves out of the colony to the West Indies.

AFRO-FLORIDIANS AND AFRO-LOUISIANANS

Whereas the North American English colonies established an elaborate system of slavery by the mid-eighteenth century, the Spanish and French North American colonies had a different experience. In Spanish Florida and French Louisiana, both characterized by racial intermingling and a more porous system of slavery, communities of free Africans began to form.

Fort Mose: The First Free Black Town

In Spanish Florida, free black people formed a fortified town—the first such community in North America. The town's founder was Francisco Menéndez. Born in a Mandinga village in Africa around 1700, Menéndez was given his Spanish name by his captors and transported to Florida in the 1720s. There his owner granted him his freedom when he demonstrated bravery in a battle against the English in 1728. Menéndez rose to the rank of captain of the free black military unit charged with protecting the Spanish foothold in Florida.

Granted land two miles north of St. Augustine, Menéndez and the rest of his unit built Pueblo de Gracia Real de Santa Terese de Mose, known simply as Mose. The fort consisted of stout walls enclosing thatched huts. Mose's Afro-Spaniards swore they would be "the most cruel enemies of the English" and would spill their "last drop of blood in defense of the great Crown of Spain and the Holy Faith." Their vow reflects their adherence to Catholicism; under Spanish rule, slaves were sometimes released if willing to convert.

Precariously perched on North America's southeastern coast, Mose was hotly contested by the Spanish and English. A group of slaves who had fled England's South Carolina—twenty-three of them, including women and children—reached Mose in late 1738. Others arrived in early 1739. The Stono Rebellion slaves had been heading to Mose when they were captured. Desperate to stanch the outflow of slaves from their colonies, English attackers, led by the governor of Georgia, drove Mose's free black people from the fort in 1740. But under Menéndez's leadership, the Afro-Hispanics regrouped and inflicted heavy losses on their attackers. Additional English attacks in 1742–1743 scattered the free Africans again. Nine years later, the Africans returned to rebuild the fort. Thoroughly intermixed with local Indians, the free Africans lived as farmers and militiamen. By 1763, when Spain ceded Florida to England, 3,000 black people lived in St. Augustine and Mose. One-quarter of them were free.

Realizing that free black people had no future under English rule, Menéndez led Mose's inhabitants to Havana, Cuba. Florida's Fort Mose stands as an important example of enslaved Africans' securing their freedom on the frontiers of European settlement. But when South Carolinians and Georgians took up land grants in northern Florida after the

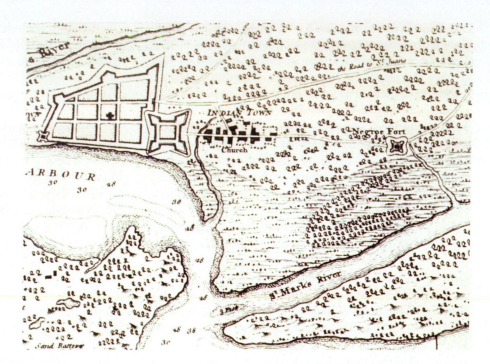

■ Drawn in 1762, this map shows "Indian Town," with the Catholic church and the "Negroe Fort" nearby. The fortifications depicted on the left of the map guarded the harbor and river. The town's name linked Mose, an old Indian place name, with Gracia Real (the king's blessing) and Teresa, the town's patron saint.

Spanish ceded the territory to England, they brought enslaved Africans with them. By the onset of the American Revolution, slaves had built profitable rice, indigo, cotton, sugar, and orange plantations along the St. Johns and St. Mary's rivers for their English masters. The free black town in Florida was only a memory. Still, many black Floridians continued to name their sons Mose.

French Louisiana: A Black Majority

Like the Spanish in Florida, the French in Louisiana treated their slaves differently than the English did. Louisiana was the only North American colony that started out with a black majority. By 1731, Louisiana had about 4,000 slaves—more than two Africans for every white French inhabitant. By 1746, Africans outnumbered the French three to one. Most slaves were imported directly from Africa, initially from Angola and the Gulf of Benin. By the 1730s, they came primarily from Senegambia, where the French had cultivated extensive trading contacts. The majority of these later arrivals were Malinka-speaking Bambaras.

In a raw frontier wilderness, French planters had to make concessions to enslaved Africans and militant Indians, who frequently joined forces against the French. In 1729, African slaves joined Natchez Indians in an uprising that killed more than 200 of the already disease-decimated French. The planters who survived offered freedom to those slaves who would retaliate against the rebels the next year. The French renewed the offer for slaves willing to fight against the Chick-

asaw Indians allied with the British in the 1730s and against the Choctaws in the 1740s. The French saw several advantages in drawing on black military skills: It enabled them to pit Africans against hostile Indians and reduce the likelihood of a disastrous Indian-African alliance. In a colony where the colonial masters had a tenuous grip on power, Africans had more opportunities to gain privileges and even positions of authority than slaves in other southeastern colonies.

Samba Bambara's story provides an example. In the 1720s, Bambara worked in West Africa as a Senegal River boatman and interpreter for France's Company of the Indies. The company sold slaves whom Bambara's people captured for the French. Perhaps he wondered whether this grisly business would someday turn against his own people. Around 1730, the French, perhaps seeing the usefulness of Bambara's talents in the New World, enslaved him and shipped him to Louisiana. There, his knowledge of French and several African languages earned him a privileged position as a court translator in Louisiana's legislative and judicial body. Later he became the overseer on the Company of the Indies' huge sugar plantation near New Orleans. But neither privilege nor position made Samba Bambara content. Aware that local Indians gave refuge to fleeing slaves, he led an African rebellion in 1731. The French crushed the revolt and executed Bambara and seven other conspirators.

Although slave revolts in Louisiana proved rare after this French crackdown, the thick swamps and forests of the lower Mississippi countryside provided cover for villages of escaped slaves, just as in English Jamaica the rugged mountains beckoned runaways. But the French used black militiamen to ferret out the renegades and suppress slave rebelliousness. Still, they never completely eliminated such villages from Louisiana.

Nor did the French manage to establish a thriving colony. Louisiana's rich soil, plentiful water, and year-round growing climate counted for little in their efforts because the French poured most of their resources—settlers, capital, and slaves—into the sugar islands of the West Indies. Few French settlers arrived after the frustrated Company of the Indies handed the colony back to the French king in 1731. Only a single slave ship arrived in the next thirty-five years to replenish Louisiana's African population. Consequently, planters tried to preserve what few slaves they had by moderating their workloads and encouraging bondspeople to form families. Catholic priests solemnized slave marriages and baptisms and permitted Africans to participate in church ceremonies. In New Orleans, where most slaves lived, white people valued their bondsmen's artisan skills highly and permitted many of them to live in their own dwellings and hire themselves out in their free time. Even more important, slaves in Louisiana slowly gained the rights to maintain their own garden plots and keep poultry and livestock. By 1763, the end of the French period in Louisiana, slaves had developed an economy of their own. They marketed their poultry and produce, gained control over more of their time, and circulated with few restraints in the New Orleans region. These conditions gave them a crucial advantage: the opportunity to save money with which to buy their freedom.

Since Louisiana had never generated a profit for its investors, French diplomats happily unloaded the colony into Spain in 1763 at the end of the Seven Years' War. By that time, because there had been almost no importation of slaves, the black population stood at less than 6,000. By contrast, more than twice as many Africans lived in the New England colonies, and Maryland and Virginia's total slave population had reached 250,000. Spain controlled the territory for only twenty years; at the conclusion of the American Revolution, it returned the region to France. Yet during those two decades of Spanish control, Afro-Louisianans acquired unique rights. New doors opened to them when the Spanish decided to set up a black militia to tighten their control over French planters resistant to Spanish rule. General Alejandro O'Reilly used free black militiamen from Havana, recommissioned the French black militia in Louisiana, and welcomed new recruits. Unheard-of in any English colony, the black militia played an indispensable role in the colonial defense system. Its ranks swelled with former slaves who had exercised the Spanish policy of *coartación* to purchase their freedom.

The French *Code Noir* (like the English slave codes) contained no policy akin to *coartación*. Only slaveowners could decide whether to free their human property. Yet in the eighteenth century, law and social custom increasingly discouraged French slaveowners from taking that step. The Spanish practice of *coartación*, however, gave slaves the right to initiate purchase of their own freedom by agreement with their master. If a master resisted, slaves could petition the governor's court to gain their freedom.

Through *coartación*, hundreds of slaves in Louisiana freed themselves during the Spanish period. Those who had raised and marketed produce for years now had the means to take advantage of this policy. Other masters freed their slaves voluntarily, particularly their slave wives and their mixed-race children for reasons of "love and affection." By the end of the Spanish era, New Orleans had a free black population of over 900. These men and women made up nearly 10 percent of the city's black people—a proportion unequaled anywhere else in North America.

BECOMING AFRICAN AMERICAN

What's in a name? For Africans recently torn from their homelands, a birth name provided not just a cherished connection to family and community but a deep mark of identity. Yet even this was stripped from them. The long

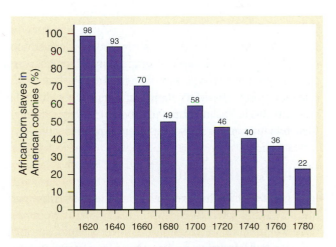

■ **FIGURE 4.2** **Percentage of African-born Slaves in American Colonies, 1620–1780**

After the Seven Years' War (1756–1763) choked off slave importations and births to slave couples, the percentage of African-born slaves in the English colonies declined. However, this varied from place to place. South Carolina and Georgia had the largest ratio of African-born to North American–born slaves.

transition from African to African American often began when a master assigned a slave a new name. Olaudah Equiano remembered vividly how his third master "named me Gustavus Vasa" (after Gustavus I, the Swedish noble who led his people from Danish rule in the sixteenth century). Struggling to learn English and disoriented by the loss of his African name, Equiano recounted, "I refused to be called so, and told him as well as I could that I would be called Jacob" (the name assigned by his Virginia master). But his new master insisted on calling him Gustavus. "When I refused to answer to my new name, . . . it gained me many a cuff; so at length I submitted, and by which I have been known ever since" (though later he published his autobiography under his African name).

Acquiring a new name was only one part of being an African in America. The transition from African to African American unfolded gradually and took on regional characteristics. Many factors influenced the course of the change, including the population density of the enslaved Africans; the ratio of imported Africans to North American–born slaves; and the type of community (town, plantation, frontier farm).

Two parallel processes also shaped the transition: encounters among people from different parts of Africa, and encounters between black slaves and white European masters. For example, when an Ibo met a Bambara, a Mandingo encountered a Koromanti, and a Fula tried to speak with an Asante in Virginia, New York, or Georgia, the brutal circumstances of their lives impelled these different peoples to fashion a collective identity out of many homeland ethnic identities. Equiano, for instance, had to overcome his revulsion at scarification—a practice among many African peoples that he considered the mark of inferior sorts who "disfigured themselves." But whatever their African ethnicities, all slaves had to adapt to European masters whose culture differed markedly from theirs. Indeed, their lives depended on their ability to adapt. This process fueled a new African American culture that slaves expressed through their religious beliefs and other cultural practices.

African Christianity

In fashioning viable lives and new identities in North America, slaves struggled to clarify their place in the cosmos. Olaudah Equiano was cut off from the Ibo people's spiritual universe in 1756 when he started his long march to West Africa's coast. Like anyone plunged into harsh, bewildering circumstances, he tried to comprehend his fate and needed spiritual solace to endure his plight. Equiano, like most slaves, gradually embraced a religion that blended African traditions with Christian practices and beliefs. In 1758, his master's ship docked in England, where two Englishwomen

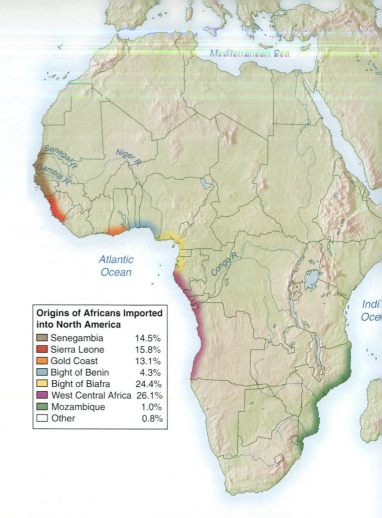

■ MAP 4.2 Origins of Africans Imported into North America

The origins of imported Africans changed markedly during the eighteenth and early nineteenth centuries. Slaves from West-Central Africa (Kongo and Angolan peoples) predominated through the 1730s, but thereafter Ibos from the Bight of Biafra made up the bulk of imported slaves.

introduced him to Christianity. The young African found the Old Testament stories of the ancient Jews especially comforting because their captivity reminded him of his own. Two years later, Equiano asked to be baptized. After he purchased his freedom in 1766 in England, he became a steadfast Christian, though his religious practice contained traces of Ibo spirituality.

Until about the time of Equiano's conversion, most Africans in the North American colonies had known little of Christianity. Instead, they clung to the religious practices and values they remembered from their homelands. Their rituals included burying a deceased person so that the body faced east. (The Christian tradition calls for the body to face west.) Africans also placed coins, porcelain plates, shoes, or treasured possessions on the stomach of the deceased to ensure a journey to an afterlife of ease in the African homeland.

With most slaves following African spiritual traditions, Christianity only slowly penetrated slave life. Many bondspeople who learned of Protestantism found little comfort in it. In Africa, most people made no sharp distinction between the sacred and the secular. But to many slaves, North American spirituality seemed confined to the church. The highly intellectual Protestant message also struck many Africans as cold and overly complex. Opposed to mysticism and stressing private devotion, silent prayer, and Sunday sermons, Protestant clergymen could offer small comfort in the strange and repressive world in which slaves found themselves.

Moreover, slave masters did little to promote Christian thinking and practice among slaves. In their view, the religion's emphasis on equality before God and a community of all humankind threatened to undercut their own authority. To be sure, northern Anglican clergy began converting slaves early in the eighteenth century, spurred by the London-centered Society for the Propagation of the Gospel in Foreign Parts. Yet the effort proved difficult. In the South, few clergymen attempted it. In 1730, following a period of unusual missionary activity in Richmond County, Virginia, a number of baptized slaves circulated the word that their acceptance of Christ entitled them to freedom. When this announcement sparked a rebellion of several hundred slaves gathered near Norfolk, masters cracked down on slave conversions.

Then a movement known as the Great Awakening whipped up new enthusiasm among people eager to Christianize slaves. A wave of evangelical fervor that began in the northern colonies in the late 1720s, the Great Awakening spread south in the 1740s. In the parish of Williamsburg, the capital of Virginia, Anglican clergymen baptized nearly a thousand slaves in a single generation. Presbyterians began conversions in the southern colonies in the 1750s and 1760s. On the eve of the American Revolution, most urban congregations in the northern colonies had black participants, many of whom married and baptized their children there.

Why did so many slaves decide that Protestantism did have something to offer them, after all? The Great Awakening gave rise to a new brand of religion that appealed strongly to Africans. For example, Methodist and Baptist preachers developed a more emotional, informal preaching style that black people appreciated. During sermons, evangelical clergymen and unschooled lay preachers spoke passionately about personal rebirth. They swayed back and forth, swept up in the power of their message. They also invited the dynamic participation of each individual. Many such preachers delivered sermons spontaneously, often in fields and barns, and encouraged ecstatic dancing, chanting, shouting, rhythmic clapping, and singing. Perhaps not surprisingly, followers—black and white alike—found the experience intensely emotional compared to the dry sermons delivered from elevated pulpits in austere Protestant churches.

For the first time in the North American colonies, slaves encountered a worship style that reminded them of African spirituality. The Awakeners stressed that Christ blessed the weak, the poor, and the humble. In the day of reckoning, "the last would be first, and the first would be last." This was a powerful, comforting message for people who had little hope of freedom in this life. Slaveowners, for their part, hoped their human property would embrace the Christian values of meekness and obedience.

Once slaves had experienced Christian doctrine, not even the most controlling master could quarantine them from the uplifting message offered in the Bible. Visiting Savannah, Georgia, in 1765, Equiano heard the spellbinding English evangelist George Whitefield preach that all souls are equal before God. In a church packed with both white and black worshipers, Equiano found Whitefield "sweating as ever I did on Montserrat beach," exhorting all present to lead Christian lives. Two years later, Equiano stepped up to "act the parson" when a slave mother in Georgia could find no white minister to bury her dead child. She was "very tenacious of the church burial service," Equiano wrote, and "she urged me very hard: I therefore complied with her entreaties." Before "a great company both of white and black people," Equiano offered words of Christian comfort to help the child into her grave. This was a God for everyone.

Africans converted to Christianity for the comfort and hope it promised. But by interweaving their own spiritual practices into the faith, they created a unique manifestation of the religion. This new entity found expression in slave spirituals, or songs. Slaves sang the melodies of Anglo-American hymns with an African rhythm. They created their own songs about biblical heroes who appealed to them, such as Daniel,

> "We sing to take away trouble."—*Nameless slave*

Joshua, Jonah, and Moses. All of these heroes had resisted their persecutors to prevail in this world rather than waiting for justice in heaven. Meanwhile, "sorrow songs" both expressed and eased the pain of enslavement. "We sing," said one slave, "to take away trouble."

Other spirituals asserted individual worth and strength. Historians have no way of determining whether slaves sang "We Are the People of God" or "I'm Born of God, I Know I Am" in the eighteenth century. However, slaves found these songs sustaining after the American Revolution, suggesting that earlier generations sang songs with similar themes. In

Redeeming Sin: A Black Christian's Account

Born to royalty about 1710 in the Lake Chad region of Central Africa, James Albert Ukawsaw Gronniosaw was captured and brought to Barbados in about 1725, where he was sold to a New Yorker. Gronniosaw viewed Christianity as offering a path forward during a long, difficult existence. The passage below comes from his autobiography. In it, his regard for a huge oak tree as a confidant and friend reflects African animism—the belief that all natural objects contain a spiritual force. The passage shows how Africans grafted their religious ideas onto Christianity.

About a quarter of a mile from my Master's house stood a large remarkably fine Oak-tree, in the midst of a wood; I often used to be employed there in cutting down trees (a work I was very fond of) and I seldom failed going to this place every day; . . . It was the greatest pleasure I ever experienced to set under this Oak, for there I used to pour out my complaints to the LORD; and when I had any particular grievance, I used to go there and talk to the tree, and tell my sorrows, as if it were to a

friend. Here I often lamented my own wicked heart, and undone state; and found more comfort and consolation than I ever was sensible of before. . . . The more I saw of the Beauty and Glory of God, the more I was humbled under a sense of my own vileness.

—from A Narrative of the Most Remarkable Particulars in the Life of James Albert Ukawsaw Gronniosaw, an African Prince, as Related by Himself, *1772.*

To view a longer version of this document, please go to *www.ablongman.com/carson/documents*.

a society where white people insisted that enslaved Africans came from a culturally impoverished continent, these songs demonstrate a sense of self-worth, a feeling of fellowship, and a commitment to life purpose.

African Muslims

While some enslaved Africans began to embrace Christianity and blend it with African religious ways, other slaves came as Muslims to North America and continued to practice Islam. Historians are only beginning to pull back the shadows that enshroud early Islam in America because the evidence is fragmentary. Most of the descendants of Muslim slaves were reluctant in later decades to discuss their Islamic background. But clearly, many slaves came from areas in West and Central Africa—especially Senegambia, Sierra Leone, the Gold Coast, and coastal Benin—where Islam had made extensive inroads. Runaway slave advertisements, especially those in South Carolina and Georgia, mention distinctly Muslim names such as Mustapha, Fatima, Mamdo, Saluma, Mousa, and Mahomet.

One such Muslim was Yarrow Mamout, who arrived aboard a slave ship around 1720. Purchased by a Maryland family, Mamout became a skilled brickmaker. He gained his

freedom after making all the bricks for his master's new mansion in Georgetown, now part of the District of Columbia. For many years, Mamout lived as a free man and eventually became a property owner of modest wealth. A faithful Muslim, he often strolled Baltimore's streets singing praises to God.

Another Muslim, Job Ben Solomon, arrived at Annapolis, Maryland, on a slave ship in 1731. He was sold to a tobacco planter, who found him resistant to field work but admired his agile mind and princely demeanor. As it turned out, Solomon was the son of a king in the land of Futa, in the Senegal River region. Captured by Mandingo enemies, he had been sold as a slave to an English slave ship captain. But once an English visitor to Maryland discovered his identity, his master sent him to England. Eventually, Solomon returned to his home in Africa, where he ascended the throne.

African American Culture: Music, Dance, and Body Adornment

Like their countrymen and women in Africa, black people in the colonies found joy in aesthetic expression. "We are almost a nation of dancers, musicians, and poets," wrote

oped innovations. How to form a pot from clay, weave a basket from sea grass, style one's hair, arrange fabric over the body, play an instrument, play with words, or use one's voice to sing or one's body to dance all came together in a unique culture developed by people determined to make life worth living.

Though given Western names and coarse clothes, slaves found ways to display their individuality. For example, they experimented with hairstyles. Drawing on homeland fashions and ideals of beauty, they braided their hair with beads, shells, and strips of material. They complemented these styles with turbans and bandanas, highly valued in West African societies. Eventually, they also began wearing beaver and raccoon-skin hats as well as flower-decked Scotch bonnets. Jaunty displays of hats, caps, and scarves cropped up throughout slave quarters in the colonies.

Though few slaves in North American practiced scarification, a common tradition throughout Africa, some developed other forms of body adornment. White authorities complained about slaves who dressed in apparel "quite gay and beyond their condition" or who dressed "so bold and impudent that

■ When the famous painter of the American Revolution, Charles Willson Peale, sought out Yarrow Mamout in Baltimore, he found the Muslim slave "healthy, active, and very full of fun." Whether Mamout was 134 years old, as he told Peale, cannot be verified. But the descendants of his first American slave master felt certain he had reached at least 100 years of age.

Equiano of his homeland. Music and dance played central roles in black slaves' spirituality and everyday life—in the fields where they toiled, in the quarters where they lived, and in the woods and along riverbanks where they gathered when they could. "Night is their day," one slaveowner remarked. When their "day" began at sunset, slaves gathered to make a world that sustained them. Dance, rhythm, rattles, and banjoes (an instrument with direct African antecedents) all testify to Africans' ability to maintain their cherished traditions. Slaves also expressed themselves through fiddling, clapping, and drumming, though some masters forbade drums because they feared slaves used them to send coded messages to each other. Above all, slaves reveled in shout songs and singing—testaments to their African spirit.

In every one of these activities, slaves fused their inherited West African knowledge with new ideas they acquired in North America. They merged what they had experienced through encounters with Native Americans and Europeans with what they remembered from African ways—and devel-

■ Sporting silk garments, Job Ben Solomon was presented to King George II in London in 1733, where this portrait was painted. Solomon wrote all 6,321 verses of the Qur'an three times from memory and won renown in London as a linguist and polished speaker.

First Person   The Character of Job Ben Solomon

Thomas Bluett, an Anglican minister, accompanied the enslaved Muslim Job Ben Solomon to England in 1734 and published Some Memoirs of the Life of Job, the Son of Solomon, the High Priest of Boonda in Africa. *Based on his extensive conversations with Solomon, Bluett's memoir provides valuable insights into the life of a black Muslim prince.*

In his reasoning there appeared nothing trifling, nothing hypocritical or over-strained; but, on the contrary, strong sense, joined with an innocent simplicity, a strict regard to truth, and a hearty desire to find it. . . . The acuteness of his genius appeared upon many occasions. . . . His memory was extraordinary; for when he was fifteen years old he could say the whole Alcoran [Qur'an] by heart, and while he was here in England he wrote three copies of it without the assistance of any other copy, and without so much as looking to one of those three when he wrote the others. He would often laugh at me when he heard me say I had

forgot anything, and told me he hardly ever forgot anything in his life, and wondered that an other body should. . . . In his natural temper there appeared a happy mixture of the grave and the cheerful, a gentle mildness, guarded by a proper warmth, and a kind and compassionate disposition towards all that were in distress.

—*from* Some Memoirs of the Life of Job, the Son of Solomon the High Priest of Boonda in Africa *by Thomas Bluett; printed for Richard Ford, 1734.*

To view a longer version of this document, please go to *www.ablongman.com/carson/documents*.

they insult every poor white person they meet with." Slaves drew on African knowledge of natural dyes to add touches of color to their clothing. They also found ways to add bright cuffs, patches, and collars to jackets, trousers, and wraparound skirts. They fashioned brass wire earrings, beaded armbands and necklaces, and cloth bands that they draped over or wrapped around the body. These forms of personal adornment were small victories to combat the humiliation of slavery.

As another cultural defense against their plight, slaves embraced humor and playfulness. Skits mimicking masters brought the liberation of laughter, and stories from Africa kept spirits alive. The tale about the trickster spider Anansi who outwits his more powerful captors was a special

■ The artist of this rare watercolor of the *juba*, a West African dance, remains unknown. On the right, a banjo player provides music, while a cross-legged man beats a drum with two twisted leather sticks. The plantation house, outbuildings, and a row of slave cabins loom in the background.
Source: The Old Plantation, c. 1790–1800. Abby Aldrich Rockefeller Folk Art Museum. Colonial Williamsburg Foundation, Williamsburg, VA

favorite. In time, this story showed up in the Aunt Nancy tales recounted in Caribbean lore. It also made an appearance in the still later animal tales of Uncle Remus, collected and published in the late nineteenth century.

Slaves sought to maintain African practices even in the way they walked. Runaway slave advertisements describe "stately" or "strutting" gaits, a "proud carriage," a "swaggering knee," or a "remarkably grand and strong" walk—evidence of Africans who refused to adopt postures of defeat.

Merging Traditions

By the eve of the American Revolution, Africans had begun to shed some aspects of their individual tribal identities and develop a new, collective identity as African Americans. Slaves in the North, outnumbered twenty to one or more by white people, understandably absorbed more European ways than those in the South. We can see the merging of traditions especially in the Pinkster holiday, an adaptation of Pentecost. Introduced by the Dutch in New Amsterdam and New Jersey, Pinkster became a sacred African and Dutch holy day as well as a joyous festival. On one occasion, slave baptisms were followed by Africans "playing upon several instruments, a dancing and a shouting so loud that they might be heard half a league off." Religious services on Pentecost Monday were followed by a Tuesday holiday during which Dutch and Africans feasted, drank, and danced together.

New England's equivalent of Pinkster Day was Negro Election Day. Like Pinkster, Negro Election Day meshed African and Yankee traditions. These annual celebrations drew slaves from the surrounding countryside for feasting, parading, dancing, and the electing of black kings, judges, and other officials. "All the various languages of Africa, mixed with broken and ludicrous English filled the air," came one report from Newport, Rhode Island, "accompanied with the music of the fiddle, tambourine, the banjo [and] drum." In a ritualized role reversal, African Americans dressed in the clothes of their masters and rode their masters' horses. They extracted money tributes from their owners, drank wine and beer, and danced exuberantly in the streets. For a day, they symbolically ruled the town. In one town, the newly elected black "governor" rode through the streets "on one of his master's horses, adorned with plaited gear, his aides on each side *a la militaire . . .* moving with a slow majestic pace."

Why did white northerners permit such celebrations? They could afford to take the risk because they vastly outnumbered black people and, like role reversals in ancient times in other parts of the world, Negro Election Day acted as a safety valve. By offering black people a chance to let off steam, the festivals discouraged rebellion. They benefited slaves as well by providing a mechanism for them to choose and honor their own leaders, who acted throughout the year as unofficial mediators of disputes and as counselors. Such festivals did not necessarily appeal to all slaves. For example, Venture Smith shunned "superfluous finery" and "expensive gatherings" and proudly claimed that he was never "at the expense of sixpence worth" of liquor. Nor could such holidays alter the cruel fact of bondage. But they did offer momentary entertainment in an otherwise grim existence.

While Africans were becoming African American, Euro-Americans were becoming African in subtle ways. For all their disparagement of African culture, white colonists knew they needed their slaves' knowledge and skills to prevail in an unpredictable environment. Only an impractical South Carolina planter would ignore the rice-growing expertise of West Africans brought to convert the marshy low country into profitable fields. Similarly, New England Puritans took advantage of Africans' medical knowledge such as inoculation against smallpox. In South Carolina, legislators who eagerly passed a slave code stripping away nearly all black rights found no contradiction in granting freedom and a lifelong pension to an African who knew how to save victims of rattlesnake bites. Many white southerners also found African conjure doctors intriguing with their knowledge of root and herbal medicine and magical cures.

Apart from such sensible borrowing of African knowledge, white people became Africanized almost without realizing it. In the South, where black people outnumbered white people in many regions, masters came to appreciate foods of African origin such as barbecued pork, fried chicken, and mustard and collard greens. Black cooks working in their master's kitchen had plentiful opportunities to carry on culinary traditions brought from West and Central Africa.

A cross-pollination of languages also occurred. Many commentators in the South reflected that after generations of living in close contact with African slaves, as Sidney Andrews put it, "the language of the common people of [South Carolina] is a curious mixture of English and African." Enslaved

> "The language of the common people of [South Carolina] is a curious mixture of English and African."
> —Sidney Andrews

Africans learned the language of their masters. But the masters also wove African nuances, tones, phraseology, and inflections into their own language. One observer described the speaking style of a wealthy plantation owner as "like a negro's." Whether influenced by African medical practices, speech patterns, music, cuisine, or even notions about death and afterlife, hardly a white colonist in the South remained untouched by African culture.

BLACK AMERICANS ON THE EVE OF THE AMERICAN REVOLUTION

African-born Olaudah Equiano and Venture Smith worked their way out of slavery by dint of extraordinary perseverance and skill. One achieved recognition as an abolitionist writer; the other, as a talented farmer and wood merchant. But few slaves transported directly from Africa won their freedom. Most of the black men and women who gained freedom were North American–born. Many were mixed-race individuals who owed their manumission to a white father.

Slaves who possessed craft skills were the best equipped to escape from bondage. Whether in towns or on farms and plantations, they had greater mobility, more thorough knowledge of the world around them, and often broader linguistic skills that served them well when they encountered patrols or constables. In making a bid for freedom, many impersonated free black sailors and hired themselves out. If they succeeded in this strategy, they hid in towns with other free black people or poor white families.

Curbing Manumission

In the early eighteenth century, white legislators turned their attention from controlling slaves to narrowing free black people's privileges. The targeted privileges included the right to hold office or vote, bear arms or serve in the militia, and employ white indentured servants. In many colonies, laws slapped special taxes on free black people and defined unusually severe punishments for crimes committed by African Americans. Only by excluding "free-negros & mulattos . . . from that great privilege of a freeman," declared Virginia's governor in 1723, could whites "make the free-Negroes sensible that a distinction ought to be made between their offspring and the descendants of an Englishman, with whom they never were to be accounted equal."

Beginning in the 1690s, colonial legislators in the South erected legal roadblocks to freedom. One provision, for example, abolished slaveowners' right to free their slaves. This change made manumission possible only through specific legislative approval. Another provision required slaveowners who managed to gain this approval to transport a newly freed man or woman out of the colony, though this ruling was not often enforced. With manumission severely curtailed, the number of free black people in the southern colonies shrank proportionally. Only a few thousand such men and women lived in the southern colonies amid more than 400,000 slaves.

Beginning in the 1720s, most northern colonies also curbed manumission by requiring slaveowners to post hefty bonds guaranteeing the good conduct of those they freed and to maintain those requiring public charity. Like Venture Smith, a few African Americans earned enough money to purchase their own liberty. However, most black men and women whose masters released them from enforced servitude were old and sickly. Their former owners, eager to dispose of a "burden," left them to fend for themselves. Masters resisted freeing young slave women most, for they had both reproductive and productive value. As in the South, lawmakers in the North barred free black people from voting, testifying in court or serving on juries, and serving in the militia.

Yet cracks were appearing in the edifice of slavery. During the Seven Years' War, the need for militia recruits convinced white northerners to set aside the ban against arming black men. Scores of slaves seized the moment by volunteering to fight in the war that drove France from Canada and the western frontier, thereby earning their freedom. Though proportionately more numerous than in the southern colonies, northern free African Americans numbered not more than 4,000 by the outbreak of the American Revolution.

Protesting Slavery

Even as slaves nurtured the hope of gaining their liberty and at least some of the privileges white colonists enjoyed, a few white men and women shared their vision. Every generation in North America contained a handful of white people who recognized slavery for what it was: an immoral system designed solely to enrich slaveowners through the brutal use of human beings. These white people refused to be swayed by biblical sanctions of the practice or examples of the widespread use of slavery throughout human history. Though slavery may have always existed, they said, that didn't mean decent people could not—and should not—stop it now.

Back in 1688, four Quakers in Germantown, Pennsylvania, had protested slavery. In the 1730s, a new breed of antislavery advocates emerged in the same colony. Whereas earlier

 **First Person**

Venture Smith Tells of Early Freedom

When he purchased his freedom around 1770, Venture Smith set out to earn enough money to purchase his wife and two sons out of slavery. In light of the difficulties he describes below, his success is all the more remarkable.

My wife and children were yet in bondage to Mr. Thomas Stanton. About this time I lost a chest containing besides clothing, about thirty-eight pounds in paper money. . . . In the space of six months I cut and corded upwards of four hundred cords of wood. . . . The money which I earned thereby amount to two hundred and seven pounds, ten shillings. This money I laid up carefully. . . . Being after this labour forty years of age, I worked at various places, . . . [and] purchased Solomon and Cuff, two sons of mine, for two hundred dollars each. . . . In my forty-fourth year, I purchased my wife Meg, and thereby prevented having another child to buy, as she was then pregnant. I gave forty pounds for her.

—*First printed by C. Holt, at the Bee-Office, 1798, as* A Narrative of the Life and Adventures of Venture, a Native of Africa: But Resident Above Sixty Years in the United States of America, Related by Himself.

To view a longer version of this document, please go to *www.ablongman.com/carson/documents*.

---

protesters occasionally spoke out against slavery, now white men such as Benjamin Lay, John Woolman, and Anthony Benezet dedicated themselves to eliminating the practice. For many such reformers, their attempts to give their cause radical force cost them their place and acceptance in society.

Benjamin Lay was an outsider from the moment of his birth in England, owing to a deformity that left him a hunchback. But his twisted body did not stop his compassionate heart and his fierce determination. After seven years at sea, Lay and his wife immigrated to Barbados. There, he witnessed the most barbaric manifestation of slavery firsthand. Arriving in Philadelphia in 1731 and seeing slavery taking hold there as well, he initiated a crusade against it.

Lay used tactics many social activists today would find impressive. In what was later known as the *free produce strategy,* he boycotted slave-produced necessities, made his own clothes from sheep's wool and flax, and publicly smashed his wife's teacups to protest the use of slave-produced sugar. By standing with one bare foot in the snow outside a Quaker meeting, he shamed those who deprived their slaves of boots. He even kidnapped a white Quaker child to teach the Society of Friends about the grief suffered by African families when their children were sold at auctions. Once he burst into a Quaker meeting brandishing a book that looked like a Bible. Unknown to the meeting participants, he had hollowed out the book and filled it with a bladder containing red pokeberry juice. Before their horri-

fied eyes, he plunged a sword into the book, splattering the startled Quakers with "blood." Thus, Lay symbolically indicted Friends who committed spiritual and physical violence against slaves in spite of their professed pacifism. Even his fellow Quakers thought Lay fanatical. But his tactics—what we might call street theater today—drew attention to the evils of slavery. However, Lay's powerful message did not gain converts for another generation.

In the 1750s, a new wave of Quaker reformers washed into view. Disturbed by what they saw as moral laxness on the part of the Society of Friends, these reformers set out to cleanse the Society's membership of slave traders and owners. John Woolman took a leading role in this effort. As a young man, he had written out a bill of sale for a slave at the behest of his employer in a New Jersey tailor shop and found the experience profoundly upsetting. In 1746, he journeyed through the southern colonies, where he saw the "many vices and corruptions" created by slavery. Heartbroken by what he witnessed, Woolman wrote *Some Considerations on the Keeping of Negroes* (1753). In the book, he argued that Africans had not forfeited "the natural right to freedom" and were equal to Europeans in God's eyes. When we "treat our inferiors with rigour, to increase our wealth and gain riches for our children," he warned, "what then shall we do when God riseth up; and when he visiteth, what shall we answer him?" Like Lay, Woolman earned the resentment of his fellow Quakers who traded or owned slaves.

■ Shown here outside his hermit's cave near Philadelphia in the 1730s, abolitionist Benjamin Lay was easy to ignore because of his eccentricity. To demonstrate his withdrawal from what he decried as a materialistic and corrupt society, he not only lived in a cave but also abstained from liquor and meat.

Another plain-spoken reformer, Anthony Benezet of Philadelphia, echoed Woolman's protests. During the day, Benezet taught poor white children; at night, he taught black children, slave and free, to read. After years of teaching, he concluded that black children were as intellectually capable as white youngsters. His published statement directly challenged the common proslavery argument that Africans were inherently inferior to Europeans, suited only for forced labor. Like Woolman, Benezet published stirring denunciations of slavery in the 1750s, inspiring a growing number of Quakers to organize antislavery blocs at meetings and to promote bans on the importation, sale, and ownership of slaves.

It took reformers a long time to get compliance from the rank and file. However, Quaker leaders in Pennsylvania and New Jersey planted the seeds of change in North America by passionately decrying slavery. Their crusade offered hope to thousands of enslaved and free African Americans and laid the foundation for a movement that, within a century, redirected the course of a fledgling nation.

CONCLUSION

By the eve of the American Revolution, slavery had made violence a way of life in the English colonies. Masters used violence to keep Africans under their thumb, and slaves struck back with violence to protest their lot. Was it true, as the Quaker John Woolman believed, that slaveholding, even among kindly masters, "depraved the mind . . . with as great

certainty as prevailing cold congeals water"? If so, many people shuddered at the implications for the North American society that had begun to take shape. Did slaves' outwardly visible degradation stem directly from what Woolman called the white colonists' "inner corruption"?

Such thought-provoking questions aside, Europeans had bound themselves to Africans in an economic system that brought wealth to the powerful and pain to the exploited. That same system gradually fused elements of European, Indian, and African cultures into a unique new entity. For their part, Africans were becoming African American. They learned to speak their master's language, whether English, Spanish, French, or German. They also acquired knowledge of the local terrain and even formed emotional attachments to the land. They came together in families, incorporated elements of Christianity into their traditional religious beliefs, and devised strategies to endure the unendurable. Some ran away, lashed out at masters, or initiated slave revolts—though masters countered with increasingly repressive laws and brutal punishments.

As tensions between white colonists and their British overlords mounted, few slaveowners perceived the parallels between their situation and that of their slaves. If the colonists had to resort to violence to keep black people under their heel, what response might these same white people expect when they tried to break the shackles their British imperial masters imposed on them? Nor did white people see the bitter irony behind their own clamoring for liberty and their subjugation of black people asking for the very same thing.

FURTHER READING

Austin, Allan D., ed. *African Muslims in Antebellum America: A Sourcebook* (New York: Garland, 1984).

Berlin, Ira. *Many Thousands Gone: The First Two Centuries of Slavery in North America* (Cambridge: Harvard University Press, 1998).

Bontemps, Alex. *The Punished Self: Surviving Slavery in the Colonial South* (Ithaca, NY: Cornell University Press, 2001).

Creel, Margaret W. *A Peculiar People: Slave Religion and Community Culture Among the Gullahs* (New York: New York University Press, 1988).

Davis, T. J. *A Rumor of Revolt: The "Great Negro Plot" in Colonial New York* (Amherst: University of Massachusetts Press, 1985).

Diouf, Sylviane A. *Servants of Allah: African Muslims Enslaved in the Americas* (New York: New York University Press, 1998).

Gomez, Michael. *Exchanging Our Country Marks: The Transformation of African Identities in the Colonial and Antebellum South* (Chapel Hill: University of North Carolina Press, 1998).

Greene, Lorenzo J. *The Negro in Colonial New England, 1620–1776* (1942; rpt. New York: Atheneum, 1968).

Hall, Gwendolyn Midlo. *Africans in Colonial Louisiana: The Development of Afro-Creole Culture in the Eighteenth Century* (Baton Rouge: Louisiana State University Press, 1992).

Ingersoll, Thomas. *Mammon and Manon in Early New Orleans: The First Slave Society in the Deep South, 1718–1819* (Knoxville: University of Tennessee Press, 1999).

Littlefield, Daniel C. *Rice and Slaves: Ethnicity and the Slave Trade in Colonial South Carolina* (Baton Rouge: Louisiana State University Press, 1985).

Morgan, Edmund S. *American Slavery, American Freedom: The Ordeal of Colonial Virginia* (New York: W. W. Norton, 1975).

Morgan, Philip D. *Slave Counterpoint: Black Culture in the Eighteenth-Century Chesapeake and Lowcountry* (Chapel Hill: University of North Carolina Press, 1998).

Mullin, Gerald W. *Flight and Rebellion: Slave Resistance in Eighteenth-Century Virginia* (New York: Oxford University Press, 1972).

Mullin, Michael. *Africa in America: Slave Acculturation and Resistance in the American South and the British Caribbean, 1736–1831* (Urbana: University of Illinois Press, 1992).

Piersen, William D. *Black Yankees: The Development of an Afro-American Subculture in Eighteenth-Century New England* (Amherst: University of Massachusetts Press, 1988).

Sobel, Mechal. *The World They Made Together: Black and White Values in Eighteenth-Century Virginia* (Princeton: Princeton University Press, 1987).

Walsh, Lorena. *From Calabar to Carter's Grove: The History of a Virginia Slave Community* (Charlottesville: University Press of Virginia, 1997).

Walvin, James. *An African's Life: The Life and Times of Olaudah Equiano, 1745–1797* (London: Cassell, 1998).

Wood, Betty. *Slavery in Colonial Georgia, 1730–1775* (Athens: University of Georgia Press, 1984).

CHAPTER 5

■ In Paul Revere's inflammatory engraving of the Boston massacre, Crispus Attacks is among the Bostonians killed by British soldiers.

The Revolutionary Era: Crossroads of Freedom

Thomas Peters Seizes His Freedom

On a steamy summer day in 1775, Thomas Peters heard rumors of a slave insurrection planned for July 8. Living in the house of his master in Wilmington, North Carolina, Peters was no stranger to feverish talk of rebellion as a way to secure a person's rights. William Campbell, Peters's owner, led Wilmington's Sons of Liberty—a citizens' group protesting the British Parliament's taxation policies. The Sons of Liberty spoke avidly about the natural rights they believed belonged to everyone at birth.

Even before the colonists began grumbling about English tyranny, Peters had fought for his own freedom. He had reached North America in 1760, at about age twenty-two, after slavers snatched him from his Yoruba homeland in what is now Nigeria. Marched to the coast like Olaudah Equiano and millions of others, Peters had been sold to a French slave trader and transported to French Louisiana. Three times he tried to escape—and three times he was recaptured and punished with whipping, branding, and ankle shackling. But his French master could not extinguish Peters's thirst for freedom, and soon gave up trying to whip his human property into obedience.

Sold from one owner to another, Peters acquired a rich array of language skills. How he came to Campbell, a Scottish immigrant in North Carolina, we do not know. But in Wilmington, a Cape Fear River town of 200 households, Peters learned his trade as a millwright, making planking and barrel staves from the pine trees that dominated the coastal forests.

When Wilmington's white citizens discovered a slave plot planned for July 8, 1775, they moved quickly to suppress it. They rounded up suspects, dealt out merciless punishments, and redoubled patrols. With American militia units and

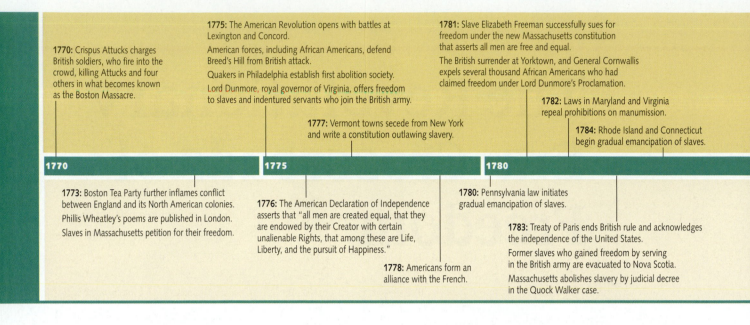

1770: Crispus Attucks charges British soldiers, who fire into the crowd, killing Attucks and four others in what becomes known as the Boston Massacre.

1775: The American Revolution opens with battles at Lexington and Concord.
American forces, including African Americans, defend Breed's Hill from British attack.
Quakers in Philadelphia establish first abolition society.
Lord Dunmore, royal governor of Virginia, offers freedom to slaves and indentured servants who join the British army.

1781: Slave Elizabeth Freeman successfully sues for freedom under the new Massachusetts constitution that asserts all men are free and equal.
The British surrender at Yorktown, and General Cornwallis expels several thousand African Americans who had claimed freedom under Lord Dunmore's Proclamation.

1782: Laws in Maryland and Virginia repeal prohibitions on manumission.

1777: Vermont towns secede from New York and write a constitution outlawing slavery.

1784: Rhode Island and Connecticut begin gradual emancipation of slaves.

1770   **1775**   **1780**

1773: Boston Tea Party further inflames conflict between England and its North American colonies.
Phillis Wheatley's poems are published in London.
Slaves in Massachusetts petition for their freedom.

1776: The American Declaration of Independence asserts that "all men are created equal, that they are endowed by their Creator with certain unalienable Rights, that among these are Life, Liberty, and the pursuit of Happiness."

1780: Pennsylvania law initiates gradual emancipation of slaves.

1783: Treaty of Paris ends British rule and acknowledges the independence of the United States.
Former slaves who gained freedom by serving in the British army are evacuated to Nova Scotia.
Massachusetts abolishes slavery by judicial decree in the Quock Walker case.

1778: Americans form an alliance with the French.

British regulars exchanging fire at Lexington and Concord in Massachusetts in the spring, the white settlers of the Cape Fear region worried about slave rebellions more than ever. As the Wilmington Committee of Safety warned, "There is much reason to fear, in these times of general tumult and confusion, that the slaves may be instigated, encouraged by our inveterate enemies, to an insurrection."

The Committee's caveat had merit. For Africans such as Peters, the colonists' rebellion prompted British military leaders to look for ways to disrupt Americans' lives—including inciting black slaves to rise up against their masters. In July, the British commander of Fort Johnston, at the mouth of the Cape Fear River, gave "encouragement to Negroes to elope from their masters" and offered protection to those who escaped. Slaves began fleeing into the woods outside Wilmington, and word spread among them that the British had promised that "every Negro that would murder his master and family . . . should have his master's plantation." Appalled, colonial authorities imposed martial law that gave militia units wide authority to impose curfews and limit the movement of slaves.

Like enslaved Africans everywhere in the colonies, Peters had to weigh his options carefully. He had married Sally, a slave, and in 1771 she had given birth to a girl the couple

■ In this French watercolor (1773), a slave ship is moored off St. Domingue, where some 200,000 Africans toiled to produce sugar and coffee.

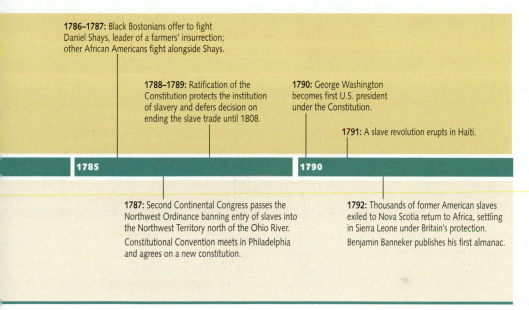

1786–1787: Black Bostonians offer to fight Daniel Shays, leader of a farmers' insurrection; other African Americans fight alongside Shays.

1788–1789: Ratification of the Constitution protects the institution of slavery and defers decision on ending the slave trade until 1808.

1790: George Washington becomes first U.S. president under the Constitution.

1791: A slave revolution erupts in Haiti.

1785

1790

1787: Second Continental Congress passes the Northwest Ordinance banning entry of slaves into the Northwest Territory north of the Ohio River. Constitutional Convention meets in Philadelphia and agrees on a new constitution.

1792: Thousands of former American slaves exiled to Nova Scotia return to Africa, settling in Sierra Leone under Britain's protection. Benjamin Banneker publishes his first almanac.

born states created constitutions that laid out the terms of how the states would govern themselves—including what they would do about slavery. When the Constitutional Convention met in Philadelphia in 1787 to hammer out the shape of a fledgling nation, slavery became a major point of contention.

When the Revolutionary War finally ground to a halt, thousands of African Americans who had been promised freedom by the British on whose side they fought had the chance to start new lives. Some migrated to Nova Scotia at the prompting of the British officials responsible for finding new homes for them. But life proved difficult there as well, and many black Nova Scotians made their way back to Africa in an unprecedented return to the motherland.

named Clairy. What chance did Peters's family have of reaching the protection of British forces? If the young father fled by himself, would his wife and child suffer the retaliation white owners and colonial lawmakers promised for runaways' kinfolk left behind? In March 1776, Peters and his family risked all. Slipping away unseen from the Campbell plantation, they headed for the British ships bobbing in the Cape Fear River. There, Peters signed up with the company of Black Guides and Pioneers, led by Captain George Martin of the British army.

The Peters family had their freedom at last. But for them and half a million other African Americans, the road ahead promised both opportunity and peril. Colonists' rhetoric about unalienable rights and Britain's crackdown on patriots in the 1760s and 1770s suggested that slavery might come to an end. But could slaves count on that? Could they wait for that day? As the American Revolution unfolded, enslaved African Americans faced difficult choices: respond to British offers of freedom, join the white patriots' cause if given the chance, or wait out the war. As this chapter reveals, all three choices gave slaves hope of liberation.

But unlike white colonists, black rebels lacked the luxury of town meetings, countywide gatherings, and state conventions to discuss their options. They had to make these difficult decisions individually or in small groups. All the while, new-

BRITISH "TYRANNY" AND A CRY FOR FREEDOM

"In every human Breast," wrote a young New England slave to her black minister friend, "God has implanted a Principle, which we call Love of Freedom; it is impatient of Oppression, and pants for Deliverance. How well, the slave asked, can whites reconcile their "Cry for Liberty" with "the Exercise of oppressive Power over others?" The plain answer was: "I humbly think it does not require the Penetration of a Philosopher to determine." With these words, nineteen-year-old Phillis Wheatley expressed the sentiments of half a million African Americans caught up in the events leading to the American Revolution. From 1764 to 1776, white colonists relentlessly proclaimed their love of freedom and their

> "In every human Breast God has implanted a Principle, which we call Love of Freedom." —*Phillis Wheatley*

impatience with British oppression—while keeping black people under the boot heel of slavery. Like Phillis Wheatley, many enslaved blacks acutely perceived the hypocrisy of the situation.

Born in Gambia in 1755 and abducted by slave traders as a small child, Wheatley arrived on North American shores in a slave ship in 1764. The slavers named her Phillis, after the vessel that had transported her. Phillis ended up serving the household of a successful Boston tailor named Wheatley, who gave her the same surname. Just eighteen months after she came to North America, the nine-year-old girl could read the most difficult biblical passages and was devouring every piece of secular and religious literature that Boston clergymen put in her hands. At age thirteen, she saw her first poem published. At sixteen, she commemorated the Boston Massacre in verse. By 1773, when her poems were published in London, Wheatley had created a sensation in the English-speaking world. This frail young African became the first woman in the American colonies to publish poetic

expressions on political events. At that time, she was arguably read more widely than any other woman in North America.

Freedom Rhetoric Exposes Colonial Enslavement

African Americans in North America, most of them enslaved, had some knowledge of the train of events that led white colonists to declare their independence from England. For example, the Stamp Act of 1765 had touched off riots across the cities. The Townshend duties of 1767 catalyzed further protests. Britain's decision to send troops to Boston instigated the Boston Massacre. The Tea Act of 1773 provoked Bostonians into dumping a shipload of tea into the harbor, an event later known as the Boston Tea Party. The British retaliated with the Coercive Acts of 1774, which further polarized the two sides. Finally, armed conflict broke out in April 1775 in the Massachusetts towns of Lexington and Concord.

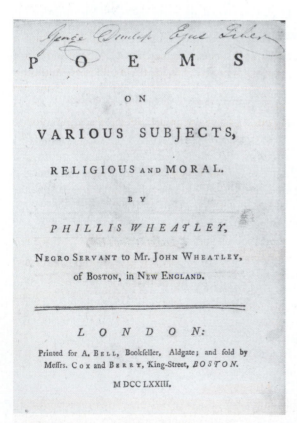

■ Frontispiece engraving of Wheatley's *Poems on Various Subjects*, with a pen drawing of Wheatley. Scipio Moorhead, a slave owned by a Boston minister, also wrote poetry and crafted this picture of Wheatley for her anthology of poems—creating the colonies' first identified African American portrait. To show her appreciation, Wheatley wrote the poem "To S. M., a young African Painter, on seeing his Works."

Each step toward revolution riveted white colonists' attention on the question of which rights and responsibilities Britain had regarding its colonies. But arguments about whether Britain had the right to tax colonists who had no representation in the British Parliament or whether royal governors could legally disband elected colonial legislatures mattered little to black Americans. What did capture their interest were the language and methods of protest white colonists used to resist the British government.

As the conflict between the colonies and Britain escalated, Africans in North America saw new opportunities to seize their own liberty. From the first colonial protests against British revenue policy in 1765 to the end of the Revolutionary War in 1783, black people staged the most widespread and protracted slave rebellion in American history. Their efforts exposed a lie that many white people believed—that most slaves were content with their lot. Though we do not know the exact number, it is likely that tens of thousands of slaves fled to the British side to gain their freedom. Meanwhile, other black people cast their lot with the Americans in the belief that they would be rewarded with liberation.

Thousands of black Americans overheard their masters' dinner-table conversations and debates, worked in taverns and coffeehouses where colonists argued about revolutionary politics, and listened to white patriots describing Britain's policies as tantamount to tyranny and enslavement. These Africans pondered the notion of unalienable rights—the idea that some privileges are not earned but rather acquired at birth. Natural rights, political theorists maintained, could not be alienated (separated) from an individual.

Black people applied the ringing phrases of the day to their own situation. Moreover, in northern towns and occasionally on southern plantations, they had the support of some white colonists who recognized the contradiction between natural rights and Africans' enslavement. For example, James Otis, a fervent pamphleteer on the rights of English-born citizens, had asserted as early as 1764 that the "colonists are by the law of nature free born, as indeed all men are, white or black. . . . Does it follow that it is right to enslave a man because he is black? Will short curl'd hair like wool, instead of Christian hair . . . help the argument? Can any logical inference in favor of slavery be drawn from a flat nose, a long or a short face?"

Enslaved Africans' spirits no doubt soared as white colonists' rhetoric of freedom and resistance to tyranny heated up. In 1768, the *Pennsylvania Chronicle* urged

COMMON SENSE;

ADDRESSED TO THE

INHABITANTS

OF

AMERICA,

On the following interesting

SUBJECTS.

I. Of the Origin and Design of Government in general, with concise Remarks on the English Constitution.
II. Of Monarchy and Hereditary Succession.
III. Thoughts on the present State of American Affairs.
IV. Of the present Ability of America, with some miscellaneous Reflections.

Man knows no Master save creating HEAVEN,
Or those whom choice and common good ordain.
THOMSON.

PHILADELPHIA;

Printed, and Sold, by R. BELL, in Third-Street.
MDCCLXXVI.

colonists to ban the African slave trade, "emancipate the whole race" of Africans, and restore "that liberty we have so long unjustly detained from them." Benjamin Rush, a young doctor in Philadelphia, penned an antislavery pamphlet in 1773 proclaiming that slavery would be dead in forty years. That same year in Massachusetts, Nathaniel Niles wrote: "For shame, let us either cease to enslave our fellow-men or else let us cease to complain of those that would enslave us." In 1775, Thomas Paine, author of the incendiary pamphlet *Common Sense*, challenged slaveholders: "With what consistency or decency [do white colonists] complain so loudly of attempts to enslave them, while they hold so many hundred thousand in slavery."

Such rhetoric ignited Africans' own revolutionary spirit. In northern colonies, where slaves had the right to petition, some black Americans couched their pleas for freedom in ways calculated to stir the conscience of their masters. At first they wrote their petitions cautiously, much as Wheatley had phrased her poetic attacks on slavery in muted terms. One 1773 petition to the Massachusetts legislature began with "The humble petition of many slaves, living in the town of Boston, and other towns in the province [rests] our Cause on your Humanity and Justice."

But petition language grew bolder as the war exploded. "We . . . ask for nothing but what we are fully persuaded is ours to claim," asserted a Connecticut slave petition in 1777, for "we are the Creatures of that God, who made of one blood, and kindred, all the nations of the earth"; hence, "there is nothing that leads to a belief . . . that we are any more obliged to serve them, than they us and . . . can never be convinced that we were made to be slaves."

Some black people also used stronger language to call attention to white patriots' ingratitude for black military assistance. In Boston, such advocates included Prince Hall, a former slave who gained his freedom in 1770 and helped found the first black Masonic lodge in North America in 1775. After African Americans took up arms at Lexington, Bunker Hill, and Charlestown, Hall and others wrote in 1777 that black people "cannot but express their astonishment that it has never been considered that every principle from which

> "We are the Creatures of that God, who made of one blood, and kindred, all the nations of the earth."
> —*Connecticut slave petition*

First Person

Lemuel Haynes Calls for Universal Liberty

The son of a white woman and an enslaved African, Lemuel Haynes grew up in a frontier town in Massachusetts. There, he showed a remarkable ability to read sermons and scripture. Enlisting as a soldier in 1774 at age twenty, Haynes saw action against the British in Boston and then at Fort Ticonderoga. Later that year he wrote a forty-six-page tract, which he titled "Liberty Further Extended." An excerpt appears below.

Every privilege that mankind enjoy have their origin from God; and whatever acts are passed in any earthly court, which are derogatory to those edicts that are passed in the court of heaven, the act is void. . . . *It hath pleased God to make of one Blood all nations of men, for to dwell upon the face of the Earth.* (Acts 17:26) And as all are of one species, so there are the same laws, and aspiring principles placed in all nations. . . . No one has the least right to take them from us without our consent; and there is not the least precept, or practice, in the sacred scriptures that constitutes a black man a slave, any more than a white one. . . . Shall a man's color be the decisive criterion whereby to judge of his natural right? Or because a man is not of the same color with his neighbour, shall he be deprived of those things that distinguish him from the beasts of the field?

—*from Lemuel Haynes, "Liberty Further Extended" (1776).*

To view a longer version of this document, please go to *www.ablongman.com/carson/documents*.

America has acted in the course of their unhappy difficulties with Great Britain pleads stronger than a thousand arguments . . . [that black people] may be restored to the enjoyments of that which is the natural right of all men." Rhetoric pressing for the end of slavery provides some of the most compelling language of the revolutionary era.

Freedom Fever in the South

In the southern colonies, laws forbade slaves from petitioning the courts. Nevertheless, black Americans stepped up demands for their liberty as the fighting between the colonists and the British regulars escalated. In Charleston, the South's largest city, enslaved Africans chanted the cry "Liberty, liberty" after a crowd of white colonists raucously celebrated the resignation of the Stamp Act distributor in 1766. Yet the same colonists promptly cracked down on agitating black slaves. "The city was thrown under arms for a week," reported an alarmed white official. For two weeks, colonial authorities dispatched messengers throughout the colony to warn of possible slave uprisings.

Still, unrest among African Americans intensified. In Georgia and South Carolina in 1773, groups of slaves fled to the country's interior. The following year, rebelling slaves killed several white people. In August 1775, another slave plot percolated in South Carolina when the free black river pilot Thomas Jeremiah planned to guide the British Royal Navy into Charleston harbor and help bondspeople win their freedom. But officials discovered Jeremiah's scheme, hanged him, and set him aflame on August 18, 1775. As one historian wrote, "Behind the bewitching rhetoric of liberty was the hideous face of slavery." White people, armed and alert to the slightest evidence of black rebelliousness, promptly crushed most uprisings.

AFRICAN AMERICANS AND THE AMERICAN REVOLUTION

By its nature, the Revolutionary War opened new doors for African Americans. With the immense movement of both civilian and military populations in and out of nearly every

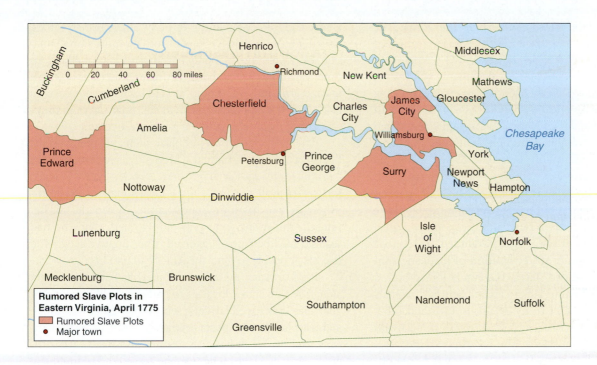

MAP 5.1 Rumored Slave Plots in Eastern Virginia Counties, April 1775

Virginia boiled with slave unrest as the colonial crisis with England climaxed. This map shows the sites of a number of reported slave plots in the same parts of Virginia where many white revolutionary leaders—George Washington, Thomas Jefferson, Patrick Henry, James Madison, George Wythe, and Richard Henry Lee—owned plantations worked by slaves.

Adapted from Woody Holton, *Forced Founders: Indians, Debtors, Slaves, and the Making of the American Revolution* (Chapel Hill, University of North Carolina Press, 1999), p. 142.

major seaport from Savannah to Boston between 1775 and 1783, urban slaves had unprecedented opportunities for seizing their independence and destabilizing the institution of slavery. In the countryside, as British and American forces criss-crossed the land, slaves fled to the British side by the thousands and disrupted plantation work routines. The few free African Americans faced a dilemma: Should they offer to fight with the American rebels in the hopes of improving their image in the minds of white patriots? Should they join the British as a means for overthrowing slavery? Or should they keep their heads down while waiting for the storm to pass? With war swirling around them, black Americans made their choices. For all of them, the hope of personal freedom guided their decisions.

Choosing the British: Black Loyalists

As Thomas Peters discovered, the British offered slaves their best chance at regaining their liberty. In November 1775, Virginia's royal governor, Lord Dunmore, issued a proclamation offering freedom for slaves and indentured servants "able and willing to bear arms" who escaped their masters and joined the British forces. Dunmore's proclamation lifted the hopes of enslaved Africans everywhere. Within just a few months, about a thousand Virginia runaway slaves reached the British lines. Many slaves who were old, infirm, very young, or pregnant decided against traveling such long distances. However, in every region, black women with children ran away from their masters in much greater proportion than they had in the colonial period. They knew that with the British offering refuge, they had a far better chance than ever before of winning—and keeping—their freedom.

Some slaves held out hope that the American patriots, prompted by their rhetoric of unalienable rights, would abolish slavery altogether. But thousands of others refused to hang their dreams on such an uncertain development. In waves, they joined the British ranks. There, they formed the Ethiopian Regiment, the Black Guides and Pioneers, and other units led by white British officers.

Thomas Peters and his family were among many slaves who chose immediate liberty over the uncertainty of being liberated by white Americans voluntarily. Peters fought with the British Black Guides and Pioneers for eight years. When escaped Virginia slaves joined his unit, he noticed that some of them wore the inscription "Liberty to Slaves" across the breast of their uniform. Peters moved north with the British forces to occupy Philadelphia in the fall of 1777, participated in the evacuation of the Pennsylvania capital in the summer of 1778, and was in New York City with the British when the war ended in 1783. Twice wounded, he received a promotion to sergeant in recognition of his leadership among his fellow escaped slaves. His family joined him in New York City by the time American and British diplomats were negotiating the peace treaty in Paris in 1782 and 1783.

Peters's wartime service brought him into contact with thousands of other black people who had obtained their freedom through a similar route. Though the war was fought primarily in the North during its first five years, African sympathy for the British cropped up in all the colonies. As the German Lutheran minister Henry Melchior Muhlenberg observed, enslaved Africans "secretly wished the British army might win, for then all Negro slaves will gain their freedom." It is difficult to know precisely how many slaves allied themselves with the British. However, many large slaveowners, such as Thomas Jefferson, acknowledged that 10 to 20 percent of their coerced labor force fled to the enemy's side.

The Lower South endured a similar exodus of slaves to the British ranks. During the southern campaigns from 1779 to 1782, when the presence of the British occupying army boosted slaves' chances of a successful break for freedom, South Carolina and Georgia in particular experienced losses of thousands of slaves.

Even in the North, where white masters exercised their rule less harshly than in the South, slaves opted for the British deal. When Thomas Peters was with the British regiments occupying Philadelphia, he observed scores of slaves flocking to the British ranks. Surveying Pennsylvania's losses in 1779, one white legislator lamented, "By the invasion of this state, and the possession the enemy obtain of this city and neighborhood, [a] great part of the slaves hereabouts were enticed away by the British army." New York City and its surrounding countryside offered numerous opportunities for slaves to escape because the British controlled the area during most of the war.

Yet British military leaders did not open their arms to all bondspeople. For example, they refused to accept white loyalists' slaves into their military machine. In 1779, Sir Henry Clinton, commander-in-chief of the British forces, issued a more restrictive version of Dunmore's proclamation; he offered freedom only to refugee slaves of rebellious Americans and warned that any African Americans captured in American uniforms would be sold back into bondage. In fact, some British officers claimed captured slaves as property rather than delivering the promised freedom.

One of the most intrepid black men enlisting with the British was the self-named Colonel Tye. A restless slave working for his master in northern New Jersey, Tye yearned for freedom all the more after local Quakers urged his owner to free his four bondspeople. When the master refused, the twenty-one-year-old Tye fled. Once he had secured his liberty, he organized other fugitive slaves and free black people to fight the American patriots.

For five years, Tye led a local guerrilla band that fought alongside New Jersey loyalists to harass patriot farmers. The guerrillas kidnapped farmers, seized their crops and cattle, and patrolled border posts between the British and Americans. Hiding out in familiar swamps and inlets, Tye gathered runaway slaves wherever he traveled. He fought in numerous battles before dying of wounds and lockjaw in 1780. A symbol of black rebellion, he inspired awe among New Jersey patriots despite the havoc he stirred up. The first notice of his death in local newspapers described Tye as "justly to be more feared and respected than any of his brethren of a fairer complexion."

Though thousands of black Americans saw the British as liberators, they discovered that fighting alongside them was anything but glorious. Soon after joining the British, many black people learned that the promise of freedom was more a military strategy than a principled commitment to abolish an immoral institution. To the British, black men and women presented a means for recruiting military laborers and disrupting the enemy's economy. Only a few former slaves, such as Peters, served in uniformed black military units with white officers. Most served as laborers, wagon drivers, cooks, and servants. They repaired roads, cleaned camp, hauled equipment, and constructed fortifications. Rations were short, clothing shabby, and barracks overcrowded. Camp fevers and contagious diseases proved more lethal than warfare, and thousands of black people who joined the British met early deaths.

Though some British royal governors and military officers genuinely believed that slaves deserved freedom, most had decidedly more pragmatic interests. How pragmatic they were became chillingly apparent during the Franco-American siege of British-occupied Yorktown in 1781. Finding his troops surrounded and short of provisions, General Charles Cornwallis expelled from his encampments several thousand African Americans who had claimed freedom

Boston King Describes the End of the War for Black Loyalists

Born about 1760 in South Carolina, Boston King fled to the British and served them throughout the war. He was among several thousand former slaves in New York City as the peace treaty was being negotiated in Paris. In 1798, he published Memoirs of the Life of Boston King, a Black Preacher. *In the book, he recounted the fear among those who received their freedom under the British that they would be forced to return to their masters.*

[In 1783] the horrors and devastation of war happily terminated, and peace was restored between America and Great Britain, which diffused universal joy among all parties, except us, who had escaped from slavery, and taken refuge in the English army; for a report prevailed at New York, that all the [former] slaves, in number 2000, were to be delivered up to their masters, altho' some of them had been three or four years among the English. This dreadful rumour filled us all with inexpressible anguish and terror, especially when we saw our old masters coming from Virginia, North-Carolina, and other parts, and seizing upon their slaves in the streets of New York, or even dragging them out of their beds. Many of the slaves had very cruel

masters, so that the thoughts of returning home with them embittered life to us. . . . The English had compassion upon us in the day of distress and issued out a Proclamation, importing that all slaves should be free, who had taken refuge in the British lines. . . . In consequence of this, each of us received a certificate . . . at New York, which dispelled all our fears and filled us with joy and gratitude. Soon after, ships were fitted out and furnished with every necessary for conveying us to Nova Scotia.

—from Boston King, Memoirs of the Life of Boston King *(London: n.p., 1798).*

To view a longer version of this document, please go to *www.ablongman.com/carson/documents*.

under Dunmore's proclamation. An embarrassed Hessian officer serving with the British wrote that Cornwallis's officers "drove back to the enemy all of our black friends, whom we had taken along to despoil the countryside. . . . We had used them to good advantage and set them free, and now, with fear and trembling they had to face the reward of their cruel masters." Cornwallis knew that if he surrendered the freed slaves to the American general George Washington, they would have been promptly reenslaved. Expelling them from the British encampments usually led to the same fate.

Fighting for Independence: Black Patriots

Choosing a different path than that of Sergeant Peters and Colonel Tye, many free African Americans and a few slaves fought for the American cause. William C. Nell, the first black American historian, honored this minority in the 1850s when, working to advance the abolitionist crusade,

he recalled the blood shed for the "glorious cause" by black Americans in the time of the nation's birth. In his *Colored Patriots of the American Revolution* (1855), Nell cited Crispus Attucks as the first person to fall during the Boston Massacre of 1770 and thus the first to lose his life in the Americans' bid for independence.

Half Wampanoag Indian and half African, Attucks was a powerfully built man who had fled slavery twenty years earlier. After regaining his freedom, he spent many years working on whaling ships that docked in the ports of New England. On the night of March 5, 1770, he led an attack in Boston—later called the Boston Massacre—against a contingent of British regulars. Brandishing a stout cordwood stick, he charged the redcoats, who earlier that evening had pummeled some loud-mouthed youths. When a squad of eight soldiers fired at nearly point-blank range, five Americans perished. "The first to defy, and the first to die," as a Boston poet wrote a century later, Attucks became a symbol of American resistance to the hated British occupation of Boston.

The story of Salem Poor provides another apt example of free black patriots' achievements. A married church member, Poor's bravery in the Battle of Charlestown in 1775 inspired fourteen Massachusetts officers to petition the Continental Congress to reward "so great and distinguished a character" and such a "brave and gallant soldier." Poor went on to fight with Washington's army at White Plains, New York, and endured the grinding winter of 1777–1778 at Valley Forge.

Some black patriots were slaves. Peter Salem, for example, a slave from Framingham, Massachusetts, served alongside his master at the Battle of Lexington. At the Battle of Bunker Hill, Salem took aim and killed Major John Pitcairn of the British Marines, the officer who led the attack on the patriots' fortifications. Salem later fought at Stony Point and Saratoga, New York. Prince Whipple, another slave patriot, pulled the stroke oar in the small boat that carried George Washington across the Delaware River. This crossing, which took place amid a piercing winter storm on Christmas night in 1776, is immortalized in a painting, where Whipple is shown, that today hangs in the U.S. Capitol. The subsequent American attack, which surprised the British at Trenton, New Jersey, handed the patriots their first major victory.

One Virginia slave, James Armistead, served as a spy under the Marquis de Lafayette, the celebrated French nobleman who came to fight with the Americans. Armistead's master, William Armistead, granted his desire to enlist when Lafayette called for the recruitment of black troops in March 1781. Lafayette soon sent James Armistead to Portsmouth, Virginia (which the British army had occupied under Benedict Arnold's command), armed with letters to other American spies. Next, Armistead infiltrated the British lines at Yorktown, posing as a runaway slave. After observing the British formations and tactical positions, he fled the camp and brought back crucial information that gave the Americans the upper hand in what became the climactic battle of the war.

Just after the war, Lafayette gave Armistead a handwritten testimonial declaring, "His intelligence from the enemy's camp were industriously collected and more faithfully delivered. He perfectly acquitted himself with some important commissions I gave him and appears to me entitled to every reward his situation can admit of." In 1786, the General Assembly of Virginia responded to Lafayette's testimonial by emancipating Armistead and appropriating money to compensate his master. The assembly record states that Armistead "at the peril of his life, found means to frequent the British camp" and provided indispensable information on behalf of the American cause. Thereafter, Armistead traded in his master's surname and called himself James Lafayette. Nearly a half-century later, when the French hero returned to the United States for a triumphal tour, he visited his namesake. James Lafayette lived poor but proud on a small farm in Virginia, a pensioner of the American Revolution.

Faithful wartime service did not always earn black Americans freedom or pensions. Even George Washington's slave, William Lee, who served the general during eight long years of combat, had to wait until his master's death in 1799 to win his liberty. Like many revolutionary leaders, Washington professed a hatred of slavery but could not bring himself to part with his human chattel. He grudgingly agreed to grant Lee's request in 1784 to transport his free black wife from Philadelphia to Mount Vernon, Washington's plantation on the Potomac River in Virginia. "I cannot refuse his request [to send for his wife]," wrote Washington, "as he has lived with me so long and followed my fortunes through the war with fidelity." The black couple lived at Mount Vernon for fifteen years—the husband a slave, the wife free—until Washington died in 1799.

Most patriot leaders refused to permit African Americans, whether slave or free, to fight at all on the American

■ This painting of James Armistead shows Armistead fitted out elaborately. During the war, the Marquis de Lafayette developed an antislavery stance and proposed to George Washington that the two men establish a small plantation in South America where Washington's freed slaves and Lafayette's could till the soil as tenant farmers.

side. The natural rights principle, which on the eve of the revolution seemed poised to inspire a broad antislavery movement, withered once the fighting erupted. By late 1775 and early 1776, the Continental Army and most state militias had decided to ban free blacks and slaves from military service. The idea of putting weapons in the hands of African Americans raised disturbing images of a broad black rebellion and of black men possessing inflated notions of equality.

Yet two years into the war, white patriots changed their minds once more—this time for pragmatic, not moral, reasons. Concerned about a worsening manpower shortage, the states began to accept free black men in militia units in 1777. At the same time, recruiting sergeants quietly accepted slaves in place of their masters, often privately promising to grant them their freedom at war's end. As the "spirit of '76" wore off among white people and the war dragged on, militias in the northern states and towns reached deeper and deeper into the reservoir of black manpower. Most African Americans serving in state militias fought alongside white soldiers, although Rhode Island, Connecticut, and Massachusetts created mostly black regiments led by white officers.

Some southern states also began tapping the African American population for military duty. Sorely pressed to fill the state quotas set by the Continental Congress each year, Maryland reluctantly recruited free black men into service. "Our recruiting business in this county goes much worse than I expected," wrote one leader from St. Mary's County to the governor in 1780. "The greatest part of those that have enlisted are free Negroes & Mulattoes." When the British army invaded the South, Maryland militias agreed to accept slaves—with their masters' consent. Not surprisingly, few slaveholders wanted to give up able-bodied black men. Farther south, Virginia permitted free black men to enlist but drew the line on slaves.

Legislatures in South Carolina and Georgia, dominated by slaveowners, banned any form of black enlistment. If the image of the revolutionary army as a refuge for runaway slaves and agitators alarmed most northerners, it terrified southerners. Especially in the Deep South and along coastal areas, where black people far outnumbered white, the thought of putting guns into the hands of any black—slave or free—struck white southerners as suicidal.

Only 1 percent of the black population was free at the outbreak of the war. Many of these African Americans viewed the chance to join the patriot cause as a means to advance their place in what they hoped would be a wholly new republic. They believed the patriots' rhetoric about natural rights and personal freedom foretold the end of slavery and the dawn of a new era of racial equality. They wanted to secure their position in this new society.

■ In this lithograph, William Lee holds Washington's white horse while the American general accepts the surrender of General Lord Cornwallis at Yorktown.

Consider the story of James Forten of Philadelphia. Forten's great-grandfather had been dragged to the Delaware River Valley in chains, probably by Dutch slavers, even before William Penn's Quakers arrived. His grandfather was one of the first Africans in Pennsylvania to purchase his freedom. His son, James's father, became a sailmaker in Philadelphia. James was born in 1766, a year after the Stamp Act riots ignited revolutionary fervor. Enjoying the advantages of Quaker schooling and rankling at the British occupation of Philadelphia in 1777–1778, young Forten cast his lot with the American cause. Just fifteen years old as the war wound down in 1781, he signed on with a privateer—a licensed merchant ship outfitted to capture British vessels. "Scarce wafted from his native shore, and periled upon the dark blue sea," wrote William Nell, "than he found himself amid the roar of cannon, the smoke of blood, the dying, and the dead." Nell was

 **First Person**   ## Jehu Grant Fights for the Patriot Cause

Many years after the American Revolution, aged black soldiers living in poverty applied to the War Department for pensions. Their application letters reveal much about black patriots' wartime experience. Jehu Grant first applied for a pension in 1832 when he was in his late seventies. Proslavery bureaucrats in Washington denied his request on the grounds that Grant had escaped his pro-British master to fight with the Americans and was therefore a "fugitive." Grant petitioned the Pension Office again in a letter in 1836, but died soon after. An excerpt from his first letter appears below, followed by an excerpt from the second petition.

[Your petitioner] was a slave to Elihu Champlen who resided at Narragansett, Rhode Island. At the time he left him, his master was called a Tory and in a secret manner furnished the enemy when shipping lay nearby with sheep, cattle, cheese, etc., and received goods from them. And this applicant being afraid his master would send him to the British ships, ran away sometime in August 1777 . . . and enlisted. [He] was put to teaming with a team of horses and wagon, drawing provisions and various other loading for the army for three or four months until winter set in, then was taken as a servant to John Skidmore, wagon master general, and served with him until spring, when the troops went to the Highlands . . . on the Hudson River, a little above the British lines . . . sometime in June, when his master either sent or

came, this applicant was given up to his master again, and he returned.

I was then grown to manhood, in the full vigor and strength of life . . . when I saw liberty poles and the people all engaged for the support of freedom. And living on the borders of Rhode Island, where whole companies of colored people enlisted, it added to my fears and dread of being sold to the British. These considerations induced me to enlist into the American army, where I served faithful about ten months, when my master found and took me home.

—*from* Index of Revolutionary War Pension Applications in the National Archives, *Washington, D.C. 1976.*

To view a longer version of this document, please go to *www.ablongman.com/carson/documents.*

---

describing a bloody engagement in 1782 in which the *Royal Louis* captured the British warship *Laurence*. Forten was the only survivor at his gun station.

But Forten continued to demonstrate his bravery and fortitude on the next voyage, when the British captured his ship after a fierce sea battle. When the British captain's young son befriended Forten, the captain offered the black youth free passage to England along with the patronage of his family. "NO, NO!" replied Forten. "I am here a prisoner for the liberties of my country; I never, NEVER, shall prove a traitor to her interests." His offer spurned, the British captain consigned Forten to the

Old Jersey—the rotting, death-trap prison ship anchored in New York harbor. Thousands of captured Americans died on such vessels, but Forten survived even this ordeal. Released seven months later as the war drew to a close, the sixteen-year-old boy made his way shoeless from New York to Philadelphia.

RHETORIC AND REALITY IN THE NEW NATION

While fighting for their independence from Britain, white Americans also worked to establish new governments and pave the way for expansion westward. Yet even as they

> **"I** am here a prisoner for the liberties of my country; I never, NEVER, shall prove a traitor to her interests."
>
> —*James Forten*

■ *The Battle of Bunker's Hill,* by John Trumbull, painter of revolutionary scenes, depicts the slave patriot Peter Salem. Gun in hand, Salem backs up Lieutenant Thomas Grosvenor, his master. After the war, Salem acquired a small amount of property and earned some income by weaving cane into chairs. He then apparently met with misfortune, dying in a poorhouse in Framingham, Massachusetts, in 1816.

argued that the British crown and Parliament had denied their unalienable rights, most white people who owned slaves exempted their human property from these same rights. Most who did not own slaves felt only a half-hearted desire to abolish the institution. The state constitutions under which the new nation operated reflected this gap between rhetoric and reality by preserving slavery. Yet African Americans pushed the agenda of freedom forward—achieving success in some states.

Continued Slavery in the South

The fighting between America and England wound down at Yorktown in 1781, and the new nation's independence was guaranteed in the Treaty of Paris in 1783. During these years, enslaved Africans in the South must have hoped the revolution's leaders would recognize the threat slavery posed to a republic founded on the notion of unalienable rights. After the war, some white officials expressed such sentiments outright. For example, leaders of the fast-growing Methodists wrote in 1784 that "the practice of holding our fellow creatures in slavery . . . [is] contrary to the golden law of God on which hang all the law and the prophets and

the unalienable rights of mankind." By 1785, even Thomas Jefferson had grown so aware of the spread of antislavery sentiment north of the Chesapeake that he maintained, "In a few years there will be no slaves Northward of Maryland." Three years later, Maryland's attorney general, Luther Martin, declared that slavery was "inconsistent with the genius of republicanism and has a tendency to destroy those principles on which it is supported, as it lessens the sense of the equal rights of mankind and habituates us to tyranny and oppression."

Yet the spread of antislavery sentiment brought only limited results in the South. Indeed, it only slightly constrained the extension of slavery into new geographic territories and the increase in the number of people in bondage in the new nation. Southern slaveholders, as well as northerners who profited from the slave trade and slave-produced goods, energetically opposed abolition.

Still, some southern lawmakers softened slightly in their attitude toward slavery. In 1782, the Virginia and Maryland legislatures repealed existing prohibitions on masters' right to manumit, or free, their slaves. Consequently, the number of free black people in Maryland soared from about 2,000 on the eve of the revolution to 8,000 by 1790, mainly through manumission. In Virginia, where about half of all American slaveowners resided, the number of free black persons expanded from about 1,800 in 1782 to more than 12,000 in 1790. By that year, about 5,000 free black persons lived in North Carolina.

What prompted some slaveholders to release their human chattel? In many cases, Enlightenment ideas about natural rights moved these white people to mercy. In other cases, planters who switched from tobacco production to less labor-intensive wheat production decided they did not need as many slaves as before.

But despite the increase in the free black population, the vast majority of African Americans in the Upper South remained trapped in bondage. Moreover, their number was climbing quickly. Slavery opponents had hoped that after the southern states stopped the importation of new bondspeople, the slave population would wither away owing to natural decrease—more slave deaths than births each year. But the opposite occurred. Slave births exceeded deaths, so the population of bondspeople expanded. Virginia's, for example, grew from about 200,000 to nearly 300,000 between 1776 and 1790. Maryland and North Carolina experienced similar trends.

In the Lower South, manumission was rare. While almost one out of every twenty African Americans in the Upper South had gained his or her freedom by 1790, only one in sixty had done so in the Lower South. The slave population of South Carolina and Georgia—the two states that

 **First Person**

Belinda Petitions for a Small Pension

Enslaved in present-day Ghana in the 1720s, Belinda served Isaac Royall, one of Boston's wealthiest slave traders and slaveowners, for many years before he fled to England as a loyalist in 1775. The revolutionary Massachusetts government confiscated his estate, including his many slaves. In 1782, at about age seventy, Belinda futilely applied for a small pension to be paid to her from the sale of her master's immense holdings.

Fifty years her faithful hands have been compelled to ignoble servitude for the benefit of an Isaac Royall, until, as if nations must be agitated and the world convulsed, for the preservation of that freedom which the Almighty Father intended for all the human race, the present war commenced. . . . The face of your petitioner is now marked with the furrows of time, and her frame feebly bending under the oppression of years, while she, by the laws of the land, is denied the enjoyment of one morsel of that immense wealth, a part whereof hath been accumulated by her own industry and the whole augmented by her servitude.

—first printed as "The Petition of Belinda an African to the General Court of Massachusetts, February 14, 1783" from the American Museum or Universal Magazine I, 1787.

To view a longer version of this document, please go to *www.ablongman.com/carson/documents*.

---

resumed importing slaves after the revolution—continued to rise. Switching from enslaved to free labor made no economic sense to planters in these states. The doctrine of unalienable rights had little meaning for them as well. Having armed themselves heavily during the war against Britain, white people in the Lower South now had the weapons to crush black rebellion and consolidate their hold on the far more numerous slaves.

Emancipation in the North

At the end of the war, only about one in ten black Americans lived in the North. Most of these were still in bondage when the British and Americans signed the Treaty of Paris that ended the American Revolution and acknowledged the independence of the United States. However, some hopeful signs, at least for African Americans in the North, began to develop when the Green Mountain towns seceded from New York in 1777 and chose delegates to write a constitution for the new state of Vermont. (The state gained admittance into the Union in 1791.) Vermont's political leaders proclaimed that nobody should serve as a slave, or even as a servant or apprentice, once he or she had reached adulthood.

In 1780, other northern states followed suit. Pennsylvania's wartime legislature passed the first state law mandating the gradual abolition of slavery. Four years later, Rhode Island and Connecticut took similar steps. Yet in New Jersey and New York, where slavery played a major role in the economy, lawmakers declined to eradicate the institution. Moreover, slavery expanded steadily in these states, despite rulings that halted slave importation. Not until 1799 and 1804, respectively, would New York and New Jersey pass gradual abolition laws. Delaware never abolished slavery. White people living in that state could legally own human chattel until the Thirteenth Amendment eliminated the practice after the Civil War.

Though the northern states' new laws must have raised African Americans' hopes, they phased out slavery only slowly. Equally frustrating to black people, abolition laws generated such heated debate that legislators sometimes watered them down even further. Pennsylvania's abolition law illustrates this point. In 1775, Quakers in Philadelphia organized the Society for the Relief of Free Negroes Unlawfully Held in Bondage. Society members moved rapidly to cleanse themselves of what they saw as the sin of slaveholding. Though not explicitly an abolition society at first,

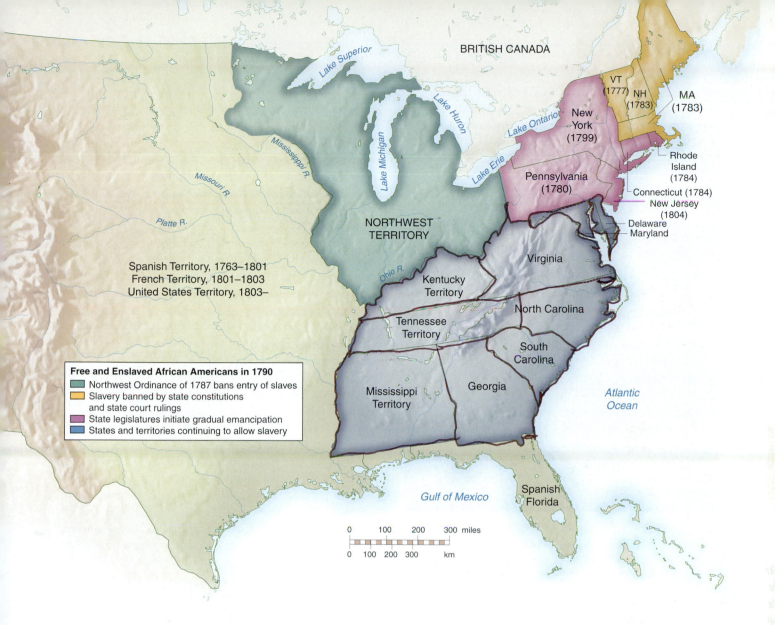

Spanish Territory, 1763–1801
French Territory, 1801–1803
United States Territory, 1803–

Free and Enslaved African Americans in 1790
- Northwest Ordinance of 1787 bans entry of slaves
- Slavery banned by state constitutions and state court rulings
- State legislatures initiate gradual emancipation
- States and territories continuing to allow slavery

■ **MAP 5.2** Free and Enslaved African Americans in 1790

Because many northern states abolished slavery only by degrees, a few African Americans remained in bondage until the mid-nineteenth century. For example, the federal censuses showed 1,129 slaves still living in northern states in 1840; 262 in 1850; and 64 in 1860.

the Quaker organization flowered after the revolution, attracting non-Quakers and becoming the first group in the English-speaking world dedicated to the eradication of human bondage.

The Society's strong stand against slavery influenced many of the state's political leaders. Building on this foundation, Pennsylvania legislators passed an abolition act in 1780—the first passed in the new nation. In the act's preamble, lawmakers wrote that by erasing slavery Pennsylvanians would regain the respect of "all Europe, who are astonished to see a people eager for liberty holding Negroes in bondage." Yet the act sparked intense debate. It did not

free a single slave and specified that all children born before the day the law took effect—March 1, 1780—would remain enslaved. Children born after that date were consigned to twenty-eight years of bondage. Hence, any child born of a slave on the last day of February 1780 could live out his or her life in slavery. If an enslaved black woman bore a child in 1820, her son or daughter would not be free until 1848. Ground down by vigorous opposition from slaveowners, the legislature amended the proposed law so it postponed full emancipation for more than half a century.

Some African Americans decided not to wait for white legislators and judges to apply the rhetoric of freedom to

---

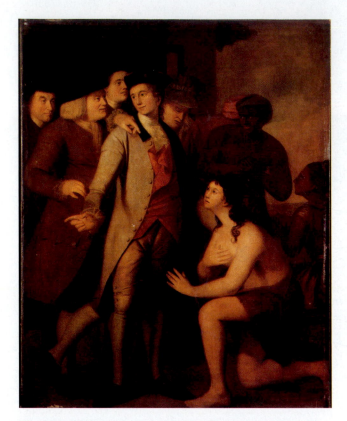

■ Dinah Neville, on bended knee, shows gratitude as the broad-hatted representative of the Pennsylvania Abolition Society drops coins into the hand of a Virginia planter who has agreed to release her from slavery.

their own lives. A slave named Elizabeth Freeman set in motion a chain of events and a judicial decision that ended slavery in Massachusetts. Her story shows that in the revolutionary era, even the humblest descendants of Africans could effect profound change.

In 1781, with the war nearing its end, Freeman and her sister served a wealthy family, the Ashleys, in the town of Sheffield, Massachusetts. One day during an argument, Mrs. Ashley swung a heated kitchen shovel at Freeman's sister. Throwing herself between her sister and their angry mistress, Freeman took the blow on her arm, "the scar of which she bore to the day of her death." She then stalked from the house and refused to return. Her master appealed to the town court for the recovery of his slave. Freeman countered by calling on Theodore Sedgwick, a lawyer from nearby Stockbridge, to take her case. She asked Sedgwick if Massachusetts's new state constitution, with its preamble stating that "all men are born free and equal," did not apply to her.

Intrigued, Sedgwick took the case. In 1781, he argued before the county court in Great Barrington that Freeman

was "not a dumb beast." Therefore, he continued, she was entitled to the same privileges other human beings enjoyed—including white ones. The all-white jury agreed that the preamble to the state constitution made no exception for skin color in its pronouncement that all humans are both free and equal. Elizabeth Freeman was released from slavery.

The widowed Freeman, whose husband had fallen on a Massachusetts battlefield during the revolution, worked as a housekeeper for the Sedgwicks for many years. She later became a noted midwife and nurse, revered for her skills in curing and calming her patients. After her death in 1829, Sedgwick's son commemorated Freeman's strength: "If there could be a practical refutation of the imagined superiority of our race to hers, the life and character of this woman would afford that refutation. . . . She uniformly . . . obtained an ascendancy over all those with whom she was associated in service. . . . Even in her humble station, she had, when occasion required it, an air of command which conferred a degree of dignity. . . . She claimed no distinction but it was yielded to her from her superior experience, energy, skill, and sagacity."

> "Is not a law of nature that all men are equal and free?"—Massachusetts Supreme Court

The Freeman decision set a precedent that influenced a similar case two years later. In that case, a runaway slave named Quock Walker sued for his freedom. The state supreme court upheld the county court jury decision, striking down 150 years of slavery in Massachusetts with these stirring words: "Is not a law of nature that all men are equal and free? Is not the laws of nature the laws of God? Is not the law of God then against slavery?"

The Northwest Ordinance of 1787

Four years after war's end, the Second Continental Congress passed the Northwest Ordinance. This law provided for the political organization of the vast region lying west of the Appalachian Mountains. With land-hungry Americans heading west in droves, many accompanied by their slaves, Congress had to decide which laws would govern this frontier territory—including what role, if any, slavery would play. The resulting decision—the Northwest Ordinance—redefined the future of slavery.

In order to stop the spread of slavery, the Ordinance in a single clause banned slaveholders from taking slaves north of the Ohio River. At the same time, the ruling allowed slaveholders who already lived in that region to

■ Susan Sedgwick, daughter of Theodore Sedgwick, painted Elizabeth Freeman's watercolor portrait in 1811 when Freeman was nearing the age of eighty. Eighteen years later, Freeman died. She left a will bequeathing to her daughter gowns belonging to Freeman's African-born parents. Freeman was buried in the Sedgwick family plot in the Stockbridge, Massachusetts, burial ground.

THE CONSTITUTIONAL SETTLEMENT

After the revolution, some Americans viewed the emerging political landscape with deep concern. Could the newly independent republic survive, they asked themselves, if one-fifth of its people were still in chains? Though the prospect of abolition loomed large at war's end, it vanished in a few sorrowful years. Reform-minded white Americans confronted two main problems in advancing their agenda: How would the nation compensate slaveowners for the immense investment they had made in their human chattel? How would free African Americans fit into the social fabric? Solutions to both problems hinged on a willingness to make economic sacrifices and to envision a biracial, republican society. To the crushing disappointment of hundreds of thousands of African Americans, white America lost its commitment to the vision. By the time members of the revolutionary generation lay in their graves, the United States had sacrificed its best opportunity to eradicate human bondage.

Roadblocks to Eradicating Slavery

Two cases illustrate the economic and social roadblocks abolition advocates encountered. In 1773, Benjamin Rush, a Philadelphia doctor, predicted an end to slavery. "National crimes," he stated in his antislavery pamphlet, "require national punishment" to be imposed on high unless "God shall cease to be just or merciful." But three years later, Rush purchased a slave, showing that a public antislavery stance did not keep men from enjoying the private advantages of a household slave. Ten years after that, while still holding William Grubber in bondage, Rush wrote that "the advocates for the poor Africans" are "considered as the benefactors of mankind and the man who dares to say a word in favor of reducing our black brethren to slavery is listened to with horror, and his company avoided by every body." Yet even after joining the Pennsylvania Abolition Society in 1784, Rush refused to release Grubber.

Rush was aware of the hypocrisy involved in publicly attacking slavery while personally owning a human being. But unwilling to lose his investment, he held Grubber for seven more years. Rush's problem was a microcosm of the nation's problem. Everyone who wanted to abolish slavery

keep their human property. Some lawmakers initially proposed a clause prohibiting slaveowners from taking bondspeople to lands south of the Ohio River as well, but a vote narrowly defeated the move.

The Ordinance gave white people living in the South what they wanted most: permission to extend slavery into a region where they knew cotton cultivation would soon spread. This area ultimately comprised the states of Kentucky, Tennessee, Alabama, and Mississippi. But antislavery northerners also got some of what they wanted: prohibition of slavery in a specified territory, which later consisted of Ohio, Indiana, Illinois, Michigan, and Wisconsin. The Northwest Ordinance thus made the first of many compromises by which leaders of the new nation determined where slavery could spread as Americans flooded west to set up homesteads.

knew that slaveowners would have to be compensated for the loss of their human property. Some called on the government to devise what they called a compensated emancipation scheme—a plan for raising taxes with which to pay slaveowners to free half a million bondspeople. But like Rush, the nation's leaders ultimately put economic interest above moral commitment and shied away from inflicting a tax burden on the citizenry.

Like Benjamin Rush, Thomas Jefferson prized liberty. He knew slavery compromised the American attempt to create the kind of republic all other nations could admire. But Jefferson also hated the thought of surrendering his own scores of slaves, who toiled on his endless renovations of his plantation, Monticello. At his death, Jefferson left so many debts that most of his slaves were sold at auction to satisfy his creditors.

Yet unlike Rush, Jefferson regarded black people as innately inferior to white people. He could not imagine the two living together in freedom. As early as 1776, he argued that the abolition of slavery would have to be followed by the recolonization of freed slaves in Africa or some remote region of the western United States. In his widely read *Notes on the State of Virginia* in 1782, Jefferson argued that freed Africans must be "removed beyond the reach of mixture." Africans were "inferior to the whites in . . . mind and body," he contended, because they were "originally a distinct race, or made distinct by time and circumstances."

While certain the new nation must somehow eradicate slavery, Jefferson worried that freed slaves would demand complete equality, which in turn would lead to a mixing of the races. This mixing would produce what a fellow Virginian called "a blended and homogenous race," a "condition of society in which the two races will be blended together; when the distinctions of colour shall be obliterated; when, like the Egyptians, we shall exhibit a dull and uniform complexion." Believing that freed slaves were "as incapable as children of taking care of themselves," Jefferson held fast to what became a widespread view among slaveholders: that an end to slavery would not only threaten racial purity and degrade white people's intellectual superiority to the level of the "inferior" Africans but also hurt newly freed black men and women.

Jefferson never overcame his "aversion . . . to the mixture of colour." In the early 1790s, he advocated banishing white Virginia women (but not black women) who bore "mulatto" children. The Virginia legislature defined the term as anyone "who shall have one-fourth part or more of Negro blood." Near the end of his long life, Jefferson maintained that "nothing is more certainly written in the book of fate than that the two races, equally free, cannot live in the same government."

Yet Jefferson had an intimate relationship with his slave Sally Hemings. Hemings was the half-sister of Jefferson's deceased wife, and her father was Jefferson's father-in-law. Hemings bore five children whose descendants trace their lineage to Jefferson. Recent DNA analysis has confirmed Jefferson's sexual liaison with his light-skinned slave.

■ Benjamin Banneker, pictured here in a woodcut from his *Almanac,* for many years kept a journal in which he recorded details about the natural world. One young white contemporary of Banneker's remembered that "he was very precise in conversation and exhibited deep reflection. . . . He seemed to be acquainted with everything of importance that was passing in the country."

Benjamin Banneker Chides Thomas Jefferson

In 1791, Benjamin Banneker implored Thomas Jefferson to change his views of African inferiority and chided him for continuing to hold slaves at Monticello. Jefferson's response, if any, has not been recorded.

We are a race of beings, who have long labored under the abuse and censure of the world, that we have long been looked upon with an eye of contempt, and that we have long been considered rather as brutish than human, and scarcely capable of mental endowments. . . . I apprehend you will embrace every opportunity to eradicate that train of absurd and false ideas and opinions which so generally prevail with respect to us, and that your sentiments are concurrent with mine, which are that one universal father hath given being to us all and that he hath not only made us all of one flesh but that he hath also without partiality afforded us all the same sensations, and endued us all with the same faculties. . . . Sir, suffer me to recall to your mind that time in which . . . you clearly saw into the injustice of a state of slavery, and in which you had just apprehensions of the horrors of its condition; it was now Sir, that your abhorrence thereof was so excited that you publicly held forth this true and invaluable

doctrine . . . : 'We hold these truths to be self evident, that all men are created equal, and that they are endowed by their creator with certain unalienable rights, that amongst these are life, liberty, and the pursuit of happiness.' . . . Sir, how pitiable is it to reflect, that although you were so fully convinced of the benevolence of the Father of Mankind, and of his equal and impartial distributions of these rights and privileges, . . . that you should at the same time counteract his mercies, in detaining by fraud and violence so numerous a part of my brethren, under groaning captivity and cruel oppression, that you should at the same time be found guilty of that most criminal act, which you professedly detested in others, with respect to yourselves.

—*"Benjamin Banneker to Thomas Jefferson, August 19, 1791."*

To view a longer version of this document, please go to *www.ablongman.com/carson/documents*.

Black Genius and Black Activism

Jefferson's staunch view of Africans as an "inferior" and "distinct" race blinded him to the examples of black genius that surfaced in the revolutionary era. For example, in reading Phillis Wheatley's poetry, Jefferson flatly dismissed her talent. "Religion, indeed, has produced a Phyllis Whately [*sic*]," Jefferson wrote, "but it could not produce a poet."

Jefferson also denigrated the work of Benjamin Banneker, a multitalented black man who used spheroid trigonometry to create an almanac that charted the heavenly bodies. The son of a freed slave from Guinea who married a

mixed-race woman, Banneker grew up near Baltimore on his parents' 100-acre farm. His English grandmother taught him to read. Banneker devoured books and developed an enviable aptitude for mathematics. At age twenty-two, he used a pocketknife to carve a wooden clock that kept accurate time and struck the hours for the next half-century. In his fifties, Banneker took up astronomy. He published almanacs with calculations charting the movement of the sun, moon, and planets throughout the year. Jefferson dismissed Banneker's calculations and surmised that he must have received help from a white patron. He concluded that Banneker "had a mind of very common stature indeed." Philadelphia's David

Rittenhouse, the nation's foremost astronomer, thought differently, praising Banneker's first almanac, published in 1792, as a "very extraordinary performance."

In the postwar turmoil, some African Americans found themselves once again on opposing sides, much as they had been during the war. This time the issue was economic. A postwar economic downturn, combined with stiff taxes levied to pay off the revolutionary debt, drove small farmers to the brink of bankruptcy. Deeming the taxes unfair in 1786, Daniel Shays led the farmers of western Massachusetts in armed protest against the court proceedings. Some free black farmers, also staggering under a grievous tax load, fought alongside the white rebels. Moses Sash, for example, served as an officer of the Shays organization and was a member of Daniel Shays's council. Meanwhile, other African Americans from Boston sided with the government in this standoff. For instance, Prince Hall offered the support of Boston's black Masons, founded by Hall in 1775. The members of the African Lodge, he wrote Governor James Bowdoin, "are willing to help and support . . . in this time of trouble and confusion, as you in your wisdom shall direct us."

Governor Bowdoin did not accept the black Masons' offer but encouraged Hall to petition the Massachusetts legislature to support a plan for their return to Africa. This ignited the first black-inspired recolonization movement in the new American republic. The movement, in turn, revealed African Americans' view of the young nation as irreparably divided by race. In a lengthy address to legislators, seventy-three "African Blacks" explained that only by finding a place of their own, beyond the reach of white power, could black people lead lives of dignity and fulfillment. The petitioners added that they wished "earnestly . . . to return to Africa, our native country . . . where we shall live among our equals and be more comfortable and happy, than we can be in our present situation." The state legislature refused to offer financial support for this scheme. Nevertheless, the petition planted the seeds for a black nationalism that resurfaced again and again in later decades.

■ Prince Hall was sixty-two years old when he authored an address to the African [Masonic] Lodge in 1797. In it, he urged an end to the "great grievance" that black Bostonians paid the same taxes as white freemen but their children were denied places in Boston's free schools. Hall died in Boston in 1807, just before Congress ended the slave trade.

A More Perfect Union?

In the torrid summer of 1787, the revolutionary generation received another chance to turn the rhetoric of liberty and equality into reality for African Americans. Meeting in Philadelphia, fifty-five delegates representing all the states except Rhode Island wrote a new constitution designed "to create a more perfect union." What emerged, however, was a compromise between large states and small states, between North and South, and between slavery opponents and slavery advocates. Many delegates who attended the convention owned human property and considered slavery a necessary evil. But others believed the time had come to put an end to the practice. For them, the question was not whether to do so, but when and how. Gouverneur Morris, representing Pennsylvania, stated his preference for "a tax paying for all the Negroes in the United States." This plan, Morris believed, would be a far better alternative to "saddl[ing] posterity" with a constitution that preserved slavery. But northern leaders, unwilling to shoulder financial responsibility for a compensated emancipation, rejected Morris's idea. Southerners concluded that the matter merited no further discussion.

Indeed, the delegates from South Carolina and Georgia exploded at the suggestion that the nation could uproot slavery from its economy and society. The "true question," argued South Carolina's John Rutledge ominously, "is whether the southern states shall or shall not be parties to the union." Was Rutledge bluffing? Georgia and South Carolina faced a precarious situation in 1787. Their white population was just one-twentieth of the nation's total, but their black population constituted about one-third of the national number. With the powerful Creek Indian confederacy and the Spanish in Florida threatening them militarily, no two states needed a strong national government more.

But no one called Rutledge's bluff. Many years later, James Madison, principal author of the Constitution, told his friend Lafayette that to try abolishing slavery in 1787 would have been akin to setting "a spark to a mass of gunpowder." Unwilling to create a national plan for freeing slaves, northern leaders simply ducked the issue.

As a result, the delegates designed a document that never explicitly mentioned slaves or slavery. Instead, they filled the Constitution with compromises designed to satisfy southerners' desire to preserve the institution. First, to determine the number of seats each state would have in the House of Representatives (which was based on a state's population), Congress decided to count three-fifths of all slaves (called "other persons") in the population calculation. This method guaranteed southern states many more votes in the House and in the Electoral College (which elected the president) than if slaves had not been counted. Second, a fugitive slave clause forbade the states from emancipating anyone who had fled bondage. The clause also required states to return such runaways to their owners. Third, another clause prohibited Congress from banning the importation of slaves (called "such persons as any of the states now existing shall think proper to admit") for twenty years. In 1807, Congress would decide whether or not to allow the slave trade to continue.

Together, these provisions protected the interests of slaveowners and their allies. In the South as well as in northern states such as New York, New Jersey, and Delaware, slaveholders acquired more and more human property. North and South Carolina, along with Georgia, kept the Atlantic slave trade open. Thus, as the new nation conducted its first experiments with democracy, slave ships continued disgorging thousands of African captives on American shores.

Under the Constitution, ratified in 1788, millions of newborn Americans entered the world as lifelong chattel. Runaway slaves—even if they managed to flee to a non–slave state—were forcibly returned to their masters if captured. A half-century later, Frederick Douglass reflected, "The Constitution of the United States—What is it? Who made it? For whom and for what was it made? Liberty and Slavery—opposite as Heaven and Hell—are both in the Constitution; and the oath to support the latter is an oath to perform that which God has made impossible. . . . If we adopt the preamble, with Liberty and Justice, we must repudiate the enacting clauses, with Kidnapping and Slave holding."

Historians have used the phrase "the compromise of 1787" to justify the revolutionary generation's accommodation of slavery. In explaining the failure of the new nation to come to grips with the institution, many historians point to the vulnerability of the newly forged union. The northern and southern states, they maintain, made a compromise in order to secure the cohesion of a constellation of states that had previously been separate colonies with distinct practices and beliefs.

But some historians argue that a national abolition plan might have strengthened rather than weakened that cohesion. Ending slavery, they contend, could have helped create a truly united nation out of loosely connected regions by eliminating a rankling sore on the body politic and enabling the United States to practice the ideological principles on which its birth was founded. Any society in which a people's behavior aligns with their principles and values is far stronger than one in which practice and principle are at odds. Moreover, those who assumed the new nation could *not* have abolished slavery make the all-too-common error of inevitability. Often, people who argue that certain regrettable historical events were inevitable are the same individuals who contributed to those events—not those who suffered their consequences.

In the end, all Americans paid a high price for the compromises that sullied the Constitution. Slavery continued to pose a painful dilemma for the new nation. Both advocates and opponents of the institution continued to cast about for a solution. When the "solution" finally came, it cost 600,000 soldiers their lives—one for each of the 600,000 black Americans whose unalienable rights the Constitution had ignored to create a more "perfect union."

Long before the Civil War broke out, some Americans continued to propose ways to end slavery. Ferdinando Fairfax, a man with ties to Virginia's largest planters, published a plan in 1790 for phasing out the institution. A protégé of George Washington, Fairfax claimed that many slaveholders were ready to release their slaves voluntarily and that many others could be induced to do so with compensation. But these planters, Fairfax said, would never agree to equal rights for free black people. Therefore, newly liberated slaves would have to be repatriated to Africa.

In 1796, St. George Tucker, another prominent Virginian, laid before the state legislature a full plan for the gradual abolition of slavery. Tucker voiced alarm over the first federal census of 1790, which showed Virginia's slave population rising rapidly. He expressed fear that the massive slave revolt that erupted in Haiti in 1791 might spread to the southern states. He also quoted the French philosopher Montesquieu that "slavery not only violates the Laws of Nature and of civil Society, it also wounds the best Forms of Government; in a Democracy, where all Men are Equal, Slavery is contrary to the Spirit of the Constitution." Tucker's comments fell on deaf ears. But a few months later, Jefferson prophetically wrote that "if something is not done, and done soon, we shall be the murderers of our own children . . . ; the revolutionary storm, now sweeping the globe, will be upon us."

> "If something is not done, and done soon, we shall be the murderers of our own children."—*Thomas Jefferson*

THE RESETTLEMENT OF AFRICAN AMERICAN LOYALISTS

For those African Americans who had joined the British side in the revolution, the Constitution mattered little because the United States was no longer their home. In 1783, just after England and the United States signed the Treaty of Paris, the British had to find new homes for these thousands of former slaves. American diplomats tried to persuade the British to surrender the freed slaves to their former masters, but the British refused. Yet where would England send the free black loyalists? Its overseas colonies, notably the West Indies sugar islands, were built on slave labor and were no place for a large community of free black people. England itself had no desire to see a wave of ex-slaves pour into the island nation. Officials in London and other major cities already lamented the growing number of impoverished black people seeking public support. Instead black loyalists were sent to Nova Scotia, the easternmost province of Canada and, unlike all other English colonies in the Americas, a free labor agricultural society.

Black Nova Scotians

Thomas Peters and his family were among the 3,000 black persons evacuated from New York City for relocation to Nova Scotia in late 1783. The journey was grueling. Gales blew the ship off course; not until the following spring did the Peterses and their fellow black settlers reach their new home. Peters led his family ashore at Annapolis Royal, a small port on the east side of the Bay of Fundy, which looked across the water to the Maine coast. In this raw, remote corner of the earth, the former American slaves sought to establish new lives based on freedom.

But their dream of life, liberty, and the pursuit of happiness soon turned into a nightmare. The refugees were segregated in impoverished villages and given scraps of rocky land they found impossible to till. Deprived of the rights normally extended to British subjects, they were forced to work on road construction in return for promised provisions. With few resources and scant support from the British, they sank into poverty. Less than a year after Peters and the others arrived from New York, British soldiers resettling in Nova Scotia attacked the black villages, burning, looting, and pulling down residents' houses.

Peters became a leader of one contingent of the New York evacuees who were settled at Digby, near Annapolis Royal. About 500 white and 100 black families competed for land there. Discouraged by his inability to get allotments of workable land and adequate support for his people, Peters traveled across the bay to St. John, New Brunswick, in search of unallocated tracts. Working as a millwright, he struggled to feed his family and to find suitable homesteads for other black settlers. He also sought to ward off the so-called bodysnatchers already at work reenslaving blacks and selling them in the United States or West Indies. To worsen matters, crop failures brought a punishing famine in 1788.

Return to Africa

By 1790, Peters and his colleagues had endured six long years of hand-to-mouth existence. Peters concluded that his people needed to move on and seek true independence elsewhere. Representing more than 200 black families in St. John and Digby, Peters composed a petition to the Secretary of State in London. Then, despite the risk of reenslavement that accompanied any black person who braved an ocean voyage, he sailed from Halifax to the English capital with little more in his pocket than the fragile piece of paper. In the document, the petitioners pleaded for fair treatment in Nova Scotia or resettlement "wherever the wisdom of government may think proper to provide for [my people] as free subjects of the British Empire."

The black leader could not have chosen a better time to head for London. English abolitionists such as Granville Sharp, Thomas Clarkson, and William Wilberforce had stepped up their activism. Though they had failed to force through Parliament a bill abolishing the English slave trade, they did win passage of a bill to charter the Sierra Leone Company for thirty-one years. The deal included a grant of trading and settlement rights on the African coast. Even better, the recruits for the new colony would consist of the former slaves from North America now living in Nova Scotia.

Peters returned to Nova Scotia a year later. There, he spread the word that the English government would provide free transport for any black Nova Scotians who wished to journey to Sierra Leone. Once on the African coast, he explained, they would receive plots of land. John Clarkson, the younger brother of one of England's best-known abolitionists, traveled with Peters to oversee the resettlement plan.

This opportunity to return to Africa excited the imaginations of most black Canadians. Nonetheless, some white Nova Scotian leaders felt reluctant to let the black people leave. Governor John Parr, for example, adamantly opposed the exodus, fearing that if too many black people headed for Sierra Leone, everyone would know he had failed to provide adequately for them in Canada. Other white Nova Scotians protested the resettlement plan because they stood to lose a considerable number of customers for their small

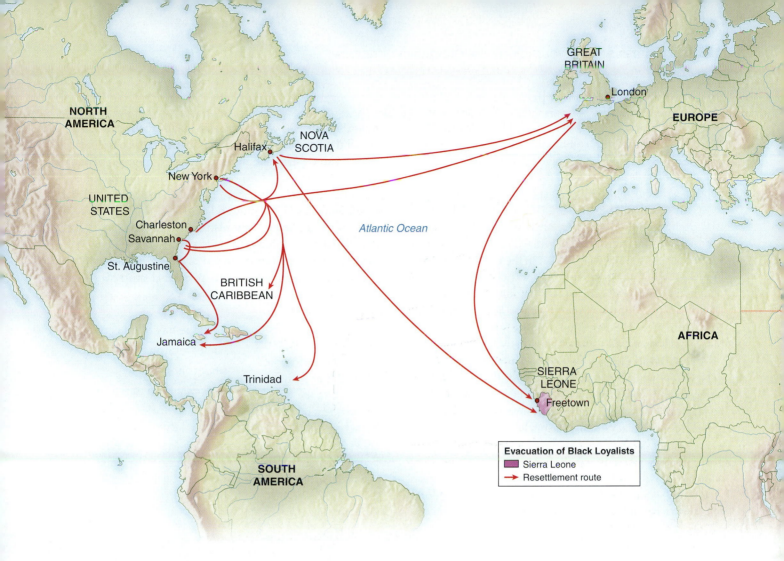

■ **MAP 5.3** **Evacuation of Black Loyalists**

At war's end, the British transported some 7,000 slaves belonging to white American loyalists to Florida, Jamaica, and other slave colonies, where they remained enslaved. Other black people who had joined the British were transported first to Nova Scotia and finally to Sierra Leone, in western Africa.

businesses. Still others forged indentures and work contracts they claimed bound black people to them. Some even refused to settle back wages and debts in hopes of discouraging black Canadians from joining the Sierra Leone venture. "The white people . . . were very unwilling that we should go," wrote one black minister from the Annapolis area, "though they had been very cruel to us, and treated many of us as though we had been slaves."

But neither white officials nor white settlers could stem the tide of black enthusiasm for resettlement to Africa. Working through black preachers—the principal leaders in the Canadian black communities—Peters and Clarkson spread the word of the Sierra Leone plan. The telling soon took on overtones of the Old Testament story about the delivery of the Israelites from bondage in Egypt. Some 350 blacks trekked through the rain to Birchtown, a black settlement near Annapolis, to hear their blind and lame preacher, Moses Wilkinson, explain the Sierra Leone Company's terms. Clark-

son wrote that "it struck me forcibly that perhaps the future welfare and happiness, nay the very lives of the individuals then before me, might depend in a great measure upon the words which I should deliver. . . . At length I rose up, and explained circumstantially the object, progress, and result of the embassy of Thomas Peters to England." Ultimately, almost 1,200 black Canadians chose to return to Africa. Only fourteen accepted an offer of army service in the British West Indies. By the end of 1791, all the prospective Sierra Leonians had made their way to the port of debarkation at Halifax. Some had trudged 340 miles around the Bay of Fundy through dense forest and snow-blanketed terrain.

Peters and Clarkson inspected each of the fifteen ships assigned for the return to Africa, ordering some decks removed, ventilation holes fitted, and berths constructed. Remembering the horrors of his own middle passage thirty-two years before, Peters resolved that the return trip would be different. As crew members prepared the fleet, the Sierra

Leone recruits made the best of barracks life in Halifax. They shared living quarters in community groups and held religious services. Moreover, they talked about how they would soon "kiss their dear Malagueta," a reference to the Malagueta pepper, or "grains of paradise," that thrived in West Africa.

Setting sail on January 15, 1792, the ships held men, women, and children whose collective experiences in North America ran the gamut of slave travail. The African-born Charles Wilkinson, a former soldier in the Black Guides and Pioneers, made the trip with his mother and two small daughters. Also on board were religious leaders such as David George, founder of the first black Baptist church in North America in Silver Bluff, South Carolina, in 1773; Moses Wilkinson, who had escaped his Virginia master in 1776; and Boston King, who had converted to Methodism in New York while serving with the British. The most elderly voyager was a woman whom Clarkson described in his shipboard journal as "an old woman of 104 years of age who had requested me to take her, that she might lay her bones in her native country." Young and old, African-born and American-born, military veterans and those too young to have seen wartime service—all shared the dream of finding a place where they could govern themselves and live in freedom. This was to be their year of jubilee.

But they had to endure additional perils before reaching Africa. Boston King, who had become a preacher in Nova Scotia, remarked that the winter gales were the worst in the seasoned crew members' history. Two of the fifteen ship captains and sixty-five black émigrés died en

route. Snow squalls and heavy gales scattered the small fleet, yet all the vessels finally reached the African coast after a two-month voyage. The ships had crossed an ocean that for nearly 300 years had borne Africans in the opposite direction as shackled captives bound for the land of misery.

Legend says that Thomas Peters, sick from shipboard fever, led his shipmates ashore in Sierra Leone singing, "The day of jubilee is come; return ye ransomed sinners home." Yet despite their joy at returning to Africa, the settlers encountered difficulties. Provisions ran short. Diseases claimed lives. The land distribution proceeded slowly. British councilors sent from London to supervise the colony acted irresponsibly. Racial discord reigned. As the elected speaker-general for the black settlers in their dealings with the white governing council, Peters tried to stem the spreading frustration among his people. Some settlers spoke of replacing the councilors appointed by the Sierra Leone Company with an elected black government. This incipient rebellion never came to pass, but

> "The day of jubilee is come; return ye ransomed sinners home."
> —Thomas Peters

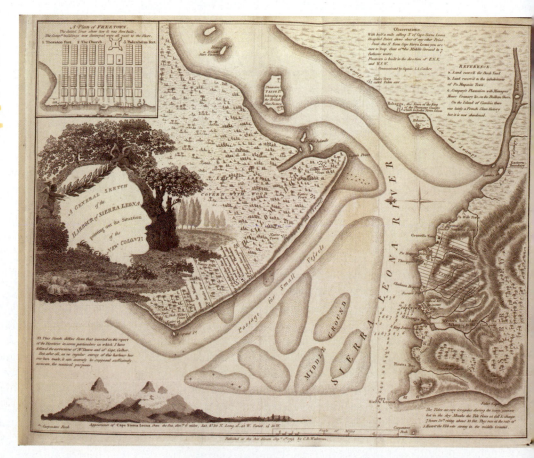

■ This map of Sierra Leone, drawn about a year after the Peters family arrived, shows the land granted to black settlers. Freetown appears at the lower left, west of the "Land granted to the Settlers." Several "Native" towns appear in the part of the country north of the Sierra Leone River. A "Town of Runaway Slaves" is marked at the lower left. "Plantation Tasso belonging to the British Slave Factory" appears on the largest island in the river. This place name indicates that while British abolitionists were settling former slaves in Sierra Leone, British merchants and investors were still engaging in the slave trade there.

Peters remained the leader of the unofficial opposition to the white government. He died in the spring of 1792—less than four months after stepping foot on Africa's shores. His family and friends buried him in Freetown, where his descendants live today.

CONCLUSION

Thomas Peters lived for fifty-four years. For most of his adult life, he struggled for both survival and freedom. He crossed the Atlantic four times. He lived in Yorubaland, French Louisiana, North Carolina, New York, Nova Scotia, New Brunswick, Bermuda, London, and Sierra Leone. He worked as a field hand, millwright, ship hand, laborer, soldier, and community leader. He also struggled against slave masters, government officials, and hostile white neighbors. He worked to secure political rights, social equity, and human dignity for himself and other former slaves.

Peters's story provides a glimpse at black Americans' lives during a pivotal time in history. When war broke out between Britain and its colonies, white revolutionaries' rhetoric about British tyranny and unalienable rights spread quickly among enslaved men and women. Taking the white colonists' cries for freedom at face value, black people petitioned for the end of slavery. Many joined white colonists who themselves lamented the contradiction between white planters' freedom claims and their continued enslavement of half a million human beings.

Thousands of bondspeople who fled their masters to claim the freedom promised by the British made the American Revolution the first large-scale slave rebellion in North America. Other enslaved blacks joined the American cause, believing their decision would win them their freedom as well. Thousands of individual acts of defiance and courage created a collective legend of black struggle, testified to black strength, and set forth a black vision of a better future.

For Peters and thousands like him, war's end meant finding new homes as British subjects—first in Nova Scotia and then in Sierra Leone in what became American slaves' first return to the ancient homeland. But back in the newborn United States, a far greater number of African Americans faced a future made uncertain by the compromise-riddled Constitution of 1787. Slavery stood on the brink of extinction in the northern states but in the South, where most bondspeople lived, black people had scant hope of regaining their freedom when George Washington assumed office in 1790 as the nation's first president.

FURTHER READING

Bedini, Silvio A. *The Life of Benajmin Banneker* (New York: Scribner, 1972).

Berlin, Ira, and Ronald Hoffman, eds. *Slavery and Freedom in the Era of the American Revolution* (Charlottesville: University Press of Virginia, 1983).

Crow, Jeffrey J. *The Black Experience in Revolutionary North Carolina* (Raleigh: North Carolina Department of Cultural Resources, 1977).

Davis, David Brion. *The Problem of Slavery in the Age of Revolution, 1770–1823* (Ithaca, NY: Cornell University Press, 1975).

Finkelman, Paul. *Slavery and the Founders: Race and Liberty in the Age of Jefferson* (Armonk, NY: M. E. Sharpe, 1996).

Frey, Sylvia. *Water from the Rock: Black Resistance in a Revolutionary Age* (Princeton, NJ: Princeton University Press, 1991).

George, Carol V. R. *Segregated Sabbaths: Richard Allen and the Rise of Independent Black Churches, 1760–1840* (New York: Oxford University Press, 1973).

Gordon-Reed, Annette. *Thomas Jefferson and Sally Hemings: An American Controversy* (Charlottesville: University Press of Virginia, 1997).

Harris, Sheldon H. *Paul Cuffe: Black America and the African Return* (New York: Simon and Schuster, 1972).

Holton, Woody. *Forced Founders: Indians, Debtors, Slaves, and the Making of the American Revolution in Virginia* (Chapel Hill: University of North Carolina Press, 1999).

Kaplan, Sidney, and Emma Nogrady Kaplan. *The Black Presence in the Era of the American Revolution* (Amherst: University of Massachusetts Press, 1989).

McLeod, Duncan. *Slavery, Race, and the American Revolution* (Cambridge: Cambridge University Press, 1974).

Nash, Gary B. *Race and Revolution* (Madison, WI: Madison House, 1990).

Nash, Gary B., and Jean R. Soderlund. *Freedom by Degrees: Emancipation in Pennsylvania and Its Aftermath* (New York: Oxford University Press, 1991).

Olwell, Robert. *Masters, Slaves, and Subjects: The Culture of Power in South Carolina Low Country, 1740–1790* (Ithaca, NY: Cornell University Press, 1998).

Patterson, Orlando. *Freedom*, vol. 1, *Freedom in the Making of Western Culture* (New York: Basic Books, 1991).

Quarles, Benjamin. *The Negro in the American Revolution* (Chapel Hill: University of North Carolina Press, 1996).

Walker, James W. St. G. *The Black Loyalists: The Search for a Promised Land in Nova Scotia and Sierra Leone, 1783–1870* (New York: Africana, 1976).

Wilson, Ellen G. *The Loyal Blacks* (New York: G. P. Putnam's Sons, 1976).

Zilversmit, Arthur. *The First Emancipation: The Abolition of Slavery in the North* (Chicago: University of Chicago Press, 1967).

CHAPTER 6

■ A female black vendor sells pepper-pot soup in Philadelphia.

After the Revolution: Constructing Free Life and Combating Slavery, 1787–1816

Richard Allen and Absalom Jones Lead Church Walkout

"Meeting had begun, and they were nearly done singing, and just as we got to the seats, the elder said, 'Let us pray.'" With these words, former slave Richard Allen remembered a momentous spring day in 1792 at St. George's Methodist church in Philadelphia. "We had not been long upon our knees before I heard considerable scuffling and low talking," Allen related. "I raised my head up and saw one of the [white] trustees, . . . having hold of the Rev. Absalom Jones, pulling him up off of his knees, and saying, 'You must get up—you must not kneel here.' Mr. Jones replied, 'Wait until prayer is over.' Mr. H_____ M_____ said, 'No you must get up now, or I will call for aid and force you away.'" Born into slavery in Philadelphia, Allen was thirty-two years old when he witnessed this scene. Nearly seventy years old when he recounted the incident, he still remembered the confrontation vividly. "Mr. Jones said, 'Wait until prayer is over, and I will get up and trouble you no more.' By this time prayer was over, and we all went out of the church in a body, and they were no more plagued with us in the church."

At St. George's, white church officials had abruptly decided to relegate black worshipers to a segregated section. The incident Allen described was a defining moment in African American history because it initiated the formation of independent northern black churches. It also sounded a foreboding note for the city of Philadelphia by heightening racial tensions there. Moreover, it proved a crucial moment for the nation, whose course Congress charted in the chambers of Philadelphia's Independence Hall only a few blocks from St. George's. Worried

129

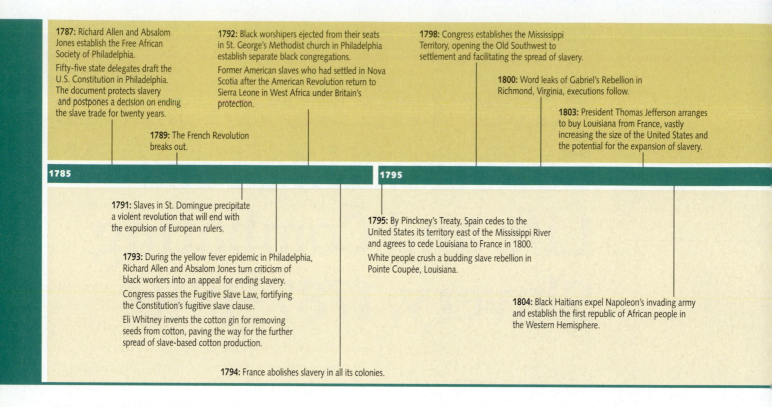

1787: Richard Allen and Absalom Jones establish the Free African Society of Philadelphia.

Fifty-five state delegates draft the U.S. Constitution in Philadelphia. The document protects slavery and postpones a decision on ending the slave trade for twenty years.

1789: The French Revolution breaks out.

1791: Slaves in St. Domingue precipitate a violent revolution that will end with the expulsion of European rulers.

1793: During the yellow fever epidemic in Philadelphia, Richard Allen and Absalom Jones turn criticism of black workers into an appeal for ending slavery.

Congress passes the Fugitive Slave Law, fortifying the Constitution's fugitive slave clause.

Eli Whitney invents the cotton gin for removing seeds from cotton, paving the way for the further spread of slave-based cotton production.

1794: France abolishes slavery in all its colonies.

1792: Black worshipers ejected from their seats in St. George's Methodist church in Philadelphia establish separate black congregations.

Former American slaves who had settled in Nova Scotia after the American Revolution return to Sierra Leone in West Africa under Britain's protection.

1795: By Pinckney's Treaty, Spain cedes to the United States its territory east of the Mississippi River and agrees to cede Louisiana to France in 1800.

White people crush a budding slave rebellion in Pointe Coupée, Louisiana.

1798: Congress establishes the Mississippi Territory, opening the Old Southwest to settlement and facilitating the spread of slavery.

1800: Word leaks of Gabriel's Rebellion in Richmond, Virginia, executions follow.

1803: President Thomas Jefferson arranges to buy Louisiana from France, vastly increasing the size of the United States and the potential for the expansion of slavery.

1804: Black Haitians expel Napoleon's invading army and establish the first republic of African people in the Western Hemisphere.

1785

1795

about a tremendous black rebellion brewing in St. Domingue, the French West Indies island later called Haiti, legislators viewed the confrontation at St. George's as a sign of similar tension in the United States.

Even before he witnessed the incident at St. George's, Allen had faced a series of tests. In 1779, he gained his freedom when his Delaware master, convinced by Methodist preachers that slaveholding was a sin, agreed to free Allen and his brother if the two men promised to pay him 60 pounds gold or silver in installments. The brothers agreed. Allen then found work sawing cordwood and hauling salt for the patriots during the American Revolution. But already he had a different kind of life's work in mind. Several years earlier, he had begun attending Methodist meetings at a nearby farm. "One night I thought hell would be my portion," Allen remembered. "I cried unto Him who delighteth to hear the prayers of a poor sinner, and all of a sudden my dungeon shook, my chains flew off, and, glory to God, I cried. My soul was filled." From this point on, he later wrote, "my lot was cast."

For the duration of the war, Allen supported himself as a wagon driver and cobbler in Wilmington, Delaware, while gradually paying off his purchase price. At the same time, he ventured into the countryside to preach the Methodist faith.

By 1783, when the Treaty of Paris concluded the American war for independence, the twenty-three-year-old former slave was delivering rousing sermons to anyone who would gather around him. Believing "it to be his Duty to Travel abroad as a Preacher of Righteousness," the young man traveled thousands of miles from New York to South Carolina, even spending two months preaching among Native Americans. Then in the autumn of 1785, he headed north to a small village west of Philadelphia. Local Methodist leaders called him to their city to preach to the small group of black Methodists attending services there. Allen had returned to the city of his birth.

Richard Allen was one of the numerous visionaries who emerged to lead the free black communities taking shape in the 1780s. The largest of these communities arose in maritime cities from Boston to New Orleans. Free black men and women congregated in these urban centers because they found work and companionship there and could attend independent black churches. Most sizable towns between Maine and Louisiana also had communities of free African Americans.

In Philadelphia, Allen lifted the spirits of hundreds of black people. "I preached in the commons, in Southwark, Northern Liberties, and wherever I could find an opening," he

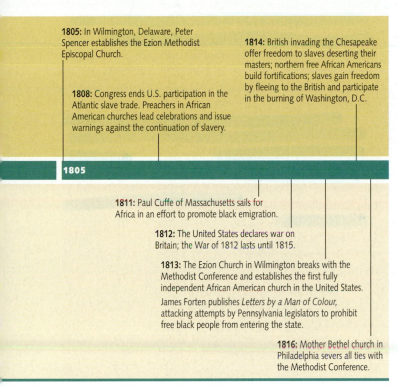

1805: In Wilmington, Delaware, Peter Spencer establishes the Ezion Methodist Episcopal Church.

1808: Congress ends U.S. participation in the Atlantic slave trade. Preachers in African American churches lead celebrations and issue warnings against the continuation of slavery.

1814: British invading the Chesapeake offer freedom to slaves deserting their masters; northern free African Americans build fortifications; slaves gain freedom by fleeing to the British and participate in the burning of Washington, D.C.

1805

1811: Paul Cuffe of Massachusetts sails for Africa in an effort to promote black emigration.

1812: The United States declares war on Britain; the War of 1812 lasts until 1815.

1813: The Ezion Church in Wilmington breaks with the Methodist Conference and establishes the first fully independent African American church in the United States. James Forten publishes *Letters by a Man of Colour*, attacking attempts by Pennsylvania legislators to prohibit free black people from entering the state.

1816: Mother Bethel church in Philadelphia severs all ties with the Methodist Conference.

remembered. "I frequently preached twice a day, at 5 o'clock in the morning and in the evening, and it was not uncommon for me to preach from four to five times a day." But that was before the white Methodists at St. George's demanded that Allen and other black worshipers sit in a separate section of the church.

Even as black worshipers endured this assault on their dignity, two profound transformations were overturning the Atlantic world. Both took inspiration from the American revolutionary ideology holding that all men are created equal and are entitled by birth to certain rights. The first of these transformations, the French Revolution, erupted in Paris in 1789 and climaxed in the bloody Reign of Terror. The second transformation, a slave rebellion that broke out in 1791 in the French sugar and coffee island of St. Domingue, compelled Americans to consider whether their experiment in democracy would include *racial* equality.

In the United States, the questions and passions stirred up by these two revolutions played out at the individual level. Though the Constitution preserved the institution of slavery, antislavery sentiment that had percolated during the revolutionary period was far from dead. The rebellion in St. Domingue demonstrated that slaves would not necessarily

resign themselves to perpetual bondage. Though slavery was dying in the North, questions remained about how free black people would fit into the dominant white society there. Would northern states confer equal rights on black citizens—as their state constitutions implied? Could black and white people live together as fellow citizens in integrated neighborhoods, churches, workplaces, and marketplaces? How would black Americans define themselves as a people? In the South, would slavery wither away as the slave trade ended, as many white leaders believed? Would Congress listen to petitioners urging the end of slavery? If the new nation became a republic for white men only, how would slaves and free black people respond?

Despite all these questions, black Americans moved energetically to enhance the quality of their lives. In this chapter, we show how the expanding free population of African Americans constructed vital communities and churches of their own as part of their struggle to gain respect and equality. We also examine how the American revolutionary ideology of unalienable rights fueled revolution in France, which ignited the slave rebellion in St. Domingue and inspired similar uprisings in Virginia. Yet twin strivings—to overthrow slavery in the South and obtain political and social equality in the North—could not halt the expansion of slavery or stop most white people's intensifying hostility toward dark-skinned Americans. Watching revolutionary egalitarianism fade, African Americans had little choice but to explore fresh options and forge new identities for themselves.

THE EMERGENCE OF FREE BLACK COMMUNITIES

"Men are more influenced by their moral equals than by their superiors" and "are more easily governed by persons chosen by themselves for that purpose than by persons who are placed over them by accidental circumstances." Richard Allen and Absalom Jones spoke these words when they set out to establish an all-black congregation in Philadelphia shortly after the U.S. Constitution was ratified. Such democratic thoughts about self-governance strongly shaped African American community life as the ranks of free black people began to swell in the new republic. The creation of free black communities during the nation's early decades laid the foundation for African Americans' later urban experience.

■ Richard Allen's earnest demeanor shows in this portrait by an unknown artist. His reputation for honesty spread just after he purchased his freedom in 1779. Finding a trunk with a small fortune in silver and gold, Allen placed newspaper notices advertising his discovery. He refused to accept a generous reward from the grateful owner who claimed the trunk. Finally, he accepted a new suit of coarse cloth.

An Expanding Free Black Population

Only a few thousand African Americans had their freedom on the eve of the American Revolution. But after the war, the numbers of free black people swelled—to nearly 60,000 by 1790, to 108,000 by 1800, and to more than 233,000 by 1820. Several forces fueled this growth. Some African

Americans purchased their own freedom or sued for it in the courts, while others won their liberty by fleeing slavery. Some slaveowners freed their bondspeople, and several state legislatures decreed the abolition of slavery. Finally, immigration of liberated people from places such as St. Domingue further expanded the ranks of free black Americans.

During the early years of the new republic, roughly 60 percent of the nation's free black people lived in the South and 40 percent in the North. However, in the South, free black people were a minority of all people of color. By contrast, freed black people in the North far exceeded the dwindling number of slaves. Free black people tended to live in the Upper South. About eight of every ten lived in Delaware, Maryland, Virginia, and Louisiana (see Figure 6.1). In 1810, for example, only 14,000 free blacks lived south of Virginia (more than half of them in Louisiana). That same year, 94,000 resided in Virginia, Maryland, Delaware, and the District of Columbia. Overall, the proportion of African Americans who were free inched upward in the South—to 5 percent in 1790, 7 percent in 1800, and 8 percent in 1820.

Throughout the country, a majority of free African Americans congregated in the cities, where they could most readily find friends, marriage partners, and work. By 1820, nine cities had more than 1,000 free African Americans. By that same year, the black communities in New York, Philadelphia, Baltimore, and New Orleans exceeded 6,000 residents (see Figure 6.2). Other cities—such as Cincinnati, Ohio; Savannah, Georgia; Providence, Rhode Island; and Albany, New York—numbered fewer than a thousand free black people but were seeing these numbers rise as well.

Free Black Work Lives

With many tasting freedom for the first time, liberated African Americans moved to establish fulfilling home and

■ **FIGURE 6.1** **Free Black Population by Region, 1790–1820**

The Upper South includes Delaware, Maryland, Virginia, District of Columbia, Kentucky, Missouri, Tennessee, and North Carolina. The Lower South comprises South Carolina, Georgia, Alabama, Mississippi, and Louisiana.

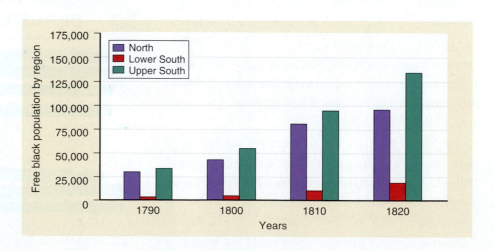

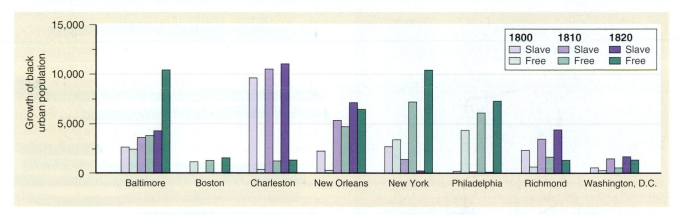

■ FIGURE 6.2 **The Growth of the Black Urban Population, 1790–1820**

By 1820, New York and Baltimore had the largest number of free black people. However, Baltimore, like New Orleans, had thousands of slaves as well. Yet Baltimore was the only southern city where free blacks outnumbered slaves.

work lives in the cities. The rise of industrialization, which depended on power-driven machinery more than human labor, might have afforded new employment opportunities for those emerging from slavery. However, many owners of textile mills, machine foundries, and boot and shoe factories refused to hire black workers. These employers preferred native-born and immigrant whites, who they saw as more reliable and educable. Thus, most free black people had to toil at unskilled labor. Even in these jobs, they faced intense competition from Irish and English immigrants. Black men typically worked as stevedores loading and unloading cargo on the wharves; as cellar-, well-, and gravediggers; as chimneysweeps and ash haulers; and as construction laborers, ragpickers who collected discarded clothing, bootblacks, stablehands, and woodcutters.

Black women, for their part, labored predominantly as washerwomen or domestic workers for white families. Many of them lived in their employers' households. But every city also had independent black seamstresses, cooks, basketmakers, confectioners, and street vendors—women who hawked pies, vegetables, fruits, fish, clothing, and handmade items from small stands. Other African American women served as proprietors of small shops, boardinghouses, and oyster cellars; some worked as midwives, teachers, and nurses. Because these women's earnings were indispensable to their families' survival, the lives of free African American women followed a different course than those of white women. While more and more middle-class white women were withdrawing from

work outside the home to serve in the emerging role of home keeper, most middle-class black women continued to work outside their homes.

Many of the available occupations offered former slaves a new sense of dignity. Many such jobs required black people to make important decisions and organize others' work. Those working for themselves, such as ragpickers, could control numerous aspects of their work life, such as which streets to walk, when to set out, and when to quit work for the day. Though most ragpickers earned sparse wages, they did not have to withstand the insulting comments of a boss, maintain a schedule set by somebody else, or face layoffs during economic downturns.

In some occupations, free African Americans not only operated independently but also developed a near monopoly on the trade. In most cases, white workers did not want these jobs. These occupations included oyster selling, carriage driving, chimneysweeping, shoe blacking, and hairdressing.

Most opportunities for black self-employment lay in service positions or the skilled crafts—for example, carting; personal services such as hairdressing, barbering, and catering; and shopkeeping and trading, especially in the clothing and food trades. Every city had its black shoemakers, carpenters, tailors, and bakers. These men and women provided valued services and crafted much-needed articles for other African Americans and sometimes for white people.

The free black Philadelphian James Forten, whom we met in Chapter 5, is an apt example. Forten joined the

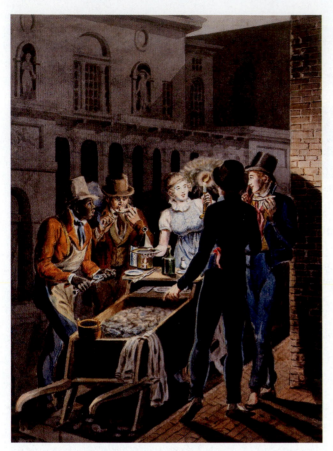

■ Pavel Petrovich Svinin, secretary to the Russian consul general in Philadelphia, painted this street scene in about 1812. Here he portrays black oystermen in top hats and aprons, selling their delicacies to theatergoers from charcoal-burning barrows.

patriot cause as a teenager and was captured by the British. He managed to escape and took to sea as a deckhand on a merchant ship bound for London in 1784. There he sewed canvas sails on the Thames River docks. Forten returned to Philadelphia a year later and apprenticed himself to white sailmaker Robert Bridges. Within a year, he was a foreman overseeing white sailmaker apprentices. When Bridges retired in 1798, Forten took over the enterprise. Business proved so brisk that by 1805 he was employing a racially mixed crew of twenty-five apprentices. His workers crafted the sails used on many of the city's largest merchant ships.

Though racism kept most free blacks from the most promising occupations, it could not stifle African American ambitions. Philadelphia's Richard Allen exemplifies this drive. Best known as a religious leader, Allen was a entrepreneur from the day of his release from slavery. Though once a farm slave in Delaware, he quickly honed his shoemaking and wagon-driving skills as a young man. He added to this reper-

toire after gaining his freedom and moving to Philadelphia. There he purchased his first piece of property in 1792. In the years that followed, he bought and sold real estate frequently. His household almost always included several servants and apprentices. Supplementing his meager minister's salary, Allen worked variously as shoemaker, housewares dealer, chimneysweep supervisor, and shoe store proprietor. He often pursued several of these occupations simultaneously while leading the black Methodist church. In 1794, he attempted to establish a nail factory with his friend Absalom Jones. Although the project never materialized, it reflected Allen's ambitious spirit—one shared by many free African Americans in their first generation of liberty.

Of all the black-dominated occupations, seafaring had special importance for free African Americans. From almost the moment the Atlantic slave trade brought the first Africans to the Americas, merchants and ship captains took enslaved African men and boys—such as Olaudah Equiano—to sea with them. After the revolution, black freedmen sailed before the mast in large numbers. As hard and dangerous as the work was, life at sea imposed far less racism on black people than life ashore did. To be sure, bigotry prevented all but a handful of black mariners from becoming captains. Nonetheless, ship captains prized any man, regardless of color, who could splice rope properly, haul down canvas quickly in a sudden storm, or scramble aloft to handle the topsails. In the early nineteenth century, black mariners usually received pay equal to that of their white messmates of the same rank and skill. Nearly one out of four mariners sailing out of New York, Philadelphia, Baltimore, New Orleans, and Newport (Rhode Island) was an African American. This proportion far exceeded free black people's share of these cities' populations. In some cases, white captains sailed with all-black crews. Moreover, the average black sailor worked at sea many more years than most white sailors because he had limited opportunities ashore. Thus, the old salts of the new nation's fleet were disproportionately black.

As free black communities burgeoned, small cadres of professionals and entrepreneurs emerged to create the nucleus of a black middle class. These communities sprang up mostly in the North but also developed in southern seaports such as New Orleans and Charleston. The search for self-employment stemmed from the same impulse that spurred the creation of independent black churches: the desire to live on one's own terms and reduce dependency on white people. At the top of the pyramid of independently employed free African Americans stood a small but influential number of landlords, doctors, ministers, musicians, and teachers. For example, Eleanor Harris—described at her death in 1797 as a "woman of character" and a "well quali-

■ Whaling captain Absalom F. Boston sat for his portrait with gold hoop earrings and a white shirt under his formal coat. Sailing out of Nantucket in 1822 in the *Industry* with an all-black crew, Boston saw his exploits widely reported in Massachusetts newspapers.

fied tutoress of children"—was one of the earliest of the female black teachers who later headed the classrooms of young African Americans. James Derham, once owned by a Quaker doctor in Philadelphia, became an accomplished physician in his own right in New Orleans. At the turn of the century, Samuel Wilson was so highly regarded for his skill in treating cancers that white Philadelphians readily sought his help. Philadelphia's Robert Bogle, a former slave, turned the idea of contracting food services at funerals, weddings, and parties into a profession, as did enterprising free black people in Charleston, South Carolina.

Family Life

In leaving slavery behind, free African Americans put a priority on reuniting families or creating new ones. Neither of these proved easy. The profound dislocation caused by the Revolutionary War, the migration of free black people north and west after the war, and the scourge of poverty made setting up a household difficult. Many black men and women postponed marriage until they could gain their financial footing; thus, black families tended to be smaller than white families in this era. In the countryside, couples who did marry usually lived in small cottages shared with relatives or friends. In the cities,

all but the most fortunate black people doubled and tripled up in crudely built houses squeezed into narrow courts and blind alleys. The most abjectly poor lived in attics and cellars. Even though African Americans competed with Irish and German immigrants for jobs, they often shared space with these struggling immigrants. Such "walking cities," where people lived near their places of work, were not segregated by race or even class. In every ward and neighborhood, black and white people of all backgrounds and classes interacted daily.

Accommodating themselves to stark reality, most free African Americans built their households step by step. For at least a few years after emancipation, many African Americans had little choice but to remain in white households. They saved their earnings, and many indentured their children to white masters and mistresses to save on food and clothing. Eventually, some could afford to do domestic work in white households by day and then go home to relatives, friends, and boarders by night. With some luck, they could establish individual households of their own. In Boston and New York, for example, about one-third of all free black people lived in white households in 1790, but thirty years later, only one-sixth did so. In southern cities, establishing independent black households took longer.

By 1820, three-quarters or more of the free black households in most major cities contained at least one adult male and one adult female. These numbers suggest that the female-centered form of slave family life—unavoidable owing to the sale and early death of many enslaved black men—gave way to the two-parent family form as more and more African Americans gained their freedom.

Prominent African American families emerged in every city and set standards that others sought to emulate. Again, the Forten family in Philadelphia exemplifies this development. The Fortens were unusual in many respects, especially in their success and accomplishments. But in their family life, they demonstrated widespread black values. As a young man, James Forten used his earnings as a sailmaker to support his widowed mother and the family of his sister, which lived meagerly on her husband's mariner wages. His sail-loft business flourishing, Forten married in 1803 at age thirty-seven, but his wife died within the year. A few months later, when his sister Abigail was widowed at age forty-two, Forten opened his three-story home to her four children. He then put two of his nephews to work in his sail loft. A year later, Forten married Charlotte Vandine, a twenty-one-year-old woman with Indian, European, and African ancestors. Between 1808 and 1823, they raised a family of nine children.

The Forten household included an assortment of relatives, apprentices, and boarders, along with children of deceased friends for whom James Forten served as guardian. Census takers recorded that Forten presided over a household

■ With its large free black population, New Orleans had more black artisans, shopkeepers, and street vendors than any other U.S. city. This 1819 painting by Benjamin Latrobe portrays "market folks" in colorful headgear and garments.

of fifteen people in 1810, eighteen in 1820, and twenty-two in 1830. Sometimes the number decreased as a son or daughter reached marriageable age and moved out—but then it grew again if the newlyweds came back to live and work in the household. With frequent comings and goings, the Forten home constantly bustled with activity. Its members also played music, read poetry, and received instruction in French as well as traditional subjects such as literature and mathematics. One of James Forten's daughters described the household as a "happy family circle." Of course, most free black families did not live as comfortably and graciously as the Fortens did. But examples of this kind gave hope to those less fortunate.

New Orleans: A Unique City

While free black communities blossomed mostly in the North, a free urban African American population also thrived in New Orleans, at the outlet of the Mississippi River. New Orleans became a city in 1803, the year the United States purchased the immense Louisiana Territory from France. When Americans began pouring into the city to pursue new opportunities, they found a unique configuration of races. In the early nineteenth century, slaves living in Louisiana were more linguistically and culturally African than anywhere else in the United States. Yet the population of free people of color was larger, better established, and more racially mixed than in other parts of the country.

Louisiana's free black population had roots reaching back to rule by the French and Spanish, who tolerated dark-skinned peoples more than Europeans elsewhere in North America did. Since the late seventeenth century, the French

explicitly endorsed mixed-race marriages in their overseas colonies. Many French garrison soldiers and colonists married female slaves, and the children of these liaisons often were freed. The number of free people of color rose after the Spanish acquired Louisiana from France in 1763 because the new rulers instituted the system of slave self-purchase called *coartación*. They did this less for humanitarian reasons than for the purpose of creating a black buffer class to align with slaveowners against rebellious bondspeople.

All of these forces coalesced to create a patchwork of peoples in New Orleans. By the time the United States acquired the Louisiana Territory in 1803, about 1,800 free black people resided in the city. Their number ballooned in 1809. That year, 3,000 free black people who had fled revolution in Haiti and then been ousted by Spanish officials in Cuba flooded New Orleans. By 1810, African Americans composed nearly two-thirds of New Orleans' population of about 17,000. Two-thirds of them were free.

Unique among U.S. cities, New Orleans became a hierarchical society with white people at the top, free people of color in the middle, and slaves at the bottom. Over time, free people of color in Louisiana became increasingly urban, lighter-skinned, and disproportionately female. Those released from slavery were mostly black women who became the wives or mistresses of white masters. The mulatto sons and daughters of these liaisons were also freed. By 1791, nearly two-thirds of all free black people in New Orleans were mulatto. Under Spanish rule, many black women managed to purchase their freedom with money they earned by setting up businesses in New Orleans.

"UNDER OUR VINE AND FIG TREE"

Finding comfort and inspiration in numbers in the cities, African Americans founded their own churches, schools, and community organizations. "We went out with our subscription paper and met with great success," wrote Richard Allen, recounting how he and Absalom Jones collected $360 on the first day of their quest to create a separate black church. This was in 1787, shortly after Allen had joined Jones to launch the Free African Society of Philadelphia (FAS). This mutual aid association used members' dues to provide assistance to needy free people.

From the beginning, the FAS had religious overtones, and soon its leaders devised plans for a black church of their own. But Allen's fervent Methodism brought him into conflict with other emerging black leaders who wished for a nondenominational "union" (denominationally blended) church. So while Jones worked to create the African Church of Philadelphia, later to be called St. Thomas's African Episcopal Church, Allen searched for the means to establish a black Methodist church. Yet both churches had the same guiding idea: that black Americans emerging from slavery required independent black houses of worship. As Jones and Allen explained it in the subscription paper they carried through the streets, there was a "necessity and propriety of separate and exclusive means, and opportunities, of worshiping God, or instructing their youth, and of taking care of their poor."

The Rise of Black Churches

The creation of "separate and exclusive" black churches expressed emancipated slaves' desire to stand on their own as a distinct *African* people. As one historian explains, the black church in these years became "the one impregnable corner of the world where consolation, solidarity, and mutual aid could be found and from which the master and the bossman—at least in the North—could be effectively barred." William Douglass, a minister at Absalom Jones's African Episcopal Church, later recalled this as an "age of a general and searching inquiry into the equity of old and established customs." Douglass also saw it as a time when "a moral earthquake had awakened the slumber of ages," causing "these humble men, just emerged from the house of bondage . . . to rise above those servile feelings which all their antecedents were calculated to cherish, and to assume,

as they did, an attitude of becoming men conscious of invaded rights." Black churches became seedbeds of black consciousness. As focal points for social and political organization, they also served as neighborhood centers where free black people could celebrate their African heritage without intrusion by white detractors.

The impulse to form all-black churches originated in the desire for self-government and self-expression. Yet often, white discrimination in interracial congregations provided just as powerful an impetus. Consider events in Wilmington, Delaware. The congregation of Asbury Methodist church was already one-third black at its founding in 1789. By 1802, it was nearly half black. The gifted young preacher Peter Spencer held separate meetings in the homes of free black worshipers or in shady groves at the city's edge. Nevertheless, the white Methodists in the congregation would not allow Spencer to preach from the church's pulpit. Representing half the congregation, black Methodists were segregated during worship services and permitted to sit only in the gallery. They were also denied communion and barred from ordination.

Matters came to a head in 1805 when the church's white members ordered black members to hold their weekday religious class meetings in the gallery rather than on the sanctuary floor. Fed up, Spencer and others led most of the black parishioners out of Asbury Methodist to found their own church. They named their all-black church Ezion Methodist Episcopal, after the port where biblical King Solomon kept his warships. Ezion's members recognized "for the time being . . . to have the directions and management of . . . spiritual concerns" under the white Methodist umbrella. But they appointed their own class leaders, lay preachers, and governing trustees. These individuals had the power to determine church membership and discipline disorderly or immoral members.

Numerous white people resented independent black churches and mutual aid societies. In their view, free black Americans should have remained subservient instead of founding their own organizations. "Their aspiring and little vanities," sneered John Fanning Watson, Philadelphia's first historian, "have been rapidly growing since they got those separate churches. [Before], they were much humbler, more esteemed in their places, and more useful to themselves and others." Comments such as these reflect a disturbing paradox facing African Americans at the end of the eighteenth century: As free black people extricated themselves from white benevolence and supervision by founding their own religious and educational institutions, white charges about innate black inferiority intensified. According to Allen and Jones, many

 **First Person**

Benjamin T. Tanner Recalls How Early Black Churches Offended White People

In 1867, many years after Richard Allen and Absalom Jones founded free black churches in Philadelphia, Benjamin T. Tanner, the bishop of the African Methodist Episcopal Church, wrote an account of the denomination's founding. The father of the painter Henry Ossawa Tanner, Benjamin Tanner was an outspoken editor of Christian journals fighting racial injustice.

The giant crime committed by the Founders of the African Methodist Episcopal Church was that they dared to organize a Church of men, men to think for themselves, men to talk for themselves, men to act for themselves: a Church of men who support from their own substance, however scanty, the ministration of the Word which they receive; men who spurn to have their churches built for them, and their pastors supported from the coffers of some charitable organization; men who prefer to live by the sweat of their own brow and be free. . . . When we were under the control of the [white] Methodist Episcopal Church, they supplied our pulpits with preachers, deacons, and elders, and these in the vast majority of instances were white men. Hence, if the instructions given were of the right kind, the merit was the white man's and his

alone. . . . The colored man was a mere hearer. . . . If the churches among the colored people were well governed, the merit was the white man's and his alone. The colored man was a mere subject. [The point was] to prove that the colored man was incapable of self-government and self-support and thereby confirm the oft-repeated assertions of his enemies, that he really is incapable of self-government and self-support. [The growth of the African Episcopal Church was] a flat contradiction and triumphant refutation of this slander, so foul in itself and so degrading in its influence.

—*from Benjamin T. Tanner,* An Apology for African Methodism *(Baltimore: n. p., 1867), pp. 16–17.*

To view a longer version of this document, please go to *www.ablongman.com/carson/documents*.

white people viewed African Americans as "men whose baseness is incurable." The two ministers freely admitted that "the vile habits often acquired in a state of servitude are not easily thrown off." In their opinion, it was unrealistic to expect too much from people who had been bent and broken by slavery. "Why," they asked, "will you look for grapes from thorns, or figs from thistles?" But speaking to white audiences, Allen and Jones insisted that black children who were born free and enjoyed "the same privileges with your own" would flourish.

In their independent churches, black Christians heard from their preachers that God had not made them inferior. Indeed, their souls were superior to those of white Christians. White people, the preachers maintained, were mired in the sins of slaveholding and trapped in the contradiction of trying to build a democratic republic whose economy hinged on the labor of human chattel. When Absalom Jones

built his African Episcopal Church, he chose words from St. Peter (1 Peter 2:9) to be inscribed on the side wall that expressed this sense of black people's greater righteousness and virtue: "But ye are a chosen generation, a royal priesthood, and an holy nation, a peculiar people; that ye should shew forth the praise of him who hath called you out of darkness into his marvelous light; which in time past were not a people, but are now the people of God."

Free African Americans in the new territory of Louisiana worshiped differently than in the northern cities. Whereas liberated people of color in the coastal North established their own religious institutions, those in Louisiana tended to stay within the interracial Catholic churches, where they married, baptized their children, and marked other turning points in their lives. Several realities prompted these differences. For one thing, church authorities in Louisiana never segregated black worshipers or

■ Richard Allen's first church, known as Mother Bethel, was a blacksmith's shop hauled to the lot he purchased in Philadelphia and then refurbished as a place of worship. Methodism's evangelical fervor and simplicity appealed to freed and fugitive southern slaves who reached northern cities.

made them feel unwelcome. In addition, New Orleans was still strongly Catholic—the Methodist and Baptist evangelical churches that thrived in the North had not yet brought diverse religious expression to this southern city.

African American Schools

After building their own churches, free African Americans felt emboldened to organize schools. In an era before public schools existed outside of New England, black parents had to create educational institutions for their own youngsters. Richard Allen organized the first black Sunday school in America at Philadelphia in 1795. Five years later, Absalom Jones, Amos White, and Ann Williams established their own school for black youth in the same city. In 1807, Allen set up the Society of Free People of Color for Promoting the Instruction and School Education of Children of African Descent. As in Philadelphia, black schools emerged alongside, or within, black churches in other parts of the country. In 1790, the Brown Fellowship Society in Charleston founded a school for black children, and in 1797 the Baltimore African Academy opened its doors.

Other emerging free black communities established separate churches and schools as well. Andrew Bryan, converted to Christianity in 1782, preached in the swamps outside Savannah after the American Revolution and became the leader of the Ethiopian Church of Jesus Christ in 1788, soon known as the First African Baptist Church. In Augusta, Georgia, Jesse Galphin led others who wanted a church of their own by founding the First African Church of Augusta in 1793. Two years later, black Methodists in Baltimore began "a distinct African, yet Methodist" church. In New York City, Peter Williams Jr., born to slavery in a cowshed, organized a separate congregation of Methodists who built their own house of worship in 1800. By 1802, the all-black Sharp Street Methodist Church was attracting members, soon led by the young Daniel Coker. By the early nineteenth century, black schools operated in all cities with sizeable free black populations.

Like white Americans, black Americans regarded education as the surest path to economic success, the key to moral improvement, and the best guarantor of personal happiness. For men and women recently released from slavery, education offered special benefits. It could restore self-confidence to those degraded under slavery. It could also undermine white claims that people of African descent were inherently inferior intellectually. But although they prized education, most black parents—like most white working-class parents—could afford only the scantiest schooling for their children. The majority of them indentured their children at an early age to white masters so as to reduce household expenses. Many of these masters would not release their young servants from work for schooling. Children fortunate enough to stay at home had to contribute to the family income by working instead of going to classes. Only the sons and daughters of the black middle class had the luxury of studying through their teenage years.

An Independent Black Denomination

In his attempts to build his flock at his African Methodist church, Allen had long met with bitter resistance from white Methodist authorities. Years before, when the white Methodist General Conference told Allen that he must sign over his new church's property to the conference, his black parishioners objected. Allen remembered how the white Methodist leader "asserted that we could not be Methodists unless we did [as he said]. We told him that he might deny us their name, but they could not deny us a seat in Heaven." The moment passed, but the struggle for control surfaced again in 1804. Allen's congregation watched uneasily as white Methodists controlled the appointment of the preacher, the licensing of lay preachers, and the administration of baptism and communion. To be sure, Allen's church's trustees were African American, and he himself occupied the pulpit at African Methodist. But he and the trustees had agreed to articles of incorporation, necessary to receive monetary gifts, without realizing that this action made their church the legal property of the white Methodist Conference.

Uncomfortable with the growing independence of Allen's church, white Methodists forced the issue in 1805. Allen remembered the moment vividly a quarter-century later. "James Smith was appointed to take the charge [pulpit] in Philadelphia; he soon waked us up by demanding the keys and books of the church, and forbid us holding any meetings except by orders from him; these propositions we told him we could not agree to." Raising the stakes, the white elder threatened expulsion of the entire black congregation from the Methodist General Conference. "We told him the house was ours," Allen replied, for "we had bought it, and paid for it."

The tug of war continued for more than ten years, compromising the notion of an interracial Methodist community. Finally, in 1816, white Methodist authorities tried to force Mother Bethel's black trustees to back down. In an appallingly offensive move, they sent white ministers to seize the black church's pulpit and preach as they desired. That day, Allen recalled, the house was so packed with black worshipers "that [the white ministers] could not get but more than half way to the pulpit." Attorneys had advised Allen's flock "to fend off" any intruders who might attempt to officiate at their church. But the determined white Methodists laid claim to the church itself and ordered it put up for auction. Allen foiled them by outbidding white Methodists at the auction, paying more than $10,000 for the brick church he had built in 1805 to replace the old refurbished blacksmith's shop. On New Year's Day in 1816, the Supreme Court of Pennsylvania finally settled the argument. Mother Bethel, the court ruled, was an independent church not subject to the authority of the white Methodist General Conference. Black Philadelphia Methodists had finally seceded from the white Methodist church.

Allen's success in achieving full independence for the African Methodist Episcopal church exemplified a broader rise of independent black denominations in the first quarter of the nineteenth century. The movement revealed a quest for autonomy fueled by the poisonous racial relations besetting free

■ Paul Svinin captured the emotionalism of black Methodist services in this painting. Evangelical outpouring soon appealed to white Methodists and helps account for the stunning rise of Methodism among white Americans in the early nineteenth century.

black communities. Even before Allen's victory, the black preacher Peter Spencer had encountered the same determination among white Methodists in Wilmington, Delaware, to keep black Methodists under their control. When the parent organization assigned a white minister permanently to Spencer's Ezion church and insisted that the church itself belonged to the white-controlled Methodist Conference, Spencer disagreed. The white minister retaliated by dismissing Ezion's black trustees and class leaders without so much as a hearing. Refusing to knuckle under to this treatment, Spencer and forty of his parishioners made a declaration of independence and created the Union Church of Africans—the United States' first fully autonomous African American church. Additional independent black denominations soon cropped up in New York City and other cities. In Baltimore, Daniel Coker led a separatist movement just a few weeks before the Supreme Court ruling in Pennsylvania.

After a generation of tension with white coreligionists, African Americans decided, as one historian has said, "to elect and be elected to church office, to ordain, and be ordained, to discipline as well as be disciplined, to preach, exhort, pray, and administer sacraments—in sum, to have their gifts and graces acknowledged by the whole community." But in fighting white suppression, black leaders had to ask themselves a hard question: Would their public assertiveness only worsen whites' antagonism and therefore jeopardize their efforts? Life in the northern cities offered free black people a cloak of anonymity. In the hustle and bustle of the urban crowds, black men and women might escape harassment while worshiping in their own way. Still, by the early nineteenth century, urban black leaders decided to take a more assertive stance. Their personal emancipation from slavery had catalyzed a psychological rebirth. The collective emancipation of black worshipers from white ecclesiastical bondage enabled them to pursue their vision of a better future from newly fortified bastions. By 1816, as Allen later recalled, his congregation was finally able "to sit down under our own vine and fig tree to worship, and none shall make us afraid."

BLACK REVOLUTION IN HAITI

In 1791, a white American writer reflecting on the astounding news of a mass slave revolt in French St. Domingue asked, "If one treats the insurrection of the negroes as rebel-lion, what name can be given to that insurrection of Americans which secured their independence?" Another white American pointed out that the black St. Dominguans were "asserting those rights by the sword which it was impossible to secure by mild measures." This same author urged Americans who had fought their own revolution to "justify those who in a cause like ours fight with equal bravery."

Self-Liberation in the Caribbean

The drama unfolding in the Caribbean captured the imagination of all Americans, but black Americans had particular interest in the massive uprising of French-speaking slaves in St. Domingue. Half a million Africans toiled on the French-owned western half of the Caribbean island. (Spain controlled the eastern half.) This number nearly matched that in the entire United States. St. Domingue also had about 50,000 *gens de couleur* (free people of color), mostly biracial, who occupied a middle caste. The 32,000 white French colonists—a significant minority—maintained an uncertain grip on power.

When revolution broke out in France in 1789, the restive free black people on St. Domingue (later called Haiti, after the indigenous Arawak name for the island) claimed their entitlement to the same "rights of man" the French revolutionaries demanded as they worked to unseat the monarchy and aristocracy in France. In 1791, a slave named Boukman led a rebellion against the most brutal slave system in the Americas. French colonists living on St. Domingue who felt repulsed by slavery and inspired by the French Revolution at home pitted themselves against French royalists who defended monarchy, the Catholic church, and slavery. By the following year, the island had erupted in violence. In the chaos, many free black people, seeking complete equality with white colonists, attacked slaves. For the most part, however, the conflict pitted white Haitians against the enslaved Africans, who outnumbered their masters fifteen to one.

In June 1793, self-liberated slaves overran the main seaport of Le Cap Français. Panicked, thousands of French planters and merchants fled the island and sought refuge in U.S. coastal cities. More than 3,000 reached Philadelphia, while thousands more poured into Norfolk, Baltimore, Charleston, New Orleans, and New York.

Many Americans initially endorsed the toppling of the brutal regime in St. Domingue, but their enthusiasm faded when French planters and merchants from the island began streaming into U.S. cities, often dragging domestic slaves with them. Their lurid stories of the Caribbean island bloodbath horrified many white Americans. Would the fever

■ **MAP 6.1** Exodus of Haitians to U.S. Seaports, 1792–1809

French slaveholders fleeing the slave revolution in 1792 (along with small numbers of free *gens de couleur*) brought thousands of slaves to U.S. coastal cities. Roughly 3,000 slaves and 3,000 free mulattoes flocked to New Orleans, further enriching that city's linguistic and cultural mix.

of black rebellion spread throughout the new nation, white Americans wondered? In 1793, newspapers circulated the report that three slaves in Albany, New York, had set a fire that destroyed twenty-six houses. People up and down the eastern seaboard soon associated black arson with the overthrow of white rule on St. Domingue. A wave of fires in 1796–1797—including one that destroyed two-thirds of Savannah, Georgia, and another that burned a million dollars' worth of property in New York City—intensified the fear of a concerted black uprising.

By this time, England and Spain had declared war against revolutionary France. Black Haitians had repulsed the 1793–1798 invasion of British forces trying to quell the revolution. The British monarch had worried the slave uprising would spread to nearby English Jamaica, where 300,000 slaves toiled in the cane fields.

While white Americans began to lose their taste for black revolution in Haiti, many black Americans began to see themselves as participants in a hemisphere-wide offensive against slavery. They applauded privately when Haitian slaves overpowered the French planters under the leadership of Toussaint L'Ouverture, formerly a trusted plantation steward. They celebrated again when black Haitians forced the withdrawal of the British army in 1798 and repulsed Napoleon's invading French army in 1801–1804. They marveled at how Haiti's half-million slaves defeated the combined might of French, English, and Spanish armies intent on reshackling them.

Know all Men by these presents that I Molineux Freres late of Capes Francois Gentleman, Have manumitted and by these presents do Manumit and Set free from Slavery my negro Boy named Lundy of the Senegal Nation aged about Twelve years and Stamped on his Breast MOLINEFS — One Condition nevertheless that he be bound by Indenture as a Servant to serve Mr Solomon Molins of the City of — Philadelphia Merchant his Executors Administrators or Assigns for & during the term of fifteen years next ensuing the day after the day of the date hereof, any thing herein before contained to the contrary in any wise notwithstanding, And I do hereby give grant and release unto the said Lundy all my rights and Title to his Person and Labour and Services as a Slave, excepting and reserving only his Services as an Indented Servant during the said Term of Sixteen years as abovementioned In Witness whereof I have hereunto set my Hand and Seal this Eighth day of July anno domini one thousand Seven hundred and Ninety five. Signed, Sealed and Delivered in the Presence of us. Beny Nones Hilary H. Baker ... I. Molineux Freres — Seal

■ Pennsylvania's Abolition Act of 1780 required French masters from St. Domingue to free their slaves within six months. However, masters and mistresses retained the labor of their former chattel by indenturing their freed slaves for long terms of service. The indenture depicted here shows that the master's surname, Molineux, had been burned into the chest of this twelve-year-old Senegalese boy.

The Haitian revolutionaries proclaimed their independence on January 1, 1804 and established a republic of African people amid the Caribbean slave regimes. Haiti was the first colony in the Americas to win its independence after the American victory over the British. Its revolutionaries had launched the first anticolonial racial war and achieved the first mass emancipation by slaves. But not until 1862 did the United States recognize the black Haitian government.

Reverberations in the United States

The revolution of Haiti cast a long shadow not only in the Caribbean but also in the United States. In Philadelphia, the latest news of Caribbean black rebellion came with yellow fever on a French ship in 1793. The virus spread, claiming 5,000 lives and turning Philadelphia into a morgue. Richard Allen and Absalom Jones, who had parted ways to start different black churches in 1792, rejoined to organize black nurses, death-cart drivers, and gravediggers. When a Philadelphia pamphleteer accused these workers of charging exorbitant fees, the two men responded with a pamphlet of their own. As they rebutted charges of black profiteering, they produced the first African American attack on slavery after the American Revolution.

In what one historian calls "a green leaf from the early scripture of black liberation," *A Narrative of the Proceedings of the Black People, During the Late Awful Calamity in Philadelphia* called attention to the slave revolt in Haiti, where black revolutionaries had turned the island's capital city into a smoldering ash heap just a few months before. "The dreadful insurrections they [the French slaves] have made . . . is enough to convince a reasonable man, that great uneasiness and not contentment, is the inhabitant of their [the slaves'] heart," wrote Allen and Jones. Take notice, they implored. "If you love your children, if you love your country, if you love the God of love, clear your hands from slaves, burden not your children or country with them."

Self-emancipation in Haiti continued to shape African Americans' thoughts about participating in a worldwide movement. In 1797, Allen, Jones, and James Forten carried a petition to Congress through the streets of Philadelphia.

■ This image of Toussaint L'Ouverture appeared in *An Historical Account of the Black Empire of Hayti*, published in London in 1805. The book spoke of the black leader's "prepossessing suavity" and remarked on his "astonishing horsemanship" and ability to travel "with inconceivable rapidity."

The document's signers implored Congress to repudiate the detested Fugitive Slave Act of 1793, which strengthened the Constitution's fugitive slave clause. Under this law, southern slaveowners and agents traveling north could seize free black people they suspected of escaping slave masters. An African American seized as a fugitive slave had no right to prove his or her status as a free person before being hauled back south. Could African Americans not expect "public justice" from the national government, the petition signers asked? When would the government end the "unconstitutional bondage" that was a "direct violation of the declared fundamental principles of the Constitution"? Black Philadelphians equated the "unconstitutional bondage in which multitudes of our fellows in complexion are held" with the "deplorable . . . situation of citizens of the United States captured and enslaved . . . in Algiers." By protecting slavery in the United States, was not Congress in the same category as

Algiers, whose Barbary pirates had seized and enslaved American sailors? With a hint of irony, Jones addressed the petition to "the President, Senate, and House of Representatives of the most free and enlightened nation in the world!!!"

In 1799, Allen and Forten composed a new petition to Congress. Steadfast to the revolutionary credo, they wrote: "Though our faces are black, yet we are men, and . . . are as anxious to enjoy the birth-right of the human race as those who [are white]." If the Declaration of Independence and the Bill of Rights "are of any validity," argued the petitioners, then black Americans should "be admitted to partake of the Liberties and inalienable Rights therein held forth." In other cities, African Americans began using the petition and other political means to hold white legislators to the standard set in their founding constitutional documents. In Boston, Prince Hall, who had led the petition-writing campaign against slavery during the American Revolution, condemned slavery again before the African Masonic Lodge in 1797. While applauding the black rebellion in St. Domingue, Hall denounced "the daily insults" suffered by black citizens on Boston's streets.

> "Though our faces are black, yet we are men."
> —*Petition to Congress*

The growing self-consciousness of free black people sometimes surfaced in unexpected ways. One such occasion occurred in Philadelphia on July 4, 1804, seven months after black Haitians had declared their independence. For years, on the Fourth of July, Philadelphians of all classes and colors had gathered in the square facing Independence Hall, where the Declaration of Independence was signed. There they feasted, toasted, and listened to stirring speeches about the blessings of liberty and the prospects of national greatness. But in 1804, several hundred black revelers also celebrated Haitian independence. Organizing themselves into military formations, electing officers, and arming themselves with bludgeons and swords, they marched through the cobblestone streets. They attacked white people who crossed their path. On the next night, they marched again. Venting their frustration and anger over growing hostility from white people, they terrorized the city, "damning the whites and saying they would shew them St. Domingo."

By 1808, when American participation in the Atlantic slave trade ended officially on January 1, black ministers in many cities turned New Year's Day into the black equivalent of the Fourth of July. African Americans needed a national day of thanksgiving and celebration that had relevance to their lives. New Year's Day served well because it marked both

First Person   New Orleans Freemen Seek Assurances from Louisiana's New Rulers

After the Louisiana Purchase of 1803, the numerous free people of color in New Orleans quickly implored the U.S. government to ensure that the rights they had enjoyed under Spanish and French rule would not be abridged. All the petitioners had French names, such as Entoine Populuse, Baptiste Rousaire, and Noel Banrepan.

We the subscribers, free citizens of Louisiana . . . are natives of the province and our dearest interests are connected with its welfare. . . . We are duly sensible that our personal and political freedom is thereby assured to us forever, and we are also impressed with the fullest confidence in the justice and liberality of the government towards every class of citizens, which they have here taken under their protection. . . . We were employed in the military service of the late government, and we hope we may be permitted to say, that our conduct in that service has ever been distinguished. . . . We therefore respectfully offer our services to the government as a corps of volunteers.

—*from* Territorial Papers of the United States: Volume IX: Territory of New Orleans, 1803–1812. *Compiled and edited by Clarence Edwin Carter.*

To view a longer version of this document, please go to *www.ablongman.com/carson/documents*.

---

the legal death of the slave trade and the birth of the free black republic of Haiti. Many of the New Year's Day sermons delivered by Richard Allen and other black ministers connected religion and politics. Such preachers often chided white leaders for not extending to black people the same rights the Declaration of Independence and many state constitutions had called unalienable to all human beings. From their pulpits, writes one historian, "God spoke out in thunder tones against chattel slavery and sharply condemned other forms of injustice inflicted upon any of His children."

Black preachers repeatedly invoked the elevated phrases of the revolutionary era, confronting white Americans with the hypocrisy of adhering to slavery when their sacred texts prohibited it. In Boston, Absalom Jones, a member of the African Society, chastised white Americans who presumed, in defiance of revolutionary principles, to exercise authority over blacks "by depriving us of our freedom, as if they had a command from heaven thus to do." "If freedom is the right of one nation," Jones asked, "why not the right of all nations of the earth?" In Philadelphia, he told his congregation, "Let the history of the suffering of our brethren, and of their deliverance, descend by this means to our children, to the remotest generations; and when they shall ask, in time to come, saying 'what mean the lessons, the psalms, the prayers, and the praises in the worship of this day?' Let us answer them by saying, the Lord, on the day of which this is the anniversary, abolished the trade which dragged your fathers from their native country, and sold them as bond men in the United States of America."

> "If freedom is the right of one nation, why not the right of all nations of the earth?"—*Absalom Jones*

THE SPREAD OF SLAVERY

The congressional prohibition of the Atlantic slave trade in 1808 did not eradicate traffic in human beings. Moreover, most southern congressmen had agreed to the ban not for humanitarian reasons but because rapid natural increase among slaves made new importations unnecessary in their states. In bold defiance of the law, slave traders in the Lower South continued to import slaves. The internal slave trade—the selling of human property from region to region within the United States—actually intensified.

In one of the greatest ironies in American history, the revolution in Haiti inadvertently aided the spread of slavery

A Black Minister Celebrates the End of the Slave Trade

Peter Williams Jr., New York City's leading black minister after the American Revolution, delivered a rousing sermon in the African Church on the day the American slave trade legally ended in 1808.

Oh, God! we thank thee, that thou didst condescend to listen to the cries of Africa's wretched sons; and that thou didst interfere in their behalf. At thy call humanity sprang forth, and espoused the cause of the oppressed: one hand she employed in drawing from their vitals the deadly arrows of injustice; and the other in holding a shield, to defend them from fresh assaults: and at that illustrious moment, when the sons of '76 pronounced these United States free and independent; when the spirit of patriotism, erected a temple sacred to liberty; when the inspired voice of Americans first uttered those noble sentiments, 'we hold these truths to be self-evident, that all men are created equal; that they are endowed by their Creator with certain unalienable rights; among which are life, liberty, and the pursuit of happiness'; and when the bleeding African, lifting his fetters, exclaimed, 'am I not a man and a brother'; then with redoubled efforts, the angel of humanity strove to restore to the African race, the inherent rights of man.

—first printed by Samuel Wood as An Oration of the Abolition of the Slave Trade: Delivered in the African Church, in the City of New York, January 1, 1808 *by Peter Williams Jr.* New York, 1808, pp. 19–21.

To view a longer version of this document, please go to *www.ablongman.com/carson/documents*.

in the United States. Having lost Haiti, France's largest source of wealth in the Americas, Napoleon no longer needed the crops produced in the lower Mississippi Valley to feed the Caribbean island's slaves. Desperate for new income, he agreed to sell the Louisiana Territory to the United States for $15 million. The Louisiana Purchase in 1803 doubled the size of the United States and vastly increased the area into which slavery could spread.

As we saw in Chapter 5, slavery deepened its roots in French Louisiana and continued after Spain reacquired the colony in 1800. Established in West Florida (including the Gulf of Mexico ports of Natchez, Mobile, and Pensacola), the Spanish had busily imported African slaves and turned the region into a slave-based plantation zone. By signing Pinckney's Treaty in 1795, the Spanish ceded to the United States all the territory they controlled east of the Mississippi River above the 31st parallel. Settling a long dispute, the treaty put in American hands much of what later became the states of Mississippi and Alabama. The agreement also gave Americans the right to transport people and goods along the Mississippi River and enabled them to launch shipments of produce from New Orleans. When the Spanish returned Louisiana to France in 1800, which made possible Napoleon's sale of the territory to the United States three years later, the Lower South became a center of slave trading and slave-based cotton production.

After Congress established the Mississippi Territory in 1798, an immense new region opened for settlement. White Americans, with their slaves in tow, streamed into the sparsely populated but racially diverse region. To carve cotton and sugar plantations out of raw land, the planters began importing additional slaves directly from Africa. When the slave trade became illegal in 1808, they started smuggling—importing thousands more Africans. Between 1790 and 1820, the slave population of the lower Mississippi valley soared almost tenfold—from 15,000 to 146,000.

The United States' purchase of Louisiana from France transformed black life in the South. Infusions of northern and southern capital and the invention of the cotton gin (see Chapter 7) accelerated the transition from an economy based on tobacco, indigo, and rice to one based on sugar and cotton. These changes paved the way for a mas-

■ Under Spanish rule, what is now called Jackson Square in New Orleans was known as the Plaza de Armas. The Catholic cathedral looms in the background; the *Cabildo* (city hall) stands on the left. The plaza served as a parade ground, a commercial center abuzz with vendors' stalls, and a ceremonial town center.

sive transfer of slaves from the Old South to the sugar and cotton lands of the lower Mississippi River region. With Americans taking over the Spanish legal system and abolishing slaves' right to self-purchase in 1807, the number of free black people leveled off. Now masters found it difficult to manumit their slaves, and the law forbade entry of free African Americans into Louisiana from other states. Between 1810 and 1860, Louisiana changed from a territory where free black people represented 13 percent of the black population to a cluster of states in which they constituted just 1 percent of the black population. By sharply restricting opportunities for black men and women to shake off the bonds of enslavement, the laws began eroding the relative freedom slaves had enjoyed under the French and Spanish system of slavery.

Even so, enslaved Louisianans continued to have some advantages over their counterparts in other parts of the new nation. Living among large numbers of freedmen and freedwomen, they could aspire to joining the ranks of free black people. In addition, many slave masters in New Orleans permitted their slaves to hire out their own time and thereby earn money. Sometimes slaves even maintained their own quarters and cultivated close contacts with free African Americans. One observer noted just after the Louisiana Purchase that slaves and dark-skinned free black people "never approach each other without displaying signs of affection and interest, without asking each other news of their relations, their friends, or their acquaintances."

Yet not all relations between free and enslaved blacks were so positive. Interactions among light-skinned free

African Americans and black slaves often proved awkward. Light-skinned free people of color were "uncomfortably sandwiched," as one historian has written, "between white free people and black slaves," making up a "third caste in a social order designed for but two." Often these free people of color saw their own well-being as dependent on white patronage, so they aligned themselves with white people in business transactions. Some even owned human property themselves, regarding slave ownership as proof of their social and political solidarity with whites.

SLAVE RESISTANCE

While some slaves hoped to win their freedom in the new nation through self-purchase or manumission by white masters, others made their bid for liberty on their own terms. The Haitian Revolution inspired many of the rebellions that struck fear into the hearts of slaveowners everywhere in the American South.

Fugitive Slave Settlements

The swamplands throughout the southern states provided advantageous hiding places for escaped slaves. Black people who fled their masters headed for nearby swamps and formed settlements that plagued slaveowners and threatened the slave regime. In North Carolina and Virginia, fleeing slaves established a community in the Great Dismal Swamp in the late 1780s. There they built cabins, planted crops, and governed themselves for many years. Farther south, former slaves who called themselves the King of England's Soldiers (indicating they had gained their freedom during the American Revolution by joining the British) also found swampy regions a staging ground for resistance. Setting up runaway camps in the swamplands of the Savannah River, slaves known as Captain Cudjoe and Captain Lewis attracted new refugees in the 1780s. With weapons acquired during the American Revolution, they led one hundred men in plundering river plantations just before the Constitutional Convention met in Philadelphia in 1787. When Georgia militia units finally destroyed their encampment, the refugee black men and women melted into the wilderness. Similarly, in the Cypress Swamp of Louisiana, black communities in the 1780s drew runaway slaves who fended off periodic attacks by militia units and free African Americans working as slave catchers.

Still other African Americans continued the effort to dismantle slavery. In 1795, slaves organized a well-planned uprising at Pointe Coupée, Louisiana, on the estate of a French planter. Inspired by the success of the black revolutionaries in Haiti and hoping to ignite a general insurrection, dozens of slaves (aided by three whites, a few Indians, and several free black men) prepared their strategy. But white authorities, alerted to the plot, seized the rebels before they could strike. A white court convicted twenty-three of them and ordered them hanged. Many others were flogged and deported for hard labor in Spanish fortresses in Mexico, Cuba, and Puerto Rico. Spanish authorities nailed the severed heads of the executed slaves to posts along the Mississippi River from Pointe Coupée to New Orleans as a warning to other would-be revolutionaries. But draconian punishments did not prevent bondspeople from planning another uprising a year later. Frustrated, the Spanish halted all importing of West Indian slaves, whom they considered prime rebels.

Gabriel's Rebellion

No severed heads or brutal crackdowns could suppress the insurrectionary spirit of slaves. That became apparent in the hot, humid summer of 1800, when a twenty-four-year-old enslaved blacksmith in Virginia prepared a strike at the heart of American slavery. Gabriel's Rebellion in Richmond, Virginia, proved the largest such plot in the republic's early decades.

Born to enslaved parents in the year the Declaration of Independence was signed, Gabriel acquired his name thanks to a midwife's prediction. As the slave midwife cut the newborn's umbilical cord, she felt the shape of the baby's head and predicted he would become a bold man. The infant's mother and father named him Gabriel after the divine messenger who appeared to Old Testament prophets and later to the Virgin Mary.

In Gabriel's youth, this choice of name seemed prophetic. He grew up among more than fifty slaves owned by Thomas Prosser, a tobacco planter and merchant in Richmond. Gabriel had the good fortune to learn to read, and Prosser kept him from the fields to teach him blacksmithing. By the mid-1790s, Gabriel had grown into a tall, muscular young man. When his master hired him out in Richmond as a capable blacksmith, he gained a measure of freedom. As Gabriel's access to the wider world expanded, he learned about the Haitian Revolution. Reported in the Richmond newspapers, the uprising was also recounted by Haitian slaves brought into Baltimore, Norfolk, Charleston, New Orleans, and other American ports. Inspired by the successful rebellion in the Caribbean, Gabriel developed a scheme to end slavery in the American South.

 **First Person**

A Virginia Slave Explains Gabriel's Rebellion

Ben Woolfolk, one of Gabriel's lieutenants, recruited many slaves for the planned insurrection. After being convicted and sentenced to die, he turned state's evidence to save his life. Below is an excerpt from his testimony, recorded by the court.

After assembling of the Negroes near Prosser's, and previous to their coming to Richmond, a company was to be sent to Gregorie's Tavern to take possession of some arms there deposited. . . . That he was present when Gabriel was appointed General and George Smith second in command. That none were to be spared of the whites except Quakers, Methodists, and French people. The prisoner and Gilbert concluded to purchase a piece of silk for a flag, on which they would have written "death or Liberty," and they would kill all except as before excepted, unless they agreed to the freedom of the Blacks, in which case they would at least cut off one of their arms.

—*from H. W. Flournoy, ed.,* Calendar of Virginia State Papers, *vol. IX (Richmond, VA: n. p., 1890), pp. 164–165.*

To view a longer version of this document, please go to *www.ablongman.com/carson/documents*.

The young man planned carefully. Whereas Richard Allen, already free in the North, chose the Bible as his instrument of change, the enslaved Gabriel in the South chose the sword. Gabriel and his chief lieutenants quietly gathered recruits for months in Richmond and surrounding counties. Governor James Monroe—a future president of the United States—later maintained that the conspiracy included most of the slaves in the Richmond area and "pervaded other parts, if not the whole, of the State." He was probably right. Gabriel and his lieutenants stealthily approached as many slaves as they could, asking "whether they would fight the white people for their freedom." Many declared their readiness to kill without compassion. When asked "if he thought he could kill White people stoutly," a slave named Jacob answered: "I will fight for my freedom as long as I have breath, and that is as much as any man can do." Another said simply, "I will kill or be killed." But other slaves declined, convinced that white people possessed insurmountable power and that rebellious slaves would die in vain. Gabriel's brother Martin, a preacher, worked to overcome this fear. In his Bible, he found comfort in the words "five of you shall conquer an hundred & a hundred thousand of our enemies." Of his life as a slave, Martin said, "I can no longer bear what I have borne."

> " **I** will fight for my freedom as long as I have breath, and that is as much as any man can do."
> —*Jacob, a slave*

Gabriel's plan centered on seizing control of Virginia's capital and killing people who supported slavery. The strategy called for 1,000 followers to meet on August 30, 1800, divide into three columns, and enter the capital after midnight with a silk flag carrying the words of the Haitian revolutionaries' battle cry, "Death or Liberty." The first column would slip through the streets of Richmond and torch the highly combustible wooden warehouses in the southeastern sector of the city. The other two columns would enter the west end of town, one seizing 4,000 rifles in the state arsenal, the other bursting into the executive mansion to take Governor James Monroe hostage. As white residents rushed out to fight the fires, freshly armed black insurgents would cut them down, sparing only poor women without slaves, Quakers and Methodists, and known opponents of slavery. Once in charge of Richmond, Gabriel's rebels intended to demand their freedom and the abolition of slavery. If the Haitian black revolutionaries had done so, they reasoned, why not slaves in Virginia?

Nature, however, conspired against the rebels. As Gabriel's army gathered, a violent storm dumped torrential rain on the area. By mid-evening, the downpour had washed out the bridges by which Gabriel's men had planned to enter Richmond. With roads impassable, morale sank. White Virginians later regarded this opening of the heavens as providential. However, a few slaves who had declined to join the conspiracy had also leaked news of the plot. We will never know whether Gabriel's plan might have succeeded barring bad weather and betrayal, or whether slaves elsewhere in Virginia and North Carolina would have rebelled if the uprising had unfolded as intended.

After the thunderstorm subsided, Virginia authorities began arresting the conspirators. Twenty slaves, including Gabriel's two brothers, were quickly rounded up. Slave masters expressed puzzlement at the fierce hatred of Gabriel and his followers and their determination to win their freedom. In many white people's view, their more moderate treatment of slaves after the American Revolution should have mollified them. Numerous slaves, whites reasoned, had gained their liberty under relaxed manumission procedures, and many masters had sold slave families together instead of breaking them up. Some masters had also allowed slaves to travel from plantation to plantation and gather on Sundays and holidays. Moreover, many slave artisans, such as Gabriel and his older brothers, had been permitted to hire themselves out in towns such as Richmond and Petersburg, where they enjoyed a degree of freedom unknown to plantation slaves. Yet slaveowners misread the temperament of even the most privileged bondsmen and women. These slaves' higher status did little to diminish their hatred of slavery. Indeed, it may well have nourished it.

Using testimony from a small number of informers, the courts tried the rebels for conspiracy and insurrection. By September 15, 1800, ten were hanged. Gabriel slipped away to Norfolk, aided by an antislavery Methodist who captained a schooner that carried the black leader down the James River. There, betrayed by two enslaved black sailors for a $300 reward and their own freedom, he was arrested. After being condemned to die, Gabriel, his brothers, and two trusted compatriots were hanged on October 10, 1800. In all, white authorities executed twenty-six conspirators and transported dozens of others out of state, selling them into slavery in French New Orleans and the West Indies.

Still, Gabriel's Rebellion survived long in the memories of Virginians. In court testimony, one of Gabriel's associates left much to ponder: "I have nothing more to offer than what General Washington would have had to offer, had he

been taken by the British and put to trial. I have adventured my life in endeavouring to obtain the liberty of my countrymen, and am a willing sacrifice in their cause." Appalled by the conspiracy and dreading a Haitian-like outbreak in the United States, white Virginians knew the "question now is a plain one," as one put it. "Shall we abolish slavery, or shall we continue it? There is no middle course to steer." Another warned that a "celestial spark" of freedom was buried in every slave and "kindles into flame" with "the breath of knowledge. . . . There have never been slaves in any country, who have not seized the first favorable opportunity to revolt." Virginia's nervous governor, James Monroe, agreed. "Unhappily, while this class of people exists among us we can never count with certainty on its tranquil submission."

Other Uprisings

Less than a year after the suppression of Gabriel's Rebellion, a slave named Sancho proved Monroe correct. A ferryman who knew upcountry Virginia well, Sancho was one of Gabriel's insurrectionists who had escaped capture. Now he plotted an "Easter rebellion"—a revolt to take place on Good Friday in 1802. By torching houses and fields, his men hoped to precipitate the collapse of slavery. They believed that a "great conflagration of houses, fodder, [hay] stacks, etc. will strike such a damp on their spirits that [white people] will be . . . willing to acknowledge liberty and equality." Word spread of an Easter uprising, even into North Carolina. But again, someone leaked news of the plan, and it quickly unraveled. White authorities sent out militia patrols, made a few arrests, and obtained evidence from other slaves. Five slaves were hanged in May 1802, Sancho among them. Other hangings followed, twenty-five in all. As in Gabriel's scheme, the rebels had not managed to strike that all-important first blow.

Southern planters fervently hoped that hangings and deportations in 1800–1802 would squelch further slave resistance. They were disappointed. In 1811, a slave named Tom was arrested in Henrico County, Virginia, and confessed that his murder of his master was part of a larger plan to kill slaveowners. Slaves "were not made to work for the white people," asserted Tom "but [white people] are made to work for themselves; and [enslaved Africans] would have it so." Later that year, one of North America's largest slave uprisings erupted just north of New Orleans. Led by Charles Deslondes, a biracial slave from Haiti, about 500 escaped men and women marched on the city, "colors displayed and full of arrogance." Two white people and sixty-six rebels lost their lives in a pitched battle with white militia and federal troops. Twenty-one were executed after a short trial.

White southerners managed to avert or defeat slave revolts, yet these uprisings reminded them that the "celestial spark" of freedom was impossible to extinguish. Rather than leading them to consider eradicating slavery, rebellion prompted whites to tighten restrictions on free black people. In 1806, Virginia passed a law ordering any newly freed slave to leave the state within one year or risk reenslavement.

BLACK IDENTITY IN THE NEW NATION

In the summer of 1792, a procession of Philadelphians filed through the streets behind the casket of the wife of the African American fruit seller William Gray. What distinguished the marchers, as one newspaper commented, was the "pleasing indifference to complexion." White and black people alike paid homage to the greatly respected deceased Widow Gray. This was "a happy presage of the time, fast approaching, when the important declaration in *holy writ* will be fully verified that 'GOD hath made of one blood, all the nations of the Earth,'" the newspaper commented. But those who believed that a new era of racial unity had dawned would soon see their hopes dashed.

In the waning years of the eighteenth century and the early decades of the nineteenth century, the growing hostility toward free African Americans led to new restrictions on people of color. Increasingly, white Americans came to regard freed African Americans as more dangerous than slaves and less useful for building the new nation. Once again, black Americans had to rethink their options, including returning to Africa. The War of 1812 raised further questions about African Americans' place in the new nation.

Rising Racial Hostility

George Washington had only recently taken office as the nation's first president when white legislators expressed their hostility toward black people with restrictive new laws. In 1790, Congress passed the Naturalization Law, which granted citizenship to only those immigrants who were "foreign whites." Two years later, the legislature limited enlistment in the state militias to white men. In 1810, it banned African

Americans from working in the U.S. postal system. States and cities added their own restrictions. In the states carved out of the Northwest Territory, new laws limited the entry of free black men and women into the region. In 1807, for example, Ohio required incoming African Americans to post a $500 bond to demonstrate their ability to support themselves. Indiana imposed a $300 annual poll tax on all adult black and mulatto men in 1815. Even Methodists and Baptists—those most ardent antislavery denominations—succumbed to the rising tide of racial hostility. Deciding that future generations should take responsibility for demolishing slavery, both denominations revoked their rule prohibiting slaveownership among members in 1793.

Philadelphia, the center of American humanitarian reform, also endured racial conflicts. Numerous working-class white people resented the influx of dark-skinned migrants, primarily from the South, who competed for jobs and agitated in densely settled neighborhoods. In 1805, the hostility of white Philadelphians toward their black neighbors surfaced during Fourth of July celebrations. White revelers unleashed a torrent of curses that drove black Philadelphians from the square facing Independence Hall. A few weeks later, a pamphlet described the city as overrun by black migrants "starving with hunger and destitute of employ."

The racial fear of white Americans dovetailed with the rise of scientifically based racism in the post-revolutionary era. Previously, many white intellectuals believed that black people were less capable than white people owing to the degradation of slavery rather than inherent inferiority. "Nurture," not "nature," they maintained, had ruined black people for any usefulness. As we saw in Chapter 5, Thomas Jefferson was among the first to revive the old argument about the supposedly immutable inferiority of people of African descent. By the early nineteenth century, some of the nation's most respected thinkers agreed with Jefferson, attacking the "nurture" theory and echoing the old idea that Africans were an inferior race even *before* slavery. For example, Charles Caldwell, a doctor and member of the medical faculty at the University of Pennsylvania, argued in 1811 that the differences between human races were innate. Therefore, he advised, the social mixing of naturally superior white people and naturally inferior black people could only lead to disaster—a mixed assortment of individuals with watered-down abilities who would not fit anywhere.

African American leaders tried to counter white people's mounting assault on egalitarianism and the promise of interracial harmony. In Philadelphia, James Forten put aside his usual reserve to publish a scorching indictment of the racism spreading in the City of Brotherly Love. He particularly

■ Racist caricatures such as the one shown here lampooned free African Americans in the North. In this image, Governor John Hancock of Massachusetts welcomes Cuffe to "the celebrated Equality Ball given to the Negroes of Boston." In mocking free African Americans, cartoons of this kind made them seem unsuitable for citizenship rights.

attacked the expulsion of black Philadelphians from the July Fourth celebration at Independence Hall Square. "Is it not wonderful," he wrote sardonically, "that the day set apart for the festival of liberty, should be abused by the advocates of freedom, in endeavoring to sully what they profess to adore?" Forten decried proposed laws that called for cordoning off Pennsylvania to keep out additional free black people seeking entry into the state. "Search the legends of tyranny and find no precedent. It has been left for Pennsylvania to raise her ponderous arm against the liberties of the black, whose greatest boast has been that he resided in a state where civil liberty and sacred justice were administered alike to all."

New Organizational and Family Names

Following the ratification of the Constitution, free African Americans struggled to define their identity in the expand-

ing white nation. Were newly freed people *African* Americans? That is, did their future lie where they had toiled most of their lives while their cultural heritage remained distinctly African? Or were they simply Americans with dark skin? If so, must they assimilate as quickly as possible into the cultural norms and social institutions of the dominant white society? Or should they regard themselves as Africans living in a strange, hostile land—a displaced people who might best return to the realms of their ancestors?

Though the rising generation of free African Americans distanced themselves from the bondage of the past, they titled their churches, schools, and social organizations in ways that suggested a shared heritage. Thoughts of the African homeland still stirred the memories of those who had been born there. The idea of Africa also served as a cultural touchstone for those who had never seen it. In 1903, the pioneering black historian W. E. B. Du Bois would call this phenomenon "double-consciousness." The black American, Du Bois observed, "ever feels his twoness—an American, a Negro; two souls, two thoughts, two unreconciled strivings; two warring ideals in one dark body, whose dogged strength alone keeps it from being torn asunder."

The African half of this double consciousness showed itself plainly in the way freed slaves named their organizations and churches. Emerging first in Newport, Rhode Island, and in Philadelphia, Pennsylvania, in 1786–1787, the first organizations of liberated black people called themselves the Free African Society. In Philadelphia, the Society's articles of incorporation made clear its members' identity: "We, the free *Africans* and their descendants, of the City of Philadelphia. . . . " The Newport organization used the same language. In naming independent black churches, congregants unvaryingly called them "African": the African Baptist Church of Boston, the African Presbyterian Church of New York, the African Union Methodist Church of Wilmington, the First African Church of Augusta.

Similarly, benevolent societies associated with black churches reflected dark-skinned people's continued identification with Africa. In Philadelphia and other cities, these organizations sometimes honored abolitionist white friends with names such as the Rush Benevolent Society and the Benezet Philanthropic Society. However, most black Philadelphians organized under such Africa-inspired names as Daughters of Ethiopia, Angola Beneficial Society, Daughters of Samaria, Sons of Africa, Daughters of Zion Angolan Ethiopian Society, and the African Friendly Society of St. Thomas.

Likewise, African Americans chose African names to represent secular organizations. African Masonic lodges cropped up in many cities. In New York, black residents joined the African Dorcas Society; in Philadelphia, black men formed the African Fire Association; and in Wilmington, parents convened the African School Society. In Boston, women attended the Afric-American Female Intelligence Society; in Pittsburgh, students signed up at the African Educational Society. Years later, in the face of mounting white hostility, some black leaders urged followers to shed the word *Africa* from such organizations' names. But for now, free black men and women used the name to reawaken the strength of their ancestors—autonomous peoples led by noble warriors and builders of a rich heritage.

After the American Revolution, free black people grappled with questions of identity at a personal as well as an organizational level: what to name themselves, and how to name their children. Inventing a family name—a surname, which most slaves did not have—enabled them to demonstrate their independence. Just as Gustavus Vasa became Olaudah Equiano and James Armistead became James Lafayette, thousands of freed people symbolically left the slave past behind by choosing a new name.

In adopting new names, most recently freed slaves disposed of their slave names altogether. Out went monikers conferred by slave masters—classical names such as Caesar, Pompey, Scipio, and Cato; mythological names such as Jupiter, Mars, Daphne, and Dionysus; place names such as London, Limerick, Hereford, and Hartford; and derisive tags such as Mistake, Moody, and Neverbegood. In acts of cultural self-definition, most liberated African Americans chose plain Anglo-American forenames such as John, Elizabeth, Benjamin, Mary, William, Dorothy, Thomas, Susanna, and Richard. Many chose biblical names—for example, Absalom, Judith, Jacob, Dinah, Isaac, Hannah, Adam, and Ruth. In Philadelphia, the slave Jacob became the freeman William Trusty; Caesar became Samuel Green; Moses became William Johnson; Susanna became Elizabeth Howell; and Pompey became James Jones.

Some freed people chose a surname that openly signified their new identity. Freemans and Newmans dot the church, census, and tax records of the North and Upper South. Others celebrated freedom with a flourish, as did Julius Caesar and Richard America in Philadelphia, Alexander the Great and Hudson Rivers in New York City, and Gowan Pamphlet, a literate black Baptist preacher, in Williamsburg, Virginia. Still others took names commemorating defining moments in their lives. A slave-born West Indian mariner who turned up in Philadelphia during the revolution and signed aboard John Paul Jones's *Bonhomme Richard* renamed himself Paul Jones. In Baltimore, John Fortune and Elisha Caution selected names that expressed their thoughts about the future. In contrast to practices farther north, freed blacks in New Orleans, Charleston, and other southern cities often tried to preserve ties with white patrons by adopting their masters' surnames.

Naming one's children represented an equally personal act for freed African Americans. As in choosing surnames, most African Americans selected ordinary English-derived first names for their sons and daughters. But tellingly, no free black parents conferred the name of Boukman or Toussaint L'Ouverture, Haiti's insurrectionist leaders, on their newborns. They knew that openly embracing the black revolution in this way would almost certainly incur the rage of white Americans already terrified of black rebellion.

The Back-to-Africa Movement

While most northern black leaders chose to stand and fight for their rights in the young nation, others considered a

 **First Person**

A Black Sailmaker Lectures White Citizens

Soon after Congress made the Atlantic slave trade illegal in 1808, northern black leaders reminded all Americans of their founding principles. Using the press to reach the public, Philadelphia's James Forten, much admired for his patriotism, benevolence, and civic spirit, published Letters from a Man of Colour *in 1813. The work included this uncompromising charge.*

We hold this truth to be self-evident, that GOD created all men equal, and is one of the most prominent features in the Declaration of Independence and in that glorious fabric of collected wisdom, our noble Constitution. This idea embraces the Indian and the European, the Savage and the Saint . . . the white Man and the African, and whatever measures are adopted subversive of this inestimable privilege, are in direct violation of the letter and spirit of our Constitution. . . . The story will fly from the north to the south, and the advocates of slavery, the traders in human blood, will smile contemptuously at the once boasted moderation and humanity of Pennsylvania. By . . . this bill, . . . the police officers are authorized to apprehend any black,

whether a vagrant or a man of reputable character, who cannot produce a certificate that he has been registered. He is to be arrayed before a justice, who is thereupon to commit him to prison!—The jailor is to advertise a Freeman, and at the expiration of six months, if no owner appear for this degraded black, he is to be *exposed to sale*, and if not sold to be confined at hard labor for seven years!!—Man of feeling, read this!—No matter who, no matter where. . . . Can anything be done more shocking to the principles of civil liberty!

—*from James Forten,* A Series of Letters by a Man of Colour, *1813.*

To view a longer version of this document, please go to *www.ablongman.com/carson/documents*.

return to Africa. Feeling strong emotional ties to the homeland and desiring to carry Christianity to Africa, aspiring emigrants assumed they had scant hope of carving out a decent life in the United States. As we saw in Chapter 5, the back-to-Africa impulse first welled up in Boston only a few years after the American Revolution. In the late 1780s, it surfaced in Newport, Rhode Island, where free African Americans reported that they were "strangers and outcasts in a strange land, attended with many disadvantages and evils which are likely to continue on us and our children while we and they live in this country."

While groups like the Free African Society in Newport advocated emigration, others urged freed men and women of color to stay. Members of Philadelphia's Free African Society contended that although the path to black acceptance and accomplishment in America was strewn with obstacles, it still offered black men and women their best prospects.

The struggle, advised Richard Allen, required patience and determination: "The holy writ" prescribed that "the race is not to the swift, nor the battle to the strong; but that one who has on the shield of faith shall chase a thousand, and two put ten thousand to flight. Here is encouragement for us of the African race [to remain in America]."

At the same time, some white leaders eagerly promoted emigration. Consider the wealthy Quaker William Thornton, who arrived from Antigua in 1786, where he had inherited a large sugar plantation worked by slaves. Thornton garnered the support of Boston's Samuel Adams and Virginia's James Madison for a plan to resettle freed slaves on the coast of Guinea. But Thornton's plan never got off the ground: He found only handfuls of free African Americans willing to leave the United States.

Paul Cuffe became the strongest proponent of emigration in the early nineteenth century. Cuffe was the seventh of ten children fathered by an enslaved African who had purchased his freedom and married a Wampanoag Indian woman from Gayhead, Massachusetts. The young man went to sea at age sixteen and was captured by the British in 1776. Sent with his shipmates to a New York prison ship, he languished there for several years. Even before the war ended, Cuffe and his brothers asked why free black men—who had no vote and could not hold office—were required to pay taxes. After the war, Cuffe married a Wampanoag woman and prospered in New Bedford, Massachusetts, as a master mariner, ship owner, and merchant. He was distinctly American, even joining the Society of Friends in New Bedford.

Yet disillusioned with the treatment of free black people in the North, Cuffe urged an exodus to Africa. In part, he hoped to bring Christianity to Africa, where repatriated free black people would serve as the principal missionaries. Supported by Philadelphia Quakers, Cuffe organized a trial voyage to West Africa in 1810 to carry out this work. He left from Philadelphia on New Year's Day in 1811 with an all-black crew. Fifty-two days later, he recorded in his ship's journal, "the dust of Africa lodged on our riggings." His voyage to Africa stirred debates about whether black Americans best future lay in Africa, in America, or in both—an argument that simmered for decades.

The War of 1812

Even as Cuffe navigated his ship across the Atlantic to West Africa in early 1811, new tensions between Britain and the United States set the stage for changing the lives of African Americans. British cruisers outside New York harbor had begun impressing white American seamen (seizing them for service on British vessels) in an escalation of a long dispute between the United States and Great Britain. The conflict provided African Americans with a fresh opportunity to secure their place in the new nation. Like other seafaring captains, Cuffe hoped the United States could preserve its neutrality while France and England clashed bitterly in the Napoleonic wars. Like other Americans, Cuffe paid the price when Congress passed the Embargo Act in 1807. The law prohibited American vessels from sailing for foreign ports and threw eastern seaports into a severe depression. Two years later, in the Non-Intercourse Act of 1809, Congress repealed the embargo and reopened trade with all nations except Great Britain and France. But this new mandate did not stop British and French attacks on U.S. ships.

For Cuffe, the dispute had personal repercussions when U.S. customs officials seized his ship in early 1812 after he returned from West Africa. He was charged with possible violations of the Non-Intercourse Act. Cuffe managed to repossess his ship and its valuable cargo only by traveling to Washington. He was back in New Bedford by June 1812—the year Congress declared war on England to protect U.S. trade links to Europe. Cuffe now had to postpone his back-to-Africa movement.

The War of 1812 gave free black men and women a chance to prove their allegiance to the new nation and slaves an opportunity to shake off their shackles. During the American Revolution, many free black men had tried to enlist in the "glorious cause." Now, in 1812, many more of them offered their services. Even before the new war, African Americans had been swept up in the forces fueling the conflict. In 1807, for example, when a British warship opened fire on the U.S. frigate *Chesapeake,* two sailors seized by the British were black. Soon English captains were impressing numerous African American sailors.

Throughout the War of 1812, free African Americans served in both black regiments and racially mixed regiments. At least one-tenth of the sailors who fought the British on the Great Lakes had dark skin. After the Battle of Lake Erie, Captain Oliver H. Perry declared that his black sailors "seemed absolute insensible to danger." One of the bravest soldiers in the Battle of North Point was William Burleigh. A Philadelphian, Burleigh positioned himself in the thick of the struggle to repulse British forces advancing to capture Baltimore in September 1814. At the Battle of New Orleans, several free black Louisiana militia units held a strategic position near General Andrew Jackson's main forces and played a gallant role in the U.S. victory.

In the summer of 1814, the conflict reached new levels of violence when the British captured and burned Washington, D.C. Many northern free black people seized the chance to display their patriotism by volunteering to fortify seaport defenses against the marauding British.

To promote the antislavery cause, abolitionists celebrated African Americans' contributions to the American effort during the War of 1812. But in truth, many more African Americans served with the British than with the Americans. Just as in the American Revolution, many slaves eagerly embraced the British offer of unconditional freedom in return for joining Britain's cause. When the British fleet conducted hit-and-run raids in the Chesapeake Bay in 1813, Marylanders and Virginians feared a wave of slave rebellions. Rather than rising against their masters, however, which carried terrible risks, bondspeople simply fled to British ships and bases. Many of them served as spies, messengers, and guides. The British, complained U.S. Brigadier General John Hungerford, "have a great advantage over us in a country where the passages and by-ways through our innumerable necks and swamps are so little known to but very few of our officers and men." Hungerford further lamented the fact that "these refugee blacks" could "penetrate [these regions] with so much ease."

Refugee slaves' knowledge of the landscape stymied American efforts to defend the nation's capital. The British troops who sailed up the Patuxent River and debarked to march through Bladensburg, Maryland, to Washington, D.C., were accompanied by at least one hundred newly liberated slaves who served with the 85th Regiment of the British Colonial Marines. These were the troops who left the capital a smoking ruin.

Before the war ended, 3,000 to 5,000 slaves of the Upper South, nearly one-third of them women, fled to the British side. Thousands more failed in the attempt. When the British invaded New Orleans in 1815, hundreds of Louisiana slaves escaped to their side as well. But because the British occupied areas in the South only briefly in the War of 1812, far fewer slaves fled to them than had done so during the American Revolution. Still, the exodus represented the largest act of slave resistance between the American Revolution and the Civil War. After the U.S.–British conflict finally petered out in 1815, the British faced the same problem they had encountered in 1783: what to do with the escaped slaves who had gained their freedom by reaching British lines. Most went to Nova Scotia; others, to Bermuda or Sierra Leone.

CONCLUSION

In the late eighteenth and early nineteenth centuries, free black leaders established autonomy for African Americans by setting up independently managed black churches, schools, and other organizations. They built free black communities from Massachusetts to Louisiana, in which many black people made the transition from chattel property to propertied families. But how would black men and women translate that autonomy into equality in the workplace, in politics, and in social life?

How could African Americans continue the fight to end slavery when so many white people believed that black people should remain subordinate and deferential? Despite African American gains, slavery was still spreading geographically, and the number of slaves was soaring—even after the slave trade officially ended in 1808. The abolitionist movement was losing steam. Even slave rebellions in Haiti and Virginia—the first successful, the second,

aborted—had not persuaded southern slaveholders to follow northern states in phasing out slavery.

Like the American Revolution, the War of 1812 gave free African Americans another chance to win white people's acceptance by showing their willingness to shed their blood for the new nation. For those still in chains, flight to the British lines offered a release from bondage. As peace returned in 1815, as Americans surged west in search of new land in recently established U.S. territories, and as tensions mounted between the North and South, what would happen to the growing population of enslaved African Americans? Bondspeople in the United States numbered about 1.3 million as James Monroe won election to the presidency in 1816. Would they follow the examples of the Haitian black insurrectionists and black rebels in the American South such as Gabriel Prosser and Charles Deslondes? Or would they continue toiling in the fields, sorrowfully bringing children into a world of enslavement—all while hoping that new white political leaders would finally set them free?

FURTHER READING

Berlin, Ira. *Slaves Without Masters: The Free Negro in the Antebellum South* (New York: New Press, 1971).

Bolster, W. Jeffrey. *Black Jacks: African American Seamen in the Age of Sail* (Cambridge: Harvard University Press, 1997).

Curry, Leonard P. *The Free Black in Urban America, 1800–1850: The Shadow of a Dream* (Chicago: University of Chicago Press, 1981).

Egerton, Douglas R. *Gabriel's Rebellion: The Virginia Slave Conspiracies of 1800 and 1802* (Chapel Hill: University of North Carolina Press, 1993).

Fields, Barbara Jean. *Slavery and Freedom on the Middle Ground: Maryland During the Nineteenth Century* (New Haven, CT: Yale University Press, 1985).

Gutman, Herbert G. *The Black Family in Slavery and Freedom, 1750–1925* (New York: Pantheon, 1977).

Hanger, Kimberly. *Bounded Lives, Bounded Places: Free Black Society in Colonial New Orleans, 1769–1803* (Durham, NC: Duke University Press, 1997).

Harding, Vincent. *There Is a River: The Black Struggle for Freedom in America* (New York: Harcourt, Brace Jovanovich, 1981).

Harris, Leslie M. *In the Shadow of Slavery: African Americans in New York City, 1626–1863* (Chicago: University of Chicago Press, 2003).

Horton, James Oliver. *Free People of Color: Inside the African American Community* (Washington, DC: Smithsonian, 1993).

Horton, James Oliver, and Lois E. Horton. *In Hope of Liberty: Culture, Community, and Protest Among Northern Free Blacks, 1700–1860* (New York: Oxford University Press, 1997).

Lebsock, Suzanne. *The Free Women of Petersburg: Status and Culture in a Southern Town, 1784–1860* (New York: W. W. Norton, 1984).

Lewis, Jan Ellen, and Peter S. Onuf, eds. *Sally Hemings and Thomas Jefferson: History, Memory, and Civic Culture* (Charlottesville: University Press of Virginia, 1999).

Melish, Joanne Pope. *Disowning Slavery: Gradual Emancipation and "Race" in New England, 1780–1860* (Ithaca, NY: Cornell University Press, 1998).

Morris, Thomas D. *Free Men All: The Personal Liberty Laws of the North, 1780–1861* (Baltimore: Johns Hopkins University Press, 1974).

Nash, Gary B. *Forging Freedom: The Formation of Philadelphia's Black Community, 1720–1840* (Cambridge: Harvard University Press, 1988).

Newman, Richard S. *The Transformation of American Abolitionism: Fighting Slavery in the New Republic* (Chapel Hill: University of North Carolina Press, 2002).

Phillips, Christopher. *Freedom's Port: The African American Community of Baltimore, 1790–1860* (Urbana: University of Illinois Press, 1997).

Sidbury, James. *Ploughshares into Swords: Race, Rebellion, and Identity in Gabriel's Virginia* (New York: Cambridge University Press, 1998).

Takagi, Midori. *"Rearing Wolves to Our Own Destruction": Slavery in Richmond, Virginia, 1782–1865* (Charlottesville: University Press of Virginia, 1999).

Wiencek, Henry. *An Imperfect God: George Washington, His Slaves, and the Creation of America* (New York: Farrar, Straus, Giroux, 2003).

White, Shane. *Somewhat More Independent: The End of Slavery in New York City, 1770–1810* (Athens: University Press of Georgia, 1991).

Winch, Julie. *A Gentleman of Color: The Life of James Forten* (New York: Oxford University Press, 2002)

CHAPTER 7

■ Eyre Crowe's *After the Sale: Slaves Going South from Richmond*, (1852–1853).

African Americans in the Antebellum Era

James Forten on Repatriation to Africa

On a wintry January evening in 1817, James Forten squeezed his way forward to the pulpit through nearly 3,000 black men who had thronged Philadelphia's Mother Bethel church. They packed the main floor, overflowed the *U*-shaped balcony, and spilled into the street in an assemblage such as the city had never seen. Representing nearly three-quarters of all African American men in Philadelphia, they had gathered to speak their minds on a hotly debated issue: a campaign initiated by white leaders to repatriate free black people to Africa.

The city's most respected black businessman, Forten opened his heart to his fellow African Americans. Forten reflected on what had happened over recent years in the lives of more than two million slaves and several hundred thousand free people of color. Though still alive, the antislavery movement had lost momentum since the slave trade ended in 1808. In the northern cities, white hostility blocked the advancement of free black people, while the federal government whittled away at their job opportunities. While Forten maintained a workforce of black and white craftsmen in his thriving sail loft, most trades excluded African Americans. White craftsmen refused to take black apprentices for training and pushed skilled black artisans out of the trades. Free black Americans had struggled mightily to establish the churches, schools, and mutual aid societies to disprove white charges of black inferiority. But this difficult road forward now seemed strewn with more obstacles than ever. Earlier hopes for racial equality—and the end of slavery—were fading in what African Americans increasingly saw as a white man's country.

A year earlier, white political leaders had founded the American Colonization Society (ACS) in Washington, D.C. Led by outgoing president James Madison and incoming president James Monroe, and including such prominent figures as Chief Justice John Marshall, Kentucky's Henry Clay, South Carolina's John C. Calhoun,

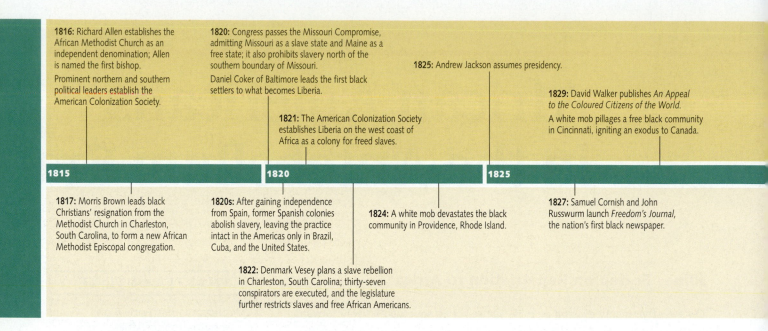

1816: Richard Allen establishes the African Methodist Church as an independent denomination; Allen is named the first bishop.

Prominent northern and southern political leaders establish the American Colonization Society.

1820: Congress passes the Missouri Compromise, admitting Missouri as a slave state and Maine as a free state; it also prohibits slavery north of the southern boundary of Missouri.

Daniel Coker of Baltimore leads the first black settlers to what becomes Liberia.

1825: Andrew Jackson assumes presidency.

1829: David Walker publishes *An Appeal to the Coloured Citizens of the World.*

A white mob pillages a free black community in Cincinnati, igniting an exodus to Canada.

1821: The American Colonization Society establishes Liberia on the west coast of Africa as a colony for freed slaves.

1815 **1820** **1825**

1817: Morris Brown leads black Christians' resignation from the Methodist Church in Charleston, South Carolina, to form a new African Methodist Episcopal congregation.

1820s: After gaining independence from Spain, former Spanish colonies abolish slavery, leaving the practice intact in the Americas only in Brazil, Cuba, and the United States.

1824: A white mob devastates the black community in Providence, Rhode Island.

1827: Samuel Cornish and John Russwurm launch *Freedom's Journal,* the nation's first black newspaper.

1822: Denmark Vesey plans a slave rebellion in Charleston, South Carolina; thirty-seven conspirators are executed, and the legislature further restricts slaves and free African Americans.

and Francis Scott Key, who wrote the lyrics of "The Star Spangled Banner," ACS members dedicated themselves to resettling free African Americans on Africa's west coast. White northerners endorsed the scheme for various reasons. Some believed white prejudice and the scars inflicted by slavery doomed any dream of racial equality in America. Many northern Protestant church leaders also saw repatriation as an opportunity to take Christianity to a continent teeming with potential new souls. Even the son of Philadelphia's Benjamin Rush, who had aided black Philadelphians' emergence from slavery, signed up for the cause. Meanwhile, numerous white southerners saw free African Americans as a threat to the continuation of slavery (and thus to their economy). In their view, free black people's emigration to Africa would remove this threat.

Long before the founding of the ACS, Forten and other northern black leaders had supported colonization. The notion appealed to African Americans who no longer believed that the United States would give up slaveholding. The vast new cotton lands opened to settlement in the Lower South and the Louisiana Territory had fueled the spread of slavery. In the North, white people prejudiced against free African Americans denied them citizenship and equal protection under the law. In a letter to Paul Cuffe, Forten expressed his belief that African Americans "will never become a people until they come out from amongst the white people." The idea of returning to Africa was Cuffe's dream, and he had already organized groups in New York and Philadelphia to support colonization. In 1811 he had transported thirty-eight black settlers to West Africa. Peter Gloucester, the black minister of Philadelphia's African Presbyterian Church, had sent his son to white ministers for training as a black missionary to Africa.

Chairing the meeting inside Mother Bethel church, Forten called on Philadelphia's three notable black ministers—Richard Allen, Absalom Jones, and Peter Gloucester—to explain to the crowd the advantages of returning to the ancestral homeland. Forten added his support. Then came time for a vote. Forten called first for "ayes" from those who favored colonization. Not one person spoke up or lifted a hand. Then he called for those opposed to colonization. The response, Forten later recalled, was one tremendous "no" that seemed "as if it would bring down the walls of the building. . . . There was not a soul that was in favor of going to Africa." Similar scenes played out in other cities in the North and Upper South.

Why did free black people oppose a plan that, on its surface, held so much promise? Ordinary black men and women understood what their leaders did not: that whatever the sincerity and good will of some ACS leaders, the repatriation project would almost certainly fall under the control of southerners seeking the deportation of free black people to

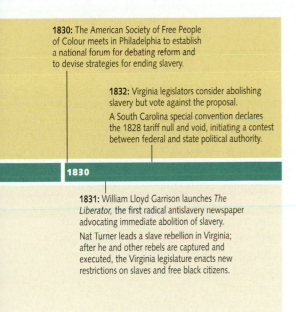

1830: The American Society of Free People of Colour meets in Philadelphia to establish a national forum for debating reform and to devise strategies for ending slavery.

1832: Virginia legislators consider abolishing slavery but vote against the proposal.
A South Carolina special convention declares the 1828 tariff null and void, initiating a contest between federal and state political authority.

1830

1831: William Lloyd Garrison launches *The Liberator,* the first radical antislavery newspaper advocating immediate abolition of slavery.
Nat Turner leads a slave rebellion in Virginia; after he and other rebels are captured and executed, the Virginia legislature enacts new restrictions on slaves and free black citizens.

protect the institution of slavery. Black Philadelphians, Forten reported, were "very much frightened . . . that all the free people would be compelled to go." They could not believe that whites wanted to do "a great good" for a people they hated. Rather, they unanimously felt certain that "the slaveholders want to get rid of [free blacks] so as to make their [slave] property more secure."

The emotional meeting at Mother Bethel church proved a defining event for black Americans. The black men who poured out of the building afterward carried with them a new commitment to the abolition of slavery and a new feeling of unity with dark-skinned peoples of different classes and religious affiliations. The resolutions they endorsed in January 1817 rejected the argument of Henry Clay, an eminent southern politician, that free black people were "a dangerous and useless part of the community" and expressed African Americans' determination to fight for freedom and equality on U.S. soil. "Whereas our ancestors (not of choice) were the first successful cultivators of the wilds of America," they announced, "we their descendants feel ourselves entitled to participate in the blessings of her luxuriant soil, which their blood and sweat manured; and that any measure . . . having the tendency to banish us from her bosom, would not only be cruel, but in direct violation of those principles which have been the boast of the republic. We never will separate ourselves voluntarily

from the slave population of this country, . . . our brethren by the ties of consanguinity, or suffering, and of wrong."

So the old battle against prejudice was rejoined. From the founding of the ACS in 1816 to a momentous Virginia slave rebellion in 1831, black Americans across the nation waged a common struggle. Free African Americans looked to build viable communities within a white-dominated land. By building independent religious denominations, establishing newspapers, and convening national conferences, they hoped to unite dozens of flourishing black communities to fight slavery and its expansion. For the vast majority of black Americans still trapped in slavery, life had grown more difficult than ever. The Louisiana Purchase and the Missouri Compromise triggered a massive transfer of slaves south and west.

Yet black people's dreams of freedom endured. Some African Americans in the South, both enslaved and free, challenged slavery through compelling words and deeds. Three inspirational figures—Denmark Vesey, David Walker, and Nat Turner—led attempts to end the nightmare of slavery, even as southerners stepped up their defense of the practice. Thomas Jefferson's comment to a friend in 1814 proved eerily predictive: "The hour of emancipation is advancing in the march of time," he wrote. Jefferson wondered if emancipation would be "brought on by the generous energy of our own minds" or perhaps would occur "by the bloody process of St. Domingo"— that is, the Haitian Revolution. Would white Americans free slaves willingly, or would oppressed African Americans grasp history by the throat? Full of premonitions, the aging author of the Declaration of Independence could not decide. It "is a leaf of our history," he wrote, "not yet turned over."

BLACK RELIGION IN THE ANTEBELLUM ERA

The black church was the rock on which all black struggles for freedom and equality rested. The more white hostility intensified, the more black people needed an independent church as a bastion of strength. In the early nineteenth century, separate black churches arose wherever a few hundred free black people lived. The next logical move was to connect these churches in regional networks.

■ This drawing of James Forten, by an unknown artist, is the only known image of the African American leader. Paul Cuffe's reply to Forten's letter quoted on p. 160 was the last he wrote. The New Bedford ship captain died on September 7, 1817.

The African Methodist Episcopal Church

Richard Allen had such networks in mind when he convened a meeting of black Methodists in April 1816. "Taking into consideration their grievances, and in order to secure their privileges, promote union and harmony among themselves," he wrote, black ministers from Maryland, Delaware, New Jersey, and Pennsylvania resolved they should "become one body under the name of the African Methodist Episcopal Church" (AME). Only by creating their own separate denomination could African Americans escape the "spiritual despotism which we have so recently experienced—remembering that we are not to lord it over God's heritage, as greedy dogs that can never have enough." Thus was born the AME. The organization became the largest denomination of black Christians in the United States and spread steadily around the world. The black ministers chose Richard Allen as their first bishop.

Such a declaration of black independence offended white Americans who wanted black subordination, not black self-assertion. Years later, one of Allen's successors as the AME's bishop stressed the importance of resisting white notions of black inferiority. Taking his cue from the scriptural passage "Stand up, I myself am also a man," Daniel Payne wrote of the psychological and political transformation that came from the creation of independent black churches. When white religious leaders controlled black churches and supplied them with preachers, deacons, and elders, most of whom were white, the merit of the churches "was the white man's and his alone. . . . The colored man was a mere hearer." The point of this paternalism, Payne believed, was "to prove that the colored man was incapable of self-government and self-support." Founding the AME was "a flat contradiction and triumphant refutation of this slander, so foul in itself and so degrading in its influence."

Charismatic Preachers

As one of his first challenges as bishop, Allen had to confront a member of his church who had a mission of her own. Jarena Lee had been born free in New Jersey, but like the children of many poor free black people, she was apprenticed to a white family as a child. She came to Philadelphia as a teenager and there experienced profound spiritual stirrings. In particular, she was transformed by a passionate sermon Allen delivered in Mother Bethel church. "That moment, though hundreds were present," she later wrote, "I did leap to my feet and declare that God, for Christ's sake, had pardoned the sins of my soul." In 1811, seven years after joining Mother Bethel, she married Joseph Lee, a black minister. Soon she heard a voice saying to her, "Go preach the Gospel!" "I immediately replied aloud, 'No one will believe me,'" Lee recalled. "Again I listened and again the same voice seemed to say, 'Preach the Gospel; I will put words in your mouth, and will turn your enemies to become your friends.'"

One night Jarena Lee had a dream. In her sleep "there stood before me a great multitude, while I expounded to them the things of religion. So violent were my exertions and so loud were my exclamations that I awoke from the sound of my own voice." Startled by her ability to preach in the dream (a power that few expected women to possess), Lee called on Allen several days later. God had spoken to her, she told him, and had commanded her to preach. Allen explained that she could not preach from Mother Bethel's pulpit because Methodism had no provision for women preachers. Lee did not back down. "If the man may preach, because the Savior died for him, why

■ This image of Jarena Lee was not included in the first edition of her *Life and Religious Experience of Jarena Lee* (1836). The several editions of her book made her one of the first women of the nineteenth century to reach a wide audience through print. In 1844 and 1852, women unsuccessfully petitioned the AME General Conference to allow ordination of black women.

to labor according to my ability. . . . I imagined, that for this indecorum, as I feared it might be called, I should be expelled from the church." Lee's outpouring convinced Allen that she "was called to that work as any of the preachers present." Though he gave her no official appointment as a minister, Allen opened Mother Bethel's pulpit to her. He also took her side against clergymen who adamantly opposed women preachers, and accepted her son into his own household for several years.

Thereafter, Lee crisscrossed the country, turning fields, farms, and city streets into sacred spaces when she could find no consecrated church in which to preach. Convinced she was safeguarded by divine protection and favor, she often delivered sermons to interracial gatherings. Traveling as far north as Canada and as far south as Maryland, she reached thousands. In one year, she journeyed more than 2,000 miles on foot and by steamboat, delivering 178 sermons.

Though never ordained, Lee served as an inspiration to AME women. Like white women in evangelical denominations, black women did the church's work: teaching in church schools, persuading wayward husbands to resume their family responsibilities, leading prayer meetings, and organizing auxiliaries that developed and maintained church programs. In gaining the pulpit, Lee broke a barrier women did not surmount in other denominations, black or white, for many decades. Across the remnants of this barrier strode other spiritually gifted Methodist women, such as Rebecca Cox Jackson, sister of a lay preacher at Richard Allen's Mother Bethel church.

THE EXPANSION OF SLAVERY

"This man came up to me, and, seizing me by the collar, shook me violently, saying I was his property, and must go with him to Georgia. . . . [He] ordered me to cross my hands behind, which were quickly bound with a strong cord; and he then told me that we must set out that very day for the south. I asked if I could not be allowed to go to see my wife and children, or if this could not be permitted, if they might not have leave to come to see me; but was told that I would be able to get another wife in Georgia." These were the words of Charles Ball, sold in 1805 by his Maryland master, who no longer needed many slaves. Like thousands of other bondspeople, Ball endured fresh pain and heartache as slavery expanded into the new southern frontier lands under development for cotton production. Passage of the

not the woman, seeing he died for her also? Is he not a whole Savior, instead of a half one?" Allen still refused to grant Lee's request, but he encouraged her to use her spiritual gifts to hold prayer meetings in her home and to take to the road as an itinerant preacher—a person without a settled church. This she did after her husband died in 1817, leaving her to support her two small children.

Two years later, Lee arose spontaneously during a Sunday service at Mother Bethel when the male minister seemed to lose the spirit. Words tumbled from her mouth, and the crowded church fell under her sway. "God made manifest His power in a manner sufficient to show the world that I was called

> "**I**f the man may preach, because the Savior died for him, why not the woman, seeing he died for her also?"—*Jarena Lee*

 **First Person**

Jarena Lee Preaches to the Downtrodden

In a journey through the Upper South, Jarena Lee encountered many slaves who had heard of the spiritual balm she dispensed. In 1836, she published her autobiography, The Life and Religious Experience of Jarena Lee, a Coloured Lady, Giving an Account of Her Call to Preach the Gospel. *She wrote of how "the Lord hath anointed me to preach good tidings unto the meek. He hath sent me to bind up the broken-hearted, to proclaim liberty to the captives, and the opening of the prison to them that are bound." In this passage, she describes her effect on some who heard her.*

In my wanderings up and down among men, preaching according to my ability, I have frequently found families who told me that they had not for several years been to a meeting, and yet, while listening to hear what God would say by his poor coloured female instrument, have believed with trembling—tears rolling down their cheeks, the signs of contrition and repentance towards God. I firmly believe that I have sown seed, in the name of the Lord, which shall appear with its increase at the great day of accounts, when Christ shall come to make up his jewels.

—*from* The Life and Religious Experience of Jarena Lee, a Colour Lady, Giving an Account of Her Call to Preach the Gospel *(1836)*.

To view a longer version of this document, please go to *www.ablongman.com/carson/documents*.

Missouri Compromise only worsened the plight of black Americans by facilitating the spread of southern slavery. Native Americans suffered as well. By the 1830s, land-hungry cotton planters had expelled Cherokees, Creeks, Choctaws, Chickasaws, and Seminoles from their ancestral homelands. White officials prodded tribe members along the "Trail of Tears" to the Arkansas Territory, to Mexican Texas, and to the unorganized region later known as the Oklahoma Territory.

King Cotton

The shipment of slaves from the Upper to the Lower South in the first half of the nineteenth century called to mind the middle passage endured by African Americans' ancestors in earlier centuries. This forced migration was triggered by the invention of a disarmingly simple machine that processed as much cotton in a single day as fifty slaves cleaned by hand. In 1793, Connecticut schoolteacher Eli Whitney had constructed an engine, or "gin"—a wooden box containing a roller equipped with wire teeth—that revolutionized cotton production. The mechanism pulled the fibers from cotton bolls through a comblike barrier to strip away their sticky green seeds. Whitney's cotton gin was operated by hand, but when built on a large scale with a giant roller driven by horses or waterpower, the machine could be tended by a single laborer. Before 1793, the time-consuming work of cleaning cotton had limited its profitability. With processing now made easy, cotton cultivation took off.

For landowners, Whitney's invention promised enormous benefits. In Britain and New England, new textile factories turned cotton into cloth coveted around the world. For southern planters, many chronically in debt, the invention slashed the costs of processing cotton and boosted profits to unprecedented heights. Southerners, along with some northerners, headed for the new frontier in the Old Southwest and Louisiana Territory to jump into the cotton business. After the War of 1812, the exodus of white planters from the seaboard states resembled a gold rush. Congress admitted Mississippi and Alabama to the Union as states in 1817 and 1819, respectively, and by 1838, their slaves were producing half the nation's cotton.

But for some 800,000 slaves sold south—about one-third of all slaves aged eighteen to thirty—Whitney's technological breakthrough spawned only heartache. Slave manumissions decreased because masters saw new opportunities to make slavery profitable. Forced marches south and west of healthy young slaves into lands previously uninhabited by white settlers broke up black families. The clearing and cultivating of new cotton fields in Tennessee, Alabama, Mississippi, Louisiana, and eventually Texas made slaves' work harsher and more backbreaking than ever.

As in Africa centuries before, slave coffles trudged south from Virginia, Maryland, Delaware, and North Carolina. Thousands of other enslaved men, women, and children were loaded onto ships in Baltimore, Washington, D.C., Alexandria, Norfolk, and Charleston and transported to Lower South ports, especially New Orleans. There, strange new masters bought them at auction and took them far away from family and friends.

The sharp rise in cotton production marked a turning point for the South and the nation. A minor commodity in 1790, cotton became an engine of economic development in both the South and North. As production of cotton

soared, so did the southern slave population (see Figure 7.1). "To sell cotton in order to buy negroes—to make more cotton to buy more negroes ad infinitum is the aim and direct tendency of all the operations of the thorough-going planter," wrote one traveler in the South. "His whole soul is wrapped up in the pursuit. It is, apparently, the principle by which he lives, moves, and has his being."

The Missouri Compromise

Cotton cultivation propelled slavery west across the Mississippi River. Now Congress could no longer tuck the smoldering issue of slavery beneath the surface of political life. Since 1789, Congress had admitted new states to the Union on an equal basis—one slave state for each free state. This strategy was crucial for maintaining the balance of congressional representatives between North and South that the Constitution's three-fifths compromise sought to ensure. But as the rapid growth of the white population in northern states gave the North a 105-to-81-member advantage in the House of Representatives, white southerners feared the scales would tip permanently against them.

Then, in 1819, the legislature of the Missouri Territory applied for statehood with explicit guarantees to permit slaveholding. Congress had allowed slavery in the old Mississippi Territory and disallowed the transportation of slaves into the Northwest Territory. However, it had never ruled on whether slavery could spread west of the Mississippi River. Now southerners implored the government to keep the trans-Mississippi West open to slavery. But admitting Missouri into the Union as a slave state—the first to be carved out of the Louisiana Purchase—would tip the balance in the Senate to the South. This was "the firebell in the night" that Thomas Jefferson claimed "awakened and filled me with terror." Nearly everyone else in the country shared the same sense of foreboding that these sectional tensions might come to a head.

Congressional lawmakers debated the issue heatedly for nearly three months. The question was not about whether to abolish slavery but about whether to allow it to spread into new territories. Both legislative houses divided sharply on two northern proposals for the gradual abolition of slavery after Missouri gained statehood. The first proposal suggested that slaves born in Missouri would be free at age twenty-five; the second, that once granted statehood, Missourians could not import any new slaves. Both proposals passed in the House of Representatives, where free African Americans in the gallery listened with approval. But in the Senate, where the northern and southern states had an even number of seats, several border-state senators sided with the South to defeat the proposal. The economic necessity and

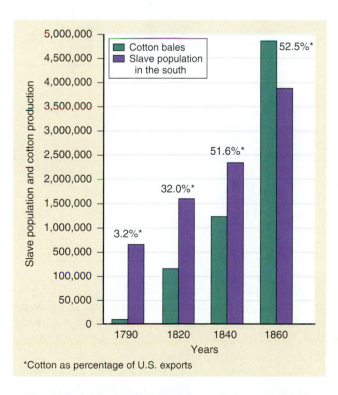

■ **FIGURE 7.1 Slave Population and Cotton Production, 1790–1860**

This chart shows why the term "King Cotton" came into use, as it became the nation's most important export.

■ **MAP 7.1** **The Internal Slave Trade, 1790–1860**

Most slaves sold in the Upper South were shipped down the Atlantic coast, around Florida, and into the Gulf of Mexico, where they were sold at auction in New Orleans and lesser slave-trading centers such as Mobile, Natchez, and Galveston. Smaller numbers went by foot or railroad. However, slave traders preferred water transportation for its speed and affordability.

moral uncertainty of slavery became a national political flashpoint, preoccupying the country's leaders and adding fuel to sectional conflicts that had been simmering for years.

By March 1820, Congress had hammered out a compromise. It admitted Maine, until now an adjunct of Massachusetts, as a free state to counterbalance the admission of Missouri as a slave state, thus maintaining the North-South balance in Senate seats. It also drew an east-west line along Missouri's southern border (36" 30') that divided the rest of the Louisiana Territory into future slave and free states. But then a second issue reared its head. A Missouri constitution,

written and passed in St. Louis in July 1820 by a proslavery convention, forbade the entry of free black Americans into the new state. Here the issue became one of citizenship. Were free black people U.S. citizens or not? Were they at liberty to go anywhere they wished?

Many northern congressmen decried the Missouri constitution's denial of free black citizenship. The law, they argued, deprived free black people everywhere of all the rights guaranteed in the U.S. Constitution—including the right to acquire property and the right to religious freedom. Southern legislators, for their part, vigorously defended

Missouri's constitution. In their view, free black people had no right to enter Missouri because they were *not* U.S. citizens. These lawmakers insisted that many northern states themselves denied free black people full citizenship rights—including the rights to vote or hold office, give evidence in court, and serve in the militia. Why should a southern state recognize the citizenship of free black people, they added, when the laws and constitutions of northern states treated African Americans, as one Delaware Congressman put it, as "a weaker caste" that could not "assimilate" with white Americans any more than "oil with water"?

Bringing the pivotal question of African American citizenship to a head, the debate embarrassed the North and heightened sectional animosity. In the end, lawmakers added a vague clause to the Missouri state constitution indicating that no citizen should be denied rights conferred by the U.S. Constitution—nearly meaningless language because no one had yet clearly defined the word *citizen*. This clause left the legal status of Missouri's free African Americans a matter for local, state, and federal courts to decide. When the Missouri legislature later passed a law banning the admission of free black people, Congress remained mute.

The Missouri Compromise temporarily shelved the issues of slavery's expansion and free black people's rights. But the issues kept simmering deep within the nation's governing bodies. Soon they resurfaced and sparked even more violent confrontations between pro- and antislavery Americans.

The Interstate Slave Trade

The expansion of slavery throughout the South increased the interstate slave trade, which burgeoned between the early 1800s and the eve of the Civil War. Interstate slave trading replaced the international form of dealing in human chattel. Large interstate slave trading firms, such as Franklin and Armfield of Virginia and Woolfolk and Slatter of Maryland, totaled hundreds of thousands of dollars in their ledgers each year. Refitting stables, warehouses, and disheveled buildings into slave pens, they herded bondsmen and women purchased from owners in the Upper South into the enclosures like cattle. From 1810 to 1860, an average of 15,000 slaves a year made the forced journey by ship or on foot through raw country to the Deep South. An estimated 300,000 Virginia slaves were sold "down the river," many from Alexandria, within view of the nation's capital, to a large depot near Natchez, Mississippi. By 1830, 825,000 slaves labored in the cotton states of South Car-

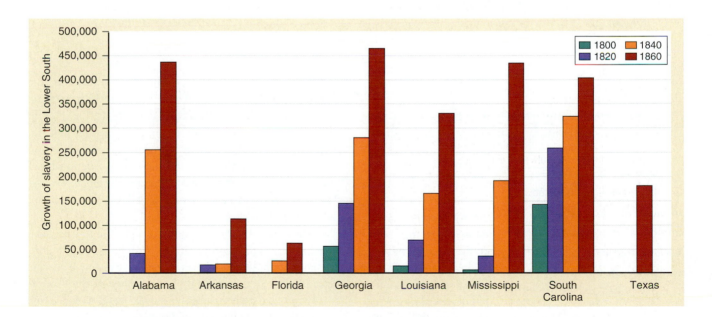

■ **FIGURE 7.2** **The Growth of Slavery in the Lower South, 1800–1860**

By 1860, about thirty African Americans for every hundred white Americans lived in the Upper South, while the Lower South contained about eighty-two African Americans for every hundred white Americans. Even as slaves were transported south, the birthrate among enslaved women rose, creating a large proportion of children born into bondage. By 1830, nearly 700,000 of the two million slaves were younger than ten.

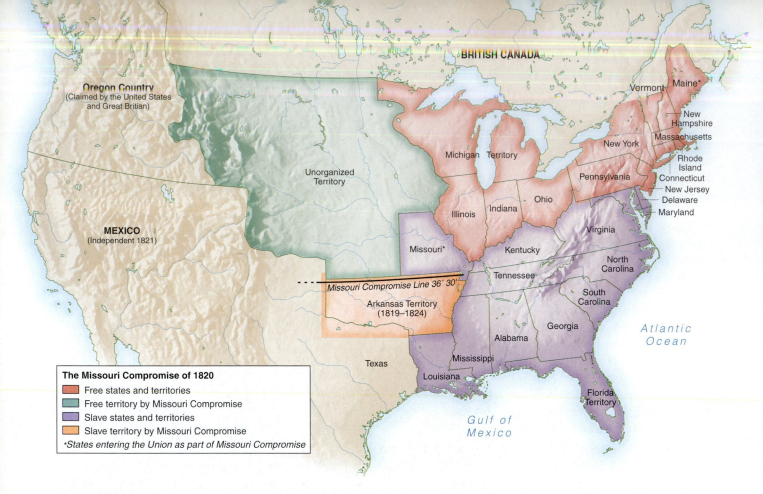

■ **MAP 7.2** **The Missouri Compromise of 1820**

Most southerners were pleased with the Missouri Compromise because it sanctioned slavery in an area where slave labor was most profitable. Out of the Arkansas Territory below the 36" 30' shown on this map, the new slave state of Arkansas was admitted to the Union.

olina, Georgia, Alabama, Louisiana, and Mississippi—four times as many as in 1800.

The vigorous commerce in human beings drove the success of the cotton industry while bringing new turmoil and terror for slaves. In addition to all the previous agonies of slave life, bondspeople now had to face the nightmare of being sold south. Human misery reached its limits in the slave pens and on auction blocks of a country on the move. "I joined fifty-one other slaves," remembered Charles Ball, "thirty-two of these were men, and nineteen women. . . . A strong iron collar was closely fitted by means of a padlock around each of our necks. . . . We were handcuffed in pairs, with iron staples and bolts, with a short chain, about a foot long, uniting the handcuffs and their

> "We were handcuffed in pairs, with iron staples and bolts, with a short chain, about a foot long, uniting the handcuffs and their wearers in pairs."
> —Charles Ball

wearers in pairs. . . . The poor man to whom I was thus ironed wept like an infant when the blacksmith, with his heavy hammer, fastened the ends of the bolts that kept the staples from slipping from our arms." Scenes like this reminded slaves that their relationship with white masters derived solely from economic motivation. Auction-block sales dehumanized men, women, and children as potential buyers prodded, inspected, and haggled over them as if at a horse or cattle auction.

The spread of cotton production south and west shattered slave families and separated kinfolk as never before. Enslaved families had never been secure, but in earlier decades they were usually broken up only on the death of an owner. In such instances, slaves were parceled out among the owner's heirs or sold outside the family to satisfy debts. Painful though this was, divided black families in neighboring areas were usually able to maintain at least some contact. But with the rise of the interstate slave trade, husbands were now sold from wives, and children, especially boys, were torn from parents they never saw again. The records of the Franklin and Armfield slave-trading firm

■ This engraving of an enslaved woman jumping from the window of a tavern in the nation's capital appeared in Jesse Torrey's *The American Slave Trade* (London, 1822), one of the first abolitionist indictments of the internal slave trade. The book relates the story of the woman's despair over the sale of her children in 1815 and her assignment to a procession of slaves chained together for shipment to the Lower South.

in Virginia from 1828 to 1836 show that three-quarters of all slaves sold south were single African Americans sold away from their families. Four-fifths of the women sold with children were shipped off without their husbands. Of the single boys and men sold, three-quarters were under age twenty-five, and of these one-third were sixteen or younger. During the antebellum era, probably one-third of all Upper South young black men and boys were sold south.

SLAVE LIFE AND LABOR

"We were worked in all weather. It was never too hot or too cold; it could never rain, blow hail, or snow too hard for us to work in the field. Work, work, work, was scarcely more the order of the day than of the night." So remembered Frederick Douglass, the man who became the most important African American abolitionist and autobiographer of the antebellum years. "It was—'Fred, come help me to cant this timber here,'" he continued. "'Hurra, Fred! Run and bring me a chisel.'—'I say, Fred, bear a hand, and get up a fire as quick as lightning under that steam box.'—'Halloo,

nigger! Come, turn this grindstone.'—'Come, come! Move, move! And *bowse* this timber forward'—'I say, darky, blast your eyes, why don't you heat up some pitch?'—'Halloo! Halloo! Halloo! (Three voices at the same time.) 'Come here!—Go there!—Hold on where you are! Damn you, if you move, I'll knock your brains out!' This was my school."

With these words, Douglass expressed the essence of slave life: the expropriation of labor from all those enslaved—young as well as old, women and children as much as men. While northern free black people struggled for their place *in the* sun, a vastly larger number of slaves struggled *under* the sun in lifelong labor. During the antebellum era, the population of enslaved Americans skyrocketed, mostly through natural increase. About 697,000 in 1790, the number of slaves reached nearly 1.2 million in 1810, more than 2 million in 1830, and 3.2 million in 1850.

> "We were worked in all weather. It was never too hot or too cold; it could never rain, blow hail, or snow too hard for us to work in the field."
> —*Frederick Douglass*

 **First Person**

Solomon Northup Describes a New Orleans Slave Auction

Solomon Northup, born free in New York, lived with his wife and children until 1841, when he was hired as a violinist to accompany a circus south to Washington, D.C. There he was seized by a slave dealer, beaten severely for protesting that he was a free man, and held in a slave pen for ten days. His captors next shipped him to the New Orleans slave market, where he was sold to a Louisiana planter. After escaping slavery twelve years later, he was interviewed by abolitionists. His account, published in 1853 as Twelve Years a Slave, *became a bestseller. In this excerpt, Northup describes a New Orleans slave auction where a young mother implored the man who bought her to also purchase her two young children.*

All the time the trade was going on, Eliza was crying aloud, and wringing her hands. She besought the man not to buy him [her young son], unless he also bought herself and Emily [her young daughter]. She promised, in that case, to be the most faithful slave that ever lived. The man answered that he could not afford it, and then Eliza burst into a paroxysm of grief, weeping plaintively. Freeman turned round to her, savagely, with his whip in his uplifted hand, ordered her to stop her noise, or he would flog her. He would not have such work—such snivelling; and unless she ceased that minute, he would take her to the yard and give her a hundred lashes. . . . Eliza shrunk before him, and tried to wipe away her tears, but it was all in vain. She wanted to be with her children, she said, the little time she had to live. All the frowns and threats of Freeman could not wholly silence the afflicted mother. She kept on begging and beseeching, most piteously, not to separate the three. Over and over again she told them how she loved her boy. A great many times she repeated her former promises—how very faithful and obedient she would be; how hard she would labor day and night, to the last moment of her life, if he would only buy them all together. . . . [The auctioneer] damned her, calling her a blubbering, bawling wench, and ordered her to go to her place and behave herself, and be some body.

—from Solomon Northup, Twelve Years a Slave, Narrative of Solomon Northup, a Citizen of New York, Kidnapped in Washington City in 1841, from a Cotton Plantation Near the Red River in Louisiana *(1853).*

To view a longer version of this document, please go to *www.ablongman.com/carson/documents*.

Sunup to Sundown: Working for the Master

Slave labor took many forms depending on the region and the crop. Slaves working in the less labor-intensive tobacco- and wheat-growing regions of the Upper South fared better than those toiling in the snake-infested, swampy rice and indigo fields of South Carolina and Georgia. Those who worked in the city enjoyed more advantages than plantation laborers, especially slaves whose masters permitted them to hire themselves out to employers on their own time. Yet plantation labor also varied depending on whether a person worked as a field hand, an artisan, or a domestic servant in the master's house. Men's, women's, and children's work differed markedly as well.

But despite all these differences, three-quarters of all slaves in the South cultivated cotton by the eve of the Civil War. In the cotton fields of Georgia, Alabama, and Mississippi, and even in upcountry Tennessee and Kentucky, slaves endured the harshest possible working conditions. Year-round, they hacked down trees and cleared land. During harvest season, the workday for cotton field hands stretched to sixteen or even eighteen hours. At any moment, a man, woman, or child could feel the lash of the master's whip.

Solomon Northup never forgot the cruelty of the cotton fields. During the hoeing season, "the overseer or driver follows the slaves on horseback with a whip. . . . The fastest hoer takes the lead row. He is usually about a rod [five and a half yards] in advance of his companions. If one of them passes him, he is whipped. If one falls behind or is a moment idle, he is whipped. In fact, the lash is flying from morning until night, the whole day long." During picking season, from "day clean to first dark" and with just minutes "to swallow their allowance of cold bacon," slaves lived in fear that they would not meet their picking quotas. The lash came down hard on those who failed.

In part, the number of slaves living on a particular plantation shaped their quality of life. On plantations with fewer than twenty bondspeople, most of them had to labor in the fields. But on the few plantations that had more than twenty slaves, there were more opportunities to work as craftsmen or domestic laborers in the big house. Many slaves gladly exchanged the backbreaking repetitiveness of cotton and rice cultivation for the more creative tasks of carpentry, blacksmithing, wagoning, river transporting, livestock tending, housekeeping, cooking, sewing, and childrearing. The most fortunate slaves had masters who not only trusted them but relied on them to supervise a farm or plantation, carry goods to market by wagon or boat, manage the master's affairs at the marketplace, or oversee other bondspeople's labor.

Slavery held special horrors for women. "[It] is terrible for men; but it is far more terrible for women," wrote Harriet Jacobs, who escaped her owner in North Carolina. "Superadded to the burden common to all," she explained, "they have wrongs, and sufferings, and mortifications peculiarly their own." In the delicate language of the day, Jacobs tried to convey the frequent sexual abuse white masters inflicted on enslaved women. She also knew that on farms and plantations, as one slave remembered, "women who do outdoor work are used as bad as men." Enslaved black women picked cotton, plowed with mule and ox teams, hoed endless rows of corn, dug ditches, spread manure fertilizer, and cut sugarcane. In the evenings, they trudged from the fields to the slave quarters, where they prepared the evening meal for their families, washed and sewed clothes, and cleaned the cabin. Women also worked in groups apart from men, spinning, weaving, and quilting. Elderly women had special responsibilities as nurses, midwives, and caretakers of a slave community's children.

In southern cities, where about one-tenth of all slaves and at least one-third of free black people lived, work regimens had greater variety than they did on the plantations. Bondsmen and women had somewhat more tolerable lives

as well. Frederick Douglass believed that "a city slave, in Baltimore, is almost a free citizen compared with a slave on [a] plantation. He is much better fed and clothed, is less dejected in his appearance, and enjoys privileges altogether unknown to the whip-driven slave on the plantation." Nonetheless, slave labor in the cities presented its own hardships. Slaves worked long, exhausting days stevedoring on the docks; chopping and hauling wood; digging wells, cellars, canals, and graves; and carrying hods of mortar and brick on house construction sites. In performing these tasks, slaves often sweated alongside free blacks and white immigrants, who by the 1830s yearned to crowd free African Americans out of urban occupations.

Despite this competition, in Lower South cities such as Charleston and New Orleans, far more free black men became skilled artisans than in Upper South and northern cities. This trend toward skilled labor continued when southern masters began to use slaves in industrial work. In sharp contrast to northern textile entrepreneurs, who froze free African Americans out of such work, southern ironmakers, textile manufacturers, and flour mill operators began shifting from paid white labor to slave and paid free African American labor in the 1820s. They did so mostly to eradicate the threat of strikes initiated by organized white workers demanding better wages and shorter hours. In Richmond, for example, the Tredegar Iron Company shifted to slave laborers after an 1847 strike by white ironworkers. Most of the workforce at the city's thirty tobacco-processing plants comprised slaves—one-third of them children. This pattern repeated itself in the flour mills and locomotive factories as well. In other southern cities, such as Charleston, South Carolina, and Lynchburg, Virginia, slaves and free African Americans composed more than half the workforce, skilled and unskilled.

Central to a slave's existence, labor was the pivot point of frequent, tense negotiations between master and bondsperson. Though slaves had limited power to negotiate the terms of their lives, they demanded customs governing work hours, holidays, and the right to maintain their own gardens. A master who made no concessions on such customs risked crop sabotage, arson, and poisoning.

This tension also characterized the system of slave hiring common in southern cities. For masters, "leasing" slaves to other white people provided a way to make quick money. Such enterprise-minded white masters established a fee for leased slaves, part of which went to the slave. They then left it to their bondsmen or women or an agent to find a hiring contract. Slaves benefited from the arrangement as well, saving money toward self-purchase and enjoying time spent away from the master's watchful eye. "After learning to caulk," wrote the young Frederick Douglass, "I sought my own employment, made my own contracts, and collected my own earnings, giving Master Hugh no trouble in any part of the transactions to which I was a party." Self-hiring became so prevalent by the 1840s that brokers and newspaper advertisements began mediating the traffic. Longstanding experience, advised one Louisville, Kentucky, broker, "renders us competent of judging and picking good homes and masters for your negroes."

Yet self-hiring had its disadvantages as well. Slaves who leased themselves out often faced hostility from white laborers who resented the competition, especially in skilled work. Douglass experienced this problem firsthand. When he hired himself out as a ship caulker in Baltimore, a white coworker beat him so badly that Douglass concluded that "the white laboring man was robbed by the slave system of the just results of his labor because he was flung into competition with a class of laborers who worked without wages."

Beyond self-hiring, urban life offered slaves other advantages, including higher-quality clothes and food, more tolerable (if still squalid) quarters, and less brutal treatment. Slaves had greater opportunities to gather and exchange news; to participate in races, fairs, gambling, and gaming; and to find companionship with fellow African Americans who could gather, largely beyond the masters' control, on evenings, Sundays, and holidays.

Urban slaves also frequently came into contact with free African Americans, for every southern city had sizable populations of former slaves who had struggled their way out of bondage. By the 1830s, in Upper South cities such as Baltimore and Washington, D.C., free black people outnumbered slaves. The changing ratio made bondage all the more galling, yet at the same time it nourished enslaved men and women's dreams of freedom. On the other hand, tensions sometimes marred relationships between enslaved and free black people. Some freedmen and women protected their legal advantages by distancing themselves from slaves or avoiding expressing sympathy for them. Moreover, a large majority of freed people were mulattoes with white fathers who had manumitted them. To continue enjoying their privileges as free men and women, they knew they had to preserve their relationships with white people.

Regardless of where they worked and what kind of labor they engaged in, slaves had to face the hard, cold fact that masters held arbitrary power over most aspects of their lives. Yet the rise of antebellum reforms in some parts of the South put constraints on how masters exercised that power. These reforms ranged from women's suffrage and penal reform to the temperance (anti-alcohol) movement and abo-

litionism. Members of evangelical churches in the South no longer advocated the dismantling of slavery, but they did urge masters to treat slaves more humanely. Thrown on the defensive, many southern slave masters adopted the notion of paternalism. According to this idea, slavery was a system of mutual obligation in which masters housed, fed, and looked after the welfare of their slaves, and slaves dutifully served their masters in return. "Inspire a negro with perfect confidence in you," wrote one planter, "and learn him to look to you for support & he is your slave."

Many slaveowners tried to apply the idea of Christian stewardship to the way they governed their slaves. However, the idea of mutual obligation between master and slave was hardly the rule. To be sure, a paternalistic approach to master-slave relations probably prevailed in settled regions like Virginia and Maryland. But in raw rural states, such as Alabama and Mississippi, large-scale selling of slaves "down the river" revealed another attitude entirely.

In addition, white men's relentless sexual assaults on enslaved women belied all talk of mutual obligation. One Virginia slave remembered what thousands of others knew: that an attractive black girl or young woman could be taken into "the big house where the young masters could have the run of her." In her *Incidents in the Life of a Slave Girl*, Harriet Jacobs revealed that her master, an Edenton, North Carolina, doctor, had fathered eleven children with slave women. The man, Jacobs said, tormented her psychologically as soon as she reached adolescence. "He peopled my young mind with unclean images, such as only a vile monster could think of," she explained. "I turned from him with disgust and hatred. But he was my master. . . . He told me I was his property; that I must be subject to his will in all things." Jacobs was one of the few black women in that household to fend off the master's sexual advances and escape to the North.

Physical, psychological, and legal cruelty held the slave system in place. In the realm of physical abuse, whipping was the most common means by which masters battered slaves into compliance. Not every slave was beaten, but all knew that at any moment they *could* feel the lash. All had seen a parent, spouse, or friend subjected to the public bloodying and humiliation that was the mainstay of the slave discipline system. The more sadistic masters advocated flogging periodically regardless of behavior. "Negroes would not bear good usage [treatment]," concluded one South Carolina master. "The best plan would be to give them 25 or 30 lashes a piece every Saturday night anyhow, which will probably keep them straight until Monday morning." The greatest psychological weapon for controlling slaves was the threat of auction. "In Maryland," recounted Charles Ball after he escaped slavery, "it had

 **First Person**

William Wells Brown Recalls Slaves Sent to Lower South

A fugitive slave who fled his master in Cincinnati in 1834, William Wells Brown found refuge with a Quaker family whose name he adopted. Brown worked as a boatman on Lake Erie for nine years, served as a conductor on the Underground Railroad in Ohio, and then became a lecturer for the Western New York Anti-Slavery Society. His Narrative of William W. Brown, a Fugitive Slave *(1848), made him a national and international figure. Here he describes his trip down the Mississippi River with other slaves to be sold in New Orleans.*

There was on the boat a large room on the lower deck, in which the slaves were kept, men and women, promiscuously—all chained two and two, and a strict watch kept that they did not get loose; for cases have occurred in which slaves have got off their chains, and made their escape at landing-places, which the boats were taking in wood;—and with all our care, we lost one woman who had been taken from her husband and children, and having no desire to live without them, in the agony of her soul jumped overboard, and drowned herself.

—*from* The Narrative of William W. Brown, a Fugitive Slave *(1847).*

To view a longer version of this document, please go to *www.ablongman.com/carson/documents*.

always been the practice of masters and mistresses, who wished to terrify their slaves, to threaten to sell them to South Carolina." Every bondsperson knew that a change in the master's moods or fortunes could mean the instant—and permanent—loss of children, spouses, and other family members through auction.

In addition to the inherently cruel nature of slavery, the close daily interactions of white and black people powerfully influenced the master-slave relationship. This was especially true for southern slaveowners who owned fewer than five slaves. Struggling themselves to make a decent living, most of these white farmers shared their housing and meager diet of cornmeal, rice, peas, and salt pork with their handful of bondspeople. On new frontiers in Alabama, Mississippi, and Louisiana, and later in Texas and Arkansas, slave and master, side by side, put broadax and saw to timber, built log houses, slept side by side on a dirt floor, trapped and hunted together, and hacked a new life out of the wilderness. But the fruits of this labor fell almost entirely into the master's hands. The "casual intimacies that had sustained them in the leaner times," one historian writes, gave way to separate slave cabins and an impressive house inhabited by only the master and his family.

Yet no matter how vast the social and psychological distance between slave and master, both parties continued exchanging cultural practices. The food on planters' tables blended African and European cuisines. Agricultural techniques reflected bot groups' longstanding knowledge of farming. Healing techniques used by black women, such as rattlesnake-bite remedies and herbal doctoring, found their way into the world of white people. Trust and distrust, intimacy and hostility, tenderness and antagonism—these paradoxes marked the master-slave relationship. At one extreme, such relations could be cordial or even affectionate. At the other extreme, they could explode into raw hatred, violence, and murder.

Sundown to Sunup: Slaves on Their Own Time

"I was not more than thirteen years old, when, in my loneliness and destitution, I longed for some one to whom I could go, as to a father and a protector. The preaching of a white Methodist minister . . . was the means of causing me to feel that in God I had such a friend. He thought that all men, great and small, bond and free, were sinners in the sight of God . . . and that they must repent of their sins. . . . Though I was a poor, broken-hearted mourner traveling through doubts and fears, I finally found my burden lightened, and my heart relieved . . . I saw the world in a new light."

With these words, Frederick Douglass recalled that the life of a slave was much more than endless travail. Though bondspeople might toil throughout the day and into the evening, they took pains to nourish their souls and spirit and maintain their dignity and humanity at every opportunity. Against terrible odds, slaves created "room for the human spirit to live." They took pleasure, as one historian expresses it, in "something good to eat, a splash of color to wear, the joy in one's body, the delight of dance and music, the ability to find love in another and to create space in which the personal self could exist and breathe." In this personal space, family and religion provided an indispensable sense of meaning, purpose, and joy.

Yet the rules governing slave life repeatedly assaulted family life—that most ancient form of human togetherness. Most slaves could not expect to find marriage partners on their own plantation, so many had "abroad" spouses—wives and husbands living at a distance. A master's whims and economic circumstances also made marriage risky. Slave unions were often sealed with the ominous words "til death or the master do you part." The birth of children brought further uncertainty; countless enslaved parents suffered the agony of seeing their sons and daughters sold away.

Equally tragic, slave women had none of the protections white women enjoyed. In the antebellum years, a new concept of the ideal female—a modest, pious woman who presided over hearth and home, raised her children, and soothed her husband when he returned from the bustling world of commerce and industry—meant little to black women. Only white women married to well-off husbands could afford to stay at home and embody this ideal. Perhaps a handful of free black women achieved it. Enslaved women, by contrast, had scant hope of escaping hard labor and were in no position to provide a domestic haven where their children could learn the virtues associated with citizenship.

Nonetheless, nature prevailed, and many enslaved women became mothers. Masters encouraged childbearing among slaves, whether a woman was married or not, because each birth constituted a capital gain. Records show that enslaved women typically had their first child at age nineteen, about two years before white women did. Most gave birth to an additional four or five babies.

For slave women, childbearing provided emotional, not economic sustenance. "When I was most sorely oppressed," Harriet Jacobs wrote of her son, "I found solace in his smiles. I loved to watch his infant slumbers; but . . . I could never forget that he was a slave. Sometimes I wished that he might die in infancy." Despite such moments of sadness, raising a family reaffirmed slave women's life force and creative power, giving them a measure of satisfaction in a world of cruelty.

In the face of huge obstacles, slave men and women made marriage commitments, brought children into the world, raised them as best they could, and maintained family connections. They kept track of kinfolk from whom they were separated. In naming their children, they remembered parents and grandparents, brothers and sisters, and aunts and uncles. Men walked long distances to be with their family on a holiday if they had been hired out or sold away from the plantation where their wives or children lived. Children sold away from parents were welcomed into new families, though no bloodline existed—gaining fictive aunts and uncles in the process. Slaves traveling from one place of work to another delivered written or spoken messages for men and women seeking to keep family and friendship ties alive.

Despite these efforts, some slaves had only memories of lost family members and friends. Lucy Tucker, a slave born in Virginia and sold into Alabama, managed to send a letter to her mother after a separation of more than ten years. "I have never heard from you but once since I left. I received a letter some year or two after I came to this country. I wish I had written to you and kept up continual correspondence. . . . My son Burrel . . . has been absent from me nine years. He is now grown, but I have not seen him since he was a boy though I hear from him now and then."

Enslaved black children's lives differed sharply from those of white youngsters. The passing down of property from parent to offspring, so vital in perpetuating white families' bloodlines, had no relevance for people who were themselves property. Slave parents had to raise their children under very different circumstances. At age seven or eight, typical childhood games of running and hiding and rhythm and rhyme gave way to carrying wood and water, cleaning cabins, tending gardens, and helping in the kitchen. At this early age, African American youngsters also had to learn how to survive in a white-run world. Mastering the rules governing black-white encounters counted among life's most crucial lessons. Every black parent in the South knew their children would soon see parents, friends, brothers, and sisters whipped, humiliated, maimed, killed, severed from family, or sold away. Children had to be prepared for this cruel world or they could not survive it.

Survival also meant knowing how to manage white people—how to play on their vanity, feign ignorance, or strategize one's way out of punishment. These practices became ingrained as enslaved girls and boys grew to young adulthood. Over and over in slave cabins, children heard stories about how to survive and outwit masters or cruel overseers. Often these stories took the form of animal tales, such as the one featuring the trickster Brer Rabbit. This clever character used guile to outwit his stronger foes, and he understood his enemies far better than they did themselves. Meant to educate and inspire, such trickster tales taught important lessons about how to use wiles and wits to survive.

If the family provided the roots for the tree of slave life, religion provided the sheltering branches. Next to family, slaves found their greatest support and solace in spirituality. Afro-Christianity took many forms and expressed itself in numerous practices. In rural areas, where most slaves lived, churches and trained black ministers were rare, so slaves gathered in a forest clearing, a slave cabin, or even a cornfield to sing, pray, and worship. In the antebellum era, more and more masters instructed their slaves in Christianity, hoping to ensure compliance.

But slaves did not necessarily practice the religion their owners taught them. Many adapted Christianity to African spiritual ways that had survived the middle passage across the Atlantic. For example, across the South, many slaves maintained a belief in the supernatural, including the existence of ghosts ("haunts")—spirits of the dead who returned to make trouble for the living. Numerous plantations also had slave conjurors, revered for their ability to cast spells on enemies and ward off evil spirits.

Slaves and masters viewed bondage through different religious lenses. White southerners used Christian teachings to encourage slaves to resign themselves to their lot. They drew extensively from the Gospel of Matthew, in which the Sermon on the Mount promises heavenly rewards for obedience. They also emphasized Genesis, in which God makes a contract to protect the heirs of the slaveholding Abraham. African Americans, on the other hand, identified with the Old Testament story of Exodus, in which Moses leads the Chosen People out of bondage. They also identified with tiny David, who overcame the giant Goliath, and Solomon, who launched warships against oppressors. Finally, they longed for the new world order as promised in Revelations.

As a slave in Arkansas observed after hearing a white preacher trying to sell obedience as the central Christian virtue: "All he say is 'bedience to de white folks, and we hears 'nough of dat without him telling us." Most slaves believed what a domestic servant told her mistress: "God never made

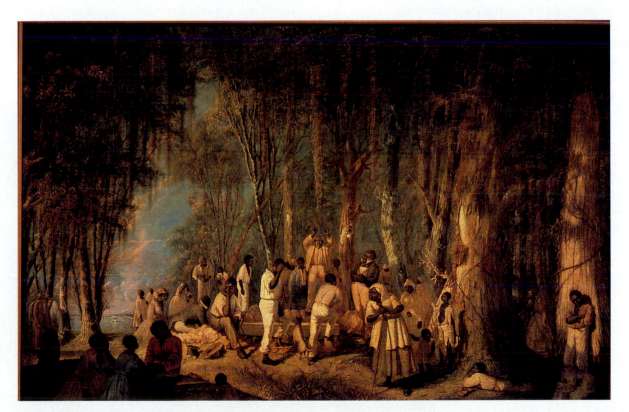

■ In this painting of an African American burial in a clearing of a Louisiana cypress forest, the black preacher, wearing a coat, conducts the service. An overseer and his horse stand at the left; white owners of the slaves watch from the right, suggesting a paternalistic plantation owner.

Source: John Antrobus, Plantation Burial, Oil Painting, The Historic New Orleans Collection.

us to be slaves for white people." In fact, no Christian idea had more resonance for slaves than divine justice. Charles Ball, for example, believed that in the Kingdom of Heaven "all distinctions of colour, and of condition, will be abolished" and that "Heaven will be no heaven" unless "those who have tormented [slaves] here will most surely be tormented in their turn hereafter."

> "God never made us to be slaves for white people."—*Anonymous*

In southern cities, where a minority of slaves but a majority of free African Americans lived, African Baptist and African Methodist churches grew rapidly. In some cities and nearby counties, these churches attracted half or more of the bondspeople living in the area. Though many urban black people maintained some West African religious practices, they tended to adopt evangelical Christianity more fully than slaves living on plantations did. In the early decades of the nineteenth century, the frequent naming of slave children after Old Testament figures—for example, Abraham and Isaac for men, Hagar and Sarah for women—reflected the spread of evangelical Christianity.

In almost all church congregations, women outnumbered men, often two to one. The male preachers played key roles in black communities and sometimes spoke before interracial congregations. Andrew Marshall, for example, who ministered the First African Baptist Church in Savannah for more than three decades, was invited to preach in white Baptist churches and even addressed the Georgia legislature. Founding schools and mutual aid societies, Marshall built a congregation of nearly 2,500 free black people and slaves by the mid-1830s. Like most other black ministers, he had to lead his congregation and community adroitly. He struck a delicate balance, remembering that white people regarded church-organized education and religion as potentially subversive while simultaneously inspiring his congregants and teaching them new skills.

Sometimes black religious and secular agendas overlapped. In one example, slaves used the songs about gaining freedom in the next world to rally comrades to seize freedom in this world. Music, like spirituality, provided crucial sustenance for slaves. Though "the songs of the slave," as Frederick Douglass explained, "represent the sorrows of his heart," music also conveyed exuberance, self-affirmation, and faith in deliverance and triumph. The mournful quality of "Nobody knows the trouble I've seen" was balanced by a refrain about finding some juicy berries hanging down "just as sweet as de honey in de comb." The same song that began with "Sometimes I feel like a motherless chile" ended with "Sometimes I feel like a eagle in de air, gonna spread my wings an' fly."

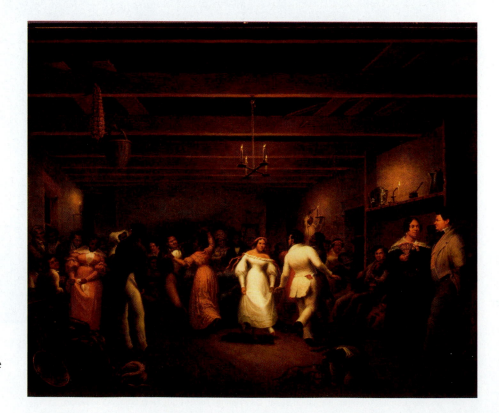

■ In this painting of a slave wedding in White Sulphur Springs, Virginia, in 1838, a black fiddler and a bone player provide the music for the festive nuptials of the resort's well-dressed domestic slaves.

Spontaneity characterized slave music. Using animal hides and gourds to fashion drums and banjoes, slaves improvised tunes and created new dances: the cakewalk, breakdown, Charleston, and "set de flo." Other dances—such as the buzzard lope, snake hips, and pigeon wing—featured moves that mimicked animals. An English musician traveling through Mississippi in the 1830s marveled at how Vicksburg slaves took a "fine old Psalm tune" and spontaneously changed the tempo and transformed it "into a kind of negro melody." "Us old heads," a former slave explained about how to create song, "use ter make 'em up on de spurn of de moment. . . . We'd all be at the 'prayer house' de Lord's day, and de white preacher he'd splain de word and read whar Ezekial done say. . . . And, honey, de Lord would come a'shinin' thoo dem pages and revive dis ole nigger's heart, and I'd jump up dar and den and holler and shout and sing and pat, and dey would all cotch de words and I'd sing it to some ole shout song I'd heard 'em sing from Africa, and dey'd all take it up and keep at it, and keep a'addin' to it, and den it would be a spiritual."

RESISTANCE AND REBELLION

In 1822, a Charleston, South Carolina, slave recalled a pivotal event from that year: "Denmark [Vesey] read at the [church] meeting different chapters from the Old Testament" and spoke of Moses' admonition that whoever steals a man "shall be put to death." White authorities later conceded that Denmark Vesey, a free black carpenter, had indeed mastered the books of the Old Testament and could "readily quote them to prove that slavery was contrary to the laws of God." The trial of Vesey and one hundred other black Charlestonians for insurrection in 1822 provided tangible evidence of a major new development: Black churches had become seedbeds of resistance to slavery as well as houses of spiritual solace.

During the 1820s, free and enslaved African Americans found a call to arms in religion. During this volatile decade, reformers across the nation, often inspired by the evangelicalism of the Second Great Awakening, launched a dizzying array of crusades. Some of these campaigns called for temperance or free public education; others, an end to imprisonment of debtors or the creation of asylums for the poor, disabled, and orphaned. All of these efforts interested African Americans, but crusades for the abolition of slavery drew their deepest commitment.

Denmark Vesey's Rebellion

Historian Vincent Harding called black Christianity a "liberation theology," one that furnished a biblical and theological justification for challenging slavery and race-based discrimination. This became apparent in Charleston, South Carolina, where black Methodists greatly outnumbered white Methodists. In this city, African Americans attended the white-controlled Methodist church for many years, but by 1815, free and enslaved black Methodists began to act independently—controlling their own Sunday collections, disciplining errant members, and holding separate black conferences.

Suspecting that even a small congregation of slaves meant trouble, slaveowners found these behaviors thoroughly alarming. White religious leaders tried to curb black ministers' autonomy and restrict their conduct of services. Black Methodists responded by launching a secession movement in 1817. Led by Morris Brown, a shoemaker and Methodist minister who had slipped away to Philadelphia to meet with Richard Allen in 1816, more than 4,300 black worshipers, enslaved and free, resigned from the old Methodist church. Later that year, they formed the new African Methodist Episcopal Church in Charleston's Hampstead district.

The leaders of this drive included a brooding free black man named Denmark Vesey. Years before, at age twenty-two, Vesey had won $1,500 at a lottery and used it to purchase his freedom from his ship-captain master. He was familiar with slavery in the West Indies, where he had traveled extensively and witnessed the black rebellion in Haiti. Literate in French, Spanish, and English, the tall, bearded Vesey became a much-respected carpenter. Among the wealthiest black men in Charleston, he was also a leader at the Methodist church.

Following the black secession from the white Methodist church, Vesey's tolerance for racial abuse wore thin while his anger at the expansion of slavery mounted. He must have fumed in 1818 when white authorities raided the black church, jailed 143 free black and slave worshipers, sentenced Morris Brown and four other church leaders to a month's imprisonment, and ordered others to pay heavy fines or receive ten lashes each. Their crime was educating slaves and holding what white authorities saw as disorderly after-dark religious meetings. Vesey certainly bristled at new South Carolina laws in 1820 that defined the teaching of slaves to read or write as a crime. These same mandates prohibited manumission, forbade free African Americans from entering South Carolina once they left the state, and slapped stiff special taxes on free black householders such as Vesey. All of this harsh treatment culminated in 1821, when white authorities shut down the AME church altogether.

Anger turned to resolution. Vesey convinced his most trusted friends that the time was approaching when the deliverance of the children of Israel from Egyptian bondage—a story told many times among black Americans—would play out in the American South. Inside Charleston and in the surrounding areas, Vesey and his comrades preached redemption and divine justice: "Behold the day of the Lord cometh, and thy spoil shall be divided in the midst of thee. For I shall gather all nations against Jerusalem to battle; and the city shall be taken . . . and they utterly destroyed all that was in the city, both man and woman, young and old, and ox and sheep, and ass, with the edge of the sword." These Old Testament stories of deliverance inspired and moved listeners. Mingling with them were African cultural practices kept alive through the influence of "Gullah Jack" Pritchard, a Vesey lieutenant who was a conjuror well known among Charleston slaves.

In 1822, Vesey and his supporters developed a plan for capturing Charleston and conquering the South Carolina countryside. How the fifty-five-year-old leader intended to implement the plan is unknown. Testimony obtained after his capture suggests that Vesey aimed to set fire to the town, seize the armory, overpower white resistance, and perhaps flee by ship to Haiti. But we must weigh such testimony carefully, because "confessions" obtained through torture often reflect what the victim thought white authorities wanted to hear.

With many white Charlestonians vacationing on nearby Sullivan's Island or other summer retreats, the city's 12,000 slaves and some 3,600 free black people outnumbered white people nearly two to one. Again, we cannot know how Vesey and his followers would have reached refuge in Haiti or carved out a territory of their own in a white-controlled country if their plan had succeeded. Still, like Gabriel before them, the rebels looked to the Haitian Revolution for inspiration. Just two decades before, they reminded themselves, slaves had overthrown their masters and then repulsed the military might of England, Spain, and France.

The conspirators carefully worked out their scheme. They chose July 14, the second Sunday of July 1822, as the fateful date for putting the plan in motion. On this day, African Americans in Massachusetts celebrated their emancipation. The date was also Bastille Day, commemorating a triumphant moment in France when revolutionaries stormed the Paris prison, a symbol of despotism. Further, on July 14, the moon would be dark, allowing armed slaves from nearby plantations to enter Charleston.

But as Vesey recruited more and more insurrectionists, the risk of betrayal increased. In May 1822, that risk became reality when one of his compatriots leaked word of the plan to white authorities. Rounding up suspects, officials began holding trials. In the end, thirty rebels were executed; all but Vesey were slaves. Thirty-seven others were condemned to die but were pardoned and transported out of the state. Morris Brown, leader of the black church, was forced to leave South Carolina. Later, white authorities discovered a letter in the trunk of one of the executed leaders' vehicles. The missive reflected biblical inspiration and measured the risks that the black insurrectionists had willingly taken on: "Fear not, the Lord God that delivered Daniel is able to deliver us."

■ Not until the civil rights movement of the 1950s and 1960s could an image of Denmark Vesey appear on a public building in Charleston, South Carolina. Vesey is now the subject of several biographies and revered as a freedom fighter.

White authorities considered black rebellion suicidal. After all, white people had managed to suppress black revolts—from the Stono Rebellion of 1739 to Gabriel's conspiracy of 1800—and execute the insurrectionists. Many white people also could not understand why well-to-do free black people as well as slaves who belonged to "the most humane and indulgent owners" would want to conduct such vicious assaults on Charleston. "It is difficult to imagine what *infatuation* could have prompted you to attempt an enterprise so wild and visionary," lectured the magistrate who sentenced Vesey to death. "You were a free man; were comparatively wealthy; and enjoyed every comfort, compatible with your situation. You had therefore, much to risk and little to gain. From your age and experience you *ought* to have known, that success was impracticable." Vesey went to the gallows silently. He apparently saw no need to explain to white authorities that freedom for a former bondsman did not mean turning one's back on enslaved brethren.

As with earlier slave conspiracies, South Carolina's authorities cracked down on African Americans after suppressing Vesey's Rebellion. Charleston's city council stiffened patrol regulations. The legislature prohibited black crew members whose ships arrived in port from coming ashore. It also criminalized efforts to teach even free black people to sign their names and forbade slaves from hiring themselves out. Even more hurtful, authorities razed the African Church in Hampstead—the heart of black religious, social, and political life. Until the end of the Civil War, black worshipers had to conduct prayer meetings and services secretly. But in 1865, Denmark Vesey's youngest son rebuilt the church.

David Walker's *Appeal*

A thousand miles north of Charleston, another free black man insisted that the fates of enslaved and free African Americans were intertwined. "They think that we do not feel for our brethren, whom they are murdering by the inches, but they are dreadfully deceived," said David Walker. Born free around 1795 in North Carolina, Walker had a white mother and enslaved black father. He traveled to Charleston in 1822, just before Vesey plotted his rebellion. Walker then headed north. What he saw and heard along the way fortified his hatred of slavery and stoked his anger at a republic that refused to live up to its founding principles. Like other African Americans, he knew about the national tumult in 1819–1821 over the Missouri Compromise. The image of slavery spreading across the continent further disheartened and angered him.

> "They think that we do not feel for our brethren, whom they are murdering by the inches, but they are dreadfully deceived."
>
> —*David Walker*

After reaching Boston in 1825, Walker became a used clothing dealer, a worshiper at the black Methodist church, and an agent for the country's first black newspaper, *Freedom's Journal.* There in the shadow of Bunker Hill, where an early battle for American independence had raged, he penned one of the nineteenth century's most provocative and prophetic essays. In his *Appeal to the Coloured Citizens of the World,* published in 1829, Walker challenged free African Americans to see themselves as part of a worldwide movement for freedom. "Your full glory and happiness," he advised, "shall never be fully consummated, but with the *entire emancipation of your enslaved brethren all over the world.* . . . When this is accomplished a burst of glory will shine upon you, which will indeed astonish you and the world. . . . There is great work for you to do."

As with Denmark Vesey, Walker regarded armed struggle as divinely sanctioned. The God he knew from the Bible hated injustice and the oppression of the weak. To resist slavery violently demonstrated obedience to God: "The man who would not fight under our Lord and Master Jesus Christ, in the glorious and heavenly cause of freedom and of God . . . ought to be kept with all of his children or family, in slavery, or in chains, to be butchered by his cruel enemies." Knowing the reprisals that had followed earlier black rebellion, Walker urged, "If you commence, make sure work—do not trifle, for they will not trifle with you—they want us for their slaves, and think nothing of murdering us in order to subject us to that wretched condition—therefore, . . . kill or be killed."

Walker also intended his *Appeal* to reach the conscience of white Americans, and he meant to break through the gradualist approach to ending slavery. Through that approach, moderate abolitionists hoped to avoid violence by waiting for moral suasion to prompt slaveowners to release bondspeople from their chains. Proud to be called "a restless disturber of the peace," Walker used his pen like a rapier. "Did not God make us all as it seemed best to himself?" he asked. "What right, then, has one of us to despise another and to treat him cruel on account of his colour . . . ? Can there be a greater absurdity in nature, and particularly in a free republican country?" Walker condemned the unprovoked white attacks on free black neighborhoods in Providence, Rhode Island, in 1825; in Boston in 1826; and in Cincinnati in 1829—the first wave of race-based riots in the nation. "I tell you Americans!" he warned, "that unless you speedily alter your course, *you*

 **First Person**

David Walker Exhorts Black Americans to Rise Against Their Oppressors

In the eyes of many white Americans, David Walker's Appeal to the Coloured Citizens of the World *made him a "restless disturber of the peace." In Boston, Walker had access to books for the first time in his life. He studied slavery in the ancient world as well as in his own time. In this passage from his* Appeal, *he called on educated free African Americans to teach, uplift, and mobilize their untutored fellows. He also urged them not to expect that compliance with white people would fend off white hostility. Those expectations, he said, would only disappoint the God of justice.*

I pray that the Lord may undeceive my ignorant brethren, and permit them to throw away pretensions, and seek after the substance of learning. I would crawl on my hands and knees through mud and mire, to the feet of a learned man, where I would sit and humbly supplicate him to instil into me that which neither devils nor tyrants could remove, only with my life—For coloured people to acquire learning in this country makes tyrants quake and tremble on their sandy foundation. Why, what is the matter? Why, they know that their infernal deeds will be made known to the world. . . . The bare name of educating the coloured people scares our cruel oppressors almost to death."

—*from David Walker,* An Appeal, in Four Articles, Together with a Preamble, to the Coloured Citizens of the World, but in Particular, and Very Expressly to Those of the United States of America, *2nd ed. (1830).*

To view a longer version of this document, please go to *www.ablongman.com/carson/documents*.

and your *Country are gone*!!!! For God Almighty will tear up the very face of the earth!!!!"

Grounded in Scripture, Walker's messianic advocacy of armed black resistance had never before appeared in print. White northerners who believed fervently in God and preached the glory of America's republicanism found Walker's words shocking. Black northerners found them inspiring. Christians were hypocrites, Walker insisted, when they indicted intemperance, infidelity, and even Sunday mail deliveries while shutting their eyes to slavery and confining black Christians to "nigger pews." Mocking Jefferson's belief that black people were born mentally inferior, Walker speculated that white people were born *morally* inferior. Perhaps black Americans could help white people gain admittance to heaven by showing them how to cleanse themselves of the national sin of slavery. "Can Americans escape God Almighty?" he asked. "If they do, can he be to us a God of justice?"

Appeal to the Coloured Citizens of the World affected Boston exactly as Walker had hoped. "It is evident," an evening newspaper reported, that African Americans "have read this pamphlet, nay, we know that the larger portion of them have read it, or heard it read, and that they glory in its principles, as if it were a star in the east, guiding them to freedom and emancipation."

To white southerners, Walker's fiery *Appeal* was printed poison. Authorities tried but failed to suppress it. Some black mariners who plied the waters between Boston and southern ports even sewed copies of the treatise inside their trousers for safekeeping. "Why do the Slave-holders or Tyrants of America and their advocates fight so hard to keep my brethren from receiving and reading my Book of Appeal to them?" asked Walker in a third edition of his *Appeal*. "Is it because they treat us so well?—is it because they are treating us like men, by compensating us all over this free country!! For our labours? . . . But perhaps the Americans do their very best to keep my Brethren from receiving and reading my 'Appeal' for fear they will find in it an extract which I made from their Declaration of Independence, which says, 'we hold these truths to be self-evident, that all men are created equal.'"

In July 1830, a few months after the *Appeal* rolled off the press, Walker died in Boston, probably of consumption.

He was just thirty-three years old. Knowing that Georgians had put a price on his head and that friends had urged him to flee to Canada, many Bostonians believed that someone had poisoned him. "I will stand my ground," he had replied to those begging him to go into hiding. *"Somebody must die in this cause. I may be doomed to the stake and the fire, or to the scaffold tree, but it is not in me to falter if I can promote the work of emancipation."*

Five months after Walker's death, another Bostonian stepped forward to demand an immediate end to slavery. Twenty-six years old, William Lloyd Garrison had joined the cause in Baltimore, Maryland. There he had worked with Benjamin Lundy, the Quaker publisher of the radical newspaper *Genius of Universal Emancipation,* which exposed the abominable internal slave traffic. Back in Boston, Garrison launched *The Liberator.* Its first issue hit the streets on January 1, 1831, after Philadelphia's James Forten loaned Garrison money to pay for the newsprint. In the premier issue, the fiery editor promised to be "as harsh as truth, and as uncompromising as justice. On this subject [of slavery], I do not wish to think, or speak, or write, with moderation. . . . No! No! Tell a man whose house is on fire to give a moderate alarm . . . but urge me not to use moderation in a cause like the present."

Nat Turner's Insurrection

A few months after the first issue of *The Liberator* rolled off the press, a slave in Southampton County, Virginia, witnessed an eclipse of the sun and decided that God had called him to lead a rebellion. Nat Turner may have known that slavery was collapsing in other parts of the world. Newspapers had reported that the new Central and South American republics that wrested their independence from Spain had abolished slavery in the 1820s. Reports also revealed that the British Parliament was debating the emancipation of the millions of slaves on Britain's West Indian colonies. A Bible-conscious man and local Baptist lay preacher to fellow slaves, Turner felt certain that an avenging God would punish white oppressors and bring divine judgment to the American republic.

In his youth, Turner had taught himself to read. For years he had searched the Bible for divine inspiration. Around 1830, he had apocalyptic visions of Christ crucified against a night sky and found what he believed was Christ's blood in a cornfield the following morning. "While labouring in the field, I discovered drops of blood on the corn as though it were dew from heaven," he recounted later. Just before this experience, Turner had been sold away from his wife—another reminder that whites measured their slaves' value only in cash. Gathering a trusted group of slaves

around him, Turner revealed his vision that the day of judgment was near. God, he proclaimed, had commanded him to take up the sword to strike down slavery.

Turner originally chose the Fourth of July to launch his uprising in 1831, but he postponed the date after taking ill. When an atmospheric condition caused the sun to appear bluish green, he and his followers agreed the time was near. Just before dawn on August 22, Turner put his religious mission into action. According to black oral tradition, he told his followers, "Remember, we do not go forth for the sake of blood and carnage; but it is necessary that, in the commencement of this revolution, all the whites we meet should die, until we have an army strong enough to carry out the war on a Christian basis. Remember that ours is not a war for robbery, nor to satisfy our passions; it is a *struggle for freedom.*"

Sixty avenging slaves struck down Turner's master and his family. Then they marched toward the small town of

> "Remember that ours is not a war for robbery, nor to satisfy our passions; it is a *struggle for freedom."*
> —Nat Turner

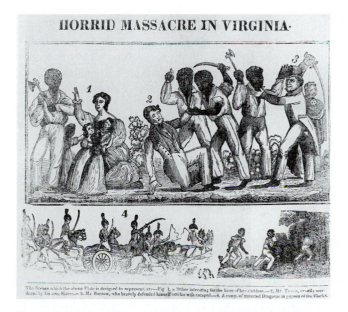

HORRID MASSACRE IN VIRGINIA.

■ Abolitionists tried to use Turner's Rebellion to tell southerners what they could expect if they did not end slavery. In this sketch, Turner attacks a white mother and her children (#1); other slaves attack Turner's master (#2); Captain John T. Barrow, a militia captain, defends himself while his wife and child retreat (#3); and the uniformed militia track down the rebels (#4).

 **First Person**

Nat Turner Tells of His Vision to Strike Against Slavery

While awaiting execution in prison, Nat Turner related the story of his life under slavery and his decision to lead a slave insurrection. Turner's Confessions *were published several months after the trial and his execution.*

Now the Holy Ghost had revealed itself to me, and made plain the miracles it had shown me; for as the blood of Christ had been shed on this earth and had ascended to heaven for the salvation of sinners, and was now returning to earth again in the form of dew,—and as the leaves on the trees bore the impression of the figures I had seen in the heavens,—it was plain to me that the Saviour was about to lay down the yoke he had bourne for the sins of men, and the great day of judgment was at hand. . . . I heard a loud noise in the heavens, and the Spirit instantly appeared to me and said the Serpent was loosened, and Christ had laid down the yoke he had borne for the sins of men, and that I should take it on and fight against the Serpent, for the time was fast approaching, when the first should be last and the last should be first.

—from Nat Turner, Confessions of Nat Turner, The Leader of the Great Insurrection in Southampton, Virginia *(1831).*

To view a longer version of this document, please go to *www.ablongman.com/carson/documents*.

Jerusalem, Virginia, where they hoped to seize a cache of arms. Storming every house in their path, they slaughtered fifty-five men, women, and children with axes and clubs. Part prophet, part general, Turner soon came face to face with white militia groups who rushed to the scene as the chilling word of black rebellion spread. Heavily outgunned, the insurrectionists scattered. Most were hunted down, captured, or killed in the woods. By the next day, only Turner and three companions remained at large. Eluding a massive manhunt for weeks, Turner was finally captured on October 30, 1831. He went to the gallows a month later, the last of eighteen executed slaves. Black insurrection had again failed.

But Turner had failed only in an immediate sense. Before he was condemned and executed, he related his "confessions" to a white slaveowning lawyer. Widely circulated as a pamphlet, *The Confessions of Nat Turner* stunned white southerners. Once regarding him as a crazed fanatic, they now found him highly articulate and rational. The *Confessions* revealed a man who felt no guilt for his actions and who insisted that he pursued the retributive justice of a Christian God. "Do you not find yourself mistaken now?" asked the white lawyer in Turner's jail cell where he was shackled and clothed in rags. "Was not Christ crucified?" replied Turner. Like David Walker and Denmark Vesey, Turner had embraced Christianity and then used it to challenge white America's own Christian con-

duct. Claiming himself a messenger of God, he warned Americans that slavery would destroy their empire of liberty. After reading Turner's *Confessions,* slave owners understood that even if they were kindly and paternal, they might perish at the hands of their slaves at any moment. Indeed, Turner himself had had a "kind master." After the carnage, one Virginia legislator suspected there was "a Nat Turner . . . in every family." Whatever steps they took to control their human property, masters now saw that slavery was a bomb with a short fuse.

White southerners were in no mood to appreciate Turner's messianic message. Yet sickened by the thought "that the same bloody deed could be acted out at any time in any place, that the materials for it were spread through the land and always ready for a like explosion," Virginia's legislature debated abolishing slavery. Motions for taking action to end slavery failed, however. Instead, state legislators enacted punishing reprisals. For example, they tried to quarantine black slaves from the radical message of literate black preachers. "The case of Nat Turner warns us," wrote the Richmond *Enquirer,* that "no black man ought to be permitted to turn a preacher through the country." All the way to Mississippi, laws entered the statute books prohibiting enslaved or free African Americans from spreading the Christian word. White ministers urgently preached obedience to authority and hope for rewards in the afterlife—

central elements of Christian faith. New laws prohibited the teaching of slaves to read or write. Other mandates prohibited black people from assembling in groups of more than two or three.

Yet beyond the reach of law was memory. A new generation of black leaders learned about Turner's work. Growing up free in Pittsburgh, Martin Delany drew inspiration from Nat Turner. Harriet Tubman, a Maryland slave, asked herself how she might continue his legacy. In 1833, white men broke up the black Sunday school class that the eighteen-year-old slave Frederick [Bailey] Douglass was organizing. If he "wanted to be another Nat Turner," they warned the young man, he would suffer Turner's fate. In every place where slaves still toiled, Turner's visionary quest for liberation would live on until the day of emancipation.

FREE BLACK ORGANIZING

"Ought we not to form ourselves into a general body, to protect, aid, and assist each other to the utmost of our power?" asked David Walker four years before Nat Turner's insurrection. Black leaders in the northern cities knew they faced an urgent task in coordinating resistance to colonization, the expansion of slavery, and discriminatory treatment and laws. In their view, organizing nationally offered them their best hope of achieving these goals. By the late 1820s, an urban-based network of educated and accomplished black leaders had taken steps to unite black leaders across the nation so all could speak with one voice.

The printed word became a powerful tool in this effort. The first black newspaper, *Freedom's Journal,* was printed in New York City in 1827. Edited by Samuel Cornish, a black Presbyterian minister, and John Russwurm, a recent graduate of Bowdoin College, the publication attacked the American Colonization Society (ACS). The journal slowly attracted writers and subscribers from all over the North, the Upper South, and the Midwest. James Forten and Richard Allen contributed articles from Philadelphia. David Walker and Thomas Paul wrote from Boston. Black New Yorkers such as Peter Williams reported on events in that city. Correspondents in Albany, Baltimore, New Haven, Wilmington, Providence, Hartford, New Bedford, Pittsburgh, and Cincinnati sent in material. *Freedom's Journal* became a clearinghouse for black people's exchange of news about the founding of new churches, schools, Masonic lodges, and mutual aid societies. Most important, it served as a forum for discussing the major problems facing African Americans.

Near the end of the paper's two-year existence, Russwurm began to promote emigration. Believing that black people had little hope of achieving better lives in white America, he took a post in the new country of Liberia on Africa's west coast. The ACS, with U.S. government funding, had founded Liberia. There Russwurm lived out his life as a newspaper editor and government official amid the few thousand African Americans who joined the experiment. Back in New York, when *Freedom's Journal* stopped publication owing to Russwurm's departure, it was replaced by *Rights for All.* This newspaper failed in the early 1830s, and *Colored American* took its place, soon to be followed by other black newspapers. Clearly, African Americans could now count on a vigorous press aimed at solidifying black opinion while tying communities together in a national network.

As black leaders stepped up organizing efforts, they began envisioning a national meeting of free African Americans. In 1829, a vicious attack by white people on black neighborhoods in Cincinnati accelerated plans for the national gathering. Though defending themselves ably, members of Cincinnati's black community—the largest west of the Appalachian Mountains—were badly shaken. Several hundred fled to Canada. Meeting in Philadelphia in 1830, black delegates from Pennsylvania, New York, Delaware, Maryland, and Virginia convened the American Society of Free People of Colour. They shared ideas and strategies for fending off white violence, for building educational and vocational institutions, for nurturing moral uplift and self-reliance, and—most essential—for confronting slavery. Seventy-year-old Richard Allen held forth as the patriarch of the 1830 gathering. Drawing on a lifetime of experience as the founder and leader of the AME Church, Allen worried about the personal and regional tensions he observed among African Americans. But he recognized that disputes and competing agendas signaled the coming of age of a new generation of black leaders. Dozens of black communities were blossoming, he noted, each with its own experiences, accomplishments, problems, and leaders.

Under Allen's leadership, the delegates decried the repatriation of free black Americans to Africa. Nevertheless, they endorsed emigration to Canada. African Americans, they reasoned, shared a common language with the Canadians. Moreover, British authorities in Canada had promised "all the rights, privileges and immunities of other citizens"—exactly what African Americans sought but could not acquire in the United States. Encouraged, many free African Americans began immigrating to Ontario, where they formed new communities.

By the time black delegates arrived in Philadelphia for a second convention in 1831, slaveholders seemed to have a firmer grip than ever on the nation's economy and political system. Congress routinely rejected antislavery petitions. White southerners, for their part, advocated that the U.S. military seize Mexican Texas—where lawmakers had abolished slavery—and add it to the American republic as a slave state. Tennessee's Andrew Jackson, the fifth slaveholder among the seven U.S. presidents who had served in office to date, held forth in the White House. Meanwhile, vice president John C. Calhoun was crafting constitutional doctrines that recognized state legislators' right to nullify federal laws they believed would adversely affect their state's vital interests.

In 1828, matters had come to a head with Congress's passage of a tariff that imposed heavier duties on manufactured goods imported from abroad. Southerners lambasted the law, calling it the Tariff of Abominations. In their view, the tariff enhanced the North's economic power and hurt their own ability to export slave-produced tobacco and cotton. Animosity between northern and southern congressmen escalated into a fiery debate in the summer of 1830. Calhoun's doctrine that southern states were entitled to protect themselves from harmful national action only worsened the conflict. According to Calhoun, if a state determined that a federal law overstepped the limits of constitutional authority, its lawmakers had the right to declare the law null and void. Everyone knew that Calhoun had far more than tariffs in mind. The doctrine sent the ominous signal that if the national government ever tampered with slavery, southern lawmakers could invoke the theory of nullification to protect their investment in human property.

Amid these gathering storm clouds, black leaders accused the ACS of "pursuing the direct road to perpetuate slavery." Leading African Americans reminded the country that "many of our fathers, and some of us, have fought and bled for the liberty, independence, and peace which you now enjoy and, surely, it would be ungenerous and unfeeling in you to deny us a humble and quiet grave in that country which gave us birth!"

> "Many of our fathers, and some of us, have fought and bled for the liberty, independence, and peace which you now enjoy."
> —James Forten

Members of the American Society of the Free People of Colour sensed that worldwide sentiment was turning sharply against slavery. Delegates to the Society's convention pointed to Denmark's recent abolition of slavery in its West Indies colonies and Britain's plans for a general emancipation in its Caribbean colonies. Encouraged by these developments, they called for the removal of the foul "stain upon the national escutcheon [shield] of this great Republic. . . . It is only when we look to our own native land, to the birthplace of our fathers, to the land for whose prosperity their blood and our sweat have been shed and cruelly extorted, that the Convention has had cause to hang its head and blush." For many years, the American Society of Free People of Colour met annually to debate strategies for reforming the North and eradicating slavery in the South.

CONCLUSION

As the delegates of the American Society of Free People of Colour left Philadelphia, they knew the generation that had come of age in the republic's early years—most of them born into slavery—was passing on. Many of the founding black ministers were dead or frail, including New York's Peter Williams, Philadelphia's Absalom Jones and Richard Allen, Wilmington's Peter Spencer, Baltimore's Daniel Coker, Charleston's Morris Brown, Augusta's Jesse Galphin, and Savannah's Andrew Bryan. Of the three great secular leaders—Prince Hall in Boston, Paul Cuffe in New Bedford, and James Forten in Philadelphia—the first two had died and the third struggled with ill health. The three great rebels—Gabriel, Denmark Vesey, and Nat Turner—had all been executed. The mightiest pen of the era, held by David Walker, would write no more.

But in many ways, these leaders had already passed the torch to the free black men and women spread across the expanding nation. These African Americans were better educated and connected than the previous generation, thanks to the printed word and national networks. These advantages enabled them to resist the ACS's back-to-Africa movement.

As free black communities proliferated during this era, slavery also expanded—as measured by the number of bondspeople and the number of states and territories whose economies depended on the practice. Earlier hopes that slavery would wither away with the halt of the slave trade faded. In fact, as cotton slavery spread throughout the Lower South and west into Texas, white slaveowners subjected their human chattel to more brutal treatment than before. At the same time, free African Americans were finding white abolitionist allies who yearned to end slavery. This development heightened tensions between northerners and southerners. The work of dismantling slavery and discrimination now lay in the hands of a new generation of black leaders who faced mounting challenges in an increasingly divided nation.

FURTHER READING

Abrahms, Roger D. *Singing the Master: The Emergence of African American Culture in the Plantation South* (New York: Pantheon, 1992).

Blassingame, John. *The Slave Community: Plantation Life in the Antebellum South* (New York: Oxford University Press, 1972; rev. ed., 1979).

Cornelius, Janet Duitsman. *"When I Can Read My Title Clear": Literacy, Slavery, and Religion in the Antebellum South* (Columbia: University of South Carolina Press, 1991).

Dubois, Laurent. *Avengers of the New World* (Cambridge: Harvard Univerity Press, 2004).

Dusinberre, William. *Them Dark Days: Slavery in the American Rice Swamps* (New York: Oxford University Press, 1996).

Egerton, Douglas R. *He Shall Go Out Free: The Lives of Denmark Vesey* (Madison, WI: Madison House, 1999).

Fogel, Robert William. *Without Consent or Contract: The Rise and Fall of American Slavery* (New York: W. W. Norton, 1989).

Frey, Sylvia R., and Betty Wood, *Come Shouting to Zion: African American Protestantism in the American South and British Caribbean to 1830* (Chapel Hill: University of North Carolina Press, 1998).

Genovese, Eugene. *Roll, Jordan, Roll: The World the Slaves Made* (1974; rpt., New York: Vintage Books, 1976).

Hinks, Peter P. *To Awaken My Afflicted Brethren: David Walker and the Problem of Antebellum Slave Resistance* (University Park: Pennsylvania State University Press, 1997).

Jeffrey, Julie Roy. *The Great Silent Army of Abolitionism: Ordinary Women in the Antislavery Movement* (Chapel Hill: University of North Carolina Press, 1998).

Johnson, Walter. *Soul by Soul: Life Inside the Antebellum Slave Market* (Cambridge: Harvard University Press, 1999).

Jones, Norrece T., Jr. *Born a Child of Freedom, Yet a Slave: Mechanisms of Control and Strategies of Resistance in Antebellum South Carolina* (Hanover, NH: University Press of New England, 1990).

Joyner, Charles. *Down by the Riverside: A South Carolina Slave Community* (Urbana: University of Illinois Press, 1984).

King, Wilma. *Stolen Childhood: Slave Youth in Nineteenth-Century America* (Bloomington: Indiana University Press, 1995).

Litwack, Leon F. *North of Slavery: The Negro in the Free States, 1790–1860* (Chicago: University of Chicago Press, 1961).

McBride, Dwight A. *Impossible Witnesses: Truth, Abolitionism, and Slave Testimony* (New York: New York University Press, 2001).

Raboteau, Albert J. *Slave Religion: The "Invisible Institution" in the Antebellum South* (New York: Oxford University Press, 1978).

Richards, Leonard. *The Slave Power: The Free North and Southern Domination, 1780–1860* (Baton Rouge: Louisiana State University Press, 2000).

Smith, M. Rogers. *Civic Ideals: Conflicting Visions of Citizenship in United States History* (New Haven, CT: Yale University Press, 1997).

Stanton, William. *The Leopard's Spots: Scientific Attitudes Toward Race in America, 1815–1859* (Chicago: University of Chicago Press, 1960).

Stevenson, Brenda. *Life in Black and White: Family and Community in the Slave South* (New York: Oxford University Press, 1996).

Tadman, Michael. *Speculators and Slaves: Masters, Traders, and Slaves in the Old South* (Madison: University of Wisconsin Press, 1996).

Tise, Larry. *Proslavery: A History of the Defense of Slavery in America, 1701–1840* (Athens: University of Georgia Press, 1987).

White, Debra. *Ar'n't I a Woman? Female Slaves in the Plantation South* (New York: W. W. Norton, 1985).

White, Shane. *Stories of Freedom in Black New York* (Cambridge: Harvard University Press, 2002).

Wood, Betty. *Women's Work, Men's Work: The Informal Slave Economies of Lowcountry Georgia, 1750–1830* (Athens: University of Georgia Press, 1995).

■ *The Fugitive's Story*, created by sculptor John Rogers in 1869, foretells the continuing hold that the drama of escaping slaves would have on the American imagination for generations after the emancipation brought about by the Civil War.

African Americans in the Reform Era, 1831–1850

James Forten Advocates an Immediate End to Slavery

"The spirit of freedom is marching with rapid strides, and causing tyrants to tremble," wrote James Forten in December 1830 to his friend and fellow abolitionist William Lloyd Garrison. Forten, a free black Philadelphian, was among many reformers exhorting Americans to renew their religious faith and their moral leadership. Such efforts, these reformers felt, were necessary to topple the slave regime and end racial hostility.

Like many abolitionists during this era of reform, Forten believed the movement required new goals and strategies. Northern states had all but eradicated slavery. However, abolitionist efforts in the past half-century had yielded scant returns in the South, where the slave population was continually expanding. Moreover, the growing number of free African Americans, mostly in northern urban areas, faced increasing oppression. "That we are not treated as freemen, in any part of the United States, is certain," Forten wrote to Garrison. "This usage . . . is in direct opposition to the Constitution; which positively declares that all men are born equal and endowed with certain inalienable rights."

Although many African Americans over the years had espoused colonization in Africa as the only real chance for black people in the United States to find freedom, Forten opposed this strategy. In the mid-1820s, he had considered a plan to help free black people gain a new life in the black republic of Haiti. But Forten—whose children counted among the first generation of African Americans born after the American slave trade ended in 1808—soon realized he was American to the core. "To separate the blacks from the whites is as impossible as to bale out the Delaware [River] with a bucket," he wrote Garrison. He would remain in America,

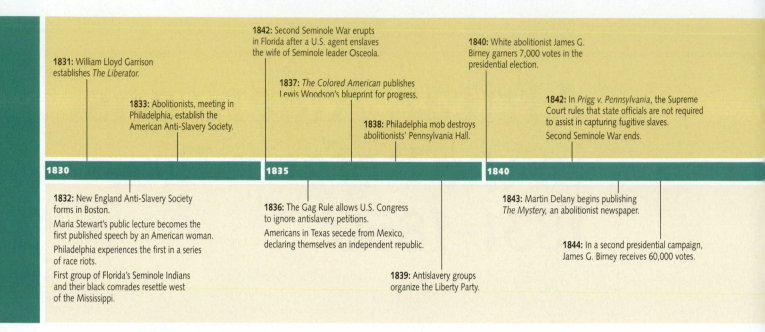

1831: William Lloyd Garrison establishes *The Liberator.*

1833: Abolitionists, meeting in Philadelphia, establish the American Anti-Slavery Society.

1842: Second Seminole War erupts in Florida after a U.S. agent enslaves the wife of Seminole leader Osceola.

1837: *The Colored American* publishes Lewis Woodson's blueprint for progress.

1838: Philadelphia mob destroys abolitionists' Pennsylvania Hall.

1840: White abolitionist James G. Birney garners 7,000 votes in the presidential election.

1842: In *Prigg v. Pennsylvania,* the Supreme Court rules that state officials are not required to assist in capturing fugitive slaves. Second Seminole War ends.

1830

1835

1840

1832: New England Anti-Slavery Society forms in Boston.
Maria Stewart's public lecture becomes the first published speech by an American woman.
Philadelphia experiences the first in a series of race riots.
First group of Florida's Seminole Indians and their black comrades resettle west of the Mississippi.

1836: The Gag Rule allows U.S. Congress to ignore antislavery petitions.
Americans in Texas secede from Mexico, declaring themselves an independent republic.

1839: Antislavery groups organize the Liberty Party.

1843: Martin Delany begins publishing *The Mystery,* an abolitionist newspaper.

1844: In a second presidential campaign, James G. Birney receives 60,000 votes.

Forten assured Garrison, and struggle in the country where his family had toiled for more than a century.

As Garrison prepared to publish the first issue of a radical newspaper entitled *The Liberator,* on January 1, 1831, Forten purchased subscriptions for his likeminded Pennsylvania friends. He believed strongly in the goal of *The Liberator:* an immediate end to slavery. *The Liberator* embodied the spirit of the reform era and a new breed of abolitionists who would not equivocate. The time of reasoning with slaveholders had ended, abolitionists agreed; the moment for direct confrontation, perhaps even violence, had arrived.

In August 1831, *The Liberator* published a piece by Forten entitled "Men Must Be Free." Forten wrote that a recent outbreak of mysterious fires in Fayetteville, North Carolina, represented a "visitation from God"—a divine warning to slaveholders. "When we . . . hear of almost every nation fighting for its liberty, is it to be expected that the African race will continue always in the degraded state they are in?" Forten asked. "No," he answered. "The time is fast approaching when the words 'Fight for liberty, or die in the attempt' will be sounded in every African ear." The day after these words were published, Nat Turner led scores of Virginia slaves in a bloody rampage to gain their liberty. Clearly, there were those willing to affirm that the moment had already arrived.

In the mid-nineteenth century, two currents were sweeping the nation. One current carried Americans, in day-to-day mingling of peoples and cultures, toward a racially blended melting pot. As white immigrants—especially from Ireland and Germany—settled in the urban North, they toiled alongside free black people in factories and shipyards and lived in the same neighborhoods. In the rural South, slaves continued to live in intimate circumstances with their masters, serving as housekeepers, valets, and nursemaids. The second current consisted of waves of intense fear and hatred stirred up as immigrants and free African Americans swelled urban populations, causing native-born white Americans to feel overwhelmed by newcomers.

Both currents reflected the new nation's complex and dynamic economic and geographic expansion. By the mid-1840s, a New York journalist declared that Americans had a "manifest destiny to overspread the continent." Americans of all backgrounds responded to the lure of the West, encountering new peoples and developing new ways of life.

In this era of reform, black leaders looked to strengthen free African American communities as a way to demonstrate to white Americans their right to full-fledged citizenship. They preached the doctrine of self-improvement and believed education was the best means of building their communities, finding work, and proving their worthiness. The African American population jumped from 2.3 million in 1830 to 3.6 million in 1850. Within this population, however, the percentage of free African Americans dropped from 15.9 to 13.6 percent. But the

1846: Mexican-American War breaks out.
Congressman David Wilmot's Proviso that slavery be prohibited in territory acquired from Mexico passes in the House but is defeated in the Senate.

1848: In the Treaty of Guadaloupe Hidalgo, Mexico cedes a large expanse of territory to the United States. Gold is discovered in California.
Frederick Douglass is the featured speaker at the Women's Rights Convention at Seneca Falls, New York.

1845

1845: United States annexes Texas, including more than 50,000 slaves.

1847: Frederick Douglass, Martin Delany, and William C. Nell establish *The North Star*.

1850: In the Compromise of 1850, Congress admits California to the Union as a free state, allows slavery in other parts of the Southwest, outlaws the slave trade in the District of Columbia, and tightens fugitive slave laws.

decrease of less than 2 percent translated into 1.3 million more slaves and fewer than 120,000 additional free black people.

The question of citizenship concerned only the shrinking number of black Americans who had their liberty. The plight of the ever-increasing slave population was of far greater concern. Among the manifold reforms under public discussion—temperance, woman suffrage, legal punishment, and public education—African Americans focused most strongly on abolition. Always a small minority, outspoken abolitionists faced scorn, violence, and the suppression of their literature. They also struggled with dissension deep within their ranks—one that often splintered friendships and alliances. Yet for all of this, free African Americans continued the struggle.

BLACK AMERICANS IN AN EXPANDING NATION

Martin Delany, who emerged as a black leader in the generation before the Civil War, had always been restless. Born in 1812 in Charleston, Virginia, Delany grew up in Pennsylvania. After studying at a black church school, he worked as a barber and a cupper and leecher—a medical practitioner who treated illness by drawing blood from the patient. In 1843, he married free-born Catherine Richards, who was from a family of well-to-do Pittsburgh cattle farmers. Richards shared

her husband's hatred of racial injustice, for she had seen her family cheated out of land by white neighbors.

A restless man, Delany traversed the country in 1839. In Philadelphia, he visited the Quaker-run Institute for Colored Youth (ICY). Established as an agricultural training school with white teachers, the ICY developed an academic curriculum and hired some black teachers at the insistence of parents of students. In New York City, Delany encountered James McCune Smith, a black doctor providing much-needed services to the city's free black community. Smith had earned a medical degree in Scotland because medical schools in the United States refused to accept him. In Boston, Delany met black abolitionist Charles Remond, whose home was a popular destination for abolitionists of all skin colors.

Delany then turned south. Earning his passage by stoking fires on Mississippi River steamboats, he traveled through Mississippi and witnessed slaves' backbreaking labor. Journeying into Louisiana, where earlier French masters had introduced the tradition of black mistresses, he found many mixed-race

■ Philadelphia's black painter Robert Douglass Jr. contributed political posters to the Female Anti-Slavery Society. He also rendered this portrait of William Lloyd Garrison.

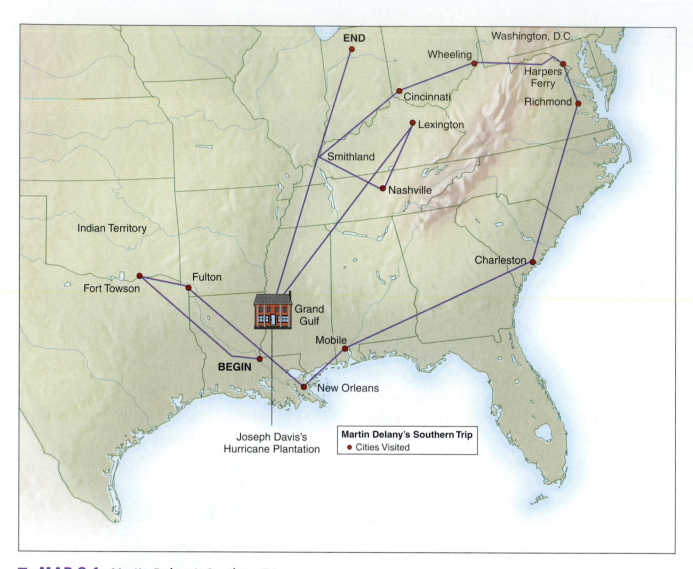

■ **MAP 8.1** **Martin Delany's Southern Trip**

In 1839, Delany toured the South, probably passing near Hurricane Plantation, where Benjamin Montgomery lived (see p. 195), and the Texas and Oklahoma Indian lands, where John Horse's family had relocated (see p. 194).

people—many slaves but also free black people, some of whom were owners of businesses and property.

Next, Delany visited Texas, where a local slave warned him that white Texans would "as like kill you as not, and they feel the same way about Mexicans and Indians." An independent republic, Texas had recently seceded from Mexico and was governed by Samuel Houston, a white American married to a Cherokee woman. Texas had attracted planters from the tobacco-worn soil of Virginia and North Carolina, who arrived with their slaves to start new lives in cotton. Texas also had free black people, whom white Texans invited there to help outnumber Mexicans and Indians. Delany continued into

Arkansas and the Indian Territory of Oklahoma, where Indians and black refugees had settled in the 1830s.

Black Population Growth

Delany witnessed an explosion in the nation's black population. In the South, the slave population grew by about 25 percent every decade from 1820 to 1860. The number of free African Americans grew more slowly; thus, while the total number of free black people increased somewhat, the *proportion* of free black people dropped dramatically after 1830 (see Figure 8.1). Why were slaves becoming an ever-

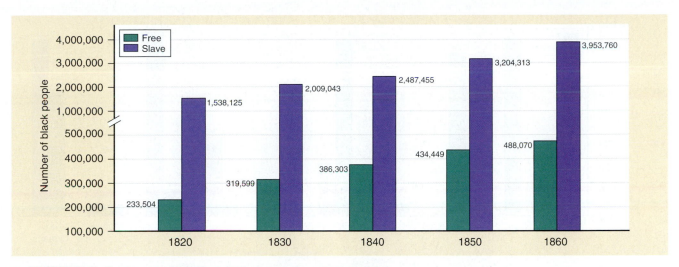

■ **FIGURE 8.1** **Free and Enslaved Black People, 1820–1860**

Though the free black population more than doubled in four decades, the number of slaves, six times greater than the free population in 1820, also doubled, dwarfing the growth in free black communities.

larger proportion of the African American population? The decrease in manumissions is a key reason. By 1820, the freeing of slaves had all but ended across most of the South. Only in the border states of Delaware, Maryland, and Kentucky could slaves gain liberty after that date. In addition, the high fertility rates of enslaved women swelled the slave population; the average black woman now bore seven children. Although the infant mortality rate was high (27 percent of black children died in the first year of life), and life expectancy was low (in 1840, life expectancy was only thirty-three years for black males and thirty-five for black females), the high birthrate helped overcome these other factors. Also, illegal importation of slaves continued.

In both the South and North, Delany saw that free African Americans preferred cities. The lure of jobs and the chance to join already established black communities made urban enters attractive. Southern black people headed to cities like Charleston, Mobile, Louisville, New Orleans, Baltimore, Savannah, and Richmond. Indeed, they were more than twice as likely to live in urban areas as white southerners. By mid-century, Baltimore had the nation's largest black community—over 20,000 free African Americans.

Black northerners were even more urbanized (see Figure 8.2 and Table 8.1). Philadelphia and New York, for example, with about 14,000 and 16,000 free black people, respectively, became thriving centers of black religious and intellectual life. Smaller black populations in

Rochester in upstate New York, Boston, Pittsburgh, and Cincinnati also established vital communities.

In the cities, especially in the South, both enslaved and free women outnumbered men. In Baltimore and Washington, for example, there were almost twice as many black women as men. The reason for this imbalance is that employers and slaveowners in cities relied on women for domestic labor, while those in rural areas depended on black men for farm labor. This gender imbalance made it difficult for black women and men to find partners and start families.

Meanwhile, slavery continued to spread during the 1830s and 1840s into the new southern states west of the Appalachian Mountains. In 1825, the vast majority of black Americans lived within a hundred miles of the ocean their

■ **TABLE 8.1** **Urbanized Americans, 1860***

Free African Americans were much more likely to be city-dwellers than were white Americans. As this table shows, free black southerners were more than twice as likely to live in cities as were white southerners. In the North and in the United States as a whole, the difference is not as dramatic, but it is still marked.

	Percentage of Free African Americans	Percentage of White Americans
North	61.4%	40.6%
South	35.2%	14.8%
United States	47.3%	32.9%

*Percentage of free African Americans and white Americans living in towns larger than 2,500.

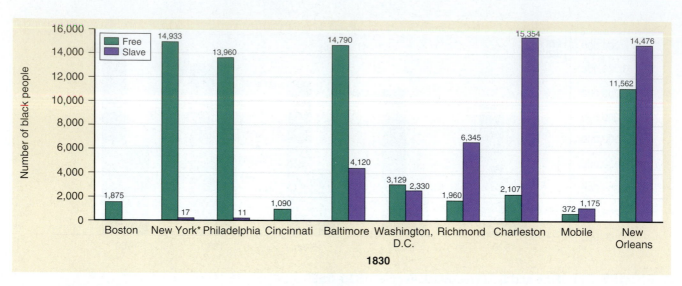

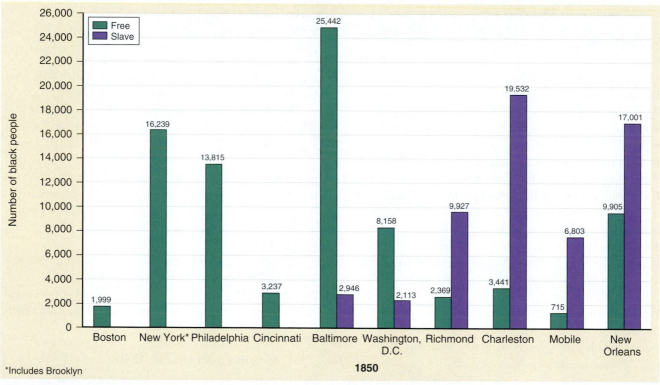

■ **FIGURE 8.2** **Free and Enslaved Black People Living in Cities, 1830 and 1850**

As slavery was abolished in the North, free black Americans preferred the cities, where they could build communities and find work. (Few had resources or opportunity to purchase farmland.) Southern cities, at first safe places for free black people, would become less so after 1850. By 1850, Baltimore and Washington, DC—the northernmost southern cities—had grown largest, and at the fastest pace.

ancestors had crossed on slave ships. But thirty years later, most slaves lived deep inside the American southern interior, thousands of miles from the borders of free states, far from easy contact with abolitionists and Underground Railroad networks. Mild climate and the labor-intensive cotton crop meant a longer and more brutal work schedule as well as far less opportunity for manumission than in the older coastal states. A few of the boldest slaves escaped into Mexico, and there were rumors of aborted slave revolts, but for most, slavery in the Lower South was brutal and relentless.

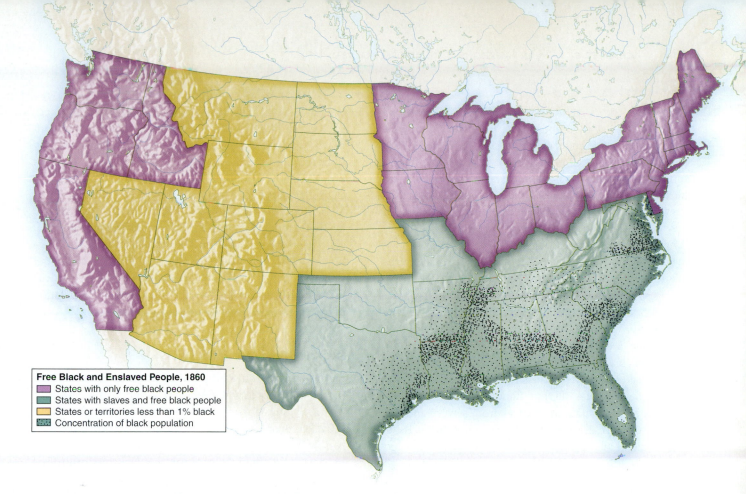

■ **MAP 8.2** Free Black and Enslaved People, 1860

Free Black and Enslaved People, 1860
- States with only free black people
- States with slaves and free black people
- States or territories less than 1% black
- Concentration of black population

By 1860, the presence or absence of slaves defined not only the labor force but also the politics of a given region. The North and Northwest, with few slaves, harbored abolitionists. The Upper South, phasing out slavery, had mixed loyalties to the institution, while the states of the Lower South, where cotton demanded large field crews, based much of their public policy on bound labor.

Racial Separation

Although the population of free black Americans was decreasing as a proportion of the total population of African Americans, free black people had tightly knit communities in which they owned land and businesses and learned practical skills. Their churches educated their children and served as the center of many of these communities.

Pittsburgh's Lewis Woodson embodied the church's promise, as he based his life's vision on his own past. Born into slavery in Virginia in 1806, he was purchased by his father (who had managed to flee the master several years earlier) when he was nineteen years old. After spending several years with his father in an all-black settlement in Clinton County, Ohio, Woodson moved to Pittsburgh. There he helped form the Pittsburgh African Education and Benevolent Society, which aimed to educate young black people. Woodson used the classroom to preach religion, industry, thrift, and temperance. The Society assembled a library and subscribed to abolitionist newspapers like Garrison's *Liberator* and *The Colored American,* which, in 1837, published some of Woodson's prescriptions for black progress.

Woodson urged free black men and women to learn artisan and farming skills, purchase land and tools, and get involved in the political process. He also urged black Americans to establish their own settlements in sparsely populated areas of Ohio, Indiana, and Illinois. There, he believed, African Americans could build safe communities and offer sanctuary to fugitive slaves. The existence of such sanctuaries, Woodson hoped, would encourage slaves to escape.

Many northern white reformers hoped to resettle black Americans in Africa. But Woodson discouraged this, arguing that if free black people left America, they would be abandoning slaves who needed their help and protection. Black Americans need "a colony in a place of our choice," insisted Woodson, and that place should be in, or near, the United States.

Some separate black communities arose in the South. These towns, which served as home to freed slaves, were usually established and sup-

> "A colony in a place of our choice."—*Lewis Woodson*

ported by the few thousand southerners who continued to hope that they could end the threat of slave revolts in the South by manumitting (freeing) their slaves and sending them to Africa. One such town was Nashoba, established in 1826 near Memphis, Tennessee. Inspired by the ideas of European idealists who envisioned communities of communal living, Nashoba was founded by British actress and reformer Frances (Fanny) Wright, who purchased 300 acres to start a cooperative farming community. There she hosted manumitted slaves whose masters hoped to educate them before sending them to Africa.

Despite insufficient funds, poor management, and local hostility, Nashoba survived for about five years. When it collapsed, Wright shipped its black members to Haiti. Meanwhile, a different kind of experiment, aimed at promoting black autonomy emerged. Several congregations of white Quakers and Methodists relocated from North Carolina to the free states of Ohio, Illinois, and Indiana. There, they hoped to insulate themselves from slavery and offer asylum to fugitives. From the 1820s through the 1850s, many individuals and communities in these states helped thousands of fugitives and manumitted slaves make the transition to freedom. Some white planters took similar action. For instance, Virginia planter Edward Coles, a secretary to President James Madison, freed a number of his slaves in 1819 and purchased land for them in Madison County, Illinois.

Dozens of white-sponsored black communities dotted the areas along waterways that linked the North and South. For example, in 1833, a Quaker community called Carthegena began in western Ohio under the leadership of Augustus Wattles. By 1838, several hundred free black farmers in Carthegena cultivated 30,000 acres and operated a school, a gristmill, and a brickyard. Silver Lake, a similar community in Susquehanna County, Pennsylvania, opened in 1836 and became home to several hundred more.

Free black people also established their own separate communities. In 1832, 300 black Virginians settled on land in Ohio that their master, John Randolph, had willed to them along with their freedom. Randolph's slaves arrived to find that some of their master's relatives had cheated them out of their land. Nonetheless, sympathetic residents in nearby Piqua welcomed them with land and employment. In 1836, Frank McWhorter, who had purchased his freedom and that of his family's, bought land in Pike County, Illinois. There he founded New Philadelphia, the first of twenty settlements in Illinois and Ohio started by free African Americans. Too isolated to attract many settlers, such towns served mostly as way stations for fugitive slaves traveling to Canada.

Most of these towns disappeared after the Civil War. Historical records contain little information about why these attempts at black settlement failed. At least one of them, however—Brooklyn, Illinois, 20 miles southeast of New Philadelphia—survived into the early twentieth century. Brooklyn grew out of a settlement started about 1830 by eleven families from Missouri. Located 30 miles east of the Mississippi River in a coal-mining and agricultural region, by 1840 Brooklyn included an African Methodist Episcopal church, a Baptist church, and a railroad connection. It was home to 200 of St. Clair County's 500 black residents. But it did not grow. In 1873, when Brooklyn became America's first incorporated majority-black town, it had a population of just 371.

Between Slave and Free

Martin Delany's tour of the United States brought him face to face with people with both African and Native American heritage. John Horse, sometimes known as John Caballo (*caballo* is Spanish for "horse"), is one such individual. Part African American, part Creek Indian, John Horse was about five years old when Colonel Andrew Jackson's brigade of American troops tried to seize part of Spanish territory in Florida inhabited by several groups of Creeks. Horse was a member of one of these groups—the Seminoles—who had many African Americans living among them.

There were many fugitives among the 15,000 slaves and 850 free black people in Florida, and Jackson wanted to eliminate this runaway sanctuary. Though the Seminoles themselves owned black slaves, they allowed their bondspeople to establish their own villages and pay only a token annual tribute in crops. Many Seminoles intermarried with African Americans, and John Horse was probably the son of a black slave woman and her Seminole master. The Seminoles also armed their slaves as warriors and prized them as translators. As black fighters joined the Seminole warriors against U.S. troops, Jackson's officers often referred to these battles as wars waged "by the negroes."

Despite Jackson's determination, Seminole communities in east Florida survived. When Jackson became president and signed into law the Indian Removal Act, some Seminoles submitted to a treaty in 1831. They agreed to abandon their Florida homes and move west to Indian territory in regions that are now Louisiana and Oklahoma. But others resisted. Their defiance initiated the First Seminole War in 1835. For more than five years, in intermittent skirmishes, they held off American soldiers.

In 1842, the United States government completed its relocation of Seminoles from Florida, but the Seminoles did not go easily. Led by Osceola, a Seminole man whose wife had been enslaved by a U.S. government agent, some Semi-

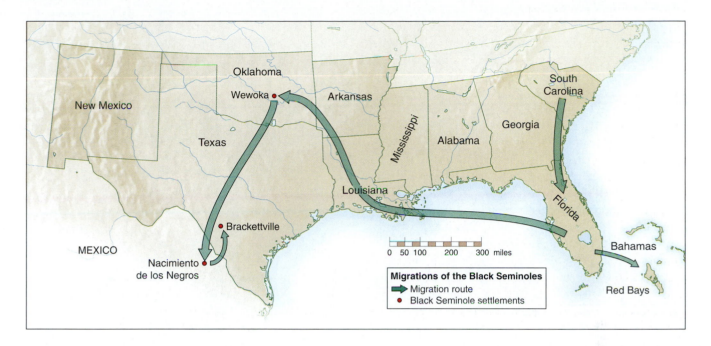

■ **MAP 8.3** Migrations of the Black Seminoles

As Seminole Indians moved west in the 1830s, African Americans accompanied them into Oklahoma, Texas, and Mexico.

noles—including John Horse—initiated a series of battles known as the Second Seminole War. When it was over, all the Florida Seminoles had been removed or subdued, but Indian resistance had cost the United States thousands of dollars and the lives of hundreds more.

Through these years, John Horse shifted his loyalties several times. Sometimes he helped the Seminoles battle white soldiers. Other times he aided the U.S. army, serving as a well-paid guide, interpreter, and, eventually, soldier. By 1840, he had married Susan, a Seminole woman, and soon the couple started a family. As the child of a slave mother, John Horse was not free, but as a slave in the Seminole community that included its slaves in armies and allowed individuals such as Horse to marry its members, he straddled the lines between black and Indian, and between slave and free. His participation in the U.S. army's campaign against the Indians indicates the instability of things such as racial loyalty.

Meanwhile, deep in the South, some slaves managed to carve out a degree of freedom. Benjamin Thornton Montgomery exemplified this situation. Though he never became free, Montgomery enjoyed many privileges usually reserved for white Americans. In 1836, Montgomery was purchased from Virginia by Joseph Davis, owner of Hurricane Plantation near Vicksburg, Mississippi. Davis, a southern reformer experimenting with crop rotation and labor management, modeled his labor system on the ideas of Scottish industri-

alist and social innovator Robert Dale Owen. Owen believed that a harmonious work setting where employers treated workers with dignity, offering them skills and responsibility, would prove more profitable than one where harsh discipline ruled. No Hurricane slave was ever punished without a hearing before a jury of peers. Davis fired overseers who violated this policy.

Soon after arriving at Hurricane, Ben Montgomery ran away. When he was captured, he negotiated an agreement that made staying more palatable. The literate Montgomery persuaded Davis to lend him books and, eventually, to give him control of the plantation store—including keeping part of the profits. Davis encouraged Montgomery to master surveying, drafting, and mechanical skills, and he gave Montgomery control over the estate's construction projects and machinery, including several steam engines.

With thrift, discipline, and his master's indulgence, Montgomery amassed broad knowledge and considerable savings. Married in 1840 to another slave, Mary Lewis, he fathered four children. He bought books, paid tutors to educate his children, and purchased his wife's time so she could stay at home to care for their family. Montgomery's family life, with his wife and children sheltered from a bruising workplace, mirrored the middle-class white ideal. His relationship with his white owner may have come as close to friendship as was possible within slavery. Indeed, Montgomery's children recalled that

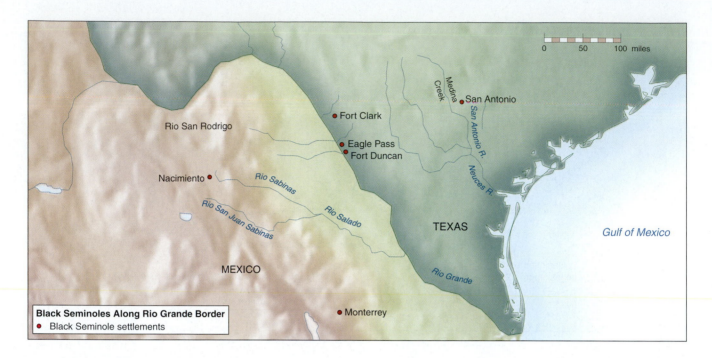

■ **MAP 8.4** Black Seminoles Along Rio Grande Border

Mixed-race Seminole leader John Horse was among the African Americans seeking a new life in Mexico. By 1849, Horse helped establish Nacimiento, a refuge for 200 black and Indian men, 100 miles west of the Rio Grande.

whenever their father entered a room, Davis pulled a chair up to the table and invited his slave to sit.

Apparently Montgomery never sought legal freedom, and Davis never offered it. Montgomery's situation was enviable compared to the other 100,000 Mississippi slaves. Still, Montgomery was constrained by a society where white people controlled black people's opportunities, and Davis' blueprint for human dignity and an efficient workplace did not include black liberation.

BLACK AMERICANS AND REFORM

"As Christ died in vain for those who will not accept his offered mercy, so will it be vain for the advocates of freedom to spend their breath in our behalf, unless [African Americans] make some mighty efforts to raise your sons and daughters from the horrible state of degradation in which they are placed." Speaking before a Boston audience in 1832, African American Maria Miller Stewart displayed the religious, intellectual, and political energy that made her one of the era's most dedicated reformers. Though her career as a public speaker was short-lived, she was nonetheless influential. Stewart used religion to inspire political and social action far broader than that of most of her peers.

Building on the reform spirit, free African Americans sought to gain skills and resources to shield themselves from racism and exploitation. They established schools and literary societies for both children and adults. They boycotted slave-produced goods to protest slavery. Black ministers preached about humility and patience. Some also taught rebellion.

Religion and Reform

Maria Miller Stewart's childhood and young adult experiences helped mold her ideas. Born to free black parents in Connecticut in 1803 but orphaned by age five, she became a servant to a white minister who taught her to read. Through this early training, she was introduced to the Second Great Awakening, a wave of religious energy that swept America in the 1820s, inspiring leaders to try to cleanse the country of sin.

In 1818 she moved to Boston, where she worked as a domestic and soon married James Stewart, a well-to-do black shipper whose income afforded her several years of leisurely reading. But her comfortable life did not last. In 1829, after just three years of marriage, Maria Stewart was widowed. Her husband left her an inheritance and a soon-to-be-born son, whom she named William. But when the white executor of the estate swindled Stewart out of her bequest, she was left to support herself again.

Stewart soon turned from reading to writing and speaking. She had applauded the fiery *Appeal to the Coloured Citizens,* published in 1829 by her friend and fellow Bostonian David Walker. Walker had hinted that God might call on slaves to violently overthrow their masters, and upon his death in 1830, Stewart took up his mixture of religion and revolution. She was encouraged in this endeavor by William Lloyd Garrison, who in 1831 helped her publish a religious pamphlet that brought her to prominence in Boston's literary circles. This pamphlet, "Religion and the Pure Principles of Morality, the Sure Foundation on Which We Must Build," began with the idea that through thrift and sobriety black citizens could earn citizenship, then continued with the importance of an underpinning of religious faith: "[I]t is the religion of Jesus alone that will constitute your happiness here, and support you in a dying hour."

Garrison also supported Stewart's advocacy of rights for black women as well as abolition. Stewart exhorted people to see that discrimination against women and African Americans were entwined, preventing black women's full development and mocking Christian virtue. She also included black men in her diatribes, insisting they were part of the oppression of black women and that African American women should refuse to be subservient to them. "How long," she asked, "shall a mean set of men flatter us with their smiles, and enrich themselves with our hard earnings; their wives' fingers sparkling with rings, and they themselves laughing at our folly?" She answered, "Until we begin to promote and patronize each other, [until women] possess [a spirit equal to that of] men, bold and enterprising, fearless and undaunted."

When Stewart unleashed her frustration at black men, they often heckled her. Nonetheless, Stewart urged black women to work together to end their oppression: "Shall it . . . be said of the daughters of Africa, [that] they have no ambition, they have no force? How long shall the fair daughters of Africa be compelled to bury their minds and talents beneath a load of iron pots and kettles? Until union, knowledge and love begin to flow among us." With barely 2,500 African Americans living in Boston in 1830, few black women heard Stewart speak. But *The Liberator's* 3,500 subscribers helped spread her words. Inspired, black New Englanders formed the Female Anti-Slavery Society of Salem, Massachusetts, in 1832.

The first female public speaker in America whose speeches were published, Stewart set an example for black women of her day. However, the hostility she encountered wore her down. She left Boston in 1833. "I am about to leave you, for I find it of no use to me to try to make myself useful among my color in this city. God has tried me as if by fire. I can now bless those who have hated me, and pray for those who have used and persecuted me." Stewart moved to New York to teach in a colored school.

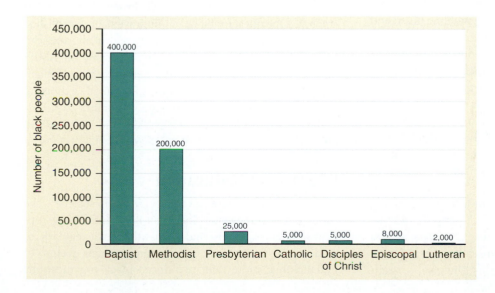

■ FIGURE 8.3 African American Church Membership, 1860

In addition to the AME church, several other Protestant groups attracted significant black membership. The few black Catholics were mostly clustered in French Louisiana.

 **Maria Stewart Challenges Her Audiences**

Lecturing in spring 1832, Maria Stewart "borrowed much of [her] language from the Bible." But Stewart often went beyond the boundaries of religion to reiterate arguments about women's rights published in her 1831 pamphlet.

It is of no use for us to sit with our hands folded, . . . lamenting our wretched condition; but let us make a mighty effort, and arise. Let every female heart become united and let us raise a fund ourselves; and at the end of one year and a half, we might be able to lay the corner-stone for the building of a High School.

Unite and build a store of your own. Fill one side with dry goods and the other side with groceries. . . . O woman, woman! Your example is powerful, your influence great; it extends over your husbands and your children, and throughout the circle of your acquaintances. . . . Cultivate among yourselves a spirit that all our goodness is as sounding brass and a tinkling cymbal.

—*from* Maria M. Stewart, Meditations from the Pen of Mrs. Maria M. Stewart *(Washington, DC: n. p., 1879).*

To view a longer version of this document, please go to *www.ablongman.com/carson/documents*.

Self-Improvement, Moral Progress, and the "Cultivated Mind"

"[A] cultivated mind is of higher consideration than dollars and cents. . . . Instead of drinking grog or smoking tobacco, we should read the newspaper." With these words, Pittsburgh teacher Lewis Woodson implored his students to use their time and money for self-improvement. Maria Stewart shared this commitment to strict self-discipline and thrift. "I would implore our men," she admonished, "and especially our rising youth, to flee from the gambling board and the dance hall; for we are poor, and have no money to throw away." Free black Americans like Woodson and Stewart hoped self-improvement would convince white Americans that black people could be responsible and productive citizens. They believed African Americans would be self-sufficient and upstanding if they learned to read and write, to work outside of slavery, and to lead lives of Christian virtue.

The Pittsburgh African Education Society, established in 1832 by Lewis Woodson and his colleagues, adopted this blueprint for self-improvement. "The intellectual capacity of the black man is equal to that of the white," said the Society's constitution, "and he is equally susceptible of improvement, all ancient history makes manifest; and modern examples put this beyond a single doubt." Persuaded that "ignorance is the cause of the present degradation and bondage of the people of color in these United States," the Society erected a building to house a school, library, and lecture hall, open to all black people, enslaved and free.

The American Moral Reform Society (AMRS) also embodied the quest for black self-improvement. Established in Philadelphia in 1835, its goal was to reform all American society. At age sixty-nine, James Forten became the AMRS president. Less than half Forten's age, the eloquent William Whipper became AMRS's leading spokesman, exhorting "every *American*," regardless of race, to commit to "EDUCATION, TEMPERANCE, ECONOMY, and UNIVERSAL LIBERTY."

Literacy and Education

The reform spirit fostered a variety of self-help societies. The Afric-Female Intelligence Society of Boston, the New York Female Literary Society, and many others met regularly to read and debate history, science, and current events. In Philadelphia, more than two dozen black organizations

> "The intellectual capacity of the black man is equal to that of the white."
> —*Pittsburgh African Education Society*

MR IRA ALDRIDGE AS AARON.

■ Cartoonist Edward Clay created many caricatures of Philadelphia's middle-class African Americans, ridiculing what he termed their tendency to "aspire too much."

■ Black leaders often applauded African American artists like actor Ira Aldridge (1805–1867) for providing evidence that African Americans had achieved the "cultivated mind." During the 1830s, Aldridge toured Europe in the lead role in Shakespeare's *Othello*; African American talent often got a better reception in Europe than at home.

modeled responsible citizenship by providing musical, educational, recreational, and burial services.

While self-help societies played a vital role, schools for black children proved even more crucial. During the 1830s, urban public schools excluded black students. To right the imbalance, dedicated teachers founded separate schools for African Americans. Most of these, of course, were established in the North. These included Margaretta Forten's school in Philadelphia, Charles L. Reason's Free African

School in New York, and the New England Union Academy in Providence, Rhode Island. Even in the South, a few free black children—often the biracial offspring of white masters—studied with black teachers such as Daniel Payne in Charleston and Marie Couvent in New Orleans.

Some philanthropic white people also set up schools for African Americans. In Philadelphia, the Quaker-run Institute for Colored Youth opened in the 1830s, becoming the nucleus of a teachers' college that still survives. In 1832, white reformer Prudence Crandall opened a school for black girls in Canterbury, Connecticut. White townspeople, however, harassed Crandall and torched the school. Despite such incidents, teachers persevered.

From "African" to "Colored"

In working for better lives, free African Americans in the mid-nineteenth century also focused on self-identity. Black

 **First Person**   Daniel Payne Abhors Slavery's Brutalization

Born free, Daniel Payne opened a school in Charleston in 1829 but was forced to abandon it when the city outlawed black education in 1834. Soon Payne moved north, working for the AME Church. In this 1839 speech, Payne condemns slavery using arguments of reason, morality, and religion.

American slavery brutalizes man—destroys his moral agency, and subverts the moral government of God. I am opposed to slavery, not because it enslaves the black man, but because it enslaves man. And were all the slaveholders in this land men of color, and the slaves white men, I would be as thorough and uncompromising an abolitionist as I now am, for . . . whenever I may see a being enslaved by his fellow man, without respect to his complexion, I shall lift up my voice to plead his cause . . . because God, . . . whom I dare not disobey, has commanded me to plead the cause of the oppressed.

Slavery brutalizes man. . . . God created [man] a little lower than the angels, and crowned him with glory and honor; but slavery hurls him down . . . to the level of brutes, and compels him to labor like an ox.

—*from Lutheran Herald and Journal of the Fort Plain, New York, Franckean Synod. 1:15 (August 1, 1839), pp. 112–114.*

To view a longer version of this document, please go to *www.ablongman.com/carson/documents*.

communities traditionally honored their origins by using the term *African* in naming their organizations. By the 1830s, some black leaders suggested discontinuing this practice in order to remind their white neighbors that they and their children were Americans, not Africans.

During these years, many Americans—regardless of skin color or region—were reassessing the meaning of the word *American*. All across the country, with new canals and railroads transporting citizens, immigrants, printed materials, and fugitive slaves to frontier communities, Americans increasingly encountered people different from themselves. As the new wave of European immigrants increased the number of Catholic congregations and Jewish synagogues, it also intensified native-born white Americans' resistance to newcomers' customs. As anti-immigrant tensions rose, many black Americans sought to remind white Americans that they were not newcomers. Rather, they were "colored *Americans.*"

Names with Meaning

Free African Americans enjoyed a luxury unavailable to most slaves: choosing their children's names. Maria Stewart named her son after white abolitionist William Lloyd Garrison. The Montgomerys bestowed the Old Testament names Rebecca and Isaiah on two of their children; they named their youngest son for an English abolitionist, William Thornton.

The Delanys also chose names reflecting black concerns as well as Christian values. In 1846, they named a son Toussaint L'Ouverture Delany, honoring the Haitian revolutionary leader. Another son, Charles Lenox Remond Delany, was named for the Massachusetts black abolitionist. Other sons' names reflected black history or literature: Alexander Dumas Delany was named after the black French author; St. Cyprian Delany honored the third-century black religious leader; Faustin Soulouque Delany was inspired by a Haitian emperor; and Ramses Placido Delany combined homage to ancient Egyptian monarchs and a Cuban revolutionary poet. In a psalm that praises God for liberating enslaved peoples, the Bible promises that in return Ethiopia will "stretch forth her hands to God." The Delanys, well versed in the Bible, named their only daughter and last child Ethiopia.

Thus, as parents have done throughout time, the Delanys, Montgomerys, and Stewarts expressed their hopes and values through their children. But these names differed from those chosen by newly freed African Americans two generations before. Those earlier generations had selected names reflecting their new status (Freeman, Newman, or Trusty) and confirming their Americanness (John, James, or

Mary). Reform-era black names often bespoke knowledge of literature, history, and current events stretching far beyond the limits of a slave world.

THE ABOLITIONIST MOVEMENT

Recounting his life story in 1845, Frederick Douglass recalled the day he decided he would never be whipped again. "Whence came the daring spirit necessary to grapple with a man who, eight-and-forty hours before, could, with his slightest word, have made me tremble like a leaf in a storm, I do not know. The fighting madness had come upon me, and I found my strong fingers firmly attached to the throat of the tyrant, as heedless of consequences as if we stood as equals before the law. My resistance was entirely unexpected and Covey [the white overseer] was taken all aback by it. He was frightened. The probability is that Covey was ashamed to have it known that he had been mastered by a boy of sixteen."

> "The fighting madness had come upon me, and I found my strong fingers firmly attached to the throat of the tyrant." —Frederick Douglass

The story of Douglass's resistance and subsequent escape and transformation from slave to abolitionist lecturer is among the most celebrated in American history. It chronicles a man's life as well as the subtleties of black-white abolitionist relationships. It also highlights the sharpened political consciousness and will to resist oppression of African Americans.

Radical Abolitionism

By 1830, the abolitionist movement turned radical as reformers were prepared to break laws, directly confront slaveholders, and even commit violence. Though the antislavery movement had long existed, a new mood of urgency infused it—symbolized by *The Liberator*'s strident masthead: "I will not retreat a single inch, and I WILL be heard." Editor William Lloyd Garrison meant to provoke Americans into imagining a radically reformed society.

Radical abolitionism solidified with the 1833 founding of the American Anti-Slavery Society (AAS) in Philadelphia. Garrison led a white delegation to the first meeting that included Arthur and Lewis Tappan from upstate New York and a group of religious revivalists from Ohio. Meeting with James Forten and other influential black Philadelphians, these men shaped AAS's mission: to complete the abolition begun in some northern states during the American Revolution. The AAS took particular offense at the clause in the Constitution counting a black person as only three-fifths of a citizen. That clause, they said, was "a criminal and dangerous relation to slavery that must be broken up." The group promised to organize "in every city, town and village in our land," to send agents, enlist the press, and circulate literature to show "the guilt of the nation's oppression" of African Americans. Members also sponsored lectures where ex-slaves gave firsthand accounts of a plantation system most northern white people—and many free black people—had never seen.

Much leadership for the abolitionist movement grew out of the black churches, particularly the African Methodist Episcopal Church, the largest black denomination. AME membership soared from 7,000 in 1836 to 20,000 by the 1850s. AME congregations, already strong in Philadelphia and Baltimore, soon arose in Mobile, Alabama; New Orleans, Louisiana; St. Louis, Missouri; and dozens of other cities. Black Baptist and Presbyterian congregations also flourished. Further, even though manumissions decreased, the natural increase in black births resulted in a growing number of free black people in the South—from 180,000 in 1830 to nearly 240,000 by 1850; this provided fertile ground for other churches. Small but tenacious Catholic, Episcopal, and Moravian

congregations took root as well. The churches became the hub of black community life, offering friendship, education, entertainment, and, sometimes, information about gaining freedom.

Sending hundreds of organizers across northern and western states to link 2,000 affiliated groups, the AAS had 150,000 members by 1840. Collecting thousands of signatures for antislavery petitions to Congress, the AAS army of traveling lecturers preached to massive audiences and published thousands of books and articles about the immorality of slavery. Their most widely read literature included Garrison's *The Liberator* and Lydia Maria Child's *An Appeal in Favor of That Class of Americans Called Africans* (1833). In *An Appeal,* Child decried slavery and the difficulty free black people had in finding work.

Child, who came from a white New England family actively involved in various reform efforts, conveyed the beliefs of many when she wrote, "We made slavery, and

William Lloyd Garrison Dreams of a Colorblind Society

In The Liberator, *William Lloyd Garrison published an account of "T. T.," a fictionalized character (probably Garrison himself) who dreamed that interracial harmony could bring about the election of a black president.*

We are . . . completely united into one people and there is as little thought of separate interests and feelings between blacks and whites, as between tall and short, or dark eyes and blue, or between men and women. . . . [At a reception for the newly elected president] nearly half the company was of the negro race, and blacks and whites were mingling with perfect ease in social intercourse. . . .

Our first black president was a man of such distinguished talents, that . . . African inferiority was heard of no more.

—*from William Lloyd Garrison, in* The Liberator *1:14, Saturday, April 2, 1831, p. 1.*

To view a longer version of this document, please go to *www.ablongman.com/carson/documents*.

slavery makes prejudice." Child argued that "our prejudice against the blacks is founded in sheer pride" arising from "the circumstance that people of their color only are universally allowed to be slaves." Echoing her mentor, William Lloyd Garrison, Child insisted that free black people were "more temperate and more industrious" than the "foreign [white] emigrants who are crowding our shores."

In addition to white reformers like Child, Garrison recruited African Americans—including Frederick Douglass—to abolitionism. Born on a Maryland plantation in 1817, Douglass was the son of a slave woman and a white father whom he never knew. The planter's wife helped him learn to read as a child. Douglass later reported that before her husband "broke her noble soul," this compassionate woman taught Douglass to seek the best in others, black and white.

Though the encounter with overseer Covey crystallized Douglass's intent to escape, it took three years and two attempts before he broke free. Finally, in 1838, disguising himself as a sailor, he made his way safely to New Bedford, Massachusetts. There he married Anna, a free woman whom he had met in Baltimore, where she had worked as a domestic servant. In New England, Douglass worked closely with Garrison for several years, later describing his "education" as resulting from contact with "Massachusetts University, Mr. Garrison, President." To avoid capture the fugitive Douglass spent two years in Eng-

land, while American abolitionists raised funds to purchase his freedom. Free by 1845, Douglass regularly traveled on abolitionist lecture tours and spoke at Conventions of Free People of Color.

The Free Produce Movement

The new mood of urgent abolitionism generated a wave of antislavery activity. Almost every northern community developed a Vigilance Committee of black people and a few white allies who harbored fugitives in their homes and bombarded local and federal legislatures with antislavery petitions. They also used connections in ports and along inland trade routes to help runaway slaves stay in touch with those left behind. Finally, they supported free produce stores, which sold only products made with nonslave labor.

The idea of boycotting slave-produced goods was not new. Eighteenth-century reformer Benjamin Lay had advocated it. In the early nineteenth century, radical Quaker Elias Hicks had published a pamphlet urging avoidance of slave-made products. The idea resurfaced in 1838, when several dozen black and white Philadelphians founded the American Free Produce Society. For almost two decades, the Society distributed literature encouraging consumers to substitute local honey for slave-grown sugar. Members bought cotton grown with free labor, had it woven into cloth, and sold it through free-produce outlets. Following

■ Frederick Douglass was twenty-nine when this daguerreotype was taken. Abolitionists displayed such images in their homes for inspiration.

The Liberator's call to be "as uncompromising as justice," they determined to drive slaveowners out of business.

Divisions Among Abolitionists

Abolitionists agreed on their primary goal: ending the sordid practice of slavery. But beyond this there was little unity about motivation or strategy. White reformers like Arthur and Lewis Tappan mostly worried that slavery compromised white Americans' morality. The Tappans would not rent to black tenants, had no desire to live near African Americans, and, like many reformers, hoped free black people would go to Africa.

William Lloyd Garrison's behavior also disturbed some black abolitionists. Garrison, who went so far as to confess shame at being part of the white race, socialized with black friends and published their writing. He also envisioned a society in which all races lived harmoniously. But he could be high-handed with abolitionists—especially black ones—who resisted doing things his way. In 1848, when he dis-

couraged Frederick Douglass from starting a newspaper, Douglass concluded that Garrison resented black leaders and wanted to make decisions for them.

Contrasting with the Tappans, who sought to avoid African Americans, and Garrison, who seemed to want to control them, were the white antislavery activists like Gerrit Smith, who embraced black Americans. In the 1840s, Smith donated a large tract of land in northern New York to start a black community, and chose to live there. In 1849, John Brown—who later tried to ignite a slave rebellion in Harper's Ferry, Virginia—moved his family to Smith's black settlement.

Those African Americans who had been slaves sometimes saw themselves as more credible voices for the abolitionist movement than those who had never known slavery. When Lydia Maria Child suggested to Frederick Douglass that his speeches sounded so polished the audience would not believe he had been a slave, Douglass replied that Child had no right to dictate how he should present his firsthand knowledge of slavery. But eventually Douglass's anger waned. In 1880, when Child died, Douglass eulogized her fondly: "Sympathetic in her nature, it was easy for her to remember those in bonds."

Even among free African Americans, there was often no abolitionist unity. Some black entrepreneurs in the North, perhaps wanting to protect thriving businesses or avoid reprisals from white people, remained silent. Others were too focused on mere survival to involve themselves in protests. Only gradually did these black Americans come to conceive of their fate as intertwined with that of slaves.

Gender became another source of division among abolitionists. The AAS leaders excluded women from decision making. Like most men of their time, they believed proper ladies should abstain from "promiscuous" gatherings—that is, groups comprising both men and women. Thus, many AAS groups were founded specifically for women, such as the Philadelphia Female Anti-Slavery Society. Women's groups raised funds for black schools or established schools of their own. But they also joined public protests: women constituted almost half of the signers of one 1837 petition to abolish slavery in the District of Columbia. In Maine and Massachusetts combined, nearly two-thirds of the 23,000 petition signers were women, as were all the signers from Rhode Island.

Appreciating that abolitionist men like Garrison and Douglass believed women's voices should be heard, some women's groups also raised money for *The Liberator*. In 1848, when radical women gathered at Seneca Falls, New York, to write a declaration of women's rights, Douglass was

First Person — James Curry Refuses to Be Whipped

James Curry's story of his flight from North Carolina in 1839, reported in The Liberator, *echoes that of Frederick Douglass. Eventually settling in Canada, Curry returned to the South in 1865 to search for his family. There he was recognized and beaten by enraged planters, but he escaped recapture. Here, he tells of the episode that prompted him to escape.*

From my childhood, I was brought up to be a domestic servant. I played with my master's children, and we loved one another like brothers. My master's oldest son . . . went to a day school, and as I had a great desire to read, I prevailed on him to teach me. My mother procured me a spelling-book. (Before Nat Turner's insurrection, a slave in our neighborhood might buy a spelling or hymn-book, but now he cannot.)

. . . Having obtained a knowledge of the course which would carry me to Pennsylvania, I only waited for an occasion to escape. . . . In May, 1839, just after I was 22 years old . . . the overseer . . . took a hickory rod and struck me some thirty or forty strokes. . . . As the strokes fell on my back, I firmly resolved that I would no longer be a slave. I would now escape or die in the attempt. They might shoot me down if they chose, but I would not live a slave.

—*from* The Liberator, *January 10, 1840.*

To view a longer version of this document, please go to *www.ablongman.com/carson/documents*.

a featured speaker. Though such male support was rare, many women found ways to make a difference. Lydia Child went on the abolitionist lecture circuit. Frederick Douglass's wife, Anna, took a job in a shoe factory to feed the family's five children and help support her husband's travels. Other black women, like the middle-class Sarah Remond, embarked on the lecture circuit themselves. Still others—such as Susan Paul, who had helped to organize the Massachusetts Female Antislavery Society, and Sarah Mapps Douglass, leader of the Philadelphia Female Antislavery Society—divided their time between teaching children, organizing women's literacy programs, and political education meetings. In Boston, black women petitioned against segregated schools. In Salem, Massachusetts, they wrote a constitution "associating ourselves for our mutual improvement and to promote the welfare of our color."

Many black women now found a new platform to celebrate both race and gender. Elleanor Eldridge's *The Memoirs of Elleanor Eldridge* (1839), describing her grandfather's noble West African heritage and her brother's leadership among black New Englanders, set an inspiring example. Jarena Lee, whom Philadelphia AME bishop Richard Allen had refused a regular pulpit, was a traveling missionary for

Allen's church (see Chapter 7). In 1839, Lee published her story, then joined the AAS, believing that after abolition "the Bible would have free course to every nation." She had spent part of her childhood working as an indentured servant, a common experience among the 150,000 African Americans living in the North, many of whom had parents who could not provide for them. Some black girls were even bound out to abolitionists such as white Philadelphian Isaac Hopper, who protected his young servant from kidnapping while benefiting from the child's labor. The AAS now provided an outlet for such black women's aspirations.

But the appointment of Abbey Kelley to the AAS executive committee in 1840 caused a rupture among abolitionists. Kelley was a tireless lecturer who advocated women's equality, exhorting abolitionists to "take a stand for all truths, because the whole are necessary to the permanent establishment of any single one." Following Garrison's lead, Kelley insisted that "moral suasion" to stir the public conscience was the only sure way to end social sins such as using race or gender to deny freedom or citizenship.

But Kelley's appointment alienated many male abolitionists who felt women should not be put forth as public leaders. The AAS splintered, with Lewis Tappan leading a

The Pennsylvania Anti-Slavery Society Executive Committee, shown in this 1851 photograph, included both free African Americans and women. Quaker minister Lucretia Coffin Mott (front row: second from right) provided an important link between abolition and women's rights. Robert Purvis (at Mott's right) was one of Philadelphia's best-known black leaders.

walkout to establish the American and Foreign Antislavery Society, which rushed delegates off to London to persuade the AAS international convention not to seat women. Sharing Tappan's conviction that women should play a subservient role, ex-slave Henry Highland Garnet became one of only six black men—all ministers—who joined the American and Foreign Antislavery Society (Garnet soon left to collaborate with black allies exclusively). Over Garrison's objections that prejudice against women was no better than prejudice against slaves, male delegates banned women from policy-making sessions, consigning them to attend only social events.

This controversy in London crystallized abolitionists' divisions. Thus, by 1840, the abolitionist movement fractured over questions of gender, leadership, the role of free African Americans in the abolitionist movement, and expectations for black people's fate should abolition succeed. After 1840, the focus on ending slavery continued to unite abolitionists, but little else did.

Violence Against Abolitionists

The AAS's confrontational posture incited violence among northerners as well as southerners who feared abolition might dislodge white people's superior social status. Yet many abolitionists welcomed public attacks, feeling it gained publicity and sympathy and ennobled their cause. Lydia Maria Child's abolitionism drove subscribers away from her children's magazine; she rose above this by starting a sugar-beet farm to promote alternatives to slave-grown sugar. As Garrison was preparing to speak before the Boston Female Antislavery Society in 1835, a white mob that feared black labor competition looped a rope around his neck and dragged him through the streets. He survived only because he was arrested for inciting a riot. The martyrdom pleased Garrison, who viewed the antislavery cause as holy and deemed it better to "have brickbats [thrown at him] in the cause of God than to have wedges of gold in the cause of sin [slavery.]"

Elijah Lovejoy was not so lucky. A New England teacher who embraced the idea of gradual emancipation, Lovejoy settled in the frontier town of Alton, Illinois, where he founded an abolitionist paper. But local white residents, worried that Lovejoy's newspaper, *The Observer*, would attract abolitionists to Alton, destroyed his printing press. Infuriated, Lovejoy vowed to defend his constitutional right to free speech. Several times the AAS replaced his equipment; several times angry mobs destroyed it.

Finally, in 1837, Lovejoy's opponents destroyed his printing press and murdered him. The *Colored American* newspaper memorialized Lovejoy in a front-page editorial, and across the North, antislavery groups mourned him. Intending mostly to defend free speech, Lovejoy became what a New York black man called "the first martyr in the holy cause of abolition in the nation."

■ **TABLE 8.2** Abolitionist Organizations

Organization/ Year Founded	Black leaders	White leaders	Goals	Strategy
American Colonization Society/1816	Paul Cuffe (died before its founding), Edward Blyden, Robert Campbell	James Madison, James Monroe, Henry Clay	Gradual abolition; black education and resettlement outside the U.S.	Encourage southern manumission; establish schools and settlements for free black people
American Anti-slavery Society (AAS)/1833	James Forten, John B. Vashon, Charles Remond	William Lloyd Garrison, Arthur and Lewis Tappan	Immediate abolition	Petition Congress to broaden the Constitution to outlaw slavery; circulate antislavery literature
Salem Female Anti-slavery Society/1832; Philadelphia Female Antislavery Society/1833	Sarah Remond, Margaretta Forten, Sarah Mapps Douglass	Lydia Maria Child, Angelina Grimké, Lucretia Mott	Support AAS; encourage black education; pursue women's rights	Raise money for AAS and for schools; confront AAS on its gender exclusion
Philadelphia Free Produce Society/1838	Robert Purvis	James Mott, Isaac T. Hopper	Freeze slaveholders out of the American economy	Produce and sell cotton cloth and sugar from free-labor growers
American and Foreign Anti-slavery Society/1840	Henry Highland Garnet, Samuel Cornish	Arthur and Lewis Tappan, James G. Birney	Agitate Congress for abolition; mount an antislavery presidential campaign	Protect American morality by denouncing slavery and refusing to have men and women work together
Liberty Party/1840	Frederick Douglass, Martin Delany	James G. Birney	Establish an antislavery political party	Challenge traditional presidential candidates
American Missionary Association/1846	Henry R. and Tamar Wilson	Lewis Tappan	Purge white churches of the sin of slavery	Dispatch missionaries to start black schools and churches

In Philadelphia, barred from meeting in most public buildings, a committee of black and white women who supported the abolitionist cause raised money and built Pennsylvania Hall. This new meeting hall opened in May 1838, with speeches by William Lloyd Garrison, black abolitionist Sarah Mapps Douglass, and Angelina Grimké, who two days earlier had married Presbyterian minister Theodore Weld. Outraged that guests at the Grimké-Weld wedding had included black people, a white crowd mobbed the building, menacing its several thousand occupants. The following day, the crowd burned the empty building to the ground while the mayor and neighbors stood idly by.

Wherever free black people agitated for citizenship, they suffered similar reprisals. Between 1833 and 1838, more than three dozen race riots in northern cities focused on symbols of black independence: churches, businesses, meeting places, and prosperous black families. An 1849 attack on Philadelphia's California House Tavern was typical. The tavern's owner, a mixed-race man and his white wife, served black and white patrons alike. This incensed white neighbors, who torched the tavern, then blocked white fire companies attempting to extinguish the blaze. For

two days, black neighborhoods were pummeled by a white mob. Newspapers reported that white laborers expressed resentment at black workers' successes. But some of the attacks came from what one historian called "gentlemen of property and standing," owners of banks, transportation, and commerce that depended on southern cotton to keep their northern textile mills profitable. White clergymen and intellectuals, armed with new pseudoscientific theories about black deficiency, added to the racist chorus. They contended that black Americans lacked the moral character or mental capacity to function as equal citizens.

In the wake of Nat Turner's Rebellion in 1831 (see Chapter 7), southern abolitionist groups dissolved. A handful of planters quietly continued manumission, but most vocal southern white abolitionists, afraid for their lives, abandoned the South. A few became leaders among northern abolitionists. James G. Birney, a slaveholder who helped to develop a manumission policy in Alabama, left the South and in 1837 became executive secretary of the AAS. Sarah Grimké, sister of Angelina Grimké Weld and daughter of a prominent South Carolina slaveholding judge, moved to Philadelphia in the 1820s, breaking ties with the South and with her family.

By 1840, few remembered that U.S. presidents Jefferson, Madison, and Monroe had suggested freeing slaves. The battle lines were drawn: Abolition was a northern movement; southerners who sympathized had best keep quiet or leave the South.

Northern Black Press, Southern White Press

"The *Advocate* will be like a chain, binding you together as ONE. It . . . will always be . . . the proper medium for laying your claims before the public." So proclaimed the New York City *Weekly Advocate,* an antislavery newspaper, in its inaugural issue of January 1837. "We . . . are opposed to colonization [and] we hold ourselves ready to combat with opposite views," the *Advocate* continued, promising also to "contain the news of the day and a variety of scientific and literary matter."

During the mid-nineteenth century, black entrepreneurs and communities raised considerable capital to launch black newssheets. These publications not only railed against slavery but also entered the debate over emigration to Africa. Bolstered by the loyalty of their mostly black readers and the increasing reliability of mail delivery, more than a half-dozen black publications appeared by the 1840s. The first of these was John Russwurm's *Freedom's Journal,* begun in 1829. When Russwurm used the paper to publicize his support for relocating to Liberia, his partner, Samuel Cornish, established an alternative publication, *The Rights of All,* against relocation. Cornish's paper asserted that while a few African Americans might benefit from relocating to Africa, they would be abandoning defenseless slaves. The *Colored American,* begun in 1837, also discouraged black Americans from going to Africa.

Martin Delany's southern travels reinforced his dedication to maintaining a black press. In 1843, he launched *The Mystery,* a paper focusing on "the moral elevation of the Africo-American and African Race." Celebrating African heritage, the masthead of *The Mystery* proclaimed "and Moses was learned in all the wisdom of the Egyptians." The newsweekly brimmed with essays, reports from national correspondents, black merchants' advertisements, letters to the editor, and, of course, tirades against slavery. Delany even publicized his support for women's education. From the start, *The Mystery* was both a source of pride and a drain on Delany's resources. While the newssheet boasted upwards of 1,000 subscribers, Delany often could not collect the subscription fees.

While the mainstream white press lamented depressed cotton prices and an economic depression that began in 1837, the white-owned *Anti-Slavery Standard* and the black-run papers reflected a debate far more important to black reformers. The *Standard* encouraged reformers to unite behind Garrison. Some black newssheets argued that racially separate organizations would allow the best hearing for those who experienced racial prejudice firsthand. Some black reformers echoed Frederick Douglass's concern that white abolitionists' efforts to control black people made these white allies little different from slaveholders. So black publications like the *Advocate* and *The Mystery* tried to remain independent of white influence.

After several years of struggling with *The Mystery,* Delany partnered with Douglass and black Boston historian William C. Nell to launch *The North Star.* (Delany later sold *The Mystery* to the AME church, which changed its name to *The Christian Recorder.* It became the only black newssheet to publish continuously into the twentieth century.) The new partnership proved just as frustrating as working alone. The newssheet's provocative writing attracted a following, but like *The Mystery, The North Star* struggled financially. Yet Delany believed in the power of the press. In 1848, he took to the road again, leaving his ailing wife and two children as he traveled through Maryland, Pennsylvania, Ohio, and Michigan seeking subscriptions to keep *The North Star* running.

Proslavery Americans also understood the power of the press. Southern post offices refused to deliver abolitionist tracts, sometimes burning them. Southern periodicals like Maryland's *American Farmer,* Virginia's *Farmer's Register,* Georgia's *Southern Cultivator,* and the widely heralded *DeBow's Review* focused on agricultural management—but all discussions were shaped by proslavery arguments. All these periodicals reminded southerners that "slave labor is the source of all our wealth and prosperity . . . the basis of the most desirable social and political system the world has ever seen."

Through such publications, southern planters exchanged advice on maximizing the value of their human property. One planter likened his slaves to livestock. "My cattle that were well cared for in winter were in better condition all the year," he wrote. Hence he was "cautious of exposing my Negroes in the winter, and to provide for them good houses, good clothing, and good food." Other planters stressed careful attention to daily work schedules, discipline, diet, housing, and religious training. With good management, advised the press, a planter could avoid such pitfalls as *drapetomania*—a mental illness they believed caused slaves to run away—and *dyaestesia aethiopica,* which they said caused slaves to become careless and break tools. Contributors to the southern press did not consider that breaking tools or fleeing bondage might be a slave's rational choice. Still other planters offered advice on

 **First Person**   Henry Highland Garnet's Call to "Strike the Blow"

At age ten, Henry Highland Garnet and his slave parents escaped from Maryland. After attending school in northern New York, he became a minister in Troy. In 1843, when Garnet presented this "Address to the Slaves of the United States of America" to the Black National Convention, Frederick Douglass opposed him, fearing it would ignite a slave rebellion that could not be won.

Brethren, the time has come when you must act for yourself. It is an old and true saying that, "if hereditary bondmen would be free, they must themselves strike the blow." . . . In the slaveholding parts of the United States, the [slave] trade is as brisk as ever. They buy and sell you as though you were brute beasts. . . . Go to your lordly enslavers and tell them plainly, that you *are determined to be free.* . . . Inform them that all you desire is FREEDOM, and that nothing else will suffice. You had better all die—die immediately, than live slaves and entail your wretchedness upon your posterity.

—from A Memorial Discourse *by Rev. Henry Highland Garnet, Delivered in the Hall of the House of Representatives, Washington, D.C., on Sabbath, February 12, 1865.*

To view a longer version of this document, please go to *www.ablongman.com/carson/documents.*

how to control slaves. Some slaves, they explained, "require stirring up, some coaxing, some flattering, and others nothing but good words."

The Gag Rule and Landmark Legal Cases

Tension about slavery underlay every congressional discussion. Though the Missouri Compromise in 1820 temporarily suppressed debate about whether slavery should spread to western territories, the controversy still percolated, bubbling up as senators Henry Clay of Kentucky, Daniel Webster of Massachusetts, and John Calhoun of South Carolina debated land policy in the West, banking policy in the East, and the division of authority between federal and state governments. Voters watched anxiously as these political stalwarts struggled over policy.

Meanwhile, the burgeoning population of the northern states foretold declining power among proslavery congressmen. As immigrants flooded into northern cities, the balance of power in the House of Representatives tipped toward the North. Radical abolitionists, though never constituting more than 5 percent of the North's population, were a strident minority. Many southerners feared that if

abolitionists were elected to Congress, they would succeed in limiting or ending slavery. Surveying their worn-out fields, southern planters yearned to take their slaves and move west, where they might establish new slave states and reclaim their majority in Congress. But some abolitionists envisioned free black settlements in the West.

Fearing incendiary debate about antislavery petitions, Congress instituted the Gag Rule. In 1836, Congress voted to receive antislavery petitions but to ignore them. Though free speech advocates like former president John Quincy Adams (now a representative) decried this ban on public discussion, the Gag Rule remained in effect for eight years.

In 1839, the debate over the fate of African Americans polarized around a dramatic court case. Its human cargo seized the *Amistad,* a Spanish slave ship, en route from one Cuban port to another. Though the mutiny occurred in international waters and involved non-American slaves, it quickly became an American *cause célèbre.* Aboard the *Amistad,* a West African man, Sengbe Pieh (who became known as Joseph Cinque), led the slaves in killing the cook and the captain and demanding the crew return them to Africa. The white crew, however, sailed the *Amistad* along the North American coast until it attracted the attention of a U.S. naval ship, which commandeered it. Charged with piracy and murder, the slaves were imprisoned, awaiting ruling on the competing claims of the *Amistad* crew, the American navy, and the Spanish government.

William Lloyd Garrison, proclaiming that this case should awaken the "sympathy of all true-hearted, impartial lovers of liberty," insisted that the slaves had done what Americans had done in their own revolution fifty years earlier: defended their rights and liberty. Abolitionist newspapers also decried Spain's disregard for international laws enacted in 1818, which banned the slave trade.

Over the next several years, the *Amistad* case slogged through the American legal system. The case was first considered in the Connecticut courts, which debated whether the U.S. naval officers who had commandeered the ship could claim the ship or its cargo as salvage and whether the slaves were guilty of a crime. In January 1840, the judge ruled that the Africans were neither criminals nor slaves but kidnapping victims. The ship, he announced, should be returned to Spain, but its human cargo should be freed and sent to Sierra Leone. Pressured by Spain and southern slaveholders, U.S. president Martin Van Buren appealed the case to the U.S. Supreme Court.

John Quincy Adams came to the defense of the mutineers. Though not an avowed abolitionist, Adams opposed slavery and was eager to use the *Amistad* case to uphold international law. In 1841, the Supreme Court upheld part of the lower court's ruling, agreeing that the *Amistad* captives should be freed. But the Court also ruled that the *Amistad* Africans themselves should decide where to live, and that the federal government was not obliged to transport them to Africa.

Abolitionists paid to ship several dozen *Amistad* passengers to Sierra Leone in November 1841. From there, Cinque wrote to Lewis Tappan, noting that Sierra Leone was not his birthplace. He nevertheless "thanked all Merica people, for them send Mendi people home. I shall never forget Merica people."

The *Amistad* episode was followed by a similar case two years later. This time, the outcome disheartened abolitionists. An American ship, the *Creole*, transporting slaves along the North American coast, was seized by the slaves and sailed to the British West Indian island of Nassau. The slaves declared themselves free because they were under British protection. Daniel Webster, now U.S. Secretary of State, claiming the ship's deck was an extension of American soil, insisted that Britain compensate the owner for his loss. Northern abolitionists felt betrayed by their government. By extending American protection for slaveholders beyond U.S. borders, they declared, the federal government implicated an unwilling North in the slave trade. Suggesting what he termed "peaceable separation for conscience sake," William Lloyd Garrison urged northern states to secede

■ To raise funds for the *Amistad* Africans' defense, abolitionists distributed lithographic copies of this painting of Joseph Cinque, leader of the mutiny, for one dollar apiece.

from the Union. To slaveholders, Garrison's recommendation provided further evidence that slavery was under siege.

Historians view the *Amistad* and *Creole* cases as landmarks, setting a precedent for extending abolitionist appeals beyond individual consciences to the reach of the courts, the Constitution, and international law. The *Amistad* case also inaugurated the American Missionary Association (AMA), an abolitionist and Christian organization. Establishing a base in Liberia, the AMA endured for many decades, supporting schools and missions for black people in Africa and the United States.

Like many Christians, the AMA urged its member churches to "purify" themselves by denying membership to slaveholding "sinners" and refusing to do business with them. AMA members did not aim to deprive southern planters of their property. Rather, they sought to cleanse Americans of the sin of slavery, even sending missionaries into the American West to preach against it. But the AMA had an additional mission: ridding America of free black people.

LIMITATIONS AND OPPORTUNITIES

"The heart of the whites must be changed, thoroughly, entirely, permanently changed," wrote New York black physician James McCune Smith to white radical abolitionist Gerrit Smith in 1846. Otherwise, the black man insisted, racial discrimination would never end. Growing restrictions on free African Americans in the South and new laws denying them the vote in the North made it clear that not enough white hearts were being changed by abolitionist agitation.

> "The heart of the whites must be changed, thoroughly, entirely, permanently changed."
> —James McCune Smith

Meanwhile, as white Americans streamed across the Appalachian Mountains and the Mississippi River, the slavery issue and racial discrimination accompanied them. In midwestern states like Ohio, Indiana, and Illinois, the 1787 Northwest Ordinance prohibited slavery. But individual state laws often barred black people from entering the state unless they could prove they had money. Some local laws prevented African Americans from owning land.

But the sparsely populated West seemed to offer greater freedom than the South or the North. The Republic of Texas, which declared its independence from Mexico in the 1830s, offered free land to any American—black or white—who would homestead there and help outnumber Mexicans.

Disfranchisement in the North

When the Liberty Party promoted abolitionist James A. Birney as a presidential candidate in 1840, Martin Delany and Frederick Douglass campaigned for him. The Liberty Party, which developed out of the AAS division in 1840, was the first antislavery political party. One *Colored American* commentator wrote of the 1840 election: "For whom shall we vote, then, is the question. All of our people who have the right to vote believe it both a right and a duty to exercise that right. We ought and must vote for the Liberty Ticket, with James G. Birney at the head, a gentleman, a philanthropist and a Christian." But the 7,000 votes cast for Birney, by white abolitionists and a small number of black

voters, only underscored the irony of black leaders like Douglass and Delany supporting a candidate for whom most black people could not vote.

By the 1840s, black political power and political participation had all but disappeared. It had not always been this way. Following the American Revolution, as northern states phased out slavery, some free black property owners had gained the franchise. But because few black men owned land, most could not exercise this right. Still, in New York, Pennsylvania, and the New England states, the presence of a few hundred black voters raised the possibility that eventually black voters could influence elections.

But even as many states began expanding the franchise after 1820 to include men without property, black voters saw their access to the polls narrowed rather than increased. New York, for example, instituted in 1821 a property requirement for black voters only. In 1838, the Pennsylvania legislature revoked African Americans' right to vote despite impassioned entreaties from black leaders who gathered massive evidence of free black people's economic and social stability. Three years later, a similar disfranchisement attempt was narrowly defeated in Rhode Island. In Ohio, Michigan, and Wisconsin, black residents repeatedly petitioned state representatives for the franchise, reminding legislators that the Constitution prohibited taxation without representation. Their pleas fell on deaf ears.

The Texas Frontier

With increasingly limited opportunities in the North and South, some African Americans looked toward the new western territories. Greenbury Logan, for example, headed for Texas. Injured in military service to the Republic of Texas, Logan wrote to the Texas legislature for tax relief in 1841: "I came here in 1831 invited by Col. [Stephen] Austin," explained Logan. "Having no family with me I got one quarter league of land instead of a third, but I love the country and did stay because I felt myself more a freeman than in the [United] states. I am on examination found permanently injured and can barely support myself now."

Logan was a free man in a territory severed from Mexico but not yet part of the United States. Indeed, Texas had a unique history. Many southern planters were among the 20,000 white Americans who accepted the Mexican government's invitation in the 1820s to settle in Texas. These planters, leaving their worn fields behind, brought 2,000 slaves to settle alongside dozens of free African Americans, including Greenbury Logan. To these black Texans, the plot of land granted by Stephen Austin gave citizenship—but without the privilege of a vote.

After Mexico achieved independence from Spain in 1821 and began abolishing slavery, Texas became a pivotal part of U.S. politics. President Andrew Jackson's unsuccessful attempt to buy Texas from Mexico led the Mexican government in 1830 to retract its invitation to American settlers. In turn, the Americans already living in Texas seceded from Mexico, inviting more Americans to help resist Mexican control. In 1836, Texans managed to wrest the territory from Mexican control. They declared it the Lone Star Republic.

Fighting for Texas secession, Greenbury Logan also unwittingly helped ensure the entrenchment of slavery. American planters petitioned Congress to annex Texas as a slave state. When President Martin Van Buren procrastinated, reluctant to risk war with Mexico, the Texans petitioned European powers for military protection against Mexico.

The question of annexing Texas dominated the 1844 U.S. presidential election. Capitalizing on northern opposition to another slave state, the Liberty Party drew support from abolitionists and others who resented southern aggressiveness. The Liberty Party and James Birney were once again defeated, prompting southerners in Congress to argue that most Americans favored annexing Texas. However, 60,000 people voted for the Liberty Party, a number that worried proslavery Americans.

Meanwhile, the U.S. government had other worries. In 1845, to prevent Texans from bringing in the French and British military, Congress granted Texas immediate statehood and allowed slavery there. In pursuit of sectional compromise, Congress stipulated that as many as four more states might be carved out of the territory gained from Mexico, and in some of those states slavery would be prohibited.

As many lawmakers feared, Mexico retaliated, sparking a two-year war that began in 1846. In 1848—only a few days after gold was discovered in California—Mexico capitulated, signing the Treaty of Guadaloupe Hidalgo. By this agreement, the United States gained more than a million square miles that eventually became Texas, Arizona, New Mexico, Utah, and California. Overnight, Greenbury Logan was demoted from a citizen in an independent republic to free black noncitizen in a slave society.

The annexation of Mexican territories had profound consequences. First, the admission of Texas to the Union strengthened slaveholders' representation in Congress. Second, with fertile soil for growing cotton, corn, sugar cane, and cattle, white Texans prospered, their exports contributing to a flourishing American economy. Third, slaves provided a stable workforce safely insulated thousands of miles beyond the reach of abolitionist agitation.

But many Americans—black and white, North and South—believed the slavery issue could tear the United States apart. As early as 1837, *The Colored American* reported a suggestion by Garrison and other abolitionists that the free states secede from the Union. They warned "should Texas be admitted into the Union, farewell to the union of the States. Ten thousand discordant clashing elements and interests will be stirred up, that will only subside with a division of the Union . . . From the Potomac to the extreme Southern boundaries, anarchy, [and] bloodshed [will] deluge the country."

Radicals like Garrison may even have welcomed such discord as a way to dramatize the evil of slavery, but most Americans hoped to avert such a clash. Pennsylvania Congressman David Wilmot tried to stop the spread of slavery, proposing in 1846 "neither slavery nor involuntary servitude shall ever exist" in any territories gained from Mexico. Known as the Wilmot Proviso, the measure passed in the northern-dominated House only to be defeated in the Senate, where the South retained a stronghold. The defeat of the Wilmot Proviso guaranteed the continuation of the controversy over extending slavery.

While war and rhetoric raged, hundreds of free black Texans worked as skilled artisans in sawmills and brickyards and as blacksmiths, tailors, tavernkeepers, and house servants. A few acquired substantial agricultural holdings. In some towns, black churches provided comradeship. But slavery was the foundation of Texas agriculture. Ten years after Greenbury Logan's plea for tax relief, the slave population in Texas had swelled to nearly 60,000; by 1860, it had more than tripled again.

The Mountain West

Texas served as just one western destination for African Americans. Lured by wagon trains or the promise of gold in California, some free black people chose the new frontier, while slaves had little choice but to accompany their owners who migrated west. Hence, many free and enslaved black Americans ended up in such places as Utah, Oregon, and California, as slaves to Mormons or as free explorers, ranchers, or entrepreneurs. James Beckwourth set out to blaze a new trail. Born in the South in 1798 to a slave mother and a white father, Beckwourth moved with his parents to St. Louis, Missouri, where he apprenticed with a blacksmith. In 1824, he signed on with the Rocky Mountain Fur Company. Through this work he was adopted into the Crow Indian community, living with them for several years. Beckwourth then assisted U.S. troops against the Seminoles in Florida. Using his scouting and translation skills, he moved easily between local Indians and white settlers.

Beckwourth next teamed up with rebel Mexicans in 1845 in an abortive attempt to wrest California from Mexico. Then he moved to New Mexico, where he joined the U.S. army's campaigns against Mexico in 1847. He was married four times—twice to Indian women, once to someone described simply as "a Spanish girl," and finally, at age sixty-two, to an African American woman in Denver, Colorado. With this last wife, he returned to the Crow community, where he died four years later.

George Washington Bush went west hoping the Mexican government would give him the political protection he could not secure from the United States. A veteran of the War of 1812, where he served under Andrew Jackson, Bush was a free man in 1844, making his living as a cattle trader in Missouri. When a wagon train bound for Oregon Territory lumbered through town, he gathered his wife, children, and four other families and joined the expedition. Years later, a fellow traveler remembered Bush's concerns: "It was not in the nature of things that he should be permitted to forget his color. He told me he would watch, when we got to Oregon, what usage was awarded to people of color, and if he could not have a freeman's rights he would seek the protection of the Mexican Government in California or New Mexico." Indeed, Bush's companions had to help him get an exemption from Oregon's anti-black laws before he received his 640-acre homestead. Once over this hurdle, Bush put down roots. He introduced the region's first sawmill, gristmill, mower, and reaper, and fathered a dynasty of local leaders known for their generosity to less well-off neighbors.

> "**I**t was not in the nature of things that he should be permitted to forget his color."—*Black traveler*

The discovery of gold in California in 1848 occasioned an influx of black easterners in search of quick wealth. Here, gold dust—not skin color—defined a man's worth. By 1850, nearly a thousand African Americans—mostly single men—had joined the flood of fortune-seekers. Even those who did not work directly in mining gained from the booming economy. As cooks, waiters, laundresses, tavern-keepers, and dockworkers in Sacramento, San Francisco, and dozens of small towns, new black wage earners enjoyed economic prosperity, even if they lacked citizenship privileges.

The Compromise of 1850

The California gold rush brought 80,000 Americans west, qualifying the territory for statehood by 1850. But admit-ting California as a free state would upset the free state/slave state balance in the U.S. Senate. Thus, when President Zachary Taylor invited California and the New Mexico Territory to apply for statehood, he touched off a bitter congressional debate over whether slavery would extend to the newly gained territory. The controversy resulted in the Compromise of 1850, the last congressional attempt to ease sectional tensions by giving something to both North and South.

The compromise contained four momentous provisions. First, the federal government admitted California to the Union as a free state, upsetting the 15-15 balance of free and slave states. Second, the government authorized the creation of territorial governments in New Mexico and Utah, letting the settlers there decide whether to permit slavery. Third, legislators abolished the internal slave trade in Washington, D.C., but not slavery itself. The compromise's fourth provision, the Fugitive Slave Act, generated the most controversy. This provision denied accused fugitive slaves a jury trial, leaving their fate to federal commissioners, who were compensated for each fugitive slave case they adjudicated. Whenever the commissioners ruled in favor of the fugitive, they received $5, but they received $10 for rul-

JAMES P. BECKWOURTH IN HUNTER'S COSTUME.

■ Trapper James Beckwourth's discovery of an obscure northern California pass through the Sierra Nevada Mountains resulted in the establishment of a town that still bears his name.

ing in favor of the owner. The Fugitive Slave Act also compelled northern citizens to help apprehend runaways. Now it was not only illegal to assist a fugitive slave; anyone who refused to assist slavecatchers could be prosecuted.

Stephen Douglass, one of the main architects of the Compromise of 1850 in Congress, saw the ruling as the "final settlement" of the slavery question. As we will see in Chapter 9, he was gravely mistaken.

CONCLUSION

When Thomas Jefferson heard about the 1820 Missouri Compromise—Congress's first attempt to balance slave states and free states—he said "like a firebell in the night, it awakened me and filled me with dread." Jefferson's anxiety was well founded. In the three decades between the Missouri Compromise and the Compromise of 1850, the controversy over slavery followed American settlers into every region of the continent and every aspect of public life. Many Americans sought reform, and for reformers, slavery was often a top priority. Shut out from public life, white and black women stepped forward not only to defend slaves but also to fight for their own rights.

During the reform era, African Americans sought ways to improve their own lives. Some negotiated a bit of latitude within the slave system; others escaped slavery altogether. Some free black people, like Martin Delany and James Forten, assumed leadership in the abolitionist struggle. Other free people sought to educate themselves, choose their own names, and shape their own communities on American soil or elsewhere. Still others, like John Horse and James Beckwourth, shifted their loyalties between enslaved people and a government that protected slavery.

Both white abolitionists and slaveholders defined black people as different from themselves, and William Lloyd Garrison's *Liberator* essay about T. T.'s dream was one of very few visions that depicted interracial society as a positive thing. But for now, the possibility of a harmonious black and white society seemed more remote than ever. With the Compromise of 1850, the nation was nearing a crisis point.

FURTHER READING

Breeden, James O. *Advice Among Masters: The Ideal in Slave Management in the Old South* (Westport, CT: Greenwood, 1980).

Browne, Stephen Howard. *Angelina Grimké: Rhetoric, Identity, and the Radical Imagination* (East Lansing: Michigan State University Press, 1999).

Cha-Jua, Sundiata Keita. *America's First Black Town: Brooklyn, Illinois, 1830–1915* (Urbana: University of Illinois Press, 2000).

Dann, Martin E. *The Black Press, 1827–1890: The Quest for National Identity* (New York: G. P. Putnam, 1971).

Eisenstadt, Peter, ed. *Black Conservatism: Essays in Intellectual and Political History* (New York: Garland, 1999).

Goodman, Paul. *Of One Blood: Abolitionism and the Origins of Racial Equality* (Berkeley: University of California Press, 1998).

Hudson, Lynn. *The Making of "Mammy Pleasant": A Black Entrepreneur in Nineteenth-Century San Francisco* (Urbana : University of Illinois Press, 2003).

Mayer, Henry. *All on Fire: William Lloyd Garrison and the Abolition of Slavery* (New York: St. Martin's, 1998).

McKivigan, John R., ed. *Antislavery Violence: Sectional, Racial, and Cultural Conflict in Antebellum America* (Knoxville: University of Tennessee Press, 1999).

Osagie, Iyunolu Folayan. *The Amistad Revolt: Memory, Slavery, and the Politics of Identity in the United States and Sierra Leone* (Athens: University of Georgia Press, 2000).

Porter, Kenneth Wiggins. *The Black Seminoles: History of a Freedom-Seeking People* (Gainesville: University Press of Florida, 1996).

Raboteau, Albert J. *Canaan Land: A Religious History of African Americans* (New York: Oxford University Press, 2001).

Schweninger, Loren D., ed., *The Southern Debate over Slavery: Petitions to Southern Legislatures, 1778–1864* (Urbana: University of Illinois Press, 2001).

Stauffer, John. *The Black Hearts of Men: Radical Abolitionists and the Transformation of Race* (Cambridge: Harvard University Press, 2002).

Sterling, Dorothy. *The Making of an Afro-American: Martin Robison Delany, 1812–1885* (New York: Da Capo, 1996).

Taylor, Quintard. *In Search of the Racial Frontier: African Americans in the American West* (New York: W. W. Norton, 1998).

Winch, Julie. *The Elite of Our People: Joseph Willson's Sketches of Black Upper-Class Life in Antebellum Philadelphia* (University Park: Pennsylvania State University Press, 2000).

Yee, Shirley. *Black Women Abolitionists: A Study in Activism, 1828–1860* (Knoxville: University of Tennessee Press, 1992).

■ In this 1852 oil painting, *Slave Market in Richmond,* E. Crowe captured the slave families' dignity, sadness, and resignation that was surely typical of hundreds of similar scenes as slaves were sold out of the Upper South into the Lower (or Deep) South.

Source: SSI85749 Slave Market, Crowe, Eyre (1824–1910) Private Collection, www.bridgeman.co.uk

A Prelude to War: The 1850s

Tragedy and Triumph at Christiana

Early on the morning of September 11, 1851, Joshua Kite and six other African American rebels crouched by the windows of a small stone farmhouse on a hill near Christiana, Pennsylvania. They were poised to resist their former owner, Edward Gorsuch. Accompanied by federal marshals, Gorsuch had journeyed more than 70 miles from Maryland to take his "boys" back "home."

Two years earlier, rather than awaiting the manumission promised by their master, twenty-one-year-old Kite and several other slaves had escaped from Gorsuch's farm. Crossing the Chesapeake Bay, they headed north. Arriving in Christiana, where they blended into a region populated by 3,000 free and fugitive African Americans, they found refuge among black neighbors and sympathy from white antislavery Quakers.

Gorsuch had hired slave-hunters to help him locate the fugitives. But by the time he arrived in Christiana, the town had been alerted to his approach. Kite and dozens of his black neighbors stationed themselves at the home of local residents William and Eliza Parker. When a federal marshal challenged him, Parker dismissed the marshal's authority: "I told him I did not care for him nor the United States." Parker's wife threatened the escaped slaves with a corn cutter lest they attempt to surrender. Within minutes of Gorsuch's arrival, he had been shot to death, and his son was badly wounded. White onlookers offered water to the injured and then left them to their fate. Kite, Parker, and a few others escaped to Canada.

The Christiana Riot, as it came to be known, struck terror in the hearts of slaveholders while inspiring hope and pride in African Americans. For once, it was black men—not white—who had prevailed. Southerners demanded hangings, hoping that public executions of black fugitives and their white supporters would deter further rebellion. Officials arrested nearly three dozen people, white and black. A recent law provided that aiding runaway slaves rather than turning them

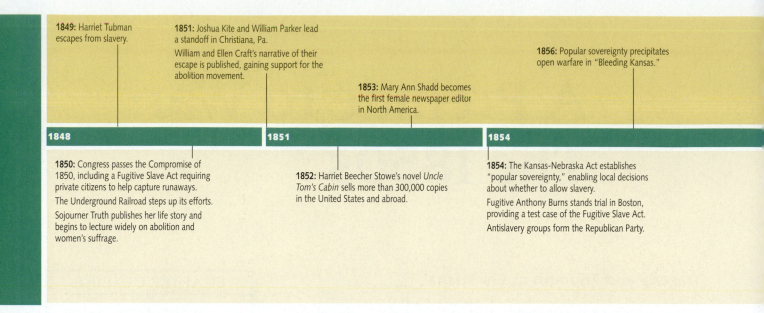

1849: Harriet Tubman escapes from slavery.

1851: Joshua Kite and William Parker lead a standoff in Christiana, Pa.

William and Ellen Craft's narrative of their escape is published, gaining support for the abolition movement.

1856: Popular sovereignty precipitates open warfare in "Bleeding Kansas."

1853: Mary Ann Shadd becomes the first female newspaper editor in North America.

1848

1851

1854

1850: Congress passes the Compromise of 1850, including a Fugitive Slave Act requiring private citizens to help capture runaways.

The Underground Railroad steps up its efforts.

Sojourner Truth publishes her life story and begins to lecture widely on abolition and women's suffrage.

1852: Harriet Beecher Stowe's novel *Uncle Tom's Cabin* sells more than 300,000 copies in the United States and abroad.

1854: The Kansas-Nebraska Act establishes "popular sovereignty," enabling local decisions about whether to allow slavery.

Fugitive Anthony Burns stands trial in Boston, providing a test case of the Fugitive Slave Act.

Antislavery groups form the Republican Party.

over to authorities was a federal crime, so the detainees were charged with conspiracy and treason—the latter punishable by death. Still, white jurors in Pennsylvania, where the trial was held, acquitted one man and dropped the charges against the rest. They viewed the slave hunt and the trial as a battle between states' rights and the federal government's attempts to erode those rights, and thus they had no interest in assisting slave hunters.

The episode dramatized the regional and racial tensions tearing at American society in the 1850s. The tensions were heightened by the Fugitive Slave Act of 1850, which required individuals to capture and return escaped slaves. Many white northerners who had been undecided or indifferent about slavery now associated antislavery action with the right to make their own laws. Meanwhile, abolitionist sentiment in the North was growing. Newspapers regularly published harrowing accounts of slavery and daring escapes—many written by escaped slaves.

In contrast, white southerners increasingly felt besieged by the federal government. With their slave-based economy and social system under attack, even white southerners who did not own slaves often felt duty-bound to defend the institution. Only a few white southerners viewed the slave system as a drag on the southern economy and a cancer on the nation.

The new militant mood of many African Americans reflected a mixture of defiance and fear. No black person, slave or free, could ignore slavery. The Underground Railroad, which provided a means of escape for slaves in the South, offered some hope to those who were enslaved, as did the growing abolitionist movement. Still, opportunities were limited even for those who were free. In Canada, former slaves could find freedom but few jobs. The American West offered dreams of gold and jobs, but efforts to extend slavery westward made it a risky place to settle. Even as reformers increased efforts to sway America's conscience, political and legal efforts tightened the grip of slavery. Convinced that Americans would never give up slavery peacefully, the boldest abolitionists joined a messianic figure, John Brown, at Harper's Ferry, Virginia, in 1859, attempting to ignite a slave rebellion.

CONTROVERSY OVER THE FUGITIVE SLAVE ACT OF 1850

The Compromise of 1850, passed by Congress in that year, addressed the issues of which states would be free or slave

1857: In *Dred Scott* v. *Sandford*, the Supreme Court rules that slaves and their descendants cannot be citizens, that slaves are property protected in every state, and that the Missouri Compromise is unconstitutional.

Hinton Rowan Helper publishes *The Impending Crisis of the South* warning of the flaws of slavery as a basis for the southern economy.

George Fitzhugh publishes *Cannibals All!* or *Slaves Without Masters,* a defense of slavery.

1857

1858: Illinois senatorial debates between Abraham Lincoln and Stephen A. Douglas dramatize sectional crisis.

1859: John Brown leads raid on a federal armory in Harper's Ferry, Virginia.

hibited the government from arbitrarily seizing citizens' houses, livestock, or land. But if slaves were freed, this would amount to the government seizing property. Should the federal government compensate owners for this seizure? If so, who should decide what constituted a fair price? If the federal government used taxpayers' money to pay slave-owners for their bondspeople, would that not be akin to northern citizens buying slaves? Should free black people be entitled to the same constitutional rights and protections as white Americans? Northerners and southerners alike agonized over these questions.

The rising sectional tension was also felt in southern slave quarters, where masters' growing anxiety about rebellion often resulted in increased repression. This, combined with the increasing frequency of slave sales from the Upper South into the Lower South, spurred a dramatic increase in the number of escapes. As the slave grapevine reported the increasing mood of resistance among some northern white abolitionists, greater numbers of slaves became willing to risk all in pursuit of freedom.

Controversy between the North and South also grew as a result of the gulf that had opened between the economies of the two regions. Many northern states had developed mills, factories, and extensive canal and railroad systems to move manufactured goods west and to transport raw materials into eastern cities. Southerners had extended their plantation system, which required many workers and vast stretches of land. People in both regions wanted to make sure their interests were adequately represented in Congress, and this too was a source of contention. Through the 1850s, immigration was swelling the North's population, thereby increasing northern membership in the House of Representatives. The balance in Congress was thus tipping to the North.

Federal Power Versus States' Rights

The U.S. Constitution protected the rights of slaveholders by providing in Article 4 that any person escaping bondage was prohibited from fleeing to another state. Federal laws passed in the 1790s provided additional protection for slaveholders by requiring local officials to return fugitives to owners. But Pennsylvania reformers had passed a "personal liberty" law in 1826 banning the forcible return of slaves. In 1842, the U.S. Supreme Court upheld personal liberty laws in *Prigg* v. *Pennsylvania,* ruling that individual states were not obliged to help enforce these federal laws. Several northern states took this decision as permission to go a step further, passing personal liberty laws *prohibiting* state officials from aiding slavecatchers.

and how that would be decided. The legislation included a provision, known as the Fugitive Slave Act, that strengthened federal regulations regarding apprehending runaways. The new policy raised tensions for many Americans, North and South, white and black. The issues included federal authority versus states' powers, constitutional protections of private property, black fugitives' anxiety over getting enough distance from slave states to avoid apprehension, and individual citizens' protests against encroaching federal power. Finally, citizens of northern states worried that southerners would outnumber them in Congress. Southerners had the same fears about the North. These concerns became either the spark or the spinoff of numerous incidents through the 1850s.

As shown in the opening story of Christiana, the tug of war between federal and states' powers stirred many white Americans. The framers of the U.S. Constitution had intended that states should retain all powers not specifically assigned to the federal government. However, this balance of power had been disputed ever since the Constitution took effect. In the 1850s, southern planters increasingly worried that if the federal government acquired too much power, it might ban slavery. Northerners feared that if the federal government could legislate how they treated fugitive slaves, it might begin controlling other facets of their lives as well. So states sought to wrest power away from the federal government.

Another constitutional issue was property rights. The prospect of abolishing slavery opened the question of how slaves, as property, might be handled. The Constitution pro-

■ First published in 1859 in *Harper's Weekly*, New York's most influential Republican voice, this engraving of the Christiana incident remained popular for decades.

THE CHRISTIANA TRAGEDY.

These northerners resented the Fugitive Slave Act provision whereby citizens who refused to help apprehend slaves could be charged with treason. This provision, they felt, overstepped federal authority. Now, as would-be fugitives could not find safety by crossing the border into a northern state, their desperation increased, as did the risks associated with escape. Fugitives would have to leave the country or find local support in standing their ground in northern border states, hoping northern resistance to federal authorities would work in their favor. The standoff at Christiana was among the most dramatic of such clashes.

Westward expansion also raised the question of states' rights, specifically whether new territories would be slave or free. As we saw in Chapter 7, Congress approved the Missouri Compromise in 1820, dividing the area acquired in the 1803 Louisiana Purchase into a northern section without slaves and a southern section where slavery was allowed. In 1848, just as Mexico was ceding to the United States new territory that included California, Utah, and New Mexico, the discovery of gold in California sparked a rush westward. Congress responded by approving the Compromise of 1850, whereby California entered the union as a free state, while leaving the possibility that the remainder of the Utah and New Mexico territories might become slave states if their citizens so chose.

As discussed in Chapter 8, the compromise gave the free states a 16–15 edge in the U.S. Senate. Although there was always the possibility that the remaining territory might end up as free states, the *potential* for expanding slavery into Utah and New Mexico calmed some southerners' worries that free states would gain the upper hand in the government.

The Compromise of 1850 established the principle of popular sovereignty, giving local residents the right to decide whether their state would be slave or free. Ultimately, however, the compromise only intensified conflict between North and South. The Fugitive Slave Act convinced even white northerners without strong abolitionist sympathies that resisting slave-hunting federal marshals was an act of patriotism. Some northern state legislatures broadened personal liberty laws to include the right of state courts to override *any* federal legislation. Massachusetts boldly nullified the Fugitive Slave Act. This was the most flagrant attack a state could make on federal power: to instruct its citizens to ignore or defy a federal law.

Northern reformers feared that a "slaveocracy" would seize congressional power and override industrialists' needs. Southerners worried that congressional antislavery sympathies would result in slaveholders losing their property. A single slave could represent an investment of as much as $2,000. Though the planters grew sugar, indigo, and other crops, the heavy dependence on cotton production in Lower South states like Alabama and Mississippi necessitated an abundance of workers who could toil long hours. The loss of even one slave meant not only the evaporation of a hefty investment but also the loss of valuable muscle to work the land.

Nevertheless, like Edward Gorsuch, many southerners in Maryland and Virginia had been preparing to release slaves for a simple reason: as the Upper South economy shifted from tobacco to grain farming, hiring seasonal field hands was far cheaper than clothing and feeding slaves all year. Nonetheless, Gorsuch's slaves represented more than

 **First Person**   ## Jermain Loguen Defies the Fugitive Slave Act

Jermain Loguen was a fugitive slave and a conductor on the Underground Railroad. He reportedly helped more than 1,500 slaves escape, including Joshua Kite, one of the slaves in the Christiana Riot. Loguen was thirty-seven years old when he spoke the words below in front of a white audience in Syracuse, New York, hoping to rally support for resistance to the Fugitive Slave Act, which had been enacted the previous week. Loguen also addressed the Liberty Party convention in 1853 and helped lead the Radical Abolitionists Party in 1855–1856.

I was a slave; I knew the dangers I was exposed to. I made up my mind as to the course I was to take [that is, to escape slavery.] . . . [I will] have my liberty or die it its defense. What is life to me if I am to be a slave in Tennessee? . . .

Now, you are assembled here . . . to proclaim to the despots in Washington whether it shall be enforced here. . . .

Whatever may be your decision, my ground is taken. I have declared it everywhere. . . . I don't respect this law—I don't fear it—I won't obey it!

It outlaws me, and I outlaw it, and the men who attempt to enforce it on me. . . . I will not live a slave, and if force is employed to re-enslave me, I will make preparations to meet the crisis as becomes a man.

—*from The Rev. J. W. Loguen*, As a Slave and a Freeman: A Narrative of Real Life *(1859)*.

To view a longer version of this document, please go to *www.ablongman.com/carson/documents*.

a financial investment. They embodied the principles of property rights, of resistance to federal control, and of personal honor. To southerners like Gorsuch, slaves themselves were less important than the principle of defending property against seemingly arbitrary federal policies.

The Underground Railroad

In 1849, the same year Joshua Kite fled from Maryland, another twenty-one-year-old slave made a similar escape. Crossing the Chesapeake Bay, Harriet Tubman made a solitary trek to Pennsylvania. After a brief rest on free soil, she retraced her steps to escort some of her family and friends over the same ground. Soon known as "Black Moses," Tubman made as many as three dozen return trips into slave territory, leading hundreds of slaves to freedom, including her own parents. Tubman seemed fearless. She was a big woman, strong and tenacious despite fragile health. Armed with a pistol, she made it clear that she would use it on anyone, white or black, who threatened to sabotage her mission. Slaves revered her. Slaveholders feared what she

represented: a new posture of black defiance. Some put a price of $40,000 on her head—equivalent to more than $1 million today. But she was never captured in her dangerous journeys.

Tubman was among the best-known members of the abolitionist network known as the Underground Railroad, a community of African Americans and their white allies who became known as railroad conductors. Originally, the Underground Railroad used secret routes along rivers, seaports, and northern border communities to transport slaves from the South to freedom in Ohio, Pennsylvania, and New York. By 1830, conductors were taking a few runaway slaves as far as New England, Canada, Britain, Europe, and Mexico. Supported by Vigilance Committees—secret local networks—the Underground Railroad was at its most active during the 1850s as the national upheaval over slavery came to a boil. Of the estimated 100,000 former slaves who passed through the Underground Railroad between 1820 and 1860, probably three-fourths of them escaped after the 1850 Fugitive Slave Act intensified slaves' desperation and Underground Railroad conductors' commitment.

Tubman was one among many conductors. William Still, a black Philadelphian, discovered that a fugitive he had aided was his own long-lost brother. Still began keeping coded records of runaways and the conductors who helped them; his records are invaluable to historians working to reconstruct this secret network. Levi Coffin, a white Quaker from North Carolina, moved to Indiana to better position himself to help. John Brown, a white New Englander, relocated his whole family to Kansas for the same reason.

Fugitives escaped by various methods. Oriented by the North Star of the Big Dipper constellation in the night sky and guided by moss on the north sides of trees, perhaps as many as 8,000 slaves per year fled the South on foot, horseback, or hidden in wagons. Some escaped by stowing away on ships leaving southern ports or by disguising themselves as crew members. At least one man had himself packed in a box and shipped as cargo from Richmond to Philadelphia. Taking advantage of bustling wharves in New Orleans, Richmond, and Charleston, slaves traveled as far as Canada and Britain, or as near as Cincinnati, Detroit, and northern ports along the Mississippi River. Some journeyed on to California, the Pacific Northwest, and Texas. Others joined Native American communities in such little-known places as Nacimiento, across the Rio Grande in Mexico, where Seminole leader John Horse established a refugee outpost in 1849.

The Escape and Trial of Anthony Burns

The experience of Anthony Burns, a slave who escaped to Boston in 1854, exemplifies how the Fugitive Slave Act played out in the North. Learning to read at a young age, Burns became a preacher in his local Baptist church in Virginia, where black and white congregants worshipped together. Hired out by Charles Suttles, his master, to work in Richmond, Burns escaped by jumping on a boat bound for Boston. Befriended by a white Quaker abolitionist, he quietly worked in a clothing shop. But he missed his family and could not resist sending a letter to his brother on the Suttles plantation. Suttles intercepted the letter and contacted Boston authorities. Burns was arrested and placed in leg irons in a federal courthouse.

Boston's abolitionists sprang to action. Lawyer Richard Henry Dana, condemning the Fugitive Slave Act as "the devil's license for kidnapping," called a public protest meeting. Several thousand angry people turned up, including hundreds of black residents from the nearby whaling town of New Bedford. In a frenzy, the crowd stormed the courthouse to free Burns, killing one federal official and wounding others. When federal marshals called for reinforcements,

President Franklin Pierce sent troops, authorizing local officials to "incur any expense" to uphold federal law. The next day, the abolitionists raised $1,200 to purchase Burns's freedom. But federal officials persuaded Suttles not to sell Burns; it was vital, they said, to use this situation as a test case in order to validate the Fugitive Slave Act in court.

Dana attempted to prove that Massachusetts' personal liberty law superseded the Fugitive Slave Act and tried a variety of other strategies to have Burns freed. When the judge ruled in Suttles's favor, armed troops escorted the slave through an aisle of sobbing abolitionists who had draped buildings in black. By the time Burns was loaded onto a boat and returned to Virginia, more than $100,000 had been spent to uphold southerners' constitutional right to federal protection of their property.

The trial deeply affected northern abolitionists. Charlotte Forten, a seventeen-year-old black Philadelphian, attended the public meetings surrounding the trial and watched Dana throw himself into Burns's defense. Forten anguished over the trial outcome, "It is impossible to be happy now." From that point, Forten rededicated herself to her own abolitionist efforts, which involved helping to organize fund-raising to aid fugitives, collecting signatures for antislavery petitions to Congress, and joining the many discussions and lectures where antislavery strategy was debated. Abolitionism was part of Forten's family tradition. The granddaughter of a prosperous black sailmaker and daughter of a widely respected abolitionist, Forten was well educated and well-to-do. Books, parties, and stimulating conversation as well as antislavery lectures and meetings filled her days. Despite her privilege, however, Charlotte Forten was still an African American in a country that dehumanized all black people, and she embraced the abolitionist cause because she empathized with slaves who suffered because of their race.

Anthony Burns's story eventually ended happily. Though Suttles sold him into North Carolina, the Boston Vigilance Committee finally purchased his freedom. By 1857, when Burns was studying at Oberlin College, abolitionists across the nation could rejoice.

THE POWER OF STORIES

In her 1987 best-selling novel *Beloved,* Toni Morrison describes a slave who so loves her child that she kills the baby rather than see the youngster grow up in bondage. Morrison's fictional character was a composite of actual enslaved women who had been driven to the same desperate act. In the 1850s, such tragic stories captured the attention of northern and southern audiences. Slave narratives were firsthand accounts from black people that exposed the details of the intolerable system of slavery. A second wave of black writing—often poetry, fiction, and historical accounts—came from northern African Americans. These works often focused on the struggles of free black people. White abolitionists such as William Lloyd Garrison, publisher of the abolitionist newspaper *The Liberator,* argued that the suffering inflicted on slaves eroded white morals, warning that unless white people destroyed slavery, they risked incurring God's wrath. Meanwhile, in their writings, most white southerners aimed to demonstrate that slavery was better than free labor systems.

Slave Narratives

In the dead of winter in 1848, William and Ellen Craft ran away from their Georgian master to freedom. William disguised himself as a servant to the light-skinned Ellen, who dressed like a man and posed as a slaveowner's son. Using money earned from William's carpentry work, the Crafts traveled as paying customers on steamboats, staying in fine hotels along the way. Who, after all, would look in such public places for runaway slaves? The following year, the Crafts toured England, explaining to spellbound audiences that although their master had not treated them harshly, they escaped because they worried they might bear a child who would be sold away from them. In 1851, the Crafts published their experiences in a London newspaper, adding their stories to those of dozens of black American abolitionists who toured England in these years, enlisting British sympathies to their cause. These African American–British networks—what one historian has called "an anti-slavery wall"—proved invaluable in coming years, demonstrating that the immediacy and humanity of these narratives could yield political power as well as emotional response.

African American fugitives—men and women alike—had dramatic stories to tell in the 1850s. The saga of former slave Henry "Box" Brown, published in 1854, provides an apt example of a popular slave narrative. Five years earlier, Brown had himself packed in a 2-foot-square crate and went on a twenty-four-hour boat ride from Richmond, Virginia, to Philadelphia. His dramatic account was illustrated by a picture of triumphant Underground Railroad conductors releasing Brown from the crate. As we saw in Chapter 7, Harriet Jacobs' *Incidents in the Life of a Slave Girl* (1861) constituted one of the most gripping stories of the cruelties inflicted on slave women. Sexual abuse and fear for their children often

■ The Crafts' narrative of their escape, published in the leading London newspaper, described how Ellen cut her hair and donned green spectacles and a top hat to complete her disguise.

heightened slave women's desperation. Some took huge risks to free or protect themselves and their youngsters; others "freed" their children from bondage by killing them. Frederick Douglass, who had published his autobiography in 1845, released an updated version entitled *My Bondage and My Freedom* in 1855. In addition to reaching a broader audience, the revised story, which included Douglass's analysis of the effect of the Fugitive Slave Act, found readers among those who had been mesmerized by the first edition. Long silenced, black Americans finally had a voice. Equally crucial, they had an audience hungry for the publications of dramatic narrators like Douglass.

Northern Black Voices

Northern African Americans told a different story of both slavery and abolition. Isabella Van Wageren was born a slave in upstate New York. After sales to a succession of masters, in 1826 she walked away from an owner who reneged on his promise to free her. There was no daring escape, no long journey, no secrecy, for both slave and master knew the

 **First Person**   **Solomon Northup Decries Planter's Cruelty**

In 1853, Solomon Northup wrote how his life as a free black New Yorker turned into a nightmare after he was kidnapped in Washington, DC, and sold to a Louisiana planter. Northup's Twelve Years as a Slave *became a best seller. This selection is typical of Northup's vivid descriptions of his master's depravity.*

When "in his cups," Master Epps was a roystering, blustering, noisy fellow, whose chief delight was in dancing with his "niggers," or lashing them about the yard with his long whip, much for the pleasure of hearing them screech and scream, as the great welts were planted on their backs. When sober, he was silent, reserved and cunning, not beating us indiscriminately, as in his drunken moments but sending the end of his rawhide to some tender spot of a lagging slave, with a sly dexterity peculiar to himself.

—*from Solomon Northup,* Twelve Years a Slave: Narrative of Solomon Northup *(1853).*

To view a longer version of this document, please go to *www.ablongman.com/carson/documents*.

gradual abolition policy instituted by New York state in 1799 would officially free Van Wageren in 1827.

After leaving her master, Van Wageren spent almost a decade in a rural commune organized by a white religious leader, Prophet Matthias. Though Matthias disapproved of racial slavery, he treated the women in his community like slaves, assigning them menial jobs and disciplining them with corporal punishment. When the commune disbanded, Van Wageren, a deeply religious woman now in her mid-forties, reported that God had called her, advising her to change her name to Sojourner Truth. A sojourner, she explained, is one who travels. She was to take to the road to tell the truth about the evil of slavery and the oppression of women.

In 1850, Truth published her life story, *Narrative of Sojourner Truth*. A spellbinding storyteller, Truth then began

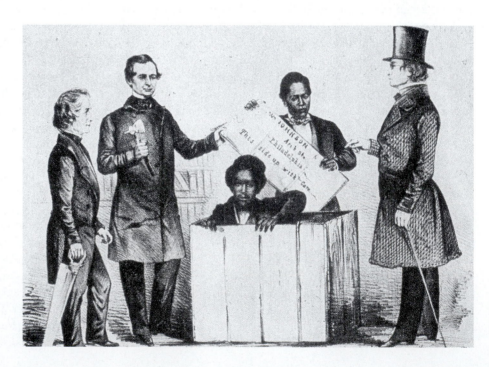

■ With help from a northern Vigilance Committee, Brown was shipped to William Johnson, a Philadelphia black abolitionist. This triumphant portrayal, using the biblical reference of "resurrection" to underscore the righteousness of Brown's escape, was published in 1854.

■ Known best as a stalwart abolitionist and crusader for women's rights, Sojourner Truth was masterful at promoting her concerns. She distributed prints of herself like this one mounted on small cards to spread her reputation and raise money for her cause.

Other black abolitionist women did their best to distribute slave stories and, as Tubman described it, "put the world right." Harriet Wilson's *Our Nig, or Sketches from the Life of a Free Black* (1859) underscored the fact that free black women also endured hardship and abuse. While Frederick Douglass traveled on abolitionist missions, his wife, Anna, remained involved in antislavery activities at home, even while she struggled to keep her family out of debt. Black and white abolitionist women banded together to help pay Anna's bills.

Most black Americans lacked the resources to publicize their plight, but others spoke for them. In 1855, Bostonian William C. Nell, America's first black historian, published two volumes documenting African Americans' participation in the American Revolution and the War of 1812. But Nell was careful about his perspective. Aiming to further the abolitionist cause by showing African Americans as patriots and citizens, he downplayed the great number of Revolutionary-period black men who fought on the British Loyalist side because the British offered them freedom.

Nell's contemporaries included novelist William Wells Brown. The first black person to publish a novel in the United States, Brown took the name William Wells in honor of the white Quaker who helped him escape from slavery. In 1847, he published the story of his own life and his escape from slavery. Six years later he published *Clotel,* a novel about Thomas Jefferson's mixed-race daughter. This novel portrayed black Americans as complex human beings rather than merely as stereotyped slaves and fugitives. In 1857, Frank Webb published *The Garies and Their Friends,* which chronicled the social life of Philadelphia's black middle class. Webb's popular novel, though somewhat melodramatic, helped white Americans put a human face on black men and women.

Francis Ellen Watkins also contributed to this black intellectual movement. Born free in 1825 and orphaned young in the slave city of Baltimore, Watkins was raised by her uncle, an abolitionist shoemaker who counted antislavery publisher William Lloyd Garrison among his close friends. The uncle encouraged his precocious niece to develop both her talent with words and her strong social conscience. Before she was twenty, Watkins had published *Forest Leaves* (1845), her first collection of poems.

In 1854, when Watkins published *Poems on Miscellaneous Subjects,* William Lloyd Garrison wrote the introduction to the book. By this time, Watkins was active in the Underground Railroad as well as in black education. In 1854, when she delivered her first public lecture before

> "**C**ould slavery exist long if it did not sit on a commercial throne?"
> —*Francis Ellen Watkins*

to travel widely on the antislavery lecture circuit. She enjoyed public speaking, she said, because "I wanted to see what God would have me say." Described by some as "the only colored woman to gain a national reputation as a speaker in the years preceding the Civil War," Truth emerged as a powerful voice for women's suffrage as well as African American rights. She secured a lasting reputation when she preached that if one woman—the biblical Eve—could turn the world upside down, then a united community of women could put it right again. Truth frequently claimed she could work as hard and eat as much as any man, yet she challenged her audience, "Ain't I a woman?" Reputedly, she shocked one audience by baring her breast to emphasize her point.

> "**A**in't I a woman?"
> —*Sojourner Truth*

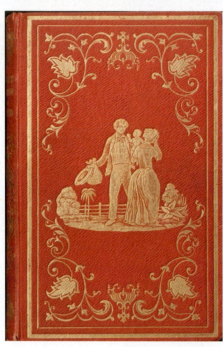

■ Many black writers took pains to demonstrate the authenticity of their narratives, as did Henry Bibb in his *Narrative of the Life and Adventures of Henry Bibb, An American Slave, Written by Himself* (1849). The flowery binding and flattering lithograph portrait of Bibb underscore that such works were designed for display as well as reading. A small sketch at the bottom of the portrait shows a fleeing slave and a pursuing slave catcher yelling: "Stop the runaway! Where is he?"

a Boston audience, she posed the rhetorical question "Could slavery exist long if it did not sit on a commercial throne?" and encouraged her listeners to boycott products resulting from slave labor. Filling lecture halls in Maine, Massachusetts, Pennsylvania, and Ohio, and by selling volumes of her poetry, the dynamic Watkins raised money for abolitionism.

White Abolitionist Appeals

White abolitionists also used stories of slavery's horror to advance the antislavery cause. A headline-grabbing story in 1856 involved Margaret Garner, who fled slavery with her husband, Simeon, their four children, and Simeon's parents and found refuge in Ohio. When U.S. marshals located the family and surrounded the home where they were staying, the distraught Garner slit the throat of her infant daughter and struck two of her sons with a shovel in an effort to prevent them from being hauled back into slavery. Before federal authorities could seize her, Garner threw herself and one or perhaps more of her children—accounts of the incident vary—into the Ohio River. Still, she was captured

before she could kill herself and sold into the Lower South. Her remaining children were taken from her and sold to different masters. Within days, abolitionists everywhere had begun recounting Margaret Garner's story.

In 1851, Harriet Beecher Stowe presented a romanticized version of slavery in a serialized newspaper story, *Life Among the Lowly*. Neither a historian nor an abolitionist, Stowe was a religious woman inflamed by the Fugitive Slave Act. In 1852, when Stowe's series was published as a novel entitled *Uncle Tom's Cabin*, it immediately sold 300,000 copies. Quickly translated into several languages, it became an international best seller. Stowe characterized most white southerners as decent God-fearing people; only the overseer, Simon Legree, was presented as heartless. She portrayed a tender friendship between Eva, an innocent white child, and Tom, a patient and loving elderly slave devoted to his master's family. Stowe depicted Tom as a spiritual man who felt a duty to serve

■ Raised in a slave-owning Kentucky family, Thomas Satterthwaite Noble painted many slave scenes, including this one depicting fugitive Margaret Garner attempting to destroy her children lest they be seized by federal authorities. The painting, done in 1867, several years after slavery's end, demonstrates the story's enduring hold on the public imagination.

his owners and to accept slavery. Comforted by his faith, he aimed to find his reward in Heaven. Stowe contrasted Tom's acceptance of slavery with the rebellious young fugitive Eliza, fleeing to freedom across the icy Ohio River.

By cautioning that southern slaveholders' benign descriptions of loving bonds between masters and their human property masked slavery's brutality, Stowe captured the sympathies of many readers who had not previously advocated abolition. Her book breathed new life into the antislavery movement. However, *Uncle Tom's Cabin* was sympathetic to southern slaveowners as well as to slaves. Stowe portrayed slaveholders as trapped in an economy supported by a tradition of bondage and cruelty. By allowing readers to empathize with many of the characters—black and white, northern and southern—Stowe reached many northern readers.

Annoyed that Stowe's hero was so passive about bondage, Martin Delany complained that Stowe "knows nothing about us." In reaction to her work, in 1852 Delany published his own reminiscences about his trip through the South in a novel, *Blake, or The Huts of Africa.* Henry Blake, the protagonist in Delany's novel, was the antithesis of Uncle Tom. A rebel who escaped from slavery, Blake has no religious qualms against killing a white man whom he fears might alert authorities. Traveling to Canada, Blake stops to talk with other African Americans, urging them to contact "one good man or woman on [each] plantation" to create a network to incite slave rebellion.

Southern Views of Slavery

As much as *Uncle Tom's Cabin* captured the imagination of some, it enraged others. Some southerners claimed that because Stowe had never visited the South, she had no authority to condemn its ways. Others argued that brutal overseers like Simon Legree were the exception. Southern novelist William Gilmore Simms described his own novel, *Woodcraft* (1854), as "probably as good an answer to Mrs. Stowe as has ever been published." Using humor, Simms portrayed a plantation life in which the sense of loyalty and responsibility on the part of slaveowners to both the land and slaves created a model society.

Other southerners joined Simms's defense of slavery. Among the most persuasive was George Fitzhugh, an aristocratic Virginia lawyer. Fitzhugh held that southern slavery offered the most moral and humane system for both white and black Americans. Although northerners were not slaveholders, he said, their system exploited weak individuals, while southern society protected them. In several works, including *Cannibals All! or Slaves Without Masters*, published in 1857, Fitzhugh argued that the North had abolished the name of slavery "but not the *thing.*"

In Fitzhugh's view, the "thing" that dehumanized the North was the wage system, which made no provisions for workers' illnesses, pregnancy, childrearing, or old age. It was to planters' economic advantage, Fitzhugh explained, to protect children, care for infirm workers, and to continue using the diminished skills of older workers. By contrast, northern industrialism forced owners to cast out all but the most efficient laborers. Applauding Fitzhugh's publications, which articulated long-held views, many southerners shifted from a defensive posture to one of defiance. Northerners like Harriet Beecher Stowe were hostile, southerners insisted, because they were uninformed about southern life.

THE CHANGING SOUTH

In 1857, North Carolinian Hinton Rowan Helper's *The Impending Crisis of the South, and How to Meet It* infuriated many southerners with the assertion that the economy was fundamentally unsound. Helper looked at slavery purely from an economic point of view and argued that the institution undermined both the livelihoods of non-slaveholding white people (such as himself), and the southern

economy at large. By depressing the employment opportunities and wages of white workers, slavery kept southern industries and ports from expanding. Because the majority of public resources, such as taxes, were organized to serve the minority of southerners who were influential planters, other public services (such as schools, hospitals, orphanages, and public works like municipal water services) were stunted. *The Impending Crisis* was banned across the South. Southern post offices refused to deliver copies of it, and Helper fled to New York. But banning *The Impending Crisis* did nothing to stop the forces transforming the South's society and economy.

Southern Society and Economy

During the 1850s, about 25 percent of the 8 million white people living in the South owned slaves, and only about 1 percent possessed as many as 300 slaves. A minority of the South's white men controlled almost all of the region's slaves. Nevertheless, they wielded disproportionate social

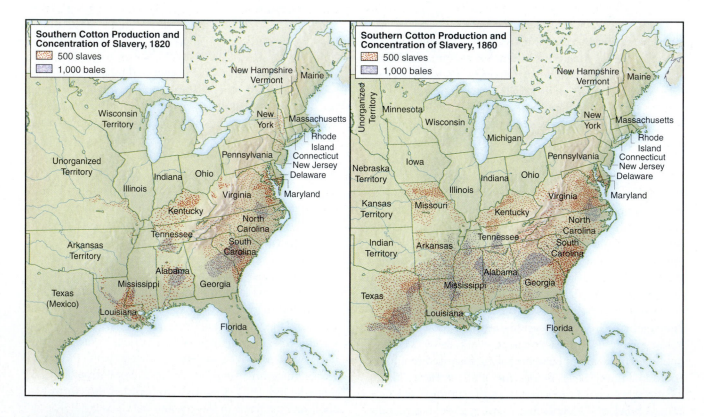

■ **MAP 9.1** **Southern Cotton Production and Concentration of Slavery, 1820 and 1860**

Between 1820 and 1860, as cotton production eclipsed tobacco, the concentration of slaves shifted from Upper South to the Lower South. Most slaves were now further isolated from the Atlantic coast and from the North.

■ **TABLE 9.1** Regional Distribution of Slaves, 1850 and 1860

Region	1850	1860
Upper South	1,634,087	1,778,700
North	236	18
Lower South	1,579,964	2,177,996
West	26	104

The westward expansion of slavery following the compromise of 1850 led to a dramatic increase in the number of slaves in the Southwest.

and political influence. The nearly 55 million bales of cotton they produced annually accounted for more than half of the dollar value of all U.S. exports. Because northern textile mills relied on southern cotton, many northern congressmen sympathized with southerners' arguments that only slave labor could sustain the U.S. economy.

The South Hinton Rowan Helper described was actually transforming into several Souths, each with its own economy and social structure. In the Upper South (Virginia, Maryland, and North Carolina), corn and wheat production was replacing tobacco, and the selling of excess slaves to the Lower South was rapidly reducing the number of African Americans. In contrast, the Lower South (from South Carolina to eastern Texas), where cotton production dominated the economy, the black population swelled rapidly. In both the Upper and Lower South, the rich soils of coastal areas supported the slave-based plantation system. Meanwhile, the forested terrain to the west remained the preserve of struggling white farmers. In North Carolina, for example, most of the slave-owning large planters were in the coastal region, while most of the 70 percent of the white population living in the hilly western parts of the state held no slaves at all, and over two-thirds of those who owned slaves had fewer than ten.

Through the 1850s, the imbalances that emerged in southern demographics worried some white southerners. The slave count climbed steadily, especially in the Lower South. Meanwhile, the free black population grew slowly—mostly in the Upper South—from 250,000 in 1850 to about 260,000 in 1860. More than one-third of free black people lived in the cities, while less than one-quarter of the white population was urban. Though the birthrate for all black Americans, enslaved and free, had decreased slightly, the free black population in the West more than quadrupled in the same decade, as free African Americans abandoned the South. (Through the 1850s, free African Americans in the South increasingly faced the risk of being kidnapped and

sold into the Lower South.) The arrival of more than 2 million European immigrants during the same years—almost all of whom settled in the North and West—complicated the situation, providing the North with labor alternatives unavailable to the South. Reports vary as to how urgent the situation was, but most white southerners felt themselves losing their control over the dependable labor systems that had once given them an economic advantage over the North.

In the *Impending Crisis,* Helper championed the cause of southern white farmers who struggled to make a living on small plots of land without sufficient labor. He lamented their dependence on large planters to help market their crops. He decried the unfairness that taxes levied on slave-less southerners were used to compensate any owner whose slave was executed for committing a crime. Using statistics (some of them exaggerated), Helper argued that slavery deprived the South of funds for schools, roads, libraries, newspapers, and industries. These policies, he added, maintained large planters' dominance and kept poor white people isolated, ignorant, and dependent on planters. Using slave labor, he noted, planters had built railroads, but most of the track covered short routes between commercial cities and did not link broad areas, as did railroads in the North. By depriving the South of industry, transportation, and diversified commerce, Helper claimed, planters forced southerners to import most finished goods from the North or from abroad.

Historians are still debating how prosperous the South really was, but Helper identified some real problems with the South's economy. Much of the land was mortgaged to banks in England or in the North. Many planters were land rich but cash poor, unable to pay wages for labor to work the land. Sometimes the cost of acquiring and maintaining a slave worker exceeded the slave's productivity.

Yet many large and small southern planters were wedded to their way of life, even if it was in crisis.

■ **TABLE 9.2** Regional Distribution of Free Black People, 1850 and 1860

Region	1850	1860
Upper South	196,542	216,821
North	194,721	219,682
Lower South	41,645	44,097
West	1,587	6,470

Westward expansion also saw an increase in the number of free black people, although these numbers are dwarfed by the number of slaves.

First Person

A Plea from James Phillips

James Phillips, a slave in Maryland, wrote this letter to his wife, Mary, who had escaped to Harrisburg, Pennsylvania. Phillips was fearful that he, like many other slaves in Maryland and Virginia in the 1850s, would be sold into the Deep South. But he knew of abolitionists, and in this letter he expresses his hope that his wife would use this appeal to entice an abolitionist group to purchase his freedom.

Dear Wife, I will now write to you to inform you where I am and my health. I am well and I am in hope when you receive this, it may find you well also. I am now in a trader's hands . . . and he is going to start South with a lot of negroes in August. I do not like that country at all, and would almost rather die than go South. Tell all of the people that if they can do anything for me, now is the time to do it. I can be bought for $900. . . . My master is willing to sell me to any gentleman who will be so kind as to come on and buy me. . . . My master gave me full consent to have this letter written, so do not feel any hesitation to come on and see about poor James Phillips. Try and do something for me as soon as you can, for I want to get back to you very bad indeed. I have nothing more to write, only I wish I may be bought and carried back to Harrisburg in a short time. My best love to you, my wife. You may depend I am almost dying to see you and my children. You must do all you can for your husband.

—*from* The Liberator, *July 16, 1852.*

To view a longer version of this document, please go to *www.ablongman.com/carson/documents*.

"The World They Made Together"

With the large black-to-white ratio in many parts of the South, African Americans—including fugitives and even some black slaveholders—often exerted surprisingly great influence. In theory, white southerners controlled black lives. Nonetheless, the interdependence between slaves and owners was so intricate that one historian concluded that black and white southerners inhabited "a world they made together."

In the summer of 1855, Lucy Skipwith, at Alabama's Hopewell plantation, wrote to her master in Virginia: "We keeps up family Prayers every morning. I does the best I can teaching the children but I can never get more than two and sometimes three little ones on week days. My little girl Maria is beginning to write very well and is very anxious to write to you." However, the child was staying in the overseer's house, to help his wife. Thus Lucy Skipwith reported, "I have very little chance to teach her."

Through the writing of Lucy Skipwith, who managed a plantation household during the 1850s, we see some of the inner workings of plantation life. Her master, John Hartwell Cocke, was a southern reformer who planned to Christianize his slaves, teach them thrift and temperance, and then free and dispatch them to be missionaries in Liberia. To that end, Cocke in 1840 established Hopewell, a cotton plantation in Greene County, Alabama. There he installed Lucy Skipwith's father, George Skipwith, as head driver and sometimes as overseer directing four dozen slaves. At Hopewell, white overseers came and went during the 1840s, many complaining about George Skipwith's refusal to acknowledge their authority. Cocke knew his black overseer was cantankerous, sometimes dishonest, and prone to incite disagreements among other overseers and slaves. Yet he trusted George Skipwith's loyalty. As long as George Skipwith's crews produced cotton, Cocke tolerated the black man's flaws. Eventually, however, when production fell, Cocke removed George Skipwith as overseer. Still, he continued to leave his household affairs in the hands of George Skipwith's daughter.

Though Cocke defined the long-range goals of the Hopewell enterprise, the plantation's day-to-day operation lay in the hands of the black Skipwiths. For over a decade, Cocke spent almost half of each year in Virginia, leaving the Skipwiths to manage Hopewell. When Cocke was at Hopewell, Lucy Skipwith was his personal servant. But when he was in Virginia, she designed her own schedule and set the household priorities—managing sewing, weaving, cooking, and religious education.

Throughout the 1850s, Cocke granted this young woman a great deal of authority. Lucy Skipwith diligently reported on life at Hopewell, including her frustration at trying to teach religion to slave children when overseers demanded their labor. By following her master's instructions to Christianize her black charges, Lucy Skipwith was able to lobby for black education and, simultaneously, undermine the white overseers' authority by complaining to Cocke when overseers interfered with her plans to teach the children. Thus Cocke's legal authority and power intertwined with the Skipwiths' *de facto* authority and power. The power was unequal, but the interdependence was inescapable.

The lives of many black slaves and their masters fell somewhere between what northern fiction readers found in Harriet Stowe's meek Uncle Tom and others found in Martin Delany's insurrectionist Henry Blake. White slaveholders believed they controlled their world, but in fact, slaveholders depended heavily on slaves' ingenuity and loyalty. Masters also encountered resistance from slaves in the form of countless small rebellions: burned meals, deliberately broken tools, pilfered livestock, sabotaged crops. Slave revolts, rumors of revolts, events such as the Christiana episode, and defiant slaves provided constant reminders of the precariousness of the slave system. Masters vacillated between denying that instability and fearing its implications. Every law, every policy, every move a master made was shaped by the desire to tighten control over potentially rebellious bondspeople.

Free Black People

By 1850, more than 200,000 free black people lived in the South. Most of them were clustered in the cities, where they worked as domestic workers or craftspeople such as carpenters, blacksmiths, or clothiers. Some of these African Americans were the children of masters. Others were slaves whose masters had allowed them to hire out their time; they had saved their money and purchased themselves or their families. It was not uncommon for a man to purchase his wife—while himself remaining enslaved—in order to protect her from sexual exploitation and to assure that his children would be born free. But the free black person's life was precarious. If captured by an unscrupulous slave hunter, a free black man or woman might be sold off to some distant location before he or she had the opportunity to produce papers proving freedom or to find a white neighbor who would vouch for his or her free status. Because black people were usually not allowed to testify in the courts, there was little recourse if a white person claimed a black person as property.

Nevertheless, some southern free African Americans made a fairly comfortable life. Often choosing not to leave the area where relatives were still enslaved, they opened schools or shops or made a living along the docks. A few even acquired substantial property—including slaves. By 1850, a few hundred black slaveholders across the South owned 9,000 bondspeople. To be sure, most southern free African Americans, even those of substantial means, did not traffic in black people. But a few purchased a labor force with the same cold-bloodedness as their white neighbors. The black men and women who did own slaves were free to exploit their human property just as their white neighbors did, and some did so.

A few black planters grew wealthy. South Carolina's William Ellison owned more than five dozen slaves. William Johnson of Natchez, Mississippi, left a diary of his career as landlord and farmer. A mixed-race man freed by his master, Johnson was twenty-three years old in 1832 when he bought his first slave. Through the next two decades, Johnson established a prosperous barbershop where he employed both free black workers and slaves to service a white-only clientele. He bought and sold real estate; at his death, he owned 400 acres. Like his white neighbors, he gambled, traveled, hunted, fished—and whipped his slaves. As he was in a position to lend money to some of his white neighbors, Johnson attained a status that was remarkable in the slave South.

In the weeks following the passage of the 1850 Fugitive Slave Act, Johnson's diary entries remained focused on produce, wool, livestock, and his white overseer and his slaves. However, a cryptic comment from late September suggests that he remained alert to local tensions: "Young Jno [Jonathan] Gains shot a Black man that had ran away from Mr. Hutcheons this morning and killed him dead. This was done in the woods." Ironically, Johnson himself was shot to death in those same woods the following year, apparently the result of a property line dispute with another biracial planter. The only witnesses were black men—who were not allowed to testify in the courts. After two years in jail and multiple trials, Johnson's killer convinced a jury he was white. Because the murder of a black man by a white man was not considered a crime, the killer was acquitted.

Viewing black planters as potential allies in the common cause of justifying bondage and suppressing slave insurrection, some white planters encouraged black slaveholding. But there were limits to what black slaveholders could do. They could not vote or escape racial insults, and they had no protection in the courts. Their status and freedom depended on not angering powerful white neighbors.

BLACK EXILES ABROAD AND AT HOME

The number of hospitable destinations for free black people in the United States shrank quickly during the 1850s. The Ohio legislature, for example, imposed a heavy tax on free black immigrants, making it difficult for all but a prosperous few to settle there. A new Illinois statute halted black immigration completely. Maryland, long home to thousands of free African Americans, began to allow slave hunters to seize *free* black people entering from other states and sell them into bondage. Virginia laid a poll tax—a tax on voting—on free black residents, intended specifically to create funds to deport them to Africa. Minnesota revoked a long-held black franchise. Other states followed suit until black men could vote only in Maine, New Hampshire, Rhode Island, Vermont, Wisconsin, and Massachusetts.

Thus, black leaders argued over the best options for free black people, with some advocating that they leave the country that was increasingly curtailing their freedoms. Some moved to Canada, others to the American frontier, and others still farther abroad—to Haiti, Africa, and elsewhere. Debates intensified over whether free African Americans should leave the country as well as where they should go.

The Debate over Emigration

The divisions between the Holly brothers over emigration exemplified the debates taking place in the free black community in the 1850s. The son of a shoemaker, James T. Holly studied mathematics and classics in black schools in his native Washington, DC, and in Brooklyn, New York. In 1850, Holly and his older brother Joseph established themselves as bootmakers in Burlington, Vermont. But James Holly dreamed of a better life outside the United States. Some leaders strongly advocated that black Americans save money to relocate to Africa or accept the offers of groups like the American Colonization Society to help finance such a move. Joseph Holly, James' brother, insisted that expatriates were traitors, as they left enslaved black people in America with no one to advocate for them. Expatriates, Joseph Holly said, were manipulated by white schemers intending to send the most talented (and therefore troublesome) black people to places where they could not incite rebellion.

By 1852, James Holly had settled in Ontario, where he met the embittered Martin Delany. Two years earlier, Delany had managed to gain admission to Harvard University's medical school. In 1850, only a few black doctors practiced in the United States, and most of them had been educated abroad. In 1849, Bowdoin College awarded medical degrees to two African American brothers, Thomas and John White, and Harvard's training would position Delany as the next black American doctor trained in his own country. However, white fellow students forced Delany to withdraw during his first year. Unable to enlist the support of Boston abolitionists, who felt they had more pressing battles to fight, the embittered Delany moved to Ontario with his wife and children. There, he became one of the leaders of the black exile community.

Together, Delany and James Holly led the formation of the American Emigration Society. At the Society's annual conventions, its leaders endorsed Canada, whose government offered citizenship and all-black communities, as a worthwhile destination. They also suggested the West Indies, Liberia, Haiti, and Central America as other havens from discrimination.

But in the years before the Civil War, views changed. At first Holly championed Canada, citing its proximity to the United States as ideal for aiding slaves. But after encountering white abolitionist James Redpath, who urged black people to leave "this bastard democracy in the United States," Holly by 1855 was recommending Haiti because he and Redpath had persuaded the government there to give free land to African American settlers. Meanwhile, Martin Delany, fearing the United States would soon annex Canada, recommended Central and South America and the British Caribbean.

Safe Haven in Canada

In a pamphlet written in 1852, a young woman named Mary Ann Shadd touted Canada as a home for free black people in a pamphlet entitled "Notes of Canada West." Shadd compared opportunities in the British West Indies and Central America and concluded that the Great Lakes region of southern Canada, a short ferry ride from Detroit, "offers stronger inducements to colored people." Indeed, the Canadian government, motivated by the hope that the new black communities would provide a buffer zone between white Canadians and rebellious Indians, offered citizenship and the franchise to black immigrants after only three years' residency.

Canada's invitation had wide appeal. During the 1850s, Ontario's black community grew dramatically. By 1860, about 5,000 black immigrants had moved to Canada. They included the principal players in the Christiana episode—William and Eliza Parker and some of the fugitive slaves—Martin Delany, and many other disaffected African Americans.

■ **MAP 9.2** **Free Black Communities in Canada, 1860**

Scattered in more than a half-dozen communities within 200 miles of Detroit, African Americans in Canada looked longingly across the Great Lakes toward their American homes and families.

While grateful for Canadian sanctuary, many resented both the exile and Canadians' treatment of them as second-class citizens. Although several thousand free black people lived in Ontario—several hundred of whom owned businesses and land—black people experienced difficulty finding work, and their wages were often lower than those of white workers.

Unlike Delany and many other Canadian immigrants, Mary Ann Shadd had never experienced slavery. Born in 1823 to free and relatively prosperous parents in Delaware, she had studied at Quaker schools. In the 1840s, the family relocated to Canada. Shadd's father, Abraham, was elected to the town council in Chatham—the first black person to win an elective office in Canada. In the late 1840s, Mary Ann Shadd returned to the United States to teach black children in Pennsylvania, Delaware, and New York. However, the passage of the Fugitive Slave Act spurred her to return to Canada in order to teach fugitive slaves.

Arriving in Ontario in 1851, Shadd accepted the support of the American Missionary Association (AMA) to open a school. But she always felt uneasy about the AMA, suspecting the organization of cheating black refugees by buying Canadian land and reselling it at inflated prices to African Americans. In 1856, when the AMA withdrew its support from her school, she was relieved to regain her autonomy.

Shadd was mentored early on by Henry Bibb, a black newspaper publisher. Bibb experienced a much more har-rowing entry into Canada than Shadd. It took five attempts before he finally escaped from his master in Kentucky in 1842. Then he spent several years lecturing for the Underground Railroad and campaigning for the antislavery Liberty Party. In 1849, settled in Detroit, Bibb published his *Narrative of the Life and Adventures of Henry Bibb, An American Slave, Written by Himself.* When the Fugitive Slave Act made him feel vulnerable in Detroit, Bibb moved to Ontario, where he felt safe enough to write to his former owner celebrating his own "work of self-emancipation." By 1852, Bibb was publishing his own newspaper, *The Voice of the Fugitive.*

Shadd and Bibb debated, however, over education for black children, reflecting the frustrations within the black communities over how to carve out lives for themselves in a new country. The Canadian government provided schools for black immigrants, but they were inferior to those provided for white students. Shadd advocated independent schools. Black and white parents alike, she insisted, could pool their resources for a good education for children of both races. In contrast, Henry Bibb, whose wife had founded an independent school for black children that had failed financially, felt African Americans could ill afford private schools, and the government-supported all-black schools were better than no schools at all. Bibb had no faith that interracial schools would work.

 **First Person** ## Mary Ann Shadd Considers Emigration

Numerous influential black leaders publicized views on emigration. In the early 1850s, Mary Ann Shadd recommended Canada. But this letter to white Philadelphia Quaker Benjamin Coates, who advocated black people moving to Africa, suggests that by the late 1850s she had reconsidered.

November 20/[18]58

I beg to acknowledge the receipt from you of a pamphlet and "Gazette" containing important matter relative to the Civilization of Africa. Upon careful examination of the book and the letter in the paper, we feel that the matter cannot be too forcibly urged upon the attention of the colored people of Canada as well as the United States.

We of the *Freeman* Office have put the views expressed by you before some of our best informed and most reliable colored men among whom I may mention Abraham D. Shadd . . . and Martin Delany. An organization should be formed at no distant day.

From the number and enterprising habits of our people of Canada I think it probable that many will emigrate to the Yoruba Country, provided the subject can be put properly before them. . . .

You may depend upon us for an organization as besides Dr. Delany's influence we are extensively known to the colored people through the paper and a school. . . . Our people need only proper information scattered among them by means of the press and schools.

—from Haverford College Library, Quaker Collection, Benjamin Coates Collection, Collection no. 1190, Mary Ann Shadd Cary to Benjamin Coates, November 20, 1858.

To view a longer version of this document, please go to *www.ablongman.com/carson/documents*.

In 1853, Shadd assumed editorship of the *Provincial Freeman*, an independent black newspaper. She was the first female newspaper editor, black or white, in North America. The paper gave her an outlet to voice her views about emigration, community life, and education. She also had an outlet for venting her frustration with Bibb. Their feud over education played out in public, in their respective newspapers. Meanwhile, though the Canadian government made no concessions, black fugitives—motivated by the stepped-up slave hunts resulting from the Fugitive Slave Act—poured into Canada in ever-increasing numbers. By 1860, there were 4,000 African Americans in communities along the northern rim of the Great Lakes, and hundreds more in western Canada and along the Atlantic coast.

The Lure of the Frontier

While several thousand African Americans sought refuge in Canada in the 1850s, a small but steady stream of black Americans joined the western migration. During the 1840s, a few fled to Texas—but by 1860, when roughly 300 free black Texans were vastly outnumbered by a slave population grown to nearly 183,000, white Texans acted swiftly to constrain their rights.

So black freedom-seekers moved on to the next frontier. By 1860, several thousand African Americans reached California. Another hundred made it to the Oregon Territory. In both regions, slavery was outlawed. Though these areas hardly extended a warm welcome, many African Americans established themselves as tavernkeepers, laundresses, haulers, and shopkeepers. Others became scouts, cooks, livestock tenders for wagon trains, or gold prospectors.

Among the most colorful black westerners was free-born Mifflin W. Gibbs. As a twenty-two-year-old Philadelphian in 1850, Gibbs was recruited to the antislavery lecture circuit by Frederick Douglass and Charles Remond. Soon, however, he was lured by the gold rush and the energy of the black-rights community in California, where leaders lectured newcomers about their rights and encouraged any who had been brought west as slaves to claim their freedom.

There Gibbs learned of Biddy Mason, whose master had brought her from Utah to California in 1851. Encouraged by free black leaders, Mason petitioned the California courts for her family's freedom. In 1855, in only three days of hearings, Gibbs saw the courts declare the Mason family free.

The abolitionist spirit in California energized Gibbs, who established *Mirror of the Times*, California's first black newspaper. Gibbs protested California's poll tax (a fee charged for the right to vote), which was imposed only on black voters. When he voted without paying the tax, local officials seized goods from the clothing store he owned. But Gibbs resisted. "With a fervor as cool as the circumstances would permit" he published his pledge "that the great State of California might annually confiscate our goods, but we would never pay the voters tax." The courts ordered his goods returned, and Gibbs basked in his victory: "No further attempts to enforce the law upon colored men were made." But soon Gibbs was on the move again—this time to a gold rush in Canada.

> " No further attempts to enforce the law upon colored men were made."
> —*Mifflin Gibbs*

SECTIONAL CRISIS

"Are we incapable of self-government?" Martin Delany asked black Americans in an 1852 essay. Answering his own question, Delany insisted that only political power, not moral argument, could assure African Americans lives of dignity. Smarting after his humiliation at Harvard, Delany poured out his discouragement at the prospects for equality and justice in the country of his birth. "No people can have political power if they do not constitute a majority," he concluded.

Delany's concern about finding a place where black people could influence government policy mirrored the concerns of other groups about representation. Across the nation, white southerners fretted about losing their majority in Congress. New western settlers worried that federal laws would favor easterners. As free black people sought to boost their influence, their leadership splintered. Meanwhile, white leaders' attempts to settle the slavery question in the West took the nation to the precipice of civil war with the Kansas-Nebraska Act of 1854. Sectional compromise seemed all but impossible.

From Moral Suasion to Political Power

While some black Americans chose emigration, others, like Frederick Douglass, began exploring political methods to end slavery and gain citizenship. For more than a decade, Douglass promoted William Lloyd Garrison's concept of "moral suasion"—appealing to Americans' consciences to end slavery. But increasingly convinced that this tactic was naive and unrealistic, Douglass moved toward political action after the 1839 founding of the Liberty Party. In 1840, he joined the Free Soil Party, a coalition of Americans in the East led by New England abolitionists who wanted any territory gained from Mexico to be non-slave. The Free Soil Party ran an antislavery candidate on the presidential ticket in 1848. Though black men could vote in only a few states, Douglass was able at least to help design the party's platform.

Douglass also began to see a value in separate black organizations. These ideas drew him away from other black leaders, who still believed biracial cooperation to change the hearts and minds of white Americans was the only way to achieve enduring racial peace.

Frederick Douglass argued that the U.S. Constitution—if it could be enforced—guaranteed African Americans citizenship. He remained committed to staying in the United States and encouraged black organizations to work with—but not within—white reform organizations. Through these differences in perspectives, black leadership splintered in the 1850s.

The Kansas-Nebraska Act

In 1854, Illinois Senator Stephen A. Douglas reopened the question of western slavery. Arguing that local people could best determine their region's needs, Douglas suggested another compromise to help all Americans remember their common interests. A railroad to the West, he argued, anchored in Chicago, would benefit the entire nation's economy. For the railroad to succeed, however, white Americans would need to settle the expanse of Kansas and Nebraska. Why not offer these new settlers popular sovereignty—that is, the right to decide, by popular referendum, whether to have slavery in their communities? Though some politicians saw this plan as a recipe for disaster because it could lead western settlers battling with each other for control of their communities, Congress passed the Kansas-Nebraska Act in May 1854.

Despite his twenty years of political experience, Douglas had misjudged how Americans' anxieties about slavery could fuel their fears of conspiracies. When fugitive Anthony Burns was apprehended in Boston just two days

 **First Person** **Frederick Douglass Reflects on "Bleeding Kansas"**

Frederick Douglass published an expanded version of his 1845 Narrative of the Life and Times of Frederick Douglass *in 1855, one year after Congress passed the Kansas-Nebraska Act. Revising the Narrative Again after the Civil War, Douglass reflected on how the Kansas-Nebraska Act intensified northern abolitionism.*

The important point to me . . . .was the effect of the Kansas battle upon the moral sentiment of the North: how it made abolitionists of people before they themselves became aware of it, and how it rekindled the zeal, stimulated the activity, and strengthened the faith of our old antislavery forces. . . . The men who went to Kansas with the purpose of making it a free state were the heroes and martyrs. One of the leaders in this holy crusade for freedom . . . was John Brown. This brave old man and his sons were amongst the first to hear and heed the trumpet of freedom calling them to battle. . . . When it became evident . . . that the war for and against slavery in Kansas was not to be decided by the peaceful means of words and ballots, but that swords and bullets were to be employed on both sides, Captain John Brown felt that now, after long years of waiting, his hour had come.

—*from Frederick Douglass,* The Life and Times of Frederick Douglass *(Revised edition, 1892).*

To view a longer version of this document, please go to *www.ablongman.com/carson/documents*.

after passage of the new act, northern reformers accused Douglas of plotting with others in the federal government to stir up southern resentment against the North. Radical white abolitionists and even many moderate northerners also worried that the proposed plan for Kansas and Nebraska would undermine the Missouri Compromise. That law, so hard won in 1820, had created a nation with an equal number of slave states and free states—but Kansas and Nebraska, both of which lay north of the Compromise line, might now become slave states. Losing their faith in Douglas's integrity, northerners deserted the Democratic Party because the Illinois senator was one of its leaders. Some switched to the antislavery Republican Party, a new coalition formed in 1854 when the remnants of the Liberty Party teamed up with the Free Soil Party. Others opted for the two-year-old Know-Nothing Party, which condemned abolitionists and proslavery advocates alike and focused its fury on Catholics and recent immigrants. The Know Nothings feared these groups would bring religion into America's carefully guarded separation between church and state.

In the wake of the Kansas-Nebraska Act, the opening of new territory, combined with the desire to stake a claim for a slave or non-slave community, sent many new settlers from both North and South rushing to the new popular sovereignty territory. By 1856, the Kansas-Nebraska territory was the tense arena for proslavery and antislavery confrontation.

"Bleeding Kansas"

The conflict in Kansas-Nebraska soon erupted in violence. Southern settlers, frustrated that the federal government refused full support for slavery, rioted in the antislavery town of Lawrence, Kansas. In retaliation, the New England Emigrant Aid Society sent a group of white radical abolitionists into the area, including abolitionist John Brown and four of his sons. Brown, who had moved many times in support of his self-proclaimed mission for racial justice, initiated several skirmishes with southerners who had brought their slaves to Kansas. In these battles, he killed several southern settlers, and two of Brown's own sons also died. Newspapers called the area "Bleeding Kansas." Hearing the reports from Kansas, Charlotte Forten, the black abolitionist in Boston, recorded her mixture of concern and exhilaration as she listened to black abolitionist Charles Remond speak about the situation. "Mr. [Charles] Remond lectured for us this evening," she wrote. "I particularly liked what he said about Kansas. Everybody has so much sympathy for the [white] sufferers there, and so little for the poor slave, who for centuries has suffered tenfold worse miseries—still I am glad that something has roused the people of the North at last. . . . [I also] went to hear Mr. [Richard Henry] Dana [a white abolitionist lawyer] who taught me more about Kansas than I ever knew before. A very great political excitement prevails."

In Washington, DC, anger about Kansas ignited chaos in Congress. As Congress debated whether to admit Kansas to statehood in May 1856, Massachusetts abolitionist senator Charles Sumner delivered an impassioned speech about the "crime against Kansas." He chided his colleagues, especially Stephen Douglas, for initiating the popular sovereignty policy that precipitated the violence. Two days later, South Carolina congressman Preston Brooks, nephew of a senator who had supported Douglas, stormed into the Senate and pounded Sumner with a cane. Disabled by the attack, Sumner could not return to Congress for three years. However, he remained useful to the Republican Party: To protest the beating, Massachusetts voters reelected him in 1857, hoping his empty chair in the Senate would symbolize abolitionist sacrifice.

The Dred Scott Decision

As blood spilled in Kansas, the U.S. Supreme Court considered a crucial suit that had meandered through the courts for more than a decade. The suit centered on Dred Scott, a Missouri slave whose master had taken him from slave territory into Illinois and free Wisconsin Territory in the 1830s and then back south. When the master died in 1846, his widow's brother, an abolitionist, helped Scott sue for his freedom on the grounds that he had lived on free soil.

Before the Fugitive Slave Act was passed, Missouri's local courts had judged Scott free. But in the post-Act hysteria, Missouri's supreme court overturned this decision in 1852. Following five more years of litigation, in March 1857 the U.S. Supreme Court handed down three important rulings. First, the judges said Scott was not free, because to free him would deprive his owner of property without due process of law. Second, the Court declared that slaves were not entitled to use the courts, as only citizens had that right. Finally, the justices maintained that neither slaves nor their descendants could ever be citizens.

The Court used Scott's case to define the Missouri Compromise as unconstitutional. Because the Constitution protects citizens from having their property arbitrarily confiscated, the Court held that Congress could not make a policy—such as the Missouri Compromise—that could deprive citizens of their property just because they moved to a different region of the United States. Many northern and western states had passed laws prohibiting slavery, and their residents feared that if a longstanding congressional policy like the Missouri Compromise could be overturned, state laws could be overturned as well.

In the face of these legal decisions that stripped away the few citizens' rights that elevated free black people above slaves, New York's radical black *Weekly Anglo-African* promised persistent opposition: "When you repeal the Fugitive Slave Law, reverse the Dred Scott decision, and give us the right of citizenship in the free states, and break up the internal slave trade between the slave states, then, and not until then, you may expect us to be silent. But just so long as the enemies of the colored men's rights are to be found skulking behind the pillars of the church, and seeking security in the strong arm of the law, we can never remain silent."

The Lincoln-Douglas Debates

Stephen Douglas remained embroiled in the slavery debate. In the 1858 Illinois congressional elections, he was pitted against Abraham Lincoln, a Republican who accused Douglas of taking contradictory positions. The principle of popular sovereignty, said Lincoln, which Douglas had espoused in pushing the Kansas-Nebraska Act, promised power to local residents. But the Dred Scott decision (which Douglas supported) gave power to the federal government. Caught between his antislavery posture and his approval of the Dred Scott decision (which supported the side of slavery), Douglas was only narrowly reelected. His attempt to bolster his political position by trying to please people in many regions had ended with many people distrusting him. Lincoln, on the other hand, gained popularity for his more moderate approach. While not suggesting that southerners do "what I would not know how to do,"—that is, abolish slavery—he warned that the nation cannot exist "half-slave and half-free."

In these debates, Lincoln took seemingly contradictory stances as well. He argued both that the Constitution protected African Americans as citizens and that only white people should settle the West. While emphasizing that slavery was morally wrong, he stopped short of suggesting it be prohibited. He condemned the Dred Scott decision, saying black people should be equal before the law, but he shied away from the question of whether African Americans were the intellectual or social equals of white people. Lincoln contended that discrimination based on race could easily become discrimination based on eye color, height, or other arbitrary characteristics, yet he offered no solution for prohibiting discrimination. But he did predict an impending crisis.

John Brown at Harper's Ferry

By 1859, Lincoln's prediction was realized, and the 1850s ended as they began—with bloody confrontation. On October 16, 1859, a fifty-nine-year-old white man ordered his twenty-one-man army, "Men, get on your arms; we will proceed to the ferry." The bearded, stooped leader was the

> "**M**en, get on your arms; we will proceed to the ferry."—*John Brown*

intensely religious John Brown. Dedicated to purging society of the sin of slavery, Brown spent months preparing for this day.

Brown represented abolitionists who believed violence was the only solution. They advocated direct action calling slaves to all-out rebellion. The loss of his sons in Kansas left Brown in deep despair. He began soliciting arms, information, recruits, and money to establish a sanctuary for runaways in the mountains along the borders of the slave South. From this sanctuary, he envisioned a slave revolt to ignite a chain reaction down into the South. If they could "conquer Virginia," Brown assured his followers, "the other southern states would nearly conquer themselves."

Arriving in Ontario in the spring of 1858, Brown had already studied guerrilla warfare and was finalizing his plans. He consulted with Harriet Tubman, an expert on the southern terrain. He received donations from white New Englanders and black New York residents who were weary of ineffectual protests. He spoke with Frederick Douglass, who offered guarded encouragement for Brown's plan to set up a free black state, but Douglass would not support violent confrontation. The Massachusetts State Kansas Committee— mostly Boston abolitionists—agreed to supply money and guns. Using passionate religious arguments to lure them away from their pacifist convictions, Brown had even recruited several young Iowa Quakers. The elderly reformer was ready to fashion an army. Martin Delany, Mary Ann Shadd, James T. Holly, and William Parker were among the Cana-

dian refugees who listened with interest to Brown. Parker, Holly, and the Shadd family made tentative plans to join the rebellion. But Delany, feeling Brown was moving too slowly, turned his attention to seeking a place to relocate in West Africa. Delany sailed for Nigeria in the spring of 1859.

Brown proceeded to Harper's Ferry, Virginia, a stopping point on the Underground Railroad, in June 1859. Harper's Ferry had a federal armory, which Brown planned to raid to get rifles to arm local slaves for an all-out uprising. An industrial village located where the Shenandoah and Potomac rivers meet, 60 miles northwest of Washington, DC, Harper's Ferry seemed well situated as a base from which to launch an attack on the South. The terminus of many trains and canals, it was a hub that would allow easy escape for slaves and rebels, and the town had a substantial

■ The U.S. Supreme Court's ruling on the Dred Scott case evoked a wave of public sympathy for Scott, as this news story highlighting his family suggests.

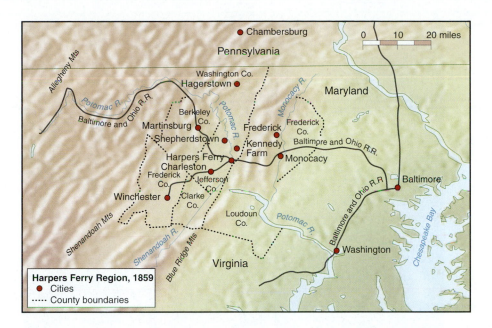

■ MAP 9.3 Harper's Ferry Region, 1859

Located at the hub of slave traffic, within 40 miles of the Pennsylvania border, Washington DC, and the tidewater region of Virginia, Harper's Ferry was also nestled in an area inhabited by many anti-slavery Quakers who condemned violence.

number of free African Americans who might be called on to lend their support.

But Harper's Ferry also had some serious disadvantages as a center for rebels. Relatively few strong black slaves were nearby to form an army; of the 18,000 slaves in the surrounding counties, most were women working as house servants. Because Harper's Ferry had no unified community, black or white, and only a small pool of black men from which to draw an army, Brown failed to win local support.

Brown's army of sixteen white men and five black men, recruited from far afield, reflected the broad geographical reach of abolitionist networks. Only Shields Green had once been a slave. John Anthony Copeland, a North Carolinian studying at Oberlin College, brought along his uncle, Sheridan Leary, a mixed-race resident of Oberlin who left behind his wife and baby daughter. Mixed-race Dangerfield Newby also joined the group, hoping to liberate his wife and children from slavery in Virginia.

When the insurrection began, the small army managed to seize a local farmer—George Washington's great-grand-nephew—as a hostage. But the campaign to seize the arsenal soon went awry. Brown had brought the wrong ammunition for the guns they carried. Holly, Parker, and the Shadd family were late in arriving from Canada. Reinforcements promised by Harriet Tubman never showed. Not one local African American joined in. Most of Brown's freedom fighters, including two more of his sons, perished in the fray. Osborne Anderson, the only black man among the five who escaped, returned to Canada. Unlike the Christiana confrontation, the raid at Harper's Ferry had no triumphant

ending. This time southerners got their hangings. On December 2, 1859, Brown and the remaining few of his band went to the gallows for treason.

Yet Brown succeeded in stirring up America. Southerners worried the Harper's Ferry raid would spark full-blown war. Because of "a good deal of talk about Harper's Ferry," wrote one slave trader, "everybody nearly wants to volunteer to go to fight. . . . But no serious danger is apprehended," he concluded. The uncertainty caused slave prices to plummet. When Congress convened on December 5, lawmakers came armed. Hoping for southern support for a presidential bid, Stephen Douglas blamed the Republicans for Brown's insurrection. Southern congressmen demanded a committee to investigate whether the Republican Party had supported Brown. But when Abraham Lincoln and other white Republicans also condemned Brown, rumors of a plot subsided.

Though Brown's mission failed, William Lloyd Garrison, who had heretofore been a pacifist, conceded the righteousness of the effort. Black and white abolitionists began describing Brown's raid as "noble." John Copeland, Brown's young black Oberlin recruit, wrote home to his mother, "Could I die in a more noble cause?" Black poet Frances Ellen Watkins

> "Could I die in a more noble cause?"—*John Copeland*

addressed Brown's wife as the "noble wife of the hero of the nineteenth century." Watkins continued: "Belonging to the race your dear husband reached forth his hand to assist, I thank you. Not in vain has your dear husband periled all.

Brown asked that his execution be attended only by the "poor little, dirty, ragged bare headed and barefooted slave boys & girls led by some old grey headed slave mother." But fearing an attempt to rescue Brown, the authorities barred the public from the abolitionist martyr's scaffold. Still, many artists painted the scene Brown had envisioned anyway, some showing him as a Christ-like avenging angel. More than two decades after the event, Thomas Hovenden, who had married an abolitionist, produced this fictional rendition of Brown kissing a black child.

From the prison comes forth a shout of triumph. Enclosed I send you a few dollars as a token of my gratitude, reverence and love." Frederick Douglass eulogized Brown as "a human soul illuminated with divine qualities," who "saw slavery through no mist or cloud but in the light of infinite wisdom" and "loved liberty for all men." Memorials, songs, and poems helped Brown accomplish in death what he could not in life: stirring abolitionists to agree that the only way to end slavery was to "purge the land with blood."

Brown's army died with a dignity and conviction that brought wide admiration, but the day of their execution was a sad one for the hundreds of thousands of black Americans who, weeping, lined the tracks as the train carried Brown's remains home from Virginia through Philadelphia to his farm in New York's Adirondack Mountains.

CONCLUSION

The congressional leaders who had created the Missouri Compromise, the Compromise of 1850 (with its Fugitive Slave Act), and the policy of popular sovereignty struggled to provide political solutions to the slavery problem ripping at the United States. Antislavery advocates sought to accomplish abolition by raising moral outrage. Proslavery forces called on constitutional and legal power to protect their property—and with the Dred Scott decision, the U.S. Supreme Court supported their claims. But both southerners and northerners knew the matter was far from settled.

The 1850s opened and closed with bloody confrontations over slavery. But the slavery debate was just one of many conflicts dividing Americans living in different sections of the country. The issue quickly spilled into bitter battles over the federal government's jurisdiction over states, federal protection of citizens' property, and the moral and religious implications of holding a person in bondage. As new settlement areas opened in the West and in Canada, Americans struggled to define how race related to citizenship and what individuals could do to defend their rights. Throughout the decade, cotton remained the nation's most profitable export crop, and the land and labor required to grow it became the subjects of hot debate and brutal skirmishes.

For black Americans, these developments had mixed implications. On the one hand, the Fugitive Slave Act increased the danger and desperation of slave life. But the same law helped create and publicize black heroes and chroniclers. Inspired by accounts of courageous actions, more and more white Americans began to perceive slaves' lives as intertwined with their own. Nonetheless, an increasing number of Americans, black and white alike, began to share Abraham Lincoln's foreboding that the country would have to reach a crisis before the controversy could finally end.

FURTHER READING

Blackett, Richard. *Building an Antislavery Wall* (Baton Rouge: Louisiana State University Press, 1983).

Fett, Sharla M. *Working Cures: Healing, Health, and Power on Southern Slave Plantations* (Chapel Hill: University of North Carolina Press, 2002).

Gould, Virginia Meacham. *Chained to the Rock of Adversity: To Be Free, Black, and Female in the Old South* (Athens: University of Georgia Press, 1998).

Haines, Michael R., and Richard H. Steckel. *A Population History of North America* (Cambridge: Cambridge University Press, 2000).

Johannsen, Robert Walter. *Stephen A. Douglas* (Urbana: University of Illinois Press, 1997).

Koger, Larry. *Black Slaveowners: Free Black Slave Masters in South Carolina, 1790–1860* (Jefferson, NC: McFarland, 1985).

Painter, Nell Irvin. *Sojourner Truth: A Life, a Symbol* (New York: W. W. Norton, 1996).

Penningroth, Dylan C. *The Claims of Kinfolk: African American Property and Community in the Nineteenth-Century South* (Chapel Hill: University of North Carolina Press, 2003).

Richards, Leonard L. *The Slave Power: The Free North and Southern Domination, 1780–1860* (Baton Rouge: Louisiana State University Press, 2000).

Rhodes, Jane. *Mary Ann Shadd Cary: The Black Press and Protest in the Nineteenth Century* (Bloomington: Indiana University Press, 1998).

Schweninger, Loren. *The Southern Debate over Slavery: Petitions to Southern Legislatures, 1778–1864* (Urbana: University of Illinois Press, 2001).

Sinha, Manisha. *The Counterrevolution of Slavery: Politics and Ideology in Antebellum South Carolina* (Chapel Hill: University of North Carolina Press, 2000).

Slaughter, Thomas P. *Bloody Dawn: The Christiana Riot and Racial Violence in the Antebellum North* (New York: Oxford University Press, 1991).

Taylor, Quintard. *In Search of the Racial Frontier: African Americans in the American West, 1528–1990* (New York: W. W. Norton, 1998).

von Frank, Albert. *The Trials of Anthony Burns: Freedom and Slavery in Emerson's Boston* (Cambridge: Harvard University Press, 1998).

■ For the regimental flag of the Sixth Colored Troops, who fought on the Union side in the Civil War, black Philadelphia artist David Bustill Bowser created a design of Liberty holding a flag and counseling a volunteer. In the background, a slave child applauding on a bale of cotton symbolizes the connection between the service of black northerners and the emancipation of southern slaves. The scroll proclaims "Freedom for All." On the reverse, an eagle in flight carries a streamer bearing the national motto "E Pluribus Unum."

Civil War and the Promises of Freedom: The Turbulent 1860s

Martin Delany Becomes First Black U.S. Army Major

The 1850s left some African Americans despairing of ever seeing the end of slavery in the United States. Abolitionist Martin Delany, who had settled in Canada in search of greater freedom, began to dream of a home for African Americans in Africa. "Africa for the African race, and black men to rule them," he proclaimed.

In December 1860, Delany returned to America from an eighteen-month visit to England and Africa during which he made plans for such a community. In spring 1859, he had founded the Niger Valley Exploring Party to sponsor his trip. The group drew up a comprehensive plan "to make a topographical, geological and geographical examination of the valley of the Niger River . . . and an inquiry into the state and condition of the people . . . for the purpose of science and general information." But its main goal was to locate the best place for black Americans to resettle. The trip was arduous, but success seemed imminent. While in Africa, Delany met with Yoruban leaders in West Africa and wrote to New York American Methodist Episcopal (AME) minister Henry Highland Garnet, "I am happy to report that I have concluded a treaty . . . , by which we secure the right of locating in common with the natives on any part of their territory not otherwise occupied." Pleased, Garnet contacted a "number of men who are willing to embark on this glorious enterprise, and who believe as I do—that there is a glorious future before Africa." But when Delany returned to the United States he found it teetering on the precipice of a civil war that delayed his Africa plans for almost two decades.

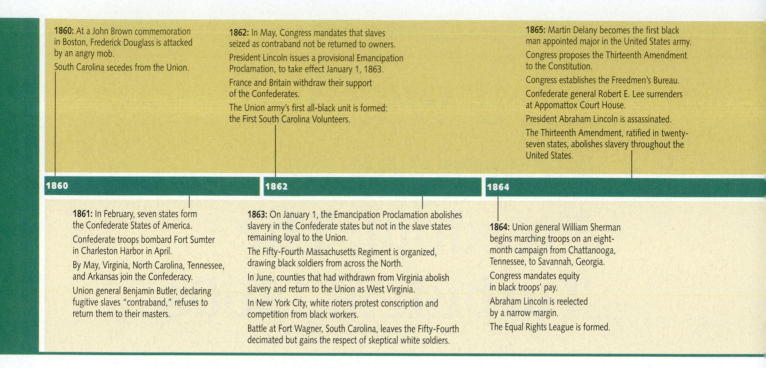

1860: At a John Brown commemoration in Boston, Frederick Douglass is attacked by an angry mob.
South Carolina secedes from the Union.

1862: In May, Congress mandates that slaves seized as contraband not be returned to owners.
President Lincoln issues a provisional Emancipation Proclamation, to take effect January 1, 1863.
France and Britain withdraw their support of the Confederates.
The Union army's first all-black unit is formed: the First South Carolina Volunteers.

1865: Martin Delany becomes the first black man appointed major in the United States army.
Congress proposes the Thirteenth Amendment to the Constitution.
Congress establishes the Freedmen's Bureau.
Confederate general Robert E. Lee surrenders at Appomattox Court House.
President Abraham Lincoln is assassinated.
The Thirteenth Amendment, ratified in twenty-seven states, abolishes slavery throughout the United States.

1860   **1862**   **1864**

1861: In February, seven states form the Confederate States of America.
Confederate troops bombard Fort Sumter in Charleston Harbor in April.
By May, Virginia, North Carolina, Tennessee, and Arkansas join the Confederacy.
Union general Benjamin Butler, declaring fugitive slaves "contraband," refuses to return them to their masters.

1863: On January 1, the Emancipation Proclamation abolishes slavery in the Confederate states but not in the slave states remaining loyal to the Union.
The Fifty-Fourth Massachusetts Regiment is organized, drawing black soldiers from across the North.
In June, counties that had withdrawn from Virginia abolish slavery and return to the Union as West Virginia.
In New York City, white rioters protest conscription and competition from black workers.
Battle at Fort Wagner, South Carolina, leaves the Fifty-Fourth decimated but gains the respect of skeptical white soldiers.

1864: Union general William Sherman begins marching troops on an eight-month campaign from Chattanooga, Tennessee, to Savannah, Georgia.
Congress mandates equity in black troops' pay.
Abraham Lincoln is reelected by a narrow margin.
The Equal Rights League is formed.

Like that of thousands of others, Delany's life was redirected by the civil war that erupted in the spring of 1861. After the federal government eventually recruited black troops, Delany petitioned to serve as a surgeon. Receiving no answer, he journeyed to Washington, DC to propose that northern black leaders help organize slaves into a fighting force. President Abraham Lincoln agreed and issued Delany a commission. Thus, in February 1865, the fifty-two-year-old Delany—who had been driven from Harvard's medical school, been an expatriate in Canada, and dreamed of life in Africa—became the U.S. army's first black major.

The Civil War set northerners to debating whether it was more important to end slavery or to hold the nation together. Some hoped to settle the controversy by allowing southerners to keep slaves in return for accepting federal authority over states. Many northerners had family, friends, and business partners in the South, and they dreaded seeing these relationships severed by war. Even as they prepared to take up arms against their southern brothers and uncles, they resented their government's asking them to do so.

Initially, northerners went to war not about slaves or black people but about preserving the Union by defending the authority of the federal government. Describing the conflict as "a white man's war," northern (Union) officials turned

away free black men who volunteered to join the army. President Lincoln envisioned resettling black people outside the United States, and slaves who escaped from the South (the Confederacy) to Union army camps were returned to their masters. But northern free black men and women insisted that the war *had* to be about black people. When the Union government could not raise enough white recruits, African Americans mustered 190,000 black volunteers whose battlefield achievements won their country's admiration.

Gradually, emancipation came to be seen as an effective military strategy by both the Union and the Confederacy, as both sides concluded that offering freedom could secure black people's loyalty. Meanwhile, free black people petitioned the Union for concessions such as equal military pay, opportunities for education, and the right to vote.

The war signaled dramatic changes for black and white people alike. In the North, it stimulated the economy but also increased political and racial tensions. In the South, white men needed little persuasion to enlist in the Confederate army, even as the war ravaged the landscape and uprooted families. White slaveowners persuaded many white men who did not own slaves that they should fight to uphold regional and family loyalty. At war's end, African Americans celebrated emancipation and embraced their new "citizenship." But they knew that without

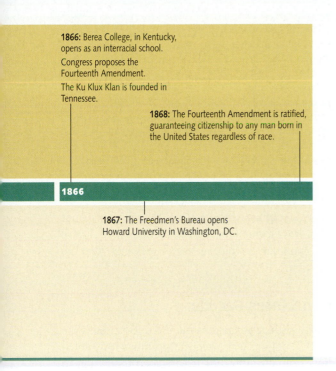

1866: Berea College, in Kentucky, opens as an interracial school.
Congress proposes the Fourteenth Amendment.
The Ku Klux Klan is founded in Tennessee.

1868: The Fourteenth Amendment is ratified, guaranteeing citizenship to any man born in the United States regardless of race.

1866

1867: The Freedmen's Bureau opens Howard University in Washington, DC.

ing "was invaded, insulted, captured by a mob of gentlemen, and thereafter broken up and dispersed by the order of the mayor." Popular opinion held that anti-abolitionists were lower-class ruffians, but Douglass knew better. These rioters, said Douglass, were not just "among the baser sort, maddened by rum and hounded on by some wily politician." Rather, "the leaders of the mob were gentlemen . . . who pride themselves upon their respect for law and order." Many of these "gentlemen" profited from slave-produced cotton, woven into coarse fabrics by northern industrialists who sold them back to the South. Abolitionist success might mean the end of their cotton supplies. But soon these northern white gentlemen would reluctantly be drawn into a war against their southern customers. If slavery was the spark that ignited the war, the election of a new president fanned the flame.

The Election of Abraham Lincoln

For the 1860 presidential election, the Republicans still had hopes of appealing to both abolitionists and southern planters. Their platform resurrected the 1846 Wilmot Proviso, which suggested prohibiting slavery in the territories while reaffirming states' right to control local institutions. The Democratic Party had fractured into southerners, who wanted slavery protected in the West, and followers of Illinois senator Stephen A. Douglas, who favored a hands-off policy. With the splintering of the Democrats, Republican Abraham Lincoln won the presidency by a narrow margin—and without the support of a single southern state.

Many southerners viewed the newly elected president as an abolitionist, but black Americans knew better. In a February 1860 speech, Lincoln condemned abolition as "extremism." Though he opposed the extension of slavery into the western territories, he also opposed interfering with regions where it already existed. One outspoken black critic of Lincoln was H. Ford Douglas. A fugitive from Virginia, Douglas had lived in Canada and worked with Henry Bibb to publish *The Voice of the Fugitive.* During the presidential campaign, Douglas delivered an impassioned speech on the Fourth of July—a day he declared he would "rather curse than bless" because he equated the founding of America with the enslavement of black people. He reminded his audience of Lincoln's disturbing political record: For example, during a brief term as an Illinois Whig in the U.S. House of Representatives (1847–1849), Lincoln had supported a draft of the Fugitive Slave Act giving planters even more latitude to pursue runaways than the law that finally passed. Douglas "did not believe in the antislavery of Abraham Lincoln, because he is on the side of this slave power . . . that has the possession of the federal government."

the right to vote, they were not yet full citizens. Only changes in the U.S. Constitution would grant them full citizenship.

While federal officials struggled to plan for 4 million freed black men, women, and children, southern states gradually granted the franchise to black men. But efforts to build a solid political structure in the South were complicated by the region's economic woes and many southern white peoples' resistance to slaves' emancipation. These circumstances left the majority of black southerners unable to attain better lives or protection from white violence.

By June 1868, southern freedmen could cast a ballot—but most northern African Americans could not. So black people confronted the next hurdle: gaining the franchise for black men in the South *and* in the North.

"A WHITE MAN'S WAR"

On December 10, 1860, while Martin Delany was crossing the Atlantic Ocean, Frederick Douglass was speaking in Boston's Music Hall, where a crowd commemorated John Brown's martyrdom. Douglass described an abolitionist meeting at the Music Hall the week before that had been disrupted by anti-abolitionists. He described how the meet-

MAJOR MARTIN R. DELANEY, U. S. A.

■ By war's end, Martin Delany—having spent the first five decades of his life as an outsider in his native United States—achieved as much honor as his government had to offer: the highly dignified rank of major.

Other black Americans also distrusted Republicans. The usually optimistic Frederick Douglass conceded, "[T]he very best that can be said of [the Republican] party . . . is that it is simply opposed to allowing slavery to go where it is not at all likely to go." In New York's *Weekly Anglo-African* newspaper, publisher Thomas Hamilton compared the hands-off policies of Republicans and northern Democrats:

> The two great political parties . . . entertain the same ideas. . . . [T]he Democratic party would make the white man the master and the black man the slave, and have them thus together occupy every foot of American soil. . . . The Republican party . . . with larger professions for humanity . . . oppose the re-opening of the slave-trade . . . oppose the progress of slavery in the territories, and . . . cry humanity to the world. [B]ut . . . their opposition to slav-

ery means opposition to the black man— nothing else. Where it is clearly in their power to do anything for the oppressed colored man, . . . they are too conservative to do it. . . . We have no hope from either [Democrats or Republicans]. We must rely on ourselves, [and on] the righteousness of our cause.

> "We must rely on ourselves, [and on] the righteousness of our cause." —*Thomas Hamilton*

Nearly a year after Lincoln's election, New Jersey AME minister Jabez Campbell despaired that "the president is not now, and never was, either an abolitionist or an anti-slavery man. He has no quarrel whatever with the South upon the slavery question."

Southern States Secede

Convinced, nevertheless, that Lincoln intended to eradicate slavery, South Carolina's legislators in December 1860 voted to withdraw from a union they felt invaded their right to hold slaves. Many South Carolinians who did not own slaves also voted to secede, as they felt excluded from a political system that could choose a president without a single southern electoral vote. They also worried about how thousands of free black people would fit into their society. Most Americans hoped a compromise would prevent war, but now that possibility vanished forever.

Cotton was also a catalyst for the sectional strife. By 1860, driven by international markets as well as demand in the northern textile industry, cotton production had expanded by 30 percent over two decades, and its value had more than doubled in the same period. Most southerners could not envision a southern economy without cotton, nor could they imagine cotton production without slaves. South Carolina and Mississippi, which depended heavily on labor-intensive cotton agriculture and thus had the most to lose if slavery were abolished, were the first to secede.

By February 1861, Florida, Alabama, Georgia, Louisiana, and Texas, which also depended heavily on slave labor, also left the Union, establishing a congress and writing a constitution for a confederacy. The Confederacy's constitution stressed each state's "sovereign and independent character" and implied that states had the right to secede. Delegates elected a president, Jefferson Davis of Mississippi, who was the brother of Hurricane Plantation owner Joseph Davis (see Chapter 8). Quickly raising an army, the Confederacy began seizing federal forts, post offices, and arsenals across the South. By April, Fort Sumter, situated at the entry to the harbor in Charleston, South Carolina, was one of only three southern forts still under Union control.

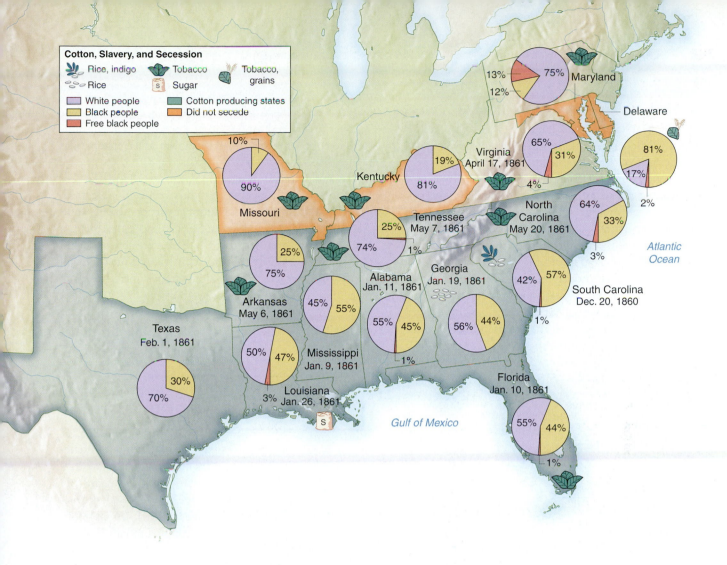

Cotton, Slavery, and Secession

Legend:
- Rice, indigo
- Rice
- White people
- Black people
- Free black people
- Tobacco
- Sugar
- Cotton producing states
- Did not secede
- Tobacco, grains

Maryland: 75% / 13% / 12%

Delaware: 81% / 17% / 2%

Missouri: 90% / 10%

Kentucky: 81% / 19%

Virginia April 17, 1861: 65% / 31% / 4%

North Carolina May 20, 1861: 64% / 33% / 3%

Tennessee May 7, 1861: 74% / 25% / 1%

Arkansas May 6, 1861: 75% / 25%

Georgia Jan. 19, 1861: 56% / 44%

South Carolina Dec. 20, 1860: 42% / 57% / 1%

Alabama Jan. 11, 1861: 45% / 55%

Mississippi Jan. 9, 1861: 55% / 45% / 1%

Texas Feb. 1, 1861: 70% / 30%

Louisiana Jan. 26, 1861: 50% / 47% / 3%

Florida Jan. 10, 1861: 55% / 44% / 1%

Atlantic Ocean

Gulf of Mexico

■ **MAP 10.1** Cotton, Slavery, and Secession

The greater the investment in slaves and cotton, the more quickly and resoundingly came the vote for secession. In the four states where cotton was unimportant and the free black population high, white soldiers chose to fight on each side. At least 40 percent of Kentucky soldiers served in the Confederate army, as did 30 percent of Maryland volunteers, 25 percent of recruits from Missouri, and about 10 percent from Delaware. More than 13,000 Delaware men fought for the Union.

In his March 1861 inaugural speech, Lincoln again promised not to interfere with slavery, but he refused to accept secession. He promised to "have no policy, [but] to get done what the people desire to have done." He seemed unsure "how to find that out exactly." He hesitated to do anything that might encourage other states to join the Confederacy. In early April, informed of supply shortages at Fort Sumter, Lincoln notified South Carolina's governor that he would send food but no arms or troops. But South Carolinians concluded that provisions would prolong the Union's control over the South. On April 12, southern militiamen fired on Fort Sumter and blockaded the harbor. The following day, the Union forces ran out of ammunition and surrendered the fort.

Lincoln's fears about the loss of additional states to the Confederacy were realized; on April 17, Virginia seceded.

With their eastern soil depleted by tobacco and their western counties too mountainous for plantations, Virginians had little incentive to support slavery. In fact, in January 1861, three-fourths of Virginia's voters decided against secession in a referendum. But after Lincoln called up troops, the number of Virginians opposed to secession dropped to one-third, and state legislators voted to join the Confederacy. (The western counties soon broke away from Virginia, declaring themselves a new state, West Virginia.) Unnerved by the clashes of arms and Lincoln's military buildup, Arkansas, Tennessee, and North Carolina followed suit in May, bringing the number of Confederate states to eleven.

Four slave states—Delaware, Maryland, Kentucky, and Missouri—did not secede and instead sent thousands of troops to the Union army. These states were not major cotton producers; rather, they grew tobacco and other crops, mostly on small farms. With large free black populations and relatively few slaves, these states had already adjusted to the presence of considerable numbers of free black people. Accepting Lincoln's claim that he was more interested in maintaining federal authority than ending slavery—a system they were beginning to phase out anyway—these states became known as the "loyal slave states" remaining committed to the Union. Yet some individuals from these states did fight on the Confederate side.

Frederick Douglass hoped the southerners' challenge to federal authority would unleash more sweeping change. "God be praised," he wrote. "The slaveholders have saved our cause. They have exposed the throat of slavery to the keen knife of liberty." Through the early summer of 1861, Douglass persisted in believing that the "inexorable logic of events will force it upon them in the end: that the war now being waged . . . is a war for and against slavery; and that it can never be . . . put down till one or the other . . .

> "The slaveholders have saved our cause. They have exposed the throat of slavery to the keen knife of liberty." —*Frederick Douglass*

is completely destroyed." Skeptics like H. Ford Douglas noted that a federal government willing to allow "loyal" slaveholders to keep their chattel hardly demonstrated a commitment to ending slavery. Yet many African Americans shared Frederick Douglass's optimism.

Black Volunteers Rejected

Like most northerners, Lincoln felt certain that the South could not wage much of a battle. After all, the North had most of the nation's banks and industry, a better railroad system, and more than twice the South's population. It outpaced the South in firearms and in the resources to repair and replace them. European immigrants, arriving in northern cities at a rate of nearly 200,000 per year, could replenish men lost to war. Expecting quick victory, Lincoln requested recruits for only three months' duty—hardly enough time to train them, much less mount sustained warfare. Even so, many eligible white men resisted leaving their homes to pursue a war they did not care about in a region they had never seen.

But thousands of free black Americans volunteered for military service—only to be turned away. African Americans sent dozens of petitions to President Lincoln. One such plea proclaimed, "We cherish a strong attachment for the land of our birth and for our Republican Government. We are strong in numbers, in courage, and in patriotism, and . . .

we offer to you and to the nation a power and a will sufficient to conquer rebellion, and establish peace on a permanent basis." Lincoln ignored them.

When African American attorney John Mercer Langston, recently elected to Ohio's board of education, offered to raise troops, Ohio's governor David Todd responded, "Do you not know, Mr. Langston, that this is a white man's government; that white men are able to defend and protect it? When we want you colored men we will notify you." In Cincinnati, Ohio, police forced a black recruiting station to remove the American flag. "We want you . . . niggers out of this," police officers retorted. "This is a white man's war."

WAR AND FREEDOM

As free black northerners experienced a mixture of excitement and humiliation in the war's first months, Union leaders hoped that blockading southern ports and using foot soldiers to seize southern cities would bring a quick resolution to the conflict. In the summer of 1861, Union troops left Washington, DC, aiming to seize Richmond, Virginia, the Confederate capital. But on July 21, Confederate soldiers stopped them cold near Manassas Junction, less than 30 miles southwest of Washington.

The Confederacy's success at this engagement, known in the North as the Battle of Bull Run, caught Union leaders off guard. On the heels of the humiliating Manassas defeat, some black Americans again hoped Lincoln would use black people to buttress the Union offense. Again, they were turned away. Not until 1863 would official black Union regiments form, even then serving under white officers who often doubted black soldiers' courage and ability.

Most white northerners shared Lincoln's conviction that assembling black troops was a bad idea. Some worried that black soldiers would be cowardly and undisciplined. Others feared that armed black men would present a threat to white civilians. Thus, when southern slaves first began escaping into Union camps, they were returned to their owners.

Slaves as Contraband

The rejection of black men by the army changed within weeks of the firing on Fort Sumter. In May 1861, fugitive slaves began arriving at Union general Benjamin Butler's camp at Fort Monroe, near Hampton Roads, Virginia.

During the Civil War, a federal power struggle ensued among the military, Congress, president, and Supreme Court on the status of slaves and Confederate lands.

Date	Military	Congress	Presidency	Supreme Court
1861	General Benjamin Butler accepts freed slaves at Union army post in Hampton Roads, Virginia, declaring them "contraband." General Benjamin Butler declares fugitive slaves in Georgia, Florida, and South Carolina to be free.	Congressional Confiscation Act seizes Confederate's farms, and frees all slaves employed by Confederate military; abolishes slavery in District of Columbia.	Lincoln reverses Butler's emancipation order.	Supreme Court rules that wartime exigency allows the president to institute a blockade of southern ports, and that the president and military can suspend the right of *habeas corpus*.
1862	Over Lincoln's disapproval, General David Hunter organizes freemen into First South Carolina volunteers.	In response to Lincoln's Constitutional concerns, Congress amends Confiscation Act, allowing confiscated land to revert to heirs of Confederates.	Lincoln objects to congressional plan to confiscate land, on grounds that it would deprive heirs of their rightful inheritance.	
1863	General John Frémont frees slaves of Missouri residents who are in rebellion.	Congress refuses to seat Arkansas and Louisiana representatives pardoned by Lincoln.	Lincoln reverses General Frémont's order freeing Missouri slaves. Lincoln issues Emancipation Proclamation, abolishing slavery in states still in rebellion, but promises amnesty to southern states where 10% of citizens take loyalty oaths, and state agrees to free slaves. Lincoln offers amnesty to states that comply with loyalty-oath requirements; Arkansas and Louisiana comply.	
1864	Sherman's "Field Order #15" designates 80,000 acres of confiscated land in South Carolina for rent or purchase by freedmen. Military field officers claim right to try civilians.	Congress passes Wade-Davis Bill, requiring that, for readmission, a majority of a Confederate states' citizens must swear allegiance to Union.	Lincoln pocket-vetoes Wade-Davis Bill.	In *Ex Parte Vallandighan*, Supreme Court refuses to rule on whether military has wartime jurisdiction in civilian offenses.
1865		Congress establishes Freedmen's Bureau. Congress refuses to seat ex-Confederates who have not sworn allegiance to the Union. Congress passes Thirteenth Amendment, abolishing slavery in *all states* and territories. It is ratified by 27 states.	Andrew Johnson grants "amnesty and pardon" to most Confederate citizens, restoring their confiscated land, and exiling thousands of black farmers from their land.	

Declaring the slaves "contraband"—enemy property seized in war—Butler put them to work. By July, the camp at Fort Monroe had more than 900 black men and women. Returning these people to their owners was counterproductive, Butler reasoned, as their labor would only assist the enemy. But Butler also had larger plans and began talking about "the effect of war upon [the slaves'] status." He suggested to the secretary of war that planters who joined the Confederate army had abandoned their human property. "Have [slaves] not assumed the condition [i.e., freedom] which we hold to be the normal one of those made in God's image?" he asked.

Butler was not alone in thinking that war transformed the status of slaves. From his command in the Army of the West, General John C. Frémont, an abolitionist, harbored similar notions. Declaring military law in Missouri in August 1861, Frémont proclaimed that "real and personal property of those who shall take up arms against the United States . . . is declared confiscated, and their slaves are hereby declared free men." Lincoln reversed this policy and promptly removed Frémont from command. But Congress soon passed the Confiscation Act, specifying that any slaves used in Confederate forces would automatically gain their freedom. Through the summer of 1861, field commanders followed Frémont's example, liberating thousands of slaves and employing them as cooks, laborers, spies, and sometimes as armed soldiers.

Meanwhile, local communities made their own military plans. By the end of 1861, the First Kansas Colored Infantry had organized, consisting of Native Americans, slaves, and black fugitives. Originally formed as a Confederate regiment, the First Kansas was led by a slaveholding Cherokee who soon concluded that the Union was the likely victor. Transferring his loyalties to the Union, he declared his unit open to "all persons, without reference to color . . . willing to fight for the American flag." In 1862, Union general David Hunter, in charge of captured coastal areas of South Carolina, ignored official orders and organized the First South Carolina Volunteers, the Union's first all-black fighting unit comprising primarily ex-slaves. In Kentucky, a "general stampede" of slaves (as one white officer described it) arrived at Hart County's Camp Nevin. The Union officers returned a few to their own-

ers but soon established contraband camps for others, putting them to work building fortifications. When the army moved on, these workers accompanied them and began to move onto the battlefield.

New Roles for Southern Slaves

In spring 1862, when Joseph Davis heard that Union forces had seized New Orleans, he abandoned Hurricane Plantation near Vicksburg, Mississippi, leaving it in the hands of his trusted slave, Ben Montgomery. Montgomery wrote regularly to Davis, who took up residence near Jackson, Mississippi. Montgomery reported that some slaves had gone to Vicksburg to help Union soldiers build fortifications; others had simply disappeared, but many remained on the plantation. In June, Union forces swept through Hurricane, destroying what remained of the previous year's cotton crop. With commerce at a standstill, food supplies dwindled, and disease ravaged the plantation. Montgomery survived by starting a small business, tanning leather and making shoes to sell to neighbors. When Union admiral David D. Porter arrived at Hurricane in the spring of 1863, he spotted Montgomery and his talented son, Isaiah, and set them to repairing machines on Union boats. But he soon judged them too valuable to risk being injured in warfare, and he sent them north to Ohio.

Some slaves cast their lot with the Confederacy. Hearing stories of Yankee cruelty, or worried about reprisals if the South won the war, many chose to remain in familiar surroundings or went to war as servants to masters they knew and trusted. Others were pressed to remain with their masters. One former Virginia slave reported that his master, seeing slaves escape across the Potomac River, shipped him from his coastal home to the Blue Ridge Mountains to help build the Confederates' Virginia Central Railroad. Another black Virginian reported being "put to work . . . felling trees across the highway [from Washington to Richmond] for the purpose of holding up the Yanks." By 1865, as Confederate leaders contemplated defeat, some grew desperate enough to recruit black regiments—promising freedom to those who helped defend the South.

Like Ben Montgomery, many black people, free and enslaved, remained in the South but undertook new endeavors. In Kentucky in 1862, a black man known only as Mr. Bradwell, who purchased his freedom years before, organized his slave neighbors to grow and sell livestock and produce. The group raised $700 to erect their own Methodist church building.

But many bondspeople took the risky step of fleeing their masters. A Georgia slave who had secretly learned to read escaped to the Union lines in 1862. Years later, she recalled how she "had been reading so much about the 'Yankees' and was . . . anxious to see them. The [southern] whites would tell their colored people not to go to the Yankees, for they would harness them to carts . . . in place of horses . . . [but] my grandmother . . . [said] that the white

 **First Person**

A Slave Remembers Choosing Freedom

In the excerpt below, Mill, a Mississippi slave, remembered her liberation day. Like many slaves, Mill weighed the risk of staying in place or fleeing with Union soldiers.

One day [my mistress] say, "Mill, I reckon that's a gunboat comin'. Now if the Yankees do stop you all run and hide, and tell all the niggers in the quarters to run to the woods an' hide, because [the Yankees] kills niggers."

I said, "I ain't feared the Yankees."

[The mistress said,] "Now Mill you won't go with them, will you?"

I felt safe and said, "I'll go if I have a chance."

[The mistress] began to wring her hands and cry. "Now, remember, I brought you up. You won't take your children away from me, will you Mill?"

"Mistress, I shall take what children I've got lef'."

Here come four sojers [soldiers] with swords hangin' at their sides, and never looked at mistress, but said to me, "Auntie, you want to go with us?"

"Yes, sir," I said. An' we all go on the boat in a hurry, and when we's fairly out in the middle of the river, we all give three times three cheers for the gunboat boys, and three times three cheers for big Yankee sojers, an' three times three cheers for gov'ment; and I tell you every one of us, big and little, cheered loud and long and strong, an' made the old river just ring ag'in.

—*from* The Liberator, *August 22, 1862.*

To view a longer version of this document, please go to *www.ablongman.com/carson/documents*.

people did not want slaves to go over to the Yankees and told them those things to frighten them. . . . I heard that the Yankee was going to set all the slaves free." One Louisiana house servant and his mother stole a mule from their master and "traveled eighteen miles to a plantation known as the Orphans' Home, where the Yankees had a camp." In May 1862, South Carolina's Robert Smalls, who had gained experience as a steamboat pilot while in slavery, stowed his family aboard the Charleston steamship *Planter* and delivered the ship to Union naval forces near Charleston. The Union converted the *Planter* to a warship and appointed Smalls captain.

The Port Royal Experiment

Early in 1862, the Union army invaded the Sea Islands off the coast of South Carolina. The few white islanders fled, abandoning meals cooking in their kitchens, crops ripening in the fields, and thousands of bewildered slaves. As Union leaders debated whether to treat the slaves as contraband or as recruits, northern abolitionists stepped into the vacuum. They estab-

lished themselves in Port Royal, the largest of the Sea Islands, bringing with them food, clothing, and volunteer teachers.

Many northern African Americans joined the effort. Twenty-four-year-old Charlotte Forten, from a free black family in Philadelphia, arrived at Port Royal in October 1862. She recorded her excitement as she "commenced teaching the children [the song] 'John Brown' . . . [and] felt the full significance of that song being sung here . . . by little negro children . . . whom the glorious old man died to save."

Federal officials encouraged educational efforts in Port Royal, but they also saw commercial opportunities. They hired the black residents to cultivate cotton, which the government could sell abroad and to northern factories. Ex-slaves were angry to discover that "freedom" meant only more of the familiar backbreaking labor. One black woman, hoeing cotton at Port Royal under the new wage system, complained to a Union agent that the New England manager of her plantation gave her *less* clothing, shoes, and food than had her former master.

The years after the war came to be known as Reconstruction—the rebuilding of the South. As one historian has

■ Organizations sponsored by northern philanthropists sent young women into the South to teach black people. Though one black volunteer wrote proudly, "We think it noble work, and will do it nobly," some observers have commented that the black teachers in this photograph seem to be marginalized as the white people take center stage.

described it, the Port Royal scenario became a "rehearsal for Reconstruction"; the regimen introduced there was repeated in numerous communities throughout the South as Union forces liberated one area after another. Northerners, both black and white, showed up to help slaves with the transition to freedom. However, these northerners envisioned what one observer called "a happy and contented peasantry; of black people working the fields by day, learning to read in the evenings, and spending weekends in prayer and domestic work." Under this strict Union regimen of education and manual labor, many slaves felt that so-called freedom had not changed their lives much.

Indeed, this perception on the part of slaves was justified. In Mississippi, in the winter of 1863, Admiral David D. Porter began setting up contraband camps similar to the Port Royal experiment. Camped a few miles from Hurricane Plantation, the admiral invited Quaker missionaries to set up schools, and he pressed black refugees into tilling confiscated land to feed Union troops. While a few freed people saw battle under Porter's supervision, most worked as unpaid or underpaid laborers. In this Mississippi outpost, more than one-third of the black population died as malnutrition and poor sanitation lowered resistance to pneumonia, smallpox, measles, and malaria.

EMANCIPATION AS MILITARY AND POLITICAL STRATEGY

In the summer of 1862, Frederick Douglass wrote to Charles Sumner, a white abolitionist and former Massa-

chusetts senator, "The events taking place seem like a dream." He was describing a series of federal policies gradually overriding Lincoln's official position that the war was not about ending slavery. As the war dragged on, undermining slavery became both a goal of the war and a strategy for weakening the South. After repeated battlefield defeats, congressional leaders agreed with General Benjamin Butler: Returning slaves to their masters only aided the enemy. In the spring of 1862, Congress forbade commanders to return captured or fugitive slaves.

Emancipation Possibilities

As the war unfolded, Union leaders confronted thorny challenges. How would they mount a long-distance military campaign to reestablish federal control over the South? How would they maintain confidence in federal authority among states loyal to the Union? How would they dissuade foreign nations—some of which depended on southern cotton—from taking the Confederate side? By 1862, Union officials concluded that African Americans could have immense strategic value in dealing with these challenges.

Throughout 1862, Lincoln tried to strike a balance between keeping northern abolitionists' support and persuading the South to cease hostilities—all while trying to avoid alienating slave states loyal to the Union. Moreover, many northern white Americans who opposed slavery made it clear they did not want black people as social or political equals. Lincoln could not afford to alienate people whose sons he needed to win the war. Walking a tightrope, Lincoln proposed that the federal government free slaves and compensate their masters. Congress voted him down.

Now dominated by strongly reformist Republicans, Congress set out to define black Americans as people rather than property. These legislators strived to impose federal power on the South and elevate black people's legal status. In a symbolic move, Congress abolished slavery in the District of Columbia—the only area of the United States where it had the power to do so. With similar symbolism, Congress established diplomatic relations with Haiti and Liberia, two black nations ruled by former slaves. Then the secretary of state, responding to British criticism of the government's treatment of black people, made a public event of issuing a passport to Henry Highland Garnet, explicitly designating this black man a *"citizen of the United States."* A well-known black Bostonian, William C. Nell, was appointed a postal clerk, becoming the first African American to hold a federal civilian appointment. Lincoln even signed a second Confiscation Act, freeing any slave entering Union-held territory and allowing Union soldiers to seize "all property"—including slaves—in areas they captured.

To be sure, each of these events was a token—one that exempted states that remained loyal to the Union. Yet each move constituted a small step toward eroding slavery and elevating free African Americans. Black hopes were raised. When slavery was banned in the nation's capital, the editor of New York's *Anglo-African* exulted, "Henceforth, whatever betide the nation, its physical heart [Washington, DC] is freed from the presence of slavery." Simultaneously, abolitionists increasingly drew encouragement from the international community—especially Britain, which had abolished slavery three decades before.

Throughout 1862, Lincoln made clumsy overtures toward African Americans. He reiterated his abhorrence of slavery but insisted his goal was holding the nation together, not ending slavery. He continued to reject black military volunteers. Frederick Douglass described the Republican administration as "fighting the war with only one hand," implying that black troops were the other hand. In August,

Lincoln invited Douglass and several other black leaders to the White House. Douglass anticipated a discussion about abolition and black soldiers, but Lincoln only suggested relocating slaves—and any interested free black people—to Central America. Feeling betrayed by that White House meeting, Douglass's hopes turned to bitterness: "Abraham Lincoln is . . . the miserable tool of traitors and rebels. . . . [He] seems to possess an ever increasing passion for making himself appear silly and ridiculous." But Douglass's son Lewis became one of several hundred African Americans who volunteered to relocate to Chiriqui, in today's Panama.

Some black Americans grew increasingly skeptical of all federal policy. They knew that Secretary of State William Henry Seward had recognized Henry Highland Garnet as a citizen only after Garnet endorsed Lincoln's plan to remove black people from the United States. Many black leaders believed William C. Nell's appointment as a postal clerk in Massachusetts came only because the state had an abolitionist governor. Disillusioned and frustrated, northern black leaders debated strategy.

A few prominent African Americans insisted black people should not fight in a war that ultimately would not free slaves. Others imagined places abroad where black people might find better opportunities. Uncharacteristically, Frederick Douglass considered moving to Haiti. But Martin Delany, declaring Haiti "a small island, with no prospect of additional territory," favored "Africa . . . a vast continent peopled by one of the great, enduring . . . absorbing races of the earth." Hoping to gather recruits for African resettlement, Delany criss-crossed the North and West, leaving his wife in Canada with their new baby. Others also supported emigration. "If this war should result in the abolition of slavery, as we hope it may . . . it will not ameliorate the condition of the free black man one iota. . . . The scanty pittance of social toleration which is here and there grudgingly doled out to us . . . illustrat[es] the more strikingly the rule which everywhere excludes us," the *Weekly Anglo African* quoted one black New Yorker.

Like Philadelphian Isaiah Wears, the majority of black people yearned to fight for justice in the America of their birth. In a black newspaper, Wears proclaimed his opinion in crystal-clear terms: "To be asked, after so many years of oppression . . . by a [white] people who have been so largely enriched by the black man's toil, to pull up stakes . . . and go . . . simply to gratify . . . [a] wicked prejudice emanating from slavery, is unreasonable and anti-Christian."

Fredrick Douglass agreed. After considering emigration, he announced his decision to stay in the United States and proclaimed publicly his right to do so. Others joined in. Sarah Remond, the fiery sister of black abolitionist Charles Remond, spent much of 1862 encouraging British abolitionists who were urging their government not to side with the South. She implored, "Let no diplomacy of statesmen, no intimidation of slaveholders, no scarcity of cotton, no fear of slave insurrections, prevent the people of Great Britain from maintaining their position as the friend of the oppressed negro."

The Emancipation Proclamation

The battle of Antietam finally prompted Lincoln to stop waffling on the fate of slaves. By mid-1862, the Union navy had blockaded southern seaports and captured Memphis and New Orleans. With Union commanders poised to control the Mississippi River, Confederate general Robert E. Lee tried to push the war into the North to disrupt railroad lines that supplied Washington, DC. On September 17, Lee's troops entered Maryland, where Union troops, led by General George McClellan, met them at Sharpsburg, on Antietam Creek. The bloodiest one-day battle of the war ensued; more than 22,000 soldiers perished or suffered injuries.

Lee retreated to Virginia. Had McClellan pursued Lee, he might have won a decisive victory. But the Union general, characteristically timid and slow to act, missed his chance. Nonetheless, in stopping Lee's advance, the Antietam battle was viewed as a defeat for the South. England and France now definitively abandoned the southern cause. More significantly, the battle moved the cautious Lincoln to action. First, he removed McClellan from duty. Second, on September 22, the president surprised the nation by issuing a proclamation offering a provisional promise of freedom to slaves in the Confederate states.

In this preliminary emancipation proclamation, Lincoln chose his words carefully. Emphasizing that he was not planning to free slaves in states loyal to the Union, he promised that any Confederate state that rejoined the Union by January 1, 1863 would also be allowed to retain slavery. The effect was the freeing of slaves only in areas where the Union had no control. Moreover, the order would not take effect if the war ended before January 1, 1863. Though aware of the promise's limitations, Frederick Douglass made the best of it: "We shout for joy that we live to record this righteous decree."

Still advocating African American emigration, Lincoln persuaded Congress to appropriate funds for implementing the plan. Yet many black men and women preferred to aid the Union and to advance the cause of black freedom in the United States. Dozens of black women labored alongside Clara Barton, nursing wounded soldiers in Baltimore. Fugitive slave leader Harriet Tubman returned to the South as both nurse and spy, her information helping secure a Union victory at the Combahee River. Tubman reported that one slave woman rejoiced, "Oh! Praise de Lord! I'd prayed seventy-three years, and now he's come and we's all free." Mary Elizabeth Bowser, a literate servant in the Confederate presidential mansion, feigned mental illness to gain access to Jefferson Davis's military secrets, which she passed to Union officers. Meanwhile, in Washington, DC, Elizabeth Keckley, a free black seamstress employed by President Lincoln's wife, helped raise relief money for southern black people. "If the white people can give festivals to raise funds for the relief of suffering soldiers, why should not the well-to-do colored people . . . do something for . . . suffering blacks? The next Sunday I made a suggestion in the colored church," Keckley said, "and in two weeks the 'Contraband Relief Association' was organized, with forty working members." This was one of dozens of black groups that raised money for southern contraband camps.

Despite its limitations, Lincoln's emancipation promise lifted black spirits. In New Orleans, where the newspaper *L'Union* served a vibrant mixed-race community, an editorial urged readers to drop "the craven behavior of bondage." The writer exhorted black people to "stand up under the noble flag of the union." One black observer recalled that in Washington, DC, "men squealed, women fainted, dogs barked, songs were sung, and cannons began to fire at the navy yard." Philadelphia's *Christian Recorder* thanked "God and President Lincoln" even while the editor expressed his hope that "Congress will do something for those poor souls [slaves] who will still remain in degradation."

Meanwhile, the fighting dragged on. In December 1862, when Union troops made another attempt to capture Richmond, they met resounding defeat at Fredericksburg, Virginia. As the year ended, southern leaders declared the Confederate states would not return to the Union; they intended to continue fighting.

On January 1, 1863, as promised, Lincoln declared that any slave living in Confederate territory was "then, thenceforward, and forever free." One Virginia slave remembered the day: "It was wintertime and mighty cold, but we danced and sang right out in the cold . . . then we [left the plantation, carrying blankets and pots and pans and chickens piled on our backs." In Port Royal, where black Americans jubilantly read aloud the new order, Charlotte Forten called this "the most glorious day this nation has yet seen." She wrote, "I was in such a state of excitement. It all seemed . . . like a brilliant dream." The news traveled throughout the slave South: Lincoln might finally liberate slaves—if the North could win the war.

"MEN OF COLOR, TO ARMS!"

Martin Delany responded to the Emancipation Proclamation by proposing the "Corps D'Afrique," a private black army to aid Union forces. But before he could organize it, Lincoln admitted that the "white man's war" lacked enough white recruits and authorized Massachusetts governor John Andrew to raise the first northern black regiment. Thus was born the Massachusetts Fifty-fourth Regiment. Andrew sent a team of black leaders to recruit in other Union states. With renewed hope, Delany joined the recruitment team.

Long sidelined, black men could now contribute to the Union effort. But many white northerners doubted African Americans could make competent soldiers. Even some white abolitionists found it easier to envision Harriet Beecher Stowe's meek Uncle Tom than rebels like Nat Turner or Denmark Vesey. One northern reformer at Port Royal, appalled at General David Hunter's plans for a southern black regiment, wrote, "Plantation negroes will never make soldiers. . . . Five white men could put a [black] regiment to flight."

Arriving at Port Royal in November 1862, Colonel Thomas Wentworth Higginson believed in the courage of black soldiers. A white Massachusetts abolitionist and Unitarian minister, Higginson ignored his West Point comrades' warning that commanding black troops would destroy his career. He insisted that "it needs but a few days to show the absurdity of doubting the equal military availability of these people, as compared with whites. There is quite as much . . . courage . . . as much previous knowledge of the gun, & there is readiness of the ear."

United after the Emancipation Proclamation, black leaders recruited black men to the war effort. Burying their philosophical differences, they carried posters summoning "Men of Color, To Arms!" A few black Americans hung back from military service, agreeing with Robert Johnson, a member of the audience at a New York City recruitment lecture who insisted that black Americans should withhold support until the government offered citizenship. Many more signed on, energized by rhetoric like this New York *Anglo-African* editorial:

> Should we not with two centuries of cruel wrong stirring our heart's blood, be but too willing to embrace any chance to settle accounts with the slaveholders? . . . Can you ask any more than a chance to drive bayonet or bullet into the slaveholders' hearts?

Across the United States, black speakers urged black men to answer the call to arms. Sarah Woodson, sister of reformer Lewis Woodson, urged listeners "to accept the means which God has placed in your power," proclaiming that "the voice of millions, who are perishing without a ray of intellectual light, call upon you." New York minister J. W. C. Pennington agreed: "The only wise and safe course is to [join the army and] press rapidly into the heart of the slave country, and [secure] the Proclamation of freedom."

Black communities sent more than 180,000 black enlisted men and over 7,000 officers to Union service; this constituted 10 percent of the North's total fighting force. Most of these volunteers came from unremarkable circumstances, but sons of renowned black leaders also came forth to stand beside sons of the unknown. Alongside Martin Delany's seventeen-year-old son Toussaint L'Ouverture Delany marched Frederick Douglass's sons Lewis and Charles. Sojourner Truth sent off her grandson James Caldwell, observing wryly that

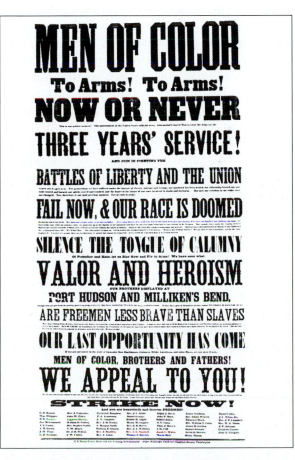

■ Recruiters carried this poster, which stood as tall as 8 feet and was endorsed by nearly five dozen nationally known black leaders, to enlist black soldiers.

this was yet another example of how "the niggers always have to clean up after the white folks." Even as they worried that if captured they would be immediately killed, black men volunteered in record numbers.

Colored Troops

At Camp Meigs near Boston, the Massachusetts Fifty-fourth received just two months' training before heading south in July 1863 to launch a night attack on Fort Wagner, in the Charleston harbor. Led into battle by their young white colonel, Robert Gould Shaw, the black regiment withstood relentless shelling that left Shaw and many others dead or wounded.

Though the Massachusetts Fifty-fourth did not win its first battle, its battlefield performance earned wide recognition. As a result of his bravery at Fort Wagner, Sergeant William Carney was the first black serviceman to be awarded the Congressional Medal of Honor, the military's new medal. To Toussaint L'Ouverture Delany, Fort Wagner brought injuries from which he never recovered. Poet Frances Ellen Watkins Harper captured the moment in a poem: "Bearers of a high commission; To break each brother's chain; With hearts aglow for freedom, They bore the toil and pain." The *New York Tribune* wrote that the regiment "made Fort Wagner such a name to the colored race as Bunker Hill has been for ninety years to the white Yankees."

Other black regiments demonstrated similar battlefield bravery. Louisiana's First and Third Native Guards helped establish Union control at Port Hudson, near Vicksburg, Mississippi, in May 1863, thereby splitting the Confederacy. Meanwhile, at Milliken's Bend, also near Vicksburg, three black regiments held off a division of Texans. These battles resoundingly demonstrated the courage and discipline of African Americans. One black observer wrote, "The bravery displayed before Port Hudson [Louisiana, 27 May] by the colored troops was applaudingly received here by persons who have not been looked upon as friendly to the movement [of raising black troops]."

By summer 1863, support for black soldiers emerged from surprising places. Sidestepping her pacifist beliefs, white Quaker abolitionist Lucretia Mott offered her farm near Philadelphia to house a training camp for black recruits. In Ohio, the same Governor Todd who had rebuffed John Mercer Langston's offer of aid now requested his help in recruiting.

Northern black soldiers took great pride in their regiments. Before setting off into battle, the Sixth Colored Infantry dedicated their regimental flag. "Soldiers," the speaker urged, "under this flag let your rallying cry be 'for God, for freedom,

and our country.' If for this you must fall, you fall the country's patriots, heroes, and martyrs." While the regimental flag served as a battlefield marker, it also held symbolic meaning, binding soldiers together. The Sixth carried its regimental flag into battle at Petersburg, Dutch Gap, and New Market Heights in Virginia; at Fort Fisher, in Wilmington, North Carolina; and at the Battle of Olustee in the Florida swamps. The flag's symbolic meaning extended beyond the battlefield and indeed far beyond the war. When the Sixth

> "Under this flag let your rallying cry be 'for God, for freedom, and our country.'"
> —*Black soldier*

mustered out at war's end, its banner had been reduced to tatters. Still, Sergeant Major Thomas Hawkins was honored to have his comrades award it to him. His country had awarded him a Congressional Medal of Honor, but he had also earned the flag, his comrades said. Though wounded in the battle at New Market Heights, Hawkins had seized the flag from a fallen soldier and borne it safely from the field. At war's end, the flag dropped out of public view, only to make a triumphant reappearance during the late twentieth century. Now residing in a museum, the regimental flag helps Americans remember the part played by African American patriots and heroes in the preservation of the Union.

Yet military service did not necessarily bring glory. Black soldiers often received the most onerous assignments, including performing longer guard duty and setting up camps and embattlements. Others were relegated to manual tasks of construction, growing food, or tending livestock. Thus, for many black men, war continued the endless drudgery they endured under slavery.

For the most unfortunate, survival on the battlefield might be followed by capture by the Confederate army, which had a policy of defining black prisoners as "insurrectionists" and killing them rather than holding them in prison camps. The most notorious case of this became known—after Congress launched an investigation—as the Fort Pillow Massacre. In this incident, which occurred on April 12, 1864, at a Union outpost in Mississippi, more than 300 Union soldiers were massacred after they surrendered.

The Fight for Equal Pay

Black recruits often earned less than half the pay of white soldiers. In August 1863, Frederick Douglass beseeched President Lincoln to countermand this blatant inequity. As Douglass later recalled, Lincoln replied that because black soldiers were "a serious offense to popular prejudice, [pay

■ These pictures show the transformation of a slave into a freedman. After Contraband Jackson fled to the Union army, he was mustered into the 79th U.S. Colored Troops as Drummer Jackson. Abolitionists produced such visual renditions to show how changes in clothing and occupation transformed African Americans' posture, facial expression, and confidence.

inequity] seemed a necessary concession to smooth the way to their employment at all as soldiers, but that ultimately they would receive the same."

Meanwhile, black soldiers at the front petitioned Secretary of War Edwin Stanton. In the fall of 1863, the Massachusetts Fifty-fourth refused to accept any pay until their earnings equaled those of white soldiers. One regiment member stated, "We were mustered in for pay [but refusing] to acknowledge ourselves different from other Massachusetts soldiers [we refused unequal pay]. Four months we have been working night and day under fire . . . patiently, waiting for justice." After more than a year of pressure from northern abolitionists and the horror of black sacrifice at Fort Pillow, Congress passed legislation equalizing pay in June 1864.

War's Impact on Black Women

As the Civil War disrupted southern households, many black women and children were set adrift. It was one thing for the Union army to offer sanctuary to able-bodied black men, who were useful to the war effort; it was quite another to offer aid to wives and children who were not. Though one black army widow reported that "the [Union] officers let me live in a tent with my husband," she was a rare exception. Most Union officers, convinced the presence of women and children undermined discipline, allowed wives to visit only occasionally, if at all. Yet as large numbers of black women, some with children, arrived at Union camps, sometimes white troops put the women to work in the fields alongside the men. Because many slave women could not read or sew, they did not conform to northern white men's idea of "ladies." Thus the military treated some of them like men, assigning them heavy labor. Other women worked as cooks, nurses, or livestock tenders. Discovering they might be separated from their husbands or assigned housekeeping duties for white people, some black women collected their families and traveled to nearby towns where Confederates paid for such services.

Single or widowed women often accepted help from northern relief agencies, or tried to fend for themselves.

 **First Person**   ## A Black Soldier Petitions for Equal Pay

In 1863, James Henry Gooding of Massachusetts, a recruit to the Massachusetts Fifty-fourth Colored Regiment, wrote to President Lincoln to demand better pay for black soldiers. His argument is based, in part, on his belief that the experience of freedom had elevated northern black men to a status above those who had recently been slaves and that the federal government should recognize this difference. Wounded in the February 1864 Battle of Olustee in Florida, Gooding was captured by Confederates and held as a prisoner of war.

Camp of the 54th Mass. Colored Reg. Morris Island Dept. of the South. Sept. 28, 1863.
Your Excellency, Abraham Lincoln:

Your Excellency will pardon the presumption of an humble individual like myself, in addressing you, but the earnest Solicitation of my Comrades in Arms beside the genuine interest felt by myself in the matter is my excuse. . . . The main question is, Are we Soldiers, or are we Labourers? We are fully armed, and equipped, have done all the various Duties pertaining to a Soldier's life, have conducted ourselves to the complete satisfaction of General Officers, who were, if anything, prejudiced against us, but who now [after Fort Wagner] afford us all the encouragement and honor due us. . . .

Now, your Excellency, we have done a Soldier's Duty. Why Can't we have a Soldier's pay?

We of this Regt. were not enlisted under any "contraband" act. But we do not wish to be understood as rating our Service of more Value to the Government than the service of the ex-slave. Their Service is undoubtedly worth much to the Nation, but Congress made express provision touching their case, as slaves freed by military necessity, and assuming the Government to be their temporary Guardian. Not so with us. Freemen by birth . . . we do not consider ourselves fit subject for the Contraband act.

We appeal to you, Sir, . . . to have us justly Dealt with. . . . We feel as though our Country spurned us, now that we are sworn to serve her. Please give this a moment's attention.

—*letter by James Henry Gooding, September 28, 1863.*

To view a longer version of this document, please go to *www.ablongman.com/carson/documents*.

Nearly 6,000 Natchez, Mississippi, black women were dependent on American Missionary Association philanthropy or on funds raised by northern black women to help with relief and education. In formal contraband camps, women seldom received the promised wages for farming, cooking, and laundry services. Other women huddled in camps outside towns, vulnerable to Confederate raids and to Union officers who might coerce them onto abandoned plantations to grow food for Union soldiers. One woman, probably typical of many, reported trading sex for pay because "we women had to make a living." Still, some women recently freed from slavery, even during the war, were able to find paid work, save money, and sometimes even buy a home.

1863: THE TIDE TURNS

After a costly loss to the Confederates at Chancellorsville, Virginia, in May 1863, Union general Ulysses Grant won five victories in a three-week period. By mid-1863, a Union victory was within reach. But soldiers were needed to solidify that victory, and a surprisingly strong resistance to the newly instituted draft emerged in the North.

Victory at Gettysburg

In July 1863, as Confederate general Richard Ewell led his cavalry north toward Pennsylvania cities, Lincoln's call for

 **First Person**   ## Joseph Miller Describes Camp Life

In joining the Union army, ex-slaves often had no choice but to take their families into the hardships of military life as well. Joseph Miller reported his family's experience at Camp Nelson, Kentucky, when Union officers decided to expel women and children.

My wife and children came with me, because my master said that if I enlisted he would not maintain them, and I knew they would be abused by him when I left. . . . On presenting myself as a recruit, I was told by the lieutenant in command to take my family into a tent within the limits of the camp. [Some days later] a mounted guard told my wife that she and her children must leave camp before early morning. . . . My wife had no place to go. I told him that I was a soldier of the United States. He told me that it did not make any difference. He told my wife and family that if

they did not get up in the wagon he would shoot the last one of them. . . . My wife and children went into the wagon. My wife carried the sick child in her arms. . . . [Later] I found my wife and children shivering with cold and famished with hunger; they had not received a morsel of food during the whole day. My son . . . died directly after getting down from the wagon.

—*from* The Liberator, *vol. 9, December 1864.*

To view a longer version of this document, please go to *www.ablongman.com/carson/documents*.

more volunteers got a quick response. In a three-day clash at Gettysburg's Cemetery Ridge, northern troops led by General George Meade shot down more than half of the Confederate troops sent into the battle. By the time Confederate forces retreated from this bloodiest battle of the war, more than 23,000 Union soldiers and 28,000 Confederates had perished or sustained grave injuries.

The Union victory at Gettysburg, which foreshadowed northern victory, shifted attitudes abroad. Now European nations definitively withdrew their support from the South. Britain canceled contracts to build warships for the Confederacy, as British dependence on northern wheat outweighed its need for southern cotton. (British merchants had begun importing cotton from India and Egypt.) Also, British popular opinion, massaged into abolitionist sympathies by dozens of antebellum black abolitionists, helped solidify this decision. Following the British lead, France, too, distanced itself from the Confederacy.

President Lincoln also bestowed symbolic importance on this battle. In November 1863, he traveled to Gettysburg to deliver his memorable address dedicating the battlefield as a cemetery. Before a somber audience, he declared the Gettysburg victory foretold "a new birth of freedom" in a

United States that had been "conceived in liberty and dedicated to the proposition that all men are created equal."

Anti-Draft Riots

Along with Union gains came setbacks, especially the difficulty finding recruits to expand the army. In the spring of 1863, Congress enacted a draft law requiring three years military service for every man between age twenty and forty-five. (Those who could pay a fee or find a substitute were exempted.) Shortly after the Gettysburg victory, when New York newspapers printed a list of draftees, hundreds of young white men rioted in New York City. Convinced that black men would take their jobs while they were off fighting, the white draftees stormed a building where a draft lottery was taking place. This fuse of unrest, once lit, smoldered for more than a week, during which mobs vandalized factories and shipyards where war supplies were manufactured or transported.

Why such resistance to the draft? The majority of the rioters were poor newcomers to the United States who also resented the draft law's provision allowing wealthier men to avoid service. Falling wages also provoked the outbursts. The military's need for supplies had inflated prices,

■ This lithograph, produced thirty years after the Battle of Olustee, attests to the conflict's enduring symbolic importance.

but earnings had not kept pace. Thus, poorly paid white factory workers, seeing their standard of living decline, were frustrated at the state of affairs. Black workers, viewed as the source of the troubles, were randomly attacked on the streets, and black neighborhoods were ravaged. Black competition lowered wages, claimed the protesters, as black workers would often settle for less money than white employees. Moreover, they resented black men and women who carved out successful lives. Mobs also vandalized factories and shipyards where war supplies were built or transported. As black New Yorkers struggled to defend themselves, more than 100 black and white people died before the government diverted troops from the battlefield to crush the uprising. In the end, Union draft officers looked the other way while fully 10 percent of young white men ignored their call or deserted after entering the army. In Detroit, Philadelphia, and other cities, as the Democratic press fanned fears of competition for

jobs, the New York scenario was played out again and again as white rioters resisted the draft and vented their anxiety on black Americans.

Grant and Sherman Lead Union Victories

By early 1864, the successes at Vicksburg and Gettysburg had solidified the North's advantage. Now black troops accompanied Union general Ulysses S. Grant when he confronted Confederate general Robert E. Lee in Virginia. "By arming the negro we have added a powerful ally," Grant told Lincoln. "They make good soldiers,

> "By arming the negro we have added a powerful ally."—*Ulysses S. Grant*

Black Soldiers on the Battlefields
- Major battle involving black soldiers
- Major city

Wrightsville
Washington DC
New Market Hts
Fort Gilmer
9/28/64
Indianapolis   Cincinnati
Richmond
Petersburg
"The Crator"
7/30/64
Louisville
Virginia   Elizabeth
City
Saltville
Island Mound
10/28/62
Mississippi
Valley
Raleigh
Sherwood
Nashville
Wilmington
Fort Pillow
4/12/64
Overton Hill
12/16/64
Columbia   Camden   Ft. Fisher
1. Cable Creek 7/1–2/63
2. Honey Springs 7/17/63   Flat Rock Creek
Moscow
Dalton   Decatur
Georgetown
Indian Territory   Fort Smith
Memphis
Brice's Crossroads
6/10/64
Atlanta
Charleston
Fort Wagner 7/18/63
Little
Rock   Tupelo
1. Poison Spring 4/18/64
2. Jenkin's Ferry 4/30/64
Camden
Montgomery
Honey Hill
11/30/64
Savannah
Mound Plantation
Jackson
Trans-Mississippi
Milliken's Bend
6/7/63
Mobile
Jacksonville
Department of the South
Pascagoula
Marianna   Tallahassee
Port Hudson
5/27/63
Baton Rouge
Fort Blakely
4/8/65
Natural Bridge
3/6/65
Olustee
2/20/64
Austin
New Orleans
San Antonio
Houston
Department of the Gulf
Indianoia
Mississippi
Valley
Brownsville
Palmitto Ranch
5/12–13/65

■ **MAP 10.2**   Black Soldiers on the Battlefields

This map shows some of the more than 200 Civil War engagements in which black soldiers participated. In all, black soldiers served in battles as far north as Maryland, as far south as Florida, and as far west as Indian Territory. A number of black men rose to the rank of sergeant during the Civil War, and more than a dozen received the Congressional Medal of Honor.

and taking them from the enemy weakens [the South] as it strengthens us." In June 1864, when Lee's forces stopped Grant's at the outskirts of Petersburg, Virginia, both sides suffered high casualties in a siege that lasted nine months.

African American soldiers also accompanied Union general William T. Sherman in May 1864 as he marched from Tennessee through Georgia to the sea and north into South Carolina in order to cut off the Upper South from the Lower South. One black Rhode Island recruit described the southern white people he encountered on this trek: "We could see signs of smothered hate [for] both our color and [our] present character as Union soldiers. But, for once [I] walked fearlessly and boldly through the streets of a southern city, without being required to take off my hat at every step, or to give all the side-walks to the planters' sons." During this eight-month campaign, Union troops systematically

destroyed everything in their path: factories, warehouses, bridges, railroads, barns, crops, and homes all went up in flames. By the time Sherman reached Savannah in December 1864, he had severed all transportation and supply routes between the Upper and the Lower South.

While Sherman swept through the South, the 1864 presidential election reminded Americans of their precarious political situation as politicians and federal officials in Washington clashed over the management of the war and slaves. Northern voters were also divided over how to handle hostilities with the Confederates. The Democratic platform called for an immediate end to the war. Even the Republicans, weary of war and worried about reelection, considered replacing Lincoln with a candidate more sympathetic to the South. Only Sherman's military victories in Georgia assured Lincoln's reelection—which he won with 55 percent of the

State	Number of Battles
Virginia	46
Louisiana	36
Mississippi	30
Arkansas	28
South Carolina	22
Tennessee	21
Alabama	13
North Carolina	12
Florida	11
Kentucky	10
Indian Territory	5
Kansas	4
Missouri	3
Georgia	2
Maryland	1
Texas	1

■ **TABLE 10.2** Black Soldiers on the Battlefield

popular vote. (Southern voters, of course, did not participate in the election.) Out of 4 million votes cast, Lincoln received just 40,000 more than his opponent, confirming that northerners had mixed feelings about the war.

"Forty Acres and a Mule"

Sherman's success marked another turning point for former slaves. In January 1865, after taking Savannah, Sherman met with a group of black ministers who petitioned for only one thing—land on which they and their people could raise food for their families. The general responded by issuing Special Field Order No. 15, granting thousands of acres of confiscated land along the Florida, Georgia, and South Carolina coast to black families in 40-acre plots. Sherman also gave them mules to work the acreage.

News of Field Order No. 15 spread quickly. Many ex-slaves and northern reformers concluded the government should provide *all* freed individuals with "40 acres and a mule." But both white and black Republican leaders disagreed. Some white leaders doubted the legality of confiscating and redistributing property. Black leaders who had worked their way up the economic ladder worried that free land grants might foster laziness and undermine the capitalist economy they now embraced. Both black and white leaders also feared that, at war's end, white resentment of land grants might reignite rioting. South Carolina's Alonzo Ransier, an African American soon to win election to the United States House of Representatives, advised people to "buy lands by saving their money, and not to expect confiscation or the possession of lands that were not theirs."

But most ex-slaves disagreed. Some suggested the states buy land at tax auction, then resell it to freedmen at reduced costs, requiring new owners to improve the land, farm it, and occupy it for a specified number of years. Modeled after the Homestead Act passed by Congress in 1862, this plan never saw the light of day. Many freed people lamented the government's lack of action. As one landless South Carolinian expressed it: "At the close of the war [we] were set free without a dollar, and without a foot of land [or] the wherewithal to get the next meal even. The labor of these people had for two hundred years cleared away the forests and produced crops that brought millions of dollars annually. . . . Did they get any portion of it? Not a cent. . . . Four million people turned loose without a dollar . . . [by those] whose duty it was to feed them. My opinion is that the government should have done it."

AN INCOMPLETE VICTORY

By the time Major Martin Delany arrived in Charleston on April 3, 1865 to organize a black fighting force, the war had nearly extinguished itself. On April 9, Confederate general Lee surrendered at Virginia's Appomattox Court House.

Across the nation, black people rejoiced. Local black soldiers hurried home with the news to West Chester, Pennsylvania, where they rang the courthouse bell. Black residents in New York celebrated with a parade. Thomas Morris Chester, the black war correspondent who had covered the war for African American newspapers, sent word to Philadelphia: "The colored population was wild with enthusiasm. Old men thanked God in a very boisterous manner, and old women shouted upon the pavement as high as they ever had done at a religious revival."

On April 14, ex-slave Robert Smalls sailed into Charleston Harbor on the steamship *Planter,* which he had stolen from Confederate ship owners early in the war. Now a gunboat captain, Smalls joined the Union flag-raising celebration at Fort Sumter—four years, almost to the day, after its fall. William Lloyd Garrison and the son of slave rebel Denmark Vesey were among the veteran abolitionists there when Martin Delany recorded the buoyant mood: "The Union flag," he said, "now symbolizes freedom for all, without distinction of race or color."

In Texas, the Union army arrived on June 19, to announce victory ("Juneteenth" celebrations still mark the day). One black Texan remembered that a woman who had fled slavery and survived in the wild for several years now had "freedom not of the swamp, but of the world." At a New Orleans Fourth of July parade in 1865, a black military officer "declared that slavery was dead and will be buried so deep that the judgment will not find it!"

First Person

Henry Highland Garnet Demands the Vote

When Henry Highland Garnet spoke before Congress—the first black man to do so—on February 12, 1865, the draft of the Thirteenth Amendment awaited state approval. In thundering tones, Garnet entreated House members to follow abolition with political rights.

[Slavery] has divided our national councils. It has engendered deadly strife between brethren. It has wasted the treasure of the Commonwealth and the lives of thousands of brave men. . . . It has caused the bloodiest civil war recorded in the book of time. It has shorn this nation of its locks of strength. . . .

It is often asked when and where will the demands of the reformers end? When emancipation shall be followed by enfranchisement, and all men holding allegiance to the government shall enjoy every right of American citizenship. When the men who endure the sufferings and the peril our country . . . shall enjoy the well-earned privilege of voting. . . . When in every respect, [the black man] shall be equal before the law, and shall be left to make his own way in the social walks of life.

—from A Memorial Discourse *by Rev. Henry Highland Garnet, Delivered in the Hall of the House of Representatives, Washington, D.C. on Sabbath, February 12, 1865.*

To view a longer version of this document, please go to *www.ablongman.com/carson/documents*.

But the idea of freedom proved more exhilarating than the reality. Freed slaves had few resources with which to provide for or protect themselves—and no power to acquire them. Across the South, state governments were in disarray, local economies had shriveled, and cities and farms lay in shambles. Black and white families alike desperately needed food, shelter, medical care, and reassurance. One black Floridian wrote, "Nobody had his bearings. The freed people had no homes and no names except such as they inherited from their owners. They [did not know] whether to rejoice because they were free or to be cast down at their new condition of . . . . responsibility and homelessness." In New Orleans, Frank Bell recalled his experience: "When war am over [the master] won't free me, says I'm valuable to him in his trade. He say, 'Nigger, you's supposed to be free but I'll pay you a dollar a week and iffen you runs off I'll kill you.'" When Nancy Johnson's master released her from his South Carolina plantation, she repeatedly sent her four hungry children back to him for food before she finally established a boardinghouse in Orangeburg, South Carolina. "I might as well stayed where I was. It 'pears we can't be free, nohow," said another black South Carolinian. "The rebs [Confederates] won't let us alone. If they can't kill us, they'll kill all our frien's."

The Assassination of President Lincoln

Within days of the South's surrender, Confederate sympathizer John Wilkes Booth shot Abraham Lincoln dead as the president attended a theater performance. Setting aside earlier disappointments with Lincoln, Martin Delany eulogized him as "the humane, the benevolent, the philanthropic, the generous, the beloved, the able, the wise, great and good President of the United States." Delany suggested a fitting memorial would be a statue depicting a kneeling African woman with tear-filled eyes cast to heaven, to be funded by a one-cent donation from every African American man, woman, and child. The work was never erected.

Other black Americans also memorialized Lincoln as their savior, helping create a legend that remained untarnished for more than a century. The black New Orleans *Tribune*, having criticized the living Lincoln, now linked him with the most radical abolitionist: "Lincoln and John Brown are two martyrs. . . . Both have willingly jeopardized their lives for the sacred cause of freedom." Black people in the South Carolina Sea Islands, where the Port Royal system still tied black people to the land, passed a resolution praising "the

Freedmen's Bureau
Locations Across the South
● Freedmen's Bureau

Ohio R.

Missouri R.

Mississippi R.

Washington, DC

Richmond ●

St. Louis ●

Raleigh ●

● Nashville

Beaufort
● ─

Atlantic
Ocean

Montgomery
●

● Vicksburg

● Tallahassee

New Orleans ●

Gulf of Mexico

■ **MAP 10.3** Freedmen's Bureau Locations Across the South

With more than two dozen regional offices and thousands of employees, the Freedmen's Bureau became the federal government's most visible presence in the postwar South.

wisdom and Christian patriotism [Lincoln] displayed" in the "most memorable act proclaiming Liberty to our race."

The Thirteenth Amendment

While Union forces seized Virginia, the Thirteenth Amendment to the U.S. Constitution, ending slavery everywhere in the United States and its territories, worked its way through Congress. By December 18, 1865, twenty-seven states (including eight in the South) had accepted the premise that "neither slavery nor involuntary servitude, except as a punishment for crime, shall exist within the United States." Congress had the "power to enforce this article." Once again, celebrations followed. In Boston, black and white abolitionists crowded into Music Hall, where William Lloyd Garrison reported being moved by the "deeply religious and moral significance" of outlawing slavery.

But the Thirteenth Amendment did not include the franchise. Even as black people celebrated, Martin Delany

exhorted them to organize for the right to vote. Augusta, Georgia's *Colored American* reported that a black convention in South Carolina called for "equal suffrage be conferred in common with white men as a protection from hostility, and because all free governments derive their power from the consent of the governed." In the North and South, Equal Rights Leagues, many led by black veterans of antebellum abolitionism, took up the franchise battle. Only the vote could safeguard the freedom promised by the Thirteenth Amendment.

Reuniting Black Families

With slavery vanquished, thousands of liberated black Americans sought lost family members. Northern and southern black newspapers published advertisements: "I have a mother somewhere in the world. I know not where. She used to belong to Philip Mathias in Elbert County, Georgia, and she left four of her children there about twenty-three years ago. . . . I ask all who read this to inquire

 **First Person**

Two Views of the Freedmen's Bureau

Freedmen's Bureau agents often viewed their mission with reverence. B. F. Randolph, whose application letter is excerpted below, is one example. An Oberlin graduate, Randolph had been chaplain of the Union army's Twenty-sixth Division. But the second letter reveals some of the flaws in the system. Black leaders petitioned in this letter for the removal of Lieutenant J. S. Powers, a white agent who had close ties to local planters.

I am desirous of obtaining a position among the freedmen where my qualifications and experience will admit of the most usefulness. I don't ask position or money. But I ask a place where I can be most useful to my race. My learning and long experience as a teacher North, and my faithful service as Chaplain demand that I seek such a place. If you should obtain for me some responsible position in the Freedmen's Bureau . . . you would never regret it.

——B. F. Randolph

We the undersigned citizens of Beaufort, S.C., believing that the Freedmen's Bureau was established for the purpose of protecting refugees and freedmen, take this opportunity to set forth the facts relative to Lieutenant J. S. Powers, officer of the Freedmen's Bureau in Beaufort. In all his dealings with freedmen, he manifests a contempt for them. . . . He uses profane language whenever they happen to get before him. He keeps them in such fear that those who have been in his office once fear to enter the second time. He kicks and strikes them whenever he desires and he thinks they will not retaliate. . . .

. . . The Freedmen have been enraged, almost to the point of rising up against him. . . . We therefore respectfully request that Lieutenant J. S. Powers be removed from our midst.

——Robert Smalls, Jonathan J. Wright, William J. Whipper. . . .

—*from* House Miscellaneous Document #52, 40th Congress, 3rd Session.

To view a longer version of this document, please go to *www.ablongman.com/carson/documents*.

---

for her. Her name was Martha and I heard that she was carried off to Mississippi by speculators."

Similar heart-wrenching appeals testified to African Americans' longing to be reunited with loved ones. Some had been separated by slave sales or war. Others hoped to locate relatives who had escaped to the North or were returning from exile. Fugitive slave James Davis, heading home from Canada, yearned to hear from his family. "Write me word how Johnny is getting on," implored his newspaper announcement. "I am in East Boston but I feel very lonesome. I don't see any colored ladies & gentlemens." From Cincinnati, Ben Montgomery and his family returned home to Hurricane Plantation in the Mississippi River delta in 1865. They reopened their old store but now served the free black farmers who leased confiscated land from the government.

The Freedmen's Bureau

In 1865, Congress established a department known as the Freedmen's Bureau. Chartered for only one year, the bureau was formed to allocate work, supplies, and abandoned and confiscated southern lands among freed black people. Bureau agents also delivered medical, educational, and legal services. Northern bureau agents helped a few white southerners set up hospitals, schools, and stores; inventory landholdings; and help black families gain their footing. The bureau assigned Martin Delany a post in South Carolina.

The federal government sent troops to impose political order in the South while the states reestablished local governments and law enforcement. But it was the Freedmen's Bureau that was charged with repairing southern social and economic order, encouraging white planters to revive their farms, urging black workers to accept the available jobs, monitoring contracts between landowners and workers, and pressing both groups to treat each other as employers and employees, not owners and property. Bureau agents followed the Port Royal model, blending education, philanthropy, and coercive labor.

As the extent of the South's devastation became clear, Congress renewed the Freedmen's Bureau charter in 1866. Bureau agents now expanded their reach, working to reunite families, helping black refugees write or read letters and newspaper advertisements for lost kin. Reuniting families sometimes involved legal battles with local and national courts, as local governments tried to replace slavery with other forms of servitude. Maryland was a typical example. The state's 1864 constitution ended slavery but established an apprenticeship system restricting black children to serving white craftsmen only and providing none of the safeguards afforded white apprentices. Craftsmen were not obliged to teach black apprentices reading, writing, or even manual skills. If a craftsman died, his apprentice could be bound to another white person without consulting the child's parents. Parents who visited apprenticed children risked arrest for trespassing. It took three years, but by 1868 the Freedmen's Bureau got the Supreme Court to outlaw Maryland's apprentice system. In the process, the bureau established African Americans' right to seek justice in the Maryland courts.

Black Codes and Sharecropping

Maryland's system of separate laws for black people was part of a larger southern legal pattern known as Black Codes. After the Civil War, the federal government restored citizenship privileges and statehood to southern states whose white leaders swore allegiance to the United States. By 1869, many Confederate states had elected new officials, returned to the Union, and begun reorganizing state governments, militia, and police. Yet most southern state officials sought to restrict black people's movement, economic and social prospects, and access to legal recourse. Alabama gave former slave owners the right of first refusal to any black child available for apprenticeship. Georgia made interracial marriage illegal. North Carolina instituted the death penalty if a black man raped a white woman; in all other instances, rapists were only fined.

Even the contracts promoted by the Freedmen's Bureau often bound black workers to repetitive tasks, long hours, low wages, or compensation in produce rather than cash. When the dream of "40 acres and a mule" evaporated, the Bureau pressured black freedmen to accept an owner-tenant relationship known as *sharecropping*. In such arrangements, a landowner provided about 40 acres and some of the seeds, farm equipment, work animals, or other supplies to plant cotton, corn, wheat, oats, or rice. In return, the tenant gave the landlord a percentage, or share, of the resulting crop.

Viewed by the Freedmen's Bureau as a way to avoid vagrancy, sharecropping encouraged blatant exploitation. Many landowners manipulated the cost of supplies to make supply prices exceed the tenant's share. This ploy kept the tenant perpetually indebted to the owner and therefore tied to the land. Other landowners found excuses to dismiss tenants just before their compensation was due. Such incidents made black people wary of entering into contracts. "I am opposed to working under a contract," wrote one black South Carolinian. "I expect to stay in the South . . . but not to hire myself to a planter. . . . I have seen some men hired who were turned off [of the land] without being paid."

Tough economic times also forced single black women into agricultural contracts. "Times are very hard, and hard to get money," wrote South Carolina ex-slave Celia Johnson in 1868, resigning herself to a farming agreement. As often as men, women suffered their employers' violent resentment of the postwar changes. One Georgia county agent reported "On the last day of January 1868 Thomas [the landowner] ordered [a freedwoman] to the field very early before she had had time to properly care of her child. She refused to go at that time and he cursed and abused her when she told him she was as free as he. On this he kicked her in the head and knocked her down seriously hurting her."

By 1869, sharecropping often worked in tandem with Black Codes. Black adults who failed to enter into contracts, or who broke them, could be arrested and imprisoned. Prisoners, in turn, were leased to farmers or commercial concerns, and the wages from their labor went to state coffers. A ball and chain attached to the ankle kept prisoners from escaping as they toiled on county roads and private railroads. Freedmen's Bureau agents declined to interfere with such practices, believing they brought order by preventing black vagrancy. But few black southerners described their new conditions as free.

Black Education

The Freedmen's Bureau was overwhelmed by land and labor issues, but it did a better job of providing some other services. Between its 1866 establishment by Congress and 1872, when Congress decided to redirect federal resources, the bureau distributed more than 21 million food rations and widespread medical care to distressed southerners, both black and white. But its most enduring influence was on

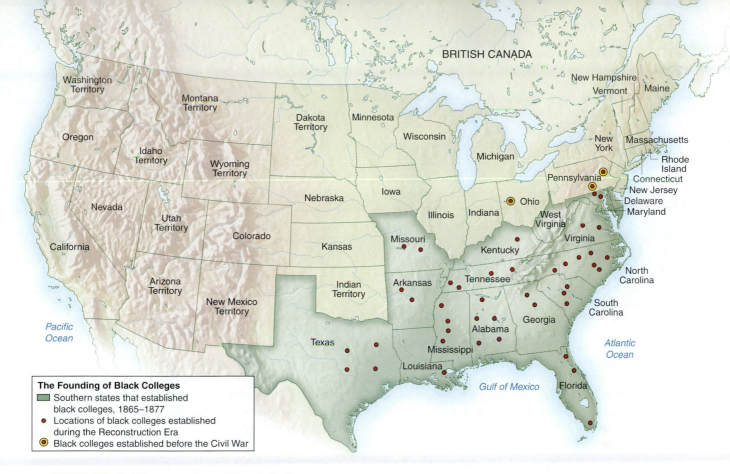

BRITISH CANADA

The Founding of Black Colleges

- Southern states that established black colleges, 1865–1877
- ● Locations of black colleges established during the Reconstruction Era
- ◉ Black colleges established before the Civil War

■ **MAP 10.4** The Founding of Black Colleges

Each of the more than three dozen black colleges founded in the postwar euphoria has a unique story. For example, when Howard University opened its "normal" (teachers) curriculum on May 1, 1867, it did so with only four students—all of them the white daughters of the school's trustees. Within three months, the student body had grown to 900—most of them black. Many black colleges, known today as HBCUs (Historically Black Colleges and Universities), still survive.

black education. Over its sixteen years of existence, it established more than 4,000 schools for former slaves, many of which survive today. One black woman reported that though she had had little interest in literacy as a slave, she was pleased to be "learning to read and figure, now."

Private organizations often helped develop black schools. In 1868, Samuel Chapman Armstrong, fresh from establishing schools for Native Americans, organized a black boarding school near Hampton Roads, Virginia. The curriculum at Hampton focused on self-discipline, hygiene, and manual skills, and aimed to produce skilled, responsible workers.

Other schools adopted the mission of developing black leaders. Established by the Freedmen's Bureau in 1867 and named for Bureau director and Union general Oliver O. Howard, Howard University in Washington, DC, offered a rigorous and varied curriculum, including degrees in law and medicine. Lincoln University in Pennsylvania and Wilberforce in Ohio, supported by the American Mis-

sionary Association, shared Howard University's focus on liberal education.

So, too, did the innovative Berea College in Kentucky. Opened in 1858, Berea was suspended during the Civil War. Reopening in 1866, it adopted a policy similar to the one that guided Hampton: Students put their manual training to immediate use in maintaining the school's buildings and grounds. Berea's abolitionist founder, Reverend John Fee, welcomed black and white students and hired an integrated faculty. To this day, tuition is free at Berea, and graduates are expected to commit their lives to social reform ideals.

The Rise of the Ku Klux Klan

Even while black southerners pursued self-improvement, they remained aware of their white neighbors' lingering bitterness over the war, the demise of slavery, and the federal military presence in the South. In Tennessee in 1866, angry

white southerners formalized their hatred in an organization known as the Ku Klux Klan. Billing itself as the protector of the Old South's noble traditions, the Klan united resentful Confederates from many walks of life. Led by a former Confederate general, the Klan used secret codes, night raids, and threats to prevent black Americans from taking advantage of their new opportunities.

White retaliation groups like the Klan spread quickly through the South. Disguised by hoods and emboldened by fiery crosses, thousands of so-called night riders systematically threatened, maimed, or killed anyone who encouraged black people to get involved in politics. But between 1867 and 1870, southern black men gained the right to vote, while most of their northern counterparts could not legally cast a ballot. They were determined to leverage this power.

The Fourteenth Amendment

Race-based hatred showed black southerners what black northerners had long understood: True equality comes from political power only. As early as February 1862, Frederick Douglass laid out his vision of the war's outcome: "No war but an Abolition war; no peace but an Abolition peace; liberty for all, chains for none; the black man a soldier in war, a laborer in peace; a voter at the South as well as at the North; America his permanent home, and all Americans his fellow countrymen. [Then] our glory as a nation will be complete."

Following Douglass's lead, black northerners began organizing for the right to vote during the war. In 1864, more than a hundred African Americans from eighteen states came together in Syracuse, New York. This group, which included seven representatives from states still in the Confederacy, created the National Equal Rights League, insisting the war was about citizenship as well as slavery.

To secure citizenship rights for black people, the Republican Congress in 1866 proposed the Fourteenth Amendment, aimed at overriding the Supreme Court's 1857 Dred Scott decision that declared African Americans were not citizens. The amendment, proposing that "no state shall make or enforce any law which shall abridge the privileges or immunities of citizens in the United States," protected citizens' rights from violation by state governments. It also promised that "when the right to vote at any election is

denied to any of the male inhabitants of such state, . . . the representation [in Congress] shall be reduced in proportion."

To regain representation in Congress, Confederate states had to first ratify the Fourteenth Amendment. Rather than submit to a Congress dominated by northerners, seven states—North Carolina, South Carolina, Florida, Alabama, Tennessee, Arkansas, and Louisiana—joined the North in ratification by July 1868. Federal troops began to trickle out of the South. Considering its job nearly done, the Freedmen's Bureau began to close down.

But black Americans did not consider the job done. The National Equal Rights League expanded rapidly, linking New York, Michigan, Pennsylvania, and Ohio with Tennessee, Louisiana, and North Carolina. Proclaiming that "it is the duty of every colored citizen to obtain a repeal of [any state] law which disfranchises him on the soil on which he was born," members repeatedly petitioned state legislatures for the franchise implied under the Fourteenth Amendment.

Thus, securing the right to vote became paramount in the postwar years. The black editor of the Atlanta paper *Loyal Georgian* spoke for many when he wrote, "The colored man owes it to the martyrs who have fallen to procure his right to—upon their graves reared to liberty—*vote* and vote *right*. Let the Republicans of the North know the strength and character of the colored voter in the South." The *Arkansas Freeman* agreed: "The colored voters hold the power to strike out for themselves" and "demand their rights." In Mississippi, black planter

> "The colored voters hold the power to strike out for themselves."—*The* Arkansas Freeman

P. B. S. Pinchback cautioned African Americans that voting was essential "if they wanted to be men." For many decades to come, black people equated manhood with the right to go to the polls.

CONCLUSION

What began as a "white man's war" in 1861 evolved over four years into a conflict where black men fought to end slavery. Former slaves assumed leadership positions in the military, and a president who wanted to deport black people issued an Emancipation Proclamation freeing them. Congress followed with the Thirteenth Amendment to the Constitution, finally eradicating slavery. Federal soldiers, the

Freedmen's Bureau, and private agencies moved into the South to build a new society that included African Americans as free people, not slaves.

Postwar freedom brought black southerners real advances—reunited families, increased land ownership (in some regions), and rising literacy rates. The Fourteenth Amendment guaranteed citizenship to anyone born in the United States. But these advances came only in the South, and only under pressure from Congress. Moreover, freedom also brought hate groups out in the South, bent on restricting black progress.

In Washington, meanwhile, the struggle over ending slavery and defining new roles for black Americans highlighted rivalries among the legislative, judicial, and executive branches of the federal government, as well as between these units and the military. For African Americans, the struggle did not end with the war's conclusion. As we'll see in the next chapter, the federal government gradually concluded that black citizens in the North should also have the right to vote. In February 1869, when Congress proposed the Fifteenth Amendment, advocating the franchise for all black men, African Americans' hopes stirred again. Nonetheless, it required intense pressure from the federal government to ratify the amendment that made the African American man "a voter at the North as well as at the South," finally fulfilling Frederick Douglass's hope.

FURTHER READING

Adams, Virginia Matzke, Ed. *On The Altar of Freedom: a Black Soldier's Civil War Letters from the Front.* (Amherst: University of Massachusetts Press, 1991).

Blight, David. *Frederick Douglass and Abraham Lincoln: a Relationship in Language, Politics, and Memory.* (Milwaukee: Marquette University Press, 2001).

Kenner, Charles L. *Buffalo Soldiers and Officers of the Ninth Cavalry, 1867–1898* (Norman: University of Oklahoma Press, 1999).

Mabee, Carlton. *Sojourner Truth: Slave, Prophet, Legend* (New York: New York University Press, 1993).

McFeely, William. *Frederick Douglass* (New York: W. W. Norton, 1991).

McPherson, James. *The Negro's Civil War: How American Negroes Felt and Acted during the War for the Union* (New York: Pantheon, 1965).

Miller, Floyd. *The Search for a Black Nationality* (Urbana: University of Illinois Press, 1975).

O'Connor, Thomas H. *Civil War Boston: Home Front and Battlefield* (Boston: Northeastern University Press, 1997).

Redkey, Edwin S., ed., *A Grand Army of Black Men: Letters from African American Soldiers in the Union Army, 1861–1865* (Cambridge: Cambridge University Press, 1992).

Richardson, Marilyn. *Maria W. Stewart: America's First Black Woman Political Writer* (Bloomington: Indiana University Press, 1987).

Rose, Willie Lee. *Rehearsal for Reconstruction: The Port Royal Experiment* (Indianapolis: Bobbs-Merrill, 1964).

Saville, Julie. *The Work of Reconstruction: From Slave to Wage Labor in South Carolina, 1860–1870* (New York: Cambridge University Press, 1994).

Sterling, Dorothy. *The Making of an Afro-American: Martin Robison Delany, 1812–1885* (New York: Da Capo, 1996).

———. *The Trouble They Seen: Black People Tell the Story of Reconstruction* (Garden City, NY: Doubleday, 1976).

Taylor, Dudley. *The Sable Arm: Black Troops in the Union Army, 1861–1865* (Lawrence: University Press of Kansas, 1987).

Vorenberg, Michael. *Final Freedom: The Civil War, The Abolition of Slavery, and the Thirteenth Amendment.* (New York: Cambridge University Press, 2001).

Wilkie, Laurie A. *Creating Freedom: Material Culture and African American Identity at Oakley Plantation, Louisiana, 1840–1950* (Baton Rouge: Louisiana State University Press, 2000).

■ *Upland Cotton*, rendered in oil by genre painter Winslow Homer in 1879, captures the lingering power of the slave South's tragic story—cotton, race, back-breaking labor.

Post–Civil War Reconstruction: A New National Era

Emanuel Fortune Testifies Before Congress

"They always spoke very bitterly against it," said Florida Republican Emanuel Fortune, describing his white neighbors' reaction to the idea of black people voting. Those neighbors told Fortune, "The damned Republican party has put niggers to rule us, and we will not suffer it." Fortune was testifying before a congressional committee assigned to investigate Ku Klux Klan threats and violence against black southerners. After the Civil War, when anger in many southern white communities erupted in violence, some white southerners targeted black men like Fortune who organized voters or ran for office. "I got information that I would be missing some day and no one would know where I was, on account of my being a leading man in politics," Fortune recalled.

Emanuel Fortune's story typified the experience of black political leaders who emerged in the postwar period. Relatively young—Fortune was thirty-nine in 1871—these leaders were new to politics. Just a few years earlier, they had been outsiders—many of them slaves. Now they had a political voice. Fortune, for example, had participated in the 1868 constitutional convention that qualified Florida—which had been part of the Confederacy during the war—to reenter the Union by guaranteeing black suffrage and ratifying the Fourteenth Amendment. That amendment defined citizens as anyone born in the United States and guaranteed them the right to vote, to use the courts, to own property, and to be protected by all the citizens' rights outlined in the Constitution. The fact that a black man could run for office and get elected by a black constituency demonstrated those new rights. But the threats Fortune received also highlighted the risks run by southern black men who dared to claim seats at the political table. He described Jackson County, Florida, in 1869 as being in "such a state of lawlessness that my life was in danger at all times."

269

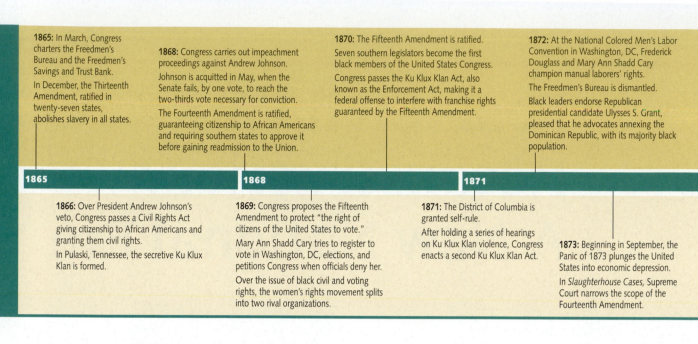

1865: In March, Congress charters the Freedmen's Bureau and the Freedmen's Savings and Trust Bank.
In December, the Thirteenth Amendment, ratified in twenty-seven states, abolishes slavery in all states.

1868: Congress carries out impeachment proceedings against Andrew Johnson. Johnson is acquitted in May, when the Senate fails, by one vote, to reach the two-thirds vote necessary for conviction.
The Fourteenth Amendment is ratified, guaranteeing citizenship to African Americans and requiring southern states to approve it before gaining readmission to the Union.

1870: The Fifteenth Amendment is ratified. Seven southern legislators become the first black members of the United States Congress.
Congress passes the Ku Klux Klan Act, also known as the Enforcement Act, making it a federal offense to interfere with franchise rights guaranteed by the Fifteenth Amendment.

1872: At the National Colored Men's Labor Convention in Washington, DC, Frederick Douglass and Mary Ann Shadd Cary champion manual laborers' rights.
The Freedmen's Bureau is dismantled.
Black leaders endorse Republican presidential candidate Ulysses S. Grant, pleased that he advocates annexing the Dominican Republic, with its majority black population.

1865 | **1868** | **1871**

1866: Over President Andrew Johnson's veto, Congress passes a Civil Rights Act giving citizenship to African Americans and granting them civil rights.
In Pulaski, Tennessee, the secretive Ku Klux Klan is formed.

1869: Congress proposes the Fifteenth Amendment to protect "the right of citizens of the United States to vote."
Mary Ann Shadd Cary tries to register to vote in Washington, DC, elections, and petitions Congress when officials deny her.
Over the issue of black civil and voting rights, the women's rights movement splits into two rival organizations.

1871: The District of Columbia is granted self-rule.
After holding a series of hearings on Ku Klux Klan violence, Congress enacts a second Ku Klux Klan Act.

1873: Beginning in September, the Panic of 1873 plunges the United States into economic depression.
In *Slaughterhouse Cases,* Supreme Court narrows the scope of the Fourteenth Amendment.

Fortune was prepared to fight back. Reputedly "a remarkably fine shot [who] practiced target shooting regularly," he was remembered by friends as a "dead shot, and he *would* shoot." He fortified his home to provide cover from an attack. Under his bedroom floor, he dug a pit from which he could open fire on intruders. Though violent threats prompted Fortune to move his family from isolated rural Jackson County to the relative safety of a black neighborhood in the city of Jacksonville, Florida, in 1870, he never relinquished his political commitment. Over the next ten years, he served as city marshal, Republican national convention delegate, county commissioner, clerk of the city market, and state congressman.

Fortune's testimony before Congress reveals the realities of the postwar South. White southerners complained bitterly about what they called "black rule" as African Americans took positions as sheriffs, justices of the peace, county clerks, and school superintendents. Yet throughout the South, only a few dozen black Americans occupied positions of real authority. Relatively few black candidates ran for office, and many black voters, intimidated by threats or actual violence in the open southern polls, where each person's vote was public knowledge, supported white politicians. Those African Americans who did run for office encountered white resentment and often threats.

With the South's return to the Union after the Civil War, race relations in that embattled region took political center stage. For the first dozen years after the Confederacy's surrender—a period that became known as Reconstruction—the federal government sent troops and agents to help restore order to the battered South and aid slaves' transition to freedom. Federal and private agencies opened schools, distributed food and medicine, and intervened in legal disputes between freed people and their white neighbors. In what many northerners considered a new national era, the federal government aimed to heal the war-torn South and to make it more like the North, physically, economically, socially and politically. While repairing fields, roads, and homes was a top priority, many northerners hoped the South would soon have new railroads, factories, banks, and wage laborers as well.

Reconstruction also extended to the national level, as black men were elected to Congress and Republican presidents appointed African Americans to positions of authority. During this era, black leaders made access to the polls their highest priority, believing African Americans could vote into office leaders who supported their goals, such as farm ownership and jobs that would allow them to move away from livelihoods that depended on white landowners. They also wanted education for their children, as literacy would, in turn,

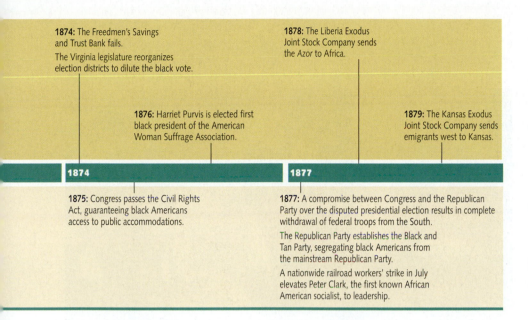

1874: The Freedmen's Savings and Trust Bank fails.

The Virginia legislature reorganizes election districts to dilute the black vote.

1878: The Liberia Exodus Joint Stock Company sends the Azor to Africa.

1876: Harriet Purvis is elected first black president of the American Woman Suffrage Association.

1879: The Kansas Exodus Joint Stock Company sends emigrants west to Kansas.

1874

1877

1875: Congress passes the Civil Rights Act, guaranteeing black Americans access to public accommodations.

1877: A compromise between Congress and the Republican Party over the disputed presidential election results in complete withdrawal of federal troops from the South.

The Republican Party establishes the Black and Tan Party, segregating black Americans from the mainstream Republican Party.

A nationwide railroad workers' strike in July elevates Peter Clark, the first known African American socialist, to leadership.

of southern and federal politics. Washington, DC—seat of the national government—symbolized the complexities of the new era. From across the nation, black Americans seeking employment and federal protection streamed into the capital city.

But federal sympathy toward freedmen and freedwomen waned after a decade of Reconstruction efforts, and federal promises went unfulfilled. Discouraged by slow progress, some black Americans again directed their hopes elsewhere—to African or western frontiers.

provide opportunities for entrepreneurship and political power to lift people out of poverty.

Meanwhile, most northern and southern white Americans hoped to "reconstruct" a system that tied black Americans to menial roles. A few white Americans envisioned former bondspeople becoming successful landowners or entrepreneurs, although certainly not equal members of society. Though slavery had been outlawed, persuasion, local statutes, intimidation, and widespread prejudice kept black people tied to agricultural and service jobs in both South and North.

As we saw in Chapter 10, resentful southern planters also began instituting laws—Black Codes—to keep black people subservient. These laws they backed up with violence, threats, or economic reprisals, such as dismissing black farm workers who tried to vote or encouraged others to do so. The presence of the federal Freedmen's Bureau in the South, which aimed to help former slaves become full citizens, infuriated many white southerners. Many of these planters hoped to reconstruct the old agricultural system in which wealthy white men made the laws, leaving both white and black poor people powerless.

But black Americans had sweeping ambitions: strengthening their communities economically, reassembling their families, and protecting themselves from violence and intimidation. All of these goals hinged on acquiring and protecting political rights, navigating the shifting and sometimes treacherous tides

POSTWAR RECONSTRUCTION

On February 25, 1870, an ambitious, urbane southerner arrived in Washington, DC, with a mission: to ensure that the federal government treated black people as full citizens. That southerner was Hiram Revels—African Methodist Episcopal Church (AME) minister, former Union recruitment officer, and advocate of improving education for black people. The first black American to be elected to Congress, Revels soon discovered how fervently white congressmen resented his presence. His public service career—beginning before the Civil War and continuing until his death in 1901—reveals much about how emancipation transformed black people and about the complexities of Reconstruction.

Radical Reconstruction

Revels found Congress dominated by a coalition of northern representatives known as Radical Republicans. These politicians aimed to protect and promote the interests of black southerners and to punish white southerners for the Civil War. Simultaneously, Congress clashed with the president over how to define and protect black rights. Though the war had ended, racial tensions between the North and South continued to simmer. The Radical Republicans constituted the majority in Congress when southern seats were vacant dur-

■ Hiram Revels helped recruit the first black Civil War regiments in Maryland and Missouri. After his U.S. Senate service, he returned to Mississippi and became president of Alcorn, a Reconstruction-era black college. This photo of Revels with his wife and five daughters was taken in about 1870.

ing the war. By the end of 1865, many southern states had ratified the Thirteenth Amendment and rejoined the Union—just in time to elect congressmen to reclaim their prewar seats. Because black men could not yet vote, the same southern white aristocrats who had ruled in Congress before the war simply returned to their former posts.

But Radical Republicans still held the majority. Led by Pennsylvania representative Thaddeus Stevens and Massachusetts senator Charles Sumner (who returned to the Senate in 1860), they asserted the right of Congress to refuse seats to southern congressmen who had not yet sworn Union allegiance. Next they strategized on how to get southern black candidates seated in Congress in order to drive southern white men from the legislature. Through the last half of the decade, Radical Republicans pounded the South with new policies. In early 1867, Congress passed three new Reconstruction acts. The first ruling divided the South into five military districts, sending federal troops to maintain order and protect freed people. The second required the former Confederate states to hold conventions to draft constitutions that guaranteed black male suffrage. The third act stipulated that former Confederate states could send congressmen to Washington, DC, only after state legislatures had ratified the Fourteenth Amendment. This amendment, ratified in 1868, was the most important product of the Reconstruction era. It affirmed black people's citizenship, removing every trace of ambiguity left from the Supreme Court's decision in the *Dred Scott* case of 1857. It also denied former slaveowners' claims that they should receive compensation for their lost "property." Emanuel Fortune, a delegate to Florida's constitutional convention, helped his state pass these provisions. Hoping to stir northern support for punishing southerners, Congress also established a Joint Committee on Reconstruction to gather information about southern anti-black violence.

Presidential Reconstruction

Black people across the nation hoped the Fourteenth Amendment would secure them a place in their nation's economic, political, and social life. However, a milder form of Reconstruction proposed by President Lincoln and favored by his successor, Andrew Johnson, enabled the white South to resist. Hoping to heal sectional bitterness, Lincoln and some northerners favored a less punitive way for the South to reenter the Union. The South, they contended, did not possess the authority to leave the United States. Hence, southern states had always remained in the Union, and thus technically did not need to rejoin.

When Lincoln was assassinated in April 1865, the presidency fell to Vice President Andrew Johnson. A former Democratic senator from Tennessee, Johnson also favored a lenient Reconstruction policy. Reversing Congress's Confiscation Act of 1862, which had allowed the federal government to seize Confederates' property without compensating them for it, Johnson offered to pardon and to restore the property of former Confederates who took an oath of allegiance to the Constitution. He also promised to restore their confiscated land. Finally, he acknowledged North Carolina's new government, which had been reconstructed with a new constitution following the Republican guidelines that provided black men with the vote. Johnson also encouraged the other Confederate states to quickly reestablish state governments.

Thus, black rights became the focal point as Johnson battled with Congress over which branch of government would wield power in the postwar era. President Johnson vetoed Congress's Civil Rights Act of 1866, which offered limited legal rights to African Americans. He also vetoed a congressional vote to renew the Freedmen's Bureau. But Radical Republicans gathered enough votes to override Johnson's veto and pass both bills. The new president still opposed the Fourteenth Amendment because he felt it violated southern states' rights to control their citizenship. During the 1866 midterm campaign, he urged the southern states not to ratify it. His opposition only deepened the rift between the White House and Congress.

Tension between Johnson and Congress reached a climax when the president tried to remove Secretary of War Edwin Stanton, who oversaw the military occupation of the unreconstructed southern states. Johnson was incensed that Stanton encouraged military officers stationed in the South to ignore communications from the president. Seeking to undermine Johnson's authority, Congress passed the Tenure of Office Act. The ruling blocked Johnson from firing Stanton and guaranteed tenure of office to anyone appointed with the Senate's approval. Johnson responded by placing strict controls on military commanders in the South and renewing efforts to dismiss Stanton and other government officials sympathetic to congressional Reconstruction. Republicans promptly called for the president's impeachment on the grounds that he had violated several recent congressional edicts meant to prevent him from removing military or cabinet appointees without congressional approval. A three-month impeachment trial failed to remove Johnson, however, because the two-thirds majority required in the Senate fell one vote short. Once more, the contest for power between the South and branches of the federal government—ostensibly about black issues—only diverted federal attention from black people's needs.

The Fifteenth Amendment

The Fourteenth Amendment should have secured black freedom everywhere, but even as Congress enacted policies ensuring southern black men the franchise, northern black men with political ambitions had to head south to fulfill them. In a bitter irony, southern black men, so recently liberated from slavery, had more opportunities for political leadership than did black northerners. The *New York Tribune* put the matter bluntly: "They who desire the Right of Suffrage for Blacks of the South oppose the extension of the same right to Blacks of the North."

> "They who desire the Right of Suffrage for Blacks of the South oppose the extension of the same right to Blacks of the North."
> —The *New York Tribune*

This pattern of exclusion appeared in numerous northern states. In 1867, white voters in Kansas and Ohio banned African Americans from the polls by referendum. The following year, white voters in Michigan promptly rejected a new Radical Republican constitution that included black suffrage. In Connecticut, New York, and Minnesota, when put to popular vote, black suffrage was defeated. Only in Iowa could Republicans procure black enfranchisement. To protest political exclusion, Equal Rights Leagues arose in the North. Consisting of alliances between black leaders and white former abolitionists, these organizations advocated for full political equality.

By the 1868 elections, northern voters had enough of the tug-of-war in Washington. They elected moderate Republicans intent on distancing themselves from the Radicals' platform, which focused not just on full civil rights for African Americans but also on women's suffrage and the rights of labor unions. Instead of expending energies in power struggles, the moderates supported the new president: military hero Ulysses S. Grant. With conservative governments victorious in Virginia by 1869 and in North Carolina and Georgia by 1871, aggressively pro-black Reconstruction all but vanished.

Now that Republican congressmen faced a conservative southern contingent, even moderate Republicans—most of whom had rejected a black suffrage amendment—began to see that northern black voters might help them win close congressional contests. So in February 1869, moderate Republicans proposed the Fifteenth Amendment, prohibiting federal and state governments from limiting the franchise because of "race, color, or previous condition of servitude." Former Confederate states wishing to return to the Union had to ratify the new amendment. Mississippi was among the first to comply. Upon its readmission, black voters sent state senator Hiram Revels to Washington to finish out the Senate term vacated by Jefferson Davis in 1861. As a black Pittsburgh teacher commented, "The Republican party had done the Negro good [in passing the Fifteenth Amendment], but they were doing themselves good at the same time." When Revels took his congressional seat, he was as much a symbol as a politician. To black Americans and Radical Republicans, he embodied victory in the battle for full black enfranchisement. (Indeed, the Fifteenth Amendment was ratified in March 1870, just as Revels took office.) His presence symbolized the South's defeat. To moderate Republicans, he represented a concession to Radical Republican schemes—one that would preserve Republican congressional dominance.

Black Suffrage and Women's Suffrage

The passage of the Fourteenth and Fifteenth amendments exposed the fragility of the northern white and black reformer alliance. With Emancipation, war's end, and the Thirteenth Amendment, many white abolitionists were

THE FIRST COLORED SENATOR AND REPRESENTATIVES.
In the 41ˢᵗ and 42ⁿᵈ Congress of the United States.

U.S. Senator H.R.REVELS, of Mississippi   BENJ.S.TURNER.M.C.of Alabama   JOSIAH T.WALLS, M.C. of Florida   JOSEPH H.RAINY, M.C. of S.Carolina   R.BROWN ELLIOT, M.C. of S.Carolina

ROBERT C.DE LARGE, M.C. of S.Carolina   JEFFERSON H.LONG, M.C. of Georgia

■ This popular portrait of the seven black congressmen, from spring of 1873, includes several who were ending their term and several just arriving. Missing is Pinckney Benton Stewart Pinchback, elected to the Senate from Louisiana in 1872.

satisfied that black rights would come in due course. While continuing to lobby for black rights, they diverted some of their energies to promoting full citizenship for women. This connection between black rights and women's rights had been marked as early as Frederick Douglass's attendance at the 1848 Women's Rights Convention at Seneca Falls, New York. Douglass and Elizabeth Cady Stanton had long been friends, as Douglass backed Stanton's claim that "the power to choose rulers and make laws was the right by which all others could be secured."

During the war, Stanton had circulated petitions supporting the Thirteenth Amendment outlawing slavery. With ratification of the amendment, she expected antislavery leaders like Wendell Phillips to support her women's agenda in return. At issue for her was the word *male* in the Fourteenth Amendment. Previously, women had assumed they were citizens. The new amendment, which specified voters as "male inhabitants," underscored women's exclusion from the political process. Furious, Stanton refused to support the Four-

teenth and Fifteenth Amendments. "My question," she challenged Phillips, "is do you believe the African race is composed entirely of males?" Stanton's friendship with Douglass also soured, as Douglass argued that the right to vote was more crucial for black men than for women. "The government of this country loves women," he contended, "but the Negro is loathed." Douglass feared a bill including enfranchisement of women could not pass, even in a Radical Republican Congress.

> "The government of this country loves women, but the Negro is loathed."
> —*Frederick Douglass*

The question of whether women had as much right to vote as freedmen found few sympathizers, even among Radical Republicans. The majority of reformers adopted a "black men first" strategy. By opposing the Fourteenth and later the Fifteenth amendments, Stanton found herself

■ TABLE 11.1 The Federal Power Struggle 1865–1877

Black newspapers recognized that often white Americans' interest in Reconstruction involved a power struggle among the three branches of government rather than the best interests of black people or the South. African American concerns frequently faded into the background. Below are some of the battles that took place during the Reconstruction years.

Date	Congress	Presidency	Supreme Court
1865	Establishes Freedmen's Bureau	Andrew Johnson grants "amnesty and pardon" to most Confederates, restoring confiscated land, and exiling thousands of black farmers from their land	
1866	Passes Thirteenth Amendment, abolishing slavery in all states and territories; ratified by 27 states Expands Freedmen's Bureau authority and over Johnson's veto empowers it to try civil cases for freedmen Over Johnson's veto, passes three Civil Rights Acts, including one that vacates 1857 *Dred Scott* decision and granting citizenship to black Americans Passes Fourteenth Amendment, guaranteeing citizenship and requiring Confederate states' approval; ratified in 1868	Johnson vetoes two-year extension for Freedmen's Bureau Johnson vetoes Civil Rights Acts	In *Ex Parte Milligan*, rules that neither the president nor Congress has legal power to allow other agencies to try civilian cases, except in theater of war
1867		Enforces provisions of Civil Rights Acts	In *Cummings* v. *Missouri*, rules that government may not require voters to take oaths of past loyalty
1868	Passes Tenure of Office Act, forbidding president to remove Secretary of War Edwin Stanton Impeaches Johnson; conviction fails by one vote	Removes military officers from duty, including Secretary of War Edwin Stanton	Agrees to hear a southern state's case regarding the constitutionality of Reconstruction Acts Outlaws Maryland's race-based apprentice system
1869	Passes Fifteenth Amendment guaranteeing suffrage, requiring Confederate states to ratify; ratified in 1870		Upholds congressional authority to shape Reconstruction In *Texas* v. *White*, rules that Confederate officials had never left Union, since secession was illegal
1870–71	Passes Ku Klux Klan Acts Moderate Republicans refuse to seat black Louisiana Senator P. B. S. Pinchback		
1872	Passes Amnesty Act Dismantles Freedmen's Bureau		
1873			In *Slaughterhouse Cases*, rules that only the rights of federal citizenship are protected under Fourteenth Amendment; other rights at state discretion
1875	Passes Civil Rights Act guaranteeing freedmen access to public accommodations		
1877	Compromise installs Rutherford B. Hayes as president; federal troops withdrawn from South		

■ A woman who made her living by words, Frances Ellen Watkins Harper (1835–1911) often canonized black heroes in poetry. A staunch advocate of temperance and the franchise for women, she agonized over the tensions tearing at reformers' alliances as rival groups argued about the Fourteenth and Fifteenth Amendments.

men will be masters over the women. . . . I am glad to see that men are getting their rights, but I want women to get theirs," said Sojourner Truth in a 1867 New York speech. Frances Ellen Watkins Harper and Mary Ann Shadd Cary agreed. They joined Stanton and Susan B. Anthony in the National Woman Suffrage Association in 1869. Cary shared Anthony's interest in divorce reform and support for women entrepreneurs. Cary drafted a woman-suffrage statement to the House of Representatives and led a group of women who attempted to register to vote in the District of Columbia elections in 1869.

But soon Cary and other black women were put off by Stanton's and Anthony's impulsive rhetoric about "black [male] beasts" gaining the ballot before white women. In 1871, Cary broke away, establishing the Colored Woman's Progressive Franchise Association, which aimed to "take an aggressive stand against the assumption that men only [should] vote]." Thus, in one of the nation's greatest ironies, the victory of enfranchisement for African Americans severed alliances between black leaders and white female reformers. When the Fifteenth Amendment was ratified in 1870, Douglass resumed his advocacy of women's suffrage, and slowly rebuilt his friendship with Stanton. But the contest between race progress and gender reform continued into the twenty-first century.

ELECTED BLACK LEADERS

Hiram Revels's election as the first black man to serve in the U.S. Senate was a mixed victory. The new senator found that northern and southern congressmen questioned his eligibility for the Senate. Had he been a citizen of the United States for the required nine years? After all, the Fourteenth Amendment granting citizenship had been ratified only two years before. By arguing that he had some white ancestors and therefore had been at least *partly* a citizen before 1868, Senator Revels succeeded in taking his seat.

Within months, six other African Americans joined Revels in Congress, thanks to the rising number of southern black voters. To represent South Carolina, Georgia, Alabama, and Mississippi came former slaves and free men born in the North and the South. All seven knew their fellow congressmen would feel—at best—ambivalent about their presence. Yet they set out to help maintain a Republican majority in Congress and to sustain their party's commitment to African Americans. Black Americans celebrated what promised to be a new national era. Frederick Douglass, who had long maintained that each black man must be "a voter in the North and in the South," reveled in the tri-

linked to anti-black forces. The issue split the women's movement. Remaining true to her abolitionist principles that black suffrage was more important than women's suffrage, Lucy Stone founded the interracial American Woman Suffrage Association (AWSA). She was soon joined by Harriet Purvis, who became its first black president in 1876. Other reformers sought to promote the cause of women and African Americans equally. "If colored men get their rights, and not colored women theirs, colored

> "If colored men get their rights, and not colored women theirs, colored men will be masters over the women."—Sojourner Truth

First Person   Frances Ellen Watkins Harper Proposes Women's Leadership

In April 1875, Frances Ellen Watkins Harper spoke before the Pennsylvania Society for Promoting the Abolition of Slavery, recommending that black Americans avoid dependence on white Americans' kindness. She maintained that black women should take leadership roles in designing African Americans' future.

The great problem to be solved by the American people, is this: Whether or not there is enough strength in democracy, virtue enough in our civilization, and power enough in our religion to have mercy and deal justly with four millions of people but lately translated from the old oligarchy of slavery to the new commonwealth of freedom. . . . The most important question before us colored people is not simply what the Democratic party may do against us or the Republican party do for us; but what are we going to do for ourselves?

Before our young men is another battle—not a battle of flashing swords and clashing steel, but a moral warfare, a battle against ignorance, poverty and low social condition. . . .

Give power and significance to your life, and in the great work of upbuilding there is room for woman's work and woman's heart. . . . .

—*from* Centennial Anniversary of the Pennsylvania Society for Promoting the Abolition of Slavery *(1876).*

To view a longer version of this document, please go to *www.ablongman.com/carson/documents.*

umph of enfranchisement for black men. He envisioned a day when black northerners also would have the voting strength to elect black representatives.

Black congressmen were pragmatic about the limits of their new power. Familiar with the ways of white southerners, they recognized the need to compromise with white men if they hoped to accomplish their goals. Revels offered reassurance to those white Americans who feared politically powerful black men: "The white race has no better friend than I. I am true to my own race. I wish to see all done that can be done . . . to assist [black men] in acquiring property, in becoming intelligent, enlightened . . . citizens . . . but at the same time, I would not have anything done which would harm the white race."

> "We all have to go armed in the South, ready at a moment's warning to sell our lives if it is necessary."
> —*Hiram Revels*

Yet along with white deference, Revels lobbied for integrated schools. "Prejudice has no cause to justify it," he stated. "We must admit that it is wicked. . . . I hold it to be the duty of this nation to discourage it, because it is wicked, because it is wrong." Recognizing the atmosphere of violence in which

black politicians operated, he recommended self-defense. "We all have to go armed in the South," he reported, "ready at a moment's warning to sell our lives if it is necessary." Delicately balancing humility, resolution, and self-protection, Revels worked for political progress.

Like Revels, fellow Mississippian Blanche K. Bruce also hoped compromise with white southerners could spur black progress. A well-educated man who had held local offices, Bruce was elected to the Senate in 1874. He joined southern white senators in lobbying for federal funds to improve Mississippi's ports. At the same time, he advocated full citizenship for Chinese and Native Americans. These groups, he figured, would increase the Republican Party's membership.

Many black congressmen looked for ways to gain white allies. Hiram Revels and Alabama's representative Benjamin Turner were among those African American politicians who voted for the Amnesty Act of 1872, which would remove restrictions on former Confederates' political participation. Revels explained to his constituency that accommodating white southerners "got colored mechanics in the United States Navy Yard for the first time." By using compromise and accommodation, Mississippi's Blanche K. Bruce negotiated alliances that brought black people jobs in post offices, customs offices, and Freedmen's Bureau offices across the South. Black representatives in Washington also

■ TABLE 11.2 The Black Men Who Went to Congress in 1870

Most African American congressmen were young, ambitious, and outspoken. All represented the South, though some were born in the North. Some brought prestigious educational credentials; others brought a wisdom born of life experience. Here is a look at the first seven black men who were elected to Congress. Most went on to fruitful careers following their terms in Congress.

Name/State/Age in 1870	Background	Prior experience	Service in Congress	Post-Congress experience
Blanche K. Bruce (1841–1898) Mississippi 29 years old	Born slave in Virginia to master and slave woman	Studied at Oberlin College; Mississippi tax assessor, superintendent of education, alderman, sheriff	Senate, 1875–1881. Supported seating of P. B. S. Pinchback, Mississippi River flood control and port development, citizenship for Chinese and Native Americans, dissolving all-black regiments	1881–1893: Register of the Treasury and DC Recorder of Deeds; trustee of Howard University
Richard H. Cain (1825–1887) South Carolina 45 years old	Born free in western Virginia to black mother, Cherokee father	Studied at Wilberforce College; delegate to SC state constitutional convention; served in SC state senate	House of Representatives 1873–1874; 1877–79. Opposed Amnesty Act; supported woman suffrage, education, and land	1878: Encouraged South Carolinians to support Liberia exodus
Robert DeLarge (1842–1874) South Carolina 28 years old	Born free in Virginia	SC constitutional convention (1868) and state legislature	House of Representatives, 1871–1873. Removed from office 2 months before his term expired because white opponent won contested election. Supported Amnesty Act, black land ownership	Magistrate in Charleston
Robert Brown Elliott (1842–1884) South Carolina 28 years old	Born in South Carolina to free black parents	Passed SC bar in 1867; editor of black Republican newspaper, the *South Carolina Leader;* SC constitutional convention; assistant adjutant-general of SC	House of Representatives, 1871–1875. Supported suppression of Ku Klux Klan, protection of black vote	Lawyer in New Orleans, Louisiana
Jefferson Long (1836–1900) Georgia 34 years old	Born a slave in Georgia to slave mother and white father	Tailor	House of Representatives, 1871–1873. Supported Ku Klux Klan Acts, opposed amnesty for ex-Confederates	Tailoring business suffered because of his continued organizing for Republican Party
John Roy Lynch (1847–1939) Mississippi 23 years old	Louisiana slave, freed when Union army seized Natchez, 1863	Elected justice of the peace; Mississippi legislature speaker of the house	House of Representatives, 1872–1876. Supported civil rights legislation	Delegate to four national Republican conventions; appointed by President Benjamin Harrison to be auditor of the U.S. Treasury for the Navy Department
Pinckney Benton Stewart Pinchback (1837–1921) Louisiana 33 years old	Born free to Georgia planter and an emancipated slave	Louisiana state senator; lieutenant governor; acting governor	Senate: elected in 1872, but never allowed to assume office. Advocated education, women's suffrage	U.S. Customs inspector; cotton planter; owner of Mississippi riverboat company; admitted to Louisiana bar in 1886; helped found Southern Normal School

cut deals that brought black cadets to West Point and the Naval Academy.

Maneuvering through Washington's corridors of power, black politicians understood that their constituents were vulnerable and their own positions fragile. They sought issues on which they could negotiate with white allies without trading away too many black political gains. The balancing act demanded constant attention and vigilance.

Some outspoken black congressmen refused to compromise or negotiate. "In my state, since emancipation there have been over five hundred loyal men shot down by the disloyal men there, and not one of those men who took part in committing those outrages has ever been brought to justice," said Congressman Jefferson Long of Georgia. "Those disloyal people still hate this Government, [and] when loyal men dare to carry the 'stars and stripes' through our streets, they are turned out of employment. When we take the men who commit these outrages before judges and juries, we find that these courts and juries remain in the hands of the very Ku Klux themselves."

Uncompromising black congressmen like Long found it difficult to push their agenda. Too few in number and too new to politics, they struggled to represent their constituents' concerns. Sometimes simply being heard was all they could hope for. For example, Long voted against the Amnesty Act, knowing this would further isolate him in a Congress bent on reconciliation. Richard Cain, a representative from South Carolina, also voted no. "I want to see a change in this country," said Cain, a northern-born minister whose calling had taken him South to fight for black justice. "Instead of colored people being always penniless, I want to see them coming in with their mule teams and ox teams, with their corn and potatoes to exchange for silks and satins. I want to see children coming to enjoy life as it ought to be enjoyed." Cain doubted that reinstating political rights to Confederates would help realize this vision. Several other black congressmen also voted no on amnesty. Even red-inked letters from the Ku Klux Klan warning of "doom sealed in blood" could not deter these men from speaking out—knowing their arguments fell on deaf ears.

Young black congressmen sought counsel from seasoned political activists like Frederick Douglass. The esteemed black leader befriended them, often hosting them at his home. Yet even Douglass misread the political realities of Reconstruction. In the 1872 presidential race, Douglass supported Republican President Ulysses S. Grant's bid for reelection. True, Grant had demonstrated only lukewarm support for black rights, but he represented the political party that had freed slaves, and he had opposed President Andrew Johnson. Grant suggested annexing the Dominican Republic—which had a large black population

and was adjacent to the black Caribbean island republic of Haiti—to provide a haven where African Americans could escape white oppression while maintaining U.S. citizenship. Douglass believed in Grant's goodwill.

Douglass did not question Grant's motives, but others—notably Douglass's abolitionist friend Senator Charles Sumner, who chaired the Senate Foreign Relations Committee—suspected that annexation was a scheme to enrich white land speculators. Douglass continued to support the president, even when Grant refused to invite black representatives to the White House dinner where legislators were to discuss annexation. The black leader counted on the president's good intentions and hoped Grant would reward him with a federal appointment. With support from the black voters Douglass helped deliver, Grant won reelection—but neither annexation of the Dominican Republic nor a federal appointment for Douglass materialized. Black people now had another reminder that their vote wielded little influence unless they could enlist support from powerful white allies.

Local Politics in the South

"When we opened the school a party of armed men came to my house, seized me, carried me out and threw me in Thompson's Creek after they had belabored me with the muzzles of their revolvers . . . [saying] they 'did not want . . . any damned nigger school in that town and were not going to have it,'" Texas state senator George Ruby recalled while testifying about obstacles facing southern black politicians at the state and local levels. Some of these challenges centered on crafting effective political strategies and alliances; others involved ensuring constituents' safety in a hostile environment. Whatever forms the difficulties took, local black  politicians had few southern white allies. In the South, local politics and politicians saw little intercession by white Radical Republicans on behalf of black concerns. Even the presence of federal troops could not deter threats such as those Ruby endured for merely opening a school.

Ruby quickly learned the Texas political terrain. Born in New York and educated in New England, he had lived for a while in Haiti but returned to the United States to work for the Freedmen's Bureau. Assigned to build schools in Texas, he also represented Galveston County at the Texas constitutional convention in 1868. This experience gained him the visibility to be elected to the state senate in 1869.

One of only two black state senators in Texas, Ruby had a constituency mainly of black voters and the minority of white politicians who were bent on securing federal assistance for rebuilding the state's infrastructure, refurbishing the Galveston port, and establishing an educational system benefiting poor Texans of all races.

Like Revels and other black leaders at the national level, Ruby used compromise and negotiation. He supported white Texans as well as black for patronage positions, and he tolerated the new state laws segregating public travel, parks, and even Republican political events. In return, he hoped to gain white support for laws that would restrain the Klan, give citizenship and the franchise to Native Americans (who would presumably increase the Republican party rolls), and promote schools and other services to improve the lives of freed people. He also hoped to contain the growing institution of Black Codes, those state or local laws restricting African Americans' employment choices, land ownership, free mobility, and other opportunities.

Ruby's strategy reflected his understanding of southern political realities. In the postwar era, southern politics took one of three forms: the political middle—which consisted of the vast majority of white southerners, the political right, and the radical left. The political middle, or "moderates," included many entrepreneurs and professionals as well as farmers. Many in this group had concluded even before the war that the South needed to modernize—to diversify their region's economy, develop technology and industry, and avail themselves of federal subsidies for geological surveys, railroads, factories, and ports. Moderate white southerners were not particularly interested in economic advancement for African Americans, but they envisioned black laborers as part of the new South, working in factories as well as in fields. They welcomed alliances with black leaders whom they felt could help persuade black communities to meet moderate white people's goals. As long as leaders like Ruby stayed "in their place"—that is, deferential to white people—white moderates supported black education and voting rights.

South Carolina planter Wade Hampton exemplified white moderates. Hampton believed black and white southerner leaders should unite in rebuilding the South. "Does not that glorious southern sun above us shine alike for both of us?" he asked. But Hampton and other moderates made no overtures toward social integration, viewing class and racial divisions as natural for society.

Black leaders like George Ruby cultivated political connections with white moderates like Wade Hampton among his constituency. With such alliances, he could build support for black people to obtain broader access to education and jobs in agriculture or factories. This was better than joblessness or the specter of black southerners migrating to the North in large numbers in search of jobs—a situation neither white southerners nor white northerners wanted.

Martin Delany also advocated black-white alliances. Filling in as editor for South Carolina's *Missionary Record,* Delany developed a blueprint for black-white cooperation. He felt certain that "the black man and the white man must work together . . . [to] bring about the redemption of the state and prosperity and happiness for the whole people." At the same time, he shuddered at the ever-increasing threats from such groups as the Ku Klux Klan, the Knights of the White Camellias, and the White Leagues. "The black men of this state are dependent on the whites, just as the whites are dependent on them," he wrote in 1873. Thus, he advised black southerners to relinquish "hatred and resentment" and to show themselves as "polite, pleasant, agreeable, ever ready and obliging."

Persuaded by Hampton's argument that "when all our troubles and trials are over, [black and white southerners] will sleep in that same soil in which we first drew breath," Delany supported Hampton's successful bid for governor of South Carolina in 1876.

At the political right stood what some might call radical reactionaries, a small but significant group of white southerners. These included dislocated plantation owners who had lost their economic system, and a few struggling white farmers who had an emotional investment in the South's old way of life, which had given even poor white people a higher status than black people. Their anger at the ravages of war prevented them from embracing any part of a new order that enabled African Americans to progress beyond a servile role. Intent on reviving the prewar agricultural economy, radical reactionaries needed laborers to work the land, and they wanted freed slaves to do the job. They had little interest in modernizing the South and were the ones who most often instigated violence against black people. Black politicians did their best to avoid them.

The South's radical left—the third political group— argued that poor black people had more in common with poor white people than with wealthy black ones. That is, class was more important than race in working to achieve goals. Their view of a postwar South included interracial politics based on unity among poor people regardless of race. Their

> "The black man and the white man must work together."—*Martin Delany*

Madison Hemings Recalls His Family History

Madison Hemings's story, published in 1873, reinforced white southerner's fears about interracial relations. In this interview, the sixty-eight-year-old Hemings describes a family with a biracial background. Born in Virginia, Hemings identified himself both as a black American and as the son of United States president Thomas Jefferson. Jefferson's white descendants denied this relationship until DNA testing in 1999 confirmed the story.

[After the death of his wife, Thomas Jefferson] left for France, taking his eldest daughter with him. . . . My mother accompanied her as her body servant. During that time my mother became Mr. Jefferson's concubine. . . . He promised her . . . that her children should be freed at the age of twenty-one years. . . . She gave birth to four [children] and Jefferson was the father of all of them. Their names were Beverly, Harriet, Madison (myself) and Eston. We all became free . . . [and] all married and have raised families.

Beverly left Monticello and went to Washington as a white man. He married a white woman in Maryland, and their only child, a daughter, was not known by the white folks to have any colored blood coursing through her veins. Beverly's wife's family were people in good circumstances.

Harriet married a white man in good standing in Washington City, whose name I could give, but will not, for prudential reasons. She raised a family of children, and so far as I know they were never suspected of being tainted with African blood in the community where she lived or lives. I have not heard from her for ten years, and do not know whether she is dead or alive. She thought it to her interest, on going to Washington, to assume the role of a white woman. . . .

Eston married a colored woman in Virginia, and moved from there to Ohio. . . .

I married Mary McCoy. Her grandmother was a slave, and lived with her master, Stephen Hughes, near Charlottesville, as his wife. She was manumitted by him, which made her children free. Mary McCoy's mother was his daughter.

—*from* The Pike County [Ohio] Republican, *March 13, 1873.*

To view a longer version of this document, please go to *www.ablongman.com/carson/documents*.

---

concerns included universal education, more equitable land policies, better contracts for renters, and politicians who advocated the rights of the poor. Some of their beliefs were based on socialism, a political philosophy for establishing a government that distributed wealth equally among all its members. This philosophy, which defined economic circumstance as more important than race or ethnicity, gained favor with many of the world's poor people in the late nineteenth century. Many black sharecroppers and laborers indeed understood they had more in common with poor white farmers than with wealthy black planters who benefited from the same exploitative sharecropping and tenant systems used by white planters.

As steel and mining industries began to bring about the hoped-for modernizing of southern cities like Birmingham, Alabama, and Atlanta, Georgia, a black laborers' movement gathered momentum in the South, taking some of its energy from alliances with white radicals. A small but vocal minority of southern white labor organizers embraced black radicals like Lucy Parsons, (an early organizer of Texas's Socialist Workingmen's Party, which advocated interracial labor unions), and Peter Clark of Cincinnati, Ohio, who traveled through the North and the South urging industrial workers to put class unity above racial division. Parsons, who was married to a white Texas socialist, exemplified much of what conservative white southerners feared: miscegenation, or sexual liaison between black and white people. Though such "race-mixing" was common under slavery, white planters feared that in post-slavery times, mixed-race people would feel entitled to the privileges of white Americans.

Only the most optimistic of black Americans joined the socialist ranks. Most soon recognized that white socialists had little power to effect real change. However, the idea of political parties that subordinated racial differences to class loyalty remained alive for decades. In the 1890s, when the Populist Party emerged to put many of these concerns on the national agenda, poor black southerners counted among its strongest supporters.

White Backlash

Even outside the South, white Americans found many ways to keep black people "in their place." Immediately after Congress introduced the Thirteenth Amendment abolishing slavery, white-on-black violence intensified in the North. The same night President Abraham Lincoln was assassinated, an Ohio mob torched the main building of the black Wilberforce University. The blaze destroyed all of Martin Delany's correspondence, manuscripts, and African art collections. "The hand that placed the torch," wrote Delany, was "leagued in sentiment with the same dastardly villains who struck down the greatest Chief Magistrate [Lincoln] of the present age."

Indeed, that hand had a broad span. In Philadelphia and San Francisco, in the late 1860s, white trolley riders forcibly repelled black ones when they tried to board the public transit system. In Rochester, New York, in the winter of 1867, Frederick Douglass's son-in-law, who operated a taxi pulled by what observers described as "a handsome span of greys [horses]," was so badly menaced by other drivers that he quit the trade. That same winter, in the Freedmen's Bureau offices in Washington, DC, General Oliver O. Howard had to threaten to fire his white clerks to get them to accept black coworkers.

In the South, members of the Ku Klux Klan, cloaked in white hoods, galloped on horseback to the homes of black political leaders and their supporters who tried to vote, or those who had become economically comfortable, or supposedly did not show due deference to whites. The attackers often dragged black people out of their homes and whipped or tortured them. Sometimes they killed them, mutilated them, set them on fire, or hanged them from trees—a practice that became known as *lynching*.

Between 1868 and 1876, while an estimated 20,000 black people were murdered by the Ku Klux Klan, southern officials looked the other way. Many of the victims had played an active role in local politics. One Alabama woman said the Klan had murdered her husband because "he just would hold up his head and say he was a strong Radical." Klan members meted out countless other brutal beatings to people who, like Ruby, did nothing more radical than build a school or exude confidence. Another woman reported that the "Ku Klux came to my house and took us out and whipped us, and then said 'don't lets hear any big talk from you, and don't sass any white ladies.'" Yet

another woman received "forty licks with a hickory and [was] kicked in the head and hit with a pistol" to ensure that she would not "sauce [be impertinent to] white women."

The Klan's tactics helped overturn Republican Party control in Georgia in 1870, as terrified black voters stayed away from the polls. The following year, Mississippi Klansmen burned dozens of black churches and schools, torturing and killing the ministers and teachers. Still, many black southerners followed the lead of the Alabaman who said, "The Republican party freed me, and I will die on top of it. I vote every time. I will stick with the Republican party and die in it."

> "The Republican party freed me, and I will die on top of it." —*Alabama black man*

Klansmen did not limit their assaults to black people. They also harassed and murdered the few poor or idealistic southern white citizens who supported socialist groups and advocated racial equality. One white South Carolina Republican reported being "thrashed" by the Ku Klux Klan because he agreed to have polls situated at his residence,

■ After Emanuel Fortune's death in 1903, his son, journalist Timothy Thomas Fortune, reported, "It was natural [for him] to take the leadership in any independent movement of Negroes."

where he welcomed black Republicans and refused entrance to two Democratic voters.

The Enforcement Acts

The Fifteenth Amendment gave all black American men the right to vote—but securing that right in practical terms presented an entirely separate challenge. Affirming the federal commitment to the Fourteenth and Fifteenth Amendments, Congress passed two Enforcement Acts in 1870 and 1871—also known as the Klan Acts, because they were an effort to protect black voters from Ku Klux Klan violence. Both acts defined interference with a person's right to vote as a federal offense punishable by fine or imprisonment. In the summer of 1871, responding to Freedmen's Bureau reports of continued attacks against black southerners, Congress collected testimony from Emanuel Fortune, Robert Meacham, and hundreds of others to learn whether southern voters indeed were still unable to express their political views safely. The hearings produced thirteen volumes of testimony. In one dramatic account, a black Arkansas Republican organizer told of relying on sentinels, coded signals, and the use of religious rhetoric to convince white passersby that a political rally was "only a nigger prayer meeting."

The Enforcement Acts did little to stop violence against black people. In Louisville, Kentucky, white people mobbed and pummeled black residents who exercised their recently court-won right to ride the trolley cars. In Colfax, Louisiana, long-simmering racial hatred led local black men to arm themselves and patrol the town to protect their families from attack by white people. In a confrontation on Easter Sunday, 1873, between the black militia and the white sheriff and a posse of white men he had pulled together, the two groups exchanged fire. The battle ended with more than a dozen white men killed or wounded and two dozen black men injured. About three dozen black men were arrested and executed without a trial. Frederick Douglass's *New National Era* reported that in the wake of the incident, the local White League, bringing in guns and cannons from neighboring states, randomly shot, stabbed, and beat black citizens. They intended, they said, to set an example for "every parish in the State [so] we shall begin to have some quiet and niggers will know their place."

Racial violence broke out in the North as well. In Philadelphia, the federal government sent in a company of marines to protect black voters in the 1870 national election. The following year, when the government failed to provide such protection, a white mob murdered Octavius Catto at his Philadelphia polling place. Catto's leadership in the Pennsylvania Equal Rights League had made him a target. Having served as a major in the Union army, Catto was a beloved school principal after the war. One of his friends lamented, "The Ku Klux of the South are not by any means the lower classes of society. The same may be said of the Ku Klux of the North. Both are industriously engaged in trying to break us down." Black Americans had witnessed yet another instance of their government's inability to protect them.

The Freedmen's Bank

If reconstructing the nation politically posed daunting challenges, establishing a firm economic foundation for African Americans proved even more difficult. In 1865, Congress chartered a new bank: the Freedmen's Savings and Trust Company. It offered black people the opportunity for leadership and to save money and it made loans to help purchase land and farm equipment.

In 1870, the *New National Era* gave glowing reports of the bank's progress. Though Congress did not assume responsibility for monitoring the bank's operations, thousands of black depositors in Washington, Baltimore, New York, Louisville, and dozens of other cities trusted the bank as they painstakingly saved for businesses, farms, equipment, and homes. Year by year, coin by coin, they accumulated nest eggs they hoped would give them financial autonomy.

But the bank soon fell on hard times. In its first years, several well-known white bankers—along with Freedmen's Bureau director Oliver Howard and a national board of four dozen trustees—oversaw operations. They upheld the congressional mandate of investing depositors' money in government securities. But in 1870, during a postwar building boom and railroad expansion, Congress amended the bank's charter, enabling the managers to invest deposits in real estate and railroads. In the next few years, several white members of the bank's board secretly made unsuccessful speculative loans in these industries. By the time the results of these investments became known, the men who managed them had resigned, leaving a core of mostly black trustees to repair the damage. As one black trustee put it, "We trustees—meeting but once a month, and then only hearing statements—could really know nothing about the affairs of the bank."

Desperate to maintain black people's confidence in the bank, the trustees called on the well-respected Frederick Douglass to replace the white bank president. Douglass did so, even investing $10,000 of his own money. Yet he could not prevent the trustees from approving more bad loans. Failing to persuade Congress to salvage the bank, Douglass presided over its closing in July 1874.

As the savings of thousands of African Americans evaporated, some blamed the bank's failure on Douglass, leaving his reputation seriously tarnished. Discouraged that Congress had offered no assistance, numerous African

Americans also lost their faith in the federal government, convinced their government had abandoned them yet again.

WASHINGTON, DC, IN THE NEW NATIONAL ERA

The seat of both hope and disappointment, Washington, DC, became a magnet for black Americans. By 1870, African Americans constituted more than 30 percent of the capital city's population of 132,000—a dramatic increase from 10 percent of the city's population just ten years before. Due in part to its proximity to the South, the black population of Washington soon eclipsed even that of Philadelphia and Baltimore both in absolute numbers and in proportion. The nation's capital offered black people greater economic and social opportunities than any other city. Along with federal protection and political power came black organizations and businesses. Churches, fraternal organizations, debate clubs, the new Preparatory High School (later renamed for black poet Paul Laurence Dunbar), black-owned stores and hotels, and the plentiful jobs generated by the federal bureaucracy all made Washington alluring for those with the resources to take advantage of them.

The Black Elite

Drawn by the federal government and Howard University, many accomplished African Americans settled in the capital city. Frederick Douglass moved to Washington during the 1870s, working with his sons to publish the *New National Era*. The news weekly chronicled the explosive political progress of the Republican Party and its new black constituency. Douglass himself had launched what would become a quarter-century-long career in government service as the District of Columbia Recorder of Deeds and as director of U.S. diplomatic relations with Haiti. John Mercer Langston, the Oberlin-educated lawyer and Equal Rights League activist, came to Washington from Ohio to direct the law curriculum at Howard University. Langston also served as counsel to the city Board of Health, collecting vital statistics and monitoring the city's health measures.

Douglass and Langston were central figures in a growing cadre of Washington intellectuals. Anticipating ties with well-read companions and enjoying sophisticated conversation with like-minded colleagues and friends, they encouraged those with similar tastes to join them.

Many black poets, essayists, novelists, and public speakers responded to the call. Literate women such as Frances Ellen Watkins Harper, Maria Stewart, and Charlotte Forten were among them. Harper became a frequent lecturer, while Stewart taught in the public schools. Stewart also served as a matron at the Freedmen's Hospital, established by the Freedmen's Bureau to provide medical care for Washington's black population. Though long retired from public speaking, she did not lose her feminist drive. In 1878 she published her speeches on women's rights. Charlotte Forten arrived in Washington from the South Carolina Sea Islands in 1864, exhausted and ill after eighteen months of teaching. In the capital city, she became one of fifteen black female clerks employed in the Treasury Department.

The black elite of Washington, DC—around 2 percent of the city's black population—consisted of lawyers, doctors, teachers, publishers, and business owners. Many were of mixed-race background, and their families had been free a generation or more. Thus they had been able to educate themselves and establish businesses or professions that gave them influence far beyond their small numbers. They provided employment for many members of the newer free black community. For example, James Wormley's hotel near the White House drew praise from European and American guests, as it provided a handsome living to its black proprietor and steady employment for black workers. These individuals led black social clubs, churches, schools, and social service agencies. Some even lived in integrated neighborhoods. They sent their children to the growing number of African American colleges and universities. A few young people attended the small number of white colleges—including Bowdoin, Amherst, Oberlin, and the University of Pennsylvania—that had begun accepting black students. Thus the black people in these wealthy, educated circles prepared their children and grandchildren to become Washington's future leaders.

Shopkeepers and service workers formed the core of Washington's black middle class. They enjoyed the chance to rub shoulders not only with Washington's black politicians and intellectuals but also with renowned social activists such as Sojourner Truth. In 1874, Truth became the first African American to take communion at the white Metropolitan Methodist Church. She also spoke before the white congregation of First Congregational Church, where General Oliver Howard called for desegregation. However, she focused her attention on the desperate situation of black people outside in the streets. Seeing black "men and women taking dry bread from the government to keep from starving," she set out to get "land for these people, where they can work and earn their own living." She had the ear of General Howard, who offered money and moral support for

 **First Person**

The *New National Era* Reports on Washington Social Life

Members of Washington's small black middle class sometimes enjoyed a luxurious social life, as evidenced by the New National Era's *report of Cordelia Downing's wedding in 1870. Her father, George T. Downing, was a caterer who ran the restaurant for the House of Representatives.*

The long-anticipated matrimonial affair in high colored circles came off this evening. About one hundred ladies and gentlemen . . . were assembled. Among the more prominent present were Senator Revels of Mississippi, Frederick Douglass, Professor Wilson, cashier of the Freedmen's Savings Bank, [and] Dr. Purvis. . . .

The bride . . . is a young lady of twenty-one years, petite in figure and of more than ordinary beauty. . . . The groom, Mark R. De Mortie, is at present engaged in business in Richmond, Virginia, where he is one of the owners of a manufactury of oil of sassafras. . . .

The guests then retired to an elaborate supper . . . [in a room] fitted up for the occasion, the ceiling being made up of American flags. . . .

—*from* The New National Era, *May 26, 1870.*

To view a longer version of this document, please go to *www.ablongman.com/carson/documents*.

---

her plan to help freedmen obtain farmland in the West by taking advantage of the 1862 Homestead Act. Truth also assisted Freedmen's Bureau agents in relocating refugees from Washington to Ohio and Michigan.

The Black Working Class and Poor

Like Sojourner Truth, Mary Ann Shadd Cary was concerned with the plight of ordinary black people. Widowed in 1860 with two children to rear, Cary moved to Washington permanently in 1869. Believing black people needed their own legal counseling, she became Howard University's first female law student. Encouraged by her family, Cary also assumed leadership in other areas where she felt black communities needed to make progress. She left Howard University in 1871 to go on the lecture circuit, speaking out about the need to ensure that young African Americans gained access to education and employment opportunities—a notion that became a theme for black leaders in the century ahead.

Cary's concern for the working class had deepened as she reflected on the experiences of her son, Linton, who worked as a messenger in the House of Representatives, and her daughter, Sarah, a dressmaker's apprentice. In 1873 she and Frederick Douglass spoke before the National Colored Men's Labor Convention, stressing again the need for educational programs that would teach job skills such as black-smithing, dressmaking, and carpentry to black youth. That year, as an economic depression—the Panic of 1873—gripped America, Cary's anxiety deepened.

The Panic of 1873, the result of overinflated railroad speculation, decreased European demand for American farm products, and the failure of powerful American banks decreased job opportunities for all Americans, especially unskilled black workers. In 1874, Cary wrote two articles to provoke black parents' thinking about employment for their sons. "I have a boy who must and shall have a trade, and yet where may he learn it, or where exercise it when learned?" she asked. "We have members of State Legislatures . . . [and] aspirants in the field of letters, all of which is enjoyably rose-tinted and gilded as compared to the past; but we, no more than others, can afford to build at the top of the house only. . . . [T]he craftsman, the architect, the civil engineer must all come through the door opened to us by the mechanic." Cary believed most young black workers would be more able to benefit from training in—and be able to find work in—man-

> "The craftsman, the architect, the civil engineer must all come through the door opened to us by the mechanic."—*Mary Ann Shadd Cary*

■ A woman of strong opinions, Mary Ann Shadd Cary caught the attention of outspoken white women, including fellow Washington lawyer Belva Lockwood. Throwing her energies into Lockwood's 1872 presidential campaign, Cary hoped to show her support not only for black rights but also for women's leadership.

ual trades rather than in intellectual or political leadership roles. In succeeding years, many black leaders shared her concern for the fate of the average worker.

Cary's concerns about the lack of economic opportunities for African Americans deepened when she saw the widespread poverty in the nation's capital. More than three-quarters of Washington's black families lived in alleys next to large houses where they served as laundresses, porters, handymen, and domestic servants. In the crowded alleys near the Capitol and along the Potomac River lived those who worked in government service. Many of these black households, teeming with family members and boarders, experienced living conditions as bleak as those under slavery. Malnutrition, poor health, violence, and alcoholism plagued them. Fish from local rivers and lakes and vegetables from urban gardens helped ward off starvation, but some black people resorted to prostitution and petty theft in order to survive. Others returned home to the familiar rural South. As black historian John Hope Franklin observed, "It was one thing to provide temporary relief for freedmen, and another to guide them along the road to economic stability and independence."

Despite these difficulties, many freed people managed to build vibrant communities in the capital city. The streets of Washington's poor black neighborhoods rang with the shouts of children playing games, adults performing music, and residents regaling each other with stories.

But there was typically a large gap between black political leaders, who were often economically well off, at least comparatively, and newly freed black people, who were mainly of the working class. Some black leaders—both social advocates and politicians—lost touch with the needs of ordi-

nary black people. While they took seriously their role as advocates for racial and economic justice, their own lives came to include second homes at summer resorts, international travel, and interracial marriages. Many seemed to forget the impact of slavery on the present generation. Cary was one leader who never forgot; she dedicated herself to working for economic stability and independence for the poor.

Political Patronage and Politics

In 1871, Congress established a local government for the District of Columbia consisting of a governor and eleven commissioners appointed by the president, and a twenty-two-member board of delegates, elected by popular vote, with the power to make local laws. Though the District had no voice in Congress or in national politics, as the states did, respected black leaders—including Frederick Douglass and AME bishop James A. Handy—were elected to the board of delegates and hence had a say in local politics. The new structure, which replaced the haphazard and inefficient older structure whereby the District was governed under several conflicting jurisdictions, was seen by many northern leaders as an improvement over the old charter that had expired in 1870.

Though African Americans were in a minority in this interracial governing group, the restructured District government signaled a friendly attitude toward black residents, and dozens of loyal black Republican supporters were rewarded with political patronage positions in such agencies as the Board of Health and the Recorder of Deeds office, Patent Office, Treasury Department, Post Office, public schools, and municipal utilities. Hundreds more found employment in the new district as government clerks and service workers. Local ordinances outlawed racial segregation in public services, and operators of hotels, restaurants, concert halls, and theaters paid fines and saw their licenses suspended if they breached these laws. The Civil Rights Act of 1875, though soon to be overturned by the Supreme Court, reinforced open access to public accommodations.

Steady cash wages—a first for most black people— allowed for middle-class lifestyles for some and elevated others to elite status. Black service workers were sometimes able to save money and buy property of their own. A government employee's income allowed Frederick Douglass to leave his urban brick rowhouse and move to Cedar Hill, an estate in nearby Anacostia. Even as she railed against segregated schools, Mary Ann Shadd Cary served as the principal at the

American Missionary Association's Lincoln School—a position that placed her among the 3 percent of Washington's black workers who held a professional job. These political and social developments mirrored a phenomenon unfolding across the nation. In staggering numbers, African Americans left the countryside, relocating to urban areas where some made economic progress and began participating in local politics. They headed for Detroit and Cincinnati, for New York, Philadelphia and Pittsburgh. Black communities flourished in Baltimore, Maryland; Charleston, South Carolina; Galveston, Texas; Jacksonville, Florida; and Richmond, Virginia.

Many cities had enough black residents to support a black press. Ambitious—if sometimes short-lived—black newspapers proliferated. Across the river from Washington, DC, Alexandria, Virginia, had the *People's Advocate*. Harrisburg, Pennsylvania, boasted the *National Progress*. At the end of the 1870s, in Evansville, Indiana, Edwin Horn was publishing *Our Age*. All of these publications kept their eyes on Washington, where they began noticing a troubling development: the waning of federal protection for African Americans. In succeeding decades, Washington remained an important destination for many black Americans, but the experience of these later arrivals differed markedly from that of Reconstruction-era black Washingtonians.

THE END OF RECONSTRUCTION

Radical Reconstruction brought important gains to black southerners: schools, varied economic possibilities, and the franchise. Efforts to diversify the economy and increase access to the polls, leadership experience, and the reuniting of many families separated by slavery also improved black lives. In 1867, in New Orleans, African Americans won the right to ride the public trolley cars. Through protests and negotiations, they persuaded the car companies to admit "our citizens into all the cars, without any distinction as to color." In many southern states, Radical Republican governments passed laws granting black people access to soda fountains, opera houses, railroads, and steamboats. In 1875, Congress sought to certify these gains with a Civil Rights Act banning discrimination in public places throughout the country. But the act constituted the last piece of civil rights legislation to make its way through Congress until 1957.

Waning Federal Sympathy

Even as civil rights legislation was passed, many reformers pulled back from the enormous effort required to remake a former slave society. The same 1870 elections that brought black congressmen to power also swept away the Republican majority in the House of Representatives. With the crumbling of Republican power in the early 1870s, African American progress began to disintegrate as well. In the South, from which federal troops were gradually withdrawn, black political organizations withered away. In 1869, Mississippi had 87,000 registered black voters; eleven years later, it had just half that number. Southern Radical Republican governments in southern states gave way to conservative white Democratic ones. White southerners called these developments "redemption." A black Louisianan saw it differently in 1877: "The whole South—every state in the South—had got into the hands of the very men that held us slaves."

> "The whole South—every state in the South—had got into the hands of the very men that held us slaves."—*Black Louisianan*

The Supreme Court joined the retreat from black causes by limiting the scope of the Fourteenth Amendment. In the *Slaughterhouse Cases* (1873), the Court drew a distinction between citizenship of the United States and citizenship of a state. It asserted that the amendment applied only to the former; states had the right to define citizenship and its accompanying rights for their residents. In 1883, the Supreme Court heard several cases in the course of which it voted to overturn the 1875 Civil Rights Act. In making their decisions, the justices distinguished between political rights—guaranteed by the Constitution—and social rights—pertaining to segregation in public places, for example—which it felt involved citizens' private lives. The Court declared the federal government had no authority over social rights. The stage was now set for the so-called Jim Crow laws, which limited the rights of African Americans for the next seventy-five years.

The Compromise of 1877

The 1876 presidential contest gave Republicans in Congress a final small victory. In an election so close that it fell to the House of Representatives to adjudicate disputed electoral votes, Republicans and Democrats worked out an agreement that became known as the Compromise of 1877.

In the Compromise, southern congressmen agreed to concede the presidency to Republican can-

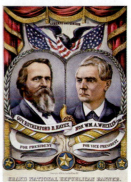

First Person   Simon Smith Laments the End of Hope

*With the 1876 presidential election, black southerners saw their political power evaporate.
Returning home to Columbia, South Carolina, Simon P. Smith, a recent graduate of Howard
University, wrote to a northern friend.*

I visited the state senate and house and the
Democrats were very jubilant; but Republicans were
in despondency. I talked with two colored
representatives . . . and two colored senators. . . .
They are all without hope. They all think that the
colored man is done in this state. Colored men who
had influence here once have no more today than I
have. The Rebels are making colored men do common
work for $.25 per day. How can they live! Labor is
worth nothing and provision higher than anywhere
else. I know not what our people will do here now.
—*from American Missionary Association Archives.*

To view a longer version of this document, please go
to *www.ablongman.com/carson/documents*.

didate Rutherford B. Hayes, while Republicans agreed to
make concessions to white southerners, allowing them to
control local elections and to make local ordinances controlling such issues as black employment contracts and racial
separation. The few remaining federal troops were withdrawn
from the South, federal intervention in southern state affairs
ceased, and the U.S. government agreed to appoint at least
one southerner to the president's cabinet. Across the South,
state governments now lay firmly in the hands of the white
"redeemers," who regained local power to deny true citizenship privileges—such as the vote—to thousands of African
Americans. The national Republican Party distanced itself
from black interests, establishing segregated "Black and Tan"
parties in an increasingly segregated South. For white Americans, the era of Reconstruction had ended.

AFRICAN AMERICANS ON THE MOVE

"I made the outside box [for Julia Haven] and her coffin,
in Smith County, Tennessee. And another young colored
lady . . . they committed an outrage on her and then shot her,
and I helped to make her coffin." In the spring of 1880, seventy-year-old Benjamin "Pap" Singleton used these two examples of women who had been raped and killed to help a Senate
committee understand why black people were fleeing the
South. The investigation had been launched in response to
claims by both Democrats and Republicans that the opposing
political party was conspiring to provoke black people to leave
the South. Republicans accused Democrats of wanting to gain
control of the South by expelling black voters; Democrats
insisted that Republicans sought to spread their influence outside the South. Singleton knew better: Black people were fleeing the South to avoid rape, murder, and mutilation.

Ho for Kansas!

Brethren, Friends, & Fellow Citizens:
I feel thankful to inform you that the
REAL ESTATE
AND
Homestead   Association,
Will Leave Here the
15th of April, 1878,
In pursuit of Homes in the Southwestern
Lands of America, at Transportation
Rates, cheaper than ever
was known before.
For full information inquire of
Benj. Singleton, better known as old Pap,
NO. 5 NORTH FRONT STREET.
Beware of Speculators and Adventurers, as it is a dangerous thing
to fall in their hands.
Nashville, Tenn., March 18, 1878.

One of the many posters calling on southern blacks to leave for Kansas.

■ Recruiters for the new black settlements took posters such
as this one to local meetings across both North and South.

The Exodusters

Benjamin Singleton, a former Tennessee slave who had escaped via the Underground Railroad through Detroit into Canada, returned to his home state after the war. Like many black Americans, Singleton soon took advantage of the 1862 Homestead Act, which offered 160 acres of government land free to anyone who would live on the property, improve it, and pay a small registration fee. With other black Tennesseeans, he started the Edgefield Real Estate and Homestead Association to establish a new black settlement in Kansas. Several families who had visited Kansas, he said, "brought back favorable reports. . . . Three or four hundred . . . went into Southern Kansas . . . and formed a colony there, and bought about a thousand acres of ground." Comparing their projects to the exodus of the biblical Hebrews from Egyptian bondage, the thousands of black Americans who went west with groups such as the Kansas Exodus Joint Stock Company in the late 1870s called themselves *Exodusters*.

The town of Nicodemus in Graham County, Kansas, on the Solomon River typifies these new African American frontier communities. By 1880, 700 black settlers had emigrated to Nicodemus, but many emigrants encountered stiff resistance even as they left home. To retain the South's cheap labor force, white southerners tried to sabotage the planned black exodus. Singleton told Congress how armed white men, positioned along the shore, blocked the Mississippi River to black travelers. They sometimes grabbed the would-be pioneers and hacked off their hands. "Now see if you can go to Kansas and work," they said. White sheriffs arrested black travelers for breach of contract (if they were contracted to a planter) or for vagrancy (if they were not). Despite these tactics, black people continued to head west. Between 1870 and 1880, the African American population in Kansas doubled to more than 40,000.

At first white Kansans welcomed the Exodusters. Eager to increase the population of farmers and defend themselves from Native Americans who resisted the white influx, some Kansas communities raised money to help black newcomers pay land fees. But many black homesteaders, with few tools or work animals, found independent farming tough going. Discouraged, many Exodusters ended up in Topeka, where they hunted for work. But this city was also home to displaced white southerners also looking for employment. Racial intimidation and lynchings became so common that the Republican mayor of Topeka, once sympathetic to African Americans, suggested the money raised for black relief might

> "We don't want to leave the South, and just as soon as we have confidence in the South I am going to persuade every man to go back."—Benjamin Singleton

better go to returning black refugees to the South—especially agitators "who were always talking politics."

Some black leaders like Frederick Douglass urged black families to stay in the South. Only with large numbers, they contended, could black voters exert power and influence. But Douglass wrote from the relative safety and comfort of Washington. It was people like Singleton who experienced the southern predicament firsthand: "We don't want to leave the South," he wrote in 1881, "and just as soon as we have confidence in the South I am going to . . . persuade every man to go back, because that is the best country; . . . we love that country . . . but [by leaving] we are going to learn the South a lesson."

The Western Frontier

Beyond Kansas, numerous African Americans found adventure and fortune in Nebraska, Colorado, North Dakota, and along the Pacific coast. Closed out of northern and southern

■ Finishing a term as a forager (raider) for the Confederate army, Isom Dart was among the cowboys who drifted west. Joining a group of cattle thieves, he was arrested in Texas, Colorado, and Wyoming. Legend has it that he was never imprisoned.

First Person — John E. Bruce Promotes Africa

Black journalist John E. Bruce was among those who envisioned Africa as a "homeland." Before a Philadelphia audience in 1877, he argued that Africa offered black Americans freedom from racial prejudice.

I shall endeavor to show tonight why the colored American should emigrate to Africa. First, because Africa is his fatherland; secondly, because before the war, in the South he was a slave, and in the North, a victim of prejudice and ostracism; and thirdly, because, since the close of the war, although he has been freed by emancipation and invested with enfranchisement, he is only nominally free; and lastly, because he is still a victim of prejudice, and practically proscribed socially, religiously, politically, educationally, and in the various industrial pursuits.

. . . The colored American should emigrate to Africa . . . because he . . . cannot enter a hotel and obtain accommodations without paying a double price, should he be successful in entering at all. If he go to the church of God in this Christian land, he is thrust into the gallery.

. . . Africa is a country rich in its productions, offering untold treasures to the adventurer who would go there. It has a peculiar claim upon the colored American.

—*excerpted from the* Christian Recorder, *November 1, 1877.*

To view a longer version of this document, please go to *www.ablongman.com/carson/documents*.

---

economy and politics, many black families headed for these new frontiers. Nancy Lewis told how she and her husband, a Civil War veteran, established their Nebraska farm in the 1870s. By 1880, they counted among 2,000 black Nebraskans. Virginia-born Barney Ford, a one-time barber and ship's steward, journeyed to Denver and by 1874 had opened a prosperous hotel. Two of Frederick Douglass's sons were also among Denver's thousand African Americans. Colorful cowboy Nat Love was among several hundred African Americans in North Dakota. His prowess in an 1876 rodeo in Deadwood City gained him the nickname "Deadwood Dick." Love's autobiography, *The Life & Adventures of Nat Love, Better Known in the Cattle Country As Deadwood Dick* (1876), promoted the escapades of black cowboys. But when the book was later published as one of many mass-market stories of the West, mention of Love's African heritage was omitted.

Some black Americans got as far west as California. By 1880, as many as 6,000 reached the coastal state. Several hundred settled in each of the other western states and territories. These pioneers included cowboys, shopkeepers, prospectors, service workers such as barbers, laundresses, and domestic servants, and farmers. A few, like Biddy Mason, found California a rewarding home. Dragged across the Rocky Mountains in the 1850s when her Mormon owner joined the gold rush, Mason remained in California after the courts declared her free. Purchasing property, she ran a successful boarding-house and grocery store, donated some of her profits to black schools, and helped establish the West's first AME church.

To Africa

Driven by the same hope and frustration that motivated western migration, other black Americans looked east to Africa. In the postwar years, Martin Delany revived his dream of claiming a black nationality there. "We have no chance to rise from beggars," Delany argued. "Men own the capital that we work who believe that my race have no more right to any of the profits of their labor than one of their mules." Richard Cain, a disillusioned ex-congressman, echoed Delany's despair: "There are thousands who are willing and ready to leave South Carolina, Georgia, Florida, and North Carolina. . . . The colored people of the South are tired of the constant struggle for life and liberty and prefer going where [there are] no obstacles . . . to . . . their liberty." Partnering with AME minister Henry McNeal Turner, Delany recruited settlers for Liberia. Turner had been born free in South Carolina in 1834, studied in the North, and served as pastor for a Washington, DC, church before the Civil War. After a stint as an army chaplain, he stayed in Georgia, working for the Republican Party and the AME church. By 1877, he shared Delany's dismay at the federal government's abandonment of black southerners.

In the spring of 1878, thousands of black Americans watched the launching of the *Azor* from Charleston's wharf.

Led by Delany and Turner, and with support from Cain, the Liberian Exodus Joint Stock Company had raised more than $6,000 to purchase the ship, which now carried roughly 200 settlers to Africa. Other black families invested thousands more. But expenses exceeded the company's limited capital, and the Exodus company soon lay in financial shambles. After delivering its first settlers, the company collapsed without establishing a permanent community. Though the Liberian Exodus Company represented yet another failed dream, the image of an African homecoming remained in the black imagination. Future generations would try again.

CONCLUSION

Emanuel Fortune's testimony in 1871 before the congressional committee investigating the Ku Klux Klan revealed the violence underlying post–Civil War southern politics. The politics of this war-torn region was no longer merely a regional concern of southerners and a few abolitionist northerners. The challenges facing African Americans now dominated the national agenda.

The federal government had outlawed slavery, extended equal rights to all citizens, and mandated that all black men could vote, but the law had little to do with reality. Though Hiram Revels and other black men represented southern states in Congress, white supremacist groups such as the Ku Klux Klan used threats, torture, and murder to scare southern black would-be voters away from the polls. Still, many black politicians sought common ground to negotiate compromises with southern white politicians. Sometimes they urged their black followers to accommodate some aspect of racial oppression in return for economic gains or political representation. At the far margin of the political spectrum, radicals tried to bridge the gap between the wealthy and the disaffected. They offered hope of a society that transcended divisions of race and class. All these strategies aimed to enable black people to move toward economic and social equality.

By 1877, African Americans seemed destined to be shunted aside again. With the Compromise of 1877, the federal government completed its withdrawal from helping freed slaves gain political rights and economic security. In the postwar era, black politicians had gained seats in Congress and in state legislatures. But with the end of Reconstruction, black politicians began leaving Washington and returning to the South to manage their personal lives and fortunes and to try to forge working relationships with white neighbors. Most white people in the North and the South expected black Americans to stay in the South, resigning themselves to menial jobs, limited political power, and continued deference to white

people. Indeed, in the coming decades, southern black laborers seemed doomed to jobs that ensured only subordination and debt, and black leaders understood these as the limitations within which they must operate.

Though Washington, DC, the federal capital, continued to attract black people seeking jobs and a strong black community, the American frontier and Africa lured others who dreamed of better opportunities and fresh ideas. By 1879, with the passing of many antebellum black leaders, the black cause desperately needed new energy and direction. The ratification of the Thirteenth, Fourteenth, and Fifteenth amendments had promised African Americans access to political participation. Now, with Black Codes, poverty, and violence circumscribing those promises, black Americans needed new leaders.

FURTHER READING

Bullock, Penelope L. *The Afro-American Periodical Press, 1838–1909* (Baton Rouge: Louisiana State University Press, 1981).

Butchart, Ronald. *Northern Schools, Southern Blacks, and Reconstruction: Freedmen's Education, 1862–1875* (Westport, CT: Greenwood, 1980).

Cimbala, Paul, and Randall Miller. *The Freedmen's Bureau and Reconstruction: Reconsiderations* (New York: Fordham University Press, 1999).

Cox, Thomas. *Blacks in Topeka, Kansas, 1865–1915* (Baton Rouge: Louisiana State University Press, 1982).

Dann, Martin. *The Black Press, 1827–1890: The Quest for National Identity* (New York: Putnam, 1971).

Foner, Eric. *Reconstruction: America's Unfinished Revolution, 1863–1877* (New York: Harper and Row, 1989).

Gutman, Herbert. *The Black Family in Slavery and Freedom, 1750–1925* (New York: Pantheon, 1976).

Hahn, Steven. *A Nation Under Our Feet: Black Political Struggles in the Rural South, From Slavery to the Great Migration.* (Cambridge, MA: Harvard Press, 2003).

Jaynes, Gerald. *Branches Without Roots: Genesis of the Black Working Class in the American South, 1682–1882* (New York: Oxford University Press, 1986).

McPherson, James. *Battle Cry of Freedom: The Civil War Era* (New York: Oxford University Press, 1988).

Rhodes, Jane. *Mary Ann Shadd Cary: The Black Press and Protest in the Nineteenth Century* (Bloomington: University of Indiana Press, 1998).

Saville, Julie. *The Work of Reconstruction: From Slave to Wage Labor in South Carolina, 1860–1870* (Cambridge: Cambridge University Press, 1996).

Sears, Richard. *A Utopian Experiment in Kentucky: Integration and Social Equality at Berea, 1866–1904* (Westport, CT: Greenwood, 1996).

Wilson, Kirt H. *The Reconstructin Desegregaton Debate: The Politics of Equality and the Rhetoric of Place, 1870–1875.* (E. Lansing: Michigan State University Press, 2002).

Appendices

THE DECLARATION OF INDEPENDENCE IN CONGRESS, JULY 4, 1776

The Unanimous Declaration of the Thirteen United States of America

When, in the course of human events, it becomes necessary for one people to dissolve the political bonds which have connected them with another, and to assume, among the powers of the earth, the separate and equal station to which the laws of nature and of nature's God entitle them, a decent respect to the opinions of mankind requires that they should declare the causes which impel them to the separation.

We hold these truths to be self-evident: That all men are created equal; that they are endowed by their Creator with certain unalienable rights; that among these are life, liberty, and the pursuit of happiness; that, to secure these rights, governments are instituted among men, deriving their just powers from the consent of the governed; that whenever any form of government becomes destructive of these ends, it is the right of the people to alter or to abolish it, and to institute new government, laying its foundation on such principles, and organizing its powers in such form, as to them shall seem most likely to effect their safety and happiness. Prudence, indeed, will dictate that governments long established should not be changed for light and transient causes; and accordingly all experience hath shown that mankind are more disposed to suffer, while evils are sufferable, than to right themselves by abolishing the forms to which they are accustomed. But when a long train of abuses and usurpations, pursuing invariably the same object, evinces a design to reduce them under absolute despotism, it is their right, it is their duty, to throw off such government, and to provide new guards for their future security. Such has been the patient sufferance of these colonies; and such is now the necessity which constrains them to alter their former systems of government. The history of the present King of Great Britain is a history of repeated injuries and usurpations, all having in direct object the establishment of an absolute tyranny over these states. To prove this, let facts be submitted to a candid world.

He has refused his assent to laws, the most whole-some and necessary for the public good.

He has forbidden his governors to pass laws of immediate and pressing importance, unless suspended in their operation till his assent should be obtained; and, when so suspended, he has utterly neglected to attend to them.

He has refused to pass other laws for the accommodation of large districts of people, unless those people would relinquish the right of representation in the legislature, a right inestimable to them, and formidable to tyrants only.

He has called together legislative bodies at places unusual, uncomfortable, and distant from the depository of their public records, for the sole purpose of fatiguing them into compliance with his measures.

He has dissolved representative houses repeatedly, for opposing, with manly firmness, his invasions on the rights of the people.

He has refused for a long time, after such dissolutions, to cause others to be elected; whereby the legislative powers, incapable of annihilation, have returned to the people at large for their exercise; the state remaining, in the mean time, exposed to all the dangers of invasions from without and convulsions within.

He has endeavored to prevent the population of these states; for that purpose obstructing the laws for naturalization of foreigners; refusing to pass others to encourage their migration hither, and raising the conditions of new appropriations of lands.

He has obstructed the administration of justice, by refusing his assent to laws for establishing judiciary powers.

He has made judges dependent on his will alone, for the tenure of their offices, and the amount and payment of their salaries.

He has erected a multitude of new offices, and sent hither swarms of officers to harass our people and eat out their substance.

He has kept among us, in times of peace, standing armies, without the consent of our legislatures.

He has affected to render the military independent of, and superior to, the civil power.

He has combined with others to subject us to a jurisdiction foreign to our constitution, and unacknowledged by our laws, giving his assent to their acts of pretended legislation:

For quartering large bodies of armed troops among us;

For protecting them, by a mock trial, from punishment for any murder which they should commit on the inhabitants of these states;

For cutting off our trade with all parts of the world;

For imposing taxes on us without our consent;

For depriving us, in many cases, of the benefits of trial by jury;

For transporting us beyond seas, to be tried for pretended offenses;

For abolishing the free system of English laws in a neighboring province, establishing therein an arbitrary government, and enlarging its boundaries, so as to render it at once an example and fit instrument for introducing the same absolute rule into these colonies;

For taking away our charters abolishing our most valuable laws, and altering fundamentally the forms of our governments;

For suspending our own legislatures, and declaring themselves invested with power to legislate for us in all cases whatsoever.

He has abdicated government here, by declaring us out of his protection and waging war against us.

He has plundered our seas, ravaged our coasts, burned our towns, and destroyed the lives of our people.

He is at this time transporting large armies of foreign mercenaries to complete the works of death, desolation, and tyranny already begun with circumstances of cruelty and perfidy scarcely paralleled in the most barbarous ages, and totally unworthy the head of a civilized nation.

He has constrained our fellow-citizens, taken captive on the high seas, to bear arms against their country, to become the executioners of their friends and brethren, or to fall themselves by their hands.

He has excited domestic insurrection among us, and has endeavored to bring on the inhabitants of our frontiers the merciless Indian savages, whose known rule of warfare is an undistinguished destruction of all ages, sexes, and conditions.

In every stage of these oppressions we have petitioned for redress in the most humble terms; our repeated petitions have been answered only by repeated injury. A prince, whose character is thus marked by every act which may define a tyrant, is unfit to be the ruler of a free people.

Nor have we been wanting in our attentions to our British brethren. We have warned them, from time to time, of attempts by their legislature to extend an unwarrantable jurisdiction over us. We have reminded them of the circumstances of our emigration and settlement here. We have appealed to their native justice and magnanimity; and we have conjured them, by the ties of our common kindred, to disavow these usurpations, which would inevitably interrupt our connections and correspondence. . . . They, too, have been deaf to the voice of justice and of consanguinity. We must, therefore, acquiesce in the necessity which denounces our separation, and hold them, as we hold the rest of mankind, enemies in war, in peace friends.

We, therefore, the representatives of the United States of America, in General Congress assembled, appealing to the Supreme Judge of the world for the rectitude of our intentions, do, in the name and by the authority of the good people of these colonies, solemnly publish and declare, that these United Colonies are, and of right, ought to be, FREE AND INDEPENDENT STATES; that they are absolved from all allegiance to the British crown, and that all political connection between them and the state of Great Britain is, and ought to be, totally dissolved; and that, as free and independent states, they have full power to levy war, conclude peace, contract alliances, establish commerce, and do all other acts and things which independent states may of right do. And for the support of this declaration, with a firm reliance on the protection of Devine Providence, we mutually pledge to each other our lives, our fortunes, and our sacred honor.

BUTTON GWENNETT	JOHN HANCOCK	JNO. WITHERSPOON
LYMAN HALL	FRANCIS LIGHTFOOT LEE	FRAS. HOPKINSON
GEO. WALTON	CARTER BRAXTON	JOHN HART
WM. HOOPER	ROBT. MORRIS	ABRA. CLARK
JOSEPH HEWES	BENJAMIN RUSH	JOSIAH BARTLETT
JOHN PENN	BENJA. FRANKLIN	WM. WHIPPLE
EDWARD RUTLEDGE	JOHN MORTON	SAML. ADAMS
THOS. HEYWARD, JUNR.	GEO. CLYMER	JOHN ADAMS
THOMAS LYNCH, JUNR.	JAS. SMITH	ROBT. TREAT PAINE
ARTHUR MIDDLETON	GEO. TAYLOR	ELBRIDGE GERRY
SAMUEL CHASE	JAMES WILSON	STEP. HOPKINS

WM. PACA
THOS. STONE
CHARLES CARROLL OF CARROLLTON
GEORGE WYTHE
RICHARD HENRY LEE
TH. JEFFERSON
BENJA. HARRISON
THS. NELSON, JR.

GEO. ROSS
CAESAR RODNEY
GEO. READ
THO. MÍKEAN
WM. FLOYD
PHIL. LIVINGSTON
FRANS. LEWIS
LEWIS MORRIS

WILLIAM ELLERY
ROGER SHERMAN
SAMÍEL. HUNTINGTON
WM. WILLIAMS
OLIVER WOLCOTT
MATHEW THORNTON
RICHD. STOCKTON

THE CONSTITUTION OF THE UNITED STATES OF AMERICA*

Preamble

We the People of the United States, in Order to form a more perfect Union, establish Justice, insure domestic Tranquility, provide for the common defence, promote the general Welfare, and secure the Blessings of Liberty to ourselves and our Posterity, do ordain and establish this Constitution for the United States of America.

Article I.

Section 1   All legislative Powers herein granted shall be vested in a Congress of the United States, which shall consist of a Senate and House of Representatives.

Section 2   The House of Representatives shall be composed of Members chosen every second Year by the People of the several States, and the Electors in each State shall have the Qualifications requisite for Electors of the most numerous Branch of the State Legislature.

No Person shall be a Representative who shall not have attained to the Age of twenty five Years, and been seven Years a Citizen of the United States, and who shall not, when elected, be an Inhabitant of that State in which he shall be chosen.

Representatives and direct Taxes shall be apportioned among the several States which may be included within this Union, according to their respective Numbers, *which shall be determined by adding to the whole Number of free Persons, including those bound to Service for a Term of Years, and excluding Indians not taxed, three fifths of all other Persons.* The actual Enumeration shall be made within three Years after the first Meeting of the Congress of the United States, and within every subsequent Term of ten Years, in such Manner as they shall by Law direct. The Number of Representatives shall not exceed one for every thirty Thousand, but each State shall have at Least one Representative; *and until such enumeration*

The constitution became effective March 4, 1789. Any portion of the text that has been amended is printed in italics.

shall be made, the State of New Hampshire shall be entitled to chuse three, Massachusetts eight, Rhode-Island and Providence Plantations one, Connecticut five, New-York six, New Jersey four, Pennsylvania eight, Delaware one, Maryland six, Virginia ten, North Carolina five, South Carolina five, and Georgia three.

When vacancies happen in the Representation from any State, the Executive Authority thereof shall issue Writs of Election to fill such Vacancies.

The House of Representatives shall chuse their Speaker and other Officers; and shall have the sole Power of Impeachment.

Section 3 The Senate of the United States shall be composed of two Senators from each State, chosen by the Legislature thereof, for six Years; and each Senator shall have one Vote.

Immediately after they shall be assembled in Consequence of the first Election, they shall be divided as equally as may be into three Classes. The Seats of the Senators of the first Class shall be vacated at the Expiration of the second Year, of the second Class at the Expiration of the fourth Year, and of the third Class at the Expiration of the sixth Year, so that one third may be chosen every second Year; and if Vacancies happen by Resignation, or otherwise, during the Recess of the Legislature of any State, the Executive thereof may make temporary Appointments until the next Meeting of the Legislature, which shall then fill such Vacancies.

No Person shall be a Senator who shall not have attained to the Age of thirty Years, and been nine Years a Citizen of the United States, and who shall not, when elected, be an Inhabitant of that State for which he shall be chosen.

The Vice President of the United States shall be President of the Senate, but shall have no Vote, unless they be equally divided.

The Senate shall choose their other Officers, and also a President *pro tempore*, in the Absence of the Vice President, or when he shall exercise the Office of President of the United States.

The Senate shall have the sole Power to try all Impeachments. When sitting for that Purpose, they shall be on Oath or Affirmation. When the President of the United States is tried the Chief Justice shall preside: And no Person shall be convicted without the Concurrence of two thirds of the Members present.

Judgment in Cases of Impeachment shall not extend further than to removal from Office, and disqualification to hold and enjoy any Office of honor, Trust or Profit under the United States: but the Party convicted shall nevertheless be liable and subject to Indictment, Trial, Judgment and Punishment, according to Law.

Section 4   The Times, Places and Manner of holding Elections for Senators and Representatives, shall be prescribed in each State by the Legislature thereof; but the Congress may at any time by Law make or alter such Regulations, except as to the Places of chusing Senators.

The Congress shall assemble at least once in every Year, and such Meeting *shall be on the first Monday in December, unless they shall by Law appoint a different Day.*

Section 5   Each House shall be the Judge of the Elections, Returns and Qualifications of its own Members, and a Majority of each shall constitute a Quorum to do Business; but a smaller Number may adjourn from day to day, and may be authorized to compel the Attendance of absent Members, in such Manner, and under such Penalties as each House may provide.

Each House may determine the Rules of its Proceedings, punish its Members for disorderly Behaviour, and, with the Concurrence of two thirds, expel a Member.

Each House shall keep a Journal of its Proceedings, and from time to time publish the same, excepting such Parts as may in their Judgment require Secrecy; and the Yeas and Nays of the Members of either House on any question shall, at the Desire of one fifth of those Present, be entered on the Journal.

Neither House, during the Session of Congress, shall, without the Consent of the other, adjourn for more than three days, nor to any other Place than that in which the two Houses shall be sitting.

Section 6   The Senators and Representatives shall receive a Compensation for their Services, to be ascertained by Law, and paid out of the Treasury of the United States. They shall in all Cases, except Treason, Felony and Breach of the Peace, be privileged from Arrest during their Attendance at the Session of their respective Houses, and in going to and returning from the same; and for any Speech or Debate in either House, they shall not be questioned in any other Place.

No Senator or Representative shall, during the Time for which he was elected, be appointed to any civil Office under the Authority of the United States, which shall have been created, or the Emoluments whereof shall have been encreased during such time; and no Person holding any Office under the United States, shall be a Member of either House during his Continuance in Office.

Section 7   All Bills for raising Revenue shall originate in the House of Representatives; but the Senate may propose or concur with Amendments as on other Bills.

Every Bill which shall have passed the House of Representatives and the Senate, shall, before it become a Law, be presented to the President of the United States; If he approve he shall sign it, but if not he shall return it, with his Objections to that House in which it shall have originated, who shall enter the Objections at large on their Journal, and proceed to reconsider it. If after such Reconsideration two thirds of that House shall agree to pass the Bill, it shall be sent, together with the Objections, to the other House, by which it shall likewise be reconsidered, and if approved by two thirds of that House, it shall become a Law. But in all such Cases the Votes of both Houses shall be determined by yeas and Nays, and the Names of the Persons voting for and against the Bill shall be entered on the Journal of each House respectively. If any Bill shall not be returned by the President within ten Days (Sundays excepted) after it shall have been presented to him, the Same shall be a Law, in like Manner as if he had signed it, unless the Congress by their Adjournment prevent its Return, in which Case it shall not be a Law.

Every Order, Resolution, or Vote to which the Concurrence of the Senate and House of Representatives may be necessary (except on a question of Adjournment) shall be presented to the President of the United States; and before the Same shall take Effect, shall be approved by him, or being disapproved by him, shall be repassed by two thirds of the Senate and House of Representatives, according to the Rules and Limitations prescribed in the Case of a Bill.

Section 8   The Congress shall have Power:

To lay and collect Taxes, Duties, Imposts and Excises, to pay the Debts and provide for the common Defence and general Welfare of the United States; but all Duties, Imposts and Excises shall be uniform throughout the United States;

To borrow Money on the credit of the United States;

To regulate Commerce with foreign Nations, and among the several States, and with the Indian Tribes;

To establish an uniform Rule of Naturalization, and uniform Laws on the subject of Bankruptcies throughout the United States;

To coin Money, regulate the Value thereof, and of foreign Coin, and fix the Standard of Weights and Measures;

To provide for the Punishment of counterfeiting the Securities and current Coin of the United States;

To establish Post Offices and post Roads;

To promote the Progress of Science and useful Arts, by securing for limited Times to Authors and Inventors the exclusive Right to their respective Writings and Discoveries;

To constitute Tribunals inferior to the supreme Court;

To define and punish Piracies and Felonies committed on the high Seas, and Offences against the Law of Nations;

To declare War, grant Letters of Marque and Reprisal, and make Rules concerning Captures on Land and Water;

To raise and support Armies, but no Appropriation of Money to that Use shall be for a longer Term than two Years;

To provide and maintain a Navy;

To make Rules for the Government and Regulation of the land and naval Forces;

To provide for calling forth the Militia to execute the Laws of the Union, suppress Insurrections and repel Invasions;

To provide for organizing, arming, and disciplining, the Militia, and for governing such Part of them as may be employed in the Service of the United States, reserving to the States respectively, the Appointment of the Officers, and the Authority of training the Militia according to the discipline prescribed by Congress;

To exercise exclusive Legislation in all Cases whatsoever, over such District (not exceeding ten Miles square) as may, by Cession of particular States, and the Acceptance of Congress, become the Seat of the Government of the United States, and to exercise like Authority over all Places purchased by the Consent of the Legislature of the State in which the Same shall be, for the Erection of Forts, Magazines, Arsenals, dock-Yards, and other needful Buildings;

To make all Laws which shall be necessary and proper for carrying into Execution the foregoing Powers, and all other Powers vested by this Constitution in the Government of the United States, or in any Department or Officer thereof.

Section 9   The Migration or Importation of such Persons as any of the States now existing shall think proper to admit, shall not be prohibited by the Congress prior to the Year one thousand eight hundred and eight, but a Tax or duty may be imposed on such Importation, not exceeding ten dollars for each Person.

The Privilege of the Writ of Habeas Corpus shall not be suspended, unless when in Cases of Rebellion or Invasion the public Safety may require it.

No Bill of Attainder or ex post facto Law shall be passed.

No Capitation, or other direct, Tax shall be laid, unless in Proportion to the Census or Enumeration herein before directed to be taken.

No Tax or Duty shall be laid on Articles exported from any State.

No Preference shall be given by any Regulation of Commerce or Revenue to the Ports of one State over those of another: nor shall Vessels bound to, or from, one State, be obliged to enter, clear, or pay Duties in another.

No Money shall be drawn from the Treasury, but in Consequence of Appropriations made by Law; and a regular Statement and Account of the Receipts and Expenditures of all public Money shall be published from time to time.

No Title of Nobility shall be granted by the United States: And no Person holding any Office of Profit or Trust under them, shall, without the Consent of the Congress, accept of any present, Emolument, Office, or Title, of any kind whatever, from any King, Prince, or foreign State.

Section 10   No State shall enter into any Treaty, Alliance, or Confederation; grant Letters of Marque and Reprisal; coin Money; emit Bills of Credit; make any Thing but gold and silver Coin a Tender in Payment of Debts; pass any Bill of Attainder, ex post facto Law, or Law impairing the Obligation of Contracts, or grant any Title of Nobility.

No State shall, without the Consent of the Congress, lay any Imposts or Duties on Imports or Exports, except what may be absolutely necessary for executing its inspection Laws: and the net Produce of all Duties and Imposts, laid by any State on Imports or Exports, shall be for the Use of the Treasury of the United States; and all such Laws shall be subject to the Revision and Controul of the Congress.

No State shall, without the Consent of Congress, lay any Duty of Tonnage, keep Troops, or Ships of War in time of Peace, enter into any Agreement or Compact with another State, or with a foreign Power, or engage in War, unless actually invaded, or in such imminent Danger as will not admit of delay.

Article II.

Section 1   The executive Power shall be vested in a President of the United States of America. He shall hold his Office during the Term of four Years, and, together with the Vice President, chosen for the same Term, be elected, as follows:

Each State shall appoint, in such Manner as the Legislature thereof may direct, a Number of Electors, equal to the whole Number of Senators and Representatives to which the State may be entitled in the Congress: but no Senator or Representative, or Person holding an Office of Trust or Profit under the United States, shall be appointed an Elector.

The Electors shall meet in their respective States, and vote by Ballot for two Persons, of whom one at least shall not be an Inhabitant of the same State with themselves. And they shall make a List of all the Persons voted for, and of the Number of Votes for each; which List they shall sign and certify, and transmit sealed to the Seat of Government of the United States, directed to the President of the Senate. The President of the Senate shall, in the Presence of the Senate and House of Representatives, open all the Certificates, and the Votes shall then be counted. The Person having the greatest Number of Votes shall be the President, if such Number be a Majority of the whole

Number of Electors appointed; and if there be more than one who have such Majority, and have an equal Number of Votes, then the House of Representatives shall immediately chuse by Ballot one of them for President; and if no Person have a Majority, then from the five highest on the List the said House shall in like Manner chuse the President. But in chusing the President, the Votes shall be taken by States, the Representation from each State having one Vote; A quorum for this Purpose shall consist of a Member or Members from two thirds of the States, and a Majority of all the States shall be necessary to a Choice. In every Case, after the Choice of the President, the Person having the greatest Number of Votes of the Electors shall be the Vice President. But if there should remain two or more who have equal Votes, the Senate shall chuse from them by Ballot the Vice President. The Congress may determine the Time of chusing the Electors, and the Day on which they shall give their Votes; which Day shall be the same throughout the United States.*

No Person except a natural born Citizen, *or a Citizen of the United States, at the time of the Adoption of this Constitution,* shall be eligible to the Office of President; neither shall any Person be eligible to that Office who shall not have attained to the Age of thirty five Years, and been fourteen Years a Resident within the United States.

In Case of the Removal of the President from Office, or of his Death, Resignation, or Inability to discharge the Powers and Duties of the said Office, the Same shall devolve on the Vice President, and the Congress may by Law provide for the Case of Removal, Death, Resignation or Inability, both of the President and Vice President declaring what Officer shall then act as President, and such Officer shall act accordingly, until the Disability be removed, or a President shall be elected.

The President shall, at stated Times, receive for his Services, a Compensation, which shall neither be increased nor diminished during the Period for which he shall have been elected, and he shall not receive within that Period any other Emolument from the United States, or any of them.

Before he enter on the Execution of his Office, he shall take the following Oath or Affirmation: "I do solemnly swear (or affirm) that I will faithfully execute the Office of President of the United States, and will to the best of my Ability, preserve, protect and defend the Constitution of the United States."

Section 2   The President shall be Commander in Chief of the Army and Navy of the United States, and of the Militia of the several States, when called into the actual Service of the United States; he may require the Opinion, in writing, of the principal Officer in each of the executive Departments, upon any Subject relating to the Duties of their respective Offices, and he shall have Power to grant Reprieves and Pardons for Offences against the United States, except in Cases of Impeachment.

He shall have Power, by and with the Advice and Consent of the Senate, to make Treaties, provided two thirds of the Senators present concur; and he shall nominate, and by and with the Advice and Consent of the Senate, shall appoint Ambassadors, other public Ministers and Consuls, Judges of the supreme Court, and all other Officers of the United States, whose Appointments are not herein otherwise provided for, and which shall be established by Law: but the Congress may by Law vest the Appointment of such inferior Officers, as they think proper, in the President alone, in the Courts of Law, or in the Heads of Departments.

The President shall have Power to fill up all Vacancies that may happen during the Recess of the Senate, by granting Commissions which shall expire at the End of their next Session.

Section 3   He shall from time to time give to the Congress Information of the State of the Union, and recommend to their Consideration such Measures as he shall judge necessary and expedient; he may, on extraordinary Occasions, convene both Houses, or either of them, and in Case of Disagreement between them, with Respect to the Time of Adjournment, he may adjourn them to such Time as he shall think proper; he shall receive Ambassadors and other public Ministers; he shall take Care that the Laws be faithfully executed, and shall Commission all the Officers of the United States.

Section 4   The President, Vice President and all civil Officers of the United States, shall be removed from Office on Impeachment for, and Conviction of, Treason, Bribery, or other high Crimes and Misdemeanors.

Article III.

Section 1   The judicial Power of the United States, shall be vested in one supreme Court, and in such inferior Courts as the Congress may from time to time ordain and establish. The Judges, both of the supreme and inferior Courts, shall hold their Offices during good Behaviour, and shall, at stated Times, receive for their Services, a Compensation which shall not be diminished during their Continuance in Office.

Section 2   The judicial Power shall extend to all Cases, in Law and Equity, arising under this Constitution, the Laws of the United States, and Treaties made, or which shall be made, under their Authority;—to all Cases affecting Ambassadors, other public Ministers and Consuls;—to all Cases of admiralty and maritime Jurisdiction;—to Controversies to which the United States shall be a Party;—to Controversies between two or more States;—*between a State and Citizens of another State;*—between Citizens of different States;—between Citizens of the same State claiming Lands under

Grants of different States, and between a State, or the Citizens thereof, and foreign States, Citizens or Subjects.

In all Cases affecting Ambassadors, other public Ministers and Consuls, and those in which a State shall be Party, the supreme Court shall have original Jurisdiction. In all the other Cases before mentioned, the supreme Court shall have appellate Jurisdiction, both as to Law and Fact, with such Exceptions, and under such Regulations as the Congress shall make.

The Trial of all Crimes, except in Cases of Impeachment, shall be by Jury; and such Trial shall be held in the State where the said Crimes shall have been committed; but when not committed within any State, the Trial shall be at such Place or Places as the Congress may by Law have directed.

Section 3   Treason against the United States shall consist only in levying War against them, or in adhering to their Enemies, giving them Aid and Comfort. No Person shall be convicted of Treason unless on the Testimony of two Witnesses to the same overt Act, or on Confession in open Court.

The Congress shall have Power to declare the Punishment of Treason, but no Attainder of Treason shall work Corruption of Blood, or Forfeiture except during the Life of the Person attained.

Article IV.

Section 1   Full Faith and Credit shall be given in each State to the public Acts, Records, and judicial Proceedings of every other State. And the Congress may by general Laws prescribe the Manner in which such Acts, Records and Proceedings shall be proved, and the Effect thereof.

Section 2   The Citizens of each State shall be entitled to all Privileges and Immunities of Citizens in the several States.

A Person charged in any State with Treason, Felony, or other Crime, who shall flee from Justice, and be found in another State, shall on Demand of the executive Authority of the State from which he fled, be delivered up, to be removed to the State having Jurisdiction of the Crime.

No Person held to Service or Labour in one State, under the Laws thereof, escaping into another, shall, in Consequence of any Law or Regulation therein, be discharged from such Service or Labour, but shall be delivered up on Claim of the Party to whom such Service or Labour may be due.

Section 3   New States may be admitted by the Congress into this Union; but no new State shall be formed or erected within the Jurisdiction of any other State; nor any State be formed by the Junction of two or more States, or Parts of States, without the Consent of the Legislatures of the States concerned as well as of the Congress.

The Congress shall have Power to dispose of and make all needful Rules and Regulations respecting the Territory or other Property belonging to the United States; and nothing in this Constitution shall be so construed as to Prejudice any Claims of the United States, or of any particular State.

Section 4   The United States shall guarantee to every State in this Union a Republican Form of Government, and shall protect each of them against Invasion; and on Application of the Legislature, or of the Executive (when the Legislature cannot be convened), against domestic Violence.

Article V.

The Congress, whenever two thirds of both Houses shall deem it necessary, shall propose Amendments to this Constitution, or, on the Application of the Legislatures of two thirds of the several States, shall call a Convention for proposing Amendments, which, in either Case, shall be valid to all Intents and Purposes, as Part of this Constitution, when ratified by the Legislatures of three fourths of the several States, or by Conventions in three fourths thereof, as the one or the other Mode of Ratification may be proposed by the Congress; *Provided that no Amendment which may be made prior to the Year One thousand eight hundred and eight shall in any Manner affect the first and fourth Clauses in the Ninth Section of the first Article; and* that no State, without its Consent, shall be deprived of its equal Suffrage in the Senate.

Article VI.

All Debts contracted and Engagements entered into, before the Adoption of this Constitution, shall be as valid against the United States under this Constitution, as under the Confederation.

This Constitution, and the Laws of the United States which shall be made in Pursuance thereof; and all Treaties made or which shall be made, under the Authority of the United States, shall be the supreme Law of the Land; and the Judges in every State shall be bound thereby, any Thing in the Constitution or Laws of any State to the Contrary notwithstanding.

The Senators and Representatives before mentioned, and the Members of the several State Legislatures, and all executive and judicial Officers, both of the United States and of the several States, shall be bound by Oath or Affirmation, to support this Constitution; but no religious Test shall ever be required as a Qualification to any Office or public Trust under the United States.

Article VII.

The Ratification of the Conventions of nine States shall be sufficient for the Establishment of this Constitution between the States so ratifying the Same.

Done in Convention by the Unanimous Consent of the States present the Seventeenth Day of September in the Year of our Lord one thousand seven hundred and Eighty seven and of the Independence of the United States of America the Twelfth IN WITNESS whereof We have hereunto subscribed our Names.

AMENDMENTS TO THE CONSTITUTION RELATING TO CIVIL RIGHTS AND CIVIL LIBERTIES.

(*Editor's note:* The first ten amendments, called the Bill of Rights, were adopted in 1791.)

Amendment I
Congress shall make no law respecting an establishment of religion, or prohibiting the free exercise thereof; or abridging the freedom of speech, or of the press; or the right of the people peaceably to assemble, and to petition the Government for a redress of grievances.

Amendment II
A well regulated Militia, being necessary to the security of a free State, the right of the people to keep and bear Arms, shall not be infringed.

Amendment III
No Soldier shall, in time of peace be quartered in any house, without the consent of the Owner, nor in time of war, but in a manner to be prescribed by law.

Amendment IV
The right of the people to be secure in their persons, houses, papers, and effects, against unreasonable searches and seizures, shall not be violated, and no Warrants shall issue, but upon probable cause, supported by Oath or affirmation, and particularly describing the place to be searched, and the persons or things to be seized.

Amendment V
No person shall be held to answer for a capital, or otherwise infamous crime, unless on a presentment or indictment of a Grand Jury, except in cases arising in the land or naval forces, or in the Militia, when in actual service in time of War or public danger; nor shall any person be subject for the same offence to be twice put in jeopardy of life or limb; nor shall be compelled in any criminal case to be a witness against himself, nor be deprived of life, liberty, or property, without due process of law; nor shall private property be taken for public use, without just compensation.

Amendment VI
In all criminal prosecutions, the accused shall enjoy the right to a speedy and public trial, by an impartial jury of the State and district wherein the crime shall have been committed, which district shall have been previously ascertained by law, and to be informed of the nature and cause of the accusation; to be confronted with the witnesses against him; to have compulsory process for obtaining witnesses in his favor, and to have the Assistance of Counsel for his defence.

Amendment VII
In Suits at common law, where the value in controversy shall exceed twenty dollars, the right of trial by jury shall be preserved, and no fact tried by a jury, shall be otherwise re-examined in any Court of the United States, than according to the rules of the common law.

Amendment VIII
Excessive bail shall not be required, nor excessive fines imposed, nor cruel and unusual punishments inflicted.

Amendment IX
The enumeration in the Constitution, of certain rights, shall not be construed to deny or disparage others retained by the people.

Amendment X
The powers not delegated to the United States by the Constitution, nor prohibited by it to the States, are reserved to the States respectively, or to the people.

Amendment XI [Adopted 1798]
The Judicial power of the United States shall not be construed to extend to any suit in law or equity, commenced or prosecuted against one of the United States by Citizens of another State, or by Citizens or Subjects of any Foreign State.

Amendment XIII [Adopted 1865]
Section 1   Neither slavery nor involuntary servitude, except as a punishment for crime whereof the party shall have been duly convicted, shall exist within the United States, or any place subject to their jurisdiction.

Section 2   Congress shall have power to enforce this article by appropriate legislation.

Amendment XIV [Adopted 1868]
Section 1   All persons born or naturalized in the United States, and subject to the jurisdiction thereof, are citizens of the United States and of the State wherein they reside. No State shall make or enforce any law which shall abridge the privileges or immunities of citizens of the United States; nor shall any State deprive any person of life, liberty, or property, without due process of law; nor deny to any person within its jurisdiction the equal protection of the laws.

Section 2   Representatives shall be apportioned among the several States according to their respective numbers, counting the whole number of persons in each State, excluding Indians not taxed. But when the right to vote at any election for the choice of electors for President and Vice-President of the United States, Representatives in Congress, the Executive and Judicial officers of a State, or the members of the Legislature thereof, is denied to any of the male inhabitants of such State, being twenty-one years of age, and citizens of the United States, or in any way abridged, except for participation in rebellion, or other crime, the basis of representation therein shall be reduced in the proportion which the number of such male citizens shall bear to the whole number of male citizens twenty-one years of age in such State.

Section 3   No person shall be a Senator or Representative in Congress, or elector of President and Vice-President, or hold any office, civil or military, under the United States, or under any State, who, having previously taken an oath, as a member of Congress, or as an officer of the United States, or as a member of any State legislature, or as an executive or judicial officer of any State, to support the Constitution of the United States, shall have engaged in insurrection or rebellion against the same, or given aid or comfort to the enemies thereof. But Congress may by a vote of two thirds of each House, remove such disability.

Section 4   The validity of the public debt of the United States, authorized by law, including debts incurred for payment of pensions and bounties for services in suppressing insurrection or rebellion, shall not be questioned. But neither the United States nor any State shall assume or pay any debt or obligation incurred in aid of insurrection or rebellion against the United States, or any claim for the loss or emancipation of any slave; but all such debts, obligations and claims shall be held illegal and void.

Section 5   The Congress shall have power to enforce, by appropriate legislation, the provisions of this article.

Amendment XV [Adopted 1870]
Section 1   The right of citizens of the United States to vote shall not be denied or abridged by the United States or by any State on account of race, color, or previous condition of servitude.

Section 2   The Congress shall have power to enforce this article by appropriate legislation.

Amendment XXIII [Adopted 1961]
Section 1   The District constituting the seat of Government of the United States shall appoint in such manner as the Congress may direct:

A number of electors of President and Vice-President equal to the whole number of Senators and Representatives in Congress to which the District would be entitled if it were a State, but in no event more than the least populous State; they shall be in addition to those appointed by the States, but they shall be considered, for the purposes of the election of President and Vice-President, to be electors appointed by a State; and they shall meet in the District and perform such duties as provided by the twelfth article of amendment.

Section 2   The Congress shall have power to enforce this article by appropriate legislation.

Amendment XXIV [Adopted 1964]
Section 1   The right of citizens of the United States to vote in any primary or other election for President or Vice-President, for electors for President or Vice-President, or for Senator or Representative in Congress, shall not be denied or abridged by the United States or any State by reason of failure to pay any poll tax or other tax.

Section 2   The Congress shall have power to enforce this article by appropriate legislation.

Amendment XXVI [Adopted 1971]
Section 1   The right of citizens of the United States, who are eighteen years of age or older, to vote shall not be denied or abridged by the United States or any state on account of age.

Section 2   The Congress shall have power to enforce this article by appropriate legislation.

Amendment XXVII [Adopted 1992]
No law, varying the compensation for the services of Senators and Representatives, shall take effect until an election of Representatives has intervened.

DRED SCOTT V. SANDFORD (1857)

With the help of abolitionist lawyers, Dred Scott spent twenty years trying to convince local, state, and national courts that he should be entitled to freedom because his master had taken him to live for a time in a northern territory where slavery had been outlawed by Congress. When the Supreme Court ruled against him, it also took the opportunity to declare that no African American could either be an American citizen or use the court system.

Chief Justice Taney delivered the opinion of the Court.

The question is simply this: Can a negro, whose ancestors were imported into this country, and sold as slaves, become a member of the political community formed and brought into existence by the Constitution of the United States, and as such become entitled to all the rights, and privileges, and immunities, guarantied by that instrument to the citizen? One of which rights is the privilege of suing in a court of the United States in the cases specified in the constitution. . . .

The words "people of the United States" and "citizens" are synonymous terms, and mean the same thing. They both describe the political body who, according to our republican institutions, form the sovereignty, and who hold the power and conduct the government through their representatives. They are what we familiarly call the "sovereign people," and every citizen is one of this people, and a constituent member of this sovereignty. The question before us is, whether the class of persons described in the plea in abatement compose a portion of this people, and are constituent members of this sovereignty? We think they are not, and that they are not included, and were not intended to be included, under the word "citizens" in the constitution, and can therefore claim none of the rights and privileges which that instrument provides for and secures to citizens of the United States. On the contrary, they were at that time considered as a subordinate and inferior class of beings, who had been subjugated by the dominant race, and, whether emancipated or not, yet remained subject to their authority, and had no rights or privileges but such as those who held the power and the government might choose to grant them.

It is not the province of the court to decide upon the justice or injustice, the policy or impolicy, of these laws. The decision of that question belonged to the political or law-making power; to those who formed the sovereignty and framed the constitution. The duty of the court is to interpret the instrument they have framed, with the best lights we can obtain on the subject, and to administer it as we find it, according to its true intent and meaning when it was adopted.

In discussing this question, we must not confound the rights of citizenship which a State may confer within its own limits, and the rights of citizenship as a member of the Union. It does not by any means follow, because he has all the rights and privileges of a citizen of a State, that he must be a citizen of the United States. He may have all of the rights and privileges of the citizen of a State, and yet not be entitled to the rights and privileges of a citizen in any other State. For, previous to the adoption of the constitution of the United States, every State had the undoubted right to confer on whomsoever it pleased the character of citizen, and to endow him with all its rights. But this character of course was confirmed to the boundaries of the State, and gave him no rights or privileges in other States beyond those secured to him by the laws of nations and the comity of

States. Nor have the several States surrendered the power of conferring these rights and privileges by adopting the constitution of the United States. . . .

It is very clear, therefore, that no State can, by any act or law of its own, passed since the adoption of the constitution, introduce a new member into the political community created by the constitution of the United States. It cannot make him a member of this community by making him a member of its own. And for the same reason it cannot introduce any person, or description of persons, who were not intended to be embraced in this new political family, which the constitution brought into existence, but were intended to be excluded from it.

The question then arises, whether the provisions of the constitution, in relation to the personal rights and privileges to which the citizen of a State should be entitled, embraced the negro African race, at that time in this country, or who might afterwards be imported, who had then or should afterwards be made free in any State; and to put it in the power of a single State to make him a citizen of the United States, and endue him with the full rights of citizenship in every other State without their consent? Does the constitution of the United States act upon him whenever he shall be made free under the laws of a State, and raised there to the rank of a citizen, and immediately clothe him with all the privileges of a citizen in every other State, and in its own courts?

The court thinks the affirmative of these propositions cannot be maintained. And if it cannot, the plaintiff in error could not be a citizen of the State of Missouri, within the meaning of the constitution of the United States, and, consequently, was not entitled to sue in its courts.

It is true, every person, and every class and description of persons, who were at the time of the adoption of the constitution recognized as citizens in the several States, became also citizens of this new political body; but none other; it was formed by them, and for them and their posterity, but for no one else. And the personal rights and privileges guaranteed to citizens of this new sovereignty were intended to embrace those only who were then members of the several State communities, or who should afterwards by birthright or otherwise become members, according to the provisions of the constitution and the principles on which it was founded. It was the union of those who were at that time members of distinct and separate political communities into one political family, whose power, for certain specified purposes, was to extend over the whole territory of the United States. And it gave to each citizen rights and privileges outside of his State which he did not before possess, and placed him in every other State upon a perfect equality with its own citizens as to rights of person and rights of property; it made him a citizen of the United States. . . .

In the opinion of the court, the legislation and histories of the times, and the language used in the declaration of independence, show, that neither the class of persons who had been imported as slaves, nor their descendants, whether they had become free or not, were then acknowledged as a part of the people, nor intended to be included in the general words used in that memorable instrument. . . .

It is too clear for dispute, that the enslaved African race were not intended to be included, and formed no part of the people who framed and adopted this declaration; for if the language, as understood in that day, would embrace them, the conduct of the distinguished men who framed the declaration of independence would have been utterly and flagrantly inconsistent with the principles they asserted; and instead of the sympathy of mankind, to which they so confidently appealed, they would have deserved and received universal rebuke and reprobation. . . .

But there are two clauses in the constitution which point directly and specifically to the negro race as a separate class of persons, and show clearly that they were not regarded as a portion of the people or citizens of the government then formed.

One of these clauses reserves to each of the thirteen States the right to import slaves until the year 1808, if it thinks proper. . . . And by the other provision the States pledge themselves to each other to maintain the right of property of the master, by delivering up to him any slave who may have escaped from his service, and be found within their respective territories. . . .

The only two provisions which point to them and include them, treat them as property, and make it the duty of the government to protect it; no other power, in relation to this race, is to be found in the constitution; and as it is a government of special, delegated powers, no authority beyond these two provisions can be constitutionally exercised. The government of the United States had no right to interfere for any other purpose but that of protecting the rights of the owner, leaving it altogether with the several States to deal with this race, whether emancipated or not, as each State may think justice, humanity, and the interests and safety of society, require. The States evidently intended to reserve this power exclusively to themselves. . . .

Upon a full and careful consideration of the subject, the court is of opinion, that, upon the facts stated . . . Dred Scott was not a citizen of Missouri within the meaning of the constitution of the United States, and not entitled as such to sue in its courts; and, consequently, that the circuit court had no jurisdiction of the case, and that the judgment on the plea in abatement is erroneous. . . .

We proceed . . . to inquire whether the facts relied on by the plaintiff entitled him to his freedom. . . .

The act of Congress, upon which the plaintiff relies, declares that slavery and involuntary servitude, except as a punishment for crime, shall be forever prohibited in all that part of the territory ceded by France, under the name of Louisiana, which lies north of thirty-six degrees thirty minutes north latitude and not included within the limits of Missouri. And the difficulty which meets us at the threshold of this part of the inquiry is whether Congress was authorized to pass this law under any of the powers granted to it by the Constitution; for, if the authority is not given by that instrument, it is the duty of this Court to declare it void and inoperative and incapable of conferring freedom upon anyone who is held as a slave under the laws of any one of the states.

The counsel for the plaintiff has laid much stress upon that article in the Constitution which confers on Congress the power "to dispose of and make all needful rules and regulations respecting the territory or other property belonging to the United States"; but, in the judgment of the Court, that provision has no bearing on the present controversy, and the power there given, whatever it may be, is confined, and was intended to be confined, to the territory which at that time belonged to, or was claimed by, the United States and was within their boundaries as settled by the treaty with Great Britain and can have no influence upon a territory afterward acquired from a foreign government. It was a special provision for a known and particular territory, and to meet a present emergency, and nothing more. . . .

We do not mean, however, to question the power of Congress in this respect. The power to expand the territory of the United States by the admission of new states is plainly given; and in the construction of this power by all the departments of the government, it has been held to authorize the acquisition of territory, not fit for admission at the time, but to be admitted as soon as its population and situation would entitle it to admission. . . .

It may be safely assumed that citizens of the United States who migrate to a territory belonging to the people of the United States cannot be ruled as mere colonists, dependent upon the will of the general government, and to be governed by any laws it may think proper to impose. The principle upon which our governments rest, and upon which alone they continue to exist, is the union of states, sovereign and independent within their own limits in their internal and domestic concerns, and bound together as one people by a general government, possessing certain enumerated and restricted powers, delegated to it by the people of the several states, and exercising supreme authority within the scope of the powers granted to it, throughout the dominion of the United States. A power, therefore, in the general government to obtain and hold colonies and dependent territories, over which they might legislate without restriction, would be inconsistent with its own existence in its present form. Whatever it acquires, it acquires for the benefit of the people of the several states who created it. It is their trustee acting for them and charged with the duty of promoting the interests of the whole people of the Union in the exercise of the powers specifically granted. . . .

But the power of Congress over the person or property of a citizen can never be a mere discretionary power under our Constitution and form of government. The powers of the government and the rights and privileges of the citizen are regulated and plainly defined by the Constitution itself. And, when the territory becomes a part of the United States, the federal government enters into possession in the character impressed upon it by those who created it. It enters upon it with its powers over the citizen strictly defined and limited by the Constitution, from which it derives its own existence, and by virtue of which alone it continues to exist and act as a government and sovereignty. It has no power of any kind beyond it; and it cannot, when it enters a territory of the United States, put off its character and assume discretionary or despotic powers which the Constitution has denied to it. It cannot create for itself a new character separated from the citizens of the United States and the duties it owes them under the provisions of the Constitution. The territory, being a part of the United States, the government and the citizen both enter it under the authority of the Constitution, with their respective rights defined and marked out; and the federal government can exercise no power over his person or property, beyond what that instrument confers, nor lawfully deny any right which it has reserved. . . .

These powers, and others, in relation to rights of person, which it is not necessary here to enumerate, are, in express and positive terms, denied to the general government; and the rights of private property have been guarded with equal care. Thus the rights of property are united with the rights of person and placed on the same ground by the Fifth Amendment to the Constitution, which provides that no person shall be deprived of life, liberty, and property without due process of law. And an act of Congress which deprives a citizen of the United States of his liberty or property, without due process of law, merely because he came himself or brought his property into a particular territory of the United States, and who had committed no offense against the laws, could hardly be dignified with the name of due process of law. . . .

It seems, however, to be supposed that there is a difference between property in a slave and other property and that different rules may be applied to it in expounding the Constitution of the United States. And the laws and usages of nations, and the writings of eminent jurists upon the rela-

tion of master and slave and their mutual rights and duties, and the powers which governments may exercise over it, have been dwelt upon in the argument.

But, in considering the question before us, it must be borne in mind that there is no law of nations standing between the people of the United States and their government and interfering with their relation to each other. The powers of the government and the rights of the citizen under it are positive and practical regulations plainly written down. The people of the United States have delegated to it certain enumerated powers and forbidden it to exercise others. It has no power over the person or property of a citizen but what the citizens of the United States have granted. And no laws or usages of other nations, or reasoning of statesmen or jurists upon the relations of master and slave, can enlarge the powers of the government or take from the citizens the rights they have reserved. And if the Constitution recognizes the right of property of the master in a slave, and makes no distinction between that description of property and other property owned by a citizen, no tribunal, acting under the authority of the United States, whether it be legislative, executive, or judicial, has a right to draw such a distinction or deny to it the benefit of the provisions and guaranties which have been provided for the protection of private property against the encroachments of the government.

Now, as we have already said in an earlier part of this opinion, upon a different point, the right of property in a slave is distinctly and expressly affirmed in the Constitution. The right to traffic in it, like an ordinary article of merchandise and property, was guaranteed to the citizens of the United States, in every state that might desire it, for twenty years. And the government in express terms is pledged to protect it in all future time if the slave escapes from his owner. That is done in plain words—too plain to be misunderstood. And no word can be found in the Constitution which gives Congress a greater power over slave property or which entitles property of that kind to less protection than property of any other description. The only power conferred is the power coupled with the duty of guarding and protecting the owner in his rights.

Upon these considerations it is the opinion of the Court that the act of Congress which prohibited a citizen from holding and owning property of this kind in the territory of the United States north of the line therein mentioned is not warranted by the Constitution and is therefore void; and that neither Dred Scott himself, nor any of his family, were made free by being carried into this territory; even if they had been carried there by the owner with the intention of becoming a permanent resident.

THE EMANCIPATION PROCLAMATION

By the President of the United States of America:

On January 1, 1863, when President Abraham Lincoln decreed that slaves within Confederate states would be free, black communities across the country gathered to read aloud the proclamation.

Whereas, on the twenty-second day of September, in the year of our Lord one thousand eight hundred and sixty-two, a proclamation was issued by the President of the United States, containing, among other things, the following, to wit:

> That on the first day of January, in the year of our Lord one thousand eight hundred and sixty-three, all persons held as slaves within any State or designated part of a State, the people whereof shall then be in rebellion against the United States, shall be then, thenceforward, and forever free; and the Executive Government of the United States, including the military and naval authority thereof, will recognize and maintain the freedom of such persons, and will do no act or acts to repress such persons, or any of them, in any efforts they may make for their actual freedom.
>
> That the Executive will, on the first day of January aforesaid, by proclamation, designate the States and parts of States, if any, in which the people thereof, respectively, shall then be in rebellion against the United States; and the fact that any State, or the people thereof, shall on that day be, in good faith, represented in the Congress of the United States by members chosen thereto at elections wherein a majority of the qualified voters of such State shall have participated, shall, in the absence of strong countervailing testimony, be deemed conclusive evidence that such State, and the people thereof, are not then in rebellion against the United States.

Now, therefore I, Abraham Lincoln, President of the United States, by virtue of the power in me vested as Commander-in-Chief, of the Army and Navy of the United States in time of actual armed rebellion against the authority and government of the United States, and as a fit and necessary war measure for suppressing said rebellion, do, on this first day of January, in the year of our Lord one thousand eight hundred and sixty-three, and in accordance with my purpose so to do publicly proclaimed for the full period of one hundred days, from the day first above mentioned, order and designate as the States and parts of States wherein the people thereof respectively, are this day in rebellion against the United States, the following, to wit:

Arkansas, Texas, Louisiana, (except the Parishes of St. Bernard, Plaquemines, Jefferson, St. John, St. Charles, St. James Ascension, Assumption, Terrebonne, Lafourche, St. Mary, St. Martin, and Orleans, including the City of New Orleans), Mississippi, Alabama, Florida, Georgia, South Carolina, North Carolina, and Virginia, (except the forty-eight counties designated as West Virginia, and also the counties of Berkley, Accomac, Northampton, Elizabeth City, York, Princess Ann, and Norfolk, including the cities of Norfolk and Portsmouth), and which excepted parts, are for the present, left precisely as if this proclamation were not issued.

And by virtue of the power, and for the purpose aforesaid, I do order and declare that all persons held as slaves within said designated States, and parts of States, are, and henceforward shall be free; and that the Executive government of the United States, including the military and naval authorities thereof, will recognize and maintain the freedom of said persons.

And I hereby enjoin upon the people so declared to be free to abstain from all violence, unless in necessary self-defense; and I recommend to them that, in all cases when allowed, they labor faithfully for reasonable wages.

And I further declare and make known, that such persons of suitable condition, will be received into the armed service of the United States to garrison forts, positions, stations, and other places, and to man vessels of all sorts in said service.

And upon this act, sincerely believed to be an act of justice, warranted by the Constitution, upon military necessity, I invoke the considerate judgment of mankind, and the gracious favor of Almighty God.

In witness whereof, I have hereunto set my hand and caused the seal of the United States to be affixed. Done at the City of Washington, this first day of January, in the year of our Lord one thousand eight hundred and sixty-three, and of the Independence of the United States of America the eighty-seventh.

By the President: Abraham Lincoln
William H. Seward, Secretary of State.

THE CIVIL RIGHTS CASES OF 1883

Over the course of several years, after Congress passed the Civil Rights Act of 1875, five separate test cases emerged from African Americans who were denied equal access to public facilities. These cases, as a group, were argued before the Supreme Court in March, 1883. After more than six months of deliberation, the Court concluded that the federal government had no authority to enforce the Civil Rights Act. Justice Harlan wrote a dissenting opinion, saying that the majority opinion had stripped the "soul" from the law.

Mr. Justice Bradley delivered the opinion of the court. After stating the facts . . . he continued:

The first section of the Fourteenth Amendment (which is the one relied on), after declaring who shall be citizens of the United States, and of the several States, is prohibitory in its character, and prohibitory upon the States. . . .

It is State action of a particular character that is prohibited. Individual invasion of individual rights is not the subject-matter of the amendment. It has a deeper and broader scope. It nullifies and makes void all State legislation, and State action of every kind, which impairs the privileges and immunities of citizens of the United States, or which injures them in life, liberty or property without due process of law, or which denies to any of them the equal protection of the laws. . . .

On the whole we are of opinion, that no countenance of authority for the passage of the law in question can be found in either the Thirteenth of Fourteenth Amendment of the Constitution; and no other ground of authority for its passage being suggested, it must necessarily be declared void, at least so far as its operation in the several States is concerned. . . . *And it is so ordered.*

Mr. Justice Harlan dissenting.

The opinion in these cases proceeds, it seems to me, upon grounds entirely too narrow and artificial. I cannot resist the conclusion that the substance and spirit of the recent amendments of the Constitution have been sacrificed by a subtle and ingenious verbal criticism. . . .

I am of the opinion that such discrimination practised by corporations and individuals in the exercise of their public or quasi-public functions is a badge of servitude the imposition of which Congress may prevent under its power, by appropriate legislation, to enforce the Thirteenth Amendment; and, consequently, without reference to its enlarged power under the Fourteenth Amendment, the act of March 1, 1875, is not, in my judgment, repugnant to the Constitution.

. . . To-day, it is the colored race which is denied, by corporations and individuals wielding public authority, rights fundamental in their freedom and citizenship. At some future time, it may be that some other race will fall under the ban of race discrimination. . . .

For the reasons stated I feel constrained to withhold my assent to the opinion of the court.

PLESSY V. FERGUSON (1896)

When Homer Plessy led a challenge to Louisiana's segregated trains, he started a series of events that led the Supreme Court, in 1896, to conclude that the races may be separated, as long as public facilities—such as trains and schools—were "equal."

Mr. Justice Brown, after stating the case, delivered the opinion of the court.

This case turns upon the constitutionality of an act of the General Assembly of the State of Louisiana passed in 1890, providing for separate railway carriages for the white and colored races. Acts 1890, No. 111, p. 152. . . .

The constitutionality of this act is attacked upon the ground that it conflicts both with the Thirteenth Amendment of the Constitution, abolishing slavery, and the Fourteenth Amendment, which prohibits certain restrictive legislation on the part of the States. . . .

A statute which implies merely a legal distinction between the white and colored races—a distinction which is founded in the color of the two races, and which must always exist so long as white men are distinguished from the other race by color—has no tendency to destroy the legal equality of the two races, or re-establish a state of involuntary servitude. Indeed, we do not understand that the Thirteenth Amendment is strenuously relied upon by the plaintiff in error in this connection. . . .

The object of the [Fourteenth] amendment was undoubtedly to enforce the absolute equality of the two races before the law, but in the nature of things it could not have been intended to abolish distinctions based upon color, or to enforce social, as distinguished from political equality, or a commingling of the two races upon terms unsatisfactory to either. Laws permitting, and even requiring, their separation in places where they are liable to be brought into contact do not necessarily imply the inferiority of either race to the other, and have been generally, if not universally, recognized as within the competency of the state legislatures in the exercise of their police power. The most common instance of this is connected with the establishment of separate schools for white and colored children, which has been held to be a valid exercise of the legislative power even by courts of States where the political rights of the colored race have been longest and most earnestly enforced. . . .

. . . Legislation is powerless to eradicate racial instincts or to abolish distinctions based upon physical differences, and the attempt to do so can only result in accentuating the difficulties of the present situation. If the civil and political rights of both races be equal one cannot be inferior to the other civilly or politically. If one race be inferior to the other socially, the Constitution of the United States cannot put them upon the same plane. . . .

Affirmed.

Mr. Justice Harlan dissenting.

. . . However apparent the injustice of such legislation may be, we have only to consider whether it is consistent with the Constitution of the United States. . . .

I am of opinion that the statute of Louisiana is inconsistent with the personal liberty of citizens, white and black, in that State, and hostile to both the spirit and letter of the Constitution of the United States. If laws of like character should be enacted in the several States of the Union, the effect would be in the highest degree mischievous. Slavery, as an institution tolerated by law would, it is true, have disappeared from our country, but there would remain a power in the States, by sinister legislation, to interfere with the full enjoyment of the blessings of freedom; to regulate civil rights, common to all citizens, upon the basis of race; and to place in a condition of legal inferiority a large body of American citizens, now constituting a part of the political community called the People of the United States, for whom, and by whom through representatives, our government is administered. Such a system is inconsistent with the guarantee given by the Constitution to each State of a republican form of government, and may be stricken down by Congressional action, or by the courts in the discharge of their solemn duty to maintain the supreme law of the land, anything in the constitution or laws of any State to the contrary notwithstanding.

For the reasons stated, I am constrained to withhold my assent from the opinion and judgment of the majority.

BROWN V. BOARD OF EDUCATION OF TOPEKA (1954)

Brown comprised five different lawsuits aimed at school desegregation. Thurgood Marshall and other NAACP attorneys argued that segregation in public schools was psychologically harmful. In May, 1954, the Supreme Court unanimously overturned the Plessy *decision and ruled that educational facilities were "inherently unequal" and thus unconstitutional under the Fourteenth Amendment.*

Mr. Chief Justice Warren delivered the opinion of the Court.

These cases come to us from the States of Kansas, South Carolina, Virginia, and Delaware. They are premised on different facts and different local conditions, but a common legal question justifies their consideration together in this consolidated opinion. . . .

Today, education is perhaps the most important function of state and local governments. Compulsory school attendance laws and the great expenditures for education both demonstrate our recognition of the importance of education to our democratic society. It is required in the performance of our most basic public responsibilities, even service in the armed forces. It is the very foundation of good citizenship. Today it is a principal instrument in awakening the child to cultural values, in preparing him for later professional training, and in helping him to adjust normally to his environment. In these days, it is doubtful that any child may reasonably be expected to succeed in life if he is denied the opportunity of an education. Such an opportunity, where the state has undertaken to provide it, is a right which must be made available to all on equal terms.

We come then to the question presented: Does segregation of children in public schools solely on the basis of race, even though the physical facilities and other "tangible" factors may be equal, deprive the children of the minority group of equal education opportunities? We believe that it does. . . .

We conclude that in the field of public education the doctrine of "separate but equal" has no place. Separate educational facilities are inherently unequal. Therefore, we hold that the plaintiffs and others similarly situated for whom the actions have been brought are, by reason of the segregation complained of, deprived of the equal protection of the laws guaranteed by the Fourteenth Amendment. . . .

KEY PROVISIONS OF THE CIVIL RIGHTS ACT OF 1964

The Civil Rights Act of 1964 outlawed racial discrimination in schools, restaurants, theaters, and other public places where Jim Crow laws had long reigned. The Act also prohibited large employers from discriminating against racial and religious minorities as well as women.

An Act

To enforce the constitutional right to vote, to confer jurisdiction upon the district courts of the United States to provide injunctive relief against discrimination in public accommodations, to authorize the Attorney General to institute suits to protect constitutional rights in public facilities and public education, to extend the Commission on Civil Rights, to prevent discrimination in federally assisted programs, to establish a Commission on Equal Employment Opportunity, and for other purposes.

Be it enacted by the Senate and House of Representatives of the United States of America in Congress assembled, that this Act may be cited as the "Civil Rights Act of 1964."

Title I—Voting Rights

Section 101.   . . .(2) No person acting under color of law shall—

(A) In determining whether any individual is qualified under State law or laws to vote in any Federal election, apply any standard, practice, or procedure different from the standards, practices, or procedures applied under such law or laws to other individuals within the same county, parish, or similar political subdivision who have been found by State officials to be qualified to vote;

(B) deny the right of any individual to vote in any Federal election because of an error or omission on any record or paper relating to any application, registration, or other act requisite to voting, if such error or

omission is not material in determining whether such individual is qualified under State law to vote in such election;

(C) employ any literacy test as a qualification for voting in any Federal election unless (i) such test is administered to each individual and is conducted wholly in writing, and (ii) a certified copy of the test and of the answers given by the individual is furnished to him within twenty-five days of the submission of his request made within the period of time during which records and papers are required to be retained and preserved pursuant to title III of the Civil Rights Act of 1960 (42 U.S.C. 1974–74e; 74 Stat. 88): Provided, however, That the Attorney General may enter into agreements with appropriate State or local authorities that preparation, conduct, and maintenance of such tests in accordance with the provisions of applicable State or local law, including such special provisions as are necessary in the preparation, conduct, and maintenance of such tests for persons who are blind or otherwise physically handicapped, meet the purposes of this subparagraph and constitute compliance therewith.

Title II—Injunctive Relief Against Discrimination in Places of Public Accommodation

Section 201.   (a) All persons shall be entitled to the full and equal enjoyment of the goods, services, facilities, and privileges, advantages and accommodations of any place of public accommodation, as defined in this section, without discrimination or segregation on the ground of race, color, religion, or national origin. (b) Each of the following establishments which serves the public is a place of public accommodation within the meaning of this title if its operations effect commerce, or if discrimination or segregation by it is supported by State action:

(1) any inn, hotel, motel, or other establishment which provides lodging to transient guests, other than an establishment located within a building which contains not more than five rooms for rent or hire and which is actually occupied by the proprietor of such establishment as his residence;

(2) any restaurant, cafeteria, lunchroom, lunch counter, soda fountain, or other facility principally engaged in selling food for consumption on the premises, including, but not limited to, any such facility located on the premises of any retail establishment; or any gasoline station;

(3) any motion picture house, theater, concert hall, sports arena, stadium or other place of exhibition or entertainment;

(4) any establishment (A) (i) which is physically located within the premises of any establishment otherwise covered by this subsection, or (ii) within the premises of which is physically located any such covered establishment, and (B) which holds itself out as serving patrons of such covered establishment. . . .

(d) Discrimination or segregation by an establishment is supported by State action within the meaning of this title if such discrimination or segregation

(1) is carried on under color of any law, statute, ordinance, or regulation; or

(2) is carried on under color of any custom or usage required or enforced by officials of the State or political subdivision thereof; or

(3) is required by action of the State or political subdivision thereof. . . .

Section 202.   All persons shall be entitled to be free, at any establishment or place, from discrimination or segregation of any kind on the ground of race, color, religion, or national origin, if such discrimination or segregation is or purports to be required by any law, statute, ordinance, regulation, rule, or order of a State or any agency or political subdivision thereof.

Section 203.   No person shall (a) withhold, deny, or attempt to withhold or deny, or deprive or attempt to deprive, any person of any right or privilege secured by section 201 or 202, or (b) intimidate, threaten, or coerce, or attempt to intimidate, threaten, or coerce any person with the purpose of interfering with any right or privilege secured by section 201 or 202, or (c) punish or attempt to punish any person

for exercising or attempting to exercise any right or privilege secured by section 201 or 202.

Section 204.   (a) Whenever any person has engaged or there are reasonable grounds to believe that any person is about to engage in any act or practice prohibited by section 203, a civil action for preventive relief, including an application for a permanent or temporary injunction, restraining order, or other order, may be instituted by the person aggrieved and, upon timely application, the court may, in its discretion, permit the Attorney General to intervene in such civil action if he certifies that the case is of general public importance. Upon application by the complainant and in such circumstances as the court may deem just, the court may appoint an attorney for such complainant and may authorize the commencement of the civil action without the payment of fees, costs, or security. . . .

Section 206.   (a) Whenever the Attorney General has reasonable cause to believe that any person or group of persons is engaged in a pattern or practice of resistance to the full enjoyment of any of the rights secured by the title, and that the pattern or practice is of such a nature and is intended to deny the full exercise of the rights herein described, the Attorney General may bring a civil action in the appropriate district court of the United States by filing with it a complaint

(1) signed by him (or in his absence the Acting Attorney General),

(2) setting forth facts pertaining to such pattern or practice, and

(3) requesting such preventive relief, including an application for a permanent or temporary injunction, restraining order or other order against the person or persons responsible for such pattern or practice, as he deems necessary to insure the full enjoyment of the rights herein described. . . .

Title III—Desegregation of Public Facilities

Section 301.   (a) Whenever the Attorney General receives a complaint in writing signed by an individual to the effect that he is being deprived of or threatened with the loss of his right to the equal protection of the laws, on account of his race, color, religion, or national origin, by being denied equal utilization of any public facility which is owned, operated, or managed by or on behalf of any State or subdivision thereof, other than a public school or public college as defined in section 401 of title IV hereof, and the Attorney General believes the complaint is meritorious and certifies that the signer or signers of such complaint are unable, in his judgment, to initiate and maintain appropriate legal proceedings for relief and that the institution of an action will materially further the orderly progress of desegregation in public facilities, the Attorney General is authorized to institute for or in the name of the United States a civil action in any appropriate district court of the United States against such parties and for such relief as may be appropriate. And such court shall have and shall exercise jurisdiction of proceedings instituted pursuant to this section. The Attorney General may implead as defendants such additional parties as are or become necessary to the grant of effective relief hereunder. . . .

Title IV—Desegregation of Public Education

Definitions

Section 401.   As used in this title—. . . .

(b) "Desegregation" means the assignment of students to public schools and within such schools without regard to their race, color, religion, or national origin, but "desegregation" shall not mean the assignment of students to public schools in order to overcome racial imbalance. . . .

Survey and Report of Educational Opportunities

Section 402.   The Commissioner shall conduct a survey and make a report to the President and the Congress, within two years of the enactment of this title, concerning the lack of availability of equal educational opportunities for individuals by reason of race, color, religion, or national origin in public educational institutions at all levels in the United States, its territories and possessions, and the District of Columbia. . . .

Title V—Commission on Civil Rights . . .

Duties of the Commission

Section 104.   (a) The Commission shall—

(1) investigate allegations in writing under oath or affirmation that certain citizens of the United States are being deprived of their right to vote and have that vote counted by reason of their color, race, religion, or national origin; which writing, under oath or affirmation, shall set forth the facts upon which such belief or beliefs are based;

(2) study and collect information concerning legal developments constituting a denial of equal protection of the laws under the Constitution because of race, color, religion, or national origin or in the administration of justice;

(3) appraise the laws and policies of the Federal Government with respect to denials of equal protection of the laws under the Constitution because of race, color, religion, or national origin or in the administration of justice;

(4) serve as a national clearinghouse for information in respect to denials of equal protection of the laws because of race, color, religion, or national origin, including but not limited to the fields of voting, education, housing, employment, the use of public facilities, and transportation, or in the administration of justice;

(5) investigate allegations, made in writing and under oath or affirmation, that citizens of the United States are unlawfully being accorded or denied the right to vote, or to have their votes properly counted, in any election of presidential electors, Members of the United States Senate, or of the House of Representatives, as a result of any patterns or practice of fraud or discrimination in the conduct of such election. . . .

Title VI—Nondiscrimination in Federally Assisted Programs

Section 601.   No person in the United States shall, on the ground of race, color, religion, or national origin, be excluded from participation in, be denied the benefits of, or be subjected to discrimination under any program or activity receiving Federal financial assistance.

Section 602.   Each Federal department and agency which is empowered to extend Federal financial assistance to any program or activity, by way of grant, loan, or contract other than a contract of insurance or guaranty, is authorized and directed to effectuate the provisions of section 601 with respect to such program or activity by issuing rules, regulations, or orders of general applicability which shall be consistent with achievement of the objectives of the statue authorizing the financial assistance in connection with which the action is taken. No such rule, regulation, or order shall become effective unless and until approved by the President. Compliance with any requirement adopted pursuant to this section may be effected

(1) by the termination of or refusal to grant or to continue assistance under such program or activity to any recipient as to whom there has been an express finding on the record, after opportunity for hearing, of a failure to comply with such requirement, but such termination or refusal shall be limited to the particular political entity, or part thereof, or other recipient as to whom such a finding has been made and, shall be limited in its effect to the particular program, or part thereof, in which such non-compliance has been so found, or

(2) by any other means authorized by law:

Provided, however, that no such action shall be taken until the department or agency concerned has advised the appropriate person or persons of the failure to comply with the requirement and has determined that compliance cannot be secured by voluntary means. In the case of any action terminating, or refusing to grant or continue, assistance because of failure to comply with a requirement imposed pursuant to this section, the head of the federal department or agency shall file with the committees of the House and Senate having legislative jurisdiction over the program or activity involved a full written report of the circumstances and the grounds for such action. No such action shall become effective until thirty days have elapsed after the filing of such report. . . .

Title VII—Equal Employment Opportunity . . .

Discrimination Because of Race, Color, Religion, Sex, or National Origin

Section 703. (a) It shall be an unlawful employment practice for an employer—

(1) to fail or refuse to hire or to discharge any individual, or otherwise to discriminate against any individual with respect to his compensation, terms, conditions, or privileges of employment, because of such individual's race, color, religion, sex, or national origin; or

(2) to limit, segregate, or classify his employees in any way which would deprive or tend to deprive any individual of employment opportunities or otherwise adversely affect his status as an employee, because of such individual's race, color, religion, sex, or national origin.

(b) It shall be an unlawful employment practice for an employment agency to fail or refuse to refer for employment, or otherwise to discriminate against, any individual because of his race, color, religion, sex, or national origin, or to classify or refer for employment any individual on the basis of his race, color, religion, sex, or national origin.

(c) It shall be an unlawful employment practice for a labor organization—

(1) to exclude or to expel from its membership, or otherwise to discriminate against, any individual because of his race, color, religion, sex, or national origin;

(2) to limit, segregate, or classify its membership, or to classify or fail or refuse to refer for employment any individual, in any way which would deprive or tend to deprive any individual of employment opportu-

nities, or would limit such employment opportunities or otherwise adversely affect his status as an employee or as an applicant for employment, because of such individual's race, color, religion, sex, or national origin; or

(3) to cause or attempt to cause an employer to discriminate against an individual in violation of this section.

(d) It shall be an unlawful employment practice for any employer, labor organization, or joint labor-management committee controlling apprenticeship or other training or retraining, including on-the-job training programs, to discriminate against any individual because of his race, color, religion, sex, or national origin in admission to, or employment in, any program established to provide apprenticeship or other training. . . .

Other Unlawful Employment Practices

Section 704. (a) It shall be an unlawful employment practice for an employer to discriminate against any of his employees or applicants for employment, for an employment agency to discriminate against any individual, or for a labor organization to discriminate against any member thereof or applicant for membership, because he has opposed any practice made an unlawful employment practice by this title, or because he has made a charge, testified, assisted, or participated in any manner in an investigation, proceeding, or hearing under this title.

(b) It shall be an unlawful employment practice for an employer, labor organization, or employment agency to print or publish or cause to be printed or published any notice or advertisement relating to employment by such an employer or membership in or any classification or referral for employment by such a labor organization, or relating to any classification or referral for employment by such an employment agency, indicating any preference, limitation, specification, or discrimination, based on race, color, religion, sex, or national origin, except that such a notice or advertisement may indicate a preference, limitation, specification, or discrimination based on religion, sex, or national origin when religion, sex, or national origin is a bona fide occupational qualification for employment.

Equal Employment Opportunity Commission

Section 705. (a) There is hereby created a Commission to be known as the Equal Employment Opportunity Commission, which shall be composed of five members, not more than three of whom shall be members of the same political party, who shall be appointed by the President by and with the advice and consent of the Senate. One of the original members shall be appointed for a term of one year, one for a term of two years, one for a term of three years, one for a term of four years, and one for a term of five years, beginning from the date of enactment of this title, but their successors shall be appointed for terms of five years each, except that any individual chosen to fill a vacancy shall be appointed only for the unexpired term of the member whom he shall succeed. The President shall designate one member to serve as Chairman of the Commission, and one member to serve as Vice Chairman. The Chairman shall be responsible on behalf of the Commission for the administrative operations of the Commission, and shall appoint, in accordance with the civil service laws, such officers, agents, attorneys, and employees as it deems necessary to assist it in the performance of its functions and to fix their compensation in accordance with Classification Act of 1949, as amended. . . .

Title VIII—Registration and Voting Statistics

Section 801.   The Secretary of Commerce shall promptly conduct a survey to compile registration and voting statistics in such geographic areas as may be recommended by the Commission on Civil Rights. Such a survey and compilation shall, to the extent recommended by the Commission on Civil Rights, only include a count of persons of voting age by race, color, and national origin, and determination of the extent to which such persons are registered to vote, and have voted in any statewide primary or general election in which the Members of the United States House of Representatives are nominated or elected, since January 1, 1960. Such information shall also be collected and compiled in connection with the Nineteenth Decennial Census, and at such other times as the Congress may prescribe. The provisions of section 9 and chapter 7 of title 13, United States Code, shall apply to any survey, collection, or compilation of registration and voting statistics carried out under this title: Provided, however, that no person shall be compelled to disclose his race, color, national origin, or questioned about his political party affiliation, how he voted, or the reasons therefore, nor shall any penalty be imposed for his failure or refusal to make such disclosure. Every person interrogated orally, by written survey or questionnaire or by any other means with respect to such information shall be fully advised with respect to his right to fail or refuse to furnish such information.

KEY PROVISIONS OF THE VOTING RIGHTS ACT OF 1965

The Voting Rights Act of 1965 forced the South to give up literacy tests, poll taxes, and other methods used to prevent black people from voting. It also empowered federal officials to register voters in areas with a history of denying black voter rights.

An Act

To enforce the fifteenth amendment to the Constitution of the United States, and for other purposes.

Be it enacted by the Senate and House of Representatives of the United States of America in Congress assembled, That this Act shall be known as the "Voting Rights Act of 1965."

Section 2.   No voting qualification or prerequisite to voting, or standard, practice, or procedure shall be imposed or applied by any State or political subdivision to deny or abridge the right of any citizen of the United States to vote on account of race or color.

Section 3.   (a) Whenever the Attorney General institutes a proceeding under any statute to enforce the guarantees of the fifteenth amendment in any State or political subdivision the court shall authorize the appointment of Federal examiners by the United States Civil Service Commission in accordance with section 6 to serve for such period of time and for such political subdivisions as the court shall determine is appropriate to enforce the guarantees of the fifteenth amendment (1) as part of any interlocutory order if the court determines that the appointment of such examiners is necessary to enforce such guarantees or (2) as part of any final judgment if the court finds that violations of the fifteenth amendment justifying equitable relief have occurred in such State or subdivision: Provided, That the court need not authorize the appointment of examiners if any incidents of denial or abridgment of the right to vote on account of race or color (1) have been few in number and have been promptly and effectively corrected by State or local action, (2) the continuing effect of such incidents has been eliminated, and (3) there is no reasonable probability of their recurrence in the future.

(b) If in a proceeding instituted by the Attorney General under any statute to enforce the guarantees of the fifteenth amendment in any State or political subdivision the court finds that a test or device has been used for the purpose or with the effect of denying or abridging the right of any citizen of the United States to vote on account of race or color, it shall suspend the use of tests and devices in such State or political subdivisions as the court shall determine is appropriate and for such period as it deems necessary. . . .

Section 4. (a) To assure that the right of citizens of the United States to vote is not denied or abridged on account of race or color, no citizen shall be denied the right to vote in any Federal, State, or local election because of his failure to comply with any test or device in any State with respect to which the determinations have been made under subsection (b). . . .

(b) The provisions of subsection (a) shall apply in any State or in any political subdivision of a state which (1) the Attorney General determines maintained on November 1, 1964, any test or device, and with respect to which (2) the Director of the Census determines that less than 50 per centum of the persons of voting age residing therein were registered on November 1, 1964, or that less than 50 per centum of such persons voted in the presidential election of November 1964. . . .

(c) The phrase "test or device" shall mean any requirement that a person as a prerequisite for voting or registration of voting (1) demonstrate the ability to read, write, understand, or interpret any matter, (2) demonstrate any educational achievement or his knowledge of any particular subject, (3) possess good moral character, or (4) prove his qualifications by the voucher of registered voters or members of any other class. . . .

Section 6. Whenever (a) a court has authorized the appointment of examiners pursuant to the provisions of section 3 (a), or (b) unless a declaratory judgment has been rendered under section 4 (a), the Attorney General certifies with respect to any political subdivision named in, or included within the scope of, determinations made under section 4 (b) that (1) he has received complaints in writing from twenty or more residents of such political subdivision alleging that they have been denied the right to vote under color of law on account of race or color, and that he believes such complaints to be meritorious, or (2) that in his judgment (considering, among other factors, whether the ratio of nonwhite persons to white persons registered to vote within such subdivision appears to him to be reasonably attributable to violations of the fifteenth amendment or whether substantial evidence exists that bona

fide efforts are being made within such subdivision to comply with the fifteenth amendment), the appointment of examiners is otherwise necessary to enforce the guarantees of the fifteenth amendment, the Civil Service Commission shall appoint as many examiners for such subdivision as it may deem appropriate to prepare and maintain lists of persons eligible to vote in Federal, State, and local elections. . . . Examiners and hearing officers shall have the power to administer oaths. . . .

Section 10. (a) The Congress finds that the requirement of the payment of a poll tax as a precondition to voting (i) precludes persons of limited means from voting or imposes unreasonable financial hardship upon such persons as a precondition to their exercise of the franchise, (ii) does not bear a reasonable relationship to any legitimate State interest in the conduct of elections, and (iii) in some areas has the purpose or effect of denying persons the right to vote because of race or color. Upon the basis of these findings, Congress declares that the constitutional right of citizens to vote is denied or abridged in some areas by the requirement of the payment of a poll tax as a precondition to voting.

(b) In the exercise of the powers of Congress under section 5 of the fourteenth amendment and section 2 of the fifteenth amendment, the Attorney General is authorized and directed to institute forthwith in the name of the United States such actions, including actions against States or political subdivisions, for declaratory judgment or injunctive relief against the enforcement of any requirement of the payment of a poll tax as a precondition to voting, or substitute thereof enacted after November 1, 1964, as will be necessary to implement the declaration of subsection (a) and the purposes of this section. . . .

Section 11. (a) No person acting under color of law shall fail or refuse to permit any person to vote who is entitled to vote under any provision of this Act or is otherwise qualified to vote, or willfully fail or refuse to tabulate, count, and report such person's vote.

(b) No person, whether acting under color of law or otherwise, shall intimidate, threaten, or coerce, or attempt to intimidate, threaten, or coerce any person for voting or attempting to vote, or intimidate, threaten, or coerce, or attempt to intimidate, threaten, or coerce any person for urging or aiding any person to vote or attempt to vote, or intimidate, threaten, or coerce any person for exercising any powers or duties under section 3 (a), 6, 8, 9, 10, or 12 (e).

Photo Credits

Boqueto de Woieseri; 147 The National Archives; 150 DK Images/National Museums of Scotland; 152 Rare Books and Manuscripts Division, New York Public Library, Astor, Lenox and Tilden Foundations.

Chapter 7

Chapter Opener 158 Chicago Historical Society, Eyre Crowe, After the Sale: Slaves Going South from Richmond; 162 The Historical Society of Pennsylvania (HSP), Portrait of James Forten, Leon Gardiner Collection; 162 Boston Athenaeum; 163 Schomburg Center for Research in Black Culture, The New York Public Library, Astor, Lenox and Tilden Foundations; 164 Dorling Kindersley Media Library; 169 Rare Book and Manuscript Division, The New York Public Library, Astor, Lenox and Tilden Foundations; 171 Erddig, Clwyd, North Wales/National Trust Photographic Library/John Hammond/The Bridgeman Art Library; 175 The Historic New Orleans Collection, Museum/Research Center, Acc. No. 1960.46; 176 North Carolina Museum of Art, Raleigh. Purchased with funds from the State of North Carolina; 178 Dorothy Wright, Vesey Talking to His People, painting, Gaillard Auditorium, Collection of City Hall, Charleston, South Carolina; 181 Library of Congress.

Chapter 8

Chapter Opener 186 John Rogers, The Fugitive's Story, Cincinnati Art Museum, (x1967.4); 189 The Historical Society of Pennsylvania (HSP), Portrait of William Lloyd Garrison, Society Portrait Collection; 193 The Metropolitan Museum of Art, Gift of Mr. and Mrs. Samuel Shore, 1978. (1978.61.6) Photograph © The Metropolitan Museum of Art; 194 Getty Images; 199 Getty Images; 199 The Library Company of Philadelphia; 201 Massachusetts Historical Society, MHS (neg. #0031); 203 Art Institute of Chicago (1996.433); 205 F. Gutekunst, Philadelphia/Sophia Smith Collec-

tion, Smith College; 209 The Library Company of Philadelphia; 211 Getty Images; 212 The Library Company of Philadelphia.

Chapter 9

Chapter Opener 214 Private Collection/The Bridgeman Art Library; 218 The Library Company of Philadelphia; 221 Schomburg Center for Research in Black Culture, The New York Public Library, Astor, Lenox and Tilden Foundations; 222 Getty Images; 223 National Portrait Gallery, Smithsonian Institution/Art Resource, NY; 224 University of Virginia Library, Special Collections; 224 The Harriet Beecher Stowe Center; 225 Library of Congress; 229 SuperStock, New York; 233 Getty Images; 235 Library of Congress; 238 Thomas Hovenden, 1840–1895, The Last Moments of John Brown, c. 1884, oil on canvas, 46 1/8 x 38 3/8 (117.2 x 97.5cm), Fine Arts Museum of San Francisco, Gift of Mr. and Mrs. John D. Rockefeller 3rd, 1979.60.

Chapter 10

Chapter Opener 240 University of Maryland, Albin O. Kuhn Library & Gallery; 244 Getty Images; 248 The Museum of the Confederacy, Richmond, Virginia, CT #495b, Photograph by Katherine Wetzel; 250 Haverford College, The Quaker Collection; 252 Library of Congress; 253 The Library Company of Philadelphia; 255 Corbis; 255 Corbis; 258 Anne S. K. Brown Military Collection, Brown University Library; 266 The Library Company of Philadelphia.

Chapter 11

Chapter Opener 268 The Granger Collection, New York; 272 Schomburg, Photos & Prints Division; 274 Getty Images; 276 Library of Congress; 279 Getty Images; 280 Antique Textile Resource; 282 Ohio State Historical Society; 286 National Archives of Canada/C-02997; 287 The Granger Collection, New York; 288 Library of Congress; 289 Corbis.

Index

Leeward Islands, 59, 71 (map)

Le Jau, Francis, 60

Lewis, Nancy, 290

Lexington, Battle of, 112

Lexington, Virginia, 87

The Liberator, 181, 188, 193, 197, 201–203, 221

Liberia: founding of, 183; American Missionary Association and, 209; African Americans settling in, 290–291

Liberian Exodus Joint Stock Company, 291

Liberty Party, 206 (illus.), 210, 211, 231, 233, 234

Libolo, 18

Life Among the Lowly (Stowe), 224

The Life & Adventures of Nat Love, Better Known in the Cattle Country as Deadwood Dick (Love), 290

Life of a Slave Girl (Jacobs), 172

Lincoln, Abraham: debates with Douglas, 236; Harper's Ferry raid and, 237; Civil War and, 242, 246, 247 (illus.), 248, 252–257; election of 1860 of, 243–244; inaugural speech of 1861, 245; Emancipation Proclamation and, 252–253; assassination of, 261–262, 272; Reconstruction and, 272

Lincoln-Douglas debates, 236

Lincoln School, 287

Lincoln University, 265

Literacy, 198–199

Literature/poetry: on political events, 106; on slavery, 221–225, 224 (illus.)

Living conditions, slave, 79–81, 79 (illus.), 229

Logan, Greenbury, 210

Logan, Rayford, 4

Loguen, Jermain, 219

Long, Jefferson, 278 (illus.), 279

Lopes, Duarta, 18

Louisiana: French settlements in, 72, 90–91; slave life in, 90–91; free blacks in, 132, 134, 136, 136 (illus.); interracial churches in, 138; Catholics in, 138–139, 197; slavery in, 147; secession of, 244; ratification of Fourteenth Amendment and, 266

Louisiana Purchase, 136, 146, 147

Louisiana Territory, 136, 164, 166

L'Ouverture, Toussaint, 142, 144 (illus.)

Love, Nat, 290

Lovejoy, Elijah, 205

Loyal Georgian, 266

Lundy, Benjamin, 181

L'Union, 252

Lynch, John Roy, 278 (illus.)

M

Madagascar, 78

Madeira Islands, 29, 30

Madison, James, 122–123, 154

Maine: admitted to union, 166; petition to end slavery in, 203

Mali: kingdom of, 14–15; art in, 16 (illus.)

Mamout, Yarrow, 94, 95 (illus.)

Mandingo people, 14, 15, 27

Mani-Kongo (Kongo king), 33–34

Mansa Musa (Mali king), 14–15

Manumission: methods to curb, 98; post–Revolution, 116, 150; decrease in, 191

Marriage: abroad, 83; among slaves, 91, 174. *See also* Family life; Interracial marriage

Marshall, Andrew, 176

Marshall, John, 159

Martin, George, 105

Martin, Luther, 115

Maryland: slavery in, 53–55, 56 (map), 80; indentured servants in, 60; rights of slaves in, 63, 64 (illus.); slave population in, 91; American Revolution and, 113–114; free blacks in, 116, 132; restrictions on free blacks in, 230; support for Union by, 245–246; post–Civil War apprenticeship system in, 264

Mason, Biddy, 232, 290

Masons, African American, 107, 122

Massachusetts: slavery in, 55; eradication of slavery in, 118, 203; Fugitive Slave Act and, 218

Massachusetts Bay Colony, 55

Massachusetts Female Antislavery Society, 204

Massachusetts Fifty-fourth Regiment, 253, 254

Massachusetts State Kansas Committee, 236

Mathematics, achievements in, 120–121

Mather, Cotton, 84

Matrilineal kinship systems, 19

Matthias, Prophet, 222

McClellan, George, 252

McWhorter, Frank, 194

Medical practices: smallpox inoculation and, 83–84, 97; free blacks in, 135; learned from slaves, 173

The Memoirs of Elleanor Eldridge (Eldridge), 204

Memphis, Tennessee: industrial development in, 300; post–Reconstruction growth of, 306

Menéndez, Francisco, 89

Methodist churches: establishment of black, 139–141, 176; black secession from white, 177–178

Methodist General Conference, 140, 141

Mexico: Spanish colonies in, 35, 36, 54; African slaves in, 48; Africans escaping to, 192, 196 (map); Texas and, 211; California and, 211–212

Mid-Atlantic colonies: Africans in, 56–58; slave life in, 83, 84. *See also* Colonies

Middle Ages, 22

Migration: to California, 232–233, 290; to Midwest, 289–290; to West, 289–290

Militias: free blacks in, 21; in colonial Louisiana, 91; during American Revolution, 113–114, 113 (illus.)

Miller, Joseph, 257

Mirror of the Times, 232

Missionaries: in Africa, 33–34; conversion of slaves by, 93

Missionary Record, 280

Mississippi Territory, 146

Missouri: as slave state, 166; support for Union by, 245–246

Missouri Compromise: effects of, 163–164, 179; creation of, 165–167, 168 (map); slavery and, 208, 218; Kansas and Nebraska and, 233–234; *Dred Scott* case and, 235

Missouri Territory, 165

Mobile, Alabama, 192 (illus.)

Monroe, James, 149, 159

Montesquieu, Baron de, 123

Montgomery, Ben, 195–196, 248

Morocco, 16

Morris, Gouverneur, 122

Morris, Lewis, 57

Morrison, Toni, 220–221

Mose (Florida), 89, 90 (map)

Mother Bethel Church, 139 (illus.), 140, 159, 161–163

Mott, Lucretia, 254

Muhammad, 11

Muhammad, Askia, 16

Mulattos: in South Carolina, 65–66; conditions for slave, 82; in New Orleans, 136. *See also* Interracial marriage

Music: in Africa, 23; religious expression through, 93–95, 97; role of slave, 95, 177; in African American celebrations, 97

Muslims: beliefs of, 11; slavery among, 22, 33; slave trade by, 33; slaves as practicing, 94. *See also* Islam

Mutual aid societies, 137

My Bondage and My Freedom (Douglass), 221

The Mystery, 207

Myths, Yoruba, 5

N

Nacimiento (Mexico), 196 (map)

Nanticoke Indians, 65

Seward, William Henry, 251
Sexual relations, between whites and slaves,
     62, 64, 65–66, 81–82, 171, 172, 221
Shabaka (Kushite monarch), 9
Shadd, Abraham, 230–231
Shadd, Mary Ann. *See* Cary, Mary Ann Shadd
Sharecroppers, 264
Sharp, Granville, 124
Sharp Street Methodist Church, 139
Shaw, Robert Gould, 254
Shays, Daniel, 121–122
Sherman, William T., 258–260
Sicily, 30
Sierra Leone: slaves from, 94; resettlement of
     African Americans in, 124–126, 126
     (map), 156, 160, 209
Sierre Leone Company, 124, 125
Silver Lake (Pennsylvania), 194
Simms, William Gilmore, 225
Singleton, Benjamin "Pap," 288, 289
Sixth Colored Infantry, 240 (illus.), 254
Skipwith, George, 228
Skipwith, Lucy, 227–228
Slaughterhouse Cases, 287
Slave and Citizen: The Negro in the Americas
     (Tannenbaum), 69
Slave auctions, 170
Slave codes: in South Carolina, 65–66; in
     New England, 66–67; purpose of, 67, 68;
     in Louisiana, 91
Slave life: in southern colonies, 79–81;
     families and, 80–81, 83, 87, 91, 174–175;
     in Mid-Atlantic colonies, 83, 84; in New
     England colonies, 83–84; in Louisiana,
     90–91; in antebellum years, 169–177
Slave trade: in Benin City, 17; England and,
     17, 36–37, 38 (map), 59, 60; Portugal
     and, 17, 28–34, 35 (illus.); origins of, 21;
     Europeans and, 28, 32–38; Africans
     leaders engaging in, 33, 36; personal
     accounts of, 40, 42, 44; conditions on
     ships during, 41–44; exchange of
     knowledge and techniques during, 54;
     New England colonies and, 56, 84; routes
     of, 56 (map); in Mid-Atlantic colonies, 57;
     interstate, 166 (map), 167–168;
     Compromise of 1850 and, 213
Slave revolts: personal accounts of, 44 (illus.);
     in Jamaica, 58; in New York, 60–61; in
     Virginia, 88, 109; background of, 88–89;
     in Louisiana, 90; suppression of,
     103–104; pre-revolutionary conflict and,
     106–108, 109 (map); in Haiti, 123,
     141–143; in St. Domingue, 130, 131;
     Gabriel's Rebellion, 148–150; in
     post–Revolution South, 150–151, 193
Slaveowners: sexual contact between slaves
     and, 62, 64, 65–66, 81–82, 171, 221;

relations between slaves and, 85, 86,
     227–229; rights to free slaves, 98; George
     Washington as, 113; protections of
     Constitution for, 123; retaliation toward,
     171; paternalism practiced by, 172;
     Constitutional rights and, 217, free blacks
     as, 229
Slavery: in African societies, 21–22; art
     depicting, 27; trauma of, 38–45; in
     English colonies, 51–53, 68, 69; English
     association between race and, 62; legal
     definitions of, 62–63; Catholic Church
     and, 69, 70; white protests against,
     98–100; Northwest Ordinance and,
     118–119; U.S. Constitution and,
     122–123, 131; expansion of, 145–148,
     163–168, 190–193, 210–211; westward
     expansion and, 145–148, 163–168, 208,
     210, 211
Slaves: storytelling tradition among, 3; of
     Muslims v. Europeans in Colonies, 33;
     population data regarding, 33, 71 (map),
     78, 91 (illus.), 165, 165 (illus.), 190–191,
     191 (illus.), 226, 226 (map), 227 (illus.);
     rights of Muslim-owned, 33; on
     plantations, 34–36, 54; in Spanish
     colonies, 35, 36, 69; statistics regarding
     Africans exported as, 36, 81–83; personal
     accounts of, 38–40, 44, 76–77, 84, 92;
     middle passage for, 40–44; sale of, 44–45;
     accompanying Spanish explorers, 47–48;
     legal rights of, 53–54, 62–63; in
     Chesapeake colonies, 54–55, 60, 63, 64
     (illus.), 80; in New England, 55–56,
     83–84; in Mid-Atlantic colonies, 56–58,
     83, 84; in South Carolina, 58; restrictions
     on, 64–65; living conditions of southern,
     79–81, 79 (illus.); fertility rate among,
     80–81; relations between slaveowners
     and, 85, 86, 227–228; resistance of,
     85–86; fugitive, 87–88, 88 (illus.), 94, 97,
     109, 148, 202; religion of, 92–94,
     175–176; origin of Africans imported as,
     92 (map); effects of conflict between
     colonies and Britain in, 106–108;
     relations between free blacks and,
     147–148, 172; settlements of fugitive,
     148; in urban settings, 171, 172; leasing
     of, 171–172; as contraband, 246, 248;
     during Civil War, 248–249. *See also*
     Fugitive slaves
Smallpox, 35, 69, 83–84
Smallpox inoculation, 83–84, 97
Smalls, Robert, 260
Smith, Gerrit, 210
Smith, James, 140
Smith, James McCune, 189, 210
Smith, Meg, 76, 77

Smith, Simon P., 288
Smith, Venture, 3, 75–77, 83 (illus.), 84,
     97–99
Socialist Party, in South, 281–282
Social organization: in West African
     kingdoms, 14; characteristics of African,
     20–22. *See also* Family life
Society for the Propagation of the Gospel in
     Foreign Parts, 93
Society for the Relief of Free Negroes
     Unlawfully Held in Bondage, 118
Society of Free People of Color for Promoting
     the Instruction and School Education of
     Children of African Descent, 139
Society of Friends, 58, 99
Sofala (Muslim city-state), 12
Solomon, Job Ben, 94, 95 (illus.), 96
Some Considerations on the Keeping of Negroes
     (Woolman), 99
Songhai, kingdom of, 15–16, 21, 27
Soninke people of Ghana, 14
Sons of Africa, 153
South: post–Revolution slavery in, 115–116;
     free blacks in, 132, 201; cotton
     production in, 164–165; expansion of
     slavery in, 167–168, 167 (illus.); African
     American population in, 190–192, 191
     (illus.); white press in, 207–208;
     economic issues and conflict between
     North and, 217; Fugitive Slave Act and,
     218–219; narratives on slavery in, 225;
     slavery and economy of, 226–227; Civil
     War and, 242, 243, 248; secession of,
     244–246, 245 (map); Freedmen's Bureau
     and, 263–264; Reconstruction era and,
     270–272; local politics in, 279–282;
     black migration from, 289–290
South America, 34–35, 54, 69
South Carolina: Africans in, 58; slavery in,
     58–60, 69, 70, 78–81; slave code on,
     65–66; slaves escaping to Florida from,
     70, 88, 89; rice cultivation in, 79; slave
     revolts in, 88, 108; American Revolution
     and, 114; slave laws in, 177; secession of,
     244; ratification of Fourteenth
     Amendment and, 266
Southern colonies: slave life in, 79–81; trade
     between Europe and, 85 (map); runaway
     slaves in, 87; conversion of slaves to
     Christianity in, 93; merging African and
     European traditions in, 97–98; methods
     to curb manumission in, 98; pre-
     revolutionary conflict in, 108; slaves
     aligning with British in, 110; in American
     Revolution, 113–114. *See also* Colonies;
     specific colonies
Southern Cultivator, 207
Southwestern Asia, 21